Time Series for Economics and F

Focusing on methods for data that are ordered in time, this textbook provides a comprehensive guide to analyzing time series data using modern techniques from data science. It is specifically tailored to economics and finance applications, aiming to provide students with rigorous training. Chapters cover Bayesian approaches, nonparametric smoothing methods, machine learning, and continuous time econometrics. Theoretical and empirical exercises, concise summaries, bolded key terms, and illustrative examples are included throughout to reinforce key concepts and bolster understanding. Ancillary materials include datasets for self-study and PowerPoint lecture slides, a solutions manual, and additional exercises for instructors. With its clear and accessible style, this textbook is an essential tool for advanced undergraduate and graduate students in economics, finance, and statistics.

Oliver Linton is Chair of the Faculty of Economics, a Fellow of Trinity College, and Professor of Political Economy at the University of Cambridge. He has published two books and nearly 200 articles on econometrics, statistics, and empirical finance. He was President of the Society for Financial Econometrics from 2021 to 2023 and is a Fellow of the Econometric Society, the Institute of Mathematical Statistics, and the British Academy.

Time Series for Economics and Finance

Oliver Linton
University of Cambridge

CAMBRIDGE
UNIVERSITY PRESS

Shaftesbury Road, Cambridge CB2 8EA, United Kingdom

One Liberty Plaza, 20th Floor, New York, NY 10006, USA

477 Williamstown Road, Port Melbourne, VIC 3207, Australia

314–321, 3rd Floor, Plot 3, Splendor Forum, Jasola District Centre, New Delhi – 110025, India

103 Penang Road, #05–06/07, Visioncrest Commercial, Singapore 238467

Cambridge University Press is part of Cambridge University Press & Assessment,
a department of the University of Cambridge.

We share the University's mission to contribute to society through the pursuit of
education, learning and research at the highest international levels of excellence.

www.cambridge.org
Information on this title: www.cambridge.org/highereducation/isbn/9781009396295

DOI: 10.1017/9781009396271

First published 2025

Printed in the United Kingdom by CPI Group Ltd, Croydon CR0 4YY, 2025

A catalogue record for this publication is available from the British Library.

A Cataloging-in-Publication data record for this book is available from the Library of Congress

ISBN 978-1-009-39629-5 Hardback
ISBN 978-1-009-39626-4 Paperback

Additional resources for this publication at www.cambridge.org/lintontimeseries

To my exceptional wife, Jianghong Song, and my children Marco, Silvia, Alexander, and Florence.

Contents

Figures

Tables

Preface

This work grew out of my teaching and research. Unfortunately, as a student I missed the glory days of the LSE Time Series School, and so this book will not cover general to specific modelling or parsimonious encompassing, but I try to cover the relevant tools of modern time series analysis as practiced by econometricians, now. There are so many excellent time series books, varying from the extremely rigorous like Brockwell and Davis (2006) to extremely practical books with only computer code and no justifications or understanding, and my book is somewhere in between. Time series is a bizarrely neglected topic in many econometrics and statistics graduate programs, and is facing new challenges from the machine learning community, whose main target of prediction is one historically treated under time series. I think an understanding of the key principles underlying dynamic models and their application is still very valuable for a lot of practical work in economics and finance. I have tried to update the classic corpus in the direction of where empirical practice is in economics and finance, including discussions about alternative inference methods like bootstrap that can be justified under weaker assumptions than in the classical setting. I also include material on smoothing methods, which are about flexible functional form where nonlinearity is potentially an issue, and so-called machine learning methods designed to accommodate large numbers of predictor variables. These methods are justly celebrated for their potential to improve predictions, and no doubt will take more central stage in graduate education in the future. I include some proofs, but in other cases refer the reader to where the original can be found. I left forecasting to the end, because it is about anticipating the future.

The book is intended to be used as a text for advanced undergraduates and graduate students in economics, finance, and statistics who are interested in time series, its applications, and the methodology needed to understand and interpret those applications. Some prerequisites include a course that covers probability, statistics, and linear regression, the ideas of which are central to the study of time series, along with some basic knowledge of matrices and linear algebra. In the interests of space I do not provide a full set of background results in linear algebra and econometrics, just the bare minimum of definitions. Likewise, I do not provide explicit help in programming. The book allows for different selections of material depending on the needs of students and instructors. One could just cover linear time series, including Chapters 2–9 and Chapter 13. One could instead cover nonlinear and nonparametric methods through Chapters 10–13. I have taught parts of this material at Yale University, the London School of Economics, the University of Cambridge, Humboldt University, Shandong University, SHUFE, Renmin University, and Minho University, and I thank the many students for their feedback over the years.

The book contains many terms in bold face, which can then be investigated further by internet search. In terms of software resources, EViews is a very useful package that does a lot of the procedures in this book, and I use it in some of the empirical illustrations included. However, it is not free and it has some limitations. R is free software with many shared user-created packages for doing everything from data scraping to Bayesian vector autoregression, and is highly recommended. A full list of available R packages can be found at https://cran.r-project.org. Ancillary materials include datasets (see Appendix D for detailed descriptions), the figures included throughout the book, some code in different languages such as MATLAB, GAUSS, and R, and an instructor's manual. They are available online at www.cambridge.org/lintontimeseries.

Acknowledgments

I would like to thank all my current and former colleagues, coauthors, PhD students, and postdocs. I would like to thank Seok Young Hong, Weiguang Liu, and anonymous referees for comments. I thank Rowan Groat at Cambridge University Press for help with the manuscript and for guiding me through the process.

Notation and Conventions

- In this book I use the dating convention yyyymmddhhmmss.
- I use $\xrightarrow{P}$ to denote convergence in probability and $\implies$ to denote weak convergence (or convergence in distribution).
- $\log(x)$ is the natural logarithm unless otherwise stated.
- $\mathbb{R}$ is the set of real numbers, $\mathbb{C}$ is the set of complex numbers including $i = \sqrt{-1}$, $\mathbb{Z}$ is the set of integers $0, \pm 1, \pm 2, \ldots$, and $\mathbb{N}$ is the set of positive integers $1, 2, \ldots$
- $'$ denotes differentiation.
- $\top$ denotes matrix transpose.
- I say $1(A) = 1$ if the event A is true and zero otherwise.
- I use $X_n = O(n)$ to mean that X_n/n is bounded for a deterministic sequence X_n as $n \to \infty$, and for a stochastic sequence I use the Landau O_P, o_P notation. Specifically, for a sequence of random variables X_n, I write $X_n = o_P(\delta_n)$ if $\delta_n^{-1} X_n \xrightarrow{P} 0$ for deterministic $\delta_n \to 0$ as $n \to \infty$. I write $X_n = O_P(\delta_n)$ if essentially there is a random variable X for which $\left| \delta_n^{-1} X_n \right| \le X$ for large n.
- I use $\simeq$ to generically denote an approximation.
- I use $\sim$ to mean to have the same distribution as.
- I do not have a bracketing convention like some journals, but I do have a preference for round curved things over square ones.

1   Introduction

This book is about time series data, that is, data that are recorded in sequence. Time series have some special features due to the ordering in time. Our analytic framework is to suppose that the outcomes we observe are realizations from some population of random variables or stochastic process. For each t in some set $\mathcal{T}$, $y_t \colon \Omega \to \mathbb{R}$ is a random variable with realization $y_t(\omega)$, where $\omega \in \Omega$ is some underlying sample space. For each ω, the set $\{y_t(\omega), t \in \mathcal{T}\}$ is called the **sample path** or trajectory. For each $t \in \mathcal{T}$, the collection $\{y_t(\omega), \omega \in \Omega\}$ is the set of potential outcomes of the random variable y_t, of which we observe precisely one. We may define the distribution of the random variable y_t and its moments for each t with respect to $\omega \in \Omega$. The key thing here is to define the joint distribution of each sequence $y_{t_1}, \ldots, y_{t_n}$, where $t_i \in \mathcal{T}$ for $i = 1, \ldots, n$, but this requires some detail about the relationship between the random variables.

We may have observation times that are not equally spaced. For example, stock markets are closed at weekends and during holidays. For some data, such as intraday financial transaction prices, the observation times themselves can be considered the outcomes of some stochastic process, which can interact with the observations themselves. For the most part we deal with equally spaced observations where the observation times are assumed without loss of generality to be integers. We also for the most part deal essentially with the case where the random variables are continuous, meaning they take values in the real line rather than in a more restricted domain. There are special issues to do with, say, binary or integer-valued time series and we will consider these toward the end.

We may observe a trajectory or orbit of values $\{y_1, \ldots, y_T\}$, which is one draw from the stochastic process, but under certain conditions we are able to use this sample to learn about the population properties of the process, which concern all $\omega \in \Omega$. The analysis usually consists of modelling, that is, describing the laws of motion of the time series in a parsimonious fashion reflecting subject knowledge and data features, estimation of the parameters of the model based on the sample of data, testing hypotheses about parameters of the model, and forecasting future values of the series. The analysis may be motivated by the quest for understanding, or there may be a concrete objective to evaluate the effects or potential effects of a government policy or some other intervention.

Many time series books start by talking about the additive decomposition of a series y_t, where y_t may be some transformation of the raw data (such as the logarithm or logistic), into components, that is,

$$y_t = T_t + S_t + C_t + E_t, \tag{1.1}$$

where T_t is the trend component, S_t is the seasonal component, C_t is the cyclical component, and E_t is the error term. We have to define what makes T a trend, what makes

S a seasonal component, and what makes C a cyclical component, otherwise this is a meaningless decomposition; we will take this up later. Roughly speaking, a trend is a persistent upward or downward movement, a seasonal component is a regular periodic variation (of known period) coinciding with specific calendar features, such as days of the week, months of the year, and so on, and a cycle is a more nebulous concept involving quasi-periodic behavior of unknown horizons. In economics, there are several named cycles: the Kitchin cycle of around 3–5 years, the Juglar cycle of around 7–11 years, the Kuznets cycle of around 15–25 years, and the Kondratiev wave of 45–60 years. The National Bureau of Economic Research (NBER) dates US business cycle peaks and troughs, according to their definition.[1] In climate science, there are many known cycles of varying lengths, from 30 days to thousands of years, such as the El Niño southern oscillation (around 2–7 years) and the glacial cycles, the Brückner–Egerson–Lockyer cycle of length 30–40 years, and so on.

Economists often want to work with "deseasonalized" data, which amounts to estimating the component S_t and subtracting it from y_t; central banks and many others have developed sophisticated methodologies to do this. In some cases, economists want to work with "detrended" data, to abstract from whatever is causing the growth over time in a variable and to focus on the short-run fluctuations, which may be influenced by macroeconomic policy. Finally, there are some applications where it is common to work with "decycled" data. For example, cyclically adjusted government budget deficits are favored by some economists as better reflecting the true balance in public finances, taking account of automatic adjustments that occur through a business cycle. Private sector companies are not allowed to decycle their earnings and costs in their public announcements; there are accounting tools at their disposal that allow them to smooth earnings and costs to some extent. Campbell and Shiller (1988) introduced the cyclically adjusted price to earnings (CAPE) ratio that tries to remove the short-term cyclical variation in announced earnings to give a more appropriate measure of the state of the stock market. In climate science, the focus has been on the trend part of the process, or indeed whether there is a trend and how big it is; this trend is usually called the anomaly and defined as the departure of the temperature from a long-term average such as the twentieth-century global average temperature.

The decomposition in (1.1) raises identification issues: Can we distinguish a trend from a long cycle? Can we distinguish a seasonal component from a trend? To implement this we need further modelling assumptions. One approach is to use deterministic trends and seasonal components. A second approach, called structural time series modelling, is to use random walks over and over and over again to model the trend and the seasonal. Both approaches involve applying different linear transformations to the data in sequence to deliver the separate components.

I view the decomposition in (1.1) really as a metaphor, reminding us that the key features of a time series are its trend (or lack thereof) and its seasonality (or periodicity more generally); we may have a more complicated and holistic model. We first show a few datasets to illustrate some of the issues.

---

[1] That is, two consecutive quarters of negative GDP growth; see www.nber.org/research/business-cycle-dating.

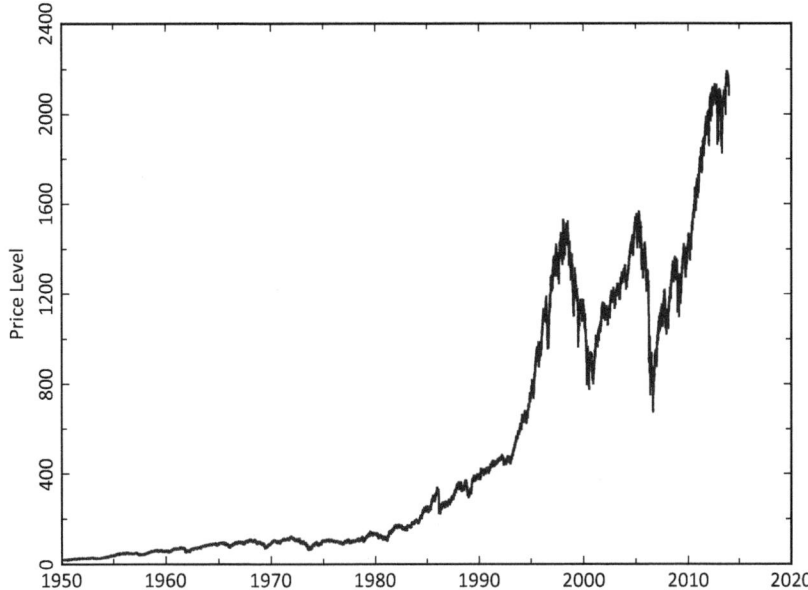

Figure 1.1 S&P500 daily stock closing price.

We next consider, in Figures 1.1–1.15, some empirical examples. The datasets are available from www.cambridge.org/lintontimeseries and are detailed in Appendix D.

The first dataset, sp500, is the Standard and Poor's (S&P) 500 index level, Figure 1.1, which shows a substantial upward trend with several visible reversals of nontrivial duration (bear markets). The key feature here is the trend.

The next series, Figure 1.2, is the daily observed short-term interest rate on US government securities, specifically the one-month T-bill, that is, the contract length is one month but the observation frequency is daily, taken from the dataset ffdaily. This series has some wandering up and down around its mean level but does not appear to have a very strong trend in comparison with stock prices; the level of this series was for a while very close to zero, which is an effective lower bound.

We next show the Chinese yuan / US dollar exchange rate from the series cnyusd along with its percentage change or return (Figure 1.3). The rate was fixed until 2005 and then effectively fixed again between 2008 and 2010, but otherwise shows some upward and downward variation in a modest range with no substantial trend in evidence. The return series (the time difference of the logarithm of price) shows the variation in more detail, as well as the occasional big movements associated with the depegging and other events.

The next series, Figure 1.4, is the daily closing price of the VIX futures contract, from the series VIX. This series also appears not to have a strong trend but rather certain cycles or waves of up and down motion along with occasional big moves such as during the financial crisis and at the beginning of the COVID-19 pandemic.

We next show the US unemployment rate (the percentage of the work force currently unemployed), which is reported monthly, taken from the series UNRATENSA (Figure 1.5).

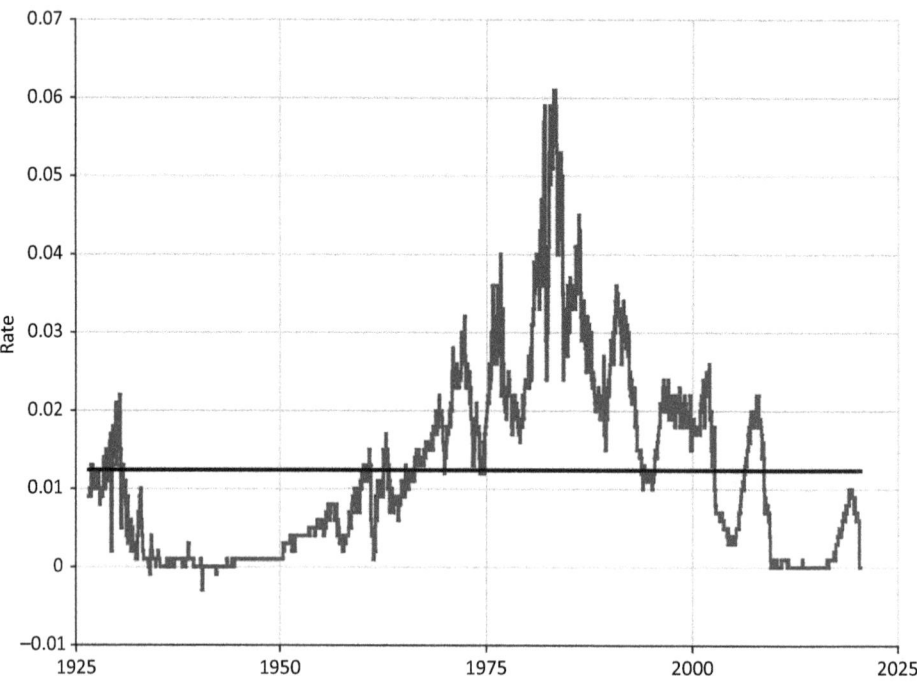

Figure 1.2 Daily one-month maturity T-bill rate.

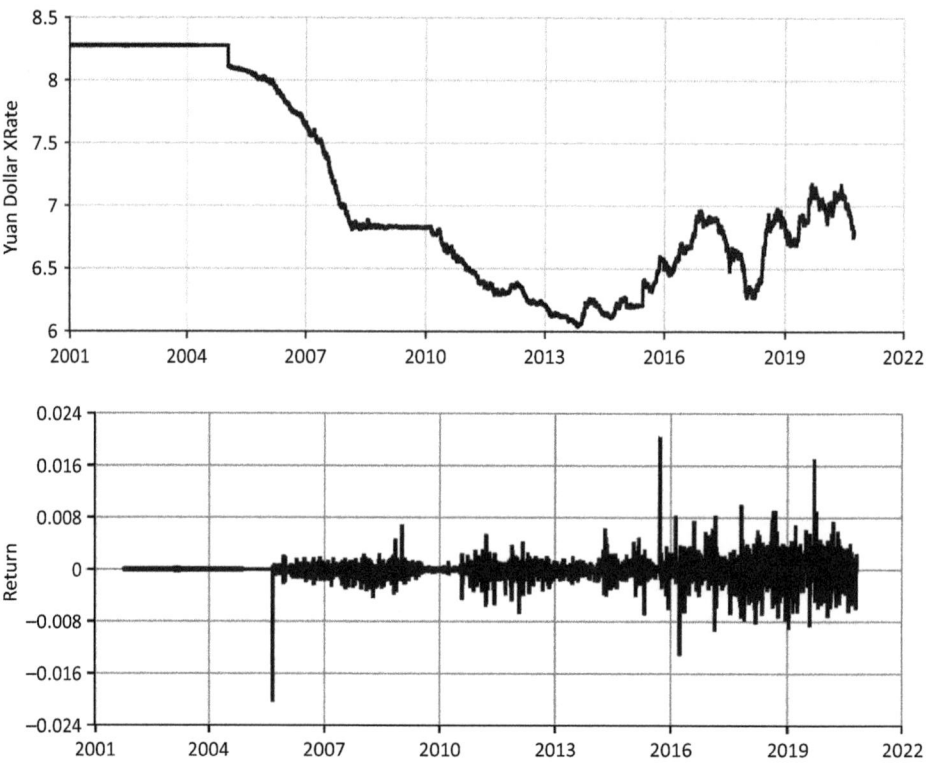

Figure 1.3 Daily yuan/dollar exchange rate and percentage change.

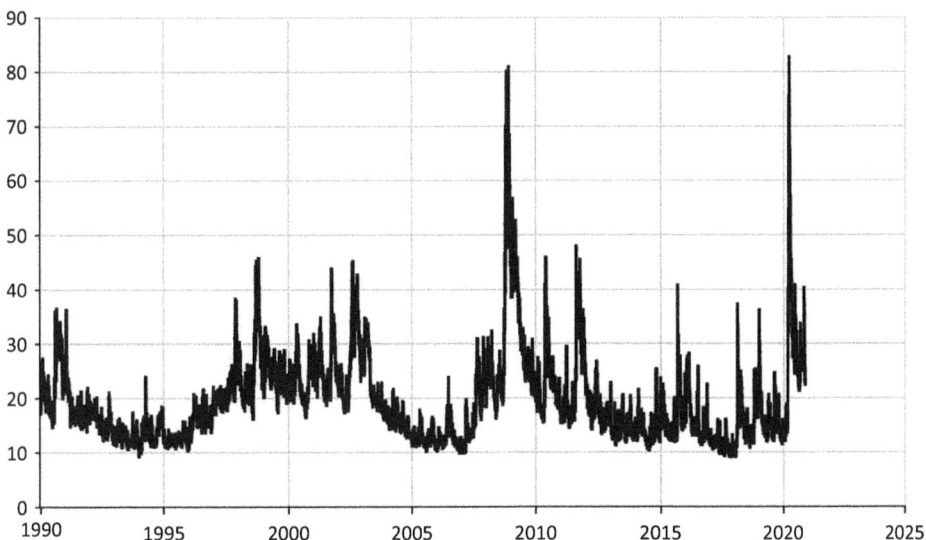

Figure 1.4 Daily level of VIX, 1990–2020.

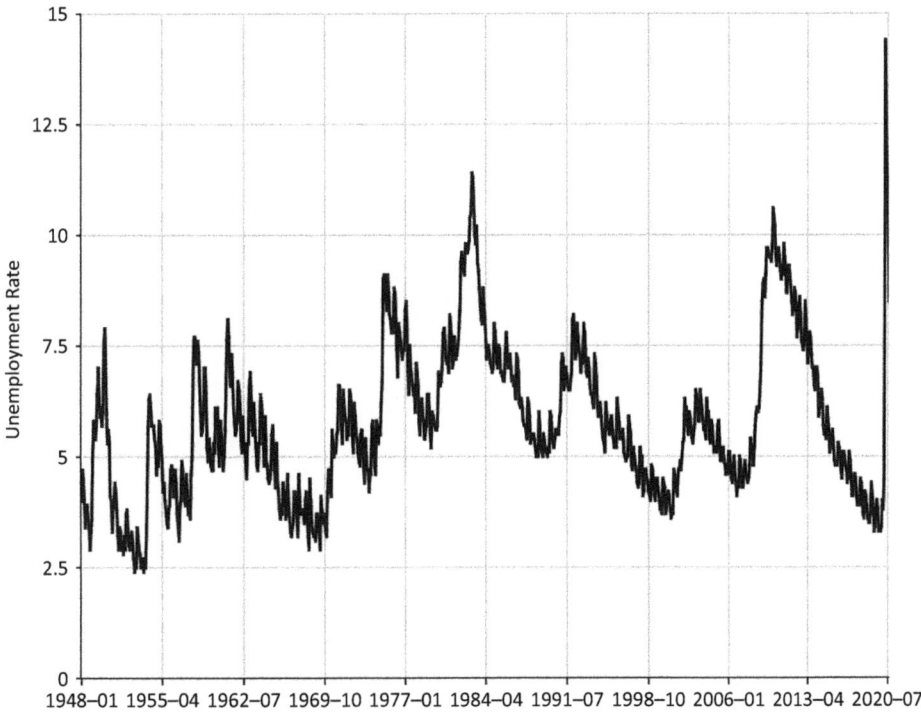

Figure 1.5 US monthly unemployment rate, not seasonally adjusted.

This series shows the recent COVID spike, along with other boom and bust periods. The series has a pronounced seasonality, because unemployment is lower in the summer and around Christmas time, which is why it is more common to show the seasonally adjusted rate.

Figure 1.6 US monthly industrial production, not seasonally adjusted.

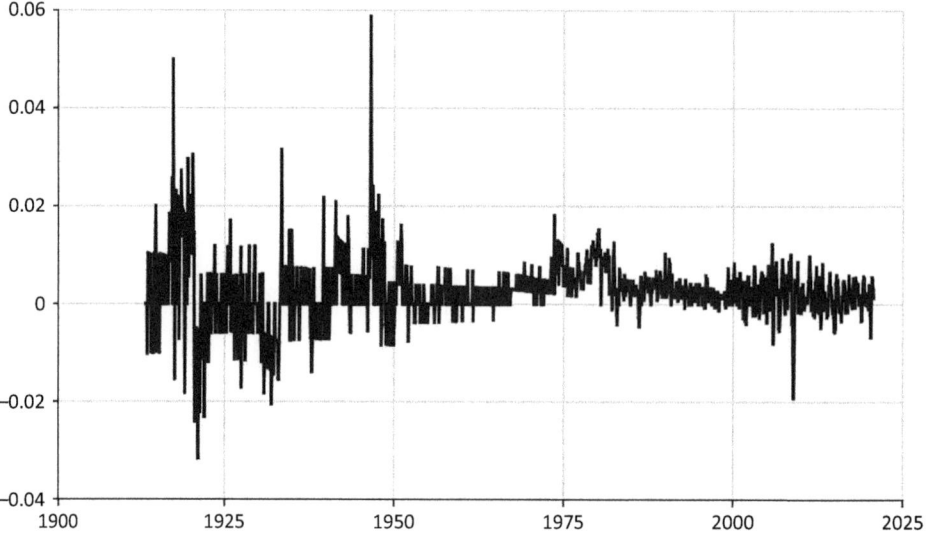

Figure 1.7 US monthly inflation rate.

Figure 1.6 shows the US monthly industrial production index, the series INDPRO. This series also shows the recent COVID spike, along with other boom and bust periods. The series has a pronounced upward trend due to economic growth and also seasonality similar to the unemployment series.

We next show the US monthly CPI inflation rate, calculated from the series CPIAUCNS (Figure 1.7). Clearly, before 1970, the series was essentially annual (apart from a few big spikes) and interpolated, in a not particularly clever way, to give a "monthly" series. The Phillips curve predicts an inverse relationship between unemployment rate and inflation. The raw correlation between contemporaneous values of the two monthly series over the

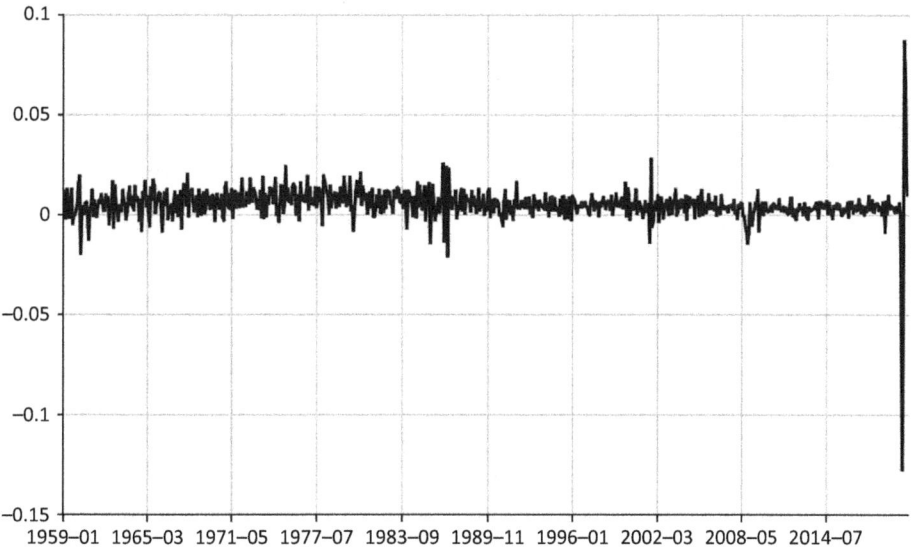

Figure 1.8 US consumption growth since 1959.

period 1948–2020 is about 0.04. One question is whether this can be improved by time series methods that adjust for seasonality and that bring in dynamics.

Figure 1.8 shows the monthly, seasonally adjusted, growth in personal consumption expenditure in the USA, the series PCE. The series is dominated by the most recent COVID-19 event. Hall (1978) argued that consumption should be a martingale, that is, the growth rate of consumption should be unpredictable.

We next show the monthly average daily maximum temperature at the Oxford weather station since 1850, from the dataset OXMT (Figure 1.9). This data shows an even more pronounced seasonality, with higher temperatures in the summer and lower temperatures in the winter. Of interest here is determining whether there is an upward trend in these temperatures due to climate change, but this is very difficult to see from the current plot, because it is dominated by the seasonal effect.

We next show, in Figure 1.10, the monthly average daily maximum temperature series for Toronto, Canada, since 1840, dataset Toronto. In this case we show the time series separately by month (January, February, etc.), the so-called seasonal subseries plot. The key thing about the graph is that every month is shown on the same vertical scale of temperature from −40 to +40 so that it is hard to perceive any change in the level of each series.

Figure 1.11 shows a higher-frequency temperature series, which is the temperature at the Cambridge University weather station recorded every 30 minutes since 1995, dataset Cam30. This data also has a pronounced seasonality, both within day (day is warmer than night) and within year (summer is warmer than winter). There does not appear to be a strong trend to this series over the time frame considered, although it is a little difficult to deal with the multiple seasonal patterns complicating things.

Next comes a weekly time series of Scottish mortality from the dataset Deadscots (Figure 1.12). This is the raw mortality unadjusted for population, which was around 5.25 million in 1974, and fell to 5.07 million in 2000 and thereafter rose to 5.46 million

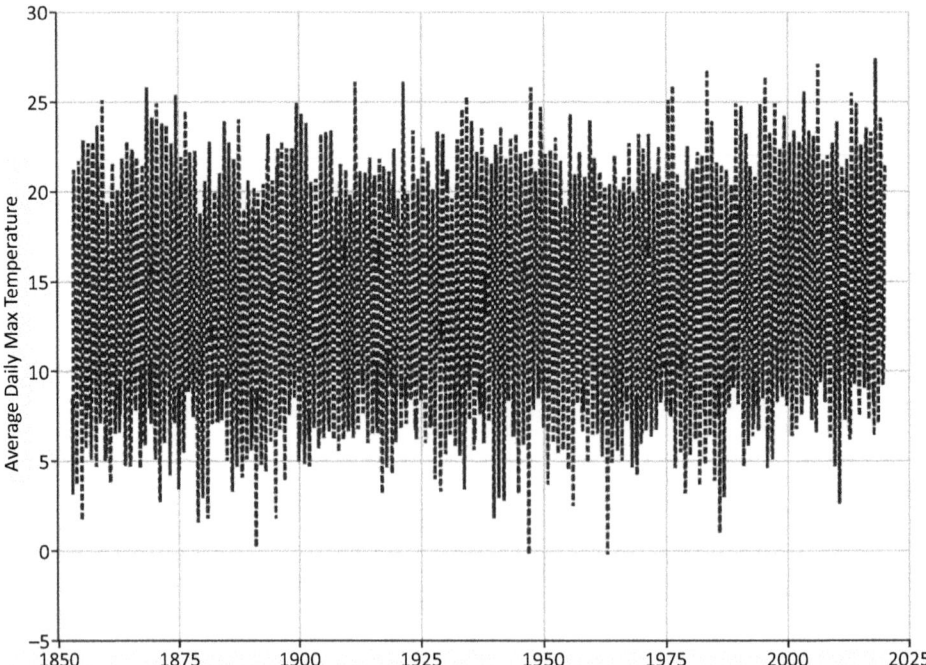

Figure 1.9 Oxford monthly average daily maximum temperature.

in 2019. This series was converted to a regular 52-week year by dividing the 53rd week between week 52 and week 1 of the following year. Modelling and forecasting mortality is important for insurance companies and public health bodies, not to mention funeral homes. There is a clear seasonality in this data since deaths are higher in the winter than in the summer. Demographers typically work with disaggregated (by age and sex) series and model these curves separately. For annual mortality, Denton *et al.* (2005) used an AR(2) process for the growth rate of Canada data from 1926 to 2000, see Chapter 3.

The next series, Figure 1.13. is of historical interest. It is data collected by John Arbuthnot on the annual number of boy and girl live births in London from 1629 to 1710, the dataset `Arbuthnot`. There appears to be first a downward trend between 1640 and 1660, which was the period of Oliver Cromwell and the Puritans, and a further, smaller, dip around 1665, caused by the Black Death, and then an upward trend in these raw numbers due to the expansion of the population of this city during the latter half of the century. The question Arbuthnot addressed was whether boys were more likely to be live-born than girls. He reported that for all 82 years there were more boys born than girls. We naturally think that the ratio should be 1, that is, boys and girls are equally likely, which we can think of as the null hypothesis. What is the probability that when you toss a coin you get heads 82 times in a row? This is $(1/2)^{82}$, which is a very small number (25 zeros). He concluded from this that boys are more likely to be born alive than girls. Can we say more? We plot in Figure 1.14 the ratio of boys to girls for each year. The ratio does not seem to have such a strong trend, but perhaps there are cycles in the ratio and short-term trends.

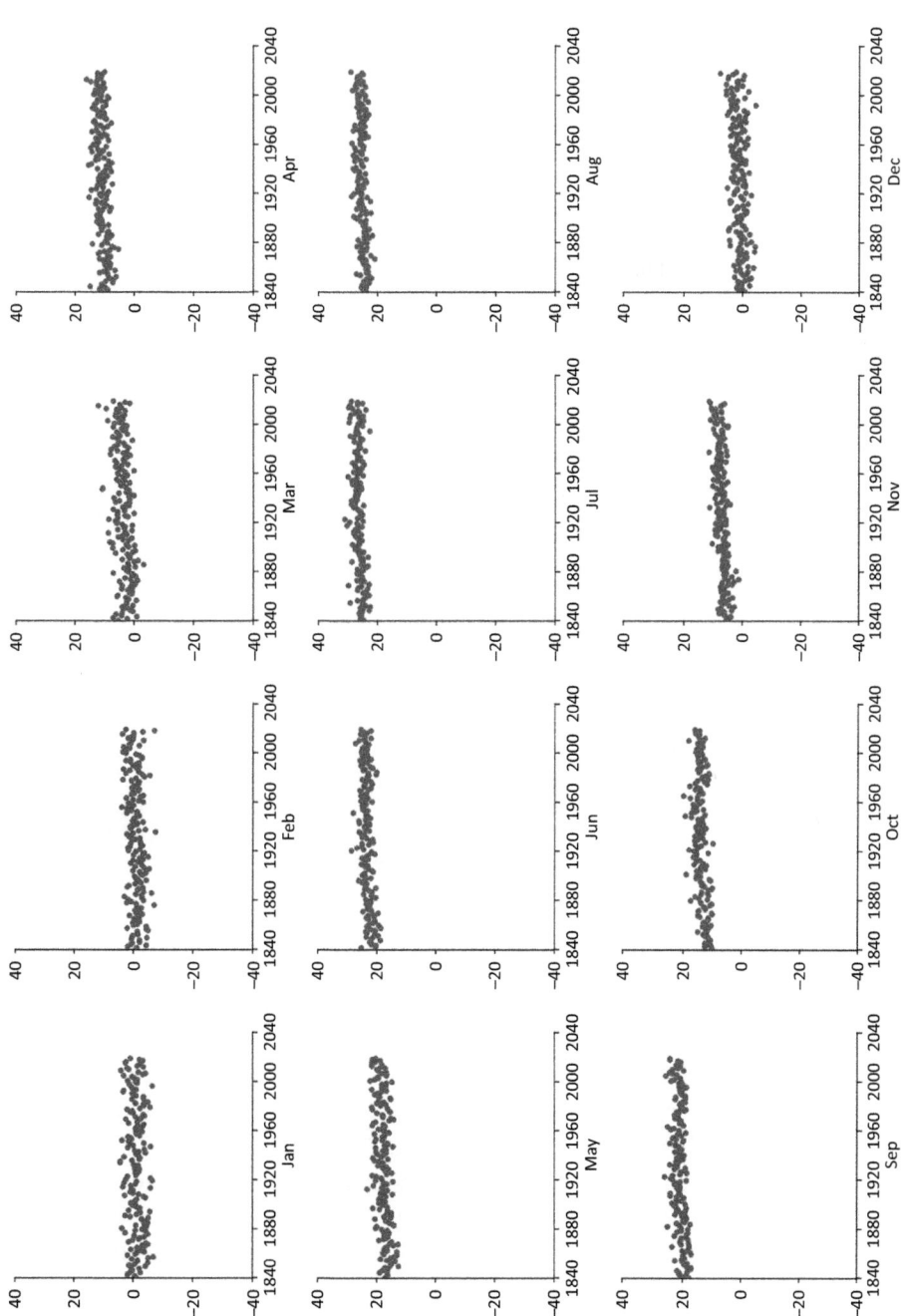

Figure 1.10 Toronto monthly average daily maximum time series by month.

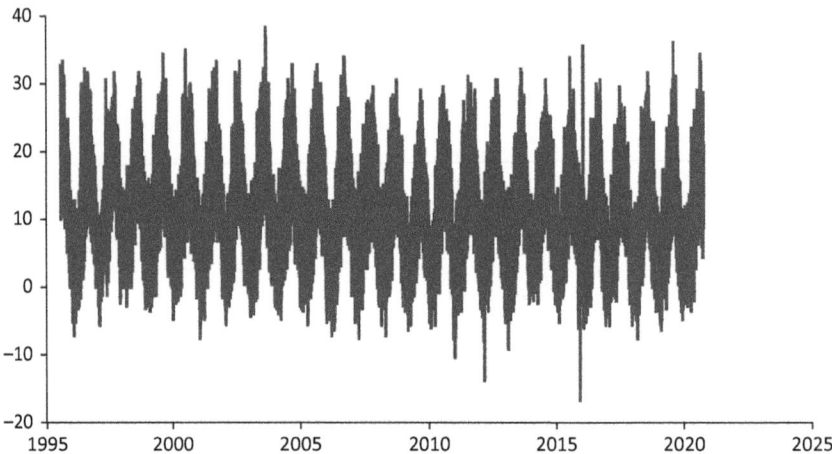

Figure 1.11 Cambridge half-hourly temperature.

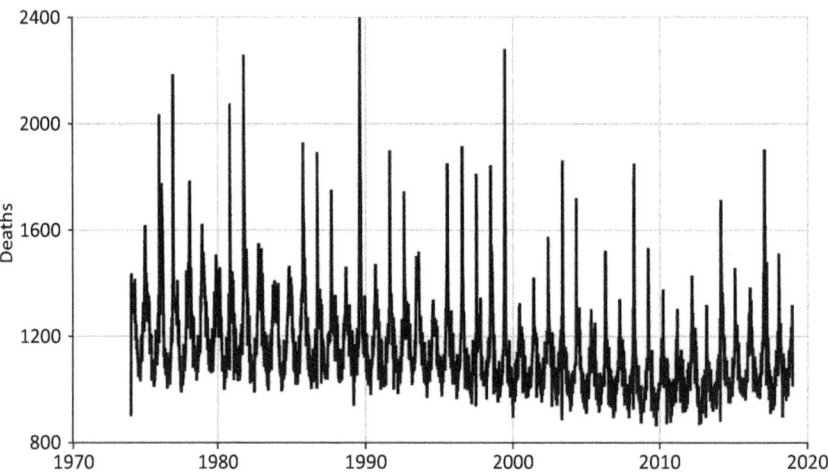

Figure 1.12 Weekly Scottish mortality, 1974–2019.

Finally, Figure 1.15 shows the daily number of new cases of COVID-19 reported in the UK during the first half of 2020, extracted from the dataset Covid19. This series has an unusual trend structure as it goes up, down, and up again; in both cases locally there is a strong trend. There is clearly a time series structure to this data as the number of new cases reported on a given day can be expected to depend on how many people were infected at the time, which itself depends on the recent numbers of new cases.

Where does economics come in? Economic theory typically involves solving some optimization problem defined by preferences, choices, information, and beliefs. This usually delivers some conditional moment restrictions that the data should satisfy. For example, the efficient markets theory says that stock returns should be unpredictable based on past information relative to a risk premium. This a fortiori suggests that stock returns should not have a seasonal component. But wait, if one is working with daily closing stock price data, then there are typically no transactions over the weekend,

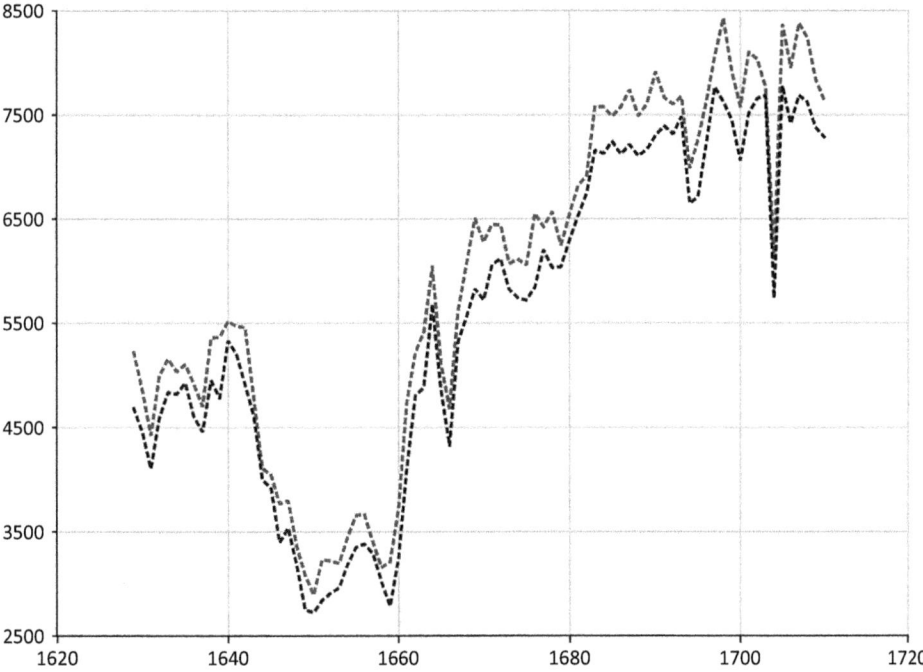

Figure 1.13 Arbuthnot data on annual live births in London.

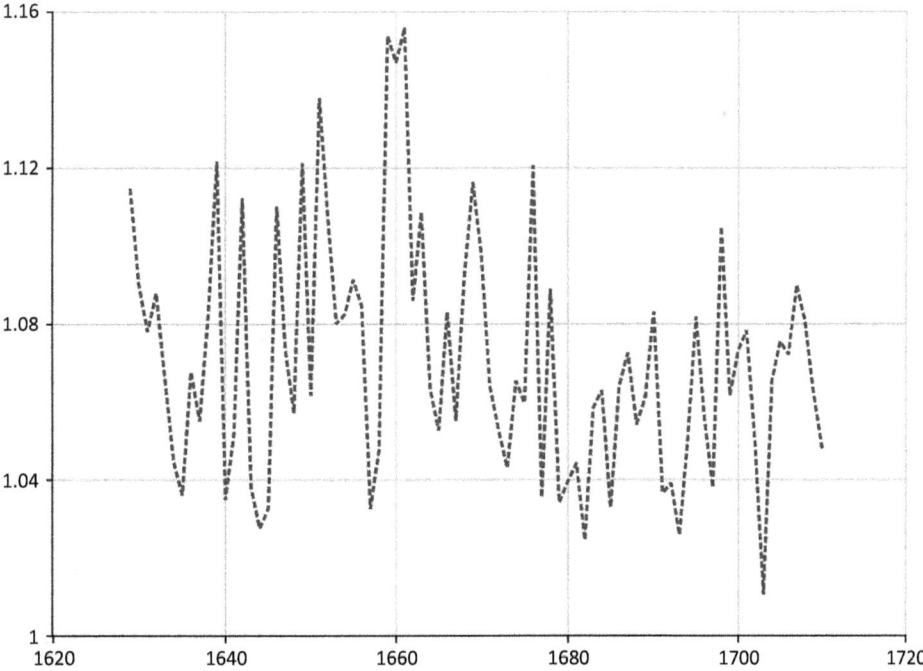

Figure 1.14 Arbuthnot's sex ratio.

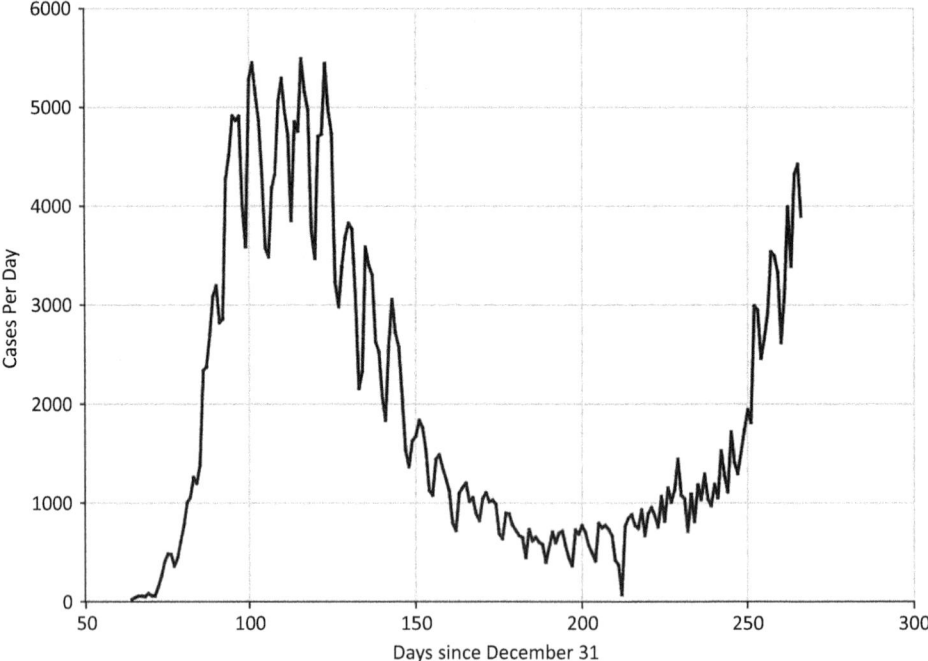

Figure 1.15 United Kingdom daily new COVID-19 cases.

so that the Monday return should be different from the Tuesday return. Furthermore, there are a number of public holidays, many of which in the USA fall on a Monday. There are also some irregular closing events such as Wednesdays during 1967 (the paperwork crisis) and the week after 9/11. The same applies to the monthly T-bill series, which is also traded on a five-day week (the COVID data, on the other hand, is collected on a seven-day week). In that case, there is the further issue that the contract it represents is of monthly duration, so the daily variation in the rate should be small. Many macroeconomic series, such as the monthly unemployment rate, are commonly presented after seasonal adjustment as the seasonal variation itself is not of primary interest; rather, the long-term trend and business-cycle variation is the focus. We will discuss common methods of delivering seasonally adjusted data. The trend is of great interest to macroeconomists, and the type of trend model adopted can make a big difference in terms of the implications of the effects of various shocks in the system.

For many series, the natural way to eliminate the trend is to work with the rate of growth. For example, stock prices may trend upwards over the long term but the rate of return is relatively stable over time. In this case the rate of return, that is, the growth rate of prices (plus perhaps some income payments), is the natural object of interest for investors who buy with a view to selling in the future. Likewise, consumption growth and GDP growth are natural objects of interest to macroeconomists. The growth rate is often defined using the "continuously compounded" growth rate, which corresponds to differencing the logarithm of the positive series, that is, we work with $y_t - y_{t-1}$, where y_t is the logarithm of the raw series. There are some cases where first-differencing fails, such as the COVID-19 data series. The first difference of that series still shows a typical nonstationarity. In this case we may need to take second or even higher-order differences to induce stationarity or closer to stationarity-like behavior. In that particular data series, differencing the data does not seem like the best solution.

One way of capturing the trend is to take the smooth moving average (SMA) "filter."[2] That is, let

$$\widehat{T}_t = \sum_{s=-k}^{k} w_s y_{t-s}, \quad t = 1, 2, \ldots, \tag{1.2}$$

where w_s, $s = -k, \ldots, k$, are weights. In many applications we may work with one-sided equal-weighted moving averages so that $w_s = 0$, $s < 0$, and $w_s = 1/(k+1)$, $s > 0$. For example, the so-called Bollinger bands work with the 20-day moving average ($k = 19$) of stock prices or exchange rates. As another example, in analyzing COVID-19 data it has been common practice to work with the seven-day moving average of new cases or new deaths, because this eliminates the day-of-the-week effect. Another special case corresponds to the differencing filter, that is, $w_0 = 1$, $w_d = -1$, and all other weights equal to zero. In both cases, the intention is that the residual $y_t - \widehat{T}_t$ be absent a trend. In financial applications, the trend is used as a guide to trading activity, where the trend represents some better measure of true value. In macroeconomics, it is common to use something called the Hodrick–Prescott filter, which is a two-sided linear filter arrived at by some optimization problem. In this case, the detrended data is easier to analyze.

The components C and E in (1.1) are assumed to be stationary, and in Chapter 2 we define what we mean by stationarity and some other related concepts. We then move on to discuss the other components, and how to model, estimate, and test for them.

---

[2] Filter: to pass (a liquid, gas, light, or sound) through a device to remove unwanted material.

2   Stationarity and Mixing

We introduce the important concept of stationarity and the two main variations of this theme that are used in time series analysis, weak and strong stationarity. We also introduce the standard measures of dependence of a time series, the autocovariance function and the autocorrelation function, and the distinction between weakly and strongly dependent time series. We define the concept of mixing, which generalizes these notions and has more general applicability in theoretical analysis. We consider the estimation of the population mean and autocovariance and autocorrelation functions from a stretch of data.

2.1   Stationarity

We suppose that $\{y_t, t \in \mathcal{T}\}$, where $\mathcal{T}$ is a subset of $\mathbb{Z}$, is a sequence of random variables defined on the same outcome space (and called a stochastic process), for now $\mathbb{R}$. Usually $\mathcal{T} = \mathbb{Z}$ or $\mathbb{Z}_+$, but for some purposes we may allow other subsets. We discuss first some notions of stationarity that are important for how we generalize from a given finite sample of data to a broader population possibly involving future and past data. When we gather a sample of cross-sectional data from a population it is easy to imagine that we could have gathered a completely different sample from that population and our calculations are based on this hypothetical alternative sample. This type of argument is a little less convincing in the time series setting: we only observe one history in which the French Revolution did take place and Manchester City are the Premier League champions (at the time of writing), and it is hard to convince ourselves that an alternative history could have taken place, but this is exactly what the mathematical framework allows for. Under some conditions including stationarity it is possible to learn from a long time series the properties of the hypothetical population and therefore obviate the need to construct a time machine.

We work with two types of stationarity in this book: strong and weak.

Definition 2.1 (Strong stationarity)   The stochastic process $\{y_t, t \in \mathcal{T}\}$ is said to be strongly stationary if the vectors of random variables $(y_t, \ldots, y_{t+r})$ and $(y_{t+s}, \ldots, y_{t+s+r})$ have the same joint distribution for all $\{t, \ldots, t+r, t+s, \ldots t+s+r\} \subset \mathcal{T}$, that is,

$$\Pr(y_t \leq x_1, \ldots, y_{t+r} \leq x_r) = \Pr(y_{t+s} \leq x_1, \ldots, y_{t+s+r} \leq x_r)$$

for all $x_1, \ldots, x_r \in \mathbb{R}$, and in particular $\Pr(y_t \leq x) = \Pr(y_{t+s} \leq x)$ for all $x \in \mathbb{R}$ and $t, t+s \in \mathcal{T}$. Equivalently, if the joint characteristic functions satisfy

$$E\left[\exp\left(i\left(u_0 y_t + \cdots + u_r y_{t+r}\right)\right)\right] = E\left[\exp\left(i\left(u_0 y_{t+s} + \cdots + u_r y_{t+s+r}\right)\right)\right]$$

for all $u_j \in \mathbb{R}, j = 0, \ldots, r$, and all $\{t, \ldots, t+r, t+s, \ldots t+s+r\} \subset \mathcal{T}$, and in particular $E\left[\exp\left(iuy_t\right)\right] = E\left[\exp\left(iuy_{t+s}\right)\right]$ for all $u \in \mathbb{R}$ and $t, s \in \mathcal{T}$.

Definition 2.2 (Weak stationarity)   The stochastic process $\{y_t, t \in \mathcal{T}\}$, is said to be weakly stationary if the vectors $(y_t, \ldots, y_{t+r})$ and $(y_{t+s}, \ldots, y_{t+s+r})$ have the same mean vector and covariance matrix for all $\{t, \ldots, t+r, t+s, \ldots, t+s+r\} \subset \mathcal{T}$. In particular, the moments $E(y_t)$ and $E(y_t y_{t-j})$ exist for all $t, j \in \mathcal{T}$, and do not depend on the time t.

Strong stationarity (also called strict stationarity) is stronger than weak stationarity (also called second-order stationary), provided the process y_t has uniformly bounded second moments, that is, if y_t is strongly stationary and $E(y_t^2) \leq C < \infty$, then y_t is also weakly stationary.[1] In fact, if further moments exist such as $E(y_t^4) \leq C < \infty$, then moments such as $E(y_t y_{t-j} y_{t-k} y_{t-l})$ for a stationary process should not depend on t, only on j, k, l. However, in the absence of the second-moment condition these definitions are not strictly nested in the sense that a process may be strictly stationary but not weakly stationary. Indeed, for a strongly stationary process $\{y_t\}$ the process $\{\tau(y_t)\}$ is also strongly stationary for any transformation $\tau(\cdot)$ (called an instantaneous transformation[2]), whereas for a weakly stationary process $\{y_t\}$ the process $\{\tau(y_t)\}$ may or may not be weakly stationary depending on the transformation $\tau(\cdot)$ (some transformed random variables may not possess moments, for example $\tau(y_t) = \exp(\exp(y_t))$). Much of what we say is restricted to (weakly) stationary series, but in the last 40 years there have been major advances in the theory of nonlinear time series where weak stationarity is a less compelling concept and where strong stationarity is central. We discuss later some of the differences between weak and strong stationarity. For simplicity, we will mostly drop explicit reference to $\mathcal{T}$ from now on.

A set of random variables $\{y_1, \ldots, y_T\}$ is said to be **independent** if all the random variables are mutually independent, that is, for all subsets $\{y_{t_1}, \ldots, y_{t_r}\}$ thereof,

$$\Pr\left(y_{t_1} \leq x_1, \ldots, y_{t_r} \leq x_r\right) = \Pr\left(y_{t_1} \leq x_1\right) \times \cdots \times \Pr\left(y_{t_r} \leq x_r\right)$$

for all $x_1, \ldots, x_r \in \mathbb{R}$. This means a little more than just what is called pairwise independence (y_t independent of y_s), since we may have y_t independent of y_s and y_s independent of y_r and even y_t independent of y_r, but the triple $\{y_t, y_s, y_r\}$ not being mutually independent. We say that a sequence is **independent and identically distributed** (i.i.d.) if in addition each y_t has the same distribution; such sequences are necessarily stationary. If $\{y_t\}$ is an i.i.d. sequence, then $\{\tau(y_t)\}$ is an i.i.d. sequence. Furthermore, more general functions of i.i.d. random variables $\{y_t\}$ such as $x_t = \tau(y_t, y_{t-1}, \ldots, y_{t-p})$, for some

---

[1] Suppose that y_t has symmetric density function

$$f_t(x) = \frac{\Gamma(2\theta_t)}{\Gamma^2(\theta_t)\left(2\sqrt{2\theta_t + 1}\right)^{2\theta_t - 1}} \left(2\theta_t + 1 - x^2\right)^{\theta_t - 1}, \quad -\sqrt{2\theta_t + 1} \leq x \leq \sqrt{2\theta_t + 1},$$

which has mean zero and variance one for all $\theta_t > 0$. Here, $\Gamma(\cdot)$ is the Gamma function. Let y_t be an independent sequence of random variables with density f_t; then clearly y_t is weakly stationary but is not strongly stationary if $t \mapsto \theta_t$ is not constant.

[2] Technically, we should restrict attention to what are called measurable transformations, but I am not going to delineate this here.

$p < \infty$ and some $\tau(\cdot)$, are stationary. We consider next the classic examples of stationary processes that fall in this category.

Example 2.1 (Gaussian process)   A process $\{y_t, t \in \mathcal{T}\}$ is Gaussian if for any vector $(y_{t_1}, \ldots, y_{t_k})^\mathsf{T}$ (evaluated at times $t_1, \ldots, t_k \in \mathcal{T}$) the distribution is Gaussian with mean vector $(\mu_1, \ldots, \mu_k)^\mathsf{T}$ and $k \times k$ covariance matrix Σ. If, for all k, $(\mu_1, \ldots, \mu_k)^\mathsf{T} = (\mu, \ldots, \mu)^\mathsf{T}$ and the i, j element of Σ satisfies $E(y_{t_i} y_{t_j}) = f(|t_i - t_j|)$ for some function $f: \mathbb{Z} \to \mathbb{R}$, then the process y_t is stationary, both in the weak sense and in the strong sense (because a Gaussian process is uniquely determined by its mean vector and covariance matrix).

Example 2.2   Suppose that $y_t = a \cos(\theta t) + b \sin(\theta t)$, where a and b are mean-zero and unit-variance random variables that are mutually independent. At first glance this process varies over time. However, we see that $E(y_t) = 0$, $\mathrm{var}(y_t) = 1$, and, using the properties of trigonometric functions,

$$
\begin{aligned}
E(y_t y_{t+k}) &= E\left[(a \cos(\theta t) + b \sin(\theta t))(a \cos(\theta(t+k)) + b \sin(\theta(t+k)))\right] \\
&= \cos(\theta t) \cos(\theta(t+k)) + \sin(\theta t) \sin(\theta(t+k)) \\
&= \cos(\theta k).
\end{aligned}
$$

It follows that y_t is weakly stationary. If a and b are Gaussian (normally distributed), then y_t is also Gaussian and so strongly stationary because for Gaussian processes weak and strong stationarity coincide. Specifically, we can show that $E\left[\exp\left(\mathrm{i}\left(u_0 y_t + \cdots + u_r y_{t+r}\right)\right)\right]$ does not depend on t. On the other hand, if a and b are independent standard Cauchy random variables, then

$$
E\left(\exp\left(\mathrm{i} u y_t\right)\right) = \exp\left(-|u|\left(|\cos(\theta t)| + |\sin(\theta t)|\right)\right),
$$

which varies with t unless $\theta = 0$. Of course, for this process the mean and variance are not even well defined so the process is neither weakly nor strongly stationary, except in the trivial case that $\theta = 0$. If a and b were standard Laplace random variables (for which the mean and variance do exist),

$$
E\left(\exp\left(\mathrm{i} u y_t\right)\right) = \frac{1}{1 + u^2 \cos^2(\theta t)} \frac{1}{1 + u^2 \sin^2(\theta t)} = \frac{1}{1 + u^2 + u^4 \sin^2(2\theta t)},
$$

which varies with t unless $\theta = 0$. In this case, the process would be weakly stationary but not strongly stationary.

For a strongly stationary process we may imagine that time runs from $-\infty$ to plus ∞, which allows us to avoid the issue of initialization. On the other hand, suppose that the process starts at time 0 with some **initial condition** y_0. If we assume that the value y_0 was a random variable that was drawn from the stationary distribution rather than being some fixed number, then we can show that the subsequent process $\{y_1, y_2, \ldots\}$ is stationary. Suppose instead that the initialization at time 0 is arbitrary, then in general the subsequent process $\{y_1, y_2, \ldots\}$ will not satisfy the definition of stationarity. However, it may be that this process converges in some well-defined sense to a stationary limit, in which case we say that the process is **asymptotically stationary**. That is, after a long time the process behaves as if it were a stationary process. In some contexts the choice of initialization matters, and in some cases it does not.

There are many different ways in which a time series y_t can be nonstationary. For example, there may be deterministic trends or fixed seasonal effects. There may be a periodic type of movement in the time series but no systematic upward or downward trend, so the type of nonstationarity can be thought of as mild. In other cases, the process could be so nonstationary that the standard tools have to be changed to yield an analysis. We will cover in subsequent chapters different types of nonstationary processes.

2.2   Dependence

Dependence is the notion that the random values of a process at some time t may depend in some sense on the random values of the process at some other time s. One measure of dependence is given by the covariance between the random variable at time t and the random variable at time s:

$$\gamma(t,s) = \operatorname{cov}(y_t, y_s) = E\left((y_t - E(y_t))\,(y_s - E(y_s))\right) = E\left(y_t y_s\right) - E(y_t)E(y_s), \quad (2.1)$$

which is called the **autocovariance** function. The autocovariance function is well defined provided $E(y_t^2) \leq C < \infty$ for all t. The autocovariance can be positive or negative or zero. Positive autocovariance can be interpreted as a tendency for subsequent values of the process to be positively related to the current value; large positive current values mean that the value of the process next period is likely to be large and positive. If y_t, y_s are independent random variables, then $\operatorname{cov}(y_t, y_s) = 0$, but not vice versa – independence is a stronger property than uncorrelatedness (except for Gaussian processes where these concepts coincide). The autocovariance function focuses on certain types of departures from independence and does not address others. Furthermore, the autocovariance is strongly affected by transformations, so we may have $\operatorname{cov}(y_t, y_s) = 0$ for all $t \neq s$, but $\operatorname{cov}(\tau(y_t), \tau(y_s)) \neq 0$ for all $t \neq s$ for some transformation $\tau(\cdot)$. Finally, the autocovariance measure is inherently a pairwise measure that is trying to capture pairwise relationships, and will not capture three-way relationships between y_t, y_s, and y_r, say.

For a stationary process, $E(y_t) = E(y_s)$ for all t, s, and the autocovariance function depends only on the time difference between t and s. In this case we may define the autocovariance function (also called the covariogram) and the **autocorrelation** function (also called the correlogram or ACF) as

$$\operatorname{cov}(y_t, y_{t-k}) = \gamma(k); \quad \rho(k) = \frac{\gamma(k)}{\gamma(0)}, \quad (2.2)$$

where y_{t-k} is the kth lag of y_t. These functions are defined for all integers $k = 0, \pm 1, \ldots$; both are **even** functions, that is, $\gamma(k) = \gamma(-k)$ and $\rho(k) = \rho(-k)$. This is because $\operatorname{cov}(y_t, y_{t-k}) = \gamma(k)$ for all t, so if we let $t \mapsto t+k$, this says that $\operatorname{cov}(y_t, y_{t+k}) = \gamma(k)$. The autocovariance function satisfies $|\gamma(k)| \leq \gamma(0)$ for all k, and hence $|\rho(k)| \leq \rho(0) = 1$. This follows by the **Cauchy–Schwarz** inequality. The functions $\gamma(\cdot)$ and $\rho(\cdot)$ are positive semidefinite in the sense that $\sum \sum_{i,j=1}^{k} \gamma(i-j)a_i a_j \geq 0$ for all vectors $a = (a_1, \ldots, a_k)^{\mathsf{T}}$

for any positive integer k. This is because $\sum\sum_{i,j=1}^{k} \gamma(i-j)a_i a_j = \text{var}\left(\sum_{j=1}^{k} a_j y_{t-j}\right)$, and a variance must be nonnegative. This property implies restrictions on the set of allowable $\gamma(\cdot)$, $\rho(\cdot)$; not all functions with $\rho(0) = 1$ and $|\rho(s)| \leq 1$ are valid autocorrelation functions.

In the stationary case we may define the $T \times T$ autocovariance matrix as

$$\Gamma_T = E\left[(y - E(y))(y - E(y))^\mathsf{T}\right] = \begin{pmatrix} \gamma(0) & \gamma(1) & \cdots & \gamma(T-1) \\ \gamma(1) & \gamma(0) & \ddots & \vdots \\ \vdots & \ddots & \ddots & \gamma(1) \\ \gamma(T-1) & \cdots & \gamma(1) & \gamma(0) \end{pmatrix}, \quad (2.3)$$

where $y = (y_1, \ldots, y_T)^\mathsf{T}$. The autocovariance matrix has a special structure called **Toeplitz**, that is, the matrix entries are constant along diagonals. In fact, we can write $\Gamma_T = \sum_{j=0}^{T-1} \gamma(j)\Delta_j$, where Δ_j are symmetric $T \times T$ matrices containing ones on the jth upper and lower diagonals and zeros elsewhere, with $\Delta_0 = I_T$. Likewise, the correlation matrix R_T is Toeplitz, where this matrix is defined as

$$R_T = \text{diag}\{\Gamma_T\}^{-1/2}\Gamma_T \text{diag}\{\Gamma_T\}^{-1/2} = \begin{pmatrix} 1 & \rho(1) & \cdots & \rho(T-1) \\ \rho(1) & 1 & \ddots & \vdots \\ \vdots & \ddots & \ddots & \rho(1) \\ \rho(T-1) & \cdots & \rho(1) & 1 \end{pmatrix}.$$

In this case $R_T = \sum_{j=0}^{T-1} \rho(j)\Delta_j$ for the same matrices Δ_j. One also encounters the notation that $\Gamma_T = \text{Toeplitz}(\gamma(0), \ldots, \gamma(T-1))$ and $R_T = \text{Toeplitz}(1, \rho(1) \ldots, \rho(T-1))$. The matrices R_T and Γ_T must be positive semidefinite for all T, meaning that $a^\mathsf{T}\Gamma_T a \geq 0$ for all vectors $a \in \mathbb{R}^T$.

The autocorrelation function can be interpreted as the slope of the **best linear predictor** (BLP) of y_t by its lag y_{t-j}, that is, we have, for any second-order stationary process and for any j,

$$E_\text{L}(y_t \mid y_{t-j}) = \alpha_j + \beta_j y_{t-j} = E(y_{t-j}) + \beta_j\left(y_{t-j} - E(y_{t-j})\right),$$

where $E_\text{L}(\cdot)$ denotes the best linear prediction and

$$\beta_j = \frac{\text{cov}(y_t, y_{t-j})}{\text{var}(y_{t-j})} = \frac{\text{cov}(y_t, y_{t-j})}{\sqrt{\text{var}(y_t)\text{var}(y_{t-j})}} = \rho(j),$$

while $\alpha_j = E(y_{t-j})(1 - \beta_j)$ and, by construction, $\text{cov}(y_t - \alpha_j - \beta_j y_{t-j}, y_{t-j}) = 0$. This says that if you are about predicting y_t and you restrict attention to linear functions of y_{t-j}, then $\rho(j)$ is the slope of that linear regression; furthermore, $\rho(j)^2$ is the R^2 of that regression so that provided $\rho(j) \neq 0$ there is some predictability. Because the slope of this regression is less than one in magnitude, we can see that there is a return toward the mean phenomenon, that is, $|E_\text{L}(y_t \mid y_{t-j}) - E(y_{t-j})| \leq |y_{t-j} - E(y_{t-j})|$.

The **partial autocorrelation** function (PACF) $\pi(j)$ represents the correlation between y_t and y_{t-j} after conditioning on or adjusting for the intermediate values $y_{t-1}, \ldots y_{t-j+1}$. Specifically, we may define $\pi(j) = \text{corr}(e_{t;1:j-1}, e_{t-j;1:j-1})$ where $e_{t;1:j-1}$ is the residual from the regression of y_t on $y_{t-1}, \ldots, y_{t-j+1}$. In other words, we may form the best linear prediction of y_t given $y_{t-1}, \ldots, y_{t-j}$,

$$E_{\mathrm{L}}(y_t \mid y_{t-1}, \ldots, y_{t-j}) = \alpha_{j,1} + \beta_{j,1} y_{t-1} + \cdots + \beta_{j,j} y_{t-j},$$

in which $\pi(j) = \beta_{j,j}, j = 1, 2, \ldots$, which in turn can be expressed as $\beta_{j,j} = e_j^{\mathsf{T}} \Gamma_j^{-1} \gamma_j$, where $\gamma_j = (\gamma(1), \ldots, \gamma(j))^{\mathsf{T}}$ and $e_j = (0, \ldots, 0, 1)^{\mathsf{T}}$ are $j \times 1$ vectors, and Γ_j is defined in (2.3).[3] The Durbin–Levinson algorithm is a common method for computing the partial autocorrelation recursively. Specifically, we have $\pi(0) = 1$, $\pi(1) = \rho(1)$, and then, for $j = 2, 3, \ldots$,

$$\pi(j) = \phi_{j,j} = \frac{\rho(j) - \sum_{k=1}^{j-1} \phi_{j-1,k} \rho(j-k)}{1 - \sum_{k=1}^{j-1} \phi_{j-1,k} \rho(k)},$$

$$\phi_{j,k} = \phi_{j-1,k} - \phi_{j,j} \phi_{j-1,j-k}, \quad k = 1, \ldots, j-1.$$

For i.i.d. series, $\gamma(j) = \rho(j) = \pi(j) = 0$ for all $j \neq 0$, while for positively (negatively) dependent series $\gamma(j), \rho(j) > (<) 0$. Economics data often appear to come from positively dependent series, but some series such as individual stock returns may have negative dependence for some horizons. We can relate the autocovariance to the probability that a process "continues in the same direction." For a zero-mean Gaussian process the probability of continuation at horizon k can be calculated exactly, it is

$$\Pr(y_t > 0, y_{t+j} > 0) + \Pr(y_t < 0, y_{t+j} < 0) = \frac{1}{2} + \frac{1}{\pi} \arcsin(\rho(j)),$$

where the arcsin function is increasing on $[-1, 1]$ and $\arcsin(0) = 0$. Therefore, for positive $\rho(j)$, the continuation probability is greater than 1/2 and the reversal probability is therefore less than 1/2.

For any stationary process with finite variance we can define the standardized process

$$z_t = \frac{y_t - E(y_t)}{\mathrm{stdev}(y_t)}, \tag{2.4}$$

which is mean zero and has variance one by construction. We then have $\rho_y(j) = E(z_t z_{t-j})$; the autocorrelation function of y_t is the autocovariance of the standardized process z_t. In earlier statistics courses one would call this the z-score of the random variable y_t, since under Gaussianity this random variable would be distributed as $N(0, 1)$.

The mean and the autocovariance constitute the second-order properties of the process y_t, hence the term second-order stationary. Such processes are defined by their mean and the sequence $\gamma_y(0), \gamma_y(1), \gamma_y(2), \ldots$ Many processes of interest will satisfy that $\gamma_y(j) \to 0$ as $j \to \infty$, which says that the covariance between the distant past and the present is small. The rate at which this decay occurs may also be of importance, and a key threshold is whether the limit

$$\lim_{n \to \infty} \sum_{j=-n}^{n} |\gamma_y(j)| = \sum_{j=-\infty}^{\infty} |\gamma_y(j)| \tag{2.5}$$

---

[3] Note that in general the conditional expectation $E(y_t \mid y_{t-j})$ is not equal to $E_{\mathrm{L}}(y_t \mid y_{t-j})$, except for example when y_t is Gaussian, and likewise $E(y_t \mid y_{t-1}, \ldots, y_{t-j})$ is not equal to $E_{\mathrm{L}}(y_t \mid y_{t-1}, \ldots, y_{t-j})$.

exists and is finite; if it does, the limit itself is called the long-run variance of the process, and is denoted by lrvar(y_t). For example, if $\gamma_y(j) = c(j) \times j^{-\alpha}$, where $|c(j)| \leq C$ and $\alpha > 1$, then $\gamma_y(j)$ satisfies (2.5). On the other hand, if $\alpha \leq 1$, then the limit does not exist and the process is said to be strongly not weakly dependent.

2.2.1   Mixing

A stochastic process is mixing if it is asymptotically independent, that is, if the mutual dependence declines as the time horizon increases. The mixing property is needed for the statistical inference question as it is a key condition for central limit theorems for sample means, autocovariances, autocorrelations, and other quantities (Herrndorf, 1984). For a Gaussian process, uncorrelatedness implies independence and hence it suffices that a condition such as (2.5) holds, but this is not the case for non-Gaussian processes such as arise in the presence of some nonlinearity or heteroskedasticity. In general the autocovariance conditions like (2.5) are necessary for mixing but by themselves are insufficient, which is why we may need to measure the dependence of a stochastic process in a more general way than autocovariance. This is more advanced material and may be avoided at first glance. Mixing can be defined in different ways.

Definition 2.3 (Wide-sense mixing)   A stationary stochastic process $\{y_t, t = 0, \pm 1, \ldots\}$ is said to be wide-sense mixing if $E\left(y_t^2\right) < \infty$ and

$$\lim_{k \to \infty} E\left(y_{t+k} - E(y_{t+k} \mid y_t, y_{t-1}, \ldots)\right)^2 = E\left(y_t - E(y_t)\right)^2 = \mathrm{var}\left(y_t\right).$$

That is, the prediction of future values approaches the unconditional prediction $E(y_t)$. For a stationary Gaussian process, the conditional expectation is linear and this statement can be related to the autocovariance function, specifically, that $\mathrm{cov}\left(y_t, y_{t-k}\right) \to 0$ as $k \to \infty$. This condition is in Yaglom (1965).

Definition 2.4 (Covariance mixing)   A stochastic process $\{y_t, t = 0, \pm 1, \ldots\}$ is said to be covariance mixing (ρ-mixing) if

$$|\mathrm{cov}(x_t, z_{t+k})| \leq \rho(k) \to 0 \quad \text{as } k \to \infty$$

for all processes x_t with $E(x_t^2) \leq C$ that are generated by (expressed as functions of) y_t and its past, and processes z_{t+k} with $E(z_t^2) \leq C$ that are generated by y_{t+k} and its future. In particular, for a stationary process this implies that $\mathrm{cov}(f(y_0), g(y_k)) \to 0$ as $k \to \infty$ for any bounded functions f, g.

If y_t is covariance mixing then perforce $\mathrm{cov}(y_t, y_{t+j}) \to 0$ as $j \to \infty$, but this also implies, for example, that $\mathrm{cov}(|y_t|, |y_{t+j}|) \to 0$ as $j \to \infty$. This says that the dependence (as measured by the covariance) on the past shrinks with horizon. This is an important property that is possessed by many models.

The covariance mixing (or ρ-mixing) property is only well defined for processes with finite variance. Some commonly used nonlinear processes (GARCH – see Section 10.3) do not necessarily possess an unconditional variance and so we need some other notions of dependence for this case.

Definition 2.5 (Strong mixing)   A stochastic process $\{y_t, \ t = 0, \pm 1, \ldots\}$ is said to be strong mixing (or α-mixing) if

$$\alpha(k) = \sup_{n \in \mathbb{N}} \sup_{A \in \mathcal{F}^n_{-\infty}, B \in \mathcal{F}^\infty_{n+k}} |\Pr(A \cap B) - \Pr(A)\Pr(B)| \to 0 \qquad (2.6)$$

as $k \to \infty$, where $\mathcal{F}^n_{-\infty}$ and $\mathcal{F}^\infty_{n+k}$ are two sigma-fields,[4] generated by $\{y_t, \ t \le n\}$ and $\{y_t, \ t \ge n + k\}$, respectively. We call $\alpha(k)$ the mixing coefficient. If the process is stationary, the first supremum is redundant. In particular, the condition (2.6) implies that uniformly over $y, y' \in \mathbb{R}$ we have, as $k \to \infty$,

$$|\Pr(y_{t+k} \le y, y_t \le y') - \Pr(y_{t+k} \le y)\Pr(y_t \le y')| \le \alpha(k) \to 0.$$

Definition 2.6 (β-mixing)   A stochastic process $\{y_t, \ t = 0, \pm 1, \ldots\}$ is said to be β-mixing if

$$\beta(k) = \sup_{n \in \mathbb{N}} \sup_{A \in \mathcal{F}^n_{-\infty}, \Pr(A) > 0, B \in \mathcal{F}^\infty_{n+k}} |\Pr(B \mid A) - \Pr(B)| \to 0$$

as $k \to \infty$. We call $\beta(k)$ the mixing coefficient. If the process is stationary, the first supremum is redundant. In particular, this implies that for any y, y' we have, as $k \to \infty$,

$$|\Pr(y_{t+k} \le y \mid y_t \le y') - \Pr(y_{t+k} \le y)| \le \beta(k) \to 0.$$

Nonstationary processes may be mixing, which is why we include the outer supremum over n in the above definitions, or they may be nonmixing, it depends on the type of nonstationarity. The mixing quantities measure the discrepancy from the benchmark independent case of certain probabilities. For independent series recall that $\Pr(A \cap B) = \Pr(A)\Pr(B)$ and $\Pr(B \mid A) = \Pr(B)$ for all events A, B, so that $\alpha(k) = \beta(k) = \gamma(k) = 0$ for all k, that is, the process is trivially mixing. For nonindependent events, $\Pr(A \cap B) \ne \Pr(A)\Pr(B)$ and $\Pr(B \mid A) \ne \Pr(B)$.

Example 2.3   An example of a non-mixing process is $y_t = \varepsilon, t = 0, \pm 1, \pm 2, \ldots$ for some random variable ε. This process is stationary, but y_t and y_s are perfectly dependent for any t, s and so definitely not mixing. In this case $\Pr(y_t \le y, y_s \le y') = \Pr(\varepsilon \le \max\{y, y'\})$. Andrews (1984) gives a nontrivial example of a process that is not strong mixing.

For general processes, $\alpha(k)$ and $\beta(k)$ are not exactly zero and they measure the magnitude of the departure from independence at the horizon k; the mixing condition requires that this magnitude declines with horizon. There are some well-known relations between different mixing concepts. We have $2\alpha(k) \le \beta(k)$ and $\alpha(k) \le \rho(k)$ (Doukhan, 1994) so that β-mixing implies strong mixing but not vice versa. If the process y_t is Gaussian, we additionally have $\alpha(k) \le \rho(k) \le 2\pi\alpha(k)$. All three measures of mixing are invariant under instantaneous transformations, that is, if $\{y_t\}$ is mixing, then $\{\tau(y_t)\}$ is mixing (with the same rate) for any transformation $\tau(\cdot)$. Indeed, $\{\tau(y_t, \ldots, y_{t-p})\}$ is also mixing for any finite p.

---

[4] A sigma-field is just a collection of events (that satisfies certain properties) upon which probability can be defined; see Davidson (1994) for a proper definition.

The rate at which the mixing coefficients decay (as $k \to \infty$) is important for the application of laws of large numbers (LLNs) and central limit theorems (CLTs). **Weakly dependent** series have $\alpha(k)$ (or $\beta(k)$ or $\rho(k)$) decay fast enough with k such that, for example, $\sum_{k=1}^{\infty} \alpha(k) < \infty$. For example, $\alpha(k) = ck^{-\alpha}$ for some positive c satisfies this definition when $\alpha > 1$ but fails when $\alpha \leq 1$. Andrews (1984) gives a simple example of a process whose autocorrelation function decays rapidly but is not α-mixing.

To try to make mixing a more friendly concept, various authors have alluded to the example of a cocktail such as the Manhattan (two ounces rye whiskey, one ounce sweet vermouth, two dashes Angostura bitters), which involves mixing quite different ingredients by stirring and shaking to blend them perfectly using a swizzle stick. The idea is that the perfect cocktail should be well mixed.

Mixing is related to **ergodicity**, which is about the equivalence of time average and space average, whereby for functions f,

$$\lim_{T \to \infty} \frac{1}{T} \sum_{t=1}^{T} f(t, \omega) = \int f(t, \omega) \, dP(\omega), \qquad (2.7)$$

where P is a probability measure. You might recognize this as a law of large numbers. Peters (2019) argues that "the prevailing formulations of economic theory – expected utility theory and its descendants – make an indiscriminate assumption of ergodicity."

Davidson (1994) discusses mixing processes in detail, and also generalizations such as near-epoch dependence, mixingales, and so on.

2.2.2   Common Classes of Processes

Definition 2.7   A **Markov process** y_t is a process for which the future is independent of the past given the present, for example, y_{t+1} is independent of y_{t-1} given y_t.

This is an important property in many areas of time series: autoregressive processes and diffusion processes are two leading examples of Markov processes. A Markov process may or may not be mixing, since the independence here is after conditioning whereas the mixing property is unconditional.

Definition 2.8   A **martingale** is a process y_t such that $E(|y_t|) \leq C < \infty$ and, with probability one, $E(y_{t+1} \mid y_t, y_{t-1}, \ldots) = y_t$. Note that by the **law of iterated expectation**, $E(y_{t+k} \mid y_t, y_{t-1}, \ldots) = y_t$ for any $k \geq 1$.

Hall (1978) argued that aggregate consumption is a martingale under the assumption that a representative agent has quadratic utility. Fama (1970) argued that stock prices are martingales after adjusting for risk. A Markov process may be a martingale or not, and vice versa.

A common framework for modelling is that $y_t = f(\varepsilon_t, \varepsilon_{t-1}, \ldots)$, where f is some mapping and ε_t are random variables. In macroeconomics the ε_t are called **shocks**, perhaps caused by policy changes or by unanticipated events, whereas in finance this terminology is less common but ε_t represents new information about, say, the stock price. The usual starting point is that ε_t are i.i.d. with mean zero and variance σ^2. This will be our principal assumption for shocks, and combined with conditions on f will deliver the properties of y_t such as stationarity and mixing.

Any random process of the form $y_t = f(\varepsilon_t, \varepsilon_{t-1}, \ldots, \varepsilon_{t-p})$ for some finite p, function f, and i.i.d. shocks ε_t is both stationary and mixing because for any $k > p$, y_t and y_{t-k} are independent and $\alpha(k) = 0$. When p is infinite, this is not necessarily the case and the answers will depend on the form of f. We next consider an important class of functions f for the $p = \infty$ case.

Definition 2.9   A **linear process** y_t satisfies

$$y_t = \mu + \sum_{j=0}^{\infty} \omega_j \varepsilon_{t-j}, \tag{2.8}$$

where $\sum_{j=0}^{\infty} |\omega_j| < \infty$, while the ε_t are i.i.d. with $E(\varepsilon_t) = 0$ and $\mathrm{var}(\varepsilon_t) = \sigma_\varepsilon^2$.

A linear process defined in this way is second-order stationary and weakly dependent with $\mathrm{var}(y_t) = \sigma_\varepsilon^2 \sum_{j=0}^{\infty} \omega_j^2 < \infty$ and $\gamma_y(k) = \sigma_\varepsilon^2 \sum_{j=0}^{\infty} \omega_j \omega_{j+k}$, which satisfies $\sum_{k=0}^{\infty} |\gamma_y(k)| < \infty$. Under some further conditions on the error distribution the process is strong mixing, although this property is not needed for inference since CLTs are satisfied for linear processes by direct arguments without invoking Herrndorf's result. If ε_t are also Gaussian, that is, $\varepsilon_t \sim N(0, \sigma^2)$, then y_t as defined in (2.8) is also Gaussian. In fact, if y_t is a Gaussian process as defined above then there exists a sequence of $\varepsilon_t \sim N(0, \sigma^2)$ such that (2.8) holds.

We also consider other, weaker, conditions on ε_t.

Definition 2.10   A **white noise** (WN) process is a process $\{\varepsilon_t\}$ that satisfies $E(\varepsilon_t) = 0$ and $E(\varepsilon_t^2) \leq C < \infty$, and is uncorrelated at all leads and lags, that is, $\mathrm{cov}(\varepsilon_t, \varepsilon_{t-j}) = 0$ for all $j \neq 0$ and all t.

WN sequences need not be i.i.d. or stationary: for example, we may have $\mathrm{var}(\varepsilon_t) = \sigma_t^2$ vary over time. Furthermore, they may not be weakly dependent. For example, we may have $\mathrm{cov}(\varepsilon_t^2, \varepsilon_{t-j}^2)$ decay very slowly with j, see Chapter 10, even though the series itself is uncorrelated. If the WN process also has constant variance σ^2 for each t we say $\varepsilon_t \sim \mathrm{WN}(0, \sigma^2)$ (a privileged white noise process). In that case, the process is indistinguishable from an i.i.d. process in terms of its second-order properties.

Definition 2.11   A **martingale difference sequence** (MDS) is a process ε_t that satisfies $E(|\varepsilon_t|) \leq C < \infty$ and, for all t, $E(\varepsilon_t \mid \varepsilon_{t-1}, \ldots) = 0$.

An MDS satisfies $\mathrm{cov}(\varepsilon_t, \varepsilon_{t-j}) = 0$ for all $j \neq 0$ and if it has a constant variance then the process is indistinguishable from an i.i.d. process in terms of its second-order properties. However, MDSs are not necessarily independent or strong mixing and can even be nonstationary (through, say, time variations in the variance). Note that for any martingale y_t, $\varepsilon_t = y_t - y_{t-1}$ is an MDS. Conversely, for any MDS ε_t, the process $y_t = \sum_{s=1}^{t} \varepsilon_s$ is a martingale.

We mostly maintain i.i.d. shocks in the presentation of specific time series processes and their properties. However, for estimation and inference it is appropriate to also consider how to proceed under the weaker WN or MDS assumptions. These conditions by themselves may not be sufficient to justify LLNs and CLTs, so we will proscribe their properties further as appropriate, for example using mixing. The cost of employing weaker conditions such as WN or MDS is that inference becomes more complicated, meaning that although we can often justify CLTs, the limiting variances are more complicated.

2.3   Estimation of Mean, Autocovariance, and Autocorrelation

We discuss here estimation of the mean, the autocovariance function, the autocorrelation function, and the partial autocorrelation function. Suppose that we have observations $\{y_1, \ldots, y_T\}$ from a stationary mixing process. Let $\mu = E(y_t)$, and suppose that $E(y_t^2) \leq C < \infty$. Then

$$\widehat{\mu} = \frac{1}{T} \sum_{t=1}^{T} y_t \tag{2.9}$$

is the usual estimator of the population mean μ. Let $\widetilde{y}_t = y_t - E(y_t)$ and $\widetilde{S}_T = \sum_{t=1}^{T} \widetilde{y}_t$, where $E(\widetilde{S}_T) = 0$. If the series is stationary (weakly so), then we may write $E(\widetilde{y}_t \widetilde{y}_s) = E(\widetilde{y}_0 \widetilde{y}_{|t-s|})$ for any t and it follows that, with i_T the $T \times 1$ vector of ones and $\widetilde{y}$ the $T \times 1$ vector of observations,

$$E(\widetilde{S}_T^2) = E\left[\left(\sum_{t=1}^{T} \widetilde{y}_t\right)^2\right]$$

$$= E\left[\left(i_T^{\mathsf{T}} \widetilde{y}\right)^2\right]$$

$$= i_T^{\mathsf{T}} \begin{pmatrix} E(\widetilde{y}_1^2) & E(\widetilde{y}_1 \widetilde{y}_2) & E(\widetilde{y}_1 \widetilde{y}_3) & \cdots & E(\widetilde{y}_1 \widetilde{y}_T) \\ E(\widetilde{y}_2 \widetilde{y}_1) & E(\widetilde{y}_2^2) & E(\widetilde{y}_2 \widetilde{y}_3) & \ddots & \vdots \\ \vdots & \ddots & \ddots & & E(\widetilde{y}_{T-2} \widetilde{y}_T) \\ & & \ddots & \ddots & E(\widetilde{y}_{T-1} \widetilde{y}_T) \\ E(\widetilde{y}_T \widetilde{y}_1) & \cdots & & E(\widetilde{y}_T \widetilde{y}_{T-1}) & E(\widetilde{y}_T^2) \end{pmatrix} i_T$$

$$= i_T^{\mathsf{T}} \Gamma_T i_T$$

$$= T E(\widetilde{y}_0^2) + 2 \sum_{k=1}^{T-1} (T - k) E(\widetilde{y}_0 \widetilde{y}_k).$$

That is, you sum all the elements of the matrix, within and across diagonals.

We have $\mathrm{var}(\widehat{\mu}) = E(\widetilde{S}_T^2)/T^2$. Therefore, for consistency of $\widehat{\mu}$, it suffices that this variance goes to zero, for which it suffices that

$$\sum_{k=1}^{T-1} (T-k) E(\widetilde{y}_0 \widetilde{y}_k)/T^2 \to 0.^5$$

If, further, the series is weakly dependent, that is, $\sum_{k=1}^{\infty} |E(\widetilde{y}_0 \widetilde{y}_k)| < \infty$, then it follows by **Kronecker's lemma** that

$$\frac{1}{T} E(\widetilde{S}_T^2) = E(\widetilde{y}_0^2) + 2 \sum_{k=1}^{T-1} E(\widetilde{y}_0 \widetilde{y}_k) - \frac{2}{T} \sum_{k=1}^{T-1} k E(\widetilde{y}_0 \widetilde{y}_k)$$

$$\to E(\widetilde{y}_0^2) + 2 \sum_{k=1}^{\infty} E(\widetilde{y}_0 \widetilde{y}_k) = \gamma(0) + 2 \sum_{k=1}^{\infty} \gamma(k)$$

$$= \mathrm{lrvar}(y_t),$$

where $\mathrm{lrvar}(y_t)$ is the **long-run variance** (as opposed to the short-run variance or just variance). Herrndorf (1984) developed a CLT for sums of α-mixing random variables that satisfy certain restrictions. A version of his theorem is given in Appendix C. Under these conditions, we have

$$\sup_{x \in \mathbb{R}} \left| \mathrm{Pr}\left(\sqrt{T}\,(\widehat{\mu} - \mu) \le x\right) - \Phi_{0,V}(x) \right| \longrightarrow 0,$$

where $V = \mathrm{lrvar}(y_t)$ and $\Phi_{0,V}(\cdot)$ is the cumulative distribution function (CDF) of a normal random variable whose mean is zero and whose variance is V. This is written less formally as

$$\sqrt{T}\,(\widehat{\mu} - \mu) \Longrightarrow N(0, V). \tag{2.10}$$

The limiting distribution does not depend on the distribution of y_t or on any other features apart from its second-order properties, so one would have the same accuracy for a Gaussian process as for a process with a different distribution. Herrndorf's conditions do not require stationarity but they do require some uniform boundedness on higher moments. The CLT holds under these conditions, although the limiting variance cannot be notationally simplified in this case (although it can be thought of as an average long-run variance).[6]

Linear processes (2.8) can be shown to satisfy the same CLT without invoking the mixing property (although under some conditions they also satisfy Herrndorf's mixing conditions), and in that case the form of the asymptotic variance simplifies. For such a linear process, we may write

---

[5] Actually, the sample mean converges to the population mean by the law of large numbers without requiring a variance to exist, although some moment condition between one and two is needed, along with mixing restrictions, in that case.

[6] In fact, it is not necessary for the long-run variance to be finite for a CLT to apply. Specifically, suppose that $E(\widetilde{S}_T^2) = Th(T)$, where $h(T)$ is a slowly varying function (e.g., $h(T) = \log T$), then one can show that $(\widehat{\mu} - \mu)/\sqrt{E(\widetilde{S}_T^2/T^2)} \Longrightarrow N(0, 1)$ if and only if $\limsup_{T \to \infty} \sqrt{E(\widetilde{S}_T^2)}/E|\widetilde{S}_T| \le \sqrt{\pi/2}$. That is, slow growth in $E(\widetilde{S}_T^2)/T$ is allowed.

$$\sqrt{T}\,(\widehat{\mu} - \mu) = \frac{1}{\sqrt{T}} \sum_{t=1}^{T} \sum_{j=0}^{\infty} \omega_j \varepsilon_{t-j}$$

$$= \sum_{j=0}^{\infty} \omega_j \frac{1}{\sqrt{T}} \sum_{t=1}^{T} \varepsilon_{t-j}$$

$$= \sum_{j=0}^{\infty} \omega_j \frac{1}{\sqrt{T}} \sum_{t=1}^{T} \varepsilon_t + \sum_{j=0}^{\infty} \omega_j \left(\frac{1}{\sqrt{T}} \sum_{t=1}^{T} \varepsilon_{t-j} - \frac{1}{\sqrt{T}} \sum_{t=1}^{T} \varepsilon_t \right)$$

$$= \sum_{j=0}^{\infty} \omega_j \frac{1}{\sqrt{T}} \sum_{t=1}^{T} \varepsilon_t + \frac{1}{\sqrt{T}} \sum_{j=0}^{\infty} \omega_j \left(\sum_{s=1-j}^{0} \varepsilon_s - \sum_{t=T-j}^{T} \varepsilon_t \right).$$

The first term on the right-hand side satisfies

$$\sum_{j=0}^{\infty} \omega_j \frac{1}{\sqrt{T}} \sum_{t=1}^{T} \varepsilon_t \Longrightarrow N\left(0, \sigma_\varepsilon^2 \left(\sum_{j=0}^{\infty} \omega_j \right)^2 \right) \tag{2.11}$$

provided $\sum_{j=0}^{\infty} \omega_j \neq 0$, and the second term is of smaller order in probability because $\mathrm{var}\left(\sum_{s=1-j}^{0} \varepsilon_s - \sum_{t=T-j}^{T} \varepsilon_t \right) = 2j\sigma_\varepsilon^2$. In fact, for the linear process y_t the long-run variance is exactly $\sigma_\varepsilon^2 \left(\sum_{j=0}^{\infty} \omega_j \right)^2$. Given the CLT, for inference we apparently require an estimator of the asymptotic variance; we will address this issue in Chapter 5.

We now turn to estimation of the population quantities $\gamma(j)$, $\rho(j)$, and $\pi(j)$. We estimate these quantities by the sample equivalents:

$$\widehat{\gamma}(j) = \frac{1}{T} \sum_{t=j+1}^{T} (y_t - \bar{y})(y_{t-j} - \bar{y}), \qquad \bar{y} = \frac{1}{T} \sum_{t=1}^{T} y_t; \tag{2.12}$$

$$\widehat{\rho}(j) = \frac{\widehat{\gamma}(j)}{\widehat{\gamma}(0)}; \qquad \widehat{\pi}(j) = e_j^{\mathsf{T}} \widehat{\Gamma}_j^{-1} \widehat{\gamma}_j,$$

where $\widehat{\gamma}_j = (\widehat{\gamma}(1), \ldots, \widehat{\gamma}(j))^{\mathsf{T}}$ and $\widehat{\Gamma}_j = (\widehat{\gamma}(i-k))_{i,k=1}^{j}$, while $e_j = (0, \ldots, 0, 1)^{\mathsf{T}}$. We may equivalently define the sample autocorrelation as $\sum_{t=j+1}^{T} \widetilde{z}_t \widetilde{z}_{t-j}/T$, where the standardized series $\widetilde{z}_t = (y_t - \bar{y})/s$, where s is the sample standard deviation of y_t. These quantities are defined for $1 - T \leq j \leq T - 1$ and are set to zero otherwise due to lack of data.

The sample autocovariance function defined in this way satisfies $|\widehat{\gamma}(j)| \leq \widehat{\gamma}(0)$ for all j, and hence $|\widehat{\rho}(j)| \leq 1$. This follows by the Cauchy–Schwarz inequality. The function $\widehat{\gamma}(\cdot)$ is also positive semidefinite in the sense that $\sum \sum_{i,j=1}^{T} \widehat{\gamma}(i-j)a_i a_j \geq 0$ for all vectors $a = (a_1, \ldots, a_T)^{\mathsf{T}}$. This is because we can write, for all $T \geq 2$,

$$\widehat{\Gamma}_T = \begin{pmatrix} \widehat{\gamma}(0) & \widehat{\gamma}(1) & \cdots & \widehat{\gamma}(T-1) \\ & \widehat{\gamma}(0) & \cdots & \widehat{\gamma}(T-2) \\ \vdots & & \ddots & \vdots \\ & & & \widehat{\gamma}(0) \end{pmatrix} = \frac{1}{T} GG^{\mathsf{T}}, \tag{2.13}$$

$$G_{T \times 2T} = \begin{pmatrix} 0 & \cdots & 0 & y_1 - \bar{y} & \cdots & y_T - \bar{y} \\ & 0 & y_1 - \bar{y} & \cdots & y_T - \bar{y} & 0 \\ \vdots & \vdots & & & & \vdots \\ 0 & y_1 - \bar{y} & \cdots & y_T - \bar{y} & \cdots & 0 \end{pmatrix}.$$

It follows that

$$\sum_{i=1}^{T}\sum_{j=1}^{T}\widehat{\gamma}(i-j)a_ia_j = a^\mathsf{T}\widehat{\Gamma}_T a = \frac{1}{T}a^\mathsf{T}GG^\mathsf{T}a \geq 0.$$

The matrix $\widehat{\Gamma}_T$ is positive definite with probability one. We can also write $\widehat{\Gamma}_T = \sum_{j=0}^{T-1}\widehat{\gamma}(j)\Delta_j$, that is, a linear combination of known zero/one matrices Δ_j; you are asked to derive these in the exercises. Note that $\widehat{\gamma}(T-1) = (y_T - \bar{y})(y_1 - \bar{y})/T$.

An alternative estimator of $\gamma(j)$ is defined as

$$\widetilde{\gamma}(j) = \frac{1}{T-j}\sum_{t=j+1}^{T}(y_t - \bar{y})(y_{t-j} - \bar{y}), \tag{2.14}$$

sometimes called the unbiased estimator, although erroneously, since it is biased in general and in fact may have higher bias than $\widehat{\gamma}(j)$ when the data are i.i.d. The nomenclature comes from the known mean case, in which $\bar{y}$ is replaced by μ (in this case this estimator is exactly unbiased, but practically much less relevant since means are rarely known). In addition, the estimator $\widetilde{\gamma}(\cdot)$ does not possess the positive-definiteness property and the implied autocorrelation $\widetilde{\rho}(j) = \widetilde{\gamma}(j)/\widetilde{\gamma}(0)$ may lie outside $[-1, 1]$. Usual practice is to work with T rather than $T-j$ normalization as in (2.12).[7] An alternative estimator of $\rho(j)$, the ordinary least squares (OLS) estimator, can be based on the linear regression of y_t on y_{t-j}, that is,

$$\widehat{\rho}_{\text{OLS}}(j) = \frac{\sum_{t=j+1}^{T}(y_t - \bar{y})(y_{t-j} - \bar{y})}{\sum_{t=j+1}^{T}(y_{t-j} - \bar{y})^2},$$

which also may lie outside $[-1, 1]$. These alternative estimators are consistent and share the same asymptotic distribution, but their finite-sample properties can vary.

We first show an important property of the sample autocovariance and autocorrelation. We have

$$\widehat{\gamma}(0) + 2\sum_{j=1}^{T-1}\widehat{\gamma}(j) \equiv 0 \quad \text{and} \quad \sum_{j=1}^{T-1}\widehat{\rho}(j) = -\frac{1}{2}. \tag{2.15}$$

This follows because

$$0 = \left(\frac{1}{T}\sum_{t=1}^{T}(y_t - \bar{y})\right)^2$$

$$= \frac{1}{T}\sum_{t=1}^{T}(y_t - \bar{y})^2 + \frac{1}{T}\sum_{\substack{t=1 \\ t \neq s}}^{T}\sum_{s=1}^{T}(y_t - \bar{y})(y_s - \bar{y})$$

$$= \frac{1}{T}\sum_{t=1}^{T}(y_t - \bar{y})^2 + \frac{2}{T}\sum_{t=1}^{T-1}\sum_{s=t+1}^{T}(y_t - \bar{y})(y_s - \bar{y}) = \widehat{\gamma}(0) + 2\sum_{j=1}^{T-1}\widehat{\gamma}(j).$$

This means that in practice we may observe positive autocorrelations for the first so many lags, but these must be followed somewhere by many negative autocorrelations to offset

---

[7] Note that $1/(T-j) = (1/T) \times (1 - j/T)^{-1} = (1/T) \times (1 + j/T + O(1/T^2))$.

the initial pattern. This is true regardless of the population autocovariance function or data-generating process. For example, suppose that $y_t = t$ for $t = 1, \ldots, 11$. Then the sample ACF is $0.727\,27, 0.463\,64, 0.218\,18, 0.000\,00, -0.181\,82, -0.318\,18, -0.400\,00,$ $-0.418\,18, -0.363\,64, -0.227\,27$.

We next note that $\widehat{\gamma}(j)$ is a quadratic form (and $\widehat{\rho}(j)$ is a ratio of quadratic forms) in the data vector $y = (y_1, \ldots, y_T)^\mathsf{T}$, that is, it is a quadratic function of all the y_t',

$$\widehat{\gamma}(j) = \frac{1}{T} y^\mathsf{T} \mathbf{Q}_j y, \qquad \mathbf{Q}_j = \mathbf{M}_T \mathbf{L}(j)^\mathsf{T} \mathbf{F}(j) \mathbf{M}_T, \tag{2.16}$$

where $\mathbf{M}_T = I_T - (1/T) i_T i_T^\mathsf{T}$ is the demeaning matrix, while $\mathbf{L}(j)$ is the j-lag matrix, a $T \times T$ matrix that consists of zeros and ones with ones on the sub-j diagonal such that $\mathbf{L}(j)y = (0, \ldots, 0, y_1, \ldots, y_{T-j})^\mathsf{T}$, and $\mathbf{F}(j)$ is the $T \times T$ matrix that consists of zeros and ones such that $\mathbf{F}(j)y = (0, \ldots, 0, y_{j+1}, \ldots, y_T)^\mathsf{T}$. For example,

$$\mathbf{L}(1) = \begin{pmatrix} 0 & \cdots & & 0 \\ 1 & & & \vdots \\ 0 & \ddots & \ddots & \\ \vdots & & 1 & 0 \end{pmatrix}, \qquad \mathbf{F}(1) = \begin{pmatrix} 0 & 0 & \cdots & 0 \\ 0 & 1 & 0 & \vdots \\ \vdots & 0 & \ddots & 0 \\ 0 & 0 & & 1 \end{pmatrix}.$$

For a Gaussian process we may write $y = \mu i_T + \Gamma_T^{1/2} z$, where z is a $T \times 1$ vector of standard normal independent random variables. In that case we may further write $\widehat{\gamma}(j) = \left(\mu i_T + \Gamma_T^{1/2} z\right)^\mathsf{T} \mathbf{Q}_j \left(\mu i_T + \Gamma_T^{1/2} z\right)/T = z^\mathsf{T} \Gamma_T^{1/2} \mathbf{Q}_j \Gamma_T^{1/2} z / T$ in terms of the vector z because of the properties of the projection matrix $\mathbf{M}_T$. Sutradhar (1994) used this representation to calculate the mean and variance of $\widehat{\gamma}(j)$; we just examine the mean.

We have, by the property $\mathrm{tr}(AB) = \mathrm{tr}(BA)$, that

$$E\left(\widehat{\gamma}(j)\right) = \frac{1}{T} \mathrm{tr}\left(\mathbf{L}(j)^\mathsf{T} \mathbf{F}(j) E(\mathbf{M}_T y y^\mathsf{T} \mathbf{M}_T)\right),$$

where

$$E(\mathbf{M}_T y y^\mathsf{T} \mathbf{M}_T) = E\left((y - \bar{y} i_T)(y - \bar{y} i_T)^\mathsf{T}\right)$$
$$= E\left((y - \mu i_T - (\bar{y} - \mu) i_T)(y - \mu i_T - (\bar{y} - \mu) i_T)^\mathsf{T}\right)$$
$$= E\left((y - \mu i_T)(y - \mu i_T)^\mathsf{T}\right) - E\left((\bar{y} - \mu)^2\right) i_T i_T^\mathsf{T}$$
$$= \Gamma_T - \mathrm{var}(\bar{y}) i_T i_T^\mathsf{T}.$$

Therefore,

$$E\left(\widehat{\gamma}(j)\right) = \frac{1}{T} \mathrm{tr}\left(\mathbf{F}(j) \Gamma_T \mathbf{L}(j)^\mathsf{T}\right) - \mathrm{var}(\bar{y}) \frac{T-j}{T} = \frac{T-j}{T}\left(\gamma(j) - \mathrm{var}(\bar{y})\right). \tag{2.17}$$

The estimation of μ leads to a (higher-order) bias in the estimation of the autocovariance function that cannot easily be corrected, because as we have seen $\mathrm{var}(\bar{y})$ itself depends on $\gamma(0), \ldots, \gamma(T-1)$. In the special case that y_t is i.i.d., $\mathrm{var}(\bar{y}) = \gamma(0)/T$ and in that case the estimator $\widetilde{\gamma}(j) = \widehat{\gamma}(j) + \widetilde{\gamma}(0)/T$ is exactly unbiased (as an estimator of zero), where $\widetilde{\gamma}(0) = T\widehat{\gamma}(0)/(T-1)$ is the unbiased variance estimator. The autocorrelation function is a ratio of two estimators and so will also have a bias, and even in the case where y_t is i.i.d., Magnus (1986) derives formulae for the moments of ratios of quadratic forms in Gaussian random variables, which can be used to further describe the properties of $\widehat{\rho}(j)$ in that special case.

Let $\widehat{\gamma} = (\widehat{\gamma}(0), \ldots, \widehat{\gamma}(T-1))^{\mathsf{T}}$ and $\gamma = (\gamma(0), \ldots, \gamma(T-1))^{\mathsf{T}}$. Then we can write

$$E(\widehat{\gamma}) = A\gamma \tag{2.18}$$

for some $T \times T$ known matrix A (whose elements depend on T but not on γ). Unfortunately, A is a singular matrix, and so one cannot obtain $A^{-1}\widehat{\gamma}$, which would be an exactly unbiased estimator of γ. Vogelsang and Yang (2016) show that when $\gamma(k) = 0$ for all $k \geq m+1$, it is possible to construct an estimator of $\gamma = (\gamma(0), \ldots, \gamma(m))^{\mathsf{T}}$ that is exactly unbiased using just the upper $(m+1) \times (m+1)$ submatrix of A, which is invertible for any fixed m and even for sequences $m \to \infty$ under some restrictions.[8] However, the implied autocorrelation estimator would be biased even in this case. In any case, from a statistical point of view bias is only one aspect of estimator performance; biased estimators are now widely used in machine learning, for example.

We now turn to the large-sample properties. We have

$$
\begin{aligned}
\widehat{\gamma}(j) &= \frac{1}{T} \sum_{t=j+1}^{T} (y_t - \mu + \mu - \bar{y})(y_{t-j} - \mu + \mu - \bar{y}) \\
&= \frac{1}{T} \sum_{t=j+1}^{T} (y_t - \mu)(y_{t-j} - \mu) - \frac{1}{T} \sum_{t=j+1}^{T} (\mu - y_t)(\mu - \bar{y}) \\
&\quad - \frac{1}{T} \sum_{t=j+1}^{T} (\mu - \bar{y})(\mu - y_{t-j}) + \frac{1}{T} \sum_{t=j+1}^{T} (\mu - \bar{y})(\mu - \bar{y}) \\
&= \frac{1}{T} \sum_{t=j+1}^{T} (y_t - \mu)(y_{t-j} - \mu) - (\mu - \bar{y})^2 \\
&\quad + (\mu - \bar{y}) \left(\frac{1}{T} \sum_{t=1}^{j} (y_t - \mu) + \frac{1}{T} \sum_{t=T-j}^{T} (y_{t-j} - \mu) - \frac{j}{T}(\mu - \bar{y}) \right) \\
&= \frac{1}{T} \sum_{t=j+1}^{T} (y_t - \mu)(y_{t-j} - \mu) - (\mu - \bar{y})^2 + o_P(T^{-1}).
\end{aligned}
$$

Since also $(\mu - \bar{y})^2 = O_P(T^{-1})$, we have

$$\sqrt{T}(\widehat{\gamma}(j) - \gamma(j)) = \frac{1}{\sqrt{T}} \sum_{t=j+1}^{T} v_{t;j} + o_P(1), \tag{2.19}$$

where $v_{t;j} = (y_t - \mu)(y_{t-j} - \mu) - E((y_t - \mu)(y_{t-j} - \mu))$. This linear approximation is all that is needed to derive a large-sample approximate distribution. One consequence of this approximation is that although μ has to be estimated from the same data, the sample autocovariance function behaves largely as if μ is known. This is a special property of

---

[8] Li (2024) generalizes these results to the multivariate case considered in Chapter 7.

autocovariance, which is not shared by other parameter estimates. It still remains to calculate the limiting distribution of $\hat{\gamma}(j)$, and specifically the limiting variance, and we use the Herrndorf (1984) result again. Note that if y_t is a strong mixing process, then $v_{t;j}$ is a strong mixing process (in t) for any j. Then, for each j, provided $v_{t;j}$ itself is a second-order stationary process (provided at least the fourth moments of y_t exist), we have

$$\sqrt{T}(\hat{\gamma}(j) - \gamma(j)) \Longrightarrow N(0, V(j)), \tag{2.20}$$

$$V(j) = \operatorname{lrvar}(v_{t;j}) = \gamma_v(0) + 2\sum_{k=1}^{\infty} \gamma_v(k),$$

where $\gamma_v(0) = \operatorname{var}(v_{t;j}) = E(\tilde{y}_t^2 \tilde{y}_{t-j}^2) - E^2(\tilde{y}_t \tilde{y}_{t-j})$ and $\gamma_v(k) = \operatorname{cov}(v_{t;j}, v_{t+k;j}) = E(\tilde{y}_t \tilde{y}_{t+k} \tilde{y}_{t-j} \tilde{y}_{t+k-j}) - E^2(\tilde{y}_t \tilde{y}_{t-j})$, where $\tilde{y}_t = y_t - \mu$. Note that the limiting properties do not depend on the entire distribution of y_t but only on the second-order properties of $v_{t;j}$, that is, the fourth-order properties of y_t.

We now turn to the sample autocorrelation function. We make a further expansion of both numerator and denominator around their probability limits, and obtain the approximation

$$\sqrt{T}(\hat{\rho}(j) - \rho(j)) = \frac{\sqrt{T}(\hat{\gamma}(j) - \gamma(j)) - \rho(j)\sqrt{T}(\hat{\gamma}(0) - \gamma(0))}{\gamma(0)} + o_P(1)$$

$$= \frac{1}{\sqrt{T}} \sum_t w_{t;j} + o_P(1),$$

with

$$w_{t;j} = \frac{(y_t - \mu)(y_{t-j} - \mu) - \gamma(j) - \rho(j)((y_t - \mu)^2 - \gamma(0))}{\gamma(0)}$$

$$= z_t z_{t-j} - \rho(j) - \rho(j)(z_t^2 - 1),$$

where $z_t = (y_t - \mu)/\sqrt{\gamma(0)}$ is the standardized series (with mean zero and variance one).[9] We have $E(w_{t;j}) = 0$; furthermore, $w_{t;j}$ is an α-mixing process in t for each j satisfying Herrndorf's conditions. Therefore, for each j,

$$\sqrt{T}(\hat{\rho}(j) - \rho(j)) \Longrightarrow N(0, V(j)), \qquad V(j) = \operatorname{lrvar}(w_{t;j}).$$

We further have joint asymptotic normality of $\hat{\rho}(j_1), \ldots, \hat{\rho}(j_p)$ for any finite collection of integers $j_1, \ldots, j_p$; in general, $\hat{\rho}(j_i)$ and $\hat{\rho}(j_k)$ are correlated in the asymptotic distribution except in the special case that the process is i.i.d.

The pointwise limiting variance is complicated in general but it simplifies in some special cases. If y_t is a linear process (no heteroskedasticity), we have

$$V_{\mathrm{LP}}(j) = \sum_{h=1}^{\infty} (\rho(h+j) + \rho(h-j) - 2\rho(j)\rho(h))^2. \tag{2.21}$$

---

[9] Specifically, we use the following approximation for $\hat{x}, \hat{y}$ close to x, y:

$$\frac{\hat{x}}{\hat{y}} = \frac{x + \hat{x} - x}{y(1 + ((\hat{y} - y)/y))} \simeq \frac{x}{y} + \frac{\hat{x} - x}{y} - \frac{x}{y}\frac{\hat{y} - y}{y}.$$

This is still very complicated unless $\rho(\cdot)$ takes certain specific forms. For example, if y_t is i.i.d., so that $\rho(j) = 0$ for $j \neq 0$, then for all $j \geq 1$, $V_{\text{LP}}(j) = 1$. We give some further special cases next.

Example 2.4   Suppose that $\rho(1) = \theta$ and $\rho(j) = 0$ for all $j \geq 2$. Then, for $j = 1$,

$$\rho(h+j) + \rho(h-j) - 2\rho(j)\rho(h) = \begin{cases} 1 - 2\theta^2, & h = 1, \\ \theta, & h = 2, \\ 0, & h \geq 3, \end{cases}$$

whereas for $j \geq 2$,

$$\rho(h+j) + \rho(h-j) - 2\rho(j)\rho(h) = \begin{cases} 1, & h = j \\ \theta, & h = j \pm 1. \end{cases}$$

Therefore, we have

$$V_{\text{LP}}(j) = \begin{cases} \left(1 - 2\theta^2\right)^2 + \theta^2 & \text{if } j = 1, \\ 1 + 2\theta^2 & \text{if } j \geq 2. \end{cases} \tag{2.22}$$

Example 2.5   Suppose that $\rho(j) = \phi^j$. Then

$$V_{\text{LP}}(j) = \frac{\phi^2}{1 - \phi^2} \left(\phi^{-j} - \phi^j\right)^2. \tag{2.23}$$

The theory for partial autocorrelation is more complicated except in the special case where y_t is i.i.d., in which case $\sqrt{T}\left(\hat{\pi}(j) - \pi(j)\right)$ is asymptotically standard normal.

2.4 Testing for the Absence of Autocorrelation

We are sometimes interested in testing the null hypothesis of no autocorrelation. For example, the efficient markets hypothesis says that stock returns should be unpredictable relative to the risk premium. Under the assumption that the risk premium is constant or small, as may be the case for daily data, this implies that the return series should have zero autocorrelation at all lags. Suppose further that y_t is i.i.d. Then, as we argued above, for any k,

$$\sqrt{T}\hat{\rho}(k) \Longrightarrow N(0, 1). \tag{2.24}$$

There are three equivalent ways of carrying out a test of the null hypothesis. First, by comparing the so-called z-scores $\sqrt{T}\hat{\rho}(k)$ with $\pm z_{\alpha/2}$; second, by comparing $\hat{\rho}(k)$ with the so-called "Bartlett intervals" $\pm z_{\alpha/2}/\sqrt{T}$, where z_α are normal critical values for level α. Finally, an alternative way of presenting the evidence is to report the two-sided p-values associated with the tests; these are $\min\{\Phi(\sqrt{T}\hat{\rho}(k)), 1 - \Phi(\sqrt{T}\hat{\rho}(k))\}$, which can be compared with α. Values of $\hat{\rho}(k)$ lying outside this interval are inconsistent with the null hypothesis. Under the alternative hypothesis that $\rho(k) \neq 0$, then $\sqrt{T}|\hat{\rho}(k)| \overset{P}{\longrightarrow} \infty$. The test is consistent against all fixed alternatives. One can also show that it has power against local alternatives of the form $\rho(k) = c/\sqrt{T}$, for any c with $-\infty < c < \infty$, since under this local hypothesis we have $\sqrt{T}\widehat{\rho}(k) \Longrightarrow N(c, 1)$. Similarly, when y_t is i.i.d., for any k, $\pi(k) = 0$ for all k and

$$\sqrt{T}\widehat{\pi}(k) \Longrightarrow N(0, 1). \tag{2.25}$$

Therefore, you can test the null hypothesis by comparing the so-called z-scores $\sqrt{T}\widehat{\pi}(k)$ with $\pm z_{\alpha/2}$, or equivalently by comparing $\widehat{\pi}(k)$ with the so-called "Bartlett intervals" $\pm z_{\alpha/2}/\sqrt{T}$, where z_α are normal critical values for level α. We will consider later the properties of $\widehat{\rho}(k)$ and $\widehat{\pi}(k)$ under weaker assumptions such as MDS and WN. Literally, this is testing the hypothesis that $\rho(k) = 0$ versus $\rho(k) \neq 0$ for a given k, but the i.i.d. assumption implies that $\rho(k) = 0$ for all k (and even stronger restrictions).

2.5   Application

In Figures 2.1–2.10 we show the ACF and PACF of some of the datasets we showed in the introduction, along with their Bartlett confidence bands, that is, the bands derived under the assumption of i.i.d., which are centered at zero. This is convention for the stock returns and exchange rate series, but it is less relevant for, say, unemployment or interest rates. We ignore the **multiple testing** issue here that we are implicitly carrying out a number of hypothesis tests simultaneously but without correcting for the consequence of

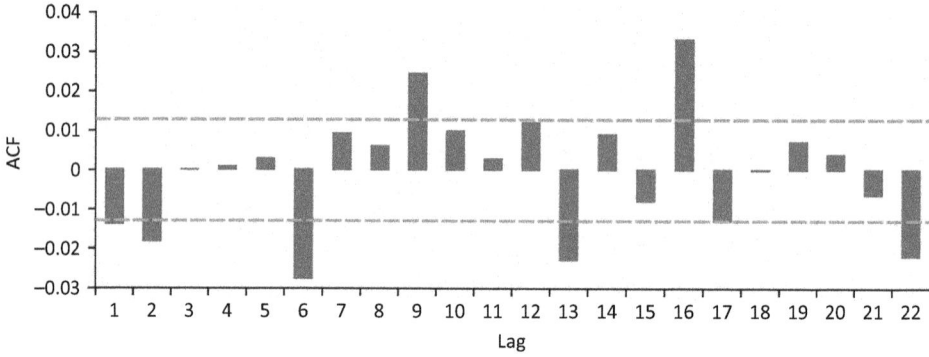

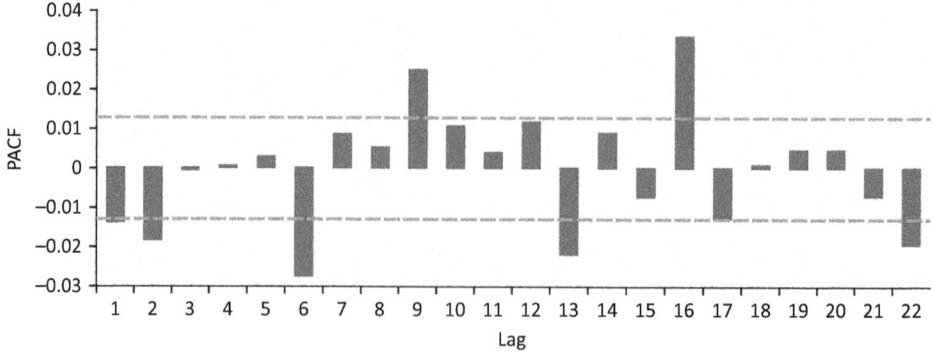

Figure 2.1 ACF and PACF of daily S&P500 stock returns along with the Bartlett 95% confidence bands.

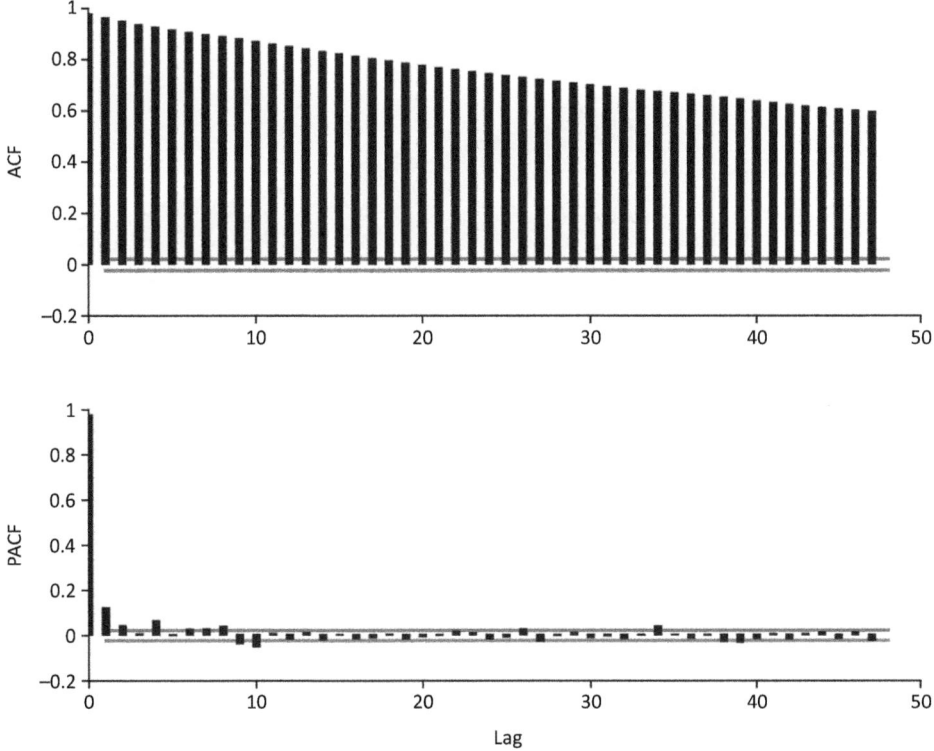

Figure 2.2 ACF and PACF of daily VIX level along with the Bartlett 95% confidence bands.

this in terms of the null rejection frequency. This is common practice. To be condemned perhaps, but common practice. The classical **Bonferroni** way of correcting for this is to work with a critical value $z_{\alpha/2p}$, where p is the number of null hypotheses (lags) under consideration, but is deemed too pessimistic. We will come back to this issue.

For the S&P500 daily return series shown in Figure 2.1 the level of the autocorrelations is small and takes both positive and negative values roughly equally. The first two lags are negative and marginally significant, so at the 5% level based on the i.i.d. confidence bands. The largest autocorrelation appears to be around +0.033 at lag 16. The partial autocorrelations follow a similar pattern to the autocorrelations, in fact almost identical (this would be expected under a white noise assumption).

For the daily VIX series, Figure 2.2, the autocorrelations are all large and positive out to many lags – they decline slowly. Furthermore, they are all strongly statistically significant. The partial autocorrelations show quite different properties: after the first lag they are much smaller and barely significant.

For the monthly USA unemployment (not seasonally adjusted) series, shown in Figure 2.3, the autocorrelations are all positive out to many lags and are strongly statistically significant; they decline slowly, albeit with a more bumpy pattern. The partial autocorrelations show quite different properties: after the first lag they are mostly much smaller and barely significant, although there are some exceptions, with lags 12, 24, and 36 being quite large and negative, and statistically significant.

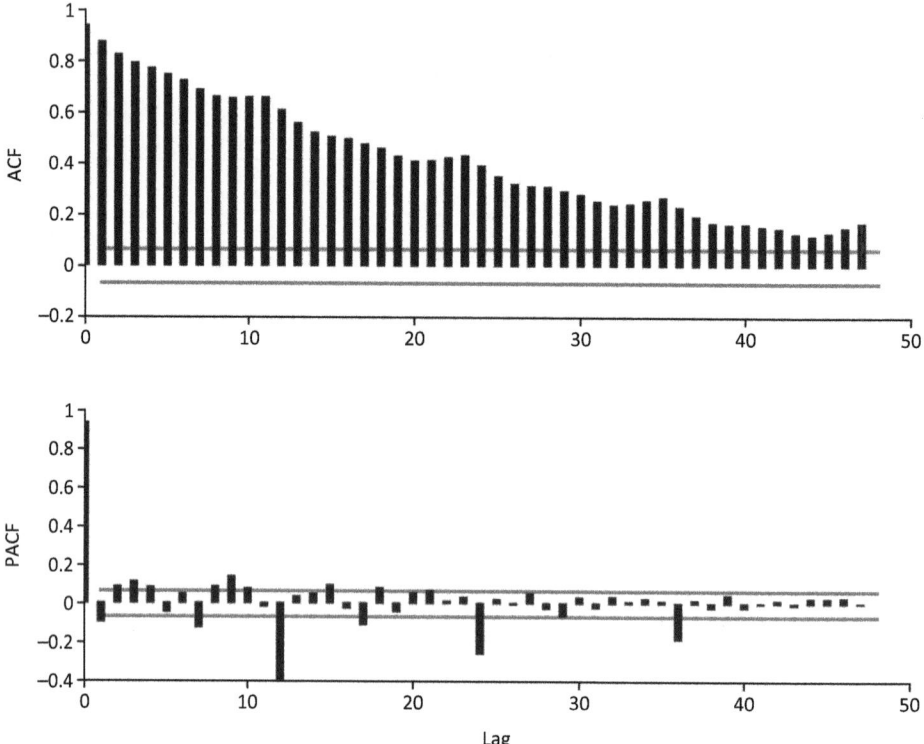

Figure 2.3 ACF and PACF of monthly unemployment in the USA, not seasonally adjusted.

For the growth in monthly personal consumption expenditure (seasonally adjusted), shown in Figure 2.4, only the second autocorrelation is statistically significant; it is negative and around −0.17. Out of many autocorrelations all but three are positive. The partial autocorrelations behave similarly to the autocorrelations with a large statistically significant negative value at lag 2, and a couple of other statistically significant but positive values at lags 11 and 16.

From Figure 2.5, for the growth in monthly industrial production (not seasonally adjusted) there is a small (around 0.1) positive first-order autocorrelation and then several large positive (around 0.45) and very significant values at lags 12, 24, 36, and 48, as well as some significant negative (but smaller) autocorrelations at assorted lags such as 10, 11, 13, 14, and 15. The partial autocorrelations show significant positive values at 12, 24, 36, and 48, and significant negative values at 13, 25, 37.

For monthly inflation (not seasonally adjusted), Figure 2.6, the first 25 lags are positive and significant, starting at around 0.5 and decaying slowly. There are some other marginally significant values at longer lags and no significant negative lags. Only the first four partial autocorrelations are positive and strongly significant. There are (marginally) significant values, both positive and negative, at longer horizons.

For the monthly average daily maximum temperature at Oxford, as shown in Figure 2.7, we find a most unusual pattern with nearly all lags being statistically significant, both positive and negative. The first two lags are positive and significant, the third lag not significant, the next five lags negative and significant, and so on. The partial

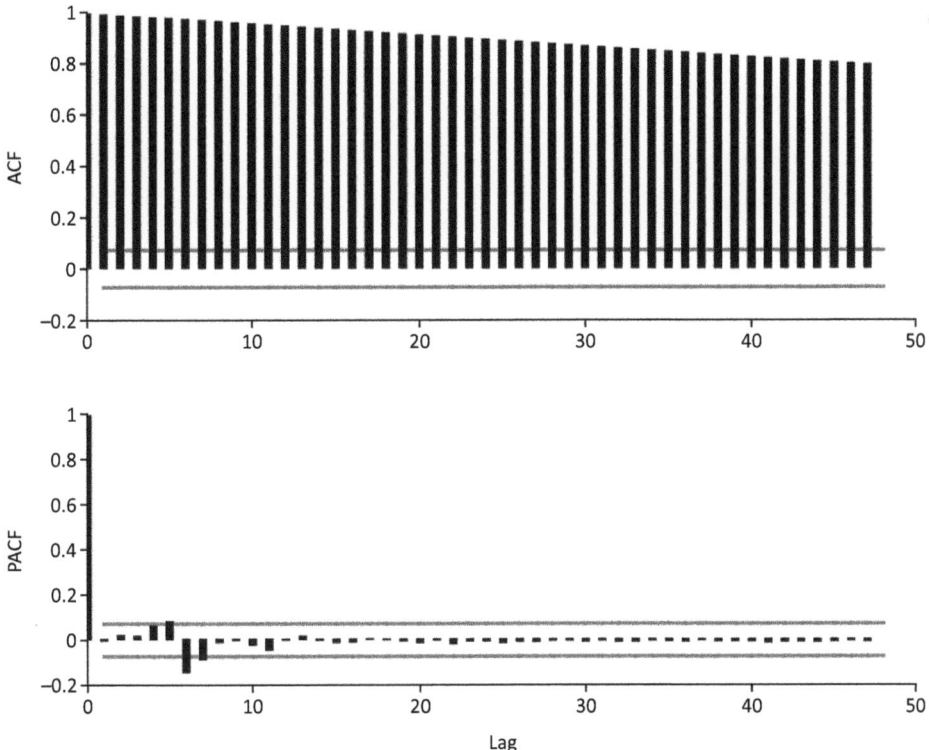

Figure 2.4 ACF and PACF of growth in monthly personal consumption expenditure, seasonally adjusted.

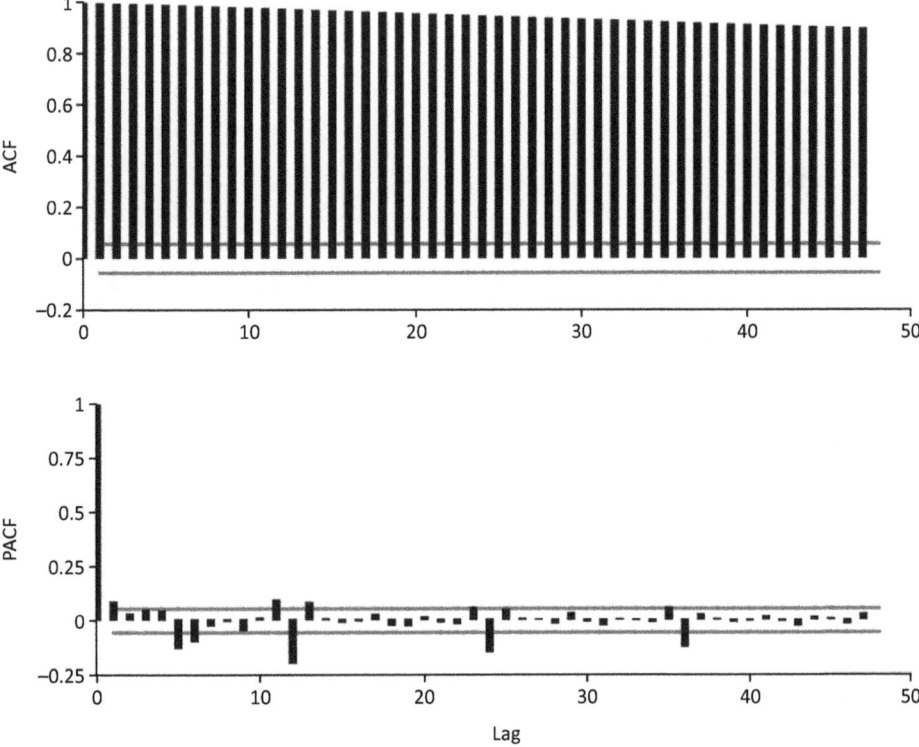

Figure 2.5 ACF and PACF of growth in monthly industrial production in USA, not seasonally adjusted.

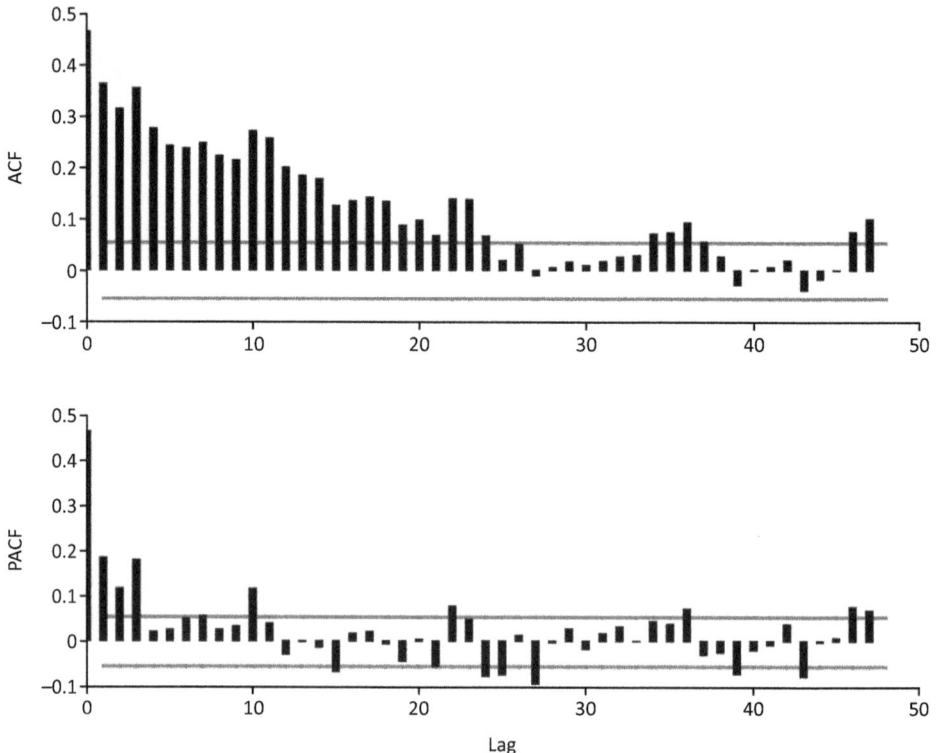

Figure 2.6 ACF and PACF of monthly inflation in USA, not seasonally adjusted.

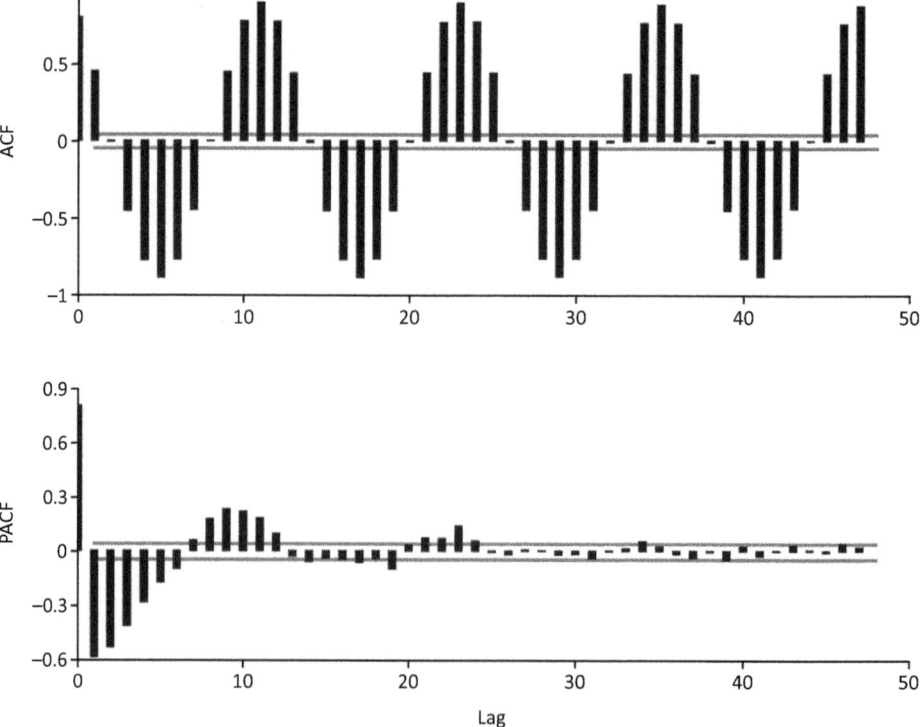

Figure 2.7 ACF and PACF of monthly average daily maximum temperature at Oxford since 1850.

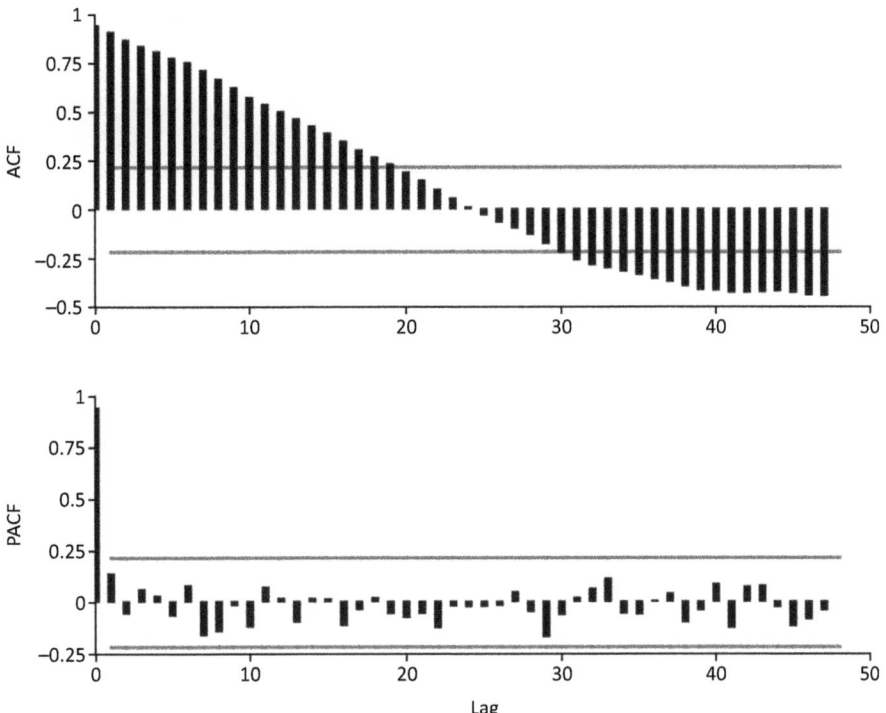

Figure 2.8 ACF and PACF of the number of female births in London, 1629–1700.

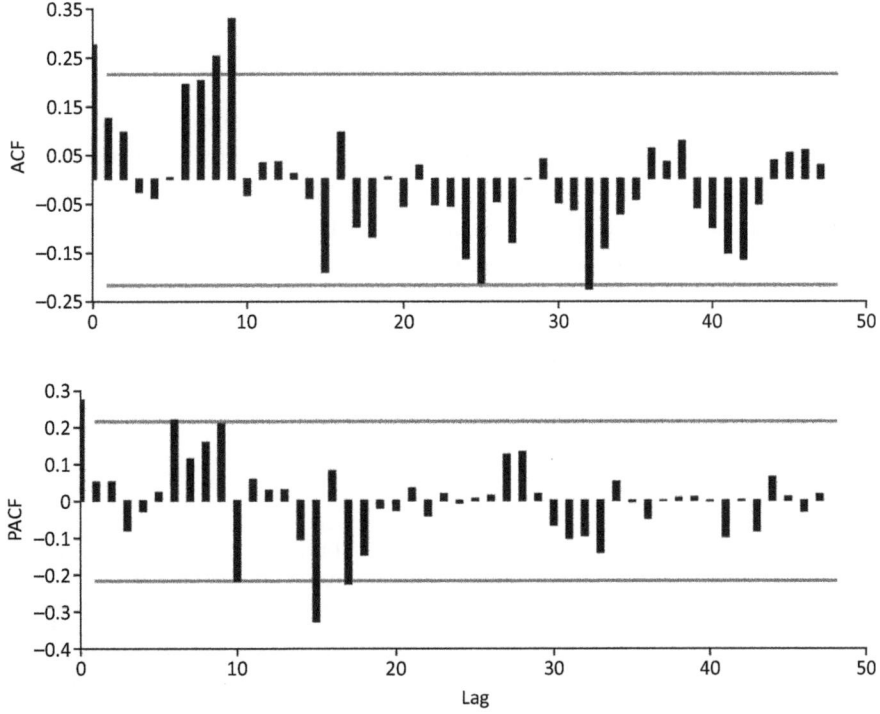

Figure 2.9 ACF and PACF of the ratio of male to female births in London, 1629–1700.

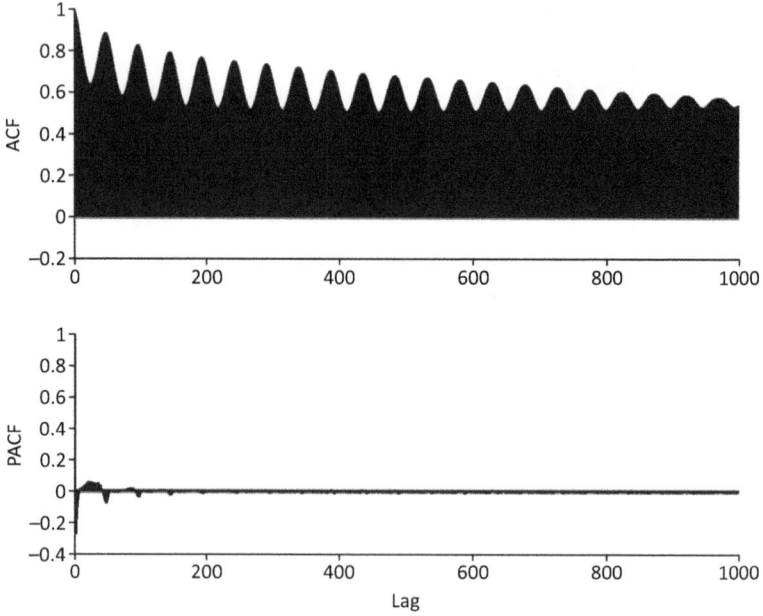

Figure 2.10 ACF and PACF of the Cambridge half-hourly temperature.

autocorrelations from lags 2 to 7 are negative and significant, lags 8–13 are positive and significant, and thereafter much smaller and sporadically significant.

For the annual number of female births in London, 1629–1700 (Figure 2.8), the first 20 lags are positive and significant, and slowly declining, and after lag 26 become negative, and significant after lag 31. The partial autocorrelations have only significance at lag 1 with a large positive value. Thereafter, there is no significance. The ratio of male to female births (Figure 2.9) shows generally positive autocorrelations out to lag 10, with lags 1, 9, and 10 being significant, and thereafter slightly more negative but not significant autocorrelations. The partial autocorrelations are equally positive and negative, with the first lag positive and significant, and lag 16 negative and significant.

For the half-hour Cambridge temperature series shown in Figure 2.10, we see very positive and significant and slowly declining autocorrelations out to a very long horizon, with a curious oscillation pattern. The partial autocorrelation series takes both positive and negative values, and its magnitude dies out very quickly.

2.6   Summary

We have introduced the main concepts of stationarity and mixing that are the foundation of the statistics of time series analysis. We defined the autocovariance function and autocorrelation function, which are the standard way of capturing the dependence of the present on the past, and showed how they can be estimated from a finite stretch of data. We gave an outline of the statistical properties of these estimators and a preliminary discussion of how to conduct inference about them, a topic we will return to. We also saw empirically the variety of dependence displayed by different time series, some containing substantial structure and others containing less. The R language has two commands, acf() and pacf(), that directly calculate and plot the ACF and PACF of the input time series. By default, these include the autocorrelation for lag zero, which is always exactly one, but there are options to suppress this. Also by default it produces the Bartlett bands.

2.7   Exercises

2.1 For the dataset CETD plot the monthly time series and calculate its autocorrelation function out to 24 lags, along with the confidence band. Calculate the sequence of linear regressions of y_t on $1, y_{t-j}$ for $j = 1, \ldots, 24$ and define $\widetilde{\rho}(j)$ as the slope in the jth regression. Compare these estimates with the standard autocorrelations $\widehat{\rho}(j)$.

2.2 For the dataset CETD calculate the sequence of linear regressions of y_t on $1, y_{t-1}, \ldots, y_{t-j}$ for $j = 1, \ldots, 24$. Define $\widetilde{\pi}(j)$ as the slope coefficient on y_{t-j}. Report this quantity for lags $1, 2, \ldots, 22$.

2.3 For the dataset GME plot the daily time series of trading volume V_t. Calculate its autocorrelation function out to 24 lags, along with the confidence band. Define the Box–Cox transformation of volume as $y_t = (V_t^\alpha - 1)/\alpha$ for $\alpha > 0$. Calculate the autocorrelation function out to 24 lags along with the confidence band for selected values of α, for example $\alpha = 1/2, \alpha = 1/4$, and $\alpha = 0$ (which we define as $y_t = \log(V_t)$. For which value of α is the autocorrelation greatest in some sense?

2.4 For the dataset GME plot the daily time series of stock returns. Calculate the sample autocovariance function $\widehat{\gamma}(k)$ for $k = 0, 1$ and define the matrix

$$\widehat{\Gamma}_2 = \begin{pmatrix} \widehat{\gamma}(0) & \widehat{\gamma}(1) \\ \widehat{\gamma}(1) & \widehat{\gamma}(0) \end{pmatrix}.$$

Show that this matrix is strictly positive definite.

2.5 Suppose that y_t is a stationary Gaussian process with mean zero and variance one, and that $\rho(1) = 0.4$, $\rho(2) = 0.4$. What is the set of possible values that $\rho(3)$ could take?

2.6 Suppose that y_t is a stationary Gaussian process. Show that the autocorrelation function of y_t^2 is the square of the autocorrelation function of y_t.

2.7 Suppose that z_t and x_t are both linear processes. Prove that $y_t = \alpha x_t + \beta z_t$ is a linear process too.

2.8 Suppose that z_t and x_t are mutually independent stationary processes with autocovariance functions $\gamma_z(\cdot)$ and $\gamma_x(\cdot)$. Show that the process $y_t = \alpha x_t + \beta z_t$ has autocovariance function $\gamma_y(\cdot)$ with $\gamma_y(k) = \alpha^2 \gamma_x(k) + \beta^2 \gamma_z(k)$ for all k.

2.9 Suppose that y_t is a Markov process. Is it necessarily the case that y_t^2 is a Markov process?

2.10 Suppose that $y_t = \cos(2\pi\theta t + \varepsilon)$, where ε is a uniform random variable on $[-\pi, \pi]$. Calculate the autocovariance function of y_t. You may find it helpful to simulate data from the series y_t and just calculate the sample autocovariance function.

2.11 Suppose that $\{\varepsilon_t, t = 0, \pm 1, \pm 2, \ldots\}$ is a white noise process with $E(\varepsilon_t) = 0$, $E(\varepsilon_t^2) = \sigma^2$, and $\text{cov}(\varepsilon_t, \varepsilon_{t-j}) = 0$ for all $t = 0, \pm 1, \ldots$ and $j \neq 0$. Let

$y_t = \varepsilon_t + \varepsilon_{-t}$, $t = \pm1, \pm2, \ldots$ Calculate var(y_2), cov(y_2, y_3), and cov(y_2, y_{-2}). Is $\{y_t, t = 0, \pm1, \pm2, \ldots\}$ a white noise process? Is $\{y_t, t = 1, 2, \ldots\}$ a white noise process?

2.12 Check the formula (2.13) for the case that $T = 4$.

2.13 Suppose that $y_t = t$, $t = 1, \ldots, T$. Calculate analytically the (sample) mean and variance of this sequence. Calculate the sample autocovariance function $\widehat{\gamma}(k)$ and autocorrelation function $\widehat{\rho}(k)$ for $k = 1, \ldots, T - 1$. You may use the facts that $\sum_{i=1}^n i = n(n+1)/2$ and $\sum_{i=1}^n i^2 = n(n+1)(2n+1)/6$ for any $n \geq 1$. Now suppose that $y_t = t^{-1}$. Calculate numerically the sample autocorrelation of this sequence and compare with the previous answer.

2.14 Suppose that

$$y_t = \sum_{j=-\infty}^{\infty} w_j \varepsilon_{t-j} = w_0 \varepsilon_t + \sum_{j=1}^{\infty} w_j \varepsilon_{t-j} + \sum_{j=1}^{\infty} w_{-j} \varepsilon_{t+j} = y_{0t} + y_{1t} + y_{2t},$$

where ε_t are i.i.d. with mean zero and variance σ^2, while $\sum_{j=-\infty}^{\infty} |w_j| < \infty$. Show that y_{0t}, y_{1t}, y_{2t} are mutually uncorrelated. What is the value of $E(y_t \mid \varepsilon_t, \varepsilon_{t-1}, \ldots)$?

2.15 Suppose that y_t is a stationary process with mean zero and autocovariance function $\gamma(j)$. Let

$$\widehat{\gamma}(j) = \frac{1}{T} \sum_{t=j+1}^{T} y_t y_{t-j}, \quad j = 0, 1, \ldots, T - 1.$$

Is it the case that $\widehat{\gamma}(0) + 2 \sum_{j=1}^{T-1} \widehat{\gamma}(j) = 0$? Compare this estimator with the estimator based on the demeaned data $y_t \mapsto y_t - \bar{y}$. Is there any efficiency gain by using the estimator based on the demeaned data versus the raw data in the case where it is known that the mean is zero?

2.16 Suppose that x_t, y_t are i.i.d. standard Gaussian with mutual correlation ρ. Let $\widehat{\rho} = \sum_{t=1}^{T} x_t y_t / T$. Show that

$$\sqrt{T}(\widehat{\rho} - \rho) \Longrightarrow N(0, 1 + \rho^2).$$

You should consult the material on Gaussian distributions in Appendix B. Suggest a confidence interval for ρ. Contrast this result with the result for sample autocorrelations of dependent non-Gaussian processes derived in this chapter. How does your answer change if x_t, y_t are Gaussian with correlation ρ but have means μ_x, μ_y and variances σ_x^2, σ_y^2? Now suppose that x_{it}, y_{it} are i.i.d. standard Gaussian with mutual correlation ρ_i, $i = 1, 2$. Derive the limiting distribution of $\widehat{\rho}_1 - \widehat{\rho}_2$ and suggest a test of the hypothesis that $\rho_1 = \rho_2$.

2.17 Suppose that x_t, y_t are i.i.d. standard Gaussian with mutual correlation ρ. Define the maximum likelihood estimator (MLE) of ρ and show that

$$\sqrt{T}(\widehat{\rho}_{\mathrm{MLE}} - \rho) \Longrightarrow N\left(0, \frac{(1 - \rho^2)^2}{1 + \rho^2}\right).$$

2.18 Suppose that y_t is a stationary Gaussian series with mean zero and autocorrelation $\rho(k) = 0$ for $k > 2$. What is the autocorrelation function of $x_t = y_t^2$? What is the autocorrelation function of $x_t = y_t y_{t-3}$? What is the autocorrelation function of $x_t = y_t y_{t-1}$ and $x_t = y_t y_{t-2}$?

2.19 Suppose that y_t is a stationary series with autocorrelation $\rho(k) = 0$ for $k > 2$. Using the formula (2.21), obtain a large-sample confidence interval for $\widehat{\rho}(3)$, $\widehat{\rho}(2)$, and $\widehat{\rho}(1)$.

2.20 The variogram is defined as

$$V(t,j) = \frac{1}{2}\text{var}(y_t - y_{t-j}), \quad j = 0, \pm 1, \ldots$$

Suppose that y_t is a stationary process with finite variance and autocovariance function $\gamma(\cdot)$.

(a) Show that $V(t,j) = V(j) = \gamma(0) - \gamma(j)$.

(b) Consider the sample estimator

$$\widehat{V}(j) = \frac{1}{2}\frac{1}{T-j}\sum_{t=j+1}^{T}(y_t - y_{t-j})^2.$$

Show that this is exactly unbiased. Derive its limiting distribution, when
  (i) y_t is i.i.d.
  (ii) y_t is a stationary martingale difference process.

(c) Now suppose that $y_{t+1} = y_t + \varepsilon_{t+1}$, where ε_t is a stationary shock process with mean zero and autocovariance function $\gamma(\cdot)$.

(d) Show that

$$V(t,j) = V(j) = j\frac{\gamma(0)}{2} + \sum_{k=1}^{j}(j-k)\gamma(k).$$

3   Linear Time Series Models

We next discuss the general class of autoregressive moving average (ARMA) models with an emphasis on the stationary and invertible case. These are a subset of the class of linear processes that are widely used in practice and form the basis of much model building. We first discuss the key properties of these models. We discuss the estimation of the parameters of specific ARMA models based on observed data and correct specification, and we discuss the associated inference questions around these parameters. We also discuss the model selection question, which allows for the order of the model to be unknown. The classic treatment of this is due to Box and Jenkins (1970) who laid out much of the methodology we will discuss here.

3.1   ARMA Models

Definition 3.1   Suppose that $y_t \in \mathbb{R}$ for $t \in \mathcal{T}$. Suppose that α, σ^2, $\phi_1, \ldots, \phi_p$, and $\theta_1, \ldots, \theta_q$ are real numbers such that

$$y_t = \alpha + \phi_1 y_{t-1} + \cdots + \phi_p y_{t-p} + \varepsilon_t - \theta_1 \varepsilon_{t-1} - \cdots - \theta_q \varepsilon_{t-q}, \tag{3.1}$$

where ε_t is i.i.d., with mean zero and variance σ^2. Then y_t is an ARMA(p, q) process.

The outcome variable y_t is defined recursively in terms of its own past and a series of random shocks; together this forms a stochastic difference equation. The model is about the dynamic response of the series to its own past, that is, the history of past values and random shocks determine the present circumstances in a recursive fashion. One can talk of the input process or shock process $\{\varepsilon_t\}$ and the output process $\{y_t\}$, in which the ARMA model is one way of converting the former into the latter. We can also just think of it as an explicit model of the dependence structure of the process $\{y_t\}$. The parameter values α, σ^2, $\phi_1, \ldots, \phi_p$, $\theta_1, \ldots, \theta_q$ determine the properties of the process $\{y_t\}$. This model class is very general since $p, q \in \mathbb{N}$, and thus we can capture a wide pattern of dynamic behavior. Indeed, for any given summable autocovariance function $\gamma(\cdot)$ and any $\epsilon > 0$, there exists an ARMA(p, q) process whose autocovariance is arbitrarily close to $\gamma(\cdot)$ in the sense that $\sum_{j=0}^{\infty} |\gamma(j) - \gamma_{p,q}(j)| \leq \epsilon$.[1]

The model (3.1) is incomplete without specifying what $\mathcal{T}$ is and when and how the process starts. There are three ways of completing this definition:

---

[1] This follows because for any integer k there exists an ARMA(p, q) process with autocovariance function identically equal to $\gamma_y(j), j = 0, 1, \ldots, k$.

1. Suppose that $y_0, \ldots, y_{1-p}$ and $\varepsilon_0, \ldots, \varepsilon_{1-q}$ are fixed nonrandom initial conditions and $\{\varepsilon_t\}_{t=1}^{\infty}$ are given random variables. Then $\{y_1, y_2, \ldots\}$ is a well-defined stochastic process.

2. Suppose that $y_0, \ldots, y_{1-p}$ and $\varepsilon_0, \ldots, \varepsilon_{1-q}$ are random initial conditions chosen from some joint distribution, and $\{\varepsilon_t\}_{t=1}^{\infty}$ are given random variables. Then $\{y_1, y_2, \ldots\}$ is a well-defined stochastic process.

3. Suppose that $\{\varepsilon_t\}_{t=-\infty}^{\infty}$ are given random variables and (3.1) is well defined for $t = 0, \pm 1, \pm 2, \ldots$

We will consider the third case, the infinite-past case, since this is in some mathematical respects simpler; we will ask later whether the process y_t is well defined in this case, which does not automatically follow, and indeed we will require restrictions on the model parameters in order to ensure this.

It is convenient to write the ARMA model using the lag polynomial notation

$$A(L)y_t = \alpha + B(L)\varepsilon_t, \tag{3.2}$$

where the lag polynomials $A(L) = 1 - \phi_1 L - \cdots - \phi_p L^p$ and $B(L) = 1 - \theta_1 L - \cdots - \theta_q L^q$. Here, the lag operator is defined through $Ly_t = y_{t-1}$, which implies, for example, that $L^k y_t = y_{t-k}$ and $L^{-1} y_t = y_{t+1}$. Some authors prefer the term "backshift operator" and use the letter B, but this sounds nasty. Usually we suppose that the ARMA representation has $\phi_p, \theta_q \neq 0$ and that the polynomials A, B have no common factors, which just asserts that the process cannot be represented by a lower-order process. It is usual to exclude common factors in the two lag polynomials because otherwise there is a redundancy. For example, suppose that $y_t = \varepsilon_t$, then we could also write $A(L)y_t = A(L)\varepsilon_t$ for any lag polynomial $A(L)$, which represents the same process as an ARMA(p,p) process. Likewise, if $A(L)y_t = B(L)\varepsilon_t$ we can also write this as $C(L)A(L)y_t = C(L)B(L)\varepsilon_t$ for another lag polynomial $C(L)$, which is a common factor of the polynomials $C(L)A(L)$ and $C(L)B(L)$. This is an important issue to bear in mind when choosing between ARMA models of different orders, and it is only an issue when both AR (autoregressive) and MA (moving average) components are present. Pure AR or pure MA models cannot be canceled in this way.

The ARMA class is very general yet easy to work with. We may rewrite the model in terms of the demeaned variable (assuming that the mean of y_t exists and is constant with respect to t), that is,

$$A(L)\widetilde{y}_t = B(L)\varepsilon_t,$$

where $\widetilde{y}_t = y_t - \mu$ with $\mu = E(y_t)$. You can think of this as an alternative parameterization of the model in terms of $\mu, \sigma^2, \phi_1, \ldots, \phi_p$, and $\theta_1, \ldots, \theta_q$. In some cases, μ is a more meaningful parameter than α; many software packages work with this parameterization.

3.1.1 Special Case: AR(1) With No Drift

Suppose that

$$y_t = \phi y_{t-1} + \varepsilon_t, \tag{3.3}$$

where ε_t is i.i.d. with mean zero and variance σ^2. In this special case, the lag polynomials are $A(L) = 1 - \phi L$ and $B(L) = 1$ in (3.2). The current value of y_t depends on its value last period times a constant plus a random disturbance around that position. In this case, $E(y_t \mid y_{t-1}, \ldots) = \phi y_{t-1}$ and $\text{var}(y_t \mid y_{t-1}, \ldots) = \sigma^2$. The size of the shock determines how far we expect y_t to deviate from ϕy_{t-1}. If $0 < \phi < 1$, then $E(y_t \mid y_{t-1}, \ldots)$ is closer to zero than y_{t-1} but with the same sign. The probability that $y_t > 0$ given that $y_{t-1} > 0$ is greater (lesser) than one-half (provided ε_t is symmetrically distributed about zero) according to whether $\phi > 0$ ($\phi < 0$); the process with $\phi > 0$ possesses what may be called momentum behavior (continues in the same direction), whereas the process with $\phi < 0$ possesses contrarian or reversal behavior, in finance terminology. Indeed, the probabilities of crossing zero decrease (increase) with the magnitude of ϕ. This property can be seen in the sample paths: as $\phi > 0$ increases, the trajectory tends to spend longer and longer sojourns above and longer sojourns below zero.

The AR(1) process is a first-order stochastic difference equation. If the process is started at time $t = 0$ with value y_0, then this is a well-defined process for each t. We suppose that the process may be defined for all time, that is, $t = 0, \pm 1, \ldots$ In this case, there is a question about whether this is a well-defined process, which we address next.

The condition $|\phi| < 1$ is necessary and sufficient for y_t to be a stationary process. Write $y_{t-1} = \phi y_{t-2} + \varepsilon_{t-1}$; substituting backwards we obtain

$$y_t = \varepsilon_t + \phi \varepsilon_{t-1} + \phi^2 y_{t-2} = \varepsilon_t + \phi \varepsilon_{t-1} + \phi^2 \varepsilon_{t-2} + \cdots$$

$$= \sum_{j=0}^{\infty} \phi^j \varepsilon_{t-j} = f(\varepsilon_t, \varepsilon_{t-1}, \ldots).$$

We claim that this implies that y_t depends on all the past shocks, and that y_t is a well-defined random variable. Clearly, we need $|\phi| < 1$ for the above sum to exist, that is, this condition is necessary and sufficient for the limit of the deterministic quantity $\lim_{k \to \infty} \sum_{j=0}^{k} |\phi|^j$ to be finite. Formally, when we consider the convergence of the random sum $\sum_{j=0}^{k} \phi^j \varepsilon_{t-j}$, we need some probabilistic notion of convergence such as mean square. Specifically, we say that

$$E\left[\left(y_t - \sum_{j=0}^{k} \phi^j \varepsilon_{t-j}\right)^2\right] = E\left[\left(\sum_{j=k+1}^{\infty} \phi^j \varepsilon_{t-j}\right)^2\right] = E\left(\varepsilon_t^2\right) \sum_{j=k+1}^{\infty} \phi^{2j} \longrightarrow 0$$

as $k \to \infty$. Note that for any bounded sequence $\{\psi_j\}$, $\sum_{j=0}^{\infty} |\psi_j|^\alpha < \infty$ implies that $\sum_{j=0}^{\infty} |\psi_j|^\beta < \infty$ for any $\beta > \alpha$ because

$$\sum_{j=0}^{\infty} |\psi_j|^\beta \leq \max_{j \geq 0} |\psi_j|^{\beta - \alpha} \sum_{j=0}^{\infty} |\psi_j|^\alpha.$$

This implies, for example, that if $\sum_{j=0}^{\infty} |\phi^j| < \infty$, then $\sum_{j=0}^{\infty} \phi^{2j} < \infty$. Alternatively, we may show convergence in probability of the sum, that is, for all $\epsilon > 0$,

$$\lim_{k \to \infty} \Pr\left(\left|y_t - \sum_{j=0}^{k} \phi^j \varepsilon_{t-j}\right| > \epsilon\right) = 0.$$

This argument does not require the existence of moments for ε_t and so would be applicable, for example, to an autoregressive process with Cauchy shocks. In practice, the mean square convergence is often the easiest to work with when we assume finite variance of the shocks, which we do.

In this case, we can verify that $y_t = \sum_{j=0}^{\infty} \phi^j \varepsilon_{t-j}$ is well defined and is a solution of the difference equation. In fact, it is the unique **causal** stationary solution, that is, it is the unique solution that depends only on $\{\varepsilon_{t-j}, j \geq 0\}$. The full proof of this can be found in Brockwell and Davis (2006). Suppose that the process is instead initialized at some value y_0; then we can establish asymptotic stationarity in the sense that the above approximations hold when $t \to \infty$, and specifically $\lim_{t \to \infty} \text{cov}(y_t, y_{t-s})$ exists and is a function only of s.

Suppose that $|\phi| > 1$; then the sum $\sum_{j=0}^{k} \phi^j$ does not converge as $k \to \infty$. However, in that case we may write

$$y_t = \frac{1}{\phi} y_{t+1} - \frac{1}{\phi} \varepsilon_{t+1}.$$

We substitute forward, replacing y_{t+1} by $y_{t+2}/\phi + \varepsilon_{t+2}/\phi$ and so on, to obtain

$$y_t = \sum_{j=0}^{\infty} \frac{(-1)^j}{\phi^{j+1}} \varepsilon_{t+1+j}, \tag{3.4}$$

which is a well-defined solution (and the unique stationary solution) of the original difference equation, but depends on future values, that is, y_t is a **noncausal** process. Note that the autocorrelation function of this noncausal process is the same as the autocorrelation function of a causal process with coefficient $1/\phi \in (-1, 1)$. Note that there are no causal solutions to the difference equation (3.3) when $|\phi| > 1$. The case where $\phi = 1$ is nonstationary, period, and we will treat this process separately in Chapter 6.

Now we calculate the moments of y_t in the case $|\phi| < 1$ using the stationarity property. Suppose that $\mu = E(y_t)$. Then by virtue of stationarity we must have $\mu = E(y_t) = \phi E(y_{t-1}) = \phi \mu$, which can be true if and only if $\mu = 0$. Furthermore, we must have $\text{var}(y_t) = \phi^2 \text{var}(y_{t-1}) + \sigma^2$, which is itself a first-order deterministic difference equation, and implies by similar logic that

$$\gamma(0) = \frac{\sigma^2}{1 - \phi^2},$$

where $\gamma(0) = \text{var}(y_t) = \text{var}(y_{t-1})$. This last calculation of course requires that $|\phi| < 1$. Next,

$$\gamma(1) = \text{cov}(y_t, y_{t-1}) = E(y_t y_{t-1}) = \phi E(y_{t-1}^2) + 0,$$

which implies that

$$\gamma(1) = \phi \gamma(0) = \phi \frac{\sigma^2}{1 - \phi^2}.$$

The higher lags of the autocovariance and autocorrelation functions satisfy the first-order difference equations

$$\gamma(k) = \phi \gamma(k-1) = \sigma^2 \frac{\phi^k}{1 - \phi^2}, \qquad \rho(k) = \phi \rho(k-1) = \phi^k. \tag{3.5}$$

If $\phi > 0$, then $\gamma(k), \rho(k)$ are positive for all k, whereas if $\phi < 0$, then $\gamma(k), \rho(k)$ oscillate between positive and negative values. This is the signature property of the AR(1) process, which Box and Jenkins (1970) emphasized. Both $\gamma(k)$ and $\rho(k)$ decay in magnitude very quickly towards zero as $k \rightarrow \infty$. This is called exponential or geometric decay, to be contrasted with algebraic or polynomial decay, which we will encounter in connection with **long-memory** processes. Note that for any t, $E(y_{t+k} \mid y_t, \ldots) = \phi^k y_t \rightarrow 0 = E(y_t)$ as $k \rightarrow \infty$, that is, the process is expected to revert to its (unconditional) mean over the long horizon (in a monotonic fashion if $\phi > 0$, or an oscillating fashion if $\phi < 0$). We also note that $E(y_t \mid y_{t-1}) = E_L(y_t \mid y_{t-1}) = \phi y_{t-1}$, and so ϕ is the slope of the best linear predictor.

The process y_t is a Markov process (assuming that ε_t is i.i.d.), and it follows that the partial autocorrelation function $\pi(1) = \rho(1)$ and $\pi(k) = 0$ for all $k > 1$, because in this case the future is independent of the past given the present. Box and Jenkins (1970) argued to use this characterization to identify the order of an autoregressive process. Furthermore, we have, for any $y \in \mathbb{R}$,

$$\Pr(y_t \leq y \mid y_{t-1}, y_{t-2}, \ldots) = \Pr(y_t \leq y \mid y_{t-1}).$$

For a Markov process, the transition CDF $F(y \mid y') = \Pr(y_t \leq y \mid y_{t-1} = y')$ expresses how the process moves from time $t - 1$ to time t. For the AR(1) process this is, for any $y, y' \in \mathbb{R}$,

$$F(y \mid y') = \Pr(\varepsilon_t \leq y - \phi y_{t-1} \mid y_{t-1} = y') = F_\varepsilon(y - \phi y'),$$

where F_ε is the CDF of ε_t. If the error process ε_t is continuously distributed with density function f_ε, then the transition density of the process $f(y \mid y')$ defined through $F(y \mid y') = \int_{-\infty}^{y} f(y_+ \mid y') \, dy_+$ satisfies $f(y \mid y') = f_\varepsilon(y - \phi y')$, and is time invariant for any value of ϕ.

We may ask what the stationary distribution of y_t is when $|\phi| < 1$. Let f_y, φ_y be the density function and characteristic function of y_t respectively, and let φ_ε be the characteristic function of ε_t; then $f_y(y)$ ($\varphi_\varepsilon(u)$) must be the unique solution to the integral (functional) equations

$$f_y(y) = \int f_\varepsilon(y - \phi y') f_y(y') \, dy', \quad y \in \mathbb{R}, \tag{3.6}$$

$$\varphi_y(u) = \varphi_y(\phi u) \varphi_\varepsilon(u), \qquad u \in \mathbb{R}.$$

There are regularity conditions that guarantee the existence and uniqueness of solutions to these types of equations – see Tong (1990). They are generally difficult to solve analytically, but there are some special cases where explicit solutions are available.

Example 3.1   Suppose that $\varphi_\varepsilon(u) = \exp(-\gamma |u|^\alpha)$ for some scale parameter $\gamma > 0$ and shape parameter $\alpha \in (0, 2]$, which is the characteristic function of a stable random variable. The Gaussian distribution is the leading special case with $\alpha = 2$. Suppose that $\varphi_y(u) = \exp(-\gamma^* |u|^\alpha)$ for some $\gamma^* > 0$, then it must be the case that

$$\exp(-\gamma^* |u|^\alpha) = \exp(-\gamma^* |\phi|^\alpha |u|^\alpha) \exp(-\gamma |u|^\alpha), \tag{3.7}$$

and this equation can be satisfied if and only if $\gamma = \gamma^* (1 - |\phi|^\alpha) > 0$. Therefore, the stationary distribution of an AR(1) process with a stably distributed innovation is stably distributed with the same shape parameter α but with a transformed scale parameter γ^*. We discuss in Chapter 11 processes with heavy tails and their applications in financial time series.

Why do we need to know the stationary distribution? Suppose that you want to simulate a stationary autoregression with an error process whose distribution is not Gaussian. To make sure that the process is exactly stationary you should initialize with a draw from the stationary distribution, which is unknown. If we assume that y_t is a stationary driftless AR(1) process, and has a stationary distribution F_y, then if $y_0 \sim F_y$, the process

$$y_t = \phi^t y_0 + \sum_{j=0}^{t-1} \phi^j \varepsilon_{t-j}$$

is stationary with marginal distribution F_y. However, to determine F_y from F_ε requires a solution to (3.6). The usual practical solution to this is to initialize in some way and then to run the process for many "burn in" periods so that the process thereafter approximates the stationary process.

Note that the process y_t possesses the property of **insensitive dependence on initial conditions**: suppose we start the process at y_0' or y_0, then the two processes y_t', y_t satisfy

$$|y_t - y_t'| = |\phi^t y_0 - \phi^t y_0'| \le |\phi^t| \times |y_0 - y_0'|,$$

and as $t \to \infty$ the discrepancy between the two processes goes to zero. This means that the initial condition issue is not so important for linear stationary processes.

3.1.2 Moving Average MA(1)

Suppose that $y_t = \mu + \varepsilon_t - \theta\varepsilon_{t-1}$, where ε_t are i.i.d. with mean zero and variance σ^2. This is not a Markov process: y_t and y_{t-2} are mutually dependent conditional on y_{t-1} (even though unconditionally y_t and y_{t-2} are mutually independent). This process is well defined for any t without any discussion of initial conditions so long as both $\varepsilon_t, \varepsilon_{t-1}$ are given random variables. In this case, $E(y_t) = \mu$ and $\gamma(0) = \sigma^2(1 + \theta^2)$. Furthermore,

$$\gamma(1) = \text{cov}(y_t, y_{t-1}) = E\left((\varepsilon_t - \theta\varepsilon_{t-1})(\varepsilon_{t-1} - \theta\varepsilon_{t-2})\right) = -\theta E(\varepsilon_{t-1}^2) = -\theta\sigma^2,$$

while $\gamma(k) = \text{cov}(y_t, y_{t-k}) = 0$ for $k \ge 2$. Therefore,

$$\rho(1) = \frac{-\theta}{1 + \theta^2}, \qquad \rho(k) = 0, \quad k = 2, 3, \ldots$$

This is a 1-dependent series, meaning that y_t, y_{t-j} are independent for any $j > 1$. In fact, even the one lag dependence is limited: the mapping $\theta \mapsto \rho(1)$ has slope $(\partial\rho(1)/\partial\theta)$ equal to $(\theta^2 - 1)/(1 + \theta^2)^2$, which decreases monotonically in θ^2 until $\theta^2 = 1$ (i.e., $\theta = \pm 1$), where $\rho(1)$ takes the values $\pm 1/2$, that is, for an MA(1) process it is impossible for the autocorrelation to exceed $1/2$ in absolute value. Exercise 3.10 considers the MA(2) case. The partial autocorrelation function is

$$\pi(k) = \frac{-\theta^k}{1 + \theta^2 + \cdots + \theta^{2k}}, \quad k = 1, 2, \ldots$$

This is nonzero for all k but tends rapidly to zero as k increases. It is also maximal at $\theta = \pm 1$ and $k = 1$, with maximal value $\pm 1/2$.

The MA(1) process is automatically stationary for any value of θ, meaning no value of θ could generate a nonstationary process when ε_t is i.i.d. Indeed, provided only ε_t is itself a stationary process, then y_t is also stationary. We may obtain a further characterization under the assumption that the shocks are i.i.d. In that case, the characteristic function of y_t satisfies

$$\varphi_y(s) = E\left(\exp\left(isy_t\right)\right)$$
$$= \exp\left(is\mu\right)\left(E\left(\exp\left(is\varepsilon_t\right)\right)E\left(\exp\left(-is\theta\varepsilon_{t-1}\right)\right)\right) = \exp\left(is\mu\right)\varphi_\varepsilon(s)\varphi_\varepsilon(-s\theta),$$

where $\varphi_\varepsilon(s)$ is the characteristic function of ε_t for any $s \in \mathbb{R}$. This does not vary over time t. Provided ε_t has a density f_ε, we may write

$$F_y(y) = \Pr\left(y_t \leq y\right) = \int F_\varepsilon(y - \mu + \theta x) f_\varepsilon(x)\, dx,$$

and the density of y_t is $f_y(y) = \int f_\varepsilon(y - \mu + \theta x) f_\varepsilon(x)\, dx$ by differentiation; this is called a convolution in the mathematical literature and is often denoted $f_\varepsilon * f_\varepsilon(y - \mu)$.

For simplicity we set $\mu = 0$ in the remainder of this section. If $|\theta| < 1$, we say that the MA(1) process is **invertible** , and we can write it as

$$y_t = -\sum_{j=1}^{\infty} \theta^j y_{t-j} + \varepsilon_t. \tag{3.8}$$

That is, $E(y_t \mid y_{t-1}, y_{t-2}, \ldots) = -\sum_{j=1}^{\infty} \theta^j y_{t-j}$. We can show this explicitly by writing $\varepsilon_{t-1} = y_{t-1} + \theta\varepsilon_{t-2}$ and substituting repeatedly to obtain

$$y_t + \theta y_{t-1} + \theta^2 y_{t-2} + \cdots + \theta^{t-1} y_1 = \varepsilon_t - \theta^t \varepsilon_0$$

and continuing backwards. Formally, $E(y_t \mid y_{t-1}, \ldots, y_1)$ converges in mean square to $E(y_t \mid y_{t-1}, y_{t-2}, \ldots)$ as $t \to \infty$, provided $\theta \in (-1, 1)$. If $\theta \geq 1$, we say the process is noninvertible (in terms of its own past) and we cannot apply this logic. Nevertheless, the process is well defined and stationary, it just cannot be expressed in this simple way in terms of past y's.

In fact, there is a question of identifiability in the MA(1) process, since the values θ and $1/\theta$ yield the same autocorrelation function and hence cannot be distinguished by estimation strategies that rely only on this function. This is easy to see from the fact that

$$\frac{-\theta}{1 + \theta^2} = \frac{-(1/\theta)}{1 + (1/\theta)^2}$$

for any $\theta \in \mathbb{R}$. Let $\varepsilon_t^* = \varepsilon_t \theta$ for each t; then the process $y_t^* = \varepsilon_t^* - \theta^{-1}\varepsilon_{t-1}^* = \theta\varepsilon_t - \varepsilon_{t-1}$ has exactly the same autocovariance function as y_t. The sibling processes y_t and y_t^* cannot be distinguished from each other based on data alone.

If $\theta \in (-1, 1)$, then $|1/\theta| > 1$ and the process with coefficient $1/\theta$ is not invertible. We will say that the invertible sibling is **fundamental** and we will have a preference for this process. The advantage of y_t is that it can be expressed as an infinite autoregression of its own past, whereas y_t^* cannot; rather, y_t^* can be expressed as an infinite autoregression of its own future, which seems rather presumptuous.

The case $\theta = 1$ is special. It is stationary but not invertible either in terms of its past or its future. Nevertheless, we may calculate the best linear predictor given one lag:

$$E_L(y_{t+1} \mid y_t) = \frac{\text{cov}(y_{t+1}, y_t)}{\text{var}(y_t)} y_t = -\frac{1}{2} y_t.$$

Conditioning on two lags, we have

$$E_L(y_{t+1} \mid y_t, y_{t-1})$$

$$= (\text{cov}(y_{t+1}, y_t), \text{cov}(y_{t+1}, y_{t-1})) \begin{bmatrix} \text{var}(y_t) & \text{cov}(y_{t+1}, y_t) \\ \text{cov}(y_{t+1}, y_t) & \text{var}(y_t) \end{bmatrix}^{-1} \begin{pmatrix} y_t \\ y_{t-1} \end{pmatrix}$$

$$= (-\sigma^2, 0) \begin{bmatrix} 2\sigma^2 & -\sigma^2 \\ -\sigma^2 & 2\sigma^2 \end{bmatrix}^{-1} \begin{pmatrix} y_t \\ y_{t-1} \end{pmatrix}$$

$$= (-1, 0) \begin{bmatrix} 2 & -1 \\ -1 & 2 \end{bmatrix}^{-1} \begin{pmatrix} y_t \\ y_{t-1} \end{pmatrix}$$

$$= -\frac{2}{3} y_t - \frac{1}{3} y_{t-1}.$$

Extending this, we find that

$$E_L(y_{t+1} \mid y_t, y_{t-1}, \dots, y_1) = -\frac{t}{t+1} y_t - \dots - \frac{1}{t+1} y_1.$$

This does not lead to a happy ending as $t \to \infty$: the coefficients on the lagged $y's$ are not square-summable; although they do decay to zero, they do not do so fast enough for this sum to converge. However, we may write

$$\frac{t}{t+1} y_t + \dots + \frac{1}{t+1} y_1 = \left(\left(1 - \frac{1}{t+1}\right) y_t + \dots + \left(1 - \frac{t}{t+1}\right) y_1 \right)$$

$$= y_t + \dots + y_1 - \frac{1}{t+1} (y_t + 2y_{t-1} + \dots + ty_1)$$

$$= \varepsilon_t - \varepsilon_0 - \left(\frac{1}{t} \sum_{k=1}^{t-1} \varepsilon_{t-k} - \varepsilon_0 \right),$$

because of the cancellation of shocks. If t is large, the right-hand side converges to a well-defined random variable (Hannan, 1970). If ε_t is Gaussian, then of course so is $y_t, y_{t-1}, \dots, y_1$ and hence $E(y_{t+1} \mid y_t, y_{t-1}, \dots, y_1)$ is Gaussian because $E(y_{t+1} \mid y_t, y_{t-1}, \dots, y_1) = E_L(y_{t+1} \mid y_t, y_{t-1}, \dots, y_1)$, a linear function of $y_t, y_{t-1}, \dots, y_1$.

On the other hand, if ε_t is not Gaussian, $E(y_{t+1} \mid y_t, y_{t-1}, \dots, y_1)$ may not equal $E_L(y_{t+1} \mid y_t, y_{t-1}, \dots, y_1)$ in the noninvertible MA case, as the following example illustrates.

Example 3.2   Suppose that $y_t = \varepsilon_t - \varepsilon_{t-1}$, where $\varepsilon_t \sim \exp(1)$, that is, $f_\varepsilon(e) = \exp(-e)$, $e \geq 0$. Here, $E(\varepsilon_t) \neq 0$ but $E(y_t) = 0$. We have

$$E(y_t \mid y_{t-1}) = E(\varepsilon_t - \varepsilon_{t-1} \mid \varepsilon_{t-1} - \varepsilon_{t-2}) = E(\varepsilon_t) - E(\varepsilon_{t-1} \mid \varepsilon_{t-1} - \varepsilon_{t-2}).$$

We can show that $E(\varepsilon_{t-1} \mid \varepsilon_{t-1} - \varepsilon_{t-2} = x) = x \times 1(x > 0) + 1/2$. It follows that

$$E(y_t \mid y_{t-1}) = \frac{1}{2} - y_{t-1} 1(y_{t-1} > 0),$$

$$E_L(y_t \mid y_{t-1}) = \frac{1}{2} + \frac{1}{2} y_{t-1}.$$

The slope of the best linear predictor is as always $+1/2$ – it does not know that $\varepsilon_{t-1} \geq 0$ but $\varepsilon_{t-1} - \varepsilon_{t-2}$ can take any value. The conditional expectation, however, uses the knowledge that $\varepsilon_t \geq 0$ and so $E(\varepsilon_{t-1} \mid \varepsilon_{t-1} - \varepsilon_{t-2} = x) \geq 0$ for all x.

3.1.3   General ARMA Case

We return to the general ARMA process (3.1). We first state the general result on stationarity and invertibility.

Theorem 3.1   *The ARMA(p, q) process $\{y_t\}$ is stationary provided the roots of the complex polynomial $A(z) = 1 - \phi_1 z - \cdots - \phi_p z^p$ (that is, the values $z_1^*, \ldots, z_p^* \in \mathbb{C}$ for which $A(z_j^*) = 0$) lie outside the unit circle on the complex plane or, equivalently, the complex polynomial $A^{\#}(w) = w^p - \phi_1 w^{p-1} - \cdots - \phi_p$ has roots $w_1^{\#}, \ldots, w_p^{\#} \in \mathbb{C}$ that lie inside the unit circle. The ARMA(p, q) process $\{y_t\}$ is invertible provided the roots of the complex polynomial $B(z) = 1 - \theta_1 z - \cdots - \theta_p z^p$ lie outside the unit circle on the complex plane or, equivalently, the roots of the complex polynomial $B^{\#}(w) = w^q - \theta_1 w^{q-1} - \cdots - \theta_p$ lie inside the unit circle.*

Note that we obtain $A^{\#}(w)$ by multiplying $A(z)$ by z^{-p} and letting $w = z^{-1}$. By the fundamental theorem of algebra there exist solutions to the equation $A^{\#}(w) = 0$ in the complex domain and there are at most p distinct complex-valued roots $w_1^{\#}, \ldots, w_p^{\#}$. The complex plain can be defined in polar coordinates as the set of points $z = r(\cos(\theta) + i \sin(\theta)) = r \exp(i\theta)$ with $0 \leq r < \infty$ and $\theta \in [-\pi, \pi]$; inside the unit circle consists of such points for which $r < 1$, while outside the unit circle consists of such points for which $r > 1$, and the unit root case consists of points on the unit circle for which $r = 1$. We have explicit formulae for the roots in the quadratic case and some cubic cases, but otherwise these roots must be found numerically (most software does this automatically). One can always search the unit circle to see whether any value of $\theta \in [-\pi, \pi]$ satisfies $A^{\#}(\exp(i\theta)) = 0$ to determine whether a given process is stationary or not. We may want to distinguish between the case where all the roots are real valued and the case where some or all of the roots are complex valued. Complex roots come in conjugate pairs, whereas real roots do not have such a twin.

For the AR(1) process, the relevant polynomials are

$$A(z) = 1 - \phi z, \qquad A^{\#}(w) = w - \phi,$$

which have roots $z^* = 1/\phi$ and $w_1^{\#} = \phi$, which are both real numbers, and we have

$$\left| \frac{1}{\phi} \right| > 1 \Longleftrightarrow |\phi| < 1.$$

We next consider the stationarity condition for the AR(2) model, which requires more complicated arguments. In this case, $A(z) = 1 - \phi_1 z - \phi_2 z^2$ is a quadratic with roots z_1^*, z_2^*, which may be real or complex. We can factor $A(z)$ around its roots as follows:

$$A(z) = 1 - \phi_1 z - \phi_2 z = (1 - z_1^* z)(1 - z_2^* z). \tag{3.9}$$

This means that we can write the AR(2) process as a first-order autoregression of a first-order autoregression, that is,

$$(1 - z_2^* L) y_t = x_t, \qquad (1 - z_1^* L) x_t = \varepsilon_t \tag{3.10}$$

for some latent variable x_t that is itself an AR(1) process. In the case where the roots are real this needs no further explanation, but in the case where the roots are complex, the process x_t is complex valued in general.

To check the stationarity conditions it is more convenient to work with the polynomial $A^{\#}(w)$, whose roots are explicitly given by

$$w_1^{\#}, w_2^{\#} = \frac{\phi_1 \pm \sqrt{\phi_1^2 + 4\phi_2}}{2}.$$

The roots are real provided $\phi_1^2 + 4\phi_2 \geq 0$, but complex valued otherwise. If the roots are complex they are conjugates, that is, $z_1^* = x + yi = r \exp(i\theta)$, $z_2^* = x - yi = r \exp(-i\theta)$, and so have the same modulus.

For stationarity we must check whether the roots of $A^{\#}(w)$ are less than one in magnitude. We consider the real and complex root cases separately:

- If the roots are real (i.e., $\phi_1^2 + 4\phi_2 \geq 0$), then the condition is equivalent to

$$\left| \frac{\phi_1 + \sqrt{\phi_1^2 + 4\phi_2}}{2} \right|, \left| \frac{\phi_1 - \sqrt{\phi_1^2 + 4\phi_2}}{2} \right| < 1. \tag{3.11}$$

- If the roots are complex (i.e., $\phi_1^2 + 4\phi_2 < 0$), then they are complex conjugates of each other and we must check whether

$$\frac{2\phi_1^2 + 4\phi_2}{4} < 1. \tag{3.12}$$

After some algebra one can show that these two conditions are implied by three inequalities:

$$\phi_2 - \phi_1 < 1, \qquad \phi_1 + \phi_2 < 1, \qquad \phi_2 > -1. \tag{3.13}$$

This defines a triangular region of values of (ϕ_1, ϕ_2) for which the process is stationary (and the region of values where it is not). Note that it is not necessary that $|\phi_1| < 1$; however, if $\phi_1, \phi_2 \geq 0$ then we must have $\phi_1 + \phi_2 < 1$. The stationary region of the AR(2) process is shown in Figure 3.1. It is the shaded triangular region, which happens to be convex (a property that is useful for optimization algorithms). Within that region there are two subregions corresponding to real and complex solutions.

How do we know whether a given AR(p) process is stationary or not? In general one has to test whether the roots of the characteristic polynomial are less than one in

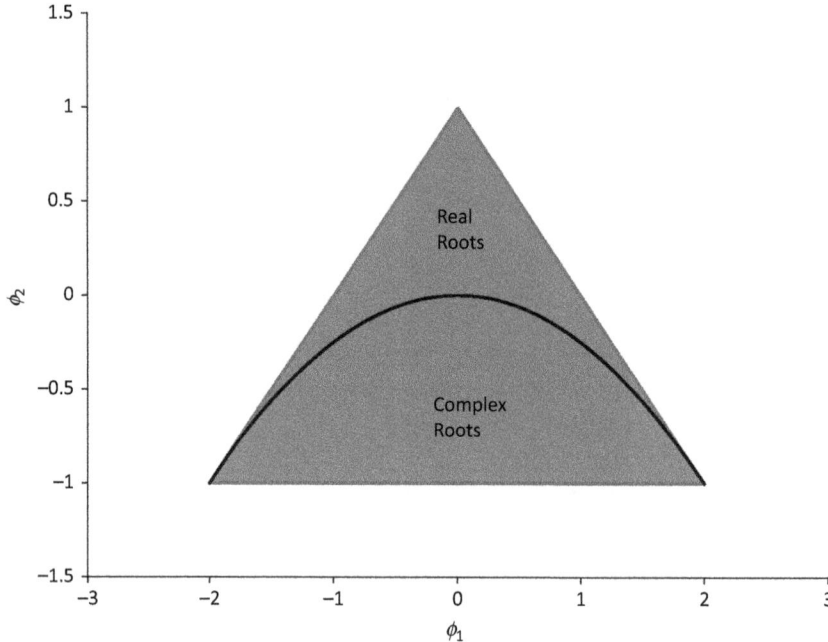

Figure 3.1 Stationary region of the AR(2) process.

magnitude; the roots of any polynomial can be found numerically using **Sturm's theorem** and the **Newton–Raphson algorithm**. Alternatively, one can identify the roots of the AR(p) process with the eigenvalues of the so-called companion matrix

$$A = \begin{pmatrix} \phi_1 & \phi_2 & \cdots & \phi_p \\ 1 & 0 & \cdots & \vdots \\ 0 & 1 & \ddots & \\ 0 & \cdots & & 0 \end{pmatrix}, \tag{3.14}$$

as we shall see later.

3.1.4   Using Stationarity to Calculate the AR(2) Autocovariance Function

If the process is stationary, then we can calculate the mean, variance, and autocovariance using this property. Specifically, we have, for any AR(2) process,

$$E(y_t) = \alpha + \phi_1 E(y_{t-1}) + \phi_2 E(y_{t-2}).$$

Stationarity implies that $E(y_t) = E(y_{t-1}) = E(y_{t-2})$, and so it follows that

$$E(y_t) = \mu = \frac{\alpha}{1 - \phi_1 - \phi_2}.$$

Furthermore,

$$\text{var}(y_t) = \phi_1^2 \text{var}(y_{t-1}) + \phi_2^2 \text{var}(y_{t-2}) + 2\phi_1\phi_2 \text{cov}(y_{t-1}, y_{t-2}) + \sigma^2,$$
$$\text{cov}(y_t, y_{t-1}) = \phi_1 \text{var}(y_{t-1}) + \phi_2 \text{cov}(y_{t-1}, y_{t-2}).$$

The last two equations can be written as

$$
\begin{pmatrix} 1 - \phi_1^2 - \phi_2^2 & -2\phi_1\phi_2 \\ -\phi_1 & 1 - \phi_2 \end{pmatrix} \begin{pmatrix} \gamma(0) \\ \gamma(1) \end{pmatrix} = \begin{pmatrix} \sigma^2 \\ 0 \end{pmatrix}. \tag{3.15}
$$

This 2×2 system can be solved explicitly (provided the determinant of the matrix is nonzero) as

$$
\gamma(0) = \sigma^2 \frac{1 - \phi_2}{(\phi_2 + 1)(1 - \phi_1 - \phi_2)(\phi_1 - \phi_2 + 1)},
$$

$$
\gamma(1) = \sigma^2 \frac{\phi_1}{(\phi_2 + 1)(1 - \phi_1 - \phi_2)(\phi_1 - \phi_2 + 1)} = \frac{\phi_1}{1 - \phi_2}\gamma(0).
$$

We further find that, for $k = 2, 3, \ldots,$

$$
\gamma(k) = \phi_1\gamma(k-1) + \phi_2\gamma(k-2), \tag{3.16}
$$

which is a linear nonstochastic difference equation whose initial conditions, $\gamma(0), \gamma(1)$, we have just determined. Dividing through by $\gamma(0)$ we obtain the following equations for the autocorrelations:

$$
\rho(0) = 1, \qquad \rho(1) = \frac{\phi_1}{1 - \phi_2},
$$

$$
\rho(k) = \phi_1\rho(k-1) + \phi_2\rho(k-2), \quad k \geq 2.
$$

We also have $\pi(1) = \rho(1)$, $\pi(2) = \phi_2$, and $\pi(k) = 0$ for all $k \geq 3$. Note that if $\phi_1, \phi_2 > 0$, then $\rho(k) > 0$ for all k. More generally, though, unlike the AR(1) case the autocovariance function is not restricted to be monotonically decreasing and can cycle around zero with alternating positive and negative values as well, depending on the values of ϕ_1, ϕ_2. Suppose that $\phi_1 = 0$ and $\phi_2 < 0$, then the roots of the AR polynomial are complex. In that case $\rho(1) = 0$, $\rho(2) = \phi_2 < 0$, $\rho(3) = 0$, $\rho(4) = \phi_2^2 > 0$, and so on. Figure 3.2 shows an example that has complex roots; it shows several cycles around zero.

3.1.5   Using Stationarity to Calculate the AR(p) Autocovariance Function

For the stationary AR(p) process we have the equations

$$
\gamma(k) = \phi_1\gamma(k-1) + \cdots + \phi_p\gamma(k-p) \tag{3.17}
$$

for all $k \geq 1$. For $k = 1, \ldots, p-1$ the equations sort of wrap around since $\gamma(k) = \gamma(-k)$, and we have, for example,

$$
\gamma(p-1) = \phi_1\gamma(p-2) + \cdots + \phi_{p-2}\gamma(1) + \phi_{p-1}\gamma(0) + \phi_p\gamma(1). \tag{3.18}
$$

In addition, we have

$$
\gamma(0) = \mathrm{var}\left(\sum_{j=1}^{p} \phi_j y_{t-j}\right) + \mathrm{var}(\varepsilon_t)
$$

$$
= \sum_{j=1}^{p} \phi_j^2\gamma(0) + 2\sum_{j=1}^{p-1} \phi_j\phi_{j+1} \times \gamma(1) + \cdots + 2\phi_1\phi_p\gamma(p-1) + \sigma^2. \tag{3.19}
$$

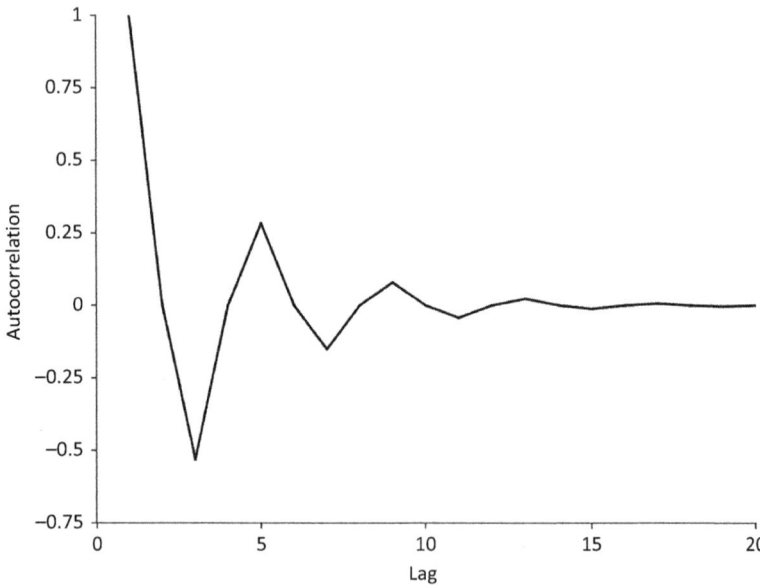

Figure 3.2 ACF of the process $y_t = -0.532 y_{t-2} + \varepsilon_t$.

Combining these relationships, we obtain the following $p \times p$ system of equations for the autocovariances $j = 0, 1, \ldots, p - 1$:

$$
\begin{pmatrix}
1 - \sum_{j=1}^{p} \phi_j^2 & -2 \sum_{j=1}^{p-1} \phi_j \phi_{j+1} & \cdots & -2\phi_1 \phi_p \\
-\phi_1 & 1 - \phi_2 & \cdots & -\phi_{p-1} \\
& & & \\
-\phi_{p-1} & -(\phi_{p-2} + \phi_p) & \cdots & 1
\end{pmatrix}
\begin{pmatrix}
\gamma(0) \\
\gamma(1) \\
\vdots \\
\gamma(p-1)
\end{pmatrix}
=
\begin{pmatrix}
\sigma^2 \\
0 \\
\vdots \\
0
\end{pmatrix}.
$$

$$(3.20)$$

This matrix equation can be uniquely inverted if and only if the process is stationary; if this is so, we can express $\gamma(0), \ldots, \gamma(p - 1)$ uniquely, albeit nonlinearly, in terms of the parameters $\phi_1, \ldots, \phi_p$ and σ^2. We then define $\gamma(k)$ for $k \geq p$ recursively by (3.17) given these initial conditions. Alternatively, we may define linear recursions for $\rho(k)$, that is, $\rho(k) = \phi_1 \rho(k - 1) + \cdots + \phi_p \rho(k - p)$, and solve the corresponding system of equations to give initial conditions. The theory of linear difference equations can be brought to bear here to express the autocovariance function in terms of the roots of the characteristic polynomial. The higher the order of the autoregressive polynomial, the more complex the behavior one can accommodate in the functions $\gamma(\cdot)$ and $\rho(\cdot)$ and the longer the cycles they may exhibit. One can understand this by considering the so-called seasonal AR process $y_t = \phi y_{t-p} + \varepsilon_t$ for integer p. We already saw that when $p = 1$ and $\phi < 1$ the ACF oscillates around zero, decaying rapidly to zero in magnitude; we might say it is periodic with period one and shrinking magnitude. For $p > 1$ and $\phi < 0$, the ACF is zero unless the lag is a multiple of p and oscillates around zero with period p and shrinking magnitude. In the general AR(p) case one can have richer behavior with cycles of length up to and including p; this is an issue for model specification – consider the cam30 data example. Finally, we note an important fact for the AR(p) process: we have $\pi(k) = 0$ for all $k > p$. This may be used to identify the order of the autoregression.

3.1.6   Using Stationarity to Calculate the Autocovariance Function of an MA Process

The argument for the MA processes is a little different. We consider a general MA(q) process. We have

$$E\left(y_t^2\right) = E\left(y_t\varepsilon_t\right) - \theta_1 E(y_t\varepsilon_{t-1}) - \cdots - \theta_q E(y_t\varepsilon_{t-q}),$$
$$E\left(y_t y_{t-1}\right) = E\left(y_{t-1}\varepsilon_t\right) - \theta_1 E(y_{t-1}\varepsilon_{t-1}) - \cdots - \theta_q E(y_{t-1}\varepsilon_{t-q}),$$
$$\vdots$$
$$E\left(y_t y_{t-q}\right) = E\left(y_{t-q}\varepsilon_t\right) - \theta_1 E(y_{t-q}\varepsilon_{t-1}) - \cdots - \theta_q E(y_{t-q}\varepsilon_{t-q}).$$

Let $\delta(j) = E(y_t\varepsilon_{t-j})$; then $\delta(j) = 0$ for $j < 0$ and $j > q$. It follows that

$$\gamma = \begin{pmatrix} \gamma(0) \\ \vdots \\ \gamma(q) \end{pmatrix} = \begin{pmatrix} \delta(0) & -\delta(1) & \cdots & -\delta(q) \\ 0 & \ddots & & -\delta(1) & 0 \\ \vdots & & \ddots & & \vdots \\ 0 & & 0 & -\delta(0) \end{pmatrix} \begin{pmatrix} 1 \\ \theta_1 \\ \vdots \\ \theta_q \end{pmatrix} = D\theta,$$

where D is a $(q+1) \times (q+1)$ matrix. We also have

$$\delta(0) = E\left(y_t\varepsilon_t\right) = E\left(\varepsilon_t^2\right) - \theta_1 E(\varepsilon_t\varepsilon_{t-1}) - \cdots - \theta_q E(\varepsilon_t\varepsilon_{t-q}) = \sigma^2,$$
$$\delta(1) = E\left(y_t\varepsilon_{t-1}\right) = E\left(y_{t-1}\varepsilon_t\right) - \theta_1 E(\varepsilon_{t-1}^2) - \cdots - \theta_q E(\varepsilon_{t-1}\varepsilon_{t-q}) = -\theta_1\sigma^2,$$
$$\vdots$$
$$\delta(q) = E\left(y_t\varepsilon_{t-q}\right) = E\left(\varepsilon_{t-q}\varepsilon_t\right) - \theta_1 E(\varepsilon_{t-q}\varepsilon_{t-1}) - \cdots - \theta_q E(\varepsilon_{t-q}^2) = -\theta_q\sigma^2.$$

Therefore, the elements of the matrix D can be expressed linearly in terms of the parameters $\theta_1, \ldots, \theta_q$:

$$d = \begin{pmatrix} \delta(0) \\ \delta(1) \\ \vdots \\ \delta(q) \end{pmatrix} = \sigma^2 \begin{pmatrix} 1 & 0 & \cdots & 0 \\ 0 & -1 & 0 & \vdots \\ \vdots & & \ddots & \\ 0 & & 0 & -1 \end{pmatrix} \begin{pmatrix} 1 \\ \theta_1 \\ \vdots \\ \theta_q \end{pmatrix}.$$

This leads to a quadratic equation for γ in terms of θ.

3.1.7   Representations for ARMA(p, q) Processes

We now return to the general case. For a stationary and invertible ARMA(p, q) process (3.2), for some $C(L)$ and $D(L)$, we can write

$$\frac{A(L)}{B(L)}y_t = C(L)y_t = \sum_{j=0}^{\infty} \gamma_j y_{t-j} = \alpha' + \varepsilon_t, \tag{3.21}$$

$$y_t = \alpha'' + \frac{B(L)}{A(L)}\varepsilon_t = \alpha'' + D(L)\varepsilon_t = \alpha'' + \sum_{j=0}^{\infty} \delta_j \varepsilon_{t-j}, \tag{3.22}$$

where $\alpha' = B(1)^{-1}\alpha$ and $\alpha'' = A(1)^{-1}\alpha$; here, $A(1) = \sum_{j=0}^{p} \phi_j$. Before discussing the meaning of these expressions, we discuss how these equations are obtained constructively.

For any polynomial $A(L)$ we may factor in terms of its roots and the roots of $A^{\#}(L)$ as follows:

$$A(L) = 1 - \phi_1 L - \cdots - \phi_p L^p = (1 - z_1^* L) \times \cdots \times \left(1 - z_p^* L^p\right)$$

$$= \left(1 - \frac{1}{w_1^{\#}} L\right) \times \cdots \times \left(1 - \frac{1}{w_p^{\#}} L^p\right).$$

We then expand each reciprocal separately, so that

$$\left(1 - \frac{1}{w_1^{\#}} L\right)^{-1} = 1 + \frac{1}{w_1^{\#}} L + \left(\frac{1}{w_1^{\#}} L\right)^2 + \cdots$$

This is true for real and complex roots. We then multiply all these infinite series together and collect terms in powers of L. For example, in the AR(2) case with real roots only we have

$$\left(1 - \phi_1 L - \phi_2 L^2\right)^{-1} = \left(1 - \frac{1}{w_1^{\#}} L\right)^{-1} \left(1 - \frac{1}{w_2^{\#}} L\right)^{-1}$$

$$= \left(\sum_{k=0}^{\infty} w_1^{\#-k} L^k\right) \left(\sum_{k=0}^{\infty} w_2^{\#-k} L^k\right) = \sum_{k=0}^{\infty} \varphi_k L^k$$

for some sequence $\{\varphi_k\}$ that can be obtained by equating coefficients. In fact,

$$\varphi_k = \begin{cases} (k+1) w^{\#-k} & \text{if } w_1^{\#} = w_2^{\#} = w^{\#}, \\ \dfrac{w_1^{\#-(k+1)} - w_2^{\#-(k+1)}}{w_1^{\#-1} - w_2^{\#-1}} & \text{if } w_1^{\#} \neq w_2^{\#}. \end{cases}$$

Equation (3.21) is called the AR(∞) representation, and expresses y_t in terms of its own past. For the sum to be well defined we require that $\sum_{j=0}^{\infty} |\gamma_j| < \infty$. This gives a specific form to the expression $E(y_t \mid y_{t-1}, y_{t-2}, \ldots)$, that is, a linear conditional expectation. This is useful when it comes to estimation and forecasting. This expression also shows that the shock ε_t can be recovered from current and past $y's$. We may also obtain from the AR representation that the conditional quantile process (for quantile $\alpha \in [0, 1]$ given the entire past $y_{t-1}, y_{t-2}, \ldots$) satisfies

$$q_t(\alpha) = \alpha' + \sum_{j=1}^{\infty} \gamma_j y_{t-j} + w_\alpha,$$

where w_α is the α-quantile of ε_t, that is, w_α is the assumed unique value that satisfies $\Pr(\varepsilon_t \leq w_\alpha) = \alpha$, and $q_t(\alpha) = \alpha' + \sum_{j=1}^{\infty} \gamma_j y_{t-j} + w_\alpha$ is the unique value that satisfies $\Pr(y_t \leq q_t(\alpha) \mid y_{t-1}, y_{t-2}, \ldots) = \alpha$.

Equation (3.22) is called the MA(∞) representation, and expresses y_t in terms of the past history of the random shocks. This is a special case of the Wold decomposition, which is discussed next. This representation is useful in terms of tracing through the consequences of shocks, which is a common application in macroeconomics.

So far we have written y_t in three different ways; in Chapter 8 we discuss a further representation. Any given process has multiple representations that lead to the same auto-covariance function. Another way of saying this is that if two processes have the same autocovariance functions they are the same process up to second order, that is, they are in an equivalence class. The second-order qualification is important when it comes to nonlinear processes. We have maintained the strong assumption above that ε_t is i.i.d., but for many purposes it suffices to assume that ε_t is $WN(0, \sigma^2)$. Specifically, the autoco-variance function and autocorrelation function only use the second-order properties, and perforce the property of weak stationarity only considers the second-order properties. However, for the purposes of establishing strict stationarity, the white noise assumption is insufficient; we discuss this further in Chapter 10.

For the general stationary and invertible $ARMA(p, q)$ case, the process y_t is strong mixing with exponential decay, that is, for some $\rho \in (0, 1)$ and $C < \infty$,

$$\alpha(k) \le C\rho^k. \tag{3.23}$$

This just says that as $k \to \infty$, $\alpha(k)$ shrinks to zero at a fast rate, and perforce $\gamma(k)$ is likewise exponentially decreasing. One consequence of the rapid decay is that the CLT for the sample mean is justified provided only $E(\varepsilon_t^2) < \infty$, and the CLT for the sample autocovariance and autocorrelation are justified provided only $E(\varepsilon_t^4) < \infty$. This shows that in some sense ARMA processes are not that general, since exponential decay is rather restrictive.

One can give simple expressions for the long-run variance of the process y_t in terms of the ARMA parameters ϕ, θ. In the AR(1) case, $\gamma(k) = \phi^k \sigma^2/(1 - \phi^2)$, so that

$$\mathrm{lrvar}(y_t) = \frac{1 + \phi}{1 - \phi} \times \frac{\sigma^2}{1 - \phi^2} = \frac{\sigma^2}{(1 - \phi)^2}.$$

The ratio of the long-run variance to the short-run variance is therefore

$$\frac{\mathrm{lrvar}(y_t)}{\mathrm{var}(y_t)} = \frac{1 + \phi}{1 - \phi}. \tag{3.24}$$

When $\phi \to 1$, we have $\mathrm{var}(y_t) \to \infty$ and the ratio $\mathrm{lrvar}(y_t)/\mathrm{var}(y_t) \to \infty$. When $\phi \to -1$, $\mathrm{var}(y_t) \to \infty$ but the ratio $\mathrm{lrvar}(y_t)/\mathrm{var}(y_t) \to 0$.

In the MA(1) case, $\mathrm{lrvar}(y_t) = \sigma^2 (1 - \theta)^2$. The ratio of the long-run variance to the short-run variance is

$$\frac{\mathrm{lrvar}(y_t)}{\mathrm{var}(y_t)} = \frac{(1 - \theta)^2}{1 + \theta^2}, \tag{3.25}$$

which can be arbitrarily large (when $\theta \to -1$) or zero (when $\theta \to 1$).

3.2 Wold Decomposition and Impulse Response

For any stationary process y_t with finite variance (but not necessarily mixing), Wold (1954) showed that there exists a representation

$$y_t = \sum_{j=0}^{\infty} \delta_j \varepsilon_{t-j} + v_t, \tag{3.26}$$

where $\{\varepsilon_t\}$ is a white noise process, that is, uncorrelated with mean zero and finite variance, while v_t is a **linearly deterministic** process, and $\sum_{j=0}^{\infty} \delta_j^2 < \infty$. By linearly deterministic we mean that v_t is perfectly forecastable by a linear combination of past y's. For example, $v_t = v$ for some mean-zero finite-variance random variable v. In this case, by the weak law of large numbers, $T^{-1} \sum_{t=1}^{T} y_t \xrightarrow{P} v$. The Wold decomposition is not unique because we can replace δ_j by $\delta_j \times \sigma$ and ε_s by ε_s / σ for all s, j without changing the value of the product $\delta_j \varepsilon_{t-j}$ and hence the sum $\sum_{j=0}^{\infty} \delta_j \varepsilon_{t-j}$. So we may without loss of generality assume that ε_t has unit variance. The shocks are defined as the errors in the best linear prediction. Some abstract mathematics (projections in a Hilbert space) is needed to justify this construction rigorously, since the conditioning is on an infinite set $\{y_{t-1}, \ldots\}$. Specifically, define, for each t,

$$\varepsilon_t = y_t - E_L(y_t \mid y_{t-1}, y_{t-2}, \ldots),$$

which has the property that $E_L(\varepsilon_t \mid y_{t-1}, \ldots) = 0$; ε_t is called the innovation in y_t. We note that the space spanned by $\{y_{t-1}, y_{t-2}, \ldots\}$ is equivalently spanned by $\{\varepsilon_{t-1}\}$ and $\{y_{t-2}, y_{t-3}, \ldots\}$. Therefore, we can write

$$E_L(y_t \mid y_{t-1}, y_{t-2}, \ldots) = E_L(y_t \mid \varepsilon_{t-1}) + E_L(y_t \mid y_{t-2}, y_{t-3}, \ldots)$$
$$= \delta_1 \varepsilon_{t-1} + E_L(y_t \mid y_{t-2}, y_{t-3}, \ldots),$$

where $\delta_1 = \mathrm{cov}(y_t, \varepsilon_{t-1}) / \mathrm{var}(\varepsilon_{t-1})$. We continue this process into the infinite past.

If the shocks $\{\varepsilon_t\}$ in (3.26) are i.i.d., then we say that $y_t - v_t$ is a linear process, cf. (2.8). The class of linear processes includes the ARMA(p, q) class (with i.i.d. shocks) for all finite p, q. For ARMA processes it may be proven that there exist $C < \infty$ and ρ with $0 < \rho < 1$ such that $|\delta_j| \leq C\rho^j$ for all j. That is, the coefficients decay exponentially fast. The class of linear processes also includes processes for which this decay rate does not hold.

Example 3.3   The **power-law process** with weights $\delta_j = c_j j^{-\theta}$, for some $\theta > 0$ with $|c_j| \leq c < \infty$. The parameter θ controls the rate of decay: when $\theta > 1/2$, this process has square-summable weights, but otherwise it does not; in the latter case it is called a **long-memory process**, which we discuss later in more detail.

The class of nonlinear processes that satisfy the Wold decomposition is of course very large.

Example 3.4   Consider the AR(1) process with $y_t = \phi y_{t-1} + \varepsilon_t$, where ε_t are i.i.d. with mean zero and finite variance, which is a stationary linear process provided $|\phi| < 1$. Let $x_t = y_t^2$ and suppose that $E(\varepsilon_t^4) < \infty$; then x_t is both weakly and strongly stationary and satisfies $x_t = \sigma^2 + \phi^2 x_{t-1} + u_t$, where $u_t = \varepsilon_t^2 - \sigma^2 + y_{t-1}\varepsilon_t$. This process has a Wold decomposition,

$$x_t = \frac{\sigma^2}{1 - \phi^2} + \sum_{j=0}^{\infty} \left(\phi^2\right)^j \varepsilon_{t-j},$$

where the shocks in that decomposition are MDS but not i.i.d. Of course, the representation $x_t = \left(\sum_{j=0}^{\infty} \phi^j u_{t-j} \right)^2$ in terms of the original i.i.d. shocks is equally valid and emphasizes the nonlinearity of the process vis à vis the i.i.d. shocks u_t.

We next use the Wold decomposition to calculate the autocovariance function of a general stationary process. Suppose that (3.26) is satisfied with $v_t = 0$. Then we have, for every k,

$$E(y_t y_{t-k}) = E(y_t y_{t+k}) = E(y_0 y_k) = E\left(\sum_{j=0}^{\infty} \delta_j \varepsilon_{-j} \sum_{j=0}^{\infty} \delta_j \varepsilon_{k-j} \right) = \sigma^2 \sum_{j=0}^{\infty} \delta_j \delta_{j+k}.$$

The long-run variance of the process is therefore

$$\mathrm{lrvar}(y_t) = \sum_{k=-\infty}^{\infty} E(y_t y_{t-k}) = \sigma^2 \sum_{k=-\infty}^{\infty} \sum_{j=0}^{\infty} \delta_j \delta_{j+k} = \sigma^2 \left(\sum_{j=0}^{\infty} \delta_j \right)^2 = \sigma^2 D(1)^2.$$

Note that in these calculations we only need the property that ε_t is WN, not that it is i.i.d. As far as the second-order properties of a process are concerned it suffices to assume that the shocks are uncorrelated. However, in that case one often has to invoke some additional properties in order to ensure that the process is strongly stationary. Under the stronger condition of i.i.d. shocks one can show further results. Specifically, we have the skewness and excess kurtosis:

$$\kappa_3(y) = \frac{E(y_t^3)}{E(y_t^2)^{3/2}} = \kappa_3(\varepsilon) \frac{\sum_{j=0}^{\infty} \delta_j^3}{\left(\sum_{j=0}^{\infty} \delta_j^2 \right)^{3/2}},$$

$$\kappa_4(y) = \frac{E(y_t^4)}{E(y_t^2)^2} - 3 = \kappa_4(\varepsilon) \frac{\sum_{j=0}^{\infty} \delta_j^4}{\left(\sum_{j=0}^{\infty} \delta_j^2 \right)^2}.$$

If ε_t is Gaussian, then the skewness and excess kurtosis of y_t are also both equal to zero (of course, since in that case y_t is itself also Gaussian). Note that

$$\sum_{j=0}^{\infty} \delta_j^4 \le \left(\sum_{j=0}^{\infty} \delta_j^2 \right)^2, \qquad \left(\sum_{j=0}^{\infty} \delta_j^3 \right)^2 \le \left(\sum_{j=0}^{\infty} \delta_j^2 \right)^3,$$

and so whatever skewness or kurtosis there is in ε_t is attenuated in magnitude for y_t, that is, $|\kappa_j(y)| \le |\kappa_j(\varepsilon)|, j = 3, 4$. The skewness of y_t could be of opposite sign to the skewness of ε_t, depending on the sign of $\sum_{j=0}^{\infty} \delta_j^3$.

For many theoretical calculations it is convenient to work with linear processes (where the Wold decomposition has i.i.d. shocks). However, Bickel and Bühlmann (1997) showed that the set of linear processes is not closed, meaning there are sequences of such processes whose limits are not linear processes, so that the boundary between linear and nonlinear processes is not contained in the set of linear processes. A consequence of this is that even with an infinitely large sample, it is impossible (with any test statistic) to distinguish perfectly between linear and nonlinear processes.

Definition 3.2   The **impulse response function** $\mathbb{I}(\cdot)$ is defined as the effect of a shock on the future trajectory of the output. Suppose that $y_t = f(\varepsilon_t, \varepsilon_{t-1}, \ldots)$ for some function f and shocks ε_t; then we may define

$$\mathbb{I}(j) = \frac{\partial y_t}{\partial \varepsilon_{t-j}} = \frac{\partial f(\varepsilon_t, \varepsilon_{t-1}, \ldots)}{\partial \varepsilon_{t-j}}, \quad j = 0, 1, 2, \ldots \tag{3.27}$$

The cumulative impulse response function is $\mathcal{I}(j) = \sum_{k=0}^{j} \mathbb{I}(k)$, and the long-run effect (provided it exists) is

$$\mathcal{I}_\infty = \lim_{j \to \infty} \mathcal{I}(j) = \sum_{k=0}^{\infty} \mathbb{I}(k).$$

In general, the impulse response function so defined is stochastic, but for the linear process case $\mathbb{I}(j) = \delta_j$ and is nonstochastic. The value of $\mathbb{I}(0)$ is the impact effect and $\mathbb{I}(\infty)$ is the long-run effect. For a stationary and mixing process, we must have $\mathbb{I}(\infty) = 0$, that is, $\mathbb{I}(j) \to 0$ as $j \to \infty$, in other words, the effects of any single shock are transitory; in fact for ARMA(p, q), $|\delta_k| \leq C\rho^k$ for some $\rho \in (0, 1)$ and $C < \infty$. The value $\mathcal{I}_\infty$ is a natural scalar measure of the persistence of the series, and for an ARMA process, $\mathcal{I}_\infty = D(1)$. Both $\mathbb{I}(\cdot)$ and $\mathcal{I}(\cdot)$ depend on the choice of representation; one convention is to assume that the shock has unit variance, in which case the corresponding impulse response function and its sum can be compared across series.

For an AR(1) process with $\phi > 0$, $\mathbb{I}(j) = \phi^j \times \sigma_\varepsilon \to 0$, monotonically and rapidly, and $\mathcal{I}_\infty = \sigma_\varepsilon / (1 - \phi)$. For an AR(2) process, $\delta_j \to 0$ rapidly but not necessarily monotonically. In fact, one can show that

$$\mathbb{I}(1) = \phi_1, \qquad \mathbb{I}(2) = \phi_1^2 + \phi_2, \qquad \mathbb{I}(k) = \phi_1 \delta_{k-1} + \phi_2 \delta_{k-2}, \quad k = 3, 4, \ldots$$

This is the same difference equation that the autocovariance function satisfies, except it has different initial conditions. If the roots are real we tend to see almost monotonic behavior, whereas if the roots are complex we tend to see oscillation. We show in Figure 3.3 the impulse response function of an AR(2) process with complex roots $\phi_1 = -1$, $\phi_2 = -0.5$.

The total cumulative impulse response for an ARMA(p, q) process is

$$\mathcal{I}_\infty = D(1) = \frac{B(1)}{A(1)} = \frac{\sum_{i=1}^{q} \theta_i}{1 - \sum_{i=1}^{p} \phi_i}. \tag{3.28}$$

For the AR(p) process, $\mathcal{I}_\infty = 1/(1 - \sum_{i=1}^{p} \phi_i)$, which is a monotonic function of the sum of the autoregressive coefficients $\sum_{i=1}^{p} \phi_i$. Consequently, it is common practice to focus on $\sum_{i=1}^{p} \phi_i$ as a measure of the **persistence** of the process. It is a necessary condition for stationarity of an AR(p) process that $\sum_{i=1}^{p} \phi_i < 1$.

Example 3.5   Suppose that $y_t = \phi y_{t-1} + \varepsilon_t$, where ε_t are i.i.d. with mean zero and finite variance, and let $x_t = y_t^2$. Then

$$\frac{\partial x_t}{\partial \varepsilon_{t-j}} = 2\phi^j \left(\sum_{k=0}^{\infty} \phi^k \varepsilon_{t-k} \right) = 2\phi^j x_t,$$

which is stochastic.

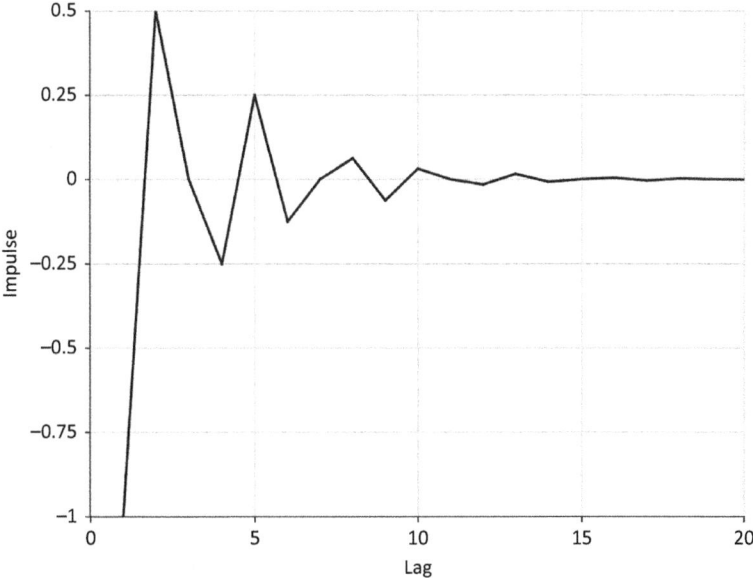

Figure 3.3 Impulse response function of an AR(2) process.

3.3   Aggregation of ARMA Processes

There are two types of aggregation we consider here: temporal aggregation and super-position or cross-sectional. First, we have a specific time series model operating at the highest frequency and the question is, what kind of process does the lower frequency (aggregated data) obey? Second, if we have some specific time series process but we observe the sum over some period of time or time difference, what are the properties of the observed process? These questions arise often in applications, and we give a brief treatment here.

3.3.1   Temporal Aggregation

In some cases we may believe that key relationships exist between series at different hori-zons. For example, our data are very high frequency but we think the relevant economic characteristics are only visible at the monthly or quarterly frequency. This might be based on an economic argument, or it may be that some of the series are only available at the lower frequency. We consider the consequences of aggregation of data from some given linear process. Suppose that x_t is an ARMA(p, q) process with i.i.d. shocks, and define the overlapping sum

$$y_t = \sum_{j=1}^{r} x_{t-j}, \quad t = 0, \pm 1, \ldots \tag{3.29}$$

If the original data was $\{x_t, t = 1, \ldots, T\}$, then we would observe a sample $\{y_t, t = 1, \ldots, T - r\}$. Suppose that x_t is an ARMA(p, q) process with i.i.d. shocks, and define the nonoverlapping sum

$$y_1 = \sum_{j=1}^{r} x_j, \qquad y_2 = \sum_{j=r+1}^{2r} x_j, \qquad \cdots$$

If the original data was $\{x_t, t = 1, \ldots, T\}$, then we would observe a sample $\{y_t, t = 1, \ldots, m\}$, assuming that $T = r \times m$ are all integers. These are both **linear filters** and are discussed in detail in Chapter 4, that is, we can obtain tractable formulae for the processes y_t in terms of the original ARMA parameters and the filter parameter r.

3.3.2 Infrequent Sampling

This issue arises in the context of stock prices and returns, and is related to the calendar time versus trading time controversy. Specifically, the stock market is closed at weekends and on holidays and we only observe daily closing prices when the market was open. The trading time approach is to just ignore this and to assume some model holds as if the data were equally spaced. According to the calendar time hypothesis the process is set every day but we miss observations when the markets are closed. For example, in January 2022, there are 20 closing prices available out of 31 days in total. The market was closed at weekends and during the Martin Luther King public holiday.

Suppose that we observe a process x_t at times $t_1 < t_2 < \cdots < t_n$, and let $y_i = x_{t_i}$. Suppose that $s_i = t_i - t_{i-1} \in \mathbb{N}$ are realizations of an i.i.d. process (that is independent of all the other randomness). Then the observed process $\{y_i, i = 1, 2, \ldots\}$ is stationary, provided that $\{x_t, t = 1, 2, \ldots\}$ is stationary. Suppose specifically that $s_i \in \{1, 2, \ldots\}$ with associated probabilities $\pi_1, \pi_2, \ldots$, and that x_t is stationary with autocovariance function $\gamma_x(k)$. Then y_i has mean zero and an autocovariance function that satisfies $\gamma_y(0) = \gamma_x(0)$, and applying the law of iterated expectation we obtain

$$\gamma_y(1) = E(x_{t_i} x_{t_{i-1}}) = E\left(E(x_{t_{i-1}+s_i} x_{t_{i-1}}) \mid t_{i-1}, \ldots\right) = E\left(\gamma_x(s_i)\right)$$

$$= \sum_{j=1}^{\infty} \pi_j \gamma_x(j),$$

and likewise $\gamma_y(2) = \sum_{j=1}^{\infty} \pi_j^* \gamma_x(j)$, where $\pi_j^* = \sum_{k=1}^{j-1} \pi_k \pi_{j-k}$. For example, suppose that x_t is a stationary AR(1) process with $x_t = \phi x_{t-1} + \varepsilon_t$, defined at discrete times $t = 0, \pm 1, \ldots$ Then $y_i = \phi^{s_i} y_{i-1} + u_i$, where $u_i = \varepsilon_{t_i} + \phi \varepsilon_{t_i-1} + \cdots + \phi^{s_i-1} \varepsilon_{t_{i-1}+1}$ has mean zero and variance $\sigma^2 \sum_{j=0}^{s_i-1} \phi^{2j}$ conditional on s_i. Therefore, unconditionally, $\text{var}(u_i) = \pi_1 \sigma^2 + \pi_2 \sigma^2 (1 + \phi^2) + \cdots$. For a sample of daily stock returns we may just work with the empirical distribution of s_i. For example, in January 2022 we had 15 days with $s_i = 1$, 4 days with $s_i = 2$, and 1 day with $s_i = 3$.

A more common and powerful framework for dealing with this issue is continuous time, which we consider later.

3.3.3 Superposition

Suppose that x_t, z_t are two stationary and invertible ARMA(p_j, q_j) processes (with i.i.d. shocks), $j = x, z$, and let $y_t = x_t + z_t$. What is the process y_t? It follows immediately that y_t is a stationary process, and indeed a linear process. We may further show that y_t is

ARMA(p, q), where $p \leq p_x + p_z$ and $q \leq \max\{p_x + q_x, p_z + q_z\}$ (Granger and Morris, 1976). In particular, if you add an i.i.d. noise to an MA(1) process you get another MA(1) process. In fact, one could say that MA processes are closed under addition (MA(p) + MA(q) = MA($\max\{p, q\}$)), whereas AR processes are closed only if one allows the order to extend.

Example 3.6   Suppose that x_t, z_t are mean zero and variance one with $x_t = \phi_x x_{t-1} + \varepsilon_{xt}$ and $z_t = \phi_z z_{t-1} + \varepsilon_{zt}$, where $\varepsilon_{xt}, \varepsilon_{zt}$ are mutually independent. We have $\rho_y(k) = (\phi_x^k + \phi_z^k)/2$. If $\phi_x = \phi_z$ then y_t is an AR(1) process, but if $\phi_x \neq \phi_z$ then it is an AR(2) process.

Granger and Joyeux (1980) showed that autoregressive mixtures can exhibit strong dependence. Specifically, suppose that we define the processes

$$x_{jt}(\phi_j) = \phi_j x_{j,t-1}(\phi_j) + \varepsilon_{jt}, \quad t = 0, \pm 1, \pm 2, \ldots,$$

where ε_{jt} are i.i.d. with zero mean and variance σ_j^2, and $|\phi_j| < 1$ for $j = 1, \ldots, n$. Each process x_{jt} is stationary in time, treating ϕ_j as fixed. Then define the aggregated process

$$y_t = \frac{1}{n} \sum_{j=1}^{n} x_{jt}(\phi_j).$$

Granger and Joyeux (1980) showed that for some choices of $\phi_1, \phi_2, \ldots$, such as random draws from a population random variable with mass near unity, the aggregated process y_t exhibits strong dependence. For example, suppose that $\sigma_j^2 = 1 - \phi_j^2$ (in which case var(y_t) = $1/n$); then, conditional on $\phi_1, \phi_2, \ldots$,

$$\text{cov}(y_t, y_{t-k}) = \text{cov}\left(\frac{1}{n}\sum_{j=1}^{n} x_{jt}(\phi_j), \frac{1}{n}\sum_{j=1}^{n} x_{j,t-k}(\phi_j)\right)$$

$$= \frac{1}{n^2}\sum_{j=1}^{n} \text{cov}\left(x_{jt}(\phi_j), x_{j,t-k}(\phi_j)\right) = \frac{1}{n^2}\sum_{j=1}^{n} \phi_j^k.$$

Therefore, by the LLN,

$$\text{corr}(y_t, y_{t-k}) = \frac{1}{n}\sum_{j=1}^{n} \phi_j^k \to E\left(\phi^k\right)$$

as $n \to \infty$. For ϕ drawn from a uniform distribution on $[0, 1]$,

$$E\left(\phi^k\right) = \frac{1}{k+1},$$

which has extremely slow decay as $k \to \infty$, and is in fact not summable. If ϕ is drawn from a Beta distribution with parameters α, β,

$$E\left(\phi^k\right) = \prod_{r=0}^{k-1} \frac{\alpha + r}{\alpha + \beta + r};$$

for some choices of α, β the ACF is summable and for others it is not and can decay even slower than for the uniform distribution.

3.3.4   Transformation of ARMA Processes

In many cases, instantaneous transformations are made to the raw data series $\{x_t, t = 1, \ldots, T\}$; that is, we work with a series $\{y_t, t = 1, \ldots, T\}$, where $y_t = \tau(x_t)$ for some transformation $\tau(\cdot)$. For example, when $x_t > 0$, such as a price series, one often takes logarithms of the data before modelling. In that case, we may assume that y_t is ARMA(p, q), say, in which case $x_t = \tau^{-1}(y_t)$ is a nonlinear process in general (although provided it is stationary it has a Wold decomposition; this will depend on the distribution of the shocks). In some cases, one may wish to consider a family of transformations such as the Box–Cox that involve unknown parameters.

Example 3.7   Suppose that x_t is a stationary Gaussian process with autocorrelation function $\rho(k)$. Then, what is the autocorrelation function of $\tau(x_t)$? For $\tau(x) = x^2$, $\rho_\tau(k) = \rho(k)^2$, while for $\tau(x) = x^3$, $\rho_\tau(k) = (2\rho(k)^3 + 3\rho(k))/5$, and so on. Any such polynomial transformation can be obtained given the moments of the normal distribution, and this argument can be extended to cover functions defined through power series expansions.

Example 3.8   Suppose that x_t is a stationary Gaussian process with mean zero, variance one, and autocorrelation function $\rho(k)$. Then, what is $\mathrm{cov}(x_t, \tau(x_{t-k}))$? By Stein's lemma we have

$$\mathrm{cov}(x_t, \tau(x_{t-k})) = \mathrm{cov}(x_t, x_{t-k}) \times E(\tau'(x_{t-k})) = \rho(k) \times E(\tau'(x_{t-k})).$$

For $\tau(x) = x^3/3$, $E(\tau'(x_{t-k})) = 1$ and $\mathrm{var}(\tau'(x_{t-k})) = 2$ so that

$$\mathrm{corr}(x_t, \tau(x_{t-k})) = \frac{\rho(k)}{\sqrt{2}}.$$

3.4   Estimation of ARMA Processes

We now consider estimation of the unknown parameters of ARMA processes based on a stretch of data $\{y_1, \ldots, y_T\}$. Let $\vartheta = (\alpha, \phi_1, \ldots, \phi_p, \theta_1, \ldots, \theta_q, \sigma^2)^\top$ denote the full parameter vector of unknown quantities. We also focus on the subvectors $\phi = (\phi_1, \ldots, \phi_p)^\top \in \mathbb{R}^p$ and $\theta = (\theta_1, \ldots, \theta_q)^\top \in \mathbb{R}^q$, and write $A_\phi(L)y_t = \alpha + B_\theta(L)\varepsilon_t$ to indicate the dependence of the lag polynomials on their parameters. We collect the mean parameters together as $\eta = (\alpha, \phi^\top, \theta^\top)^\top \in \mathbb{R}^{p+q+1}$ and the shock variance parameter $\sigma^2 \in \mathbb{R}_+$. The parameter values ϑ are assumed to lie in some parameter space $\Xi = \mathbb{R} \times \Phi \times \Theta \times \mathbb{R}_+ \subset \mathbb{R}^{p+q+2}$, that is, $\phi \in \Phi$ and $\theta \in \Theta$. We may wish to impose stationarity and invertibility on the process, which will imply restrictions on $\Phi \times \Theta$. For example, in the AR(1) case we may assume that $\Phi = (-1, 1)$; in the MA(1) case we may assume that $\Theta = (-1, 1)$. In the higher-order models these restrictions amount to systems of inequality restrictions, which can be quite complicated to invoke. We assume that $A_\phi(L)$ and $B_\theta(L)$ have no common factors, which also imposes some restrictions on $\Phi \times \Theta$, and without loss of generality that $\phi_p, \theta_q \neq 0$. We note that some software implementations do and some do not impose these restrictions in estimation.

In this section we consider two different assumptions for the shock process. First, that ε_t is i.i.d. with zero mean and variance σ^2, a special case of which is that ε_t is Gaussian.

Second, that ε_t is a martingale difference sequence with $E(\varepsilon_t \mid y_{t-1}, \ldots) = 0$ and $\mathrm{var}(\varepsilon_t \mid y_{t-1}, \ldots) \leq C < \infty$ (in this case we still have $\mathrm{var}(\varepsilon_t) = \sigma^2$). In fact, we usually require fourth moments on ε_t for least squares–based procedures that exploit the autocovariance function.

We may or may not need to take a position on the initial conditions. One possibility is that we just assume that $\{y_1, \ldots, y_T\}$ is a realization from a stationary process and make no use of explicit initializations. This is equivalent to assuming that $y_0, \ldots, y_{1-p}$ and $\varepsilon_0, \ldots, \varepsilon_{1-q}$ are random initial conditions chosen from the assumed stationary joint distribution of the process and shocks, and we do not observe them or make use of them. Assuming stationarity is the most preferred option from a statistical point of view, at least when there is high confidence that the process is stationary. On the other hand, if the process is not stationary then imposing this assumption would be undesirable, as we shall see. Imposing stationarity can also be demanding from a computational point of view. Alternatively, we may make use of initial conditions, and here there are two possibilities:

(i) Suppose that $y_0, \ldots, y_{1-p}$ and $\varepsilon_0, \ldots, \varepsilon_{1-q}$ are fixed nonrandom initial conditions that are taken as given.
(ii) Suppose that $y_0, \ldots, y_{1-p}$ and $\varepsilon_0, \ldots, \varepsilon_{1-q}$ are fixed nonrandom initial conditions that are to be estimated jointly with ϑ.

The first case is the most common in practice as this leads to much simpler estimation and inference. Although the process defined by (i) is not stationary, it may be asymptotically stationary provided the parameters obey the stationarity conditions. The weakness of this approach is that the initial conditions may be far away from the stationary distribution of the process and may thereby adversely affect estimation as the choice of parameter value tries to fit all the data, including the initial part of the trajectory, which may be skewed by the initial conditions. The second case tries to remedy this defect by making the initial conditions more compatible with the observed data. The cost of this approach is that one has to estimate an additional $p + q$ unknown quantities.

We may alternatively parameterize the model, replacing α by $\mu = E(y_t)$, in which case we have $A_\phi(L)(y_t - \mu) = B_\theta(L)\varepsilon_t$. In this case one can directly estimate μ by the sample mean $\bar{y}$, which can be shown to be the maximum likelihood estimator.

3.4.1 The Autoregressive Special Case

We first consider the AR(p) case, for which there are several alternative paradigms that yield more or less the same method. The mean of y_t can be estimated by the sample average, so we will for now assume that the mean is zero and ignore it.

3.4.1.1 Yule–Walker Equations

The first idea is to "invert" the autocovariance/autocorrelation function to compute an estimate of the vector ϕ. For example, in the AR(1) case the parameter ϕ is precisely the first-order autocorrelation. More generally, we can obtain the so-called Yule–Walker equations , which are, in the general AR(p) case, a system of linear equations for the AR parameters in terms of the autocovariance function or the autocorrelation function:

$$
\begin{pmatrix} \gamma(1) \\ \vdots \\ \gamma(p) \end{pmatrix} = \begin{pmatrix} \gamma(0) & \gamma(1) & \cdots & \gamma(p-1) \\ \gamma(1) & \ddots & & \gamma(1) \\ & & \ddots & \\ & & & \gamma(0) \end{pmatrix} \begin{pmatrix} \phi_1 \\ \vdots \\ \phi_p \end{pmatrix} = \Gamma_p \begin{pmatrix} \phi_1 \\ \vdots \\ \phi_p \end{pmatrix}, \qquad (3.30)
$$

$$
\begin{pmatrix} \rho(1) \\ \vdots \\ \rho(p) \end{pmatrix} = \begin{pmatrix} 1 & \rho(1) & \cdots & \rho(p-1) \\ \rho(1) & \ddots & & \rho(1) \\ & & \ddots & \\ & & & 1 \end{pmatrix} \begin{pmatrix} \phi_1 \\ \vdots \\ \phi_p \end{pmatrix} = R_p \begin{pmatrix} \phi_1 \\ \vdots \\ \phi_p \end{pmatrix},
$$

where Γ_p, R_p are the $p \times p$ autocovariance and autocorrelation matrices of the process y. This gives p linear equations in the p unknowns ϕ. The matrix R_p is nonsingular (under stationarity) and so we may invert it to express the vector ϕ uniquely in terms of the first p autocorrelations. In the AR(2) case we have explicit solutions:

$$
\frac{\rho(1)\,(1 - \rho(2))}{1 + \rho(1)^2} = \phi_1, \qquad \phi_2 = \rho(2) - \phi_1 \rho(1).
$$

However, in the general AR(p) case the solutions are hard to write down in a simple form, although this is not needed.

For estimation we replace the population autocorrelations by the sample autocorrelations and solve the sample versions of the equations. This requires that the sample matrix

$$
\widehat{R} = \begin{pmatrix} 1 & \widehat{\rho}(1) & \cdots & \widehat{\rho}(p-1) \\ \widehat{\rho}(1) & \ddots & & \widehat{\rho}(1) \\ & & \ddots & \\ & & & 1 \end{pmatrix} \qquad (3.31)
$$

be nonsingular, which it is with probability one provided that $\widehat{\gamma}(0) > 0$ (Brockwell and Davis, 2006, Problem 7.11). Numerical calculation of the inverse of $\widehat{R}$ is straightforward unless p is large. Furthermore, because $\widehat{R}$ is a proper correlation matrix, the solution vector $\widehat{\phi}$ automatically satisfies the stationarity conditions. This approach assumes stationarity and does not make use of initial conditions.

3.4.1.2 Linear Regression

A second idea is to consider the AR(p) model as a regression equation, that is, write $y = X\vartheta + \varepsilon$, where $\vartheta = (\alpha, \phi_1, \ldots, \phi_p)$, $y = (y_{p+1}, \ldots, y_T)^\mathsf{T} \in \mathbb{R}^{T-p}$, $\varepsilon = (\varepsilon_{p+1}, \ldots, \varepsilon_T)^\mathsf{T} \in \mathbb{R}^{T-p}$, and

$$
X = \begin{pmatrix} 1 & y_{p+1} & & y_1 \\ \vdots & \vdots & \cdots & \vdots \\ 1 & y_{T-1} & & y_{T-p} \end{pmatrix}.
$$

Note that we have dropped the first p observations. Some authors (and many software implementations) advocate padding the data series with some initial values $y_0^*, y_{-1}^*, \ldots, y_{1-p}^*$ and thereby obtaining a regression with T observations; a common choice is to use the sample mean of the y values themselves or, in the no-intercept case, zero values. An equivalent way of proceeding is to estimate μ by the sample mean $\bar{y}$ and then work with the demeaned variables to estimate ϕ. Note that in the classical treatment of linear regression we assume that $E(\varepsilon \mid X) = 0$, but this assumption does not make sense here. However, the MDS assumption on ε_t says that $E\left(\varepsilon_t \mid y_{t-1}, y_{t-2}, \ldots\right) = 0$, which is sufficient for estimation theory.

The OLS estimator satisfies the vector of first-order conditions

$$
G_T(\alpha, \phi) = \begin{pmatrix} \sum_{t=p+1}^{T} \left(y_t - \alpha - \phi_1 y_{t-1} - \ldots - \phi_p y_{t-p}\right) \\ \sum_{t=p+1}^{T} y_{t-1} \left(y_t - \alpha - \phi_1 y_{t-1} - \ldots - \phi_p y_{t-p}\right) \\ \vdots \\ \sum_{t=p+1}^{T} y_{t-p} \left(y_t - \alpha - \phi_1 y_{t-1} - \ldots - \phi_p y_{t-p}\right) \end{pmatrix} = 0, \qquad (3.32)
$$

which can be uniquely solved to give

$$
\begin{aligned}
\widehat{\vartheta} &= (X^{\mathsf{T}} X)^{-1} X^{\mathsf{T}} y \\
&= \begin{pmatrix} T-p & \sum_{t=p+1}^{T} y_t & & \\ \sum_{t=p+1}^{T} y_{t-1} & \sum_{t=p+1}^{T} y_{t-1} y_{t-2} & & \\ & & \ddots & \\ & & & \sum_{t=p+1}^{T} y_{t-p}^2 \end{pmatrix}^{-1} \\
&\quad \times \begin{pmatrix} \sum_{t=p+1}^{T} y_t \\ \sum_{t=p+1}^{T} y_t y_{t-1} \\ \vdots \\ \sum_{t=p+1}^{T} y_t y_{t-p} \end{pmatrix},
\end{aligned} \qquad (3.33)
$$

assuming that the matrix X is full rank, which it will be provided $p < T$. Using the Frisch–Waugh–Lovell (FWL) theorem, we can write separate formulae for the slope and intercepts:

$$
\widehat{\phi} = \begin{pmatrix} \sum_{t=p+1}^{T} \widetilde{y}_{t-1}^2 & \sum_{t=p+1}^{T} \widetilde{y}_{t-1} \widetilde{y}_{t-2} & \\ & \ddots & \\ & & \sum_{t=p+1}^{T} \widetilde{y}_{t-p}^2 \end{pmatrix}^{-1} \begin{pmatrix} \sum_{t=p+1}^{T} \widetilde{y}_t \widetilde{y}_{t-1} \\ \vdots \\ \sum_{t=p+1}^{T} \widetilde{y}_t \widetilde{y}_{t-p} \end{pmatrix},
$$

$$
\widehat{\alpha} = \frac{1}{T} \sum_{t=p+1}^{T} \widehat{\varepsilon}_t,
$$

where $\widetilde{y}_t = y_t - \bar{y}$ and $\widehat{\varepsilon}_t = y_t - \widehat{\phi}_1 y_{t-1} - cldots - \widehat{\phi}_1 y_{t-1}$. Furthermore, we may define $\widehat{\sigma}^2 = \sum_{t=p+1}^{T} \widehat{\varepsilon}_t^2 / T$; some authors argue in favor of the "unbiased" estimator $\widehat{\sigma}_*^2 = \sum_{t=p+1}^{T} \widehat{\varepsilon}_t^2 / (T-p)$, although it is not unbiased and even not necessarily less biased than $\widehat{\sigma}^2$.

In the AR(1) case without an intercept we have

$$\widehat{\phi} = \frac{\sum_{t=2}^{T} y_{t-1} y_t}{\sum_{t=2}^{T} y_{t-1}^2}. \tag{3.34}$$

This is similar to the sample autocorrelation at lag one except that the denominator does not include y_T^2; in fact, this difference is of some importance because the $\widehat{\phi}$ of (3.34) need not lie inside $(-1, 1)$, whereas the sample autocovariance function does lie inside the unit interval. More generally, the Yule–Walker estimators are similar to but not identical with the regression estimators, the difference being around the initial or terminal values.

Suppose that, actually, $y_t = \phi y_{t-1} + u_t$, where u_t is a mean-zero but autocorrelated series, for example $u_t = \varepsilon_t - \theta \varepsilon_{t-1}$. Then the least squares estimator $\widehat{\phi}$ is a biased and inconsistent estimator of ϕ because, in general, $E(y_{t-1} u_t) \neq 0$. In that case, one could use an instrumental variable estimator,

$$\widetilde{\phi} = \frac{\sum_{t=2}^{T} z_{t-1} y_t}{\sum_{t=2}^{T} z_{t-1} y_{t-1}}, \tag{3.35}$$

where z_t satisfies $E(z_{t-1} u_t) = 0$ and $E(z_{t-1} y_{t-1}) \neq 0$. For example, when $u_t = \varepsilon_t - \theta \varepsilon_{t-1}$, take $z_{t-1} = y_{t-2}$ or more generally $z_{t-1} = f(y_{t-2}, \ldots)$. The instrumental variable method can be applied to the estimation of ARMA(p, q) models to deliver estimates of the AR parameters ignoring the MA part. However, this will be inefficient in general and we may also be interested in the MA parameters, and so we turn to maximum likelihood.

3.4.2   Gaussian Likelihood for the General ARMA(p, q) Case

A popular estimation criterion in many contexts is the Gaussian likelihood because it is easy to specify and has a sort of universal property that it works even if the true distribution is not Gaussian itself (under some conditions, of course). Some authors refer to this as the Gaussian quasi-likelihood and the estimator as the **quasi-maximum likelihood estimator** or QMLE to emphasize that although we are using Gaussianity to define an estimation procedure, we are not fundamentalist believers in this assumption.

Suppose that the shock process is i.i.d. and $\varepsilon_t \sim N(0, \sigma^2)$ for all t; then it follows that for any stationary linear mean-zero process $y = (y_1, \ldots, y_T)^\mathsf{T}$, $y \sim N(\mu i_T, \Sigma)$ for some $T \times T$ matrix Σ with typical element $\sigma_{ts} = \operatorname{cov}(y_t, y_s)$. For a stationary process, the matrix Σ has the particular Toeplitz structure, namely, it is constant along all its diagonals because $\sigma_{ts} = \gamma(|t - s|)$. It may be convenient to write $\Sigma(\sigma^2, \phi, \theta) = \sigma^2 \Omega(\phi, \theta)$ for Toeplitz matrix Ω, or as $\Sigma(\sigma^2, \phi, \theta) = \gamma(0; \sigma^2, \phi, \theta) R(\phi, \theta)$, where R is the autocorrelation matrix, also Toeplitz. The log likelihood function for y is

$$\mathcal{L}(\vartheta \mid y) = -\frac{T}{2} \log 2\pi - \frac{1}{2} \log \det(\Sigma(\vartheta)) - \frac{1}{2}(y - \mu(\vartheta) i_T)^\mathsf{T} \Sigma(\vartheta)^{-1}(y - \mu(\vartheta) i_T). \tag{3.36}$$

The QMLE is defined as

$$\arg \max_{\vartheta \in \Xi} \mathcal{L}(\vartheta \mid y). \tag{3.37}$$

In general this is a nonlinear optimization; there are many suitable algorithms for finding the maximum, usually based on the derivatives $\partial \mathcal{L}(\vartheta)/\partial \vartheta$ and $\partial^2 \mathcal{L}(\vartheta)/\partial \vartheta \partial \vartheta^\mathsf{T}$.

Differences arise regarding the set Ξ, that is, which restrictions are imposed on the parameter set Ξ. Of course, whether y_t is Gaussian or not is irrelevant to this computation.

We may instead parameterize in terms of μ, ϕ, θ, and σ^2, and it is easy to see that the QMLE for μ is $\bar{y}$ no matter what. Furthermore, because of the separability of σ^2, we can see that, for given ϕ, θ,

$$\hat{\sigma}^2(\phi, \theta) = \frac{1}{T}(y - \bar{y}i_T)^\mathsf{T}\Omega(\phi, \theta)^{-1}(y - \bar{y}i_T). \tag{3.38}$$

In that case, we can rewrite the **profile likelihood** for the other parameters as

$$\mathcal{L}(\phi, \theta \mid y) = -\frac{T}{2}\log 2\pi - \frac{T}{2}\log(\hat{\sigma}^2(\phi, \theta)) - \frac{1}{2}\log\det(\Omega(\phi, \theta)) - \frac{T}{2},$$

where $\det(\cdot)$ is the matrix determinant (see Appendix B). The determinant of the covariance matrix and its inverse are nonlinear functions of the underlying parameters. In practice, calculating $\det\Omega$ and Ω^{-1} and their derivatives with respect to ϑ numerically can be time consuming, especially when the sample size is large, since this computation generally scales with T^3. In some special cases these quantities are known explicitly, as we discuss next.

For an AR(1) process,

$$\Sigma = \frac{\sigma^2}{1 - \phi^2}R, \qquad R = \begin{bmatrix} 1 & \phi & \phi^2 & \cdots & \phi^{T-1} \\ \phi & 1 & \ddots & \ddots & \vdots \\ \vdots & & \ddots & \ddots & \phi^2 \\ & & & \ddots & \phi \\ \phi^{T-1} & \cdots & & & 1 \end{bmatrix}, \tag{3.39}$$

where R is the population autocorrelation matrix. In this case, there is a simple closed-form expression for the inverse matrix:

$$R^{-1} = \frac{1}{1 - \phi^2} \begin{bmatrix} 1 & -\phi & 0 & & 0 \\ -\phi & 1+\phi^2 & \ddots & \ddots & \vdots \\ 0 & \ddots & \ddots & \ddots & 0 \\ \vdots & & \ddots & 1+\phi^2 & -\phi \\ 0 & & 0 & -\phi & 1 \end{bmatrix}. \tag{3.40}$$

This matrix is sparse, with only $O(T)$ nonzero elements; furthermore, it is not exactly Toeplitz since the first and last diagonal elements do not behave. In this case, the log likelihood can easily be obtained. For the AR(2) case we also have a closed-form expression for the inverse:

$$R^{-1} = \begin{bmatrix} 1 & -\phi_1 & -\phi_2 & 0 & \cdots \\ -\phi_1 & 1+\phi_1^2 & -\phi_1+\phi_1\phi_2 & \ddots & \\ -\phi_2 & \ddots & 1+\phi_1^2+\phi_2^2 & \ddots & 0 \\ & \ddots & & \ddots & -\phi_1 \\ 0 & \cdots & 0 & -\phi_1 & 1 \end{bmatrix}.$$

For the MA(1) process the covariance matrix itself is sparse:

$$\Sigma = \sigma^2(1+\theta^2)R, \qquad R = \begin{bmatrix} 1 & \frac{-\theta}{1+\theta^2} & 0 & & & 0 \\ \frac{-\theta}{1+\theta^2} & & \ddots & & \cdots & \\ 0 & \ddots & & \ddots & & 0 \\ & & \ddots & \ddots & & \frac{-\theta}{1+\theta^2} \\ 0 & & & 0 & \frac{-\theta}{1+\theta^2} & 1 \end{bmatrix}. \tag{3.41}$$

If $T = 2$, the inverse of R can be calculated simply and we obtain an expression for the log likelihood:

$$\mathcal{L}(\theta, \sigma^2 \mid y_1, y_2) = -\log 2\pi - \log(\sigma^2) - \frac{1}{2}\log\left(\theta^4 + \theta^2 + 1\right)$$
$$- \frac{1}{2\sigma^2}\frac{(1+\theta^2)(y_1^2 + y_2^2) - 2\theta y_1 y_2}{\theta^4 + \theta^2 + 1}.$$

In the general T case, however, R^{-1} is very complicated and is not sparse, that is, every element is nonzero. In particular, it has elements (t, s) (provided $|\theta| < 1$) given by

$$\frac{1+\theta^2}{1-\theta^2}\left\{\theta^{|t-s|} - \theta^{2(T+2)-t-s-2}\right\}$$
$$- \frac{\theta^{t+s}}{1-\theta^{2(T+2)-2}}\left\{\left(1 - \theta^{2(T+2)-t-2}\right)\left(1 - \theta^{2(T+2)-s-2}\right)\right\},$$

(Sutradhar and Kumar, 2003).

For the general ARMA(p, q) process we have

$$\frac{\partial\mathcal{L}(\vartheta \mid y)}{\partial\vartheta_j} = \frac{-1}{2}\mathrm{tr}\left(\left(\Sigma^{-1} - \Sigma^{-1}S\Sigma^{-1}\right)\frac{\partial\Sigma}{\partial\vartheta_j}\right),$$
$$\frac{\partial^2\mathcal{L}(\vartheta|y)}{\partial\vartheta_j\partial\vartheta_k} = \mathrm{tr}\left(\left(\Sigma^{-1} - 2\Sigma^{-1}S\Sigma^{-1}\right)\left(\frac{\partial\Sigma}{\partial\vartheta_j}\Sigma^{-1}\frac{\partial\Sigma}{\partial\vartheta_k} + \frac{\partial^2\Sigma}{\partial\vartheta_j\partial\vartheta_k}\right)\right).$$

For given values of ϑ one can numerically calculate all these quantities, which can be used to implement the **gradient descent** algorithms that are usually used for computation of the MLE. For example, compute sequentially

$$\vartheta^{(r+1)} = \vartheta^{(r)} - \lambda\left(\frac{\partial^2\mathcal{L}(\vartheta^{(r)} \mid y)}{\partial\vartheta\partial\vartheta^{\mathsf{T}}}\right)^{-1}\frac{\partial\mathcal{L}(\vartheta \mid y)}{\partial\vartheta}, \tag{3.42}$$

where λ is a variable step length (perhaps chosen to maximize $\mathcal{L}(\vartheta^{(r+1)}(\lambda) \mid y)$) given some starting values $\vartheta^{(0)}$. Robinson (1988) showed that if $\vartheta^{(0)}$ is chosen as an initial consistent estimator then, for some finite r, $\vartheta^{(r)}$ will be asymptotically equivalent to the full MLE.

We seek an alternative approach to computing the likelihood and an approximation to it that is even easier to work with. We note that any joint density function can be factorized into the product of the conditional and the marginal density, so that $f(x, z) = f(x \mid z)f(z)$. We use this factorization repeatedly to obtain, for any $m \geq 1$,

$$f(y_1, \ldots, y_T) = f(y_1, \ldots, y_m)f(y_{m+1} \mid y_m, \ldots, y_1)\cdots f(y_T \mid y_{T-1}, \ldots, y_1).$$

It follows that we can write the log likelihood function as

$$\mathcal{L}(\vartheta \mid y) = \sum_{t=m+1}^{T} \log f(y_t \mid y_{t-1}, \ldots, y_1) + \log f(y_1, \ldots, y_m) \tag{3.43}$$

for any $T > m \geq 1$. This writes the log likelihood in terms of conditional distributions and a single marginal distribution for the first m values, or initial conditions. In the Gaussian AR(p) case the distribution of $y_t \mid y_{t-1}, \ldots, y_1$ is easy to find, it is $y_t \mid y_{t-1}, \ldots, y_1 \sim N(\alpha + \phi_1 y_{t-1} + \cdots + \phi_p y_{t-p}, \sigma^2)$, which only depends on the first p lags. The distribution of $y_1, \ldots, y_p$ is just the unconditional (assuming stationarity) distribution of this vector and this is $N(\mu i_p, \Sigma_p)$, where i_p is a $p \times 1$ vector of ones, and Σ_p is the $p \times p$ first submatrix of the full $T \times T$ covariance matrix Σ. In the AR(p) case the log likelihood is, apart from a constant,

$$\mathcal{L}(\vartheta \mid y) = -\frac{T-p}{2} \log \sigma^2 - \frac{1}{2\sigma^2} \sum_{t=2}^{T} (y_t - \alpha - \phi_1 y_{t-1} - \cdots - \phi_p y_{t-p})^2$$

$$- \frac{1}{2} \log \det(\Sigma_p) - \frac{1}{2} \left(y_{1:p} - \mu(\alpha, \phi)\right)^\mathsf{T} \Sigma_p^{-1} \left(y_{1:p} - \mu(\alpha, \phi)\right),$$

where $y_{1:p} = (y_1, \ldots, y_p)^\mathsf{T}$ and $\mu(\alpha, \phi) = \alpha/(1 - \phi_1 - \cdots - \phi_p)$. The computation and hence optimization of this likelihood is easier because it only involves the $p \times p$ covariance matrix $\Sigma_p(\sigma^2, \phi) = \sigma^2 \text{Toeplitz}(1 \mid \rho(1), \ldots, \rho(p-1))$, rather than the $T \times T$ covariance matrix Σ.

In the AR(1) case with zero mean the conditional distribution of $y_t \mid y_{t-1}, \ldots, y_1$ is $N(\phi y_{t-1}, \sigma^2)$ so that

$$\log f(y_t \mid y_{t-1}, \ldots, y_1) = -\frac{1}{2} \log 2\pi - \frac{1}{2} \log \sigma^2 - \frac{1}{2\sigma^2} (y_t - \phi_1 y_{t-1})^2.$$

The marginal distribution of y_1 is $N(0, \sigma^2/(1 - \phi^2))$, which means that

$$\mathcal{L}(\sigma^2, \phi \mid y_1) = -\frac{1}{2} \log 2\pi - \frac{1}{2} \log \frac{\sigma^2}{1 - \phi^2} - \frac{(1 - \phi^2)}{2\sigma^2} y_1^2.$$

Therefore, the full likelihood in the AR(1) case is

$$\mathcal{L}(\vartheta \mid y) = -\frac{T}{2} \log 2\pi - \frac{T-1}{2} \log \sigma^2 - \frac{1}{2\sigma^2} \sum_{t=2}^{T} (y_t - \phi y_{t-1})^2$$

$$- \frac{1}{2} \log \frac{\sigma^2}{1 - \phi^2} - \frac{1 - \phi^2}{2\sigma^2} y_1^2. \tag{3.44}$$

The maximum is to be found over the set $\Xi = (-1, 1) \times \mathbb{R}_+$, which is a noncompact set.

We may find the maximum of $\mathcal{L}(\vartheta \mid y)$ by looking at the first-order conditions. The **score functions** can be written as

$$\frac{\partial \mathcal{L}}{\partial \phi}(\vartheta \mid y) = \frac{1}{\sigma^2} \sum_{t=2}^{T} (y_t - \phi y_{t-1}) y_{t-1} + \phi \left(\frac{y_1^2}{\sigma^2/(1 - \phi^2)} - 1\right), \tag{3.45}$$

$$\frac{\partial \mathcal{L}}{\partial \sigma^2}(\vartheta \mid y) = \frac{1}{2\sigma^4} \left[\sum_{t=2}^{T} \left((y_t - \phi y_{t-1})^2 - \sigma^2\right) + \left((1 - \phi^2) y_1^2 - \sigma^2\right)\right]. \tag{3.46}$$

The second equation can be solved explicitly for σ^2 given ϕ to give

$$\widehat{\sigma}^2(\phi) = \frac{1}{T}\left[\sum_{t=2}^{T}(y_t - \phi y_{t-1})^2 + y_1^2(1 - \phi^2)\right]. \tag{3.47}$$

The logic here is that $E(y_1^2) = \sigma^2/(1 - \phi^2)$, that is, $y_1^2(1 - \phi^2)$ has expectation σ^2. The initial value y_1 has some value for estimation of both parameters. The score equation for ϕ is nonlinear due to the second term. In fact, Hasza (1980) shows that $\widehat{\phi}_{\mathrm{MLE}}$ solves a cubic equation and gives an explicit expression for it (the unique solution in $(-1, 1)$) in terms of $\sum_{t=2}^{T} y_t^2$, y_1^2, y_T^2, and $\sum_{t=2}^{T} y_t y_{t-1}$. We next write the profile likelihood,

$$\mathcal{L}_P(\phi \mid y) = -\frac{T-1}{2}\log\widehat{\sigma}^2(\phi) - \frac{1}{2\widehat{\sigma}^2(\phi)}\sum_{t=2}^{T}(y_t - \phi y_{t-1})^2 - \frac{1}{2}\log\frac{\widehat{\sigma}^2(\phi)}{1 - \phi^2}$$
$$- \frac{1-\phi^2}{2\widehat{\sigma}^2(\phi)}y_1^2, \tag{3.48}$$

and search over $\phi \in (0, 1)$ for the maximum, which is denoted $\widehat{\phi}_{\mathrm{MLE}}$, in which case $\widehat{\sigma}^2_{\mathrm{MLE}} = \widehat{\sigma}^2(\widehat{\phi}_{\mathrm{MLE}})$, which is the MLE.

It is often argued that for a stationary process $\log f(y_1)$ is small relative to $\sum_{t=2}^{T}\log f(y_t \mid y_{t-1}, \ldots, y_1)$ (technically, this needs to hold uniformly over the allowed parameter space), in which case the conditional likelihood (denoted with subscript C),

$$\mathcal{L}_C(\phi, \sigma^2 \mid y) = \sum_{t=2}^{T}\log f(y_t \mid y_{t-1}, \ldots, y_1)$$
$$= -\frac{T-1}{2}\log\sigma^2 - \frac{1}{2\sigma^2}\sum_{t=2}^{T}(y_t - \phi y_{t-1})^2, \tag{3.49}$$

is approximately equal to the full likelihood. This criterion is equivalent to the least squares criterion, and has a unique maximum at

$$\widehat{\phi} = \frac{\sum_{t=2}^{T} y_t y_{t-1}}{\sum_{t=2}^{T} y_{t-1}^2}, \qquad \widehat{\sigma}^2 = \frac{1}{T-1}\sum_{t=2}^{T}(y_t - \widehat{\phi} y_{t-1})^2.$$

The estimator $\widehat{\phi}$ is just the OLS estimator of y_t on y_{t-1}.

Alternatively, we may suppose that there is an initial condition y_0. In this case the likelihood is

$$\mathcal{L}(\vartheta \mid y, y_0) = -\frac{T}{2}\log\sigma^2 - \frac{1}{2\sigma^2}\sum_{t=1}^{T}(y_t - \phi y_{t-1})^2.$$

If $y_0 = 0$, then $(y_1 - \phi y_0)^2 = y_1^2$ does not depend on ϕ and so the MLE of ϕ is as before, although the variance estimator makes use of y_1^2. If y_0 is treated as an unknown parameter and to be estimated, then we also need a first-order condition for it. This is $\partial\mathcal{L}/\partial y_0 = (y_1 - \phi y_0)\phi/\sigma^2$, which yields $\widehat{y}_0 = y_1/\widehat{\phi}$ for given $\widehat{\phi}$. The quantities $\widehat{y}_0$ and $\widehat{\phi}$ are jointly determined from the two first-order conditions; in practice, one can first use the least squares estimator of ϕ to calculate $\widehat{y}_0$ and then update the estimate of ϕ, and so on.

The full MLE will be slightly different from the approximate MLE. In terms of asymptotic properties, the difference is negligible (in the stationary case). However, in a finite sample there can be significant differences. Also, the MLE procedure imposes that $\hat{\phi}$ be less than one, because as $\phi \to \pm 1$, $\mathcal{L}(\phi) \to -\infty$. The OLS estimator, however, can be on either side of the unit circle. This may be a plus or a minus depending on one's point of view. The higher-order AR process can be treated in a similar manner.

The moving average processes are even more complicated when it comes to estimation, and much work was devoted to finding good and stable algorithms for computing the exact MLE or good approximations to it. We discuss one such approach for the general ARMA(p, q) process. Under the Gaussian assumption one can calculate exactly $\mu_t(\eta) = E(y_t \mid y_{t-1}, \ldots, y_1)$ and $\sigma_t^2(\vartheta) = \text{var}(y_t \mid y_{t-1}, \ldots, y_1)$ based on the properties of the normal distribution (this calculation is particularly well undertaken by the Kalman filter discussed in Chapter 8). We then obtain the conditional likelihood :

$$\mathcal{L}_C(\vartheta \mid y) = -\frac{T}{2}\log 2\pi - \frac{1}{2}\sum_{t=1}^{T}\log \sigma_t^2(\vartheta) - \frac{1}{2}\sum_{t=1}^{T}\left(\frac{y_t - \mu_t(\eta)}{\sigma_t(\vartheta)}\right)^2.$$

For the MA(1) process, for example,

$$E(y_2 \mid y_1) = \frac{\theta}{1+\theta^2}y_1, \qquad \text{var}(y_2 \mid y_1) = \sigma^2\left(1 + \frac{\theta^4}{1+\theta^2}\right).$$

One can likewise calculate $E(y_3 \mid y_2, y_1)$ and $\text{var}(y_3 \mid y_2, y_1)$, and so on. These calculations become prohibitive in the general case and so we seek a simple approximation. This is based on the autoregressive representation $C(L)y_t = \varepsilon_t$, and the truncation of $C(L)$, denoted $C_t^+(L) = 1 + \sum_{j=1}^{t-1}\gamma_j L^j$. We have formally that $E(y_t \mid y_{t-1}, \ldots) = -\sum_{j=1}^{\infty}\gamma_j y_{t-j}$ and $\text{var}(y_t \mid y_{t-1}, \ldots) = \sigma^2$. We can show that

$$E(y_t \mid y_{t-1}, \ldots, y_1) \simeq -\sum_{j=1}^{t-1}\gamma_j y_{t-j}, \qquad \text{var}(y_t \mid y_{t-1}, \ldots, y_1) \simeq \sigma^2,$$

where the approximation is valid for large t since $\gamma_j \to 0$ rapidly as $j \to \infty$. This result holds without Gaussianity. Therefore, the approximate conditional likelihood (denoted with subscript AC) is, apart from constants,

$$\mathcal{L}_{AC}(\vartheta) = -\frac{T}{2}\log \sigma^2 - \frac{1}{2\sigma^2}\sum_{t=1}^{T}\varepsilon_t^2(\eta), \qquad (3.50)$$

where $\varepsilon_t(\eta) = y_t - \alpha(\eta) - c_1(\eta)y_{t-1} - c_2(\eta)y_{t-2} - \cdots - c_{t-1}(\eta)y_1$, where $\alpha(\eta) = B_\theta(1)^{-1}\alpha$. Note that $\varepsilon_t(\eta)$ is linear in the data but nonlinear in the parameters η. We can estimate ϑ by the maximizer of $\mathcal{L}^*(\vartheta)$ over the parameter space Ξ. The residual can be computed recursively assuming the initial values are set at zero. The difficulty here is the calculation of $c_j(\eta)$ from $A(\cdot)$ amd $B(\cdot)$, but also the nonlinear optimization involved in the maximization of $\mathcal{L}^*(\vartheta)$. There are several approaches that have been suggested to avoid the nonlinear optimization and reduce computation time.

Durbin (1960) suggested estimating ARMA(p, q) models by fitting a long autoregression, that is, fitting an AR(n) with parameters $c_1, c_2, \ldots, c_n$ by unrestricted OLS, where $n = \log T$; an explicit calculation. Then finding the parameters of $A(L)$ and $B(L)$ by solving the implied system relating them. For example, suppose that $y_t = \varepsilon_t - \theta\varepsilon_{t-1}$; then we have

$$y_t = -\theta y_{t-1} - \theta^2 y_{t-2} - \cdots - \theta^n y_{t-n} + \varepsilon_t + R_{t,n}(\theta),$$

where $R_{t,n}(\theta)$ is a remainder term that is small when n is large and $|\theta| < 1$. In that case, $c_j = -\theta^j$. We may just set $\theta = -c_1$, that is, regress y_t on $y_{t-1}, y_{t-2}, \ldots, y_{t-n}$ and then estimate θ by the negative of the coefficient on y_{t-1}. For the ARMA(1,1) case we have

$$y_t = (\phi - 1)\theta y_{t-1} + (\phi - 1)\theta^2 y_{t-2} + \cdots + (\phi - 1)\theta^n y_{t-n} + \varepsilon_t + R_{t,n}(\theta),$$

and in this case, $c_1 = (\phi - 1)\theta$ and $c_2 = (\phi - 1)\theta^2$ so that $\theta = c_2/c_1$ and $\phi = 1 + c_1^2/c_2$. The long autoregression can be considered an approximation to the autoregressive representation of the process, and so under some assumptions this will approximate $E(y_t \mid y_{t-1}, y_{t-2}, \ldots)$.

Hannan and Rissanen (1982) went one step further. They proposed for the general ARMA(p, q) case using the initial autoregressive fit to construct residuals, that is, estimates of ε_t, and then fitting the linear model of y_t on $y_{t-1}, \ldots, y_{t-p}, \widehat{\varepsilon}_{t-1}, \ldots, \widehat{\varepsilon}_{t-q}$. Since the initial fit approximates $E(y_t \mid y_{t-1}, y_{t-2}, \ldots)$, the residuals $\widehat{\varepsilon}_t$ approximate the unobservable errors ε_t and so this latter regression is as if we were regressing y_t on $y_{t-1}, \ldots, y_{t-p}, \varepsilon_{t-1}, \ldots, \varepsilon_{t-q}$. Hannan and Rissanen (1982) showed that their estimator is asymptotically equivalent to the Gaussian MLE under some assumptions. In the days before the sort of powerful computers and software we have now, these algorithms were very helpful.

3.4.3   Method of Moments

An alternative estimation strategy is the method of moments (MoM) based on the autocovariance or autocorrelation function. That is, for any ARMA(p, q) process we have, for $k = 0, 1, 2, \ldots, \gamma(k) = f_k(\phi, \theta, \sigma^2)$ for some known functions $f_k: \mathbb{R}^{p+q+1} \to \mathbb{R}$. Likewise, we have $\rho(k) = g_k(\phi, \theta)$ for $k = 1, 2, \ldots$ for some known functions $g_k: \mathbb{R}^{p+q} \to \mathbb{R}$. Given the estimates $\widehat{\gamma}(k), \widehat{\rho}(k)$ we can define estimators of the parameters by inverting the corresponding system of equations. For identification it is necessary that we have at least as many equations as unknowns, so for estimation of ϕ, θ, σ^2 we need at least $p + q + 1$ autocovariances. In the pure autoregressive case these are called the Yule–Walker equations and have explicit solutions, as we have seen. In the general ARMA case, we no longer have this exact solution and would generally have to use all the autocovariances to achieve full efficiency. This is more elegantly treated in the frequency domain under the rubric of the Whittle likelihood.

We next work through the MA case, for which we can give simple explicit expressions for the functions f_k, g_k. Suppose that

$$y_t = \varepsilon_t - \theta_1\varepsilon_{t-1} - \cdots - \theta_q\varepsilon_{t-q}.$$

We have the following moment conditions:

$$\gamma(0) = \sigma^2\left(1 + \theta_1^2 + \cdots + \theta_q^2\right),$$
$$\gamma(1) = -\sigma^2\left(\theta_1 - \theta_1\theta_2 - \cdots - \theta_{q-1}\theta_q\right),$$

$$\gamma(2) = -\sigma^2 \left(\theta_2 - \theta_1 \theta_3 - \cdots - \theta_{q-2} \theta_q \right),$$

$$\vdots$$

$$\gamma(q) = -\sigma^2 \theta_q,$$

which are $q+1$ moment conditions in $q+1$ unknown parameters (note that $\gamma(j) = 0$ for all $j > q$ so these are the only usable equations). The dependence on $\theta_1, \ldots, \theta_q$ is nonlinear, specifically quadratic. We can write $\gamma = f(\sigma^2, \theta)$, where $\gamma = (\gamma(0), \ldots, \gamma(q))^{\mathsf{T}}$, $\theta = (\theta_1, \ldots, \theta_q)^{\mathsf{T}}$, and $f \colon \mathbb{R}^{q+1} \to \mathbb{R}^{q+1}$ is a known smooth (quadratic) function.

Dividing through by $\gamma(0)$ we eliminate σ^2 and obtain q equations in the q unknown MA parameters, and after multiplying both sides by $1 + \theta_1^2 + \cdots + \theta_q^2$ these can be expressed as

$$\left(1 + \theta_1^2 + \cdots + \theta_q^2 \right) \rho(1) + \left(\theta_1 - \theta_1 \theta_2 - \cdots - \theta_q \theta_{q-1} \right) = 0,$$

$$\vdots$$

$$\left(1 + \theta_1^2 + \cdots + \theta_q^2 \right) \rho(q) + \theta_q = 0.$$

That is, we can write $\rho = g(\theta)$, where $\rho = (\rho(1), \ldots, \rho(q))^{\mathsf{T}}$ and $g \colon \mathbb{R}^q \to \mathbb{R}^q$ is a known smooth function.

Regarding estimation, we may solve, for σ^2 and $\theta_j, j = 1, \ldots, q$, the empirical system in which we replace $\gamma(j)$ by $\widehat{\gamma}(j), j = 0, 1, \ldots, q$; that is, we find the values of σ^2 and θ that solve the $q + 1$ equations

$$\widehat{\gamma} = f(\sigma^2, \theta). \tag{3.51}$$

Alternatively, we may solve the corresponding system for the sample autocorrelations $\widehat{\rho}(j), j = 1, \ldots, q$, which only depend on $\theta_1, \ldots, \theta_q$; that is, find θ to solve the system $\widehat{\rho} = g(\theta)$ (then we obtain $\widehat{\sigma}^2 = \widehat{\gamma}(0)/(1 + \widehat{\theta}_1^2 + \cdots + \widehat{\theta}_q^2)$). In general, these are non-linear equations without explicit solution and we must use numerical methods to find approximate solutions.

In the special case of the MA(1) process we have $\rho(1) = -\theta / \left(1 + \theta^2 \right)$, which leads to the quadratic equation $\rho(1) + \theta + \rho(1)\theta^2 = 0$, which has two real solutions provided $1 - 4\rho(1)^2 > 0$, that is, $\rho(1) < 1/2$. In that case the solutions are

$$\theta = \frac{-1 \pm \sqrt{1 - 4\rho(1)^2}}{2\rho(1)}.$$

The solutions are self reciprocal so that they take the form $\theta, 1/\theta$. We can estimate θ by the solution of this equation based on the sample $\widehat{\rho}(1)$; it is conventional to take the root that lies inside $(-1, 1)$.

3.4.3.1 Pairwise Pseudo-Likelihood

These MoM estimators can also be interpreted as so-called pseudo-likelihoods (Cox and Reid, 2004). For example, in the MA(1) case, the pairs y_t, y_{t+1} may be assumed to be jointly normal with an unknown covariance matrix that has constant diagonals. That is,

$$y_{t:t+1} = \begin{pmatrix} y_{t+1} \\ y_t \end{pmatrix} \sim N\left(0, \sigma^2 \Omega(\theta) \right), \qquad \Omega(\theta) = \begin{pmatrix} 1 + \theta^2 & -\theta \\ -\theta & 1 + \theta^2 \end{pmatrix}.$$

We may equivalently parameterize the log likelihood in terms of the autocovariance function so that

$$\mathcal{L}(\gamma_0, \gamma_1; y_{t+1}, y_t) = -\log 2\pi - \frac{1}{2}\log\left(\gamma_0^2 - \gamma_1^2\right) - \frac{1}{2}\left(\frac{\left(y_t^2 + y_{t+1}^2\right)\gamma_0 - 2y_t y_{t+1}\gamma_1}{\gamma_0^2 - \gamma_1^2}\right).$$

Then define the consecutive pairwise likelihood

$$\mathcal{L}_{\mathrm{CPL}}(\gamma_0, \gamma_1) = \sum_{t=1}^{T-1} \mathcal{L}(\gamma_0, \gamma_1; y_{t+1}, y_t).$$

The maximizing values of this objective function are $\widehat{\gamma}_0 = \widehat{\gamma}(0)$ and $\widehat{\gamma}_1 = \widehat{\gamma}(1)$, so the maximizing values in the original parameterization σ^2, θ are just the MoM estimators defined above.

3.4.4   Other Estimation Methods

Suppose that we do not require ε_t to be mean zero or even possess a mean, but suppose instead that it has median zero conditional on the past information. We note that for the general ARMA(p, q) process we have

$$\mathrm{med}(y_t \mid y_{t-1}, \dots, y_1) = \alpha(\eta_0) + C_1(\eta_0)y_{t-1} + C_2(\eta_0)y_{t-2} + \cdots + C_{t-1}(\eta_0)y_1,$$

which suffices for estimation. There is a long tradition in econometrics of using robust procedures, and the least absolute deviation (LAD) estimator is robust to heavy-tailed errors and other data features. We can define

$$Q_T(\eta) = \sum_{t=1}^{T} |y_t - \alpha(\eta) - C_1(\eta)y_{t-1} - C_2(\eta)y_{t-2} - \cdots - C_{t-1}(\eta)y_1|$$

and let $\widehat{\eta} = \arg\min_{\eta \in \mathbb{R} \times \Theta \times \Upsilon} Q_T(\eta)$. For AR($p$) processes this can be interpreted as standard linear-in-parameters quantile regression (Koenker, 2005).

3.5   Properties of Estimators

In general, all the above estimators are biased in small samples. This is true even in the AR(p) case, which we wrote as a linear regression in lagged values. This is because of the failure of the condition $E(\varepsilon \mid X) = 0$, which is at the heart of the Gauss–Markov theorem (old and new) . Nevertheless, the least squares estimating equations $G_T(\alpha, \phi)$ defined in (3.32) are exactly unbiased, meaning $E(G_T(\alpha_0, \phi_0)) = 0$ at the true values. In fact, it can be shown that these are the optimal estimating equations in the sense of Godambe and Thompson (1978). This is not true in the general ARMA(p, q) case, though, if some approximation is used to construct the likelihood and its score functions.

Brockwell and Davis (2006, Theorem 10.8.2) proves the consistency and asymptotic normality of the (Gaussian) MLE for a stationary invertible ARMA(p, q) process under the assumption that the shocks are i.i.d. with finite variance. Although the estimators are biased, the bias is of order T^{-1}, and does not affect the limiting distribution. First, note that in this theory it is not necessary to assume that the shock distribution be Gaussian.

Indeed, the limiting distribution of the estimates of the mean parameters η does not depend on the distribution of ε_t beyond its unconditional moments up to the fourth power.[2] However, the limiting distribution is affected by the assumption that the shock is i.i.d., and if we only assume that the error term be a martingale difference sequence, then although the estimates of the mean parameters are still consistent in this case, the limiting variance changes. In that case, robust standard errors should be used. In this section we consider the two cases: first, where the shock is i.i.d., and second, where the shock process is MDS.

For simplicity, and to present the heuristics, we consider the approximate quasi-likelihood for the general ARMA(p, q) process. This is, apart from constants, approximately equal to

$$\mathcal{L}^*(\vartheta \mid y) = -\frac{T}{2}\log \sigma^2 - \frac{1}{2\sigma^2}\sum_{t=1}^{T}\varepsilon_t(\eta)^2, \qquad (3.52)$$

where $\varepsilon_t(\eta) = y_t - \alpha(\eta) - C_1(\eta)y_{t-1} - C_2(\eta)y_{t-2} - \cdots - C_{t-1}(\eta)y_1$ and $\alpha(\eta) = B_\theta(1)^{-1}\alpha$. An approximation is involved because we truncate the autoregressive representation (or equivalently set pre-sample values to zero) to reflect that we do not observe $y_0, y_{-1}, \ldots$ The score function and the Hessian are

$$\frac{\partial \mathcal{L}(\vartheta)}{\partial \eta} = -\frac{1}{\sigma^2}\sum_{t=1}^{T}\varepsilon_t(\eta)\frac{\partial \varepsilon_t(\eta)}{\partial \eta},$$

$$\frac{\partial \mathcal{L}(\vartheta)}{\partial \sigma^2} = -\frac{T}{2\sigma^2} - \frac{1}{2\sigma^4}\sum_{t=1}^{T}\varepsilon_t^2(\eta),$$

$$\frac{\partial^2 \mathcal{L}(\vartheta)}{\partial \eta \partial \eta^{\mathsf{T}}} = -\frac{1}{\sigma^2}\sum_{t=1}^{T}\left(\varepsilon_t(\eta)\frac{\partial^2 \varepsilon_t(\eta)}{\partial \eta \partial \eta^{\mathsf{T}}} + \frac{\partial \varepsilon_t(\eta)}{\partial \eta}\frac{\partial \varepsilon_t(\eta)}{\partial \eta^{\mathsf{T}}}\right),$$

$$\frac{\partial^2 \mathcal{L}(\vartheta)}{\partial (\sigma^2)^2} = -\left(\frac{T}{2\sigma^4} + \frac{2}{2\sigma^6}\sum_{t=1}^{T}\varepsilon_t^2(\eta)\right),$$

$$\frac{\partial^2 \mathcal{L}(\vartheta)}{\partial \sigma^2 \partial \eta} = -\frac{1}{\sigma^4}\sum_{t=1}^{T}\varepsilon_t(\eta)\frac{\partial \varepsilon_t(\eta)}{\partial \eta}.$$

The residual derivatives are

$$\frac{\partial \varepsilon_t(\eta)}{\partial \eta} = -\frac{\partial \alpha(\eta)}{\partial \eta} - \frac{\partial C_1(\eta)}{\partial \eta}y_{t-1} - \frac{\partial C_2(\eta)}{\partial \eta}y_{t-2} - \cdots - \frac{\partial C_{t-1}(\eta)}{\partial \eta}y_1.$$

These can be defined recursively using the model structure, that is, they satisfy linear difference equations with given initial conditions. The quantity

$$\mathcal{I}_T(\vartheta) = -\frac{\partial^2 \mathcal{L}(\vartheta)}{\partial \vartheta \partial \vartheta^{\mathsf{T}}} = \begin{pmatrix} \mathcal{I}_{T;\eta\eta}(\vartheta) & \mathcal{I}_{T;\eta\sigma^2}(\vartheta) \\ \mathcal{I}_{T;\sigma^2\eta}(\vartheta) & \mathcal{I}_{T;\sigma^2\sigma^2}(\vartheta) \end{pmatrix} \qquad (3.53)$$

is called the observed information in the context of classical likelihood theory.

The key property for the theory is that $\partial \varepsilon_t(\eta)/\partial \eta$ only depends on past values of y_t. Therefore, $\partial \mathcal{L}(\vartheta_0)/\partial \eta$ is a martingale (a sum of MDSs) when $\eta = \eta_0$, that is, evaluated

---

[2] Although if the error density f is non-Gaussian, one can obtain higher efficiency by using a log likelihood based on $\log f$.

at the true parameters, and this holds even when ε_t itself is not i.i.d. but only an MDS. It follows that $\partial \mathcal{L}(\vartheta_0)/\partial \eta$ satisfies a CLT (Hall and Heyde, 1980):

$$\frac{1}{\sqrt{T}}\frac{\partial \mathcal{L}(\vartheta_0)}{\partial \eta} \Longrightarrow N(0, \mathcal{I}_{\eta\eta}), \qquad \mathcal{I}_{\eta\eta} = \frac{1}{\sigma^4}\lim_{T\to\infty}\frac{1}{T}\sum_{t=1}^{T}E\left(\varepsilon_t^2(\eta)\frac{\partial \varepsilon_t(\eta)}{\partial \eta}\frac{\partial \varepsilon_t(\eta)}{\partial \eta^{\mathsf{T}}}\right).$$

(3.54)

If ε_t is i.i.d. and if $\partial \varepsilon_t(\eta_0)/\partial \eta$ is stationary, then this limit simplifies to

$$\mathcal{I}_{\eta\eta} = E(\mathcal{I}_{T;\eta\eta}) = \frac{1}{\sigma^2}E\left(\frac{\partial \varepsilon_t(\eta)}{\partial \eta}\frac{\partial \varepsilon_t(\eta)}{\partial \eta^{\mathsf{T}}}\right).$$

The Hessian (aka observed information) satisfies an LLN (note that the first term drops out) as follows:

$$\frac{1}{T}\frac{\partial^2 \mathcal{L}(\vartheta)}{\partial \eta \partial \eta^{\mathsf{T}}} \xrightarrow{P} \mathcal{J} = \frac{1}{\sigma^2}\lim_{T\to\infty}\frac{1}{T}\sum_{t=1}^{T}E\left(\frac{\partial \varepsilon_t(\eta)}{\partial \eta}\frac{\partial \varepsilon_t(\eta)}{\partial \eta^{\mathsf{T}}}\right). \qquad (3.55)$$

Therefore, one can obtain by Taylor expansion that

$$\sqrt{T}(\widehat{\eta} - \eta) \Longrightarrow N(0, V), \qquad V = \mathcal{J}^{-1}\mathcal{I}\mathcal{J}^{-1}. \qquad (3.56)$$

In the i.i.d. case, we have

$$V = \mathcal{J}^{-1} = \sigma^2 E\left(\frac{\partial \varepsilon_t(\eta_0)}{\partial \eta}\frac{\partial \varepsilon_t(\eta_0)}{\partial \eta^{\mathsf{T}}}\right)^{-1}, \qquad (3.57)$$

which is the asymptotic Cramer–Rao efficiency bound. If ε_t is truly Gaussian, the Gaussian MLE is asymptotically efficient in the sense that its asymptotic variance is minimal amongst all (locally regular) asymptotically normal estimators.

The form of the asymptotic variance of $\widehat{\eta}$ can be given some interpretation. First of all, note that the sandwich form of the variance is reminiscent of linear regression under heteroskedasticity, and one can indeed equate $\partial \varepsilon_t(\eta_0)/\partial \eta$ with a vector of covariates, a connection we will exploit below in constructing standard errors. Furthermore, if $A_\phi(L)y_t = B_\theta(L)\varepsilon_t$, then

$$\frac{\partial \varepsilon_t}{\partial \phi} = \frac{(\partial A_\phi/\partial \phi)(L)}{B_\theta(L)}y_t = \frac{(\partial A_\phi/\partial \phi)(L)}{B_\theta(L)}\frac{B_\theta(L)}{A_\phi(L)}\varepsilon_t = \frac{(\partial A_\phi/\partial \phi)(L)}{A_\phi(L)}\varepsilon_t,$$

where $\partial A_\phi(L)/\partial \phi_j = -L^j, j = 1,\ldots,p$. Therefore, by differentiation and substitution,

$$A_\phi(L)\frac{\partial \varepsilon_t}{\partial \phi} = -\begin{pmatrix} \varepsilon_{t-1} \\ \vdots \\ \varepsilon_{t-p} \end{pmatrix}, \quad j = 1,\ldots,p, \qquad (3.58)$$

that is, $\partial \varepsilon_t/\partial \phi_j$ is an AR(p) process with shock ε_{t-j} and lag polynomial $A_\phi(L)$. That is,

$$E\left(\frac{\partial \varepsilon_t}{\partial \phi}\frac{\partial \varepsilon_t}{\partial \phi^{\mathsf{T}}}\right) = \Gamma_p,$$

where Γ_p is the autocovariance matrix of the AR(p) process with $A_\phi(L)$. Likewise,

$$\frac{\partial \varepsilon_t}{\partial \theta} = -\frac{A_\phi(L)}{B_\theta(L)}\frac{(\partial B_\theta/\partial \theta)(L)}{B_\theta(L)}y_t = -\frac{(\partial B_\theta/\partial \theta)(L)}{B_\theta(L)}\varepsilon_t,$$

where $\partial B_\theta(L)/\partial\theta_j = -L^j$ and so $\partial\varepsilon_t/\partial\theta_j$ is an AR(q) process in ε_{t-j}. In conclusion, the asymptotic variance V involves the inverse of a matrix involving the covariance matrices of two AR processes.

We next consider the distribution theory for $\widehat\sigma^2$. In this case, $\partial\mathcal{L}(\vartheta)/\partial\sigma^2$ is not a sum of MDSs unless the error process is i.i.d. and the theory is more complex. We have, by Taylor expansion,

$$\widehat\sigma^2 = \frac{1}{T}\sum_{t=1}^{T}\varepsilon_t^2(\widehat\eta) = \frac{1}{T}\sum_{t=1}^{T}\varepsilon_t^2(\eta_0) - \frac{2}{T}\sum_{t=1}^{T}\varepsilon_t(\eta_0)\frac{\partial\varepsilon_t(\eta_0)}{\partial\eta}(\widehat\eta - \eta_0) + \cdots$$

$$= \frac{1}{T}\sum_{t=1}^{T}\varepsilon_t^2 + o_P(T^{-1/2}),$$

because of the MDS property of ε_t and perforce under the i.i.d. assumption. Under the assumption that ε_t is i.i.d., we further have

$$\sqrt{T}\left(\widehat\sigma^2 - \sigma^2\right) \implies N\left(0, \mathrm{var}(\varepsilon_t^2)\right),$$

and $\mathrm{var}(\varepsilon_t^2) = \sigma^4(\kappa_4 + 2)$, where κ_4 is the (excess) kurtosis of the error term; in the Gaussian case $\kappa_4 = 0$ and the variance of the variance is $2\sigma^4$, which is of course minimal since the MLE is efficient. Here, the distribution of ε_t matters to the limiting distribution, or at least its kurtosis does.

Suppose instead that ε_t is only an MDS process. Then, $\varepsilon_t^2 - \sigma^2$ need not be an MDS process at all, and in this more general setting the asymptotic variance of $\widehat\sigma^2$ is more complicated; in particular, it equals the long-run variance of ε_t^2, that is,

$$\sqrt{T}\left(\widehat\sigma^2 - \sigma^2\right) \implies N\left(0, \mathrm{lrvar}(\varepsilon_t^2)\right). \tag{3.59}$$

Note that even in the general case where ε_t is i.i.d., $\sqrt{T}(\widehat\sigma^2 - \sigma^2)$ and $\sqrt{T}(\widehat\eta - \eta)$ are not asymptotically independent either, because ε_t^3 is not an MDS or even mean zero in general. Under the stationarity assumption the asymptotic covariance between the two sets of estimators can be expressed as

$$\mathrm{cov}\left(\sqrt{T}(\widehat\sigma^2 - \sigma^2), \sqrt{T}(\widehat\eta - \eta)\right)$$

$$\simeq E\left(\frac{\partial\varepsilon_t(\vartheta_0)}{\partial\vartheta}\frac{\partial\varepsilon_t(\vartheta_0)}{\partial\vartheta^\mathsf{T}}\right)^{-1} E\left(\varepsilon_t^3\frac{\partial\varepsilon_t(\eta_0)}{\partial\eta}\right) E\left(\frac{\partial\varepsilon_t(\vartheta_0)}{\partial\vartheta}\frac{\partial\varepsilon_t(\vartheta_0)}{\partial\vartheta^\mathsf{T}}\right)^{-1},$$

which is zero if $E(\varepsilon_t^3 \mid y_{t-1}, y_{t-2}, \ldots) = 0$, but otherwise is nonzero.

3.5.1 The AR(1) Special Case

We consider the AR(1) case. In this case, the least squares estimator is exactly defined as a ratio of two averages,

$$\widehat\phi - \phi = \frac{\sum_{t=2}^{T}\varepsilon_t(y_{t-1} - \bar{y})}{\sum_{t=2}^{T}(y_{t-1} - \bar{y})^2} \simeq \frac{\sum_{t=2}^{T}\varepsilon_t(y_{t-1} - \mu)}{\sum_{t=2}^{T}(y_{t-1} - \mu)^2},$$

where the approximation step follows from the arguments before (2.19). We may apply an LLN to $\sum_{t=2}^{T}\varepsilon_t(y_{t-1} - \mu)/T$ and $\sum_{t=2}^{T}(y_{t-1} - \mu)^2/T$, with limits zero and

$\gamma_y(0) = \sigma^2/(1 - \phi^2) > 0$, respectively. Therefore, $\widehat{\phi}$ is consistent. Furthermore, by the CLT we have

$$\frac{1}{\sqrt{T}} \sum_{t=2}^{T} \varepsilon_t(y_{t-1} - \mu) \Longrightarrow N\left(0, \sigma^2 \gamma_y(0)\right),$$

and consequently

$$\sqrt{T}(\widehat{\phi} - \phi) \Longrightarrow N(0, 1 - \phi^2). \tag{3.60}$$

Note that the error variance cancels out and does not appear in the limit distribution, just the dynamic coefficient ϕ. The limiting variance decreases with the magnitude of ϕ, with a maximum of one at $\phi = 0$ (the case where the data are i.i.d.) and a minimum of zero at $\phi = 1$ (the distribution theory breaks down when $\phi = 1$ because then y_t is nonstationary, see Chapter 6). The MLE, in the case where $|\phi| < 1$, has the same asymptotic distribution, although the arguments to establish this are more involved. We note that $\widehat{\alpha} = \bar{y}(1 - \widehat{\phi})$ and so $\widehat{\alpha} - \alpha \simeq (\bar{y} - \mu)(1 - \phi) - \mu(\widehat{\phi} - \phi)$, whence we obtain

$$\sqrt{T}(\widehat{\alpha} - \alpha) \Longrightarrow N(0, \sigma^2 + \mu^2(1 - \phi^2)),$$

because $\bar{y} - \mu$ and $\widehat{\phi} - \phi$ are asymptotically independent, and the asymptotic variance of $\bar{y}$ is the long-run variance of the AR(1) process $\sigma^2/(1 - \phi)^2$. Note that the asymptotic covariance between $\widehat{\alpha}$ and $\widehat{\phi}$ is $-\mu(1 - \phi^2)$.

In the case where the error term is only an MDS but not i.i.d., the CLT still applies but the specific limiting variance is different. In that case, although ε_t is a martingale difference sequence, it may be that $E(y_{t-1}^2 \varepsilon_t^2) \neq E(y_{t-1}^2)E(\varepsilon_t^2)$. We show some examples of this in Chapter 10. More generally, we may have a limit

$$V = \frac{\lim_{T \to \infty}(1/T) \sum_{t=2}^{T} E\left(y_{t-1}^2 \varepsilon_t^2\right)}{\left(\lim_{T \to \infty}(1/T) \sum_{t=2}^{T} E\left(y_{t-1}^2\right)\right)^2}, \tag{3.61}$$

which may be different from $1 - \phi^2$. In particular, $E(y_{t-1}^2 \varepsilon_t^2) = E(y_{t-1}^2 E(\varepsilon_t^2 \mid y_{t-1}))$ and $E(\varepsilon_t^2 \mid y_{t-1})$ may vary with y_{t-1}.

In the i.i.d. case, the estimators $\sqrt{T}(\widehat{\sigma}^2 - \sigma^2)$ and $T^{1/2}(\widehat{\phi} - \phi)$ are asymptotically independent because $E\left[\left(\varepsilon_t^2 - \sigma^2\right) y_{t-1}\varepsilon_t\right] = E(\varepsilon_t^3)E(y_{t-1}) = 0$. This holds regardless of the shape of the error distribution. However, if ε_t is only MDS, then the limiting variance of $\widehat{\sigma}^2$ is much more complicated, being the long-run variance of ε_t^2. Furthermore, the two estimators may be correlated because $E\left(\left(\varepsilon_s^2 - \sigma^2\right) y_{t-1}\varepsilon_t\right) = E(\varepsilon_s^2 y_{t-1}\varepsilon_t)$ may not be zero when $s \geq t$, that is, $E(\varepsilon_s^2 \varepsilon_t \mid y_{t-1}, y_{t-2}, \ldots)$ may be nonzero. The autoregression is special because its analysis follows the approach for linear regression with some minor differences.

3.5.2 The MA(1) Special Case

3.5.2.1 The QMLE

For the MA(1) process we have the autoregressive representation $y_t - \mu = \varepsilon_t + \theta(y_{t-1} - \mu) + \theta^2(y_{t-2} - \mu) + \ldots$ In this case, the autoregressive coefficients are $C_j = \theta^j$ so that

$\partial C_j / \partial \theta = j \theta^{j-1}$. The asymptotic variance of the QMLE, $\widehat{\theta}$, is the same as that of an AR(1) process with parameter θ, that is, in the i.i.d. error case,

$$\sqrt{T}(\widehat{\theta} - \theta) \Longrightarrow N\left(0, 1 - \theta^2\right). \tag{3.62}$$

Therefore, standard errors for the MLE here are straightforward. The intercept of an MA(1) process is equal to the mean of the process and so the large-sample properties of the estimated intercept are the same as those already derived for the sample mean of a stationary mixing process, namely the asymptotic variance is $\sigma^2(1 - \theta)^2$.

We have

$$\frac{\partial \varepsilon_t}{\partial \theta} = \frac{\varepsilon_{t-1}}{1 - \theta L} = \frac{y_{t-1}}{(1 - \theta L)^2},$$

which is an AR(1) process. Under the assumption that ε_t is an MDS, the large-sample variance of the MLE $\widehat{\theta}$ is

$$V = \lim_{T \to \infty} \frac{(1/T) \sum_t E\left(\varepsilon_t^2 \left(\varepsilon_{t-1}/(1 - \theta L)\right)^2\right)}{\left((1/T) \sum_t E\left(\left(\varepsilon_{t-1}/(1 - \theta L)\right)^2\right)\right)^2}. \tag{3.63}$$

In general, $E(\varepsilon_t^2(\varepsilon_{t-1}/(1 - \theta L)))^2 \neq E\left(\varepsilon_t^2\right) E((\varepsilon_{t-1}/(1 - \theta L))^2)$.

3.5.2.2 The Method of Moments

We compare with the MoM estimator based on $\rho(1) = g(\theta) = -\theta / \left(1 + \theta^2\right)$. The sampling properties of $\widehat{\rho}(1)$ have already been presented under i.i.d. and MDS assumptions. We have $\widehat{\rho}(1) - \rho(1) \simeq g'(\theta)\left(\widehat{\theta} - \theta\right)$, where $g'(\theta) = (\theta^2 - 1)/(\theta^2 + 1)^2$. Therefore,

$$\sqrt{T}(\widehat{\theta} - \theta) \Longrightarrow N(0, V), \qquad V = \frac{(\theta^2 + 1)^4}{(\theta^2 - 1)^2} \lim_{T \to \infty} T \times \mathrm{var}(\widehat{\rho}(1)). \tag{3.64}$$

For the MA(1) process, we have

$$T\mathrm{var}(\widehat{\rho}(1)) \simeq \frac{1 + \theta^2 + 4\theta^4 + \theta^6 + \theta^8}{(\theta^2 + 1)^4},$$

so that

$$V = \frac{1 + \theta^2 + 4\theta^4 + \theta^6 + \theta^8}{(1 - \theta^2)^2}. \tag{3.65}$$

Clearly, $V \geq 1 - \theta^2$, so that the QMLE is more efficient in the i.i.d. case.

We next consider the behavior of $\widehat{\theta}$ under the weaker MDS assumption, again using the relationship between $\widehat{\theta}$ and $\widehat{\rho}(1)$. We use the fact that, for $f(x) = (-1 \pm \sqrt{1 - 4x^2})/2x$,

$$f'_\pm(x) = \frac{1}{2x^2}\left(1 \pm \frac{1}{\sqrt{1 - 4x^2}}\right).$$

Therefore, by the delta method,

$$\sqrt{T}(\widehat{\theta} - \theta) \Longrightarrow N(0, V_{\mathrm{MDS}}), \qquad V_{\mathrm{MDS}} = \left(\frac{1}{2\rho(1)^2}\left(1 - \frac{1}{\sqrt{1 - 4\rho(1)^2}}\right)\right)^2$$

$$\times \lim_{T \to \infty} T\mathrm{var}(\widehat{\rho}(1)).$$

The limiting distribution of $\widehat{\theta}$ follows from the limiting distribution of $\widehat{\rho}(1)$.

3.5.3   Standard Errors and Inference for the ARMA(p, q) Case

We consider the i.i.d. shock case, which is the default of most statistical passages, and the MDS shock case, which is more general and usually requires a modification of the standard errors.

3.5.3.1   The I.I.D. Shock Case

Under the i.i.d. assumption, the usual standard errors for $\widehat{\eta}$ can be obtained from the diagonal entries of the matrix

$$\widehat{V}_{\text{IID}}(\widehat{\eta}) = \widehat{\sigma}^2 \left(\frac{1}{T} \sum_t \frac{\partial \varepsilon_t(\widehat{\eta})}{\partial \eta} \frac{\partial \varepsilon_t(\widehat{\eta})}{\partial \eta^{\mathsf{T}}} \right)^{-1}. \tag{3.66}$$

Standard errors for $\widehat{\sigma}^2$ are also simple in this case and are based on

$$\widehat{V}_{\text{IID}}(\widehat{\sigma}^2) = \frac{1}{T} \sum_{t=1}^{T} \left(\widehat{\varepsilon}_t^2 - \widehat{\sigma}^2 \right)^2.$$

Suppose we wish to test linear restrictions on the parameters η, that is,

$$R\eta = r \tag{3.67}$$

for some $h \times (p+q+1)$ known full-rank matrix R and $h \times 1$ vector r, where $h \leq p+q+1$. Examples include the heterogeneous autoregressive (HAR) model restrictions, see (7.19). The Wald statistic is given by

$$W = T (R\widehat{\eta} - r)^{\mathsf{T}} \widehat{V}_{\text{IID}}(\widehat{\eta})^{-1} (R\widehat{\eta} - r),$$

and under the null hypothesis it is asymptotically chi-squared with degrees of freedom h. Under the alternative hypothesis that $R\eta \neq r$, we have $W \xrightarrow{P} \infty$ and the test will reject with probability tending to one.

The likelihood ratio and score / Lagrange multiplier (LM) tests are also available in this case based on the working assumption that ε_t is Gaussian (Engle, 1984). In this case, the (conditional) likelihood function at the estimated parameters is

$$L(\widehat{\alpha}, \widehat{\phi}, \widehat{\sigma}^2) = -\frac{T}{2} \log 2\pi - \frac{T}{2} \log(\widehat{\sigma}^2) - \frac{T}{2}. \tag{3.68}$$

Suppose we wish to test a general hypothesis about θ; this could be a linear restriction on ϕ, but it could also involve restrictions on the other parameters. The likelihood ratio statistic is

$$\text{LR} = T \left(\log(\widetilde{\sigma}^2) - \log(\widehat{\sigma}^2) \right),$$

where $\widetilde{\sigma}^2$ is the MLE of σ^2 under the constraints (restricted model). The limiting null distribution is chi-squared with degrees of freedom given by the number of restrictions. Of course, the computation of the restricted estimators $\widetilde{\alpha}, \widetilde{\phi}, \widetilde{\sigma}^2$ can be quite tricksy, except in special cases such as the linear restriction case. Furthermore, it is harder to robustify these tests to heteroskedasticity.

3.5.3.2 The MDS Shock Case

Under the MDS assumption instead, we take

$$
\widehat{V}_{\text{MDS}}(\eta) = \left(\frac{1}{T} \sum_t \frac{\partial \varepsilon_t(\widehat{\eta})}{\partial \eta} \frac{\partial \varepsilon_t(\widehat{\eta})}{\partial \eta^{\mathsf{T}}} \right)^{-1} \frac{1}{T} \sum_{t=1}^{T} \left(\varepsilon_t^2(\widehat{\eta}) \frac{\partial \varepsilon_t(\widehat{\eta})}{\partial \eta} \frac{\partial \varepsilon_t(\widehat{\eta})}{\partial \eta^{\mathsf{T}}} \right)
$$
$$
\times \left(\frac{1}{T} \sum_t \frac{\partial \varepsilon_t(\widehat{\eta})}{\partial \eta} \frac{\partial \varepsilon_t(\widehat{\eta})}{\partial \eta^{\mathsf{T}}} \right)^{-1}, \tag{3.69}
$$

which just depend on the residuals and their first derivatives. We can interpret this as a form of White's heteroskedasticity-consistent covariance matrix estimator (HCCME) for linear regression, where the corresponding X matrix contains the elements $\partial \varepsilon_t(\widehat{\eta})/\partial \eta$ (so is $T + (p+q)$ or $T - (p+q) \times (p+q)$ depending on how one treats initial observations). Robust standard errors are obtained as the square root of the diagonal elements of this matrix (divided by $\sqrt{T}$). For example, in the AR(p) case we have $\partial \varepsilon_t(\widehat{\eta})/\partial \eta = (1, y_{t-1}, \ldots, y_{t-p})^{\mathsf{T}} \equiv x_t$, and letting $X = (x_t^{\mathsf{T}})$ we can write the matrix in White's formulation: $\widehat{V} = (X^{\mathsf{T}}X)^{-1} (X^{\mathsf{T}}DX) (X^{\mathsf{T}}X)^{-1}$, $D = \text{diag}\{\widehat{\varepsilon}_t^2\}$. For the MA(1) process $\partial \varepsilon_t(\widehat{\eta})/\partial \theta = \widehat{\varepsilon}_{t-1}/(1 - \widehat{\theta}L)$, where $\widehat{\varepsilon}_t = y_t/(1 - \widehat{\theta}L) = y_t + \widehat{\theta}y_{t-1} + \cdots$.

Standard errors for $\widehat{\sigma}^2$ involve long-run variance estimation because although ε_t is an MDS, there is no reason for ε_t^2 to be an MDS, so we will defer discussion of this case until the next chapter.

3.6   Testing for the Absence of Autocorrelation Again

We have already discussed some simple ways of testing for the absence of autocorrelation under the null hypothesis that the data are i.i.d. Suppose that y_t is i.i.d.; then it can be shown that

$$
\sqrt{T}(\widehat{\rho}(1), \ldots, \widehat{\rho}(p))^{\mathsf{T}} \Longrightarrow N(0, I_p)
$$

for any p. The Box–Pierce Q statistic ,

$$
Q = T \sum_{j=1}^{p} \widehat{\rho}(j)^2, \tag{3.70}
$$

can be used to test the joint hypothesis that $\rho(1) = 0, \ldots, \rho(p) = 0$ versus the general alternative. We have $Q \Longrightarrow \chi_p^2$ under the null hypothesis. The test is done by rejecting when the realized value $Q > \chi_p^2(\alpha)$ for an α-level test. Under the alternative that $\rho(k) \neq 0$ for some k with $1 \leq k \leq p$ we have $Q \overset{P}{\longrightarrow} \infty$, and so the test has power one against these type of alternatives. The Ljung–Box version,

$$
Q^* = T(T+2) \sum_{j=1}^{p} \frac{\widehat{\rho}(j)^2}{T-j}, \tag{3.71}
$$

is known to have better small-sample performance (smaller bias) and is widely used. In principle, the Box–Pierce approach addresses the multiple testing issue raised by the sample autocorrelation function, but of course authors often report multiple values of this statistic (Q_5, Q_{10}, Q_{12}, etc.) which then contains the same issue.

Variance ratio statistics (Lo and MacKinlay, 1988; Poterba and Summers, 1988) are widely used in empirical finance as a way of testing the efficient markets hypothesis (EMH) and to measure the degree and (cumulative) direction of departures from the null hypothesis of no predictability in financial time series. Indeed, this work has been extremely influential in understanding predictability in asset prices and in measuring market quality. A key advantage of this methodology relative to, say, Box–Pierce statistics is that variance ratios give information about the direction of departures from the null hypothesis that can be interpreted in meaningful economic terms (i.e., momentum versus contrarian). The population variance ratio is defined for $p = 2, 3, \ldots$ as

$$\text{VR}(p) = \frac{\text{var}(y_t + \cdots + y_{t+p-1})}{p \times \text{var}(y_t)} = 1 + 2 \sum_{k=1}^{p-1} \left(1 - \frac{k}{p}\right) \rho(k),$$

and it can be estimated for a stationary process based on the second relation as

$$\widehat{\text{VR}}(p) = 1 + 2 \sum_{k=1}^{p-1} \left(1 - \frac{k}{p}\right) \widehat{\rho}(k), \tag{3.72}$$

where $\widehat{\rho}(k)$ are the sample autocorrelations (Campbell, Lo, and MacKinlay, 1997; Hong, Linton, and Zhang, 2017). Under the i.i.d. assumption this is asymptotically normal with variance $1/T$ times

$$V_{\text{IID}}(p) = 4 \sum_{k=1}^{p-1} \left(1 - \frac{k}{p}\right)^2 = \frac{4}{6p} \left(2p^2 - 3p + 1\right).$$

This variance increases linearly with p. This null limiting distribution is therefore known and simple tests can be provided. The test only has power against alternatives for which $\sum_{k=1}^{p-1} (1 - (k/p)) \rho(k) \neq 0$, which is a one-dimensional alternative. Faust (1992) embeds the variance ratio statistic in a more general class that also includes the Durbin–Watson statistic. He shows that such tests are asymptotically equivalent to likelihood ratio tests against certain autoregressive alternatives.

3.6.1   Martingale Difference Sequence Shocks

We next consider what happens to these classical test statistics when we only assume that $\widetilde{y}_t = y_t - \mu$ is an MDS. In that case we have

$$\sqrt{T}(\widehat{\rho}(1), \ldots, \widehat{\rho}(p))^\mathsf{T} \Longrightarrow u \sim N(0, V), \quad V_{ij} = \lim_{T \to \infty} \frac{(1/T) \sum_t E\left(\widetilde{y}_t^2 \widetilde{y}_{t-i} \widetilde{y}_{t-j}\right)}{\left((1/T) \sum_t E\left(\widetilde{y}_t^2\right)\right)^2}.$$

Under stationarity, we have

$$V_{jj} = \frac{E(\widetilde{y}_t^2 \widetilde{y}_{t-j}^2)}{E(\widetilde{y}_t^2) E(\widetilde{y}_{t-j}^2)} = \frac{E(\widetilde{y}_t^2) E(\widetilde{y}_{t-j}^2) + \text{cov}(\widetilde{y}_t^2, \widetilde{y}_{t-j}^2)}{E(\widetilde{y}_t^2) E(\widetilde{y}_{t-j}^2)}$$

$$= 1 + \frac{\text{cov}(\widetilde{y}_t^2, \widetilde{y}_{t-j}^2)}{\text{var}(y_t)^2} = 1 + \frac{\text{var}(\widetilde{y}_t^2)}{\text{var}(y_t)^2} \text{corr}(\widetilde{y}_t^2, \widetilde{y}_{t-j}^2)$$

$$= 1 + \overbrace{(\kappa_4(y_t) - 1)}^{\textit{heavy} \text{ tails}} \quad \times \quad \overbrace{\text{corr}(\widetilde{y}_t^2, \widetilde{y}_{t-j}^2)}^{\textit{dependent} \text{ heteroskedasticity}},$$

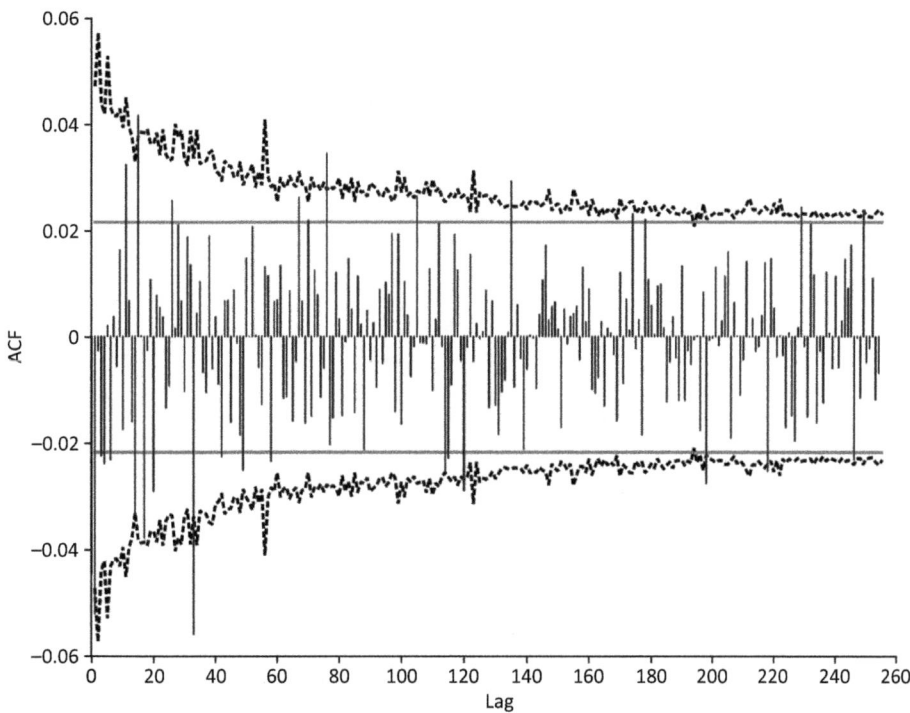

Figure 3.4 ACF of daily S&P500 returns along with Bartlett bands (solid) and heteroskedasticity-consistent bands (dashed).

where $\kappa_4(y_t) = E(\tilde{y}_t^4)/E^2(\tilde{y}_t^2) = 1 + \text{var}(\tilde{y}_t^2)/\text{var}(y_t)^2 \geq 1$ is the kurtosis of the series y_t. The asymptotic variance of $\widehat{\rho}(j)$ can be arbitrarily large due to the kurtosis factor. In practice, we expect that $\text{corr}(\tilde{y}_t^2, \tilde{y}_{t-j}^2) > 0$ and $\kappa_4(y_t) > 3$. We present these heteroskedasticity-robust confidence intervals for the ACF of the S&P500 daily return series in Figure 3.4. In comparison with the Bartlett bands, these bands are wider at the shortest horizon but the magnitude declines with lags.

Furthermore, the sample autocorrelations are mutually correlated even in large samples. Under stationarity, we have $V_{ij} = E(\tilde{y}_t^2 \tilde{y}_{t-i} \tilde{y}_{t-j})/E(\tilde{y}_t^2)^2$, and this is not in general equal to zero. It follows that the asymptotic distribution of Q is not chi-squared, however we do have

$$Q \Longrightarrow u^\mathsf{T} u = z^\mathsf{T} V z, \tag{3.73}$$

where $u = (u_1, \ldots, u_p)^\mathsf{T} \sim N(0, V)$, while z is a vector of independent standard normal random variables. In this case we may simulate the limit distribution based on the consistent estimator $\widehat{V}$ of V, where

$$\widehat{V}_{ij} = \frac{(1/T) \sum_t (y_t - \bar{y})^2 (y_{t-i} - \bar{y})(y_{t-j} - \bar{y})}{\left((1/T) \sum_t (y_t - \bar{y})^2\right)^2}.$$

That is, generate standard normal random vectors z and compute $z^\mathsf{T} \widehat{V} z$, then repeat.

Alternatively, one can modify the test by taking the robust Box–Pierce statistic

$$Q_{\text{robust}} = T(\widehat{\rho}(1), \ldots, \widehat{\rho}(p))^\mathsf{T} \widehat{V}^{-1} (\widehat{\rho}(1), \ldots, \widehat{\rho}(p)), \tag{3.74}$$

which is asymptotically chi-squared with p degrees of freedom under the null hypothesis. The robust autocorrelation and Box–Pierce tests are also consistent against the same class of alternatives; they do suffer some loss of power against certain local alternatives in comparison with the standard tests when the assumptions of the standard tests (i.i.d.) are valid. For example, if $y_t = \varepsilon_t - \theta_T \varepsilon_{t-1}$ with ε_t i.i.d. with mean zero, and $\theta_T = c/\sqrt{T}$.

For the variance ratio statistic the limiting distribution under the MDS assumption is more complicated. Let

$$\widehat{V}_{\text{MDS}}(p) = 4 \sum_{j=1}^{p-1} \sum_{k=1}^{p-1} \left(1 - \frac{j}{p}\right)\left(1 - \frac{k}{p}\right) \widehat{V}_{jk}. \tag{3.75}$$

Then it follows that

$$\widehat{V}_{\text{MDS}}(p)^{-1/2}\sqrt{T}\,(\text{VR}\,(p) - 1) \Longrightarrow N(0, 1) \tag{3.76}$$

(Hong, Linton, and Zhang, 2017).

The above tests are not based on any particular alternative. We may instead embed the null hypothesis within a general family of alternatives. Suppose that we observe y_t, which is generated from the AR(1) process $y_t = \phi y_{t-1} + \varepsilon_t$, where ε_t are i.i.d. The null hypothesis is $H_0: \phi = 0$, with $H_A: \phi \neq 0$. Under this null hypothesis y_t is i.i.d., but the alternative has a particular character. The general strategy here is to use likelihood-based tests such as the LR, Wald, or LM tests. The Wald statistic is based on the MLE estimator of ϕ. The LM test is easiest, it is based on the score function, which is

$$\left.\frac{\partial \mathcal{L}}{\partial \phi}\right|_{\phi=0} = \frac{1}{\sigma^2} \sum_{t=2}^{T} y_t y_{t-1},$$

and the estimator of σ^2 under the null hypothesis is $\widetilde{\sigma}^2 = \sum_{t=1}^{T} y_{t-1}^2 / T$, so that

$$\text{LM} = T \left(\frac{\sum_{t=2}^{T} y_t y_{t-1}}{\sum_{t=1}^{T} y_{t-1}^2}\right)^2 = T\widehat{\rho}(1)^2.$$

Under the null hypothesis $\text{LM} \Longrightarrow \chi_1^2$, and we reject the null hypothesis when LM is large relative to the critical value from χ_1^2. This approach is limited to two-sided alternatives. We can, however, also use the signed version, which is $T^{1/2}\widehat{\rho}(1)$, which has already been treated.

The Durbin–Watson d statistic was widely used a generation ago to test for serial correlation in regression residuals. The statistic based on observable data is $d = \sum_{t=2}^{T}(y_t - y_{t-1})^2 / \sum_{t=1}^{T} y_t^2$, and is a bit like the variance ratio. Using the approximation $d \approx 2(1 - \widehat{\rho}(1))$, we have under the i.i.d. null hypothesis $\sqrt{T}(1 - (d/2)) \Longrightarrow N(0, 1)$.

3.6.2   Nonstationarity in Mean and Variance

So far we have emphasized stationarity, or at least second-order stationarity. Here, we consider what happens when this assumption is violated. Specifically, suppose that $y_t = \mu_t + \sigma_t u_t$, where u_t is a stationary mean-zero process with unit variance, while μ_t, σ_t are bounded deterministic sequences. We observe the sequence $\{y_t, t = 1, \ldots, T\}$ and assume that it is from a stationary process. We have, in this case,

$$\bar{y} = \frac{1}{T} \sum_{t=1}^{T} y_t = \frac{1}{T} \sum_{t=1}^{T} \mu_t + \frac{1}{T} \sum_{t=1}^{T} \sigma_t u_t = \frac{1}{T} \sum_{t=1}^{T} \mu_t + o_P(1).$$

Furthermore, for $k = 0, 1, 2, \ldots,$

$$\frac{1}{T} \sum_{t=k+1}^{T} y_t y_{t-k} = \frac{1}{T} \sum_{t=k+1}^{T} \mu_t \mu_{t-k} + \frac{1}{T} \sum_{t=k+1}^{T} \sigma_t \sigma_{t-k} \rho_u(k)$$

$$+ \frac{1}{T} \sum_{t=k+1}^{T} \sigma_t \sigma_{t-k} \left(u_t u_{t-k} - \rho_u(k) \right) + \frac{1}{T} \sum_{t=k+1}^{T} \mu_t \sigma_{t-k} u_{t-k}$$

$$+ \frac{1}{T} \sum_{t=k+1}^{T} \mu_{t-k} \sigma_t u_t$$

$$= \frac{1}{T} \sum_{t=k+1}^{T} \mu_t \mu_{t-k} + \frac{1}{T} \sum_{t=k+1}^{T} \sigma_t \sigma_{t-k} \rho_u(k) + o_P(1).$$

Therefore, for $k = 0, 1, 2, \ldots,$

$$\widehat{\gamma}_y(k) = \frac{1}{T} \sum_{t=k+1}^{T} y_t y_{t-k} - \bar{y}^2$$

$$= \frac{1}{T} \sum_{t=k+1}^{T} \mu_t \mu_{t-k} - \left(\frac{1}{T} \sum_{t=1}^{T} \mu_t \right)^2 + \frac{1}{T} \sum_{t=k+1}^{T} \sigma_t \sigma_{t-k} \rho_u(k) + o_P(1).$$

The limiting behavior of $\widehat{\gamma}_y(k)$ depends on the values of $\mu_t, \sigma_t,\ t = 1, \ldots, T$. We next consider two alternative specifications.

Example 3.9   Suppose that $\mu_t = \mu(t/T)$ and $\sigma_t = \sigma(t/T)$ for $\mu(\cdot), \sigma(\cdot)$ smooth functions. Then, we have $\bar{y} \xrightarrow{P} \int_0^1 \mu(u)\, du$ and, for any fixed $k = 0, 1, \ldots,$

$$\frac{1}{T} \sum_{t=k+1}^{T} \mu_t \mu_{t-k} - \left(\frac{1}{T} \sum_{t=1}^{T} \mu_t \right)^2 \to \int_0^1 \mu^2(u)\, du - \left(\int_0^1 \mu(u)\, du \right)^2,$$

$$\frac{1}{T} \sum_{t=k+1}^{T} \sigma_t \sigma_{t-k} \to \int_0^1 \sigma^2(u)\, du,$$

and so, for any fixed k,

$$\widehat{\gamma}_y(k) \xrightarrow{P} \int_0^1 \mu^2(u)\, du - \left(\int_0^1 \mu(u)\, du \right)^2 + \int_0^1 \sigma^2(u)\, du \times \rho_u(k),$$

$$\widehat{\rho}_y(k) \xrightarrow{P} \bar{\rho}_y(k) = \frac{\int_0^1 \mu^2(u)\, du - \left(\int_0^1 \mu(u)\, du \right)^2 + \int_0^1 \sigma^2(u)\, du \times \rho_u(k)}{\int_0^1 \mu^2(u)\, du - \left(\int_0^1 \mu(u)\, du \right)^2 + \int_0^1 \sigma^2(u)\, du}.$$

If $\rho_u(k) = 0$, then $\bar{\rho}_y(k) = \bar{\rho}_y \in (0, 1)$.

Example 3.10   Suppose instead that μ_t and σ_t are themselves behaving like stationary stochastic processes independent of $\{u_t\}$ and each other and with autocovariance functions $\gamma_\mu(\cdot), \gamma_\sigma(\cdot)$. Then

$$\widehat{\gamma}_y(k) \xrightarrow{P} \gamma_\mu(k) + \left(\gamma_\sigma(k) + E^2(\sigma_t)\right) \times \rho_u(k),$$

$$\widehat{\rho}_y(k) \xrightarrow{P} \overline{\rho}_y(k) = \frac{\gamma_\mu(k) + \left(\gamma_\sigma(k) + E^2(\sigma_t)\right) \times \rho_u(k)}{\gamma_\mu(0) + \left(\gamma_\sigma(0) + E^2(\sigma_t)\right)}.$$

If $\rho_u(k) = 0$, then $\overline{\rho}_y(k) = \gamma_\mu(k)/(\gamma_\mu(0) + (\gamma_\sigma(0) + E^2(\sigma_t)))$, which could be negative depending on the value of $\gamma_\mu(k)$.

The calendar-time model for stock returns implies that the mean and standard deviation should be proportional to the number of days between closing prices. In a regular cycle this would be $1, 1, 1, 1, 1, 3, 1, \ldots$, with occasional holidays and longer closings such as during World War 2 and 9/11. Empirically, in the US market this sequence has a sample mean of 1.39 and standard deviation of 0.79, and autocorrelations of -0.212, -0.218, -0.208, and so on, quite large and negative. This implies that under the calendar-time model we expect the autocorrelation of returns to be negative, consistent with the stale pricing model of Lo and MacKinlay (1990). In this case, though, we may expect the level and variation of σ_t to be large relative to the variations in μ_t, so this effect may not be meaningful.

3.6.3   Testing of Residual Autocorrelation

We may be interested in testing that the residuals from some estimated model are free of autocorrelation. This may be part of the model specification process or it may be a formal requirement of our framework that we want to validate or not. Here, we just focus on pure time series models, that is, ARMA(p, q); we consider the situation of regression models later.

Suppose that we fit an autoregression $y_t = \phi y_{t-1} + \varepsilon_t$, where we assume that ε_t is i.i.d. with mean zero and variance σ^2, but we wish to test for possible misspecification, which amounts to the possibility that ε_t may be a general stationary process. There are several approaches. The sample partial autocorrelations $\widehat{\pi}(k)$, $k \geq 2$, are asymptotically standard normal and mutually independent under the i.i.d. shock assumption, and this may be used as a test of this model. An alternative strategy is to test for residual autocorrelation after fitting the model, an approach that we investigate next.

Let $\widehat{\phi}$ be the OLS estimator of ϕ and let $\widehat{\varepsilon}_t = y_t - \widehat{\phi} y_{t-1}$. Then define the residual autocovariance and autocorrelation as

$$\widehat{\gamma}_{\widehat{\varepsilon}}(k) = \frac{1}{T} \sum_{t=k+1}^{T} \widehat{\varepsilon}_t \widehat{\varepsilon}_{t-k}, \qquad \widehat{\rho}_{\widehat{\varepsilon}}(k) = \frac{\widehat{\gamma}_{\widehat{\varepsilon}}(k)}{\widehat{\gamma}_{\widehat{\varepsilon}}(0)}, \qquad k = 1, 2, \ldots \qquad (3.77)$$

The null hypothesis here is that $\rho_\varepsilon(k) = 0$ for each k (with no restriction on the value of ϕ). We next consider the limiting null distribution of $\widehat{\rho}_{\widehat{\varepsilon}}(k)$ under this null hypothesis.

We write the residuals as $\widehat{\varepsilon}_t = \varepsilon_t - y_{t-1}(\widehat{\phi} - \phi)$, so that under the null hypothesis, for any $k \geq 0$,

$$\sqrt{T}\widehat{\gamma}_{\widehat{\varepsilon}}(k) = \frac{1}{\sqrt{T}} \sum_{t=k+1}^{T} \varepsilon_t \varepsilon_{t-k} - \frac{1}{T} \sum_{t=k+1}^{T} \varepsilon_t y_{t-k-1} \times \sqrt{T}(\widehat{\phi} - \phi)$$

$$- \frac{1}{T} \sum_{t=k+1}^{T} y_{t-1} \varepsilon_{t-k} \sqrt{T}(\widehat{\phi} - \phi)$$

$$+ \frac{1}{T} \sum_{t=k+1}^{T} y_{t-1} y_{t-k-1} \times \frac{1}{\sqrt{T}} \left[\sqrt{T}(\widehat{\phi} - \phi) \right]^2.$$

We next apply the LLN to eliminate the second and last terms, and obtain

$$\sqrt{T}\widehat{\gamma}_{\widehat{\varepsilon}}(k) = \frac{1}{\sqrt{T}} \sum_{t=k+1}^{T} \varepsilon_t \varepsilon_{t-k} - E(y_{t-1}\varepsilon_{t-k})\sqrt{T}(\widehat{\phi} - \phi) + o_P(1)$$

$$= \frac{1}{\sqrt{T}} \sum_{t=k+1}^{T} \varepsilon_t \varepsilon_{t-k} - E(y_{t-1}\varepsilon_{t-k})\frac{1 - \phi^2}{\sigma^2} \frac{1}{\sqrt{T}} \sum_{t=2}^{T} y_{t-1}\varepsilon_t + o_P(1)$$

$$= \frac{1}{\sqrt{T}} \sum_{t=k+1}^{T} \left\{ \varepsilon_t \left(\varepsilon_{t-k} - \phi^{k-1}(1 - \phi^2)y_{t-1} \right) \right\} + o_P(1),$$

which follows because $E(\varepsilon_t y_{t-k-1}) = 0$ for any $k \geq 0$ and $E(y_{t-1}\varepsilon_{t-k}) = \phi^{k-1}\sigma^2$ for any $k \geq 1$. In conclusion, we have:

$$\sqrt{T}\widehat{\gamma}_{\widehat{\varepsilon}}(k) = \frac{1}{\sqrt{T}} \sum_{t=k+1}^{T} \left\{ \varepsilon_t \left(\varepsilon_{t-k} - \phi^{k-1}(1 - \phi^2)y_{t-1} \right) \right\} + o_P(1), \quad k \neq 0,$$

$$\sqrt{T}(\widehat{\gamma}_{\widehat{\varepsilon}}(0) - \gamma_\varepsilon(0)) = \frac{1}{\sqrt{T}} \sum_{t=1}^{T} (\varepsilon_t^2 - \gamma(0)) + o_P(1).$$

It follows that $\sqrt{T}\widehat{\gamma}_{\widehat{\varepsilon}}(k)$ is asymptotically normal with mean zero and variance $\sigma^4(1 - \phi^{2(k-1)}(1 - \phi^2))$ for $k \geq 1$, while for $k = 0$, $\sqrt{T}(\widehat{\gamma}_{\widehat{\varepsilon}}(0) - \gamma_\varepsilon(0))$ is asymptotically normally distributed with mean zero and variance $E(\varepsilon_t^4) - \sigma^4$ (i.e., it is not affected by the preliminary estimation). Therefore, under the null hypothesis that $\rho_\varepsilon(k) = 0$, we have

$$\sqrt{T}\widehat{\rho}_{\widehat{\varepsilon}}(k) \Longrightarrow N\big(0, 1 - \phi^{2(k-1)}(1 - \phi^2)\big), \quad k \geq 1.$$

The limiting distribution is affected by the value of ϕ for $k \neq 0$. If $\phi \neq 0$ and $k = 1$, then the limiting variance is ϕ^2, which can be much smaller than when the series ε_t is observed (in which case the limiting variance is one). For $k = 2$, the limiting variance of the sample residual autocorrelation is $1 - \phi^2(1 - \phi^2)$. As $k \to \infty$, the limiting variance approaches one.

We now consider the general case. Suppose that we fit an ARMA(p, q) model and we wish to test the validity of this specification. Let $\varepsilon_t(\widehat{\eta})$ denote the first-stage residuals. We apply the fact that

$$\varepsilon_t(\widehat{\eta}) = \varepsilon_t(\eta) + \frac{\partial \varepsilon_t}{\partial \eta}(\eta)(\widehat{\eta} - \eta) + o_P(T^{-1/2}),$$

and obtain

$$
\sqrt{T}\widehat{\gamma}_{\widehat{\varepsilon}}(k) = \frac{1}{\sqrt{T}} \sum_{t=k+1}^{T} \varepsilon_t(\widehat{\eta})\varepsilon_{t-k}(\widehat{\eta})
$$

$$
= \frac{1}{\sqrt{T}} \sum_{t=k+1}^{T} \varepsilon_t(\eta)\varepsilon_{t-k}(\eta) + E\left[\frac{\partial \varepsilon_t}{\partial \eta}(\eta)\varepsilon_{t-k}(\eta)\right] \times \sqrt{T}(\widehat{\eta} - \eta) + o_P(1)
$$

$$
= \frac{1}{\sqrt{T}} \sum_{t=k+1}^{T} \varepsilon_t(\eta)\Bigg[\varepsilon_{t-k}(\eta)
$$

$$
- E\left[\frac{\partial \varepsilon_t}{\partial \eta}(\eta)\varepsilon_{t-k}(\eta)\right] \times \left[E\left(\frac{\partial \varepsilon_t}{\partial \eta}(\eta)\frac{\partial \varepsilon_t}{\partial \eta^{\mathsf{T}}}(\eta)\right)\right]^{-1}\frac{\partial \varepsilon_t(\eta)}{\partial \eta}\Bigg]
$$

$$
+ o_P(1)
$$

$$
= \frac{1}{\sqrt{T}} \sum_{t=k+1}^{T} \varepsilon_t(\eta)w_{t,k}(\eta) + o_P(1),
$$

where

$$
w_{t,k}(\eta) = \varepsilon_{t-k}(\eta) - E\left[\frac{\partial \varepsilon_t}{\partial \eta}(\eta)\varepsilon_{t-k}(\eta)\right] \times \left[E\left(\frac{\partial \varepsilon_t}{\partial \eta}(\eta)\frac{\partial \varepsilon_t}{\partial \eta^{\mathsf{T}}}(\eta)\right)\right]^{-1}\frac{\partial \varepsilon_t(\eta)}{\partial \eta}.
$$

Note that $w_{t,k}(\eta)$ is determined purely by $y_{t-1}, y_{t-2}, \ldots$, and so $\varepsilon_t(\eta_0)w_{t,k}(\eta_0)$ is mean zero conditionally and unconditionally. Box and Pierce (1970) derived the joint distribution of the autocovariances and autocorrelations in this case. In particular, they showed that under the null hypothesis that $\rho_\varepsilon(k) = 0$,

$$
\sqrt{T}\widehat{\rho}_{\widehat{\varepsilon}}(k) \Longrightarrow N(0, V), \qquad V = \frac{E\left(\varepsilon_t^2(\eta)w_{t,k}^2(\eta)\right)}{E\left(\varepsilon_t^2(\eta)\right)^2}.
$$

The asymptotic variance can be estimated by

$$
\widehat{V} = \frac{\frac{1}{T}\sum_{t=1}^{T} \widehat{\varepsilon}_t^2\widehat{w}_{t,k}^2(\widehat{\eta})}{\frac{1}{T}\sum_{t=1}^{T} \widehat{\varepsilon}_t^2},
$$

where the expectations in $w_{t,k}(\eta)$ are replaced by sample averages, that is,

$$
\widehat{w}_{t,k}(\widehat{\eta}) = \varepsilon_{t-k}(\widehat{\eta}) - \frac{1}{T}\sum_t \frac{\partial \varepsilon_t}{\partial \eta}(\widehat{\eta})\varepsilon_{t-k}(\widehat{\eta}) \times \left[\frac{1}{T}\sum_t \frac{\partial \varepsilon_t}{\partial \eta}(\widehat{\eta})\frac{\partial \varepsilon_t}{\partial \eta^{\mathsf{T}}}(\widehat{\eta})\right]^{-1}\frac{\partial \varepsilon_t(\widehat{\eta})}{\partial \eta}.
$$

That is, we can compare $\widehat{\rho}_{\widehat{\varepsilon}}(k)$ with $\pm z_{\alpha/2}(\widehat{V}/T)^{1/2}$. The joint asymptotic distribution of $\sqrt{T}(\widehat{\rho}_{\widehat{\varepsilon}}(1), \ldots, \widehat{\rho}_{\widehat{\varepsilon}}(m))$ can be of deficient rank. Taken together, the Box–Pierce statistic $T\sum_{k=1}^{m}\widehat{\rho}_{\widehat{\varepsilon}}^2(k)$ does not have a $\chi^2(m)$ limiting distribution. However, Box and Pierce (1970) argued that provided m is large compared to $p + q$, under some circumstance the $\chi^2(m-p-q)$ distribution can provide a reasonable approximation to the null distribution.

3.7   Goodness of Fit and Model Selection

We have assumed so far that the integer orders p, q are known, and now is the time to address how to choose the model order. We first consider model selection for linear regression models. Suppose that y is the $T \times 1$ vector of responses and X is a $T \times K$ matrix of predictors. Let $\mathcal{M}$ be a collection of *linear* regression models obtained from the given set of K regressors $X = (X_1, \ldots, X_K)$, for example, $X, X_1, (X_2, X_{27}), \ldots$ Suppose that the true model lies in $\mathcal{M}$. There are a total of $(2^K - 1)$ different subsets of X (i.e., models). How do we choose the appropriate model? Just calculating the goodness of fit like the sum of squared residuals or regression R^2 will favor the largest model. In practice we should trade off the (in-sample) fit of the model against the size of the model, that is, how many parameters are estimated. The adjusted R^2, denoted R_j^{*2}, is a simple way of penalizing overfitting in regression settings, but researchers also use the model selection procedures listed below for this purpose. Let K_j be the number of explanatory variables in a given regression (there may be many different models with K_j regressors but we do not make this explicit for now for notational simplicity) and let $\widehat{u}_j$ be the OLS residuals from that model, let $\widehat{u}$ be the OLS residuals from the full model, and let $\bar{u}$ be the deviation of y from its mean. Then define the model selection measures we denote generically by MS_j:

$$R_j^{*2} = 1 - \frac{T-1}{T-K_j}(1 - R_j^2) = 1 - \frac{T-1}{T-K_j}\frac{\widehat{u}_j^{\mathsf{T}}\widehat{u}_j}{\bar{u}^{\mathsf{T}}\bar{u}},$$

$$C_j = T\frac{\widehat{u}_j^{\mathsf{T}}\widehat{u}_j}{\widehat{u}^{\mathsf{T}}\widehat{u}} - T + 2(K_j + 1),$$

$$\text{PC}_j = \frac{\widehat{u}_j^{\mathsf{T}}\widehat{u}_j}{T-K_j}\left(1 + \frac{K_j}{T}\right),$$

$$\text{AIC}_j = \log\left(\frac{\widehat{u}_j'\widehat{u}_j}{T}\right) + \frac{2K_j}{T},$$

$$\text{BIC}_j = \log\left(\frac{\widehat{u}_j'\widehat{u}_j}{T}\right) + \frac{K_j \log T}{T},$$

$$\text{CV}_j = -\frac{1}{T}\sum_{t=1}^{T}(y_t - \widehat{y}_{j,t})^2,$$

where $\widehat{y}_{j,t}$ is the predictor of the tth observation given model j but not using the observation t, that is, $\widehat{y}_{j,t} = x_{j,t}^{\mathsf{T}}(X_{j,-t}^{\mathsf{T}}X_{j,-t})^{-1}X_{j,-t}^{\mathsf{T}}y_{-t}$, where y_{-t} is the $(T-1) \times 1$ vector of observations on the dependent variable excluding the tth observation, and $X_{j,-t}$ is the $(T-1) \times K_j$ matrix of observations on the covariates of the K_j model excluding the tth observation, and $x_{j,t}$ is the K_j vector of regressors at time t. For each estimated model we obtain the model selection measure MS_j and then choose the model in $\mathcal{M}$ that maximizes this quantity – that is our selected model. Note that maximizing $\overline{R}_j^2$ is equivalent to minimizing the unbiased variance estimate $\widehat{u}_j\widehat{u}_j/(T-K_j)$. Note that maximizing the (negative) cross-validation criterion CV_j is equivalent to minimizing $\sum_{t=1}^{T}\widehat{u}_{jt}^2/(1-w_{jt})$, where w_{jt} is the tth diagonal element of the projection matrix $P_j = X_j(X_j^{\mathsf{T}}X_j)^{-1}X_j^{\mathsf{T}}$. Other well-known model selection criteria include the focused information criterion (FIC) and Spiegelhalter's DIC (deviance information criterion).

There are two main properties that justify model selection procedures. The first is efficiency, which arises in the case where the set of candidate models does not include the true model. The goal is to select the model that best approximates the truth from a set of finite-dimensional models. The AIC method (Akaike, 1974) possesses this property.

A second property is called consistency, which arises when the true model is of finite dimension and is included in the set of candidate models. The BIC (or SIC as it is sometimes called; Schwarz, 1978) correctly selects the true model with probability tending to one. There are some issues. First, $\mathcal{M}$ may be large and computing all $2^K - 1$ regressions is infeasible. Second, the true model may not be in $\mathcal{M}$, but the procedure is guaranteed to find a best model (data mining). Regarding the first issue there are many different algorithms for searching through the model class in a directed way. Recent work has proposed a variety of new methodologies to solve the selection problem. For example, LASSO (least absolute shrinkage and selection operator) is the best-known method; this involves finding parameters by penalized least squares, an L_1 penalty. We consider this method in more detail in Chapter 11.

We next turn to the AR special case (with intercept), which we can view as a regression model, as per our previous discussion. We may use all the above methods to select the order p of the autoregression. In this case, it is natural to define the model space through the largest conceivable order $p_{\max}$ and then the task is somewhat simpler. In this case, there is a natural ordering and it perhaps makes sense only to estimate the AR(1), ..., AR($p_{\max}$) models, and compare them according to the model selection criteria; it is generally thought that the most recent lags are the most important. This is not always convincing because we may have pronounced seasonal effects at specific lags but no effects at other lags in between. The other difference from the usual regression setting is that the number of observations is $T - p$ and depends on the model being estimated. In this case, let

$$\text{FPE}_p = \widehat{\sigma}_p^2 \frac{T + p}{T - p},$$

$$C_p = \frac{\sum_{t=p+1}^{T} \widehat{\varepsilon}_t^2(p)}{\sum_{t=p_{\max}+1}^{T} \widehat{\varepsilon}_t^2(p_{\max})} - T + 2p,$$

$$\text{AIC}_p = \log(\widehat{\sigma}_p^2) + \frac{2(p + 1)}{T},$$

$$\text{BIC}_p = \log(\widehat{\sigma}_p^2) + \frac{p \log(T)}{T},$$

$$\text{HQ}_p = \log(\widehat{\sigma}_p^2) + 2c \frac{p \log \log(T)}{T},$$

with $\widehat{\sigma}_p^2 = \sum_{t=p+1}^{T} \widehat{\varepsilon}_t^2(p)/T$, where $\widehat{\varepsilon}_t(p)$ are the residuals from fitting the AR(p) model. The last one is the Hannan and Quinn (1979) model selection criterion, and common practice is to choose $c = 1$. Some "small-sample" adjustments to these model selection procedures have been proposed in the literature, see McQuarrie and Tsai (1998).

These methods can be extended to the ARMA(p, q) and other time series models as follows. We suppose that there is a Gaussian log likelihood $\mathcal{L}$ defined for each model M_j, and define $\mathcal{L}_{\max}(M_j)$ to be the maximized value of the log likelihood for model M_j (with respect to the parameters of the model). Then we may define

$$\text{AIC}(M_j) = 2\mathcal{L}_{\max}(M_j) - 2\dim(M_j),$$

$$\text{BIC}(M_j) = 2\mathcal{L}_{\max}(M_j) - \log(T)\dim(M_j).$$

The definitions we gave for linear regression are equivalent to this. Note that $\dim(M_j)$ is sometimes called the L_0 norm of the parameter vector. In the ARMA(p, q) class, the maximized log likelihood is, apart from constants, $-(T/2) \log \widehat{\sigma}^2$, where $\widehat{\sigma}^2 = \sum_{t=1}^{T} \varepsilon_t^2(\widehat{\eta})/T$ and $\widehat{\eta}$ is the MLE (or approximate MLE) for the given model.[3] We usually take the dimensionality of the model to be $p + q$, ignoring the presence of σ^2. The question of how to do inference after model selection is a thorny one, see Leeb and Pötscher (2005).

3.8   Application

We estimated an AR(5) model to the Oxford Tmax data by MLE and by OLS, and show the results for MLE, OLS, and White's standard errors in Table 3.1. The MLE and OLS point estimates differ by very little and in this case the standard errors are also in quite close agreement. The parameter values show an oscillating pattern out to this order with both positive and negative values that overall leave $\sum_{j=1}^{5} \phi_j = 0.21$.

We also fitted an AR(5) to the VIX data, with the results shown in Table 3.2. In this case, the first lag is very positive and statistically significant, whereas the other coefficients are smaller and, except for ϕ_4, also positive. In total, $\sum_{j=1}^{5} \phi_j \simeq 0.98$, very close to one, indicating a great deal of persistence in this time series. According to the MLE and OLS standard errors, all coefficients are statistically significant. However, the robust standard errors are quite a bit larger than the OLS or MLE ones and according to these standard errors only the first and fifth lags are significant.

Table 3.1 AR(5) model estimates for Tmax data and different standard errors.

	MLE	MLE S.E.	OLS	OLS S.E.	Robust S.E.
ϕ_1	0.6579	0.0213	0.6637	0.0213	0.0225
ϕ_2	0.0964	0.0254	0.0912	0.0255	0.0254
ϕ_3	−0.0846	0.0254	−0.0859	0.0255	0.0253
ϕ_4	−0.2029	0.0254	−0.2004	0.0255	0.0245
ϕ_5	−0.2691	0.0213	−0.2676	0.0213	0.0214

Table 3.2 AR(5) model estimates for VIX data and different standard errors.

	MLE	MLE S.E.	OLS	OLS S.E.	Robust S.E.
ϕ_1	0.8508	0.0108	0.8509	0.0108	0.0303
ϕ_2	0.0787	0.0141	0.0786	0.0141	0.0498
ϕ_3	0.0291	0.0141	0.0291	0.0141	0.0404
ϕ_4	−0.0429	0.0141	−0.0428	0.0141	0.0338
ϕ_5	0.0677	0.0108	0.0678	0.0108	0.0247

---

[3] In the ARMA(p, q) class we do not have this simple ordering but we may consider only looking at pq models rather than $2^{p+q} - 1$.

Table 3.3 AR(5) model estimates for `Arbuthnot` sex ratio data and different standard errors.

	MLE	MLE S.E.	OLS	OLS S.E.	Robust S.E.
ϕ_1	0.2660	0.1148	0.2637	0.1115	0.1299
ϕ_2	0.0479	0.1190	0.0466	0.1150	0.1335
ϕ_3	0.0744	0.1186	0.0758	0.1148	0.1178
ϕ_4	−0.0677	0.1191	−0.0717	0.1153	0.1081
ϕ_5	−0.0251	0.1154	−0.0247	0.1119	0.1000

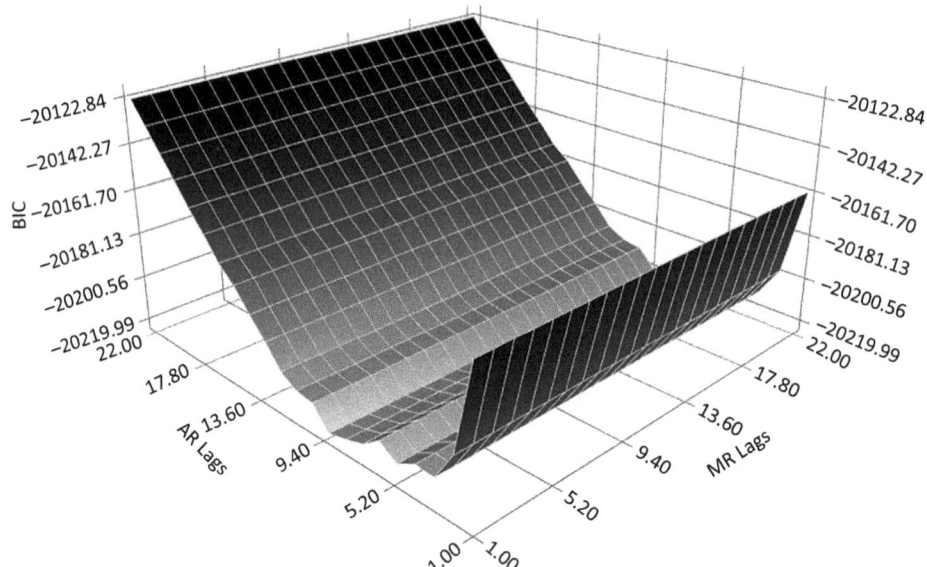

Figure 3.5 Plot of BIC against AR and MA orders.

Finally, we did this for the `Arbuthnot` sex ratio data and found the results presented in Table 3.3. We found an unconditional mean value of 1.0708 (0.0048). The ratio is significantly larger than one. The first-order autocorrelation is positive and significant, but the other coefficients are not significant. The sum of the coefficients is around 0.3, which is a modest amount of persistence.

We consider the model selection question for the daily `VIX` time series. We consider the series itself, its natural logarithm, and its square root, and we estimate ARMA(p, q) models with $p, q \in \{1, \ldots, 22\}$. In Figure 3.5 we show the graph of BIC(p, q) for the natural logarithm of `VIX`. The minimum is achieved at the AR(9,q) process for any $q = 0, 1, \ldots, 22$, so we just concentrate on the AR(9) fit. The parameter estimates and their associated standard errors are shown in Table 3.4. ϕ_1 and ϕ_9 are significantly estimated, but the other coefficients are not significantly different from zero. The sum of coefficients is close to but not exceeding one. The process is very persistent. The error variance is estimated at 0.004 308 430, whereas the variance of the response is 0.125 94, so the model reduces the variability substantially.

Table 3.4 Model-selected AR(9) model estimates for VIX data and standard errors.

Parameter	Estimate	S.E.
ϕ_1	0.8939	0.0113
ϕ_2	0.0273	0.0152
ϕ_3	0.0219	0.0152
ϕ_4	−0.0067	0.0152
ϕ_5	0.0185	0.0152
ϕ_6	−0.0174	0.0152
ϕ_7	0.0080	0.0152
ϕ_8	0.0051	0.0152
ϕ_9	0.0370	0.0113
Mean	−2.9035	0.0590

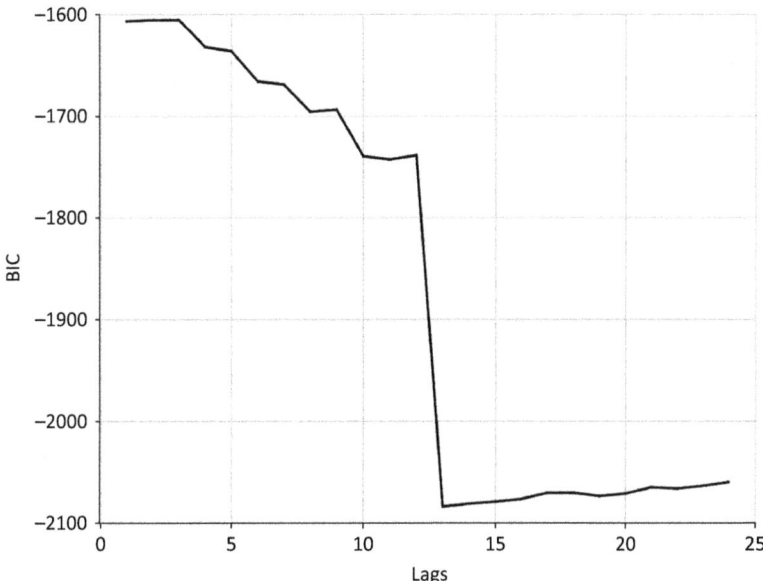

Figure 3.6 BIC criterion for AR(p) models.

In Figure 3.6 we show the BIC objective function against AR order for the monthly unemployment series; the criterion chooses order 13. The parameter estimates are shown in Table 3.5. The error variance is estimated at 0.00483, whereas the variance of the response is 0.0905, so the model reduces the variability substantially. There are strongly significant coefficients at lags 1, 5, 6, 11, 12, and 13. The roots of the AR(13) polynomial all have modulus greater than one. Ten of the roots have significant complex components, and three are either exclusively real or nearly exclusively real. This suggests very complex dynamics but overall stability of the process. Clearly, this model is not very interpretable: it does not separate seasonal components from trend from cycle . Furthermore, it is just explaining the series by its own history, which from a policy point of view is not very helpful.

Table 3.5 Model-selected AR(13) model estimates for unemployment and standard errors.

Parameter	Estimate	SE
ϕ_1	1.0093	0.0274
ϕ_2	−0.0449	0.0400
ϕ_3	−0.0247	0.0400
ϕ_4	−0.0126	0.0399
ϕ_5	0.1393	0.0433
ϕ_6	−0.1757	0.0454
ϕ_7	0.0808	0.0451
ϕ_8	−0.0426	0.0447
ϕ_9	−0.0499	0.0446
ϕ_{10}	0.0079	0.0446
ϕ_{11}	0.1001	0.0451
ϕ_{12}	0.6350	0.0458
ϕ_{13}	−0.6667	0.0314
Mean	1.7134	0.0518

3.9   Summary

We defined the class of autoregressive moving average processes and discussed their properties as stochastic processes; in particular the conditions under which a given process is stationary, invertible, and possesses autoregressive-only or moving average–only representations. We gave a full account of different estimation methods for ARMA processes and methods for conducting inference about the parameters of a given process. We also considered the question of model selection, that is, how to choose the order of a process for a given dataset. The R language has two commands, `arma()` and `arima()`, to estimate ARMA models (the latter command allows for integration, which we treat in Chapter 6). The classic reference for ARMA models is Box and Jenkins (1970).

3.10   Exercises

3.1 For the GME dataset, define $y_t = \log(V_t)$, where V_t is the daily trading volume. Estimate an AR(p) model to y_t for $p = 1, 2, \ldots, 22$. You may use either software-defined MLE or linear regression. Comment on the degree of persistence in this series as measured by the sum of the autoregressive coefficients. Examine the residuals

$$\widehat{\varepsilon}_t = y_t - \widehat{\alpha} - \sum_{j=1}^{p} \widehat{\phi}_j y_{t-j}$$

from this model and check whether they are:
(a) approximately uncorrelated
(b) homoskedastic
(c) normally distributed.

3.2 Calculate the multiple R^2 and adjusted R^2 for the linear regression estimator defined above. What percentage of the variability of the log of trading volume is explained by its own past? Which value of p maximizes the adjusted R^2?

3.3 For the GME dataset, define $y_t = \log(V_t)$, where V_t is the daily trading volume. Estimate an MA(q) model to y_t for $q = 1, 2, \ldots, 22$. Given the parameter estimates $\widehat{\theta}_j, j = 1, \ldots, q$, explain how to construct the residuals $\widehat{\varepsilon}_t$ and do it for the dataset. Check whether the residuals are:

(a) approximately uncorrelated

(b) homoskedastic

(c) normally distributed

3.4 For the GME dataset, define $y_t = \log(V_t)$, where V_t is the daily trading volume. Estimate an ARMA(11,11) model for y_t. Calculate the cumulative impulse responses and compare with the models in questions 3.1 and 3.3.

3.5 Consider the time series model

$$y_t = 10^{18} - \frac{1}{3}y_{t-1} - \frac{1}{4}y_{t-2} + \varepsilon_t - \frac{1}{2}\varepsilon_{t-1},$$

where ε_t is i.i.d. $N(0, 8)$.

(a) Write this process in terms of the lag operator L.

(b) Show that this process is stationary and invertible, and express ε_t in terms of $y_t, y_{t-1}, \ldots$

(c) Find the mean of y_t.

(d) Find the variance of y_t.

3.6 Suppose that $y_t = \phi y_{t-p} + \varepsilon_t$, where ε_t is i.i.d. with mean zero and variance σ^2, and $\phi \in (-1, 1)$. What are the roots of the autoregressive polynomial? Calculate the autocorrelation function of y_t.

3.7 Suppose that $y_t = \phi y_{t-1} + \varepsilon_t$, where ε_t is i.i.d. with mean zero and variance σ^2. Let $x_t = \Delta y_t = y_t - y_{t-1}$. Show that x_t can be represented as an ARMA(1,1) process and give the details.

3.8 Suppose that $y_t = \varepsilon_t - \theta \varepsilon_{t-1}$, where ε_t is i.i.d. with mean zero and variance σ^2. Let $x_t = \Delta y_t = y_t - y_{t-1}$. Show that x_t can be represented as an MA(2) process and give the details.

3.9 Suppose that $y_t^B = \varepsilon_t - \theta \varepsilon_{t-1}$ and $y_t^F = \varepsilon_t - \theta \varepsilon_{t+1}$, where ε_t are i.i.d. with mean zero and variance σ^2. Show that the joint distributions of (y_t^B, y_{t+1}^B) and (y_{t+1}^F, y_t^F) are the same.

3.10 Consider the MA(2) process $y_t = \varepsilon_t - \theta_1 \varepsilon_{t-1} - \theta_2 \varepsilon_{t-2}$, where ε_t is i.i.d. with mean zero and variance σ^2.

(a) Calculate the autocovariance function and autocorrelation function of y_t.

(b) What is the maximum value the autocorrelation function can take?

(c) What are the conditions for invertibility of the process? Suppose that $\theta_1 = -2\tau$ and $\theta_2 = -\tau^2$ for some τ. What are the invertibility conditions in this case?

3.11 In this question we consider weak autocorrelation.

(a) Suppose that $y_t = \phi_T y_{t-1} + \varepsilon_t$, where ε_t is i.i.d. with mean zero and variance σ^2, while ϕ_T is a sequence of constants such that $\phi_T = \phi_0/\sqrt{T}$. Derive the autocorrelation function of y_t.

(b) Suppose that $y_t = \varepsilon_t - \theta_T \varepsilon_{t-1}$, where ε_t is i.i.d. with mean zero and variance σ^2, while θ_T is a sequence of constants such that $\theta_T = \theta_0/\sqrt{T}$. Derive the autocorrelation function of y_t and compare with the autocorrelation of part (a). In particular, calculate the ratio of autocorrelations,

$$\lim_{T \to \infty} \frac{\rho_{AR,T}(k)}{\rho_{MA,T}(k)}, \quad k = 1, 2, \ldots$$

3.12 Consider the MA(2) process $y_t = \varepsilon_t - \theta_1 \varepsilon_{t-1} - \theta_2 \varepsilon_{t-2}$, where ε_t is i.i.d. with mean zero and variance σ^2. Show that σ^2 obeys a quadratic equation involving $\gamma(j), j = 0, 1, 2$, and then derive an explicit formula for θ_1 and θ_2 in terms of $\gamma(j), j = 0, 1, 2$.

3.13 Consider the MA(2) process

$$y_t = \varepsilon_t - \theta_1 \varepsilon_{t-1} - \theta_2 \varepsilon_{t-2}, \tag{3.78}$$

where ε_t is i.i.d. with mean zero and variance σ^2. Let

$$\Gamma_2 = \begin{pmatrix} \gamma(0) & \gamma(1) \\ \gamma(1) & \gamma(0) \end{pmatrix}$$

be the autocovariance matrix of the process $y_t = \theta_1 y_{t-1} + \theta_2 y_{t-2} + \varepsilon_t$, and hence show that the MLE of $\theta_1 \varepsilon_{t-1} - \theta_2$ in (3.78) satisfies

$$\begin{pmatrix} \sqrt{T}(\hat{\theta}_1 - \theta_1) \\ \sqrt{T}(\hat{\theta}_2 - \theta_2) \end{pmatrix} \Longrightarrow N \left(0, \begin{pmatrix} 1 - \theta_2^2 & \theta_1(1 - \theta_2) \\ \theta_1(1 - \theta_2) & 1 - \theta_2^2 \end{pmatrix} \right).$$

3.14 Suppose that $y_t = \frac{1}{2} y_{t-1} + \varepsilon_t$, where ε_t is i.i.d. with

$$\varepsilon_t = \begin{cases} \frac{1}{2} & \text{with probability } \frac{1}{2}, \\ 0 & \text{with probability } \frac{1}{2}. \end{cases}$$

Show that if $y_0 \in (0, 1)$, then $y_t \in (0, 1)$ for all t. Show that $E(y_t \mid y_{t-1}) = y_t/2 + 1/4$ but $E(y_{t-1} \mid y_t) = 2y_t$ (modulo 1).

3.15 Suppose that $y_t = 1 - \phi + \phi y_{t-1} + \sqrt{1 - \phi^2} \varepsilon_t$, where $\varepsilon_t \sim N(0, 1)$. Show that $E(y_t) = 1$, $\text{var}(y_t) = 1$, and $\text{cov}(y_t) = \phi^k$. Write down the log likelihood function for the single parameter ϕ based on the data $\{y_1, \ldots, y_T\}$. Alternatively, let $\hat{\alpha}, \hat{\phi}, \hat{\sigma}^2$ be the usual least squares estimators of the unrestricted parameters α, ϕ, σ^2. Show how to combine these unrestricted estimators to deliver fully efficient estimators of ϕ in the restricted model.

3.16 Suppose that $y_s^* = \phi y_{s-1}^* + \varepsilon_s$, where ε_s is i.i.d. with mean zero and variance σ^2, while time is daily. Suppose that we only observe weekly observations (five days in a week) $y_1 = \sum_{s=1}^{5} y_s^*$, $y_2 = \sum_{s=6}^{10} y_s^*$, and so on. Derive a representation for y_t as an ARMA process.

3.17 Suppose that $y_t = x_t + z_t$, where $x_t = \varepsilon_t - \theta \varepsilon_{t-1}$ with ε_t i.i.d. with mean zero and variance σ_ε^2. Calculate the autocovariance and autocorrelation functions when
(a) z_t is i.i.d. with mean zero and variance σ_z^2.
(b) $z_t = u_t - \delta u_{t-1}$, where u_t is i.i.d. with mean zero and variance σ_u^2.
(c) $z_t = \varepsilon_t - \delta u_{t-1}$, where u_t is i.i.d. with mean zero and variance σ_u^2.
(d) $z_t = \varepsilon_t - \delta \varepsilon_{t-1}$.

3.18 Suppose that $y_t = A\cos(t) + B\sin(t)$, where A, B are standard normal random variables. Using trigonometric identities, show that

$$y_t = \frac{\sin(2)}{\sin(1)}y_{t-1} - y_{t-2}.$$

3.19 This exercise is meant to familiarize you with the formula (2.21). For the following processes, obtain $V_{LP}(s)$. In each case, ε_t is i.i.d. with mean zero and variance σ^2.
   (a) $y_t = \phi y_{t-1} + \varepsilon_t$
   (b) $y_t = \phi y_{t-4} + \varepsilon_t$
   (c) $y_t = \varepsilon_t - \theta\varepsilon_{t-1}$
   (d) $y_t = \phi y_{t-1} + \varepsilon_t - \theta\varepsilon_{t-1}$

3.20 Suppose that $y_t = \phi_1 y_{t-1} + \phi_2 y_{t-2} + \phi_3 y_{t-3} + \varepsilon_t$, where ε_t is i.i.d. with mean zero and variance σ^2, while $\phi_1, \phi_2, \phi_3 > 0$ and $\phi_1 + \phi_2 + \phi_3 < 1$, which is part of the stationary region. Show that the autocorrelation function is strictly positive for all lags. For different choices of ϕ_j plot the autocorrelation function.

3.21 Suppose that time runs backwards and that $y_t = \phi y_{t+1} + \varepsilon_t$, where ε_t is i.i.d. with mean zero and variance σ^2, and $\phi \in (-1, 1)$. Is this a stationary process? Calculate the autocorrelation function of y_t. Compare the estimators

$$\widehat{\phi}_F = \frac{\sum_{t=1}^{T-1} y_{t+1}y_t}{\sum_{t=1}^{T-1} y_{t+1}^2}, \qquad \widehat{\phi}_B = \frac{\sum_{t=2}^{T} y_{t-1}^2}{\sum_{t=2}^{T} y_{t-1}y_t}.$$

3.22 Suppose that $y_t = \phi y_{t-1} + \varepsilon_t$, where ε_t is i.i.d. with mean zero and variance σ^2, and $\phi \in (-1, 1)$. Compare the following two estimators of $\rho(2)$ according to their asymptotic variance:

$$\widehat{\rho}(2) = \frac{\sum_{t=3}^{T} y_t y_{t-2}}{\sum_{t=3}^{T} y_{t-2}^2}, \qquad \widehat{\rho}(2) = \widehat{\rho}(1)^2, \qquad \widehat{\rho}(1) = \frac{\sum_{t=2}^{T} y_t y_{t-1}}{\sum_{t=2}^{T} y_{t-1}^2}.$$

3.23 Suppose that $y_t = \mu + \varepsilon_t - \theta\varepsilon_{t-1}$, where ε_t is i.i.d. with mean zero and variance σ^2. Define the familiar linear regression measure of fit in the population:

$$R^2 = 1 - \frac{\text{var}(\varepsilon_t)}{\text{var}(y_t)}.$$

What is the maximal value that this can take theoretically in the population. Does this mean that a moving average model is bad?

3.24 (Backcasting) Suppose that $y_t = \phi y_{t-1} + \varepsilon_t - \theta\varepsilon_{t-1}$, where ε_t is i.i.d. Gaussian with mean zero and variance σ^2, and $|\phi| < 1, |\theta| < 1$. Calculate expressions for $E(y_{-r} \mid y_1), \ldots, E(y_{-r} \mid y_1, \ldots, y_T), r = 0, 1, 2, \ldots,$
   (a) when $\phi = 0$
   (b) when $\theta = 0$
   (c) in the general case.

3.25 Suppose that $y_t = \phi y_{t-1} + \varepsilon_t - \theta\varepsilon_{t-1}$, where ε_t is i.i.d. with mean zero and variance σ^2, and $\theta, \phi \in (-1, 1)$. Consider the instrumental variable estimator

$$\widetilde{\phi} = \frac{\sum_{t=3}^{T} y_{t-2}y_t}{\sum_{t=3}^{T} y_{t-2}y_{t-1}}.$$

Derive the limiting distribution of $\widetilde{\phi}$, stating clearly any additional assumptions you need. Then let $\widetilde{\varepsilon}_t = y_t - \widetilde{\phi}y_{t-1}$, and propose an estimator of θ, σ^2.

3.26 Suppose that $y_t = \phi_1 y_{t-1} + \varepsilon_t - \theta_1 \varepsilon_{t-1} - \theta_1 \varepsilon_{t-2}$, where ε_t is i.i.d. with mean zero and variance σ^2. Calculate the autocovariance function of y_t.

3.27 Suppose that $y_t = \phi y_{t-1} + \varepsilon_t + \theta \varepsilon_{t-1}$, where ε_t is i.i.d. with mean zero and variance σ^2.

(a) Write down the log likelihood of the parameters ϕ, θ, σ^2 based on the data $\{y_1, \ldots, y_T\}$ conditional on $y_0 = 0$.

(b) Define $Q_T(\phi, \theta) = \sum_{t=2}^{T}(y_t - \phi y_{t-1} - \theta \varepsilon_{t-1})^2$ and show that the minimizing values of this objective function are

$$\widehat{\phi} = \frac{\sum_{t=2}^{T} y_t y_{t-1} \sum_{t=2}^{T} \varepsilon_{t-1}^2 - \sum_{t=2}^{T} y_t \varepsilon_{t-1} \sum_{t=2}^{T} y_{t-1} \varepsilon_{t-1}}{\sum_{t=2}^{T} y_{t-1}^2 \sum_{t=2}^{T} \varepsilon_{t-1}^2 - \left(\sum_{t=2}^{T} y_{t-1} \varepsilon_{t-1}\right)^2},$$

$$\widehat{\theta} = \frac{\sum_{t=2}^{T} y_{t-1}^2 \sum_{t=2}^{T} y_t \varepsilon_{t-1} - \sum_{t=2}^{T} y_{t-1} \varepsilon_{t-1} \sum_{t=2}^{T} y_{t-1} y_t}{\sum_{t=2}^{T} y_{t-1}^2 \sum_{t=2}^{T} \varepsilon_{t-1}^2 - \left(\sum_{t=2}^{T} y_{t-1} \varepsilon_{t-1}\right)^2}.$$

(c) How can one use this to estimate ϕ and θ?

3.28 Suppose that $y_t = \varepsilon_t - \theta \varepsilon_{t-1}$, where ε_t is i.i.d. with mean zero with variance σ_ε^2, and $|\theta| < 1$. Let

$$\widehat{\phi} = \frac{\sum_{t=2}^{T} y_{t-1} y_t}{\sum_{t=2}^{T} y_{t-1}^2}.$$

(a) Show that $\widehat{\phi} \overset{P}{\longrightarrow} \phi = m(\theta)$ for some function m.

(b) Derive the limiting distribution of $\widehat{\phi}$.

(c) Consider $\widehat{\theta} = m^{-1}(\widehat{\phi})$. Is this a consistent estimator of θ? Find its asymptotic distribution.

3.29 Suppose that $y_t = \alpha + \phi y_{t-1} + \varepsilon_t$, where ε_t is i.i.d. with mean zero and variance σ^2, and $\phi \in (-1, 1)$. Let $\mu = E(y_{t-1})$, where $\mu = \alpha/(1 - \phi)$.

(a) Show that the (approximate) QMLE of $\mu, \alpha, \phi, \sigma^2$ are

$$\widehat{\mu} = \frac{\widehat{\alpha}}{1 - \widehat{\phi}} \simeq \bar{y}, \qquad \widehat{\alpha} = \frac{1}{T} \sum_{t=2}^{T} (y_t - \widehat{\phi} y_{t-1}),$$

$$\widehat{\phi} = \frac{\sum_{t=2}^{T}(y_{t-1} - \bar{y})(y_t - \bar{y})}{\sum_{t=2}^{T}(y_{t-1} - \bar{y})^2}, \qquad \widehat{\sigma}^2 = \frac{1}{T} \sum_{t=2}^{T}(y_t - \widehat{\alpha} - \widehat{\phi} y_{t-1})^2.$$

(b) What is the joint asymptotic distribution of $\widehat{\alpha}, \widehat{\phi}$
   (i) in the case where $\alpha = \phi = 0$?
   (ii) in the general case?

(c) What is the joint asymptotic distribution of $\widehat{\mu}, \widehat{\phi}$
   (i) in the case where $\mu = \phi = 0$?
   (ii) in the general case?

3.30 Suppose that $y_t = \alpha + \phi_1 y_{t-1} + \phi_2 y_{t-2} + \varepsilon_t - \theta_1 \varepsilon_{t-1}$, where ε_t is i.i.d. with mean zero and variance σ^2. Consider the OLS estimator $\widehat{\beta}$ of $\beta = (\alpha, \phi_1, \phi_2)^\mathsf{T}$ from the regression of y_t on a constant and y_{t-1}, y_{t-2}.

(a) Show that $\widehat{\beta}$ is biased and inconsistent whenever $\theta_1 \neq 0$.

(b) Show that $E(u_t y_{t-j}) = 0, j \geq 2$, and thereby define a consistent estimator of β.

(c) Given consistent estimates of β, how could you define a consistent estimator of θ_1, σ^2?

3.31 Suppose that $y_t = \alpha + \phi_1 y_{t-1} + \phi_2 y_{t-2} + \varepsilon_t - \theta_1 \varepsilon_{t-1}$, where ε_t is a stationary MDS.

(a) Write an expression for ε_t in terms of $1 - \theta_1 L$ and $u_t = y_t - \alpha - \phi_1 y_{t-1} - \phi_2 y_{t-2}$.

(b) Derive expressions for

$$\frac{\partial \varepsilon_t}{\partial \alpha}, \quad \frac{\partial \varepsilon_t}{\partial \phi_1}, \quad \frac{\partial \varepsilon_t}{\partial \phi_2}, \quad \frac{\partial \varepsilon_t}{\partial \theta_1}$$

using the fact that the lag operator and the differential operator are interchangeable and that $\partial(1 - \theta L)^{-1}/\partial \theta = -L(1 - \theta L)^2$ for any θ.

(c) Therefore, show how you might estimate

$$E\left(\frac{\partial \varepsilon_t}{\partial \eta} \frac{\partial \varepsilon_t}{\partial \eta^\mathsf{T}}\right) \quad \text{and} \quad E\left(\varepsilon_t^2 \frac{\partial \varepsilon_t}{\partial \eta} \frac{\partial \varepsilon_t}{\partial \eta^\mathsf{T}}\right)$$

given estimates $\widehat{\eta}$ of $\eta = (\alpha, \phi_1, \phi_2, \theta_1)^\mathsf{T}$.

4   Spectral Analysis

In this chapter we consider spectral analysis, which is also called frequency domain analysis or Fourier analysis, in contrast with time domain analysis (which is what we have so far concerned ourselves with). This is about a transformation of a time series indexed by time $t \in \mathbb{Z}$ to a function whose real-valued argument is λ, called the frequency. Frequency is the number of occurrences of a repeating event per unit of time and so the focus of this material is on detecting and measuring such features of the data. Fourier analysis is about writing functions in terms of "waves" of different length and identifying the most important wavelengths at play. Frequency is the inverse of wavelength: long waves have low frequency and short waves have high frequency. There is a duality between time domain and frequency domain analysis in the sense that one can often find parallel analyses in these two languages.

Our purpose for using frequency domain analysis is to try to answer the following questions:

1. How important are the seasonal or cycle components in a series y_t, and at which frequencies do they occur?
2. Can we measure the variability of a series at a particular frequency? Frequency zero will be particularly important as this concerns the very long run, about which some economic theories have predictions. Also, standard error construction often involves the zero-frequency variation.
3. Can we isolate or eliminate the seasonal or cycle components? Many empirical studies proceed with seasonally adjusted data to avoid the issue of modelling the seasonal variation so that they can focus on the variation of interest to the study.
4. Can we estimate the "business cycle" component of macroeconomic data? If so, how accurate is our estimate? Some economic policies call for action that depends on the position in the business cycle, and so identifying this is useful.

There are some famous historical contributions to economics based on this methodology. Beveridge (1921) looked at the price of wheat from 1500 to 1869 and found evidence of a 15-year cycle using spectral analysis. Granger and Hughes (1971) extended the analysis and found slightly different results. Nerlove (1964) and Sims (1974) argued that the seasonal adjustment procedures commonly used by central banks and their ilk change the relationship between series, especially if different adjustments are made to each variable. According to this view one should be cautious about interpreting relationships found between seasonally adjusted variables. Since then, of course, many deaf ears have been cast to this question and it is not even observed in footnotes.

4.1   Periodic Functions and the Spectral Representation

In this chapter we will be using complex numbers so we first introduce some notation. We let $i = \sqrt{-1}$. For complex numbers $z = x + iy$, the modulus $|x + iy|^2 = z\bar{z} = x^2 + y^2$, where $\bar{z} = x - iy$; we can write $z = r\exp(i\theta)$, where $r = |z|$ and $\exp(i\theta) = \cos(\theta) + i\sin(\theta)$ (the sum of a real part, $\mathrm{Re}(z)$, and an imaginary part, $\mathrm{Im}(z)$).

Definition 4.1   A real-valued function $g\colon \mathbb{R} \to \mathbb{R}$ is periodic of period (or wavelength) α if $g(t + k\alpha) = g(t)$ for all integers k and all values of t.

The prototypical periodic functions are the trigonometric polynomials $\sin(t)$ and $\cos(t)$, which both have period 2π. We can build a more general class of periodic functions from these trigonometric functions. The function

$$g(t) = A\sin(\lambda t + \theta) \tag{4.1}$$

is periodic too, but in a more flexible way that is useful for modelling. Specifically, $g(\cdot)$ has **amplitude** A not necessarily equal to one, it has period $2\pi/\lambda$ (for $\lambda \neq 0$), and it has **phase** θ. The phase determines the value of $g(0)$, that is, where the process starts. By the properties of trigonometric functions we can write

$$g(t) = A\sin(\lambda t + \theta) = a\sin(\lambda t) + b\cos(\lambda t),$$

where $a = A\cos(\theta)$ and $b = A\sin(\theta)$. This alternative representation is more egalitarian with respect to the cosine but takes more print space. Note that $A = (a^2 + b^2)^{1/2}$ and $\theta = \arctan(b/a)$ provided $a \neq 0$.

Now consider the random process $y_t = a\sin(\lambda t) + b\cos(\lambda t)$, where a, b are mean-zero random variables with common variance σ^2 and are mutually uncorrelated. This process y_t is periodic, since $y_{t+2\pi/\lambda} = a\sin(\lambda t + 2\pi) + b\cos(\lambda t + 2\pi) = y_t$ for any t (note that this is strictly speaking about a process defined continuously in time, or at least that $2\pi/\lambda$ is an integer). We considered this process in Chapter 2, where we derived

$$E(y_t) = 0, \qquad \mathrm{var}(y_t) = \sigma^2, \qquad \mathrm{cov}(y_t, y_{t-k}) = \sigma^2\cos(\lambda k).$$

This is a (second-order) stationary process because the autocovariance function does not depend on t. Furthermore, the autocovariance function is periodic with period $2\pi/\lambda$, and hence $\sum_{k=0}^{\infty} |\gamma_y(k)| = \infty$, that is, y_t is not a mixing process. The sample autocovariance, based on a sample $\{y_1, \ldots, y_T\}$, is

$$\frac{1}{T}\sum_{t=k+1}^{T} y_t y_{t-k}$$

$$= \frac{1}{T}\sum_{t=k+1}^{T} \left(a\sin(\lambda t) + b\cos(\lambda t)\right)\left(a\sin(\lambda(t-k)) + b\cos(\lambda(t-k))\right)$$

$$= a^2\frac{1}{T}\sum_{t=k+1}^{T} \sin(\lambda t)\sin(\lambda(t-k)) + b^2\frac{1}{T}\sum_{t=k+1}^{T} \cos(\lambda t)\cos(\lambda(t-k))$$

$$+ ab\frac{1}{T}\sum_{t=k+1}^{T} \sin(\lambda t)\cos(\lambda(t-k)) + ab\frac{1}{T}\sum_{t=k+1}^{T} \cos(\lambda t)\sin(\lambda(t-k)).$$

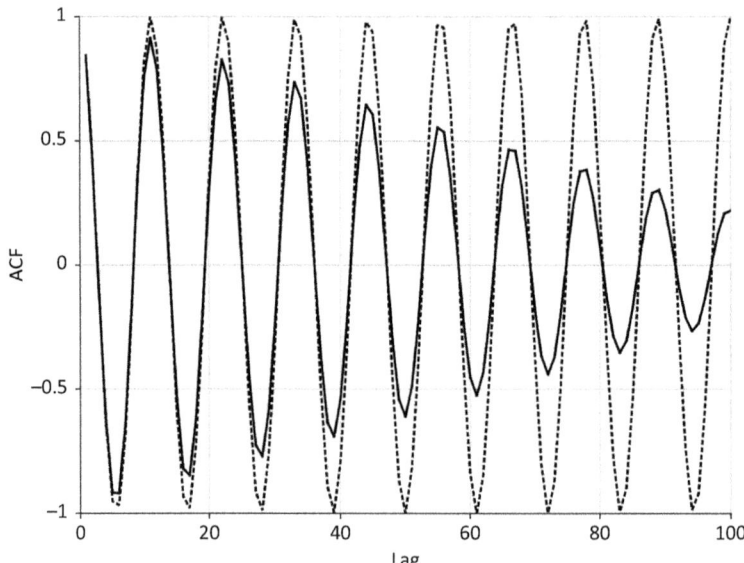

Figure 4.1 Theoretical ACF (dashed) and sample ACF (solid) for particular realizations of a, b for $T = 128$.

The deterministic quantities such as $\sum_{t=k+1}^{T} \sin(\lambda t) \sin(\lambda(t-k))/T$ converge as $T \to \infty$ to fixed numbers that depend on λ and k and are not everywhere zero. For example,

$$\frac{1}{T} \sum_{t=1}^{T} \sin(t) \sin((t-1)) \to \frac{\cos(1)}{2}.$$

Therefore, the limit of the sample autocovariance is random and depends on the realization of the random variables a, b, so the process y_t is not ergodic. In Figure 4.1 we show the theoretical ACF in an example.

We next consider a richer class of processes that may have multiple periodic components. Suppose that

$$y_t = \sum_{j=1}^{n} (a_j \sin(\lambda_j t) + b_j \cos(\lambda_j t)) = \sum_{j=1}^{n} A_j \sin(\lambda_j t + \theta_j), \tag{4.2}$$

where a_j, b_j are mean-zero random variables with common variance σ_j^2 and are mutually uncorrelated, while $\{\lambda_j, j = 1, \ldots, n\}$, are real valued. Here, $A_j = (a_j^2 + b_j^2)^{1/2}$ and $\theta_j = \arctan(b_j/a_j)$, assuming these are well defined. We have

$$E(y_t) = 0, \qquad \operatorname{var}(y_t) = \sum_{j=1}^{n} \sigma_j^2, \qquad \gamma_y(k) = \sum_{j=1}^{n} \sigma_j^2 \cos(\lambda_j k). \tag{4.3}$$

This process is also weakly stationary. It possesses a more flexible autocovariance function than the single-component $n = 1$ case. Specifically, this class of autocovariance functions can approximate any autocovariance function arbitrarily closely up to some fixed horizon. Let L be finite and let $\gamma(0), \ldots, \gamma(L)$ be the autocovariance to be approximated, then we can find a series of the form (4.2) for some finite n whose implied autocovariance function exactly equals the given autocovariances. For example, suppose $\gamma(0) = 1$ and $\gamma(1) = 1/2$. Then $n = 1$ with $\sigma_1^2 = 1$ and $\lambda_1 = \arccos(1/2)$ works.

We can rewrite the real process y_t in terms of complex numbers using the identity $A_j \sin(\lambda_j t + \theta_j) = c_j \exp(i\lambda_j t) + \bar{c}_j \exp(-i\lambda_j t)$, where $c_0 = 0$ and, for $\lambda_j > 0$, $c_j = A_j \exp(i\theta_j)/2i = -iA_j \exp(i\theta_j)/2$. Specifically, the process (4.2) can be written in the complex form

$$y_t = \sum_{j=1}^{n}(c_j + \bar{c}_j)\exp(i\lambda_j t) = \sum_{j=-n}^{n} c_j \exp(i\lambda_j t), \qquad (4.4)$$

where $c_{-j} = \bar{c}_j$. This guarantees that the right-hand side is real valued and defined for all t. We can even further write the right-hand side of (4.4) as an integral with respect to a specific random distribution $Z_n(\lambda)$: informally, $y_t = \int_{-\pi}^{\pi} \exp(i\lambda t)\, dZ_n(\lambda)$. If we pass to the limit as $n \to \infty$ we obtain the even more general result discussed in the next paragraph.

The **spectral representation theorem** says that for any stationary process $\{y_t\}$ (including mixing and nonmixing processes), we can represent it as an integral with respect to a continuous-parameter complex-valued stochastic process $Z(\lambda)$, that is, for a mean-zero y_t,

$$y_t = \int_{-\pi}^{\pi} \exp(i\lambda t)\, dZ(\lambda), \qquad (4.5)$$

where $Z(\lambda)$ is a continuous-parameter stochastic process with mean zero and orthogonal increments with $\mathrm{var}(dZ(\lambda)) = dF_y(\lambda)$, where $F_y(\lambda)$ is called the spectral distribution function of the process y_t.[1] The continuous process $Z(\lambda)$ in some sense contains more complexity than the discrete-time process y_t so the representation itself is perhaps not surprising. It shows how any stationary process can be interpreted in terms of frequency components. In the next section we focus on the second-order properties of the stationary process y_t.

4.2   The Power Spectrum

For a second-order stationary real-valued discrete-time series y_t with autocovariance function $\gamma_y(\cdot)$, Wiener (1930) and others established that there is a bounded nondecreasing function F_y such that

$$\gamma_y(k) = \int_{-\pi}^{\pi} \exp(i\lambda k)\, dF_y(\lambda), \quad k = 0, \pm 1, \pm 2, \ldots, \qquad (4.6)$$

where F_y is called the spectral distribution function and integration here is by the classical Lebesgue method. In the leading case of interest where $\sum_{k=-\infty}^{\infty} |\gamma_y(k)| < \infty$, there exists a positive function f_y such that $F_y(\lambda) = \int^{\lambda} f_y(\omega)\, d\omega$, that is, F_y is absolutely continuous. In that case, the power spectrum is defined as the discrete Fourier transform of the autocovariance function $\gamma_y(\cdot)$ of the process y_t, that is,

$$f_y(\lambda) = \mathcal{F}(\gamma_y)(\lambda) = \frac{1}{2\pi} \sum_{k=-\infty}^{\infty} \gamma_y(k)\exp(-i\lambda k),$$

---

[1] To be rigorous here we would have to talk about stochastic integrals, which we discuss in Chapter 12.

where λ is a real-valued frequency. In particular, $f_y(0) = \sum_{k=-\infty}^{\infty} \gamma_y(k)/2\pi$, which shows that the spectral density at frequency zero is proportional to the long-run variance. The function $f_y(\cdot)$ is periodic, specifically $f_y(\lambda) = f_y(\lambda + 2\pi)$ for all λ, and so without loss of generality we confine its definition to $[-\pi, \pi]$. The Fourier transform has a unique inverse,

$$\gamma_y(k) = \mathcal{F}^{-1}(f_y)(k) = \frac{1}{2\pi} \int_{-\pi}^{\pi} \exp{(i\lambda k)} f_y(\lambda) \, d\lambda,$$

for any integer $k \in \mathbb{Z}$. We have, in particular, $\gamma_y(0) = (1/2\pi) \int_{-\pi}^{\pi} f_y(\lambda) \, d\lambda$, which shows how the variance of a process can be decomposed into the sum of contributions from each frequency in $[-\pi, \pi]$, that is, we can interpret $f_y(\lambda)$ as the variance of the λ-frequency component. In fact, the function f is real valued and positive (because $\gamma_y(k) = \gamma_y(-k)$) and so it can be written more simply without complex numbers:

$$f_y(\lambda) = \frac{1}{2\pi} \left(\gamma_y(0) + 2 \sum_{k=1}^{\infty} \gamma_y(k) \cos{(\lambda k)} \right). \tag{4.7}$$

Furthermore, the function $f_y(\lambda)$ is even ($f_y(\lambda) = f_y(-\lambda)$), that is, symmetric about zero, and so when trying to describe the shape of f we need only consider $\lambda \in [0, \pi]$. Define the infinite vectors $\gamma = (\gamma_y(0), \gamma_y(1), \ldots)^\mathsf{T}$ and $c_\lambda = (1, \cos{(\lambda)}, \cos{(2\lambda)}, \ldots)^\mathsf{T}$; then we may write $f_y(\lambda) = \gamma^\mathsf{T} c_\lambda / 2\pi$, which one can think of like the covariance of the function $\gamma_y(\cdot)$ with the periodic function $\cos{(\lambda \cdot)}$ for given λ. The frequency λ that yields the largest value of $f_y(\lambda)$ is the frequency with the most power. The normalization of the spectrum is somewhat arbitrary and we can normalize it by its integral, in which case it integrates to one, that is, $f_y(\lambda) \mapsto f_y(\lambda) / \int_{-\pi}^{\pi} f_y(\lambda) \, dy$, which can be considered a proper density function on $[-\pi, \pi]$. We define the cumulated spectral density as $F_y(\lambda) = \int_{-\pi}^{\lambda} f_y(\omega) \, d\omega$, which behaves like a CDF. In some cases $f_y(\lambda)$ may be zero or infinity; the values of λ for which $f_y(\lambda) = \infty$ are called **poles** (equivalently $1/f_y(\lambda) = 0$), whereas the values of λ for which $f_y(\lambda) = 0$ are called **zeros** (equivalently $1/f_y(\lambda) = \infty$). Note further that the smoothness of $f_y(\lambda)$ is linked to the decay rate of $\gamma_y(k)$, that is, provided $\sum_{k=1}^{\infty} |\gamma_y(k)| k^{2m} < \infty$, the $(2m)$th derivative of $f_y(\lambda)$ with respect to λ exists, and

$$\frac{d^{2m} f_y(\lambda)}{d\lambda^{2m}} = \frac{1}{\pi} \sum_{k=1}^{\infty} \gamma_y(k) k^{2m} \cos{(\lambda k)}.$$

For example, if $|\gamma_y(k)| \leq c\rho^k$ for some $\rho \in (0, 1)$ and $c < \infty$, then the function $f_y(\lambda)$ is analytic (Ibragimov, 2001), meaning it possesses all derivatives.

We next consider some examples.

Example 4.1 The spectrum of a white noise process ε_t with variance σ^2 is $f_\varepsilon(\lambda) = \sigma^2/2\pi$ for all $\lambda \in [-\pi, \pi]$, that is, it is flat across frequency. Each frequency contributes equally.

Example 4.2 Suppose that $y_t = a \sin(\lambda_0 t) + b \cos(\lambda_0 t)$, where a, b are mean-zero mutually independent random variables with variance σ^2, and $\lambda_0 \in \mathbb{R}$. This process is not mixing, that is, its autocovariance function is not integrable and so strictly speaking we cannot talk about the spectral density. In this case it makes more sense to talk of the spectral distribution function, which is

$$F_y(\lambda) = \begin{cases} \sigma^2/2\pi & \text{if } \lambda \geq \lambda_0, \\ 0 & \text{if } \lambda < \lambda_0, \end{cases}$$

which has a jump or discontinuity at $\lambda = \lambda_0$. Informally, we may say that the spectrum of the process has a pole at $\lambda = \lambda_0$, and is

$$f_y(\lambda) = \begin{cases} \infty & \text{if } \lambda = \lambda_0 \\ 0 & \text{otherwise} \end{cases} = \delta_{\lambda_0}(\cdot).$$

The Dirac delta function $\delta_\lambda(\cdot)$ has the defining property that $\int g(s)\delta_{\lambda_0}(s)\,ds = g(\lambda_0)$, so that

$$\frac{1}{2\pi} \int_{-\pi}^{\pi} \exp\left(i\lambda k\right) \delta_{\lambda_0}(\lambda)\,d\lambda = \sigma^2 \cos(\lambda_0 k).$$

This perfectly periodic process is completely identified by its frequency domain properties.

Example 4.3   The MA(1) process with mean zero shocks, $y_t = \varepsilon_t - \theta\varepsilon_{t-1}$, has, for $\lambda \in [-\pi, \pi]$,

$$\begin{aligned} f_y(\lambda) &= \frac{1}{2\pi} \left(\gamma_y(0) + 2\gamma_y(1)\cos\left(\lambda\right)\right) \\ &= \frac{1}{2\pi} \left(\sigma^2(1 + \theta^2) - 2\theta\sigma^2 \cos\left(\lambda\right)\right) \\ &= \frac{\sigma^2}{2\pi} \left(1 + \theta^2 - 2\theta \cos\left(\lambda\right)\right), \end{aligned}$$

and in particular $f_y(0) = \sigma^2 (1 - \theta)^2 /2\pi$. The spectrum is monotonic on the interval $[0, \pi]$, and in particular

$$\frac{\partial f_y(\lambda)}{\partial \lambda} = \frac{\sigma^2}{\pi} \times \theta \sin(\lambda),$$

where $\sin(\lambda) \geq 0$ for all $\lambda \in [0, \pi]$. If $\theta > 0$, the spectral density increases as λ increases on $[0, \pi]$. If $\theta < 0$, the spectral density decreases as λ increases on $[0, \pi]$. For $-1 < \theta < 1$, $0 < |d_m f_y(\lambda)/d\lambda^m| < \infty$ for all λ and all $m = 0, 1, 2, \ldots$, but as $\theta \to 1$, $f_y(0) = \sigma^2(1 - \theta)^2/2\pi \to 0$.

Example 4.4   The AR(1) process $y_t = \phi y_{t-1} + \varepsilon_t$ has, for $-\pi \leq \lambda \leq \pi$,

$$\begin{aligned} f_y(\lambda) &= \frac{1}{2\pi} \sum_{k=-\infty}^{\infty} \gamma_y(k) \exp\left(-i\lambda k\right) \\ &= \frac{1}{2\pi} \frac{\sigma^2}{1 - \phi^2} \sum_{k=-\infty}^{\infty} \phi^{|k|} \exp\left(-i\lambda k\right) \\ &= \frac{\sigma^2}{2\pi} \left(1 + \phi^2 - 2\phi \cos(\lambda)\right)^{-1}, \end{aligned}$$

as we show in Appendix B, where $f_y(0) = (\sigma^2/2\pi)(1 - \phi)^2$. This is essentially the reciprocal of the MA spectral density and so behaves in the opposite way to the MA process: for $-1 < \phi < 1$, $0 < f_y(\lambda) < \infty$ for all λ, but as $\phi \to +1$, $f_y(0) \to \infty$ and the spectrum has infinite power at the origin. On the other hand, as $\phi \to -1$, $f_y(\pi) = \sigma^2 (1 + \phi)^{-2}/2\pi \to 0$.

Example 4.5   The AR(2) process has spectral density, for $-\pi \leq \lambda \leq \pi$,

$$f_y(\lambda) = \frac{\sigma^2}{2\pi} \frac{1}{1 + \phi_1^2 + \phi_2^2 - 2\phi_1(1 - \phi_2)\cos(\lambda) - 2\phi_2 \cos(2\lambda)}.$$

This can be shown by direct integration given the autocovariance function we obtained for this process. When $\phi_1 > 0$, f_y has a peak at $\lambda = 0$. When $\phi_1 < 0$, this has a spectral peak at $\lambda = 1/2$. This spectrum is generally not monotonic throughout $[0, \pi]$.

Example 4.6   The seasonal AR(m) process $y_t = \phi y_{t-m} + \varepsilon_t$ has spectral density

$$f_y(\lambda) = \frac{\sigma^2}{2\pi} \frac{1}{1 - 2\phi \cos(\lambda m) + \phi^2},$$

which is a periodic function with period π/m.

Example 4.7   Let y_t be an ARMA(p, q) process satisfying $A(L)y_t = B(L)\varepsilon_t$, where ε_t is WN($0, \sigma^2$), while $A(z) = 1 - a_1 z - \cdots - a_p z^p$ and $B(z) = 1 - b_1 z - \cdots - b_q z^q$ are complex polynomials that have common zeros and $A(z)$ has no zeros on the unit circle. Then $y_t = D(L)\varepsilon_t$, where $D(L) = B(L)/A(L)$. Applying the result of the next section, it follows that y_t has spectral density, for $-\pi \leq \lambda \leq \pi$,

$$f_y(\lambda) = \frac{\sigma^2}{2\pi} |D(\exp(-i\lambda))|^2 = \frac{\sigma^2}{2\pi} \frac{\left|1 - \sum_{j=1}^q b_j \exp(-i\lambda j)\right|^2}{\left|1 - \sum_{k=1}^p a_k \exp(-i\lambda k)\right|^2}. \tag{4.8}$$

Here, we are using $|z_1/z_2| = |z_1|/|z_2|$ for complex numbers z_1, z_2. This is a ratio of trigonometric polynomials, sometimes called a rational function. When $\lambda = 0$ this simplifies to

$$f_y(0) = \frac{\sigma^2}{2\pi} \frac{\left|1 - \sum_{j=1}^q b_j\right|^2}{\left|1 - \sum_{k=1}^p a_k\right|^2}.$$

4.3   Filters

We next define a general class of linear transformations of a data series, called filters, and trace through the consequences of the filter, that is, derive the resulting process and its properties. We have already used such transformations in defining the class of linear processes where the input is an i.i.d. shock process. One applies transformations and filters to raw time series for many reasons. For example, to reduce the autocorrelation in the series, which is called **prewhitening**, or to eliminate a trend or a seasonal component, which is called detrending or seasonal adjustment.

Definition 4.2   A general class of linearly filtered time series is of the form (for $t = 0, \pm 1, \pm 2, \ldots$) $x_t = \sum_{k=-\infty}^{\infty} \psi_{t,k} y_{t-k} = \psi_t(L) y_t$, where $\{y_t\}$ is the input or raw series, while $\{x_t\}$ is the output series, and $\{\psi_{t,k}\}$ are the filter coefficients that satisfy, for all t, $\sum_{k=-\infty}^{\infty} |\psi_{t,k}| \leq C < \infty$. If the coefficients $\psi_{t,k}$ do not depend on time t, that is, $\psi_{t,k} = \psi_k$, then we call it a time-invariant linear filter. A filter with $\psi_k = 0$ for $k < 0$ is called a one-sided (backwards) filter; a filter with $\psi_k = \psi_{-k}$ for all k is called a (two-sided) symmetric filter.

We are mostly concerned here with time-invariant filters, and we drop the t subscript in the following. These filters have the useful property that $\psi(L)(\sum_{j=1}^n \alpha_j y_{jt}) = \sum_{j=1}^n \alpha_j \psi(L) y_{jt}$ for any series y_{jt} and scalars $\alpha_j, j = 1, \ldots, n$; under some circumstances we can allow $n \to \infty$. If we apply a time-invariant filter $\psi(L)$ to the deterministic sequence $y_t = \exp(i\lambda t)$, we obtain

$$\psi(L) \exp(i\lambda t) = \sum_{k=-\infty}^{\infty} \psi_k \exp(i\lambda(t-k)) = \exp(i\lambda t) \times \sum_{k=-\infty}^{\infty} \psi_k \exp(-i\lambda k),$$

that is, the filter applied to a complex exponential returns the same complex exponential multiplied by a function of frequency that depends on $\{\psi_k\}$, which we identify in the following definition.

Definition 4.3   Define, for any filter ψ, $B_\psi(\lambda) = \sum_{k=-\infty}^{\infty} \psi_k \exp(-i\lambda k) = \psi(z)$ with $z = \exp(-i\lambda)$. The function $B_\psi(\lambda)$ is called the **transfer function** of the filter $\psi(L)$. Note that $B_\psi(\lambda + 2\pi) = B_\psi(\lambda)$. The **gain** of the filter and the **phase** of the filter are defined as

$$g(\lambda) = |B_\psi(\lambda)|^2 = \psi(\exp(i\lambda))\psi(\exp(-i\lambda)), \qquad \theta(\lambda) = \tan^{-1}\left(\frac{\text{Im}(B_\psi(\lambda))}{\text{Re}(B_\psi(\lambda))}\right). \tag{4.9}$$

We next give an interpretation of the gain and phase. The transfer function is, in general, complex valued and so can be written in standard form or polar form:

$$B_\psi(\lambda) = \sum_{k=-\infty}^{\infty} \psi_k \cos(\lambda k) - i \sum_{k=-\infty}^{\infty} \psi_k \sin(\lambda k) = g(\lambda) \exp(i\theta(\lambda)),$$

where the functions $g(\cdot)$ and $\theta(\cdot)$ are the gain and phase. It follows that we can write $\psi(L) \exp(i\lambda t) = g(\lambda) \exp(i(\lambda t + \theta(\lambda)))$, so that the input complex exponential is expanded in magnitude by $g(\lambda)$ and shifted by $\theta(\lambda)$. Some authors label $\partial\theta(\lambda)/\partial\lambda$ as the lag displacement or group delay. For example, suppose that $x_t = \alpha y_{t-k}$ for some scalar $\alpha > 0$ and integer k. In this case the gain is $g(\lambda) = |\alpha|$ and the phase is $\theta(\lambda) = -\lambda k$, so that $\partial\theta(\lambda)/\partial\lambda = -k$.

We next exhibit the effect of the filter on the power spectrum of a stationary time series, that is, its frequency domain effect.

Theorem 4.1   *Suppose that $\sum_{k=-\infty}^{\infty} \psi_k^2 < \infty$. Then the spectrum of the series $\{x_t\}$ is*

$$f_x(\lambda) = |B_\psi(\lambda)|^2 f_y(\lambda). \tag{4.10}$$

The argument for this is based on the spectral representation theorem. We have already used this argument for the case in which the input $\{y_t\}$ is a white noise process as in the ARMA class of models, but this relationship holds much more generally, as stated here. The transfer function is the key feature in going between the spectral density of y_t and the spectral density of x_t. We can view the effects of the filter through its transfer function; indeed, one can start with an ideal transfer function and try to figure out what this corresponds to in the time domain. For this latter purpose we have the result that, for any integrable function $B_\psi(\lambda)$,

$$\psi_k = \frac{1}{2\pi} \int_{-\pi}^{\pi} B_\psi(\lambda) \exp(-i\lambda k)\, d\lambda, \quad k = 0, \pm 1, \pm 2, \dots, \tag{4.11}$$

so there is a one-to-one relationship between the transfer function and the filter coefficients.

One can design filters with the purpose of obtaining a series with a particular spectral density, and this is a common endeavour in engineering, for example. We consider three types of filters that are designed to zero out different parts of the spectral density, that is, to eliminate (or at least attenuate) high-, low-, or medium-frequency variation; these are generically called **band-pass** filters:

- (The tweeter) If $g(\lambda) = 0$ for $\lambda \in [-\lambda_0, \lambda_0]$, where λ_0 is called the cut-off frequency, then $f_x(\lambda) = 0$ for $\lambda \in [-\lambda_0, \lambda_0]$. This is called an ideal **high-pass** filter: completely eliminates low-frequency variation.
- (The woofer) If $g(\lambda) = 0$ for $\lambda \notin [-\lambda_1, \lambda_1]$, where λ_1 is called the cut-off frequency, then $f_x(\lambda) = 0$ for $\lambda \notin [-\lambda_1, \lambda_1]$. This is called an ideal **low-pass** filter: completely eliminates high-frequency variation.
- (The midrange) If $g(\lambda) = 0$ for $\lambda \notin [\lambda_0, \lambda_1]$, where $\lambda_0 < \lambda_1$, this could be called an ideal **mid-pass** filter.

A mid-pass filter may be obtained from sequential application of low- and high-pass filters. For example, if $B_1(\lambda) = 1$ for $|\lambda| \le \lambda_1$ and $B_1(\lambda) = 0$ otherwise, and $B_2(\lambda) = 0$ for $|\lambda| \le \lambda_0$ and $B_2(\lambda) = 1$ otherwise, where $0 < \lambda_0 < \lambda_1$, then

$$B(\lambda) = B_2(\lambda)B_1(\lambda) = B_1(\lambda)B_2(\lambda) = \begin{cases} 1 & \text{if } \lambda_0 \le |\lambda| \le \lambda_1, \\ 0 & \text{otherwise.} \end{cases}$$

This is a symmetric band-pass filter.

To implement this in practice, one has to derive the implied time domain weights. The question is, what are the time domain coefficients $\{\psi_k\}_{k=-\infty}^{\infty}$ that deliver a given transfer function $B(\lambda)$?

Example 4.8   Suppose that

$$B(\lambda) = \frac{1}{1 - \phi z},$$

where $z = \exp(-i\lambda)$. Then $\psi_k = \phi^k$ for $k \ge 0$, provided $|\phi| < 1$. That is, $x_t = \sum_{k=0}^{\infty} \phi^k y_{t-k}$.

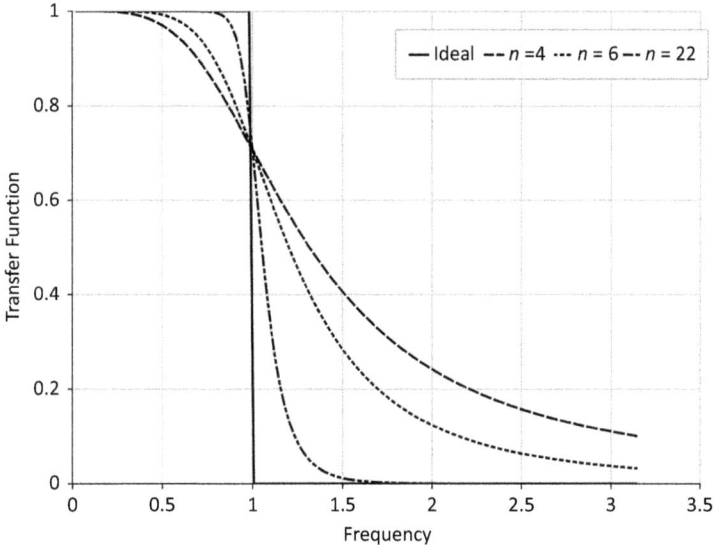

Figure 4.2 Transfer functions of Butterworth filters for different values of n.

Example 4.9   Suppose that $B(\lambda) = 1$ if $\lambda \in [-\lambda_0, \lambda_0]$, $B(\lambda) = 0$ otherwise. Then

$$\psi_k = \frac{1}{2\pi} \int_{-\lambda_0}^{\lambda_0} \exp(i\lambda k)\, d\lambda = \frac{\sin(\lambda_0 k)}{\pi k}, \quad k = 0, \pm 1, \ldots \tag{4.12}$$

In general, the implied impulse response of the ideal band-pass filter has infinitely many nonzero components, is noncausal, and is not summable, that is, $\sum_k |\psi_k| = \infty$. We only have a finite stretch of data $\{y_1, \ldots, y_T\}$, so this is not implementable. What do we do? We use approximations, that is, approximate band-pass filters.

Example 4.10 (Butterworth filter)   This class of filters is defined through its transfer function, which has gain

$$|B_n(\lambda)|^2 = \frac{1}{\sqrt{1 + (\lambda/\lambda_0)^n}},$$

where λ_0 is the cut-off frequency and n is the filter order. For large n, this is an approximate low-pass filter. As $n \to \infty$, $|B_n(\lambda)|^2 \to 0$ for $\lambda > \lambda_0$, $|B_n(\lambda)|^2 \to 1$ for $\lambda < \lambda_0$, and $|B_n(\lambda_0)|^2 = 1/\sqrt{2}$. For given n, the function is smooth, and positive and finite everywhere. The filter is causal and its time domain implementation can be computed from an ARMA(n,n) recursion. MATLAB has a script `butterworth.m` for computing this. Figure 4.2 shows the ideal filter along with some examples for finite n.

We next describe a more general approach based on approximating the ideal transfer function. Let $B_\psi^{(n)}(\lambda) = \sum_{k=-n}^{n} \psi_k \exp(-i\lambda k)$, which is based on a finite stretch of coefficients, say $T = 2n + 1$. We have

$$B_\psi^{(n)}(\lambda) = \sum_{k=-n}^{n} \left(\frac{1}{2\pi} \int_{-\pi}^{\pi} \exp(i\omega k)\, B_\psi(\omega)\, d\omega \right) \exp(-i\lambda k)$$

$$= \int_{-\pi}^{\pi} \frac{1}{2\pi} \sum_{k=-n}^{n} (\exp(i(\omega - \lambda)k))\, B_\psi(\omega)\, d\omega$$

$$= \int_{-\pi}^{\pi} D_n(\lambda - \omega) B_\psi(\omega)\, d\omega, \quad D_n(\lambda - \omega) = \frac{1}{2\pi} \frac{\sin\left(\left(n + \frac{1}{2}\right)(\lambda - \omega)\right)}{\sin\left(\frac{1}{2}(\lambda - \omega)\right)},$$

where $D_n(x)$ is the Dirchlet kernel. For many transfer functions, we have $B_\psi^{(n)}(\lambda) \to B_\psi(\lambda)$ as $n \to \infty$, and so we can interpret $B_\psi^{(n)}(\lambda)$ as the target for which we have a finite implementation $\{\psi_k, k = -n, \ldots, n\}$. However, there are continuous functions $B_\psi(\lambda)$ for which convergence does not hold. Introducing tapering can solve this problem; for example, take the Fejer kernel for which

$$B_\psi^{(n)}(\lambda) = \sum_{k=-n}^{n} \left(1 - \frac{|k|}{n} \right) \psi_k \exp(-i\lambda k)$$

$$= \int_{-\pi}^{\pi} F_n(\lambda - \omega) B_\psi(\omega)\, d\omega, \quad F_n(\lambda - \omega) = \frac{1}{2\pi n} \left(\frac{\sin(n(\lambda - \omega))}{\sin\left(\frac{1}{2}(\lambda - \omega)\right)} \right)^2.$$

In this case, $F_n(\lambda - \omega) \geq 0$, $\int_{-\pi}^{\pi} F_n(\lambda - \omega)\, d\omega = 1$, and $B_\psi^{(n)}(\lambda) \to B_\psi(\lambda)$ as $n \to \infty$ for all continuous functions. The corresponding filter coefficients are of finite length $\widetilde{\psi}_k = (1 - (|k|/n))\psi_k$ for $k = -n, \ldots, n$, where $\psi_k = \sin(\lambda_0 k)/\pi k$, say.

We next consider some popular filters in economics and finance, designed with different purposes in mind.

Example 4.11 (SMA filter)   We consider the special case where $r = s$ and $\psi_j = 1/(2r + 1)$,

$$x_t = \frac{1}{2r + 1} \sum_{j=-r}^{r} y_{t-j}, \tag{4.13}$$

which is the classic (two-sided) symmetric moving average filter. In this case, the phase shift is exactly zero, while

$$B_\psi(\lambda) = \frac{1}{2r + 1} \sum_{j=-r}^{r} \exp(-i\lambda j) = \begin{cases} 1 & \text{if } \lambda = 0, \\ \dfrac{1}{2r + 1} \dfrac{\sin((2r + 1)\lambda/2)}{\sin(\lambda/2)} & \text{if } \lambda \neq 0. \end{cases}$$

Notice that $\exp(-i\lambda j) = \exp(-i\lambda)^j$, so we are summing a geometric series. This is an (approximate) low-pass filter: it diminishes high frequencies and preserves low frequencies. Figure 4.3 shows an example.

Example 4.12 (Differencing filter)   The difference operator $\Delta = 1 - L$ is an important filter. It has the transfer function $B_\Delta(\lambda) = 1 - \exp(-i\lambda)$, which has gain

$$g(\lambda) = (1 - \cos(\lambda))^2 + \sin^2(\lambda) = 2(1 - \cos(\lambda))$$

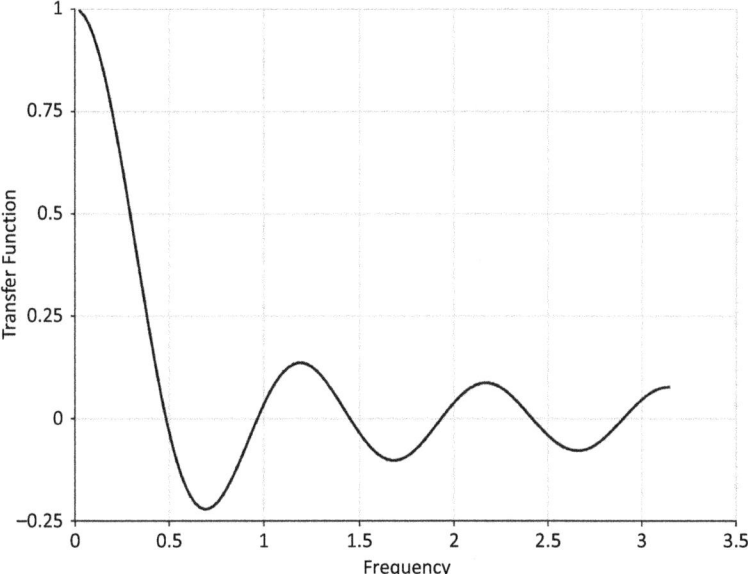

Figure 4.3 Transfer function of a moving average filter.

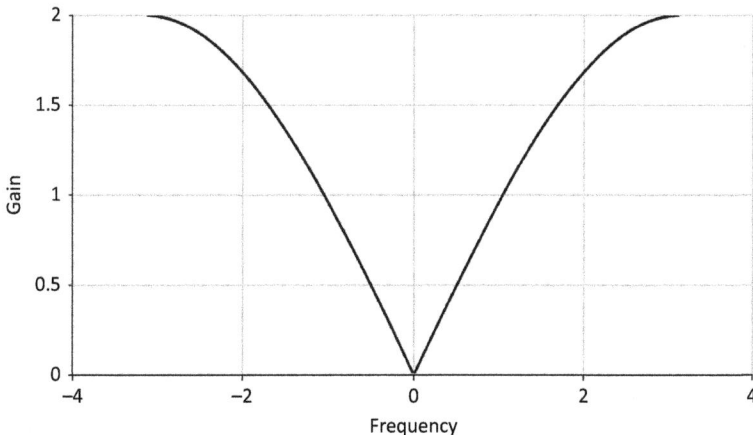

Figure 4.4 Gain of the differencing filter.

and phase

$$\theta(\lambda) = \tan^{-1}\left(\frac{\sin(\lambda)}{1 - \cos(\lambda)}\right).$$

It is a high-pass filter, it diminishes low frequencies and preserves high frequencies. This is shown in Figure 4.4.

Example 4.13 (Exponentially weighted moving average (EWMA) filter)   This filter is usually defined in a recursive fashion, specifically

$$x_t = \theta x_{t-1} + (1 - \theta)y_t$$

for a parameter $\theta \in (0, 1)$. By substitution we have

$$x_t = (1 - \theta) \sum_{j=0}^{\infty} \theta^j y_{t-j}.$$

This is a one-sided filter with exponentially decaying weights. The transfer function is $B_{\text{EWMA}}(\lambda) = (1 - \theta)/(1 - \theta \exp(-i\lambda))$.

Example 4.14 (Gaussian filter)   Suppose that $\psi_k = c \exp(-k^2/2\sigma^2)$, $k = 1, \ldots, K$, where c is chosen such that $\sum \psi_k = 1$. This filter implies rapid downweighting. We have $B_{\text{G}}(\lambda) = \exp(-\sigma^2 \lambda^2/2)$.

Example 4.15 (Baxter and King, 1995)   Symmetric, time-invariant filter. For some small $\underline{\omega}$ and given $K < T$,

$$\psi_0 = \frac{\underline{\omega}}{\pi}, \qquad \psi_k = \frac{\sin(k\underline{\omega})}{k\pi}, \quad k = \pm 1, \ldots, \pm K.$$

Example 4.16 (Christiano and Fitzgerald, 2003)   This filter is neither symmetric nor time invariant, and thereby covers the whole sample. For given $p_l < p_u$, with $2 \leq p_l < p_u < \infty$, we define

$$x_t = \psi_0 y_t + \psi_1 y_{t+1} + \cdots + \psi_{T-1} y_{T-1} + \widetilde{\psi}_{T-t} y_T + \psi_1 y_{t-1} + \cdots + \psi_{t-2} y_2 + \widetilde{\psi}_{t-1} y_1,$$

where $\psi_j = (\sin(jb) - \sin(ja))/j\pi$ for $j \geq 1$ and $\psi_0 = (b - a)/\pi$, where $a = 2\pi/p_u$ and $b = 2\pi/p_l$, while

$$\widetilde{\psi}_{T-t} = -\frac{1}{2}\psi_0 - \sum_{j=1}^{T-t-1} \psi_j, \qquad\qquad t = 3, \ldots, T - 2,$$

$$\widetilde{\psi}_{t-1} = -\psi_0 - \widetilde{\psi}_{T-t} - \sum_{j=1}^{T-1-t} \psi_j - \sum_{j=1}^{t-2} \psi_j, \quad t = 3, \ldots, T - 2.$$

We next consider the inversion process from $x \mapsto y$, which is sometimes called **decoding**. Of course, for a transfer function that is zero at some λ we cannot invert the operation, that is, we can only define $f_y(\lambda) = f_x(\lambda)/|B_\psi(\lambda)|^2$ when $B(\lambda) \neq 0$ for all λ, so that bandpass filters, which eliminate power on an interval of frequencies, cannot be inverted on the whole range of frequencies. This means that the filter $\psi(L)$ cannot be inverted so we cannot obtain the raw series y_t from the filtered series. For example, $\psi(L) = 1 - L$ corresponds to a unit-root moving average (with transfer function zero at the origin) and cannot be inverted, that is, we cannot express y_t as a convergent weighted sum of x_t.

4.3.1   Trend

We can understand the effect of filters when applied to stationary series using the transfer function. This gives us an intuition about how it works on nonstationary processes where such quantities as spectrum and the autocovariance function are not strictly defined. In fact, differencing and SMA are often applied to nonstationary processes. In

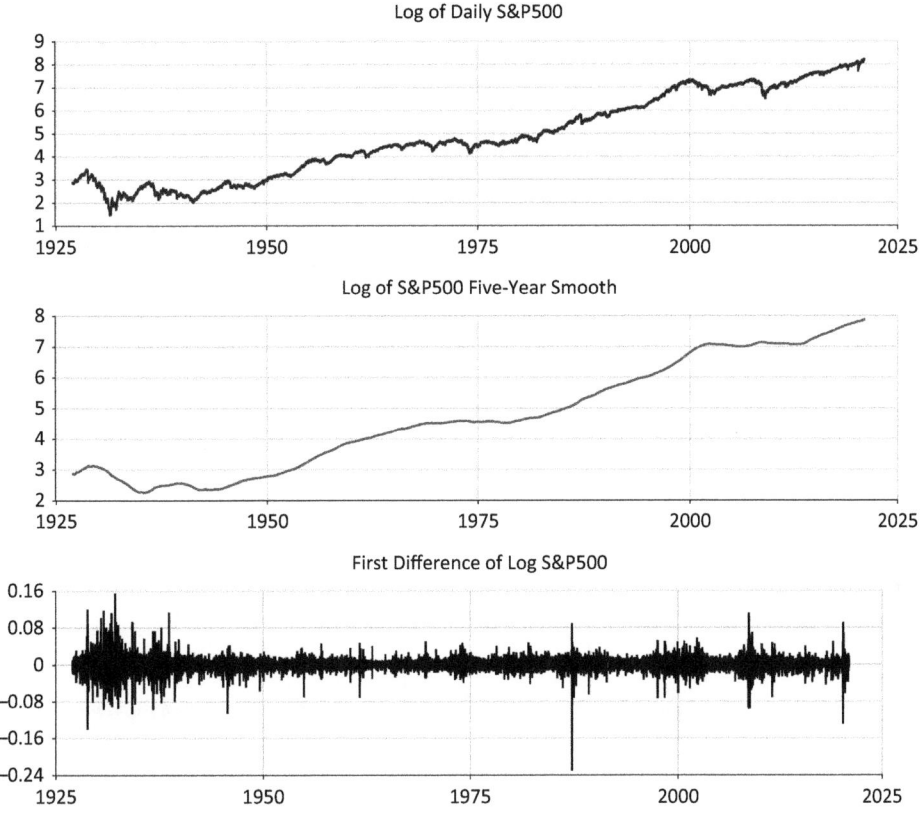

Figure 4.5 Logarithm of daily closing price of S&P500 along with five-year smooth and first difference.

Figures 4.5–4.8 we show the effect of smoothing and differencing on four of our example series.

4.3.2   Economic Cycles

Climate data has many documented cycles of different frequencies, such as El Niño and ice ages. Several authors have documented long-term cycles in economic activity: the Kitchin cycle (inventory), 3–5 years; the Juglar cycle (fixed investment), 7–11 years; the Kuznets swing (infrastructural investment), 15–25 years; the Kondratiev wave (technological basis), 45–60 years. In particular, Kuznets (1930) analyzed macro data and found evidence of a cycle after transforming the data by what we would now call a linear filter. Some authors have argued that these cycles may be spurious rather than real. For example, Slutzky (1927, 1937) applied a moving average filter to random numbers drawn from a lottery to produce a sequence that had the characteristics of a macroeconomic business cycle. Howrey (1968) argued that the Kuznets cycle itself was a consequence of the filter Kuznets used; this was $K(L) = b(L)a(L)$, with

$$a(L) = \frac{1}{5}\left(L^{-2} + L^{-1} + L^0 + L + L^2\right), \qquad b(L) = L^{-5} - L^5.$$

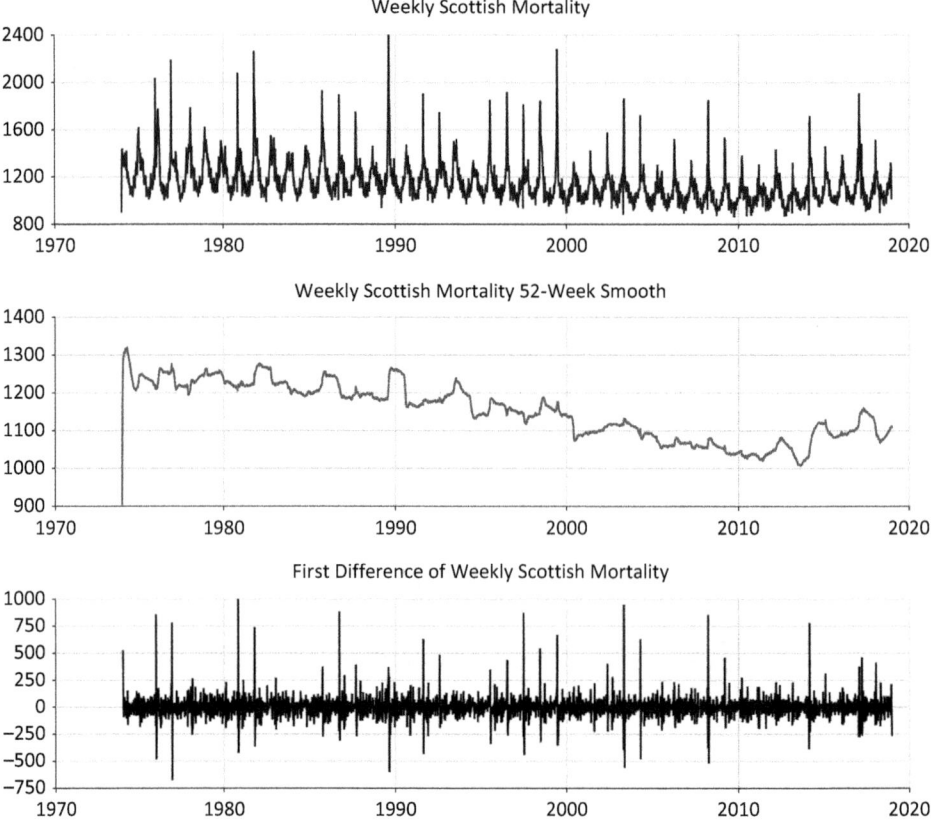

Figure 4.6 Weekly Scottish mortality along with 52-week smooth and first difference.

In the Fourier domain this filter has gain

$$g(\lambda) = \frac{2\sin(5\lambda/2)\sin(5\lambda)}{5\sin(\lambda/2)}.$$

This has a peak at the frequency $\pi/10$, which corresponds to around 20 years. The interpretation is that possibly the cycle itself is an artifact produced by the methodology.

4.3.3   Seasonality

Most seasonal adjustment is developed using time domain methods, but frequency domain methods give an understanding of and motivation for what they are doing to the data. Seasonality corresponds to a peak in the spectral density at a certain frequency, which is easy to understand and manipulate in the frequency domain. Seasonal adjustment methods aim to eliminate this peak or reduce it such that the spectrum of the transformed series is smoother across the seasonal frequencies. The implementation often involves a band-pass filter with a very narrow band around the seasonal frequency.

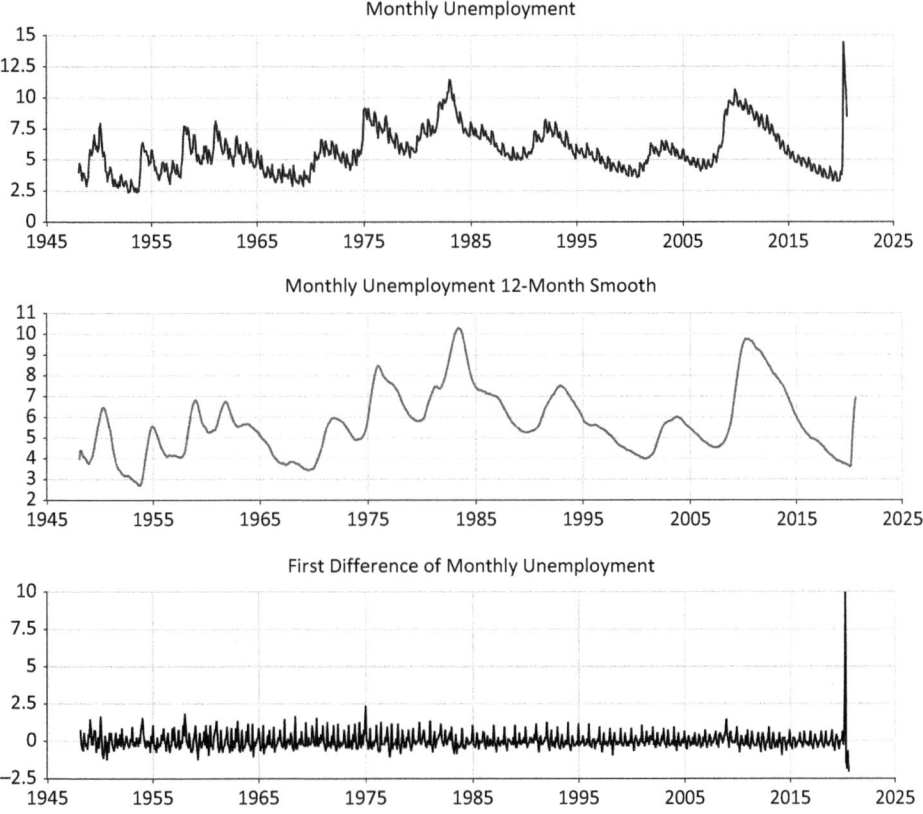

Figure 4.7 Monthly unemployment along with 12-month smooth and first difference.

Nerlove (1964) investigated the effects of seasonal adjustment on the spectrum of various series and discussed the consequences for other features. This arises because as we have seen it is impossible with a finite set of data to construct the perfect filter that mimics what we would like to do in the frequency domain. With imperfect filters we have leakage that can affect nearby frequencies and distort the properties of the transformed process. Sims (1974) argued that the relationship between two series y, x can be changed by seasonal adjustment, especially if different seasonal adjustment procedures are applied to each series to give $y^{\text{filter}}, x^{\text{filter}}$.

For any discrete-time series the number of frequencies at which the data can vary will be limited by the Nyquist frequency, which is the highest frequency of variation that the observed data can provide. For example, with a daily series, the data cannot provide any information about variation in the data at a time scale of less than 24 hours or daily. If there is a diurnal pattern in the data (maybe it is always hotter at 4pm than at 4am), we cannot learn this from the data. If we have T observations, then the largest number of cycles that we can observe in the time series is $T/2$, or one cycle every other data point. Another way of saying that is that the Nyquist frequency is $\lambda = 1/2$, that is, half a cycle per day or one cycle per two days. If we wanted information about higher-frequency

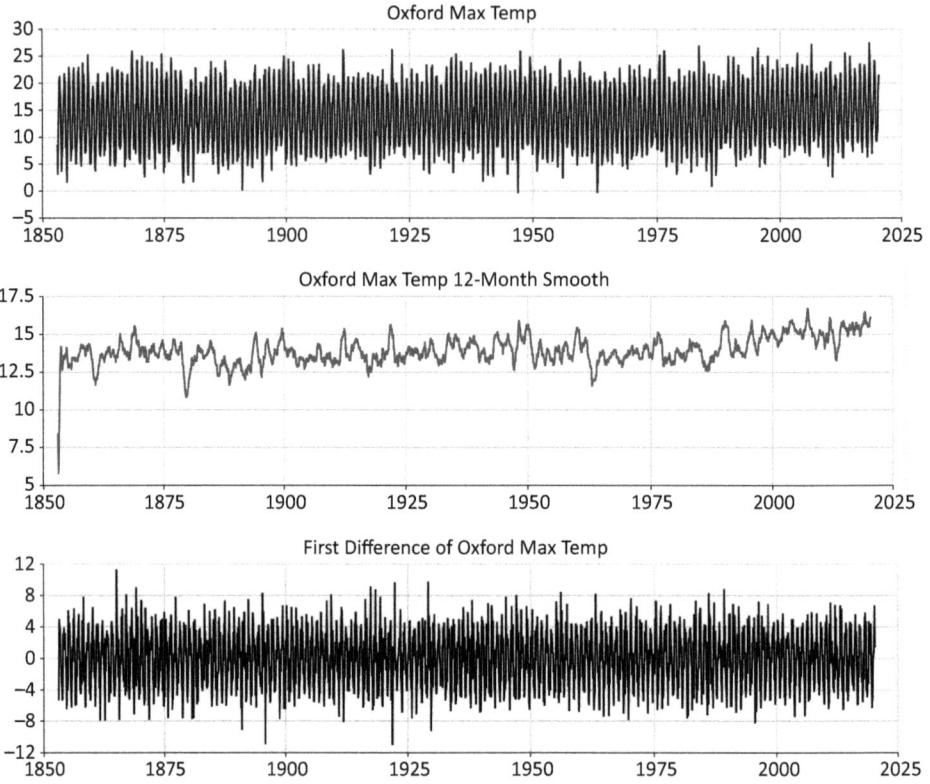

Figure 4.8 Oxford monthly maximum temperature along with 12-month smooth and first difference.

variation in temperature, we would need to make more observations. For example, if we had hourly measurements of temperature, then we would have information about the within-day variation in temperature. If the Nyquist frequency is the highest frequency about which the data can inform us, then on the other side of the spectrum is the lowest frequency, which is simply one cycle per T observations. In the full stock return dataset, we have daily observations for 93 years. Therefore, the lowest frequency we can observe is one cycle per 93 years.

4.4   The Periodogram and Estimation of the Spectral Density

We next discuss the estimation of $f_y(\lambda)$ from a sample of data $\{y_0, \dots, y_{T-1}\}$ (note the change of time origin, which is for convenience). The discrete Fourier transform (DFT) of the series is

$$d_T(y)(\lambda) = \sum_{t=0}^{T-1} y_t \exp\left(-it\lambda\right) \tag{4.14}$$

for any $\lambda \in \mathbb{R}$. Note that $d_T(y)(0) = \sum_{t=0}^{T-1} y_t$ is real valued, but $d_T(y)(\lambda)$ is in general complex valued. We often work with special frequencies called the **harmonic frequencies**, which are $\lambda_j = \pm 2\pi j/T \in [-\pi, \pi]$, that is, $j = -n, \dots, n$ with $T = 2n + 1$.

Define the vector $D_T = (d_T(y)(\lambda_{-n}), \ldots, d_T(y)(0), \ldots, d_T(y)(\lambda_n))$; then we can also write the vector of DFTs as

$$D_T = (d_{-n}, \ldots, d_n)^\mathsf{T} = \mathcal{Z}_T y, \tag{4.15}$$

where $\mathcal{Z}_T$ is the $T \times T$ Fourier matrix, which is a deterministic matrix with elements $\exp(-it\lambda_j)$. For $T = 3$ and 4, this matrix is

$$\begin{pmatrix} 1 & 1 & 1 \\ 1 & -\frac{1}{2} - \frac{\sqrt{3}}{2}i & -\frac{1}{2} + \frac{\sqrt{3}}{2}i \\ 1 & -\frac{1}{2} + \frac{\sqrt{3}}{2}i & -\frac{1}{2} - \frac{\sqrt{3}}{2}i \end{pmatrix} \quad \text{and} \quad \begin{pmatrix} 1 & 1 & 1 & 1 \\ 1 & -i & -1 & i \\ 1 & -1 & 1 & -1 \\ 1 & i & -1 & -i \end{pmatrix}.$$

If y_t is a stationary process, then the vector D_T is a $T \times 1$ vector of complex-valued random variables that are approximately mean zero and mutually uncorrelated. Furthermore,

$$E(D_T D_T^\mathsf{T}) \simeq \mathcal{Z}_T \Gamma_T \mathcal{Z}_T = \Delta + o(1), \tag{4.16}$$

where Δ is a diagonal matrix, that is, the matrix $\mathcal{Z}_T$ approximately diagonalizes any Toeplitz matrix. There are some important statistical consequences and applications of this result, which we discuss later.

The periodogram of $\{y_0, \ldots, y_{T-1}\}$ is the modulus of the scaled Fourier transform of the data,

$$I_T(\lambda) = \frac{1}{2\pi T} |d_T(y)(\lambda)|^2 = \frac{1}{2\pi T} \left| \sum_{t=0}^{T-1} y_t \exp(-it\lambda) \right|^2$$

$$= \frac{1}{2\pi T} \left(\left(\sum_{t=0}^{T-1} y_t \cos(t\lambda) \right)^2 + \left(\sum_{t=0}^{T-1} y_t \sin(t\lambda) \right)^2 \right),$$

which is real valued and nonnegative, symmetric about zero, and periodic with period 2π. The periodogram was introduced by Schuster in 1898. We have $I_T(0) = T|\bar{y}|^2/2\pi$, while if $\lambda_j = 2\pi j/T$ with $j > 0$, using the fact that $\sum_{t=-n}^n \exp(-it\lambda) = \sin((n + 1/2)\lambda)/\sin(\lambda/2)$, $\lambda \neq 0$,

$$I_T(\lambda_j) \simeq \frac{1}{2\pi T} \left| \sum_{t=0}^{T-1} (y_t - \bar{y}) \exp(-it\lambda_j) \right|^2$$

$$= \frac{1}{2\pi T} \sum_{t=0}^{T-1} \sum_{s=0}^{T-1} (y_t - \bar{y})(y_s - \bar{y}) \exp(-i(t - s)\lambda_j)$$

$$= \frac{1}{2\pi} \sum_{k=-T+1}^{T-1} \widehat{\gamma}(k) \exp(-ik\lambda_j),$$

where $\widehat{\gamma}(k) = \sum_t (y_t - \bar{y})(y_{t-k} - \bar{y})/T$. This can be interpreted as the Fourier transform of all the available autocovariances. Common practice is to use the fast Fourier transform (FFT) to do this calculation, which reduces the calculation time from $O(T^2)$ to potentially $O(T \log T)$ by exploiting the prime factorization of T to replace $T \times T$ matrix calculations by $p_j \times p_j$ matrix calculations, where p_j are the prime factors of T.

The periodogram is an asymptotically unbiased estimator of $f(\lambda)$, that is, as $T \to \infty$,

$$E(I_T(\lambda)) \to f(\lambda), \quad \lambda \neq 0. \tag{4.17}$$

This follows because

$$E(I_T(\lambda)) \simeq \frac{1}{2\pi T} \sum_{t=0}^{T-1} \sum_{s=0}^{T-1} \gamma_y(t-s) \exp(-i\lambda(t-s))$$

$$= \frac{1}{2\pi T} \sum_{k=-T+1}^{T-1} (T - |k|) \gamma_y(k) \exp(-i\lambda k)$$

$$= \frac{1}{2\pi} \sum_{k=-(T-1)}^{T-1} \left(1 - \frac{|k|}{T}\right) \gamma_y(k) \exp(-i\lambda k)$$

$$= \frac{1}{2\pi} \sum_{k=-\infty}^{\infty} \gamma_y(k) \exp(-i\lambda k) - \frac{1}{2\pi} \sum_{k=\pm|T-1|}^{\pm\infty} \gamma_y(k) \exp(-i\lambda k)$$

$$- \frac{1}{T} \frac{1}{2\pi} \sum_{k=-(T-1)}^{T-1} |k| \gamma_y(k) \exp(-i\lambda k)$$

$$\longrightarrow \frac{1}{2\pi} \sum_{k=-\infty}^{\infty} \gamma_y(k) \exp(-i\lambda k) = f_y(\lambda).$$

In fact, for a WN process $I_T(\lambda)$ is exactly unbiased. However, $I_T(\lambda)$ is an inconsistent estimator of $f(\lambda)$ because its variance does not shrink with sample size. Nevertheless, it can provide useful graphical information about the periodicity in the data. For example, if $y_t = \sum_j A_j \cos(\lambda_j t + \theta_j)$, then $I_T(\lambda)$ has peaks at $\lambda = \pm\lambda_j \pmod{2\pi}$. Various modifications of the periodogram have been considered, including tapering and smoothing.

There are two ways to obtain a consistent estimator of f:

- Frequency domain: linear smoothing of the periodogram. Define

$$\widehat{f}(\lambda) = \frac{1}{T} \sum_{j=-n}^{n} w_b(\lambda - \lambda_j) I_T(\lambda_j),$$

where $w_b(\cdot) = w(\cdot/b)/b$, where $b > 0$ is a bandwidth parameter and w is a smooth function on some domain, usually $[-1, 1]$, with $\int w(s)\,ds = 1$ and $\int w(s)s\,ds = 0$. Provided $b \to 0$ as $T \to \infty$ and $Tb \to \infty$, then $\widehat{f}(\lambda)$ consistently estimates $f(\lambda)$ provided f is smooth at λ.

- Time domain: truncation of the ACF representation of f. Define

$$\widehat{f}(\lambda) = \frac{1}{2\pi} \left(\widehat{\gamma}(0) + 2 \sum_{k=1}^{M} \kappa(k/M) \widehat{\gamma}(k) \cos(\lambda k) \right),$$

where $M = M(T) \in \mathbb{Z}$ is an integer lag truncation parameter satisfying $M \to \infty$ and $M/T \to 0$, while κ is a weight function defined on the compact support $[-1, 1]$ such as $\kappa(u) = 1 - u$. Bartlett (1948, 1950) considered the case $\kappa(u) = 1 - |u|$ for $u \in [-1, 1]$. Parzen (1957) established the consistency of this estimator for a general weighting function $\kappa(\cdot)$ at all λ in the case where y_t are residuals from a linear regression.

These estimators are approximately equivalent, that is, there is a correspondence $(w, b) \longleftrightarrow (\kappa, M)$. In particular, we may define a time domain weight κ in terms of a frequency domain weighting function and vice versa:

$$w(\lambda) = \sum_{s=-\infty}^{\infty} \kappa(s) \exp(-i\lambda s), \qquad \kappa(s) = \int w(\lambda) \exp(i\lambda s) \, d\lambda.$$

The theoretical spectral density is positive, whereas the estimated spectral density may be negative unless $w > 0$.

These estimators are biased in small samples with a bias depending on the choice of b, M and on the shape of the underlying spectrum. We face a bias/variance trade-off: In order to reduce the variability of the estimate we have to smear the mass away from the true location, which tends to attenuate the peakiness. We have, for $\lambda_j \notin \{0, \pm\pi\}$, $I_T(\lambda_j) = f(\lambda_j) + U_j f(\lambda_j)$, where U_j is a random sequence that is approximately WN$(0, 1)$. This explains why the local smoothing averages out U_j.

Theorem 4.2 *As $T \to \infty$,*

$$\frac{I_T(\lambda)}{f(\lambda)} \implies \begin{cases} \chi_2^2, & \lambda \notin \{0, \pi\}, \\ \chi_1^2, & \lambda \in \{0, \pi\}. \end{cases}$$

Theorem 4.3 *Provided $M \to \infty$ and $M/T \to 0$,*

$$\sqrt{\frac{T}{M_T}} \left(\widehat{f}(\lambda) - f(\lambda) \right) \implies \begin{cases} N\left(0, \|\kappa\|^2 f(\lambda)^2\right), & \lambda \notin \{0, \pi\}, \\ N\left(0, 2\|\kappa\|^2 f(\lambda)^2\right), & \lambda \in \{0, \pi\}, \end{cases}$$

where $\|\kappa\|^2 = \int \kappa(u)^2 \, du$.

This theory may be used for testing hypotheses about and constructing confidence intervals for $f(\lambda)$. For example, when the process is white noise we have $f(\lambda) = \sigma^2/2\pi$ and we may compare $\widehat{f}(\lambda)$ with the pointwise confidence bands

$$\frac{\widehat{\sigma}^2}{2\pi} \left(1 \pm z_{\alpha/2} \|\kappa\| \sqrt{\frac{M_T}{T}} \right)$$

for $\lambda \in (0, \pi)$. A formal test of the hypothesis that $f(\lambda) = f_0(\lambda; \vartheta)$ for some parametric model f_0 is based on test statistics such as $\max_{1 \leq j \leq T} |\widehat{f}(\lambda_j) - f_0(\lambda_j; \widehat{\vartheta})|$.

The spectral density can be used in estimation and testing of ARMA(p, q) processes and other time series models. We can estimate ARMA(p, q) models using the so-called Whittle likelihood. Suppose that $E(y_t) = 0$; then

$$\mathcal{L}_W(\vartheta) = -\frac{1}{2} \sum_j \log f_y(\lambda_j; \vartheta) - \frac{I_T(\lambda_j)}{f_y(\lambda_j; \vartheta)}, \tag{4.18}$$

where $\lambda_j = \pi j/T$ and where the sum runs over the range $-n < j < 0$ and $0 < j \leq n$, under the assumption that $T = 2n+1$. This can be seen as a heteroskedastic model for $\mathcal{F}_T(y)(\lambda_j)$. Hannan (1973) showed that this is a valid approximation to the full Gaussian likelihood, and argued that it is easier to work with, in particular reducing the computational time from $O(T^3)$ to $O(T \log T)$. Furthermore, the large-sample distribution of the Gaussian QMLE or equivalently the Whittle likelihood estimator is normal with mean zero and variance V, where

$$V = \left(\int_{-\pi}^{\pi} \frac{\partial \log f(\lambda; \eta)}{\partial \eta} \frac{\partial \log f(\lambda; \eta)}{\partial \eta^{\mathsf{T}}} \, d\lambda \right)^{-1}. \tag{4.19}$$

This suggests some alternative standard errors based on the estimated spectral density $f(\lambda; \widehat{\eta})$, that is,

$$\widehat{V} = \left(\int_{-\pi}^{\pi} \frac{\partial \log f(\lambda; \widehat{\eta})}{\partial \eta} \frac{\partial \log f(\lambda; \widehat{\eta})}{\partial \eta^{\mathsf{T}}} \, d\lambda \right)^{-1}. \tag{4.20}$$

Example 4.17   The MA(1) process $y_t = \varepsilon_t - \theta \varepsilon_{t-1}$ has, for $\lambda \in [-\pi, \pi]$,

$$f_y(\lambda) = \frac{\sigma^2}{2\pi} \left(1 + \theta^2 - 2\theta \cos(\lambda) \right).$$

The Whittle likelihood is, apart from a constant,

$$\mathcal{L}_W(\vartheta) = -\frac{T}{2} \log \sigma^2$$
$$- \frac{1}{2} \sum_j \left(\log \left(1 + \theta^2 - 2\theta \cos(\lambda_j) \right) - \frac{2\pi I_T(\lambda_j)}{\sigma^2 \left(1 + \theta^2 - 2\theta \cos(\lambda_j) \right)} \right).$$

Hong (1996) developed a test for the absence of serial correlation for a general class of time series models based on the spectral density estimate.

4.5   Application

We first show the periodogram computed from the series $y_t = a \sin(\lambda t) + b \cos(\lambda t)$ with a, b standard normal random variables, mutually independent. We take $T = 512$ and consider two cases: $\lambda = 0.75\pi$ and $\lambda = 0.01\pi$. The results are shown in Figures 4.9 and 4.10. The first case corresponds to a very high frequency with a cycle of length $2\pi/\lambda \sim 3$ periods, whereas the second corresponds to a very low frequency with a cycle of length $2\pi/\lambda \sim 200$ periods. The periodogram peak coincides very closely with the value of λ in each case.

In Figure 4.11 we show the periodogram of growth in industrial production, which shows six spikes at different frequencies, corresponding to seasonal and business cycle variation. In Figure 4.12 we show the periodogram for daily stock returns, which shows no dominant peak, with the highest value in the high-frequency range. The smoothed periodograms in Figures 4.13 and 4.14 show the same information but somewhat attenuated, due to the smearing effect of smoothing across frequencies.

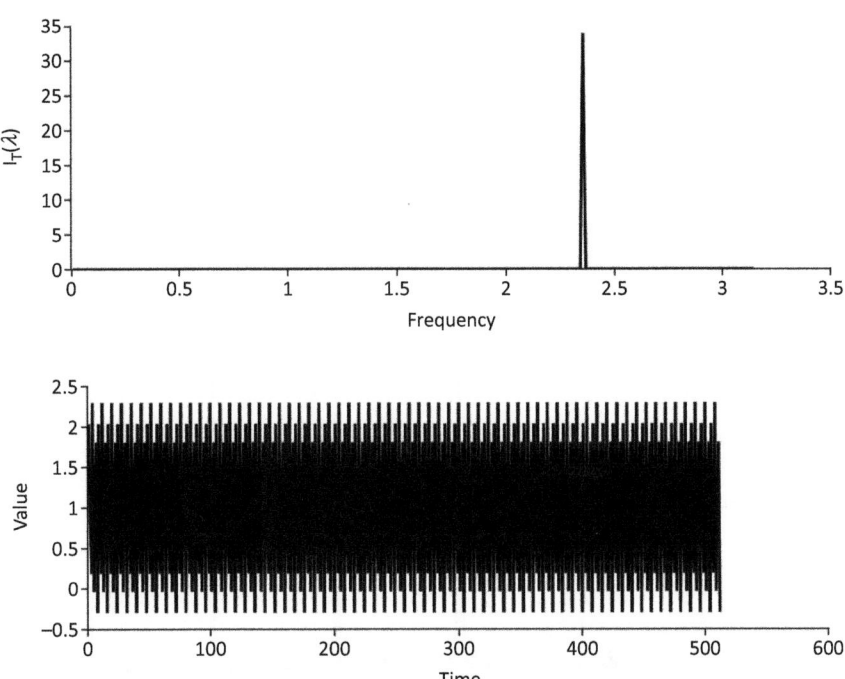

Figure 4.9 Periodogram and raw data in the case that $\lambda = 0.75\pi$.

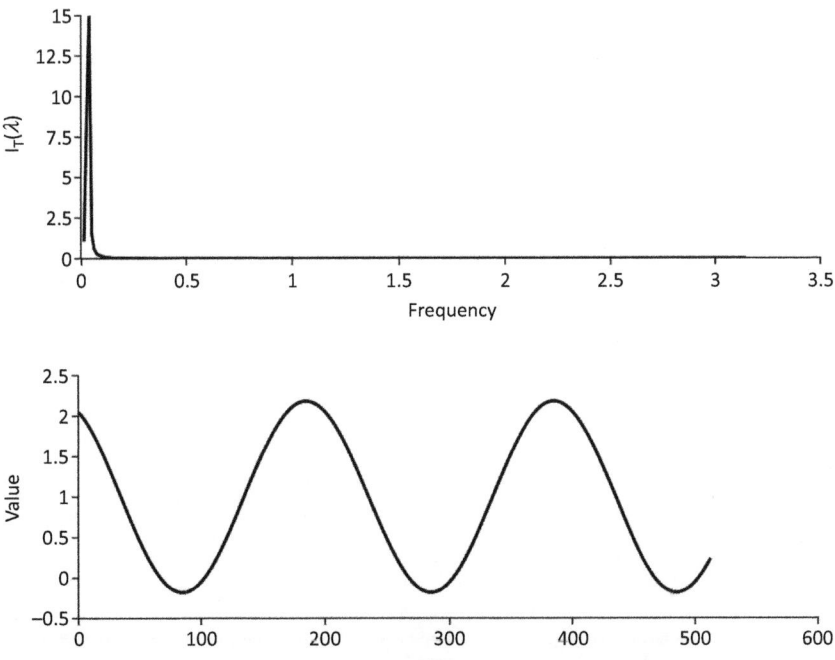

Figure 4.10 Periodogram and raw data in the case that $\lambda = 0.01\pi$.

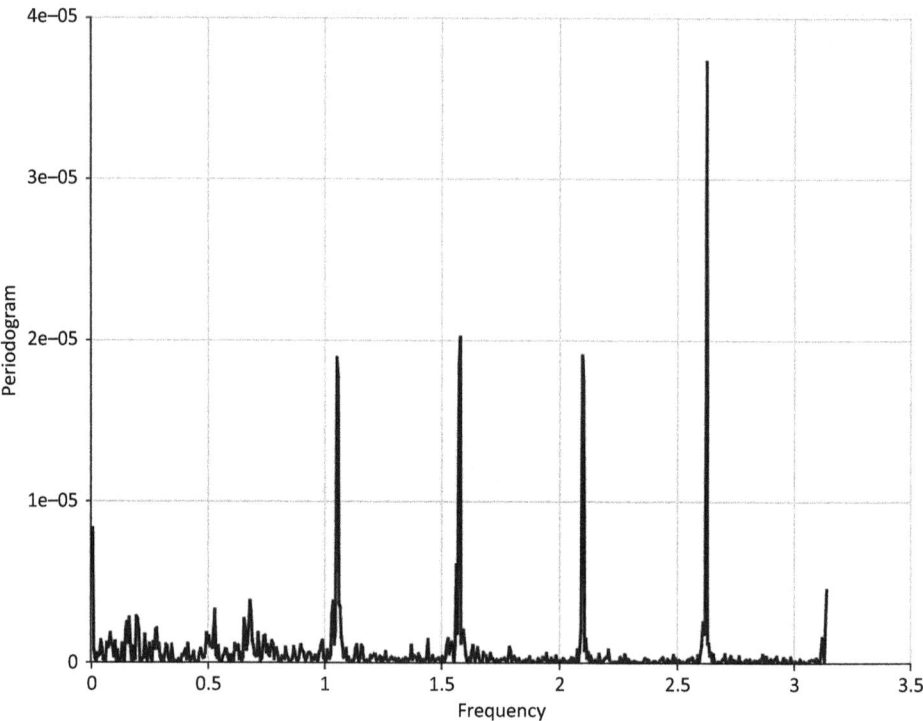

Figure 4.11 Periodogram of monthly growth in industrial production.

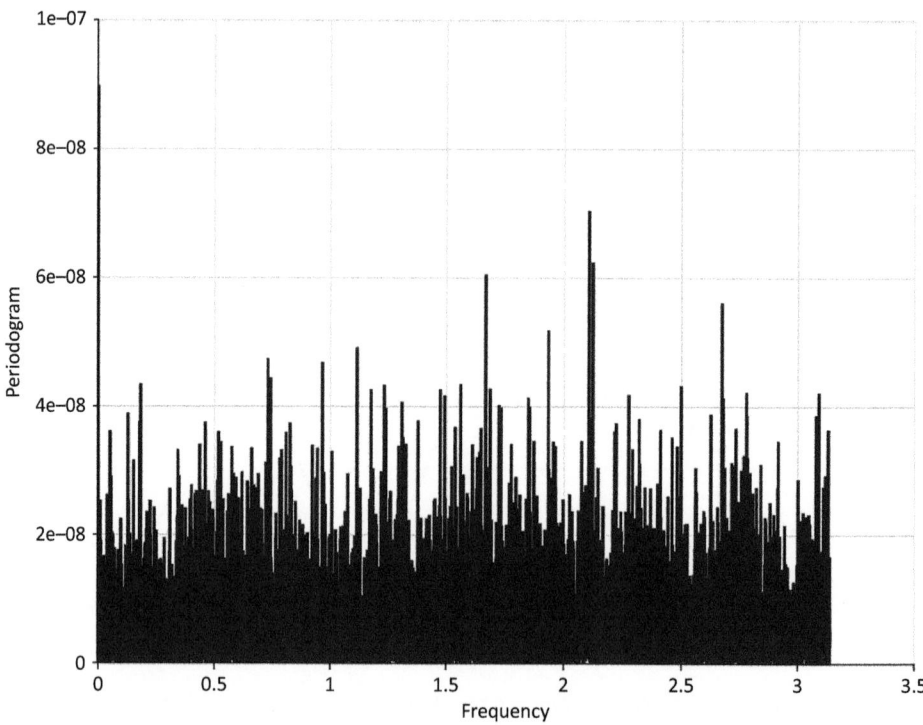

Figure 4.12 Periodogram of daily return on the S&P500, 1927–2020.

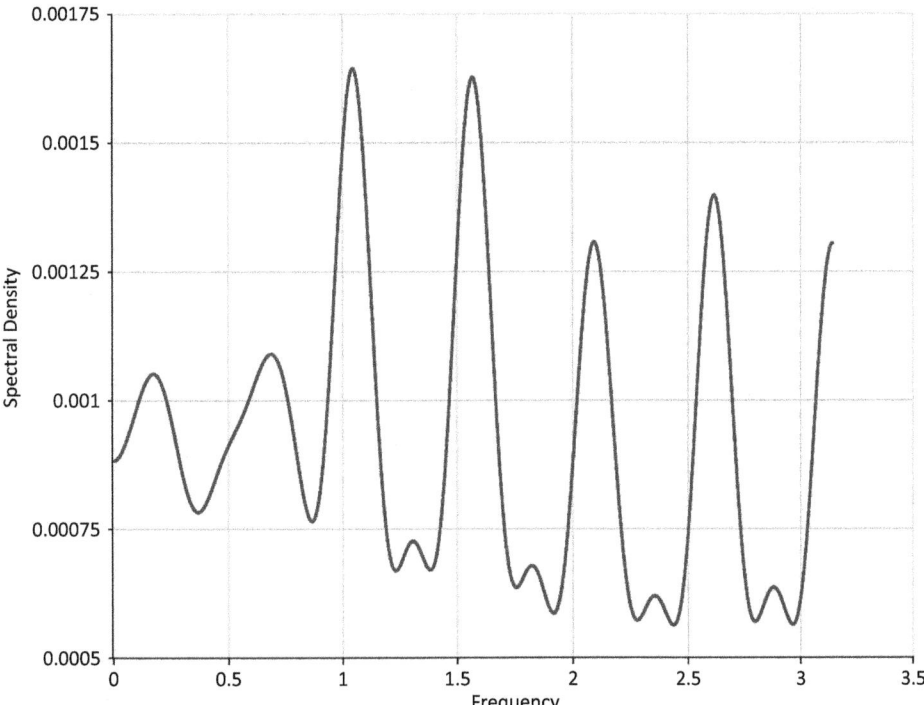

Figure 4.13 Estimated spectral density of monthly growth in industrial production.

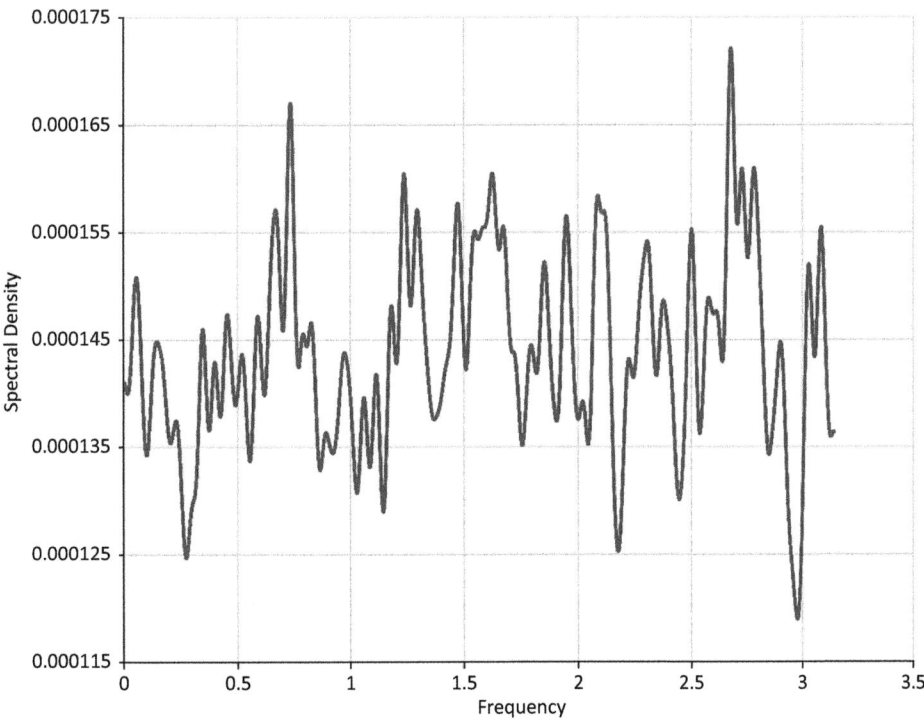

Figure 4.14 Estimated spectral density of daily return on the S&P500, 1927–2020.

4.6   Summary

We introduced spectral analysis and its use in describing periodic or repetitive phenomena such as the business cycle and seasonal variation. We focused on the spectral density function and its definition as the Fourier transform of the autocovariance function. One concrete application is in deriving the properties of filtered or aggregated time series as the analysis is much easier to handle in the frequency domain. We also discussed estimation of the spectral density function and how to conduct inference about it.

The R language has the function spectrum, which computes the spectrum of a time series using certain convenient default choices that can be modified. An alternative is to base the estimation on parametric estimation via the spec.ar function. Hannan (1970) and Brillinger (1980) are classic references on the use of frequency domain methods.

4.7   Exercises

4.1 For the data GME, define $y_t = (V_t^\alpha - 1)/\alpha$, where V_t is the daily trading volume. For $\alpha = 0$ ($y_t = \log(V_t)$) and $\alpha = 1/2$, calculate the periodogram of y_t, $I_T(\lambda_j)$, in each case at the frequencies $\lambda_j = \pi j/T, j = 0, 1, \ldots, T$, and plot the results.

4.2 Consider the two monthly unemployment time series UNRATENSA and UNRATE. Calculate the periodogram $I_T(\lambda_j)$ for these two series and compare them. Estimate the power spectrum $f_y(\lambda_j)$ by computing the equally weighted average

$$\widehat{f}_y(\lambda_j) = \frac{1}{2M+1} \sum_{k=j-M}^{j+M} I_T(\lambda_k)$$

for some choice of M with $M < T$.

4.3 Now suppose that y_t is an AR(5) process. Derive an expression for $f_y(\lambda_j)$ in terms of the parameters $\phi_j, j = 1, \ldots, 5$. Estimate the parameters from the UNRATE data and compute an alternative estimator of $f_y(\lambda_j)$. How does this compare with the nonparametric estimator from the previous question?

4.4 For the sp500 data calculate the daily stock returns y_t. Calculate the EWMA filter of y_t with parameter θ and plot the results, where:

(a) $\theta = 0.9$
(b) $\theta = 0.95$
(c) $\theta = 0.99$
(d) θ is chosen to minimize

$$Q_T(\theta) = \sum_{t=1}^{T-1} \left(y_{t+1} - (1-\theta) \sum_{j=0}^{t} \theta^j y_{t-j} \right)^2.$$

4.5 Suppose that

$$y_t = \sum_{j=1}^{3} (a_j \sin(\lambda_j t) + b_j \cos(\lambda_j t)),$$

where a_j, b_j are (mutually independent) random variables with mean zero and variance $\sigma_j^2, j = 1, 2, 3$. Let $\gamma(\cdot)$ be the autocovariance function of y. Show that

$$\gamma(0) = \sigma_1^2 + \sigma_2^2 + \sigma_3^2,$$
$$\gamma(1) = \sigma_1^2 \cos(\lambda_1) + \sigma_2^2 \cos(\lambda_2) + \sigma_3^2 \cos(\lambda_3),$$
$$\gamma(2) = \sigma_1^2 \cos(2\lambda_1) + \sigma_2^2 \cos(2\lambda_2) + \sigma_3^2 \cos(2\lambda_3).$$

Suppose that λ_1, λ_2, and λ_3 are known. Explain how you might estimate σ_1^2, σ_2^2, and σ_3^2 given a sample of data $\{y_1, \ldots, y_T\}$. Next, discuss how you might go about estimating λ_1, λ_2, and λ_3.

4.6 Suppose that z_t, x_t are mutually independent stationary processes with power spectra $f_z(\cdot)$ and $f_x(\cdot)$. Show that the process $y_t = \alpha x_t + \beta z_t$ has power spectrum $f_y(\cdot)$ with $f_y(\lambda) = \alpha^2 f_x(\lambda) + \beta^2 f_z(\lambda)$ for all $\lambda \in [-\pi, \pi]$.

4.7 Suppose that $y_t = \varepsilon_t - \theta_1 \varepsilon_{t-1} - \theta_2 \varepsilon_{t-2}$, where ε_t is i.i.d. with mean zero and variance σ^2. Calculate the power spectrum $f_y(\lambda)$ of y_t and plot it against λ. For which values of θ_1, θ_2 does $f_y(\lambda) = 0$ for some λ? Calculate $F_y(\lambda) = \int_{-\pi}^{\lambda} f_y(\lambda') \, d\lambda'$ and plot this against λ.

4.8 Suppose that y_t is an i.i.d. series with mean zero and variance σ^2, and let $x_1 = y_1, x_2 = y_{K+1}, \ldots,$

$$z_1 = \frac{1}{2K+1} (y_1 + \cdots + y_{2K+1}),$$

$$z_2 = \frac{1}{2K+1} (y_{2K+2} + \cdots + y_{4K+2}),$$

$$\vdots$$

where K is a fixed integer. Are x_t, z_t weakly stationary processes? What are their autocovariance functions and their spectra? If y_t is a general stationary process with autocovariance function γ_y and spectrum f_y, what are the corresponding counterparts for x_t, z_t?

4.9 Suppose that $\psi(z) = \psi_{-r} z^{-r} + \cdots + \psi_s z^s$ is a two-sided filter and that $x_t = \psi(L) y_t$, where

$$y_t = 2 \cos(\omega t) = \exp(i\omega t) + \exp(-i\omega t)$$

is a deterministic process that is periodic with period $p = 2\pi/\omega$. Show that

$$x_t = 2g \cos \left(\omega \left(t - \frac{\theta}{\omega} \right) \right), \tag{4.21}$$

where $g = (\psi(\exp(i\omega)) \psi(\exp(-i\omega)))^{1/2}$ is the gain of the filter and

$$\theta = \tan^{-1} \left(\frac{\text{Im} \left(\psi(\exp(i\omega)) \right)}{\text{Re} \left(\psi(\exp(i\omega)) \right)} \right)$$

is the phase.

4.10 Suppose that $x_t = y_t + \alpha y_{t-K}$, where α is a real number and K is a positive integer. Derive the transfer function, its gain, and its phase for this filter.

4.11 Suppose that $y_t = \phi_5 y_{t-5} + \phi_{22} y_{t-22} + \varepsilon_t$, where ε_t are i.i.d. random variables with mean zero and variance σ^2. Calculate the power spectrum of y_t.

4.12 Suppose that $y_t = a\sin(\lambda t) + b\cos(\lambda t)$, where a, b are mean-zero random variables with common variance σ^2 and mutually uncorrelated. Show that

$$\bar{y} = \frac{1}{T}\sum_{t=1}^{T} y_t \xrightarrow{P} 0$$

even though the process $\{y_t\}$ is not mixing.

4.13 Suppose that $y_t = a\sin(\lambda t) + b\cos(\lambda t) + \varepsilon_t$, where a, b are mean-zero random variables with common variance σ^2 and mutually uncorrelated, while ε_t is i.i.d. with mean zero and variance σ_ε^2 and independent of a, b. Derive the power spectrum of y_t.

4.14 Consider the symmetric filter $y_t = \frac{1}{2}(x_{t+1} + x_{t-1})$.
   (a) Write down the impulse response function of this filter.
   (b) Write down the transfer function of this filter.
   (c) Describe in general terms the effect this filter will have on the time series it is applied to.
   (d) Suppose that $x_t = \phi x_{t-1} + \varepsilon_t$, where $|\phi| < 1$ and ε_t is mean zero with a finite variance.
      (i) Write down the power spectrum of x_t.
      (ii) Write down the power spectrum of y_t.

4.15 Consider the symmetric filter $y_t = \frac{1}{3}(x_{t+1} + x_t + x_{t-1})$.
   (a) Write down the impulse response function of this filter.
   (b) Write down the transfer function of this filter.
   (c) Describe in general terms the effect this filter will have on the time series it is applied to.
   (d) Suppose that $x_t = \varepsilon_t - \theta\varepsilon_{t-1}$, where $|\theta| < 1$ and ε_t is mean zero with a finite variance.
      (i) Write down the power spectrum of x_t.
      (ii) Write down the power spectrum of y_t.

4.16 Suppose that $y_t = \varepsilon_t - \theta\varepsilon_{t-1}$, where ε_t is i.i.d. with mean zero and variance σ^2. Suppose that we have the periodogram of a sample $\{y_0, \ldots, y_{T-1}\}$, $I_T(\lambda_j)$, at the frequencies $\lambda_j = 2\pi j/T$, $j = 0, 1, \ldots, n$ (where $T = 2n + 1$), and consider the periodogram regression

$$I_T(\lambda_j) = \alpha + \beta\cos(\lambda_j) + e_j.$$

Suppose we knew α, β. Explain how we could obtain estimates of θ, σ^2.

5 Inference under Heterogeneity and Weak Dependence

In this chapter we consider the question of how to conduct inference about parameters of interest under weak conditions. In particular, we suppose that the observed data, or more generally an unobserved shock process inside an otherwise specified model, has a general dependence structure not characterized by a specific model. We do suppose that the process possesses the property of weak dependence, that is, α-mixing with sufficiently rapid decay of the mixing coefficients such that they are summable, which focuses attention on the case where a CLT is at least possible. We consider different approaches to conducting inference about parameter values in such cases. The question is important because relying on parametric specification of dependence structure may lead to biased inferences when the specification is incorrect. In cases where building a full model is not desirable, we may prefer instead to have an inference method that would be robust to different specifications.

Example 5.1 Hansen and Singleton (1982) considered a representative agent model where the agent has to choose investments and consumption to maximize discounted expected utility. The first-order condition is

$$E\left((1 + R_{it+1})\delta \left(\frac{C_{t+1}}{C_t} \right)^{-\gamma} - 1 \mid \mathcal{F}_t \right) = 0,$$

where $\mathcal{F}_t$ is the agent's information set. Here, γ is the coefficient of relative risk aversion and δ is the time discount function. Let $\theta = (\delta, \gamma)^{\mathsf{T}}$. We can estimate θ by the **generalized method of moments** (GMM), which is in general nonlinear in the data. We have not specified any assumptions about consumption and stock returns, there is no explicit dynamic model. Provided $C_{t+1}/C_t, R_{1t}, \ldots, R_{nt}, Z_t$ is stationary and mixing (weakly dependent), then we can justify a CLT for $\widehat{\theta}$. However, the limiting distribution will involve a long-run variance. To conduct inference about θ (e.g., confidence interval for δ, γ) we need to estimate this long-run variance or consider other methods of doing inference.

We consider three general approaches to inference: long-run variance estimation, self normalization, and bootstrap. These methods all work under similar conditions and have strengths and weaknesses.

5.1 Estimation of Mean and Autocovariance Function

We first consider the properties of the sample mean of a time series, which is important in many contexts, and is the prototypical estimation problem. Suppose that we have observations $\{y_1, \ldots, y_T\}$ taken from a mixing process. Suppose that $E(y_t^2) \leq C < \infty$, and let

$\mu_t = E(y_t)$, $t = 1, 2, \ldots$ Then, let $\widehat{\mu} = \sum_{t=1}^{T} y_t/T$ and $\mu_T = \sum_{t=1}^{T} \mu_t/T$. Here, we allow μ_t to vary just to shake things up a bit. Under the conditions of Herrndorf's theorem we have

$$\sqrt{T}\left(\widehat{\mu} - \mu_T\right) \Longrightarrow N(0, V), \qquad V = \lim_{T \to \infty} \mathrm{var}\left(\frac{1}{\sqrt{T}} S_T\right). \qquad (5.1)$$

In the stationary case, $\mu_T = \mu$ and $V = \mathrm{lrvar}(y_t)$, and in this case $\mathrm{lrvar}(y_t) = 2\pi \times f(0)$, the spectral density at frequency zero. In some cases of interest there is a special structure.

Example 5.2   Suppose that x_t are i.i.d. with mean μ and variance σ^2, and

$$y_t = \frac{1}{K}(x_t + x_{t-1} + \cdots + x_{t+1-K})$$

is an SMA of x_t. Then with $\varepsilon_t = x_t - \mu$ we have

$$y_t = \mu + u_t, \qquad u_t = \frac{1}{K}(\varepsilon_t + \varepsilon_{t-1} + \cdots + \varepsilon_{t+1-K}).$$

The error term is serially correlated, an MA$(K-1)$ process in fact. This arises in many practical situations. For example, many authors aggregate daily data to a lower frequency such as monthly, sometimes using overlapping data to create a sample of monthly data. The advantage of using overlapping data is that it produces more low-frequency observations, albeit with the cost that they are correlated. Let

$$\widehat{\mu} = \frac{1}{T} \sum_{t=K+1}^{T} y_t.$$

Then this statistic satisfies the conditions of the CLT with the limiting variance

$$V = \mathrm{lrvar}(u_t) = \gamma_u(0) + 2\left(\gamma_u(1) + \cdots + \gamma_u(K-1)\right)$$
$$= \frac{1}{K^2}\left(K\sigma^2 + 2\left((K-1)\sigma^2 + \cdots + \sigma^2\right)\right),$$

which has a special structure. In this case,

$$\widehat{\mathrm{lrvar}} = \widehat{\gamma}_y(0) + 2\left(\widehat{\gamma}_y(1) + \cdots + \widehat{\gamma}_y(K-1)\right) \qquad (5.2)$$

is a consistent estimator of V. Hansen and Hodrick (1980) and Hansen and Singleton (1982) used these estimates. One issue is that (5.2) is not guaranteed to be positive. Suppose that we also observe $\{x_t\}$, then let

$$\widehat{V} = \frac{1}{T} \sum_{t=1}^{T} w_t^2 \widehat{\varepsilon}_t^2,$$

where $\widehat{\varepsilon}_t = x_t - \bar{x}$ and $w_t = 1$ if $K \leq t \leq T-K$ and $w_t = 1 - (t-1)/K$ for $t = 1, \ldots, K-1$. These are essentially the Hodrick (1992) standard errors for aggregated data (for $\widehat{\mu}$), also known as clustered standard errors. It is not clear why one would estimate μ by $\widehat{\mu}$ instead of $\bar{x}$, but if you really must do that, then $\widehat{V}$ seems like a better source of standard errors.

We next discuss how to estimate the asymptotic variance of the sample mean in the general case of autocorrelated data. Bartlett (1950, 22) proposed an estimator of the spectral density of a linear time series process at any frequency λ multiplied by 2π; at $\lambda = 0$ this is

$$\widehat{\text{lrvar}} = \sum_{|k| \leq M_T} \left(1 - \frac{|k|}{M_T} \right) \widehat{\gamma}(k), \tag{5.3}$$

where $\widehat{\gamma}(k)$ is the sample autocovariance, where M_T is an integer sequence with $M_T \to \infty$ and $M_T/T \to 0$. The weighting function $\omega(u) = 1 - |u|$ is called the Bartlett window for exactly this reason. Parzen (1957, Theorem 5A) established the consistency of this estimator for residuals from a linear regression. This methodology was extended by Newey and West (1987) to allow y_t to be residuals from a more general estimation problem and to allow some kinds of nonstationarity compatible with the Herrndorf CLT.

Andrews (1991a) developed a methodology for choosing the sequence M_T. He considered the more general class of estimators of the form

$$\widehat{\text{lrvar}} = \sum_{k=-T+1}^{T-1} \omega \left(\frac{k}{M_T} \right) \widehat{\gamma}(k),$$

where ω is a weighting function. He showed that an optimal weighting function is the quadratic spectral kernel, that is, the kernel whose Fourier transform is quadratic. He proposed a rule-of-thumb method of bandwidth choice, see Chapter 11, which involves estimating a parametric model and computing the implied bias and variance of the estimator, which then yields a formula for the optimal bandwidth according to the mean squared error of the variance estimator. The simplest version of his methodology involves estimating an AR(1) model on the residuals and then letting

$$M_T = \left(\frac{q k_q \widehat{\alpha}(q) T}{\|\omega\|_2^2} \right)^{1/(2q+1)}, \tag{5.4}$$

where q is the order of the kernel and $\|\omega\|_2^2 = \int \omega^2(u)\, du$. He considered the cases $q = 1$ and $q = 2$, in which case

$$\widehat{\alpha}(2) = \frac{4\widehat{\phi}^2}{\left(1 - \widehat{\phi}\right)^4}, \qquad \widehat{\alpha}(1) = \frac{4\widehat{\phi}^2}{\left(1 - \widehat{\phi}\right)^2 \left(1 + \widehat{\phi}\right)^2},$$

where $\widehat{\phi}$ is the estimated autoregressive parameter. This methodology is widely used in economics applications because the software is available to automatically carry out the computations in a general class of models.

Under the Herrndorf conditions it follows that, as $T \to \infty$,

$$\tau_T = \frac{\sqrt{T}\left(\widehat{\mu} - \mu\right)}{\sqrt{\widehat{\text{lrvar}}}} \Longrightarrow N(0, 1). \tag{5.5}$$

This result allows standard inference about μ. To test the null hypothesis that $\mu = \mu_0$ we reject if the absolute value of τ_T computed with $\mu = \mu_0$ exceeds $z_{\alpha/2}$. This can be shown to be a consistent test against all alternative μs in the sense that the probability of rejection tends to one with sample size.

We may also use the long-run variance estimate to construct asymptotically valid confidence intervals that express our knowledge or lack of knowledge about the parameter. Specifically, we have

$$I_\alpha = \left\{ \mu : \widehat{\mu} - z_{\alpha/2} \sqrt{\frac{\widehat{\text{lrvar}}}{T}} \leq \mu \leq \widehat{\mu} + z_{\alpha/2} \sqrt{\frac{\widehat{\text{lrvar}}}{T}} \right\},$$

which satisfies $\Pr(\mu \in I_\alpha) \longrightarrow 1 - \alpha.$[1]

The same approach can be used to provide a confidence interval for any estimator that is asymptotically normal. Specifically, suppose that an estimator $\widehat{\theta}$ of a scalar parameter θ_0 satisfies

$$\sqrt{T}(\widehat{\theta} - \theta_0) = \frac{1}{\sqrt{T}} \sum_{t=1}^{T} \rho_t(\theta_0, \eta_0) + o_p(1) \tag{5.6}$$

for some residual $\rho_t(\theta, \eta)$ that depends on the data but is mean zero and satisfies a CLT where η is a vector of parameters that can also be estimated consistently. The limiting distribution is normal with mean zero and variance given by the long-run variance of the sequence ρ_t. One can estimate this long-run variance by using the series $\{\rho_t(\widehat{\theta}, \widehat{\eta})\}$. If additional structure is present, such as MDS, the limiting variance simplifies, and one can estimate it consistently without the full technology. One leading example of this case is the sample autocovariance and sample autocorrelation, which we discuss next.

Recall that for the sample autocovariance and autocorrelation functions we have the approximations

$$\sqrt{T}(\widehat{\gamma}(k) - \gamma(k)) = \frac{1}{\sqrt{T}} \sum_{t=k+1}^{T} v_{t;k} + o_p(1),$$

$$\sqrt{T}(\widehat{\rho}(k) - \rho(k)) = \frac{1}{\sqrt{T}} \sum_{t=k+1}^{T} w_{t;k} + o_P(1),$$

where $v_{t;k} = (y_t - \mu)(y_{t-k} - \mu) - \gamma(k)$ and

$$w_{t;k} = \{(y_t - \mu)(y_{t-k} - \mu) - \gamma(k) - \rho(k)((y_t - \mu)^2 - \gamma(0))\}/\gamma(0).$$

These two centered statistics satisfy the CLT under Herrndorf's conditions, with asymptotic variances $\sigma_j^2(k), j = \gamma, \rho$. Let

$$\widehat{v}_{t;k} = (y_t - \widehat{\mu})(y_{t-k} - \widehat{\mu}) - \widehat{\gamma}(k),$$

$$\widehat{w}_{t;k} = \{(y_t - \widehat{\mu})(y_{t-k} - \widehat{\mu}) - \widehat{\gamma}(k) - \widehat{\rho}(k)((y_t - \widehat{\mu})^2 - \widehat{\gamma}(0))\}/\widehat{\gamma}(0).$$

In the special case that $v_{t;k}, w_{t;k}$ are MDS ($v_{t;k}$ is so when $y_t - \mu$ is an MDS), one may construct an estimate of the asymptotic variances by

---

[1] Bayesians used to be triggered by such statements since it seems to be making μ a random variable, which they would like, but in the frequentist interpretation I_α is a random set and the probability statement can be rearranged in terms of the random variables $\widehat{\mu}, \widehat{\text{lrvar}}$ themselves.

$$\widehat{\sigma}^2_\gamma(k) = \frac{1}{T} \sum_{t=k+1}^{T} \widehat{v}^2_{t;k}, \qquad \widehat{\sigma}^2_\rho(k) = \frac{1}{T} \sum_{t=k+1}^{T} \widehat{w}^2_{t;k}, \tag{5.7}$$

as already discussed. In the absence of the MDS structure, we define $\widehat{\sigma}^2_\gamma(k), \widehat{\sigma}^2_\rho(k)$ as the estimated long-run variance using the series $\{\widehat{v}_{t;k}, t = k+1, \ldots, T\}$ and $\{\widehat{w}_{t;k}, t = k+1, \ldots, T\}$. It follows that, for example,

$$I_\alpha = \left\{ \rho \colon \widehat{\rho}(k) - z_{\alpha/2} \sqrt{\frac{\widehat{\sigma}^2_\rho(k)}{T}} \le \rho \le \widehat{\rho}(k) + z_{\alpha/2} \sqrt{\frac{\widehat{\sigma}^2_\rho(k)}{T}} \right\}$$

is a valid $1 - \alpha$ confidence interval for $\rho(k)$ under the corresponding conditions.

One issue with this construction may arise when $\rho(k)$ is near either boundary and the sample size is relatively small, namely that the confidence interval may extend outside the permissible values $[-1, 1]$. One solution to that is to use a transform of $\widehat{\rho}(k)$ and then invert the confidence interval for the transform. Specifically, define the Fisher z-transform,

$$\widehat{z}(k) = \frac{1}{2} \log\left(\frac{1 + \widehat{\rho}(k)}{1 - \widehat{\rho}(k)} \right), \qquad z(k) = \frac{1}{2} \log\left(\frac{1 + \rho(k)}{1 - \rho(k)} \right),$$

which can take any value in $\mathbb{R}$. We may apply the delta method to show that

$$\sqrt{T} \left(\widehat{z}(k) - z(k) \right) \Longrightarrow N\left(0, \Delta(k)^2 \sigma^2_\rho(k) \right),$$

where $\Delta(k) = 1/(1 - \rho(k)^2)$, which is the derivative of the transform with respect to $\rho(k)$. In the special case where y_t is an AR(1) process and $k = 1$, the asymptotic variance here is equal to one, that is, the Fisher z-transform is variance stabilizing, since it does not depend on the value of $\rho(1)$.

We then construct a symmetric confidence interval for $z(k)$,

$$\widehat{z}(k) \pm z_{\alpha/2} \sqrt{\frac{\widehat{\Delta}(k) \widehat{\sigma}^2_\rho(k)}{T}},$$

where $\widehat{\Delta}(k) = 1/(1 - \widehat{\rho}(k)^2)$. Then, since quantiles are equivariant under monotonic transformations, the implied confidence interval for $\rho(k)$ is

$$I_\alpha = \left\{ \rho \colon \tau\left(\widehat{z}(k) - z_{\alpha/2} \sqrt{\frac{\widehat{\Delta}(k) \widehat{\sigma}^2_\rho(k)}{T}} \right) \le \rho \le \tau\left(\widehat{z}(k) + z_{\alpha/2} \sqrt{\frac{\widehat{\Delta}(k) \widehat{\sigma}^2_\rho(k)}{T}} \right) \right\},$$

where τ is the inverse transformation $\tau(z) = (\exp(2z) - 1)/(\exp(2z) + 1)$. The inverse transformation maps $\mathbb{R}$ into $[-1, 1]$, so the resulting confidence interval for ρ contains only valid parameter values. Trigger warning: this interval will not be symmetrically centered around the parameter estimate. Alternative transformations include the inverse trigonometric functions like the arctangent ($\tan^{-1}(\cdot)$) or the arcsine ($\sin^{-1}(\cdot)$) transform (Giraitis, Li, and Phillips, 2023).

If one wants a simultaneous confidence set for say $\rho(1), \ldots, \rho(k)$, then there are several options. One can invert the Box–Pierce statistic or one can take the union of the individual intervals at a level that corrects for the multiple testing issue. In practice, such intervals are rarely used.

Table 5.1 Test of zero mean of S&P500 stock returns and zero autocorrelations.

Parameter	i.i.d.	$M_T = 5$	$M_T = 22$	$M_T = 255$	$M_T = T - 1$
μ	3.835	3.875	3.852	3.799	4.883
$\rho(1)$	−2.089	−0.338	−0.251	−0.127	−0.012
$\rho_{r2}(1)$	40.690	64\,749	63\,312	57\,237	63\,276

We consider the S&P500 daily return from 1927 to 2020, $T = 23\,345$. For these data $\widehat{\mu} = 0.000\,301\,119\,74$, $\widehat{\rho}(1) = -0.013\,673\,125$, and $\widehat{\rho}_{r2}(1) = 0.266\,313\,49$. In Table 5.1 we report the test statistics for the null hypothesis that the parameter $\theta = 0$, $\tau = \sqrt{T}\widehat{\theta}/\sqrt{\widehat{\text{lrvar}}}$.

5.2   Self Normalization

We present the self-normalization approach due to Kiefer, Vogelsang, and Bunzel (2000). This can be interpreted as an (inconsistent) estimator of the long-run variance but without any abrupt downweighting, that is, including all sample autocovariances. This apparently avoids the need to specify a bandwidth as in Andrews (1991a), although one could just say that one has chosen an extreme bandwidth.

Let $M_T = T$ in (5.3), in which case, with $C_T = \widehat{\text{lrvar}}$, we have

$$
\begin{aligned}
C_T &= \frac{1}{T}\sum_{t=1}^{T}(y_t - \bar{y})^2 + \frac{2}{T}\sum_{k=1}^{T-1}\left(1 - \frac{k}{T}\right)\frac{1}{T}\sum_{t=k+1}^{T}(y_t - \bar{y})(y_{t-k} - \bar{y}) \\
&= \frac{1}{T}\sum_{t=1}^{T}\sum_{s=1}^{T}\left(1 - \frac{|t-s|}{T}\right)(y_t - \bar{y})(y_s - \bar{y}) \\
&= 2\frac{1}{T}\sum_{t=1}^{T-1}\left(\frac{1}{\sqrt{T}}\sum_{s=1}^{t}(y_s - \bar{y})\right)\left(\frac{1}{\sqrt{T}}\sum_{s'=1}^{t}(y_{s'} - \bar{y})\right) = 2\frac{1}{T}\sum_{t=1}^{T}S_t^2,
\end{aligned}
$$

where $S_t = T^{-1/2}\sum_{s=1}^{t}(y_s - \bar{y})$. Kiefer, Vogelsang, and Bunzel (2000) showed that C_T is proportional to the long-run variance, and in particular $C_T \Longrightarrow \text{lrvar} \times 2\int_0^1 \mathbb{B}(s)^2\,ds$, where $\mathbb{B}(s) = B(s) - sB(1)$ is the standard Brownian bridge based on standard Brownian motion $B(s)$. These processes are defined and discussed in Chapters 6 and 12. Furthermore, the t-statistic satisfies

$$
\frac{\sqrt{T}(\bar{y} - \mu)}{\sqrt{C_T}} \Longrightarrow \frac{B(1)}{\sqrt{\int \mathbb{B}(s)^2\,ds}}, \tag{5.8}
$$

where $B(1) \sim N(0, 1)$. This limiting distribution is not Gaussian, but it is pivotal, meaning that it does not depend on any unknown quantities, and indeed its quantiles have been calculated and tabulated. The critical values of this distribution are given in Kiefer,

Vogelsang, and Bunzel (2000). If w_α is the α-quantile of this distribution, then a $1 - \alpha$ confidence interval for μ is

$$I_\alpha = \left\{ \mu : \widehat{\mu} + w_{\alpha/2} \sqrt{\frac{C_T}{T}} \le \mu \le \widehat{\mu} + w_{1-\alpha/2} \sqrt{\frac{C_T}{T}} \right\}.$$

We may also think of this as follows. We can write

$$S_t = \frac{t}{\sqrt{T}} (\widehat{\mu}_t - \widehat{\mu}) = \sqrt{\frac{t}{T}} \sqrt{t} (\widehat{\mu}_t - \mu) - \frac{t}{T} \sqrt{T} (\widehat{\mu} - \mu).$$

Then $\sqrt{T}(\widehat{\mu} - \mu)$ and $\sqrt{t}\,(\widehat{\mu}_t - \mu)$ are both asymptotically normal (for large t, T) with mean zero and the same variance lrvar; let us write this as

$$S_t^2 \simeq \text{lrvar} \times \left(\sqrt{\frac{t}{T}} Z_t - \frac{t}{T} Z_T \right)^2,$$

where Z_t, Z_T are jointly asymptotically normal with mean zero and variance one (but are mutually correlated). Then it is clear that, for large T, t, C_T is proportional to the long-run variance where the proportionality is stochastic, that is, it depends on the limiting values of the stochastic multiplying factor. In other words, $\lim_{T \to \infty} E(C_T) = \text{lrvar}(y_t)$, but C_T is not a consistent estimator of lrvar because $\text{var}(C_T) \nrightarrow 0$.

Lobato (2001) provided some theoretical and empirical results for the sample mean and sample autocovariance. That is, let

$$S_{t,j} = \frac{1}{\sqrt{T}} \sum_{s=1}^{t} \left((y_s - \bar{y}) (y_{s+j} - \bar{y}) - \widehat{\gamma}(j) \right), \qquad C_{T,j} = \frac{1}{T} \sum_{t=1}^{T} S_{t,j}^2.$$

Then he showed that under the null hypothesis $\gamma(j) = 0$ (and the usual restrictions for the CLT),

$$\frac{\sqrt{T} \widehat{\gamma}(j)}{\sqrt{C_{T,j}}} \Longrightarrow \frac{B(1)}{\sqrt{\int_0^1 \mathbb{B}(s)^2 \, ds}}. \tag{5.9}$$

Lazarus, Lewis, and Stock (2021) proposed a hybrid testing approach that uses a long-run variance estimator with $M_T = 1.3 T^{1/2}$ and the critical values from (5.8). They argued that this delivers a better type I/type II error trade-off.

5.3 Bootstrap Standard Errors

We outline the bootstrap approach and define it for a number of time series settings, including parametric ARMA models and nonparametric settings where we do not specify the dependence structure beyond restricting its strength.

5.3.1 The Basic Idea

The bootstrap of Efron (1982) is counted as one of the major advances in statistics of the twentieth century, and has widely affected practice. There can be computational reasons why this method is preferred to the usual approach based on estimating the unknown quantities of the asymptotic distribution. There can also be statistical reasons why the bootstrap is better than the asymptotic plug-in approach (Hall, 1992).

Suppose that $y_1, \ldots, y_T$ are i.i.d. with distribution function F. We have a statistic (root) $R_T(\tau; y_1, \ldots, y_T)$, which is a function of the data $y_1, \ldots, y_T$, and a parameter value τ. For example, R_T could be an estimator or a test statistic. Let $H_T(x, F) = \Pr(R_T \le x)$, where the probability is calculated under the true distribution F. The question is, how to estimate $H_T(x, F)$ and functions thereof?

The "asymptotic" approach uses the fact that $H_T(x, F) \longrightarrow H(x, F)$ as $T \to \infty$ by the CLT or other method. Then, estimate $H_T(x, F)$ by $\widehat{H}_A(x) = H(x, F_T)$, where F_T is some estimate of F like the empirical distribution. For example, we have $R_T = T^{1/2}(\bar{y} - \mu) \implies N(0, \sigma^2)$. We approximate the distribution of R_T by the distribution of $N(0, \widehat{\sigma}^2)$, where $\widehat{\sigma}^2$ is some consistent estimate of σ^2. In some cases the distribution function H does not depend on F and then R_T is a pivot or asymptotic pivot; for example, if $R_T = T^{1/2}(\bar{y} - \mu)/\widehat{\sigma}$ we have $R_T \implies N(0, 1)$.

Instead, the bootstrap approach is based on using $\widehat{H}_B(x) = H_T(x, F_T)$ as an estimator of $H_T(x, F)$. In fact, we usually calculate $H_T(x, F_T)$ using Monte Carlo methods. The empirical distribution of the data $y_1, \ldots, y_T$ is denoted F_T; this distribution is discrete with probability $1/T$ at each sample point. Let $y_1^*, \ldots, y_m^*$ be a sample from F_T, let $\widehat{\tau}_T$ be the estimated value of τ from the sample data, and let $R_T^* = R_T(\widehat{\tau}_T; y_1^*, \ldots, y_m^*)$. Then

$$\Pr(R_T^* \le x \mid y_1, \ldots, y_T) = \widehat{H}_B(x).$$

We actually use S replications to approximate this distribution by an "empirical" distribution. Usually, we take $m = T$ but this is not necessary; in some cases we choose $m < T$ to deal with certain types of nonregularity.

Note that F_T could be the empirical distribution, that is, $F_T(y) = \sum_{t=1}^{T} 1(y_t \le y)/T$, or an estimated parametric CDF $F_{\widehat{\theta}}$, such as the CDF of an $N(0, \widehat{\sigma}^2)$ random variable. In the latter case, the resampling is from the distribution $F_{\widehat{\theta}}$.

The bootstrap principle is to treat the distribution F_T as the population and then to sample from the new population, which we know.

The Bootstrap Algorithm

1. Generate a sample of data $\mathcal{Y}^{T*} = \{y_1^*, \ldots, y_T^*\}$ from the empirical distribution F_T, that is, drawn with replacement from $\{y_1, \ldots, y_T\}$.
2. Compute $R_T^*(\widehat{\tau}; y_1^*, \ldots, y_T^*)$, where $\widehat{\tau}$ is the sample estimate.
3. Repeat S times and let T_s^* denote the value of R_T^* for the sth sample.
4. Calculate the (empirical) distribution of $\{T_1^*, \ldots, T_S^*\}$ and use this distribution in place of $H_T(x, F)$, that is,

$$\widehat{H}_B(x) = \frac{1}{S} \sum_{s=1}^{S} 1\,(T_s^* \le x). \tag{5.10}$$

For example, a critical value can be calculated as quantiles of this distribution, that is, $\widehat{Q}_B(\alpha) = \widehat{H}_B^{-1}(\alpha)$ for $\alpha \in (0, 1)$.

Theorem 5.1 (Bickel and Freedman, 1981) *Suppose that $y_1, \ldots, y_T$ are i.i.d. with finite mean μ and positive variance σ^2, and let $\overline{\mu}_m^* = m^{-1} \sum_{i=1}^m y_i^*$ and $\overline{\mu} = T^{-1} \sum_{i=1}^T y_i$. Then, along almost all sample sequences $\{y_1, \ldots, y_T\}$, as $T, m \to \infty$ we have, for all $x \in \mathbb{R}$,*

$$\sup_{x \in \mathbb{R}} \left| \Pr\left(m^{1/2}(\overline{\mu}_m^* - \overline{\mu}) \le x \mid y_1, \ldots, y_T \right) - \Phi\left(\frac{x}{\sigma}\right) \right| \longrightarrow 0,$$

where Φ is the CDF of a standard normal random variable. In addition, $m \times \mathrm{var}(\overline{\mu}_m^* \mid y_1, \ldots, y_T) \to \sigma^2$.

In conclusion, we have found an alternative way to approximate the distribution of $T^{1/2}(\overline{\mu} - \mu)$: just tabulate the distribution of $m^{1/2}(\overline{\mu}_m^* - \overline{\mu})$ conditional on $y_1, \ldots, y_T$. In some cases this can be done exactly, but more often one approximates this distribution by a further step based on resampling.

5.3.2   Bootstrap for Time Series

In the time series case, several alternative bootstrap resampling schemes are widely used. The key issue is how to take account of the dependence in the data. The standard i.i.d. resampling above generally does not work because it fails in this regard. We consider three different resampling schemes that work for time series under certain conditions: ARMA, block bootstrap, and subsampling.

5.3.2.1   Parametric Bootstrap

Suppose that our data is generated by an ARMA process, that is,

$$A(L)y_t = \mu + B(L)\varepsilon_t,$$

where ε_t is i.i.d. with mean zero and variance σ^2. Suppose that initial values $y_0, y_{-1}, \ldots, y_{-p}, \varepsilon_0, \varepsilon_{-1}, \ldots, \varepsilon_{-q}$ are specified and fixed. We consider a general class of roots that depend on the ARMA parameters ϑ and on a vector of moments of the error process, which we denote by M, that is,

$$R_T(\tau; y_1, \ldots, y_T) = \sqrt{T}(f(\widehat{\vartheta}, \widehat{M}) - f(\vartheta, M))$$

for some smooth scalar-valued function f; here, $\tau = (\vartheta^\mathsf{T}, M^\mathsf{T})^\mathsf{T}$. For example, $M_j = E(|\varepsilon_t|^j)$. We suppose that R_T is asymptotically normal with mean zero and variance v, where v will generally depend on the time series dependence of the process y_t. For example, the root $R_T(\tau; y_1, \ldots, y_T) = \sqrt{T}(\overline{y} - \tau)$, $\tau = E(y_t)$, in which case the variance v is the long-run variance of y_t.

We next define an algorithm that can be used to obtain critical values for this root.

1. Let $\widehat{\vartheta}$ be the given estimates of the unknown parameters ϑ, say QMLE, and let $\widehat{M}$ be the sample estimate of M. Then let $\widehat{\varepsilon}_t$ be the residual defined implicitly through

$$A_{\widehat{\phi}}(L)y_t = \widehat{\mu} + B_{\widehat{\theta}}(L)\widehat{\varepsilon}_t, \quad t = 1, \ldots, T,$$

that is, we solve recursively for $\widehat{\varepsilon}_t = B_{\widehat{\theta}}(L)^{-1}(A_{\widehat{\phi}}(L)y_t - \widehat{\mu})$ using the estimated lag polynomials conditioning on the initial values. Then let $\widetilde{\varepsilon}_t = \widehat{\varepsilon}_t - \sum_{t=1}^T \widehat{\varepsilon}_t / T$ be the recentered residuals.

2. Let ε_t^*, $t = 1, \ldots, T$, be a sample drawn with replacement from $\{\widetilde{\varepsilon}_t\}_{t=1}^T$, that is, from its empirical distribution function $\widetilde{F}_\varepsilon(x) = \sum_{t=1}^T 1(\widetilde{\varepsilon}_t \leq x)/T$.

3. Then let $\{y_t^*\}_{t=1}^T$ be defined recursively through

$$A_{\widehat{\varphi}}(L)y_t^* = \widehat{\mu} + B_{\widehat{\theta}}(L)\varepsilon_t^*$$

using the same initial values. Compute $\widehat{\vartheta}^*$ using the dataset $\{y_t^*\}_{t=1}^T$ and $\widehat{M}^*$ using the dataset $\{\varepsilon_t^*\}_{t=1}^T$.

4. Repeat S times and calculate the empirical distribution of $R_T^* = \sqrt{T}\big(f(\widehat{\vartheta}^*, \widehat{M}^*) - f(\widehat{\vartheta}, \widehat{M})\big)$ across the samples as above.

See Kreiss and Franke (1992) for a discussion of this algorithm and a proof of its validity. The resampling can instead be done from a normal distribution in the case where the limiting distribution of the parameter of interest only depends on the error variance rather than other features of its distribution. In that case we can draw z_t^* from a standard normal distribution and let $\varepsilon_t^* = \widehat{\sigma}z_t^*$ in step 2, where $\widehat{\sigma}^2$ is the estimate of the error variance.

Consider the special case of an AR(1) process $y_t = \phi y_{t-1} + \varepsilon_t$, where $\phi \in (-1, 1)$ and the root is $R_T(\tau; y_1, \ldots, y_T) = \sqrt{T}(\widehat{\phi} - \phi)$. In this case, the algorithm is simpler because the estimation step is simpler and because the residuals are easy to obtain.

1. Let $\widehat{\phi}$ be the OLS estimate of ϕ (we make use of the initial value $y_0 = 0$ in this case). Then let $\widehat{\varepsilon}_t = y_t - \widehat{\phi}y_{t-1}$ be the residual for $t = 1, \ldots, T$ and let $\widetilde{\varepsilon}_t = \widehat{\varepsilon}_t - \sum_{t=1}^T \widehat{\varepsilon}_t/T$, $t = 1, \ldots, T$, be the recentered residuals (if an intercept were included this would not be necessary).

2. Let ε_t^*, $t = 1, \ldots, T$, be a sample drawn with replacement from $\{\widetilde{\varepsilon}_t\}_{t=1}^T$, that is, from its empirical distribution function $\widetilde{F}_\varepsilon$.

3. Then let $\{y_t^*\}_{t=1}^T$ be defined by $y_t^* = \widehat{\phi}y_{t-1}^* + \varepsilon_t^*$, with $y_0^* = 0$; compute $\widehat{\phi}^*$ using OLS on the dataset $\{y_t^*\}_{t=1}^T$.

4. Repeat S times and calculate the empirical distribution of $R_T^* = \sqrt{T}(\widehat{\phi}^* - \widehat{\phi})$ across the samples as above.

This method works under the assumption that the shocks are i.i.d. What if we are happy with a parametric model for dependence (such as ARMA(p, q)) but we want to allow for heteroskedasticity in the shocks? This is easy to accommodate using the **wild bootstrap**, (Mammen, 1993). This involves sampling independent z_t^* from any distribution with $E(z_t^*) = 0$ and $\mathrm{var}(z_t^*) = 1$, and then letting $\varepsilon_t^* = z_t^* \times \widehat{\varepsilon}_t$ in stage 2. This has the feature that

$$E\left(\varepsilon_t^* \mid y_1, \ldots, y_T\right) = 0, \qquad E\left((\varepsilon_t^*)^2 \mid y_1, \ldots, y_T\right) = \widehat{\varepsilon}_t^2.$$

The rest of the algorithm is as before. Some authors argued for also matching the third moment by requiring that z_t^* also satisfies $E((z_t^*)^3) = 1$.

5.3.2.2 Block Bootstrap

A second bootstrap approach is called the **block bootstrap**, which is valid without any specific model under stationarity and weak dependence conditions. The idea is to divide the data $Y = \{y_1, \ldots, y_T\}$ into contiguous long blocks within which the dependence is preserved, that is, let

$$Y_{(1)} = \{y_1, \ldots, y_b\}, \ldots, Y_{(m)} = \{y_{(m-1)b+1}, \ldots, y_T\},$$

where we assume that $T = b \times m$ exactly. We have m blocks each of length b. We consider the root

$$R_T(\tau; y_1, \ldots, y_T) = \sqrt{T}(f(\widehat{M}) - f(M)),$$

where now M is a vector of moments of $\{y_t\}$ and $\widehat{M}$ is a vector of estimates. The method can also be applied to the ARMA model case where ε_t is no longer assumed to be i.i.d., only an MDS that is weakly dependent.

The algorithm is as follows.

1. Resample the blocks randomly with replacement, and let

$$Y^* = \{Y^*_{(1)}, \ldots, Y^*_{(m)}\} = \{y_1^*, \ldots, y_T^*\}$$

   be the bootstrap data (that is, pick random integers $i = 1, \ldots, m$ with replacement from $\{1, 2, \ldots m\}$).
2. Compute $\widehat{M}^*$ using the dataset $\{y_t^*\}_{t=1}^T$.
3. Repeat S times and calculate the empirical distribution of $R_T^* = \sqrt{T}(f(\widehat{M}^*) - f(\widehat{M}))$ across the samples as above.

This method is consistent provided $b(T) \to \infty$ and $m(T) = b(T)/T \to 0$, and that some other technical conditions are satisfied.

5.3.2.3 Subsampling

A third bootstrap approach is called **subsampling**. Let b be an integer with $1 < b < T$.

1. For each subsample $Y^*_{(j)} = \{y_{j+1}, \ldots, y_{j+b}\}$, compute $\widehat{M}^*_{(j)}$.
2. Repeat for each feasible j, that is, $j = 1, \ldots, T - b$.
3. Calculate the empirical distribution of $R^*_{(j)} = \sqrt{b}(f(\widehat{M}^*_{(j)}) - f(\widehat{M}))$ across $j = 1, \ldots, T - b$.

No random number generator is needed for this algorithm, but otherwise it has some similarities with the block bootstrap. It involves essentially looking at the rolling window estimates as a distribution. This method is consistent under some conditions on the degree of dependence, provided $b(T) \to \infty$ and $b(T)/T \to 0$.

We next illustrate how these different inference methods work on S&P500 daily returns from 1927 to 2020. In all three cases the sample statistic is shown in solid black along with the histogram of the subsample statistic, where the subsample size was set at five years. Figure 5.1 shows the result for the sample mean, which shows strong rejection of the null hypothesis that the mean stock return is zero. Figure 5.2 shows the result for the first-order autocorrelation of returns, which shows weak evidence against the null hypothesis that stock returns are not autocorrelated. Figure 5.3 shows the result for the first-order autocorrelation of squared stock returns, which shows strong rejection of the null hypothesis that squared returns are not autocorrelated.

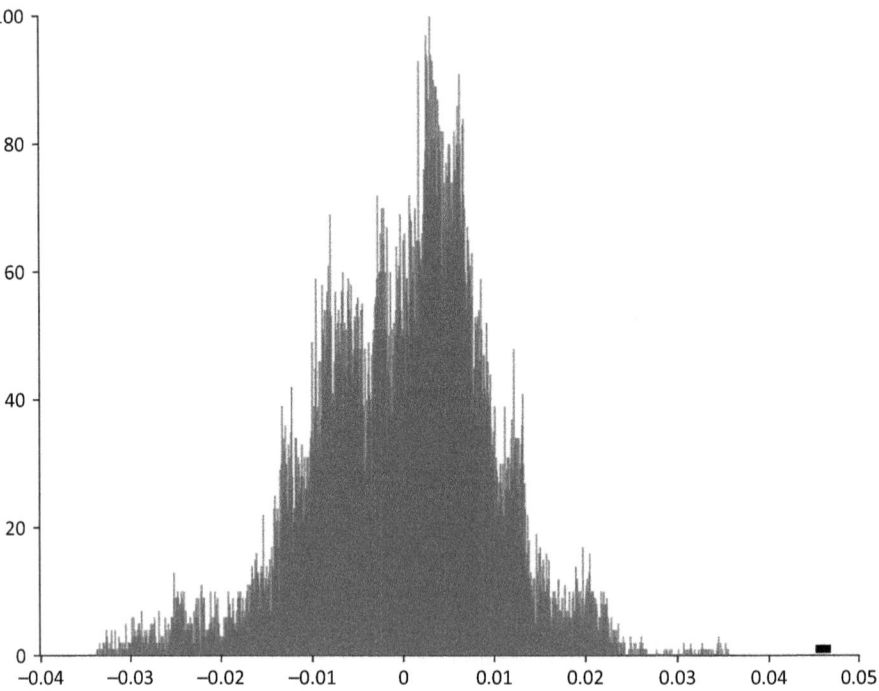

Figure 5.1 Subsample distribution of sample mean of stock returns.

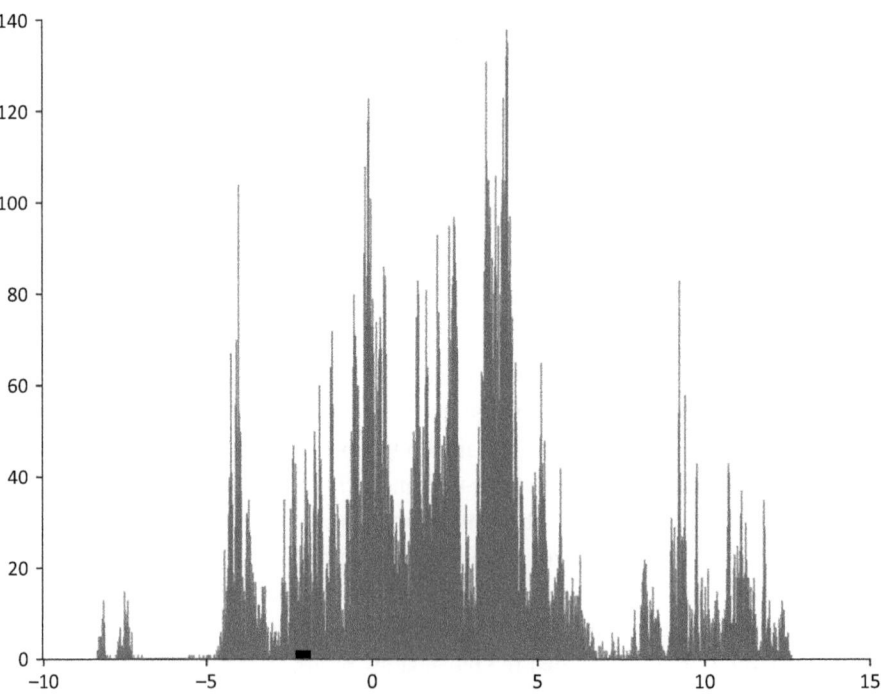

Figure 5.2 Subsample distribution of the first-order autocorrelation.

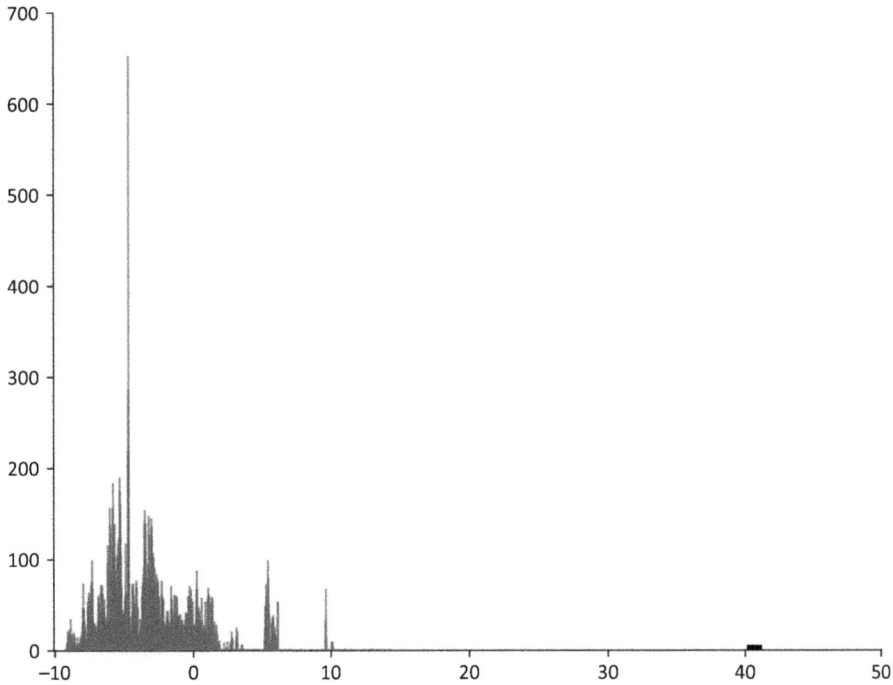

Figure 5.3 Subsample distribution of the first-order autocorrelation of squared returns.

5.4   Autocorrelation and Regression

We next consider regression models with autocorrelated disturbances. Suppose that $y_t = \beta^\mathsf{T} x_t + u_t$, where $y_t \in \mathbb{R}$ and $x_t \in \mathbb{R}^K$ are observed series. We can distinguish several cases of interest around the process generating x_t, u_t. The simplest and easiest case is to suppose that x_t is **exogenous**, roughly speaking meaning that it is determined outside the system. There are a number of different variations on this theme: **strongly exogenous** and **weakly exogenous**. A weakly exogenous process could include lagged dependent variables, which allows feedback from past values of u to x. We suppose in that case that $E(u_t \mid x_t, x_{t-1}, \ldots) = 0$.

We will for now assume strong exogeneity, meaning that

$$E(u_t \mid x_t, t = 0, \pm 1, \ldots) = 0. \tag{5.11}$$

In the matrix notation this implies that $E(u \mid X) = 0$, where u, X are a $T \times 1$ vector and $T \times K$ matrix respectively. For example, we may suppose that quarterly GDP satisfies the following trend plus seasonal regression:

$$\log \mathrm{GDP}_t = \beta_1 + \beta_2 t + \sum_{j=1}^{4} D_{jt} \gamma_j + u_t,$$

where D_{jt} are quarterly dummy variables; see Chapter 6. In this model there is no meaningful feedback from past values of u to the values of x, and the regressors are strongly exogenous. In this case, we expect the deviation from trend, u_t, to be positively autocorrelated, reflecting the business cycle, that is, not i.i.d. – recession quarter tends to be followed by recession quarter.

We can write the model in matrix form, $y = X\beta + u$, where u_t satisfies $E(u_t \mid X) = 0$ but may be heteroskedastic and autocorrelated. In this case,

$$E(uu^\mathsf{T} \mid X) = \Sigma = \left(E(u_t u_s \mid X)\right)_{t,s=1}^T.$$

In the regression context it is common practice to allow for heteroskedasticity in both cross-sectional and time series contexts. For example, suppose that the error process is multiplicative, $u_t = \omega_t z_t$, where $\omega_t(X) > 0$ is a deterministic process conditional on X, while z_t is a mean-zero, stationary, and weakly dependent process independent of X. In this case, the error covariance matrix separates into

$$\Sigma = D_\omega \begin{pmatrix} \gamma_z(0) & \gamma_z(1) & \cdots & \gamma_z(T-1) \\ \gamma_z(1) & \gamma_z(0) & \ddots & \vdots \\ \vdots & \ddots & \ddots & \gamma_z(1) \\ \gamma_z(T-1) & & \gamma_z(1) & \gamma_z(0) \end{pmatrix} D_\omega, \quad D_\omega = \mathrm{diag}(\omega_1, \ldots, \omega_T).$$

The OLS estimator of β, $\widehat{\beta} = (X^\mathsf{T}X)^{-1}X^\mathsf{T}y$, is consistent and asymptotically normal under some conditions; however, it is inefficient, and the usual standard errors are wrong. In fact, under strong exogeneity, $\widehat{\beta}$ is exactly unbiased, that is, $E(\widehat{\beta} \mid X) = \beta$ for all β. Furthermore, we have exactly

$$\mathrm{var}(\widehat{\beta} \mid X) = V_T = (X^\mathsf{T}X)^{-1}\Psi_T(X^\mathsf{T}X)^{-1},$$

$$\Psi_T = X^\mathsf{T}\Sigma X = \sum_{t=1}^T \sum_{s=1}^T x_t x_s^\mathsf{T} \sigma_{ts}.$$

In the case that u_t is a martingale difference sequence, $\Psi_T = \sum_{t=1}^T x_t x_t^\mathsf{T} \sigma_{tt}$. In the case that u_t is a stationary MDS, $\sigma_{tt} = \mathrm{var}(u_t)$ does not vary with t, and $\mathrm{var}(\widehat{\beta} \mid X) = \sigma^2(X^\mathsf{T}X)^{-1}$, the OLS story.

We now relax the strong exogeneity assumption. We suppose only that

$$E(x_t u_t) = 0, \tag{5.12}$$

but not the stronger assumption $E(u \mid X) = 0$. If x_t contains lagged dependent variables then this condition may not hold, depending on the parameters of interest.

Example 5.3   Suppose that y_t is a stationary process with autocorrelation function $\rho(\cdot)$. Then we can write $y_t = \alpha + \phi y_{t-j} + u_t$, where $\phi = \rho(j)$ and by construction $E(y_{t-j}u_t) = 0$. Furthermore, we can write

$$y_t = \alpha + \beta_1 y_{t-1} + \cdots + \beta_j y_{t-j} + u_t,$$

where $\beta_j = \pi(j)$ and by construction $E(y_{t-i}u_t) = 0$ for $i = 1, \ldots, j$. In both cases, the derived error process u_t may be autocorrelated.

Under the condition (5.12), the OLS estimator is generally biased in finite samples, but under some conditions it will be consistent and asymptotically normal so that

$$V_T^{-1/2}(\widehat{\beta} - \beta) \Longrightarrow N(0, I_K),$$

where in this case $V_T = \Omega_T^{-1} \Psi_T^{-1} \Omega_T^{-1}$ with

$$\Omega_T = \sum_{t=1}^{T} E\left(x_t x_t^{\mathsf{T}}\right), \qquad \Psi_T = \sum_{t=1}^{T} \sum_{s=1}^{T} E\left(x_t x_s^{\mathsf{T}} u_t u_s\right).$$

The question we address here is how to conduct inference about β without making further assumptions about Σ beyond those in Herndorrf's theorem. Under some conditions we may expect that $T^{-1} \Psi_T \xrightarrow{P} \Psi_\infty$, where Ψ_∞ is finite (and nonsingular), for example if $z_t = x_t u_t$, where z_t is a scalar stationary and mixing process. In this case, Ψ_∞ is the long-run variance of z_t. However, the limit Ψ_∞ may exist even when the process z_t is not stationary. We define the following estimator:

$$\widehat{\Psi}_T = \sum_{t,s:|t-s|\leq M_T} x_t x_s^{\mathsf{T}} w\left(|t-s|\right) \widehat{u}_t \widehat{u}_s, \tag{5.13}$$

where $\widehat{u}_t = y_t - \widehat{\beta}^{\mathsf{T}} x_t$ are the least squares residuals, while $w(k) = 1 - k/(M+1)$ for $|k| \leq M_T$, for some M_T. For example, suppose that $x_t = 1$, then

$$\frac{1}{T} \sum_{t,s:|t-s|\leq M_T} w\left(|t-s|\right) \widehat{u}_t \widehat{u}_s = \sum_{k=-M_T}^{M_T} w(|k|) \frac{1}{T} \sum_t \widehat{u}_t \widehat{u}_{t-k}$$

$$= \sum_{k=-M_T}^{M_T} w(|k|) \widehat{\gamma}_u(k),$$

which is essentially the long-run variance estimate of the previous section. We can show that $\widehat{\Psi}_T$ is a positive-definite covariance matrix with probability one for this choice of weighting. Then let

$$\widehat{V}_T = (X^{\mathsf{T}} X)^{-1} X^{\mathsf{T}} \widehat{\Psi}_T X (X^{\mathsf{T}} X)^{-1}.$$

Newey and West (1987) showed that under some conditions $(\widehat{V}_T - V_T)/T \xrightarrow{P} 0$, and furthermore,

$$\widehat{V}_T^{-1/2} \left(\widehat{\beta} - \beta\right) \Longrightarrow N(0, I_K).$$

This result allows one to construct confidence intervals based on the matrix $\widehat{V}_T$. Let $\widehat{V}_T^{ii}$ denote the ith diagonal element of $\widehat{V}_T^{-1}$; then $\widehat{\beta}_i \pm z_{\alpha/2} \sqrt{\widehat{V}_T^{ii}}$ is a symmetric confidence interval with asymptotic coverage $1 - \alpha$. These results can be used to derive confidence bands for the estimated autocorrelation and partial autocorrelation of a time series using the regression formulation.

An alternative strategy is to model the autocorrelation and take account of it in both estimation and inference. For example, we may assume that the error process u_t follows an ARMA(p, q) model with parameters ϑ, and use the Gaussian maximum likelihood (ML)

$$\mathcal{L}(\beta, \vartheta) = -\frac{1}{2} \log |\Sigma(\vartheta)| - \frac{1}{2} (y - X\beta)^{\mathsf{T}} \Sigma(\vartheta)^{-1} (y - X\beta)$$

to jointly estimate the parameters θ of the u process and β. An efficient estimate of β (under Gaussianity) is a sort of generalized least squares (GLS),

$$\widehat{\beta}_{\mathrm{ML}} = \left(X^{\mathsf{T}} \Sigma(\widehat{\vartheta})^{-1} X\right)^{-1} X^{\mathsf{T}} \Sigma(\widehat{\vartheta})^{-1} y,$$

where $\widehat{\vartheta}$ is the MLE of ϑ. This will be asymptotically efficient when the chosen parametric model is correct and satisfies

$$\left(X^{\mathsf{T}}\Sigma(\widehat{\vartheta})^{-1}X\right)^{-1/2}\left(\widehat{\beta}_{\mathrm{ML}} - \beta\right) \Longrightarrow N\left(0, I_K\right),$$

provided the error model is correctly specified. The advantage of this approach is that the model itself gives us a way of calculating standard errors without resorting to bandwidth parameters $n(T)$ and weighting functions w. The weakness is that it relies on the ARMA model assumption and requires estimation of those parameters, which can be quite time consuming and is perhaps not in itself of interest. Most empirical practice in economics takes the former approach.

5.4.1   Bootstrap for Regression

We consider first the algorithm for the strongly exogenous case. Suppose that

$$y_t = \beta^{\mathsf{T}} x_t + \varepsilon_t, \tag{5.14}$$

where ε_t are stationary and mixing with $E(\varepsilon \mid X) = 0$. We next give a bootstrap algorithm.

1. Calculate the OLS estimator $\widehat{\beta}$ and the residuals $\widehat{\varepsilon}_t = y_t - \widehat{\beta}^{\mathsf{T}} x_t$, $t = 1, \ldots, T$. If an intercept is not included, then recenter the residuals, that is, let $\widetilde{\varepsilon}_t = \widehat{\varepsilon}_t - \overline{\widehat{\varepsilon}}_t$.
2. Resample $\{\varepsilon_1^*, \ldots, \varepsilon_T^*\}$ from $\{\widetilde{\varepsilon}_1, \ldots, \widetilde{\varepsilon}_T\}$; we may do either parametric bootstrap based on an ARMA model for the errors, block bootstrap, or subsampling.
3. Define, for $t = 1, \ldots, T$, $y_t^* = \widehat{\beta}^{\mathsf{T}} x_t + \varepsilon_t^*$.
4. Calculate the bootstrap estimate $\widehat{\beta}^* = (X^{\mathsf{T}}X)^{-1}X^{\mathsf{T}}Y^*$.
5. To approximate the distribution of any function of $\widehat{\beta} - \beta$ use the computable conditional distribution of $\widehat{\beta}^* - \widehat{\beta}$.

Now suppose that the regression model (5.14) holds but that y_t, x_t are stationary and mixing with $E(\varepsilon_t \mid x_t) = 0$.

1. Calculate the OLS estimator $\widehat{\beta}$ and the residuals $\widehat{\varepsilon}_t = y_t - \widehat{\beta}^{\mathsf{T}} x_t$, $t = 1, \ldots, T$. If an intercept is not included, then recenter the residuals, that is, let $\widetilde{\varepsilon}_t = \widehat{\varepsilon}_t - \overline{\widehat{\varepsilon}}_t$.
2. Resample $\{\varepsilon_1^*, x_1^* \ldots, \varepsilon_T^*, x_T^*\}$ from $\{(\widetilde{\varepsilon}_1, x_1), \ldots, (\widetilde{\varepsilon}_T, x_T)\}$; we may do one of parametric bootstrap based on an ARMA model for the errors, block bootstrap, or subsampling.
3. Define, for $t = 1, \ldots, T$, $y_t^* = \widehat{\beta}^{\mathsf{T}} x_t^* + \varepsilon_t^*$.
4. Calculate the bootstrap estimate $\widehat{\beta}^* = (X^{*\mathsf{T}}X^*)^{-1}X^{*\mathsf{T}}Y^*$.
5. To approximate the distribution of any functional of $\widehat{\beta} - \beta$ use the computable conditional distribution of $\widehat{\beta}^* - \widehat{\beta}$ given the data.

5.4.2   Generalized Method of Moments

We now consider the general GMM estimation method developed by Hansen (1982). Suppose that the unconditional moment restrictions must hold, that is, the function $G(\theta) = 0$ if and only if $\theta = \theta_0$, where

$$G(\theta) = E\left(g(X_t, \theta)\right), \tag{5.15}$$

where g is a $q \times 1$ vector of functions of the $d \times 1$ vector of observed variables X_t and the $p \times 1$ vector of unknown parameters θ. We can approximate the unconditional expectation by the sample average, so long as the data are stationary, and this is the basis for estimation. We estimate the parameters θ by the GMM method using q sample moments,

$$G_T(\theta) = \frac{1}{T} \sum_{t=1}^{T} g(X_t, \theta),$$

and a possibly stochastic $q \times q$ weighting matrix W_T. For example, $W_T = I_q$.

Definition 5.1   Let $\widehat{\theta}_{\text{GMM}}$ solve the following optimization problem:

$$\widehat{\theta}_{\text{GMM}} = \arg \min_{\theta \in \Theta} G_T(\theta)^\mathsf{T} W_T G_T(\theta). \tag{5.16}$$

This objective function is nonlinear in θ. In many theoretical treatments (Pakes and Pollard, 1989) it suffices to let $\widehat{\theta}_{\text{GMM}}$ be only an approximate minimizer, which allows for the case that $G_T(\theta)$ may not be a continuous function of θ, but we shall assume that $G_T(\theta)$ is continuously differentiable for simplicity. See Ai and Chen (2003) for an upgraded theory allowing for high-dimensional nuisance parameters.

Under some conditions this method is consistent and the estimators are normally distributed in large samples. We suppose that $W_T \xrightarrow{P} W$ for some positive-definite matrix W. First, we assume *identification*, in this case

$$\text{for all } \delta > 0, \quad \inf_{\|\theta - \theta_0\| > \delta} G(\theta)^\mathsf{T} W G(\theta) \geq \epsilon(\delta) > 0.$$

This condition is really about the population model. Second, we have the uniform law of large numbers (ULLN) condition that

$$\sup_{\theta \in \Theta} \|G_T(\theta) - G(\theta)\| \xrightarrow{P} 0.$$

These conditions imply consistency of the GMM estimator. The ULLN result has been established for a number of settings, including stationary and mixing processes; the result is a slight strengthening of the usual LLN that we have discussed. We next turn to the limiting distribution.

Define the positive-definite matrix

$$V(W) = (\Gamma^\mathsf{T} W \Gamma)^{-1} \Gamma^\mathsf{T} W \Omega W \Gamma (\Gamma^\mathsf{T} W \Gamma)^{-1}.$$

Theorem 5.2   *Suppose that θ_0 is in the interior of Θ. Suppose that G_T, G are both continuously differentiable and that, for all sequences of positive numbers δ_T such that $\delta_T \to 0$,*

$$\sup_{\|\theta - \theta_0\| \leq \delta_T} \left\| \frac{\partial G_T(\theta)}{\partial \theta} - \frac{\partial G(\theta)}{\partial \theta} \right\| \xrightarrow{P} 0. \tag{5.17}$$

Suppose that $\Gamma = \partial G(\theta_0)/\partial \theta$ is of full rank and that $\sqrt{T} G_T(\theta_0) \Longrightarrow N(0, \Omega)$, where Ω is of full rank. Then, as $T \to \infty$,

$$T^{1/2}(\widehat{\theta}_{\text{GMM}} - \theta_0) \Longrightarrow N(0, V(W)).$$

If we take $W_{\text{opt}} = \Omega^{-1}$, then the asymptotic variance of $\widehat{\theta}_{\text{GMM}}$ is $V(W_{\text{opt}}) = (\Gamma^{\mathsf{T}}\Omega^{-1}\Gamma)^{-1}$ and satisfies

$$(\Gamma^{\mathsf{T}}\Omega^{-1}\Gamma)^{-1} \leq (\Gamma^{\mathsf{T}}W\Gamma)^{-1}\Gamma^{\mathsf{T}}W\Omega W\Gamma(\Gamma^{\mathsf{T}}W\Gamma)^{-1}$$

for all weighting matrices W. In practice, we take W_T to be a consistent estimator of Ω^{-1}. The resulting estimator is consistent and asymptotically normal, and optimal within this class.

One can construct confidence intervals for θ using t-statistics or Wald statistics based on a consistent estimator $\widehat{V}$ of V. Specifically, let

$$\widehat{\theta}_{\text{GMM},i} = \pm z_{\alpha/2}\sqrt{\frac{\widehat{V}_{ii}}{T}},$$

where $\widehat{V}_{ii}$ is a consistent estimator of V_{ii}, the component of V corresponding to θ_i. This is a symmetric, coverage $(1-\alpha)$ confidence interval for θ_i.

We take

$$\widehat{\Gamma} = \frac{\partial G_T(\widehat{\theta}_{\text{GMM}})}{\partial\theta}, \quad \widehat{\Omega} = \frac{1}{T}\sum_{t,s:|t-s|\leq n(T)}\sum w\left(|t-s|\right)g(X_t,\widehat{\theta}_{\text{GMM}})g(X_s,\widehat{\theta}_{\text{GMM}})^{\mathsf{T}},$$

which are consistent estimates under (5.18).

Example 5.4 (Hansen and Singleton, 1982, again)   The first-order condition is

$$E\left((1+R_{it+1})\delta\left(\frac{C_{t+1}}{C_t}\right)^{-\gamma} - 1 \mid \mathcal{F}_t\right) = 0, \tag{5.18}$$

where $\mathcal{F}_t$ is the agent's information set. If we replace $\mathcal{F}_t$ by any coarser information set (of observed data) $\mathcal{F}_t^*$, then this conditional moment restriction continues to hold. We will suppose that returns and consumption are observable, along with some other data. Let $\theta = (\delta, \gamma)^{\mathsf{T}}$, and define the vector

$$g(X_{t+1},\theta) = \left(\left(\begin{array}{c} 1+R_{1,t+1} \\ \vdots \\ 1+R_{n,t+1} \end{array}\right)\delta\left(\frac{C_{t+1}}{C_t}\right)^{-\gamma} - 1\right) \otimes Z_t \in \mathbb{R}^q$$

for each parameter value θ. Here, Z_t are observed **instruments** included in $\mathcal{F}_t^*$, and X_t denotes the observed data including returns, consumption, and instruments, while $\otimes$ is the Kronecker product, which basically means multiply all elements together. In practice, there are many, many instruments $Z_t \in \mathcal{F}_t^*$ that could be used, so that the parameters θ are overidentified, that is, $q > 2$.

Hansen and Singleton (1982) estimated their model by GMM (and by ML under stronger restrictions). They used seasonally adjusted real per capita monthly consumption data and a single stock market index return (value weighted or equal weighted) from 1958:2–1978:1. For the GMM standard errors they assumed that the process is

n-dependent with $n = 1, 2, 6$, and they chose $w(u) = 1$ (which does not guarantee positive variance). They found

$$\widehat{\alpha} = \widehat{\gamma} - 1 = \underset{(0.3355)}{-0.9457}, \qquad \widehat{\delta} = \underset{(0.0031)}{0.9931},$$

where the standard errors are in parentheses below.

5.4.3 Self-Normalization Approach

Compute the recursive GMM estimates $\widehat{\theta}_t$ based on the sample $X_1, \ldots, X_t$ and let

$$C_T = \frac{1}{T^2} \sum_{t=1}^{T} t^2 \left(\widehat{\theta}_t - \widehat{\theta}\right) \left(\widehat{\theta}_t - \widehat{\theta}\right)^{\mathsf{T}}.$$

Then define the statistic $R_T(\widehat{\theta}_{\text{GMM}}, \theta) = T(\widehat{\theta}_{\text{GMM}} - \theta)^{\mathsf{T}} C_T^{-1} (\widehat{\theta}_{\text{GMM}} - \theta)$. It follows that, as $T \to \infty$,

$$R_T \Longrightarrow U_p = B_p(1)^{\mathsf{T}} V_p^{-1} B_p(1). \tag{5.19}$$

where $V_p = \int_0^1 \left(B_p(r) - rB_p(1)\right) \left(B_p(r) - rB_p(1)\right)^{\mathsf{T}} dr$ and B_p is a vector of independent Brownian motions. A confidence set for θ can be computed as $\{\theta : R_T(\widehat{\theta}_{\text{GMM}}, \theta) \leq w_{1-\alpha}\}$, where $w_{1-\alpha}$ is the value computed such that $\Pr(U_p \leq w_{1-\alpha}) = 1 - \alpha$. This can be found numerically: Choose a grid of points $\{\theta_j, j = 1, \ldots, J\}$ and determine whether the condition $R_T(\widehat{\theta}_{\text{GMM}}, \theta_j) \leq w_{1-\alpha}$ is satisfied or not for each member of the grid.

5.4.4 Bootstrap Approach

1. Generate a sample of data $\{X_1^*, \ldots, X_T^*\}$ by the block bootstrap method.
2. Compute the GMM estimator $\widehat{\theta}^*$ with the bootstrap data, and compute $\sqrt{T}(\widehat{\theta}^* - \widehat{\theta})$.
3. Repeat S times and calculate the (empirical) distribution of $\sqrt{T}(\widehat{\theta}^* - \widehat{\theta})$ across replications.

Recomputing the GMM estimator for each new sample can be computationally demanding. However, one can use $\widehat{\theta}$ as starting values for any derivative-based algorithm, which should cut down the time. In fact, authors have suggested instead working with the two-step estimator or the influence function. That is, since

$$\sqrt{T}(\widehat{\theta} - \theta) = \frac{1}{\sqrt{T}} \sum_{t=1}^{T} \psi(X_t, \theta_0) + o_P(1),$$

and we can resample

$$\sqrt{T}(\widehat{\theta}^* - \widehat{\theta}) = \frac{1}{\sqrt{T}} \sum_{t=1}^{T} \psi(X_t^*, \widehat{\theta}) + o_{P^*}(1).$$

5.5 Summary

We have discussed the main approaches to conducting inference in situations characterized by dependence and heteroskedasticity. These include estimation of a long-run variance, self normalization, and different forms of the bootstrap. We considered a general class of estimation problems including linear regression and GMM.

The R language has the command `tsboot` to perform a variety of bootstrap resampling for time series, including model based, block bootstrap, and subsampling. Härdle, Horowitz, and Kreiss (2003) is a good reference for resampling methods. For long-run variance estimation, I recommend Parzen (1957).

5.6   Exercises

5.1 For the dataset GME, define $y_t = \log(V_t)$, where V_t is the daily trading volume. Calculate the sample mean of trading volume and provide a confidence interval for the population mean based on
   (a) i.i.d. standard errors
   (b) MDS standard errors
   (c) long-run variance estimation
   (d) self normalization
   (e) bootstrap.

5.2 Now divide the data by day of the week, so you have a Monday time series, a Tuesday time series, and so on. Test the hypothesis that the mean volume is the same for every day of the week based on
   (a) i.i.d. standard errors
   (b) MDS standard errors
   (c) long-run variance estimation
   (d) self normalization
   (e) bootstrap.

5.3 For the GME data, define $y_t = \log(V_t)$, where V_t is the daily trading volume. Fit an AR(5) model to this data and construct t-statistics for each coefficient using
   (a) i.i.d. (errors) standard errors
   (b) MDS (errors) standard errors.

5.4 Using the datasets `sp500stocks` and `sp500` calculate OLS estimates of market model parameters, where $R_t = \alpha + \beta R_{mt} + \varepsilon_t$ and $E(\varepsilon_t \mid R_{mt}) = 0$. You may take one stock to start with and extend. Discuss different methods of inference about the parameters α, β.

5.5 Suppose that $y_t = \phi_1 y_{t-1} + \phi_2 y_{t-2} + \varepsilon_t$, where ε_t is i.i.d. with mean zero and variance σ^2. Calculate the Fisher z-transform of the autocorrelation function
$$z(k) = \frac{1}{2} \log\left(\frac{1 + \rho(k)}{1 - \rho(k)}\right).$$
Derive the limiting distribution of
$$\widehat{z}(k) = \frac{1}{2} \log\left(\frac{1 + \widehat{\rho}(k)}{1 - \widehat{\rho}(k)}\right),$$
where $\widehat{\rho}(k)$ is the sample autocorrelation function, and use this to obtain a confidence interval for $\rho(k)$, $k = 1, 2, 3$.

5.6 Suppose that $y_t = \varepsilon_t - \theta\varepsilon_{t-1}$, where ε_t is i.i.d. with mean zero and variance σ^2, and $|\theta| < 1$. Define a bootstrap algorithm for inference about the parameter θ. Compare the numerical performance of this algorithm with the performance of the asymptotic approach.

5.7 Suppose that $y_t = (y_{1t}, y_{2t})^\mathsf{T}$ is a bivariate stationary and mixing process with $E(y_t) = \mu = (\mu_1, \mu_2)^\mathsf{T}$ and suppose that the component processes are mutually independent with autocovariance functions $\gamma_1(\cdot)$ and $\gamma_2(\cdot)$.

(a) Show how to test the hypothesis that $\mu_1 = \mu_2$ versus $\mu_1 \neq \mu_2$.

(b) Show how to test the hypothesis that $\mu_1 = \mu_2 = 0$ versus the general alternative.

(c) Show how to test the hypothesis that $\mu_1/\sigma_1 = \mu_2/\sigma_2$ versus the general alternative, where $\sigma_j^2 = \gamma_j(0)$. In your answer, discuss several alternative ways of doing this.

5.8 Suppose that y_t is a stationary process, and define

$$y_t = \beta_0 + \beta_1 y_{t-1} + \cdots + \beta_k y_{t-k} + \varepsilon_t,$$

where $E(\varepsilon_t) = 0$ and $E(\varepsilon_t y_{t-j}) = 0$ for $j = 1, \ldots, k$. Let $\beta = (\beta_0, \beta_1, \ldots, \beta_k)^\mathsf{T}$ and $\widehat{\beta} = (\widehat{\beta}_0, \widehat{\beta}_1, \ldots, \widehat{\beta}_k)^\mathsf{T}$, and let $\widehat{\pi}(k) = \widehat{\beta}_k$ be the partial autocorrelation of order k. Explain how to construct confidence intervals for $\pi(k) = \beta_k$ when:

(a) y_t is i.i.d.

(b) ε_t is an MDS

(c) ε_t is only restricted by the unconditional moment restrictions and so may be autocorrelated.

5.9 Suppose that $y_t = \frac{1}{2} y_{t-1} + \varepsilon_t$, where $\varepsilon_t \sim N(0, 3/4)$ so that y_t is a stationary process with marginal distribution $N(0, 1)$. Suppose that we observe $\{y_1, y_2, y_3, y_4\}$. Let $\bar{y} = (y_1 + y_2 + y_3 + y_4)/4$.

(a) Consider the block bootstrap method with $b = 2$, that is, we resample the blocks $\{y_1, y_2\}$ and $\{y_3, y_4\}$ with replacement. What are the possible samples one can get? What are the possible values of $\bar{y}^*$ one can get and what are their relative frequencies (i.e., their distribution conditional on the data)?

(b) Consider the subsampling method with $b = 2$. What are the possible samples one can get? What are the possible values of $\bar{y}^*$ one can get and what are their relative frequencies (i.e., their distribution conditional on the data)?

(c) Calculate analytically $\mathrm{var}(\bar{y})$ and $\mathrm{var}(\bar{y}^* \mid y_1, y_2, y_3, y_4)$ for the two resampling procedures.

5.10 For the dataset PCE let $y_t = \log(\mathrm{PCE}_t) - \log(\mathrm{PCE}_{t-1})$ be the growth rate of consumption. Estimate the mean value of this series by the sample average. Construct a confidence interval for the population mean value using the subsampling method.

5.11 For the dataset PCE let $y_t = \log(\mathrm{PCE}_t) - \log(\mathrm{PCE}_{t-1})$ be the growth rate of consumption. Estimate the partial autocorrelation $\pi(k)$ by fitting the linear regression

$$y_t = \alpha_k + \beta_{k,1} y_{t-1} + \cdots + \beta_{k,k} y_{t-k} + e_{t,k}$$

and let $\widehat{\pi}(k) = \widehat{\beta}_{k,k}$. Describe how you would construct inference about $\pi(k)$ under different assumptions using asymptotic theory, self normalization, or resampling methods.

5.12 Suppose that we consider the following model for quarterly PCE and GDP:

$$\Delta \log \text{PCE}_t = \alpha + \beta \Delta \log \text{GDP}_t + u_t,$$

where u_t is a stationary and mixing error process. Using the data from USGDPQSA and PCE, construct a confidence interval for the parameter β using the OLS estimator and three different methods.

6   Nonstationary Processes, Trends, and Seasonality

In this chapter we consider different approaches to modelling nonstationarity and seasonality, and to providing tests about their presence or absence. Some datasets cover a very long span of time, for example the FRED CPI series goes back to 1913, and the level of this series has increased substantially over time as have many macroeconomics series like GDP, industrial production, and the level of exports and imports. Climate change is nowadays a fashionable topic and many methodologies have been deployed to determine the rate of increase of global and local temperatures, as well as the variability around that projected increase. The main approaches can be grouped around deterministic and stochastic components, and we present both types of analysis.

6.1   Ad Hoc Practical Approaches

A common, but crude, way of handling potential nonstationarity is to divide the sample into subperiods and to assume stationarity within subperiods but allow for variation across subperiods. For example, we may suppose that

$$A^{(j)}(L)y_t = \alpha^{(j)} + B^{(j)}(L)\varepsilon_t^{(j)} \tag{6.1}$$

for $t \in I_j$ and $j = 1, \ldots, J$. The mathematical assumption here is that the number T_j of observations in each subperiod I_j is large, that is, $T_j \to \infty$, but that the number of subperiods J is fixed. Within each subperiod the process is a stationary ARMA(p, q) process with its own mean, error variance, and dynamic parameters, but these parameters are allowed to change from subperiod to subperiod in a free way. For example, one may divide the 107-year period from 1913 to 2020 into 11 subperiods of length 10 years (with the last period or the first period a bit shorter in this case), or one may choose 22 periods of length 5 years.

A common application is to test whether a series is uncorrelated. In this case, the null hypothesis is that the process has means $\mu^{(j)}$ and variances $\sigma^{2(j)}$, $j = 1, \ldots, J$, which are allowed to vary across subperiod, whereas for all subperiods $A^{(j)}(L), B^{(j)}(L) = 0$. This allows the null hypothesis to be more general than assuming a constant mean and variance throughout the whole data series. Another nice feature of this framework is that estimates of the parameters $\vartheta^{(j)}$ are asymptotically independent of estimates of the parameters $\vartheta^{(k)}$ for $j \neq k$. This means, for example, that if a test statistic from period j, $\tau^{(j)}$, is asymptotically standard normal, then $\tau = \sum_{j=1}^{J} \tau^{(j)}$ is asymptotically $N(0, J)$. If

Table 6.1 Rolling window Box–Pierce statistic for daily S&P500 stock returns.

Period	T	m	s	Q_5	VR_5
1926–1929	1037	0.0482	1.2161	193.9802	0.9060
1930–1939	2988	0.0128	1.7513	9.5884	1.0868
1940–1949	2918	0.0329	0.7962	95.3058	1.1964
1950–1959	2598	0.0597	0.6329	78.3424	1.0984
1960–1969	2489	0.0186	0.6252	119.9787	1.3704
1970–1979	2526	0.0023	0.8371	212.5605	1.5056
1980–1989	2528	0.0324	0.9654	57.3417	1.1576
1990–1999	2528	0.0500	0.8399	21.4128	1.0979
2000–2009	2515	−0.0027	1.4050	34.4606	0.8329
2010–2020	2727	0.0530	1.1283	93.6373	0.8462
1926–2020	24 854	0.0297	1.0785	88.0338	1.0552

$\tau^{(j)}$ is asymptotically chi-squared p_j, then τ is asymptotically chi-squared with degrees of freedom $\sum_{j=1}^{J} p_j$.

We illustrate these principles on the daily Fama–French market factor (the market stock return minus the risk-free rate) over the period 1927–2020. In Table 6.1 we show the mean, standard deviation, Q_5 statistic, and VR_t statistic for different subperiods. The critical values for $Q_5 = T\sum_{k=1}^{5} \widehat{\rho}(k)^2 \sim \chi^2(5)$, where $\chi^2_{0.95}(5) = 11.07$, while the sum over 10 decades $\sum_{j=1}^{10} Q_5^{(j)} \sim \chi^2(50)$, where $\chi^2_{0.95}(50) = 67.51$. Most decades have significant departures from the null, and in the full sample this statistic is strongly significant; the aggregation of the subperiods yields even stronger significance. The variance ratio statistic is sometimes above one and sometimes below one, indicating a change in the direction of predictability across subsamples.

This approach is often taken without explicitly spelling out what the model is, perhaps for the good reason that it is a little implausible that the parameters change values exactly on the dates chosen by the classification into subperiods. A lot of work has been done on the more general setting where the subperiods I_j themselves are unknown and are to be determined from the data. This structural change literature is discussed below. Another approach is to allow the parameters $\vartheta^{(j)}$ to vary smoothly rather than abruptly; this framework is now widely associated with the term "local stationarity," discussed below. An informal approach consistent with that setting is to use a **rolling window**, where we choose the window size N smaller than the sample size. The first window has observations $1, \dots, N$, the second window has observations $2, \dots, N+1$, and so on to the last window observations at $T - N + 1, \dots, T$.

In Figure 6.1 we show the 10-year rolling window Q_5 statistics for the Fama–French market factor excess return. It seems hard to argue that market efficiency has improved over time based on this. The degree of short-term predictability seems to go up and down and up and down rather than following a secular improvement to EMH heaven. This methodology allows for smooth variation in the mean return and variance of return, that is, the risk premium is allowed to vary over time in a general way but without attaching the driving forces of that change.

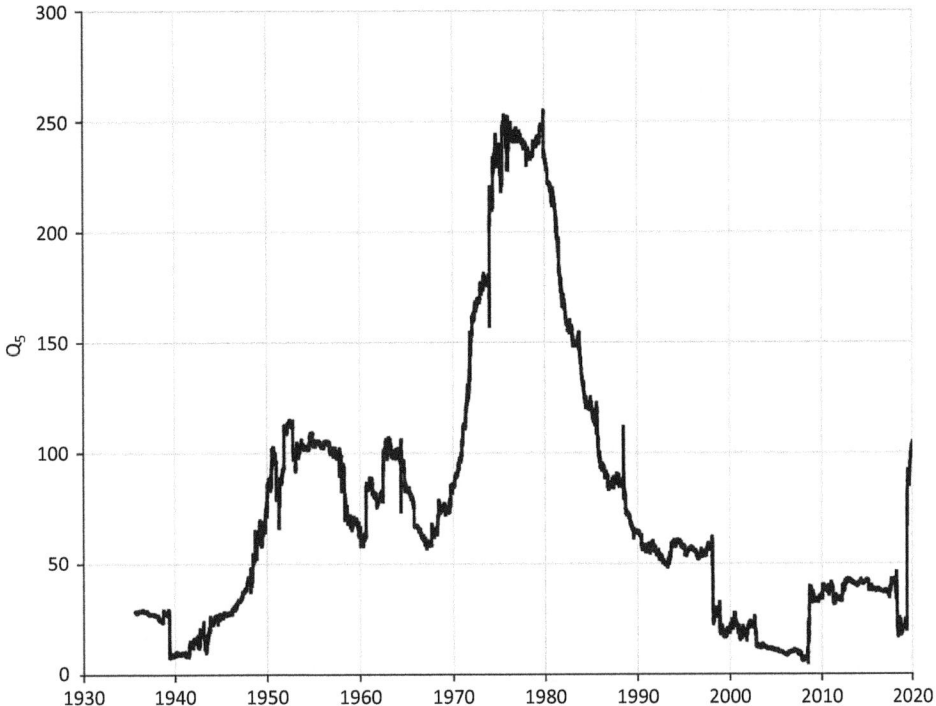

Figure 6.1 Rolling window Box–Pierce statistic for market factor excess return.

6.2   Deterministic Trend Models

There are two general philosophies in trend modelling, the "stochastic process approach" and the "deterministic approach." We first consider the deterministic approach based on parametric models or nonparametric models.

6.2.1   Polynomial Trend Models

Consider the process

$$y_t = \beta_0 + \beta_1 t + \cdots + \beta_p t^p + u_t = Q_p(t; \beta) + u_t, \tag{6.2}$$

where $\beta = (\beta_0, \beta_1, \ldots, \beta_p)^\mathsf{T}$, p is an integer, and Q_p is a pth-order polynomial, while $\{u_t\}$ is a stationary mean-zero process, for example

$$A(L)u_t = B(L)\varepsilon_t, \tag{6.3}$$

where the polynomials A and B satisfy the usual conditions required for stationarity and invertibility. This is a trend + stationary decomposition, where the trend is called a strong trend or a global trend and is captured by the polynomial Q_p in time. Specifically, we have $Q_p(t) \to \pm\infty$ (depending on the sign of β_p) as $t \to \infty$. In this model, the shocks u_t are transitory – they last for some period of time and then are forgotten as y_t returns to the deterministic trend. A traditional example is gross national product (GNP), which we may suppose grows at 3% per year (on average) for happily ever after. The linear case $p = 1$ is the most commonly employed, although quadratic and higher trends are also sometimes used. An alternative (and more general) class of models allows the dynamics to enter through y, for example $C(L)y_t = Q_p(t, \beta) + u_t$; you are asked to compare this class of models in the exercises. Under the model (6.2) and (6.3) we have

$$E(y_t) = \beta_0 + \beta_1 t + \cdots + \beta_p t^p, \qquad \text{var}(y_t) = \sigma_u^2$$

for all t. The lack of stationarity comes only through the mean, but that is only because we have only defined a mean effect. More generally, suppose that $y_t = \alpha + \beta t + \sqrt{\omega + \gamma t}\varepsilon_t$, where ε_t is i.i.d., which has $E(y_t) = \alpha + \beta t$ and $\text{var}(y_t) = (\omega + \gamma t)\sigma_\varepsilon^2$. In this case, both mean and variance go to infinity with t (and at the same linear rate as the unit root process, see below). Polynomial trend functions are very smooth in t (thinking of t as real valued) and so reflect the properties of sluggishly varying time series such as climate and macroeconomy. However, for higher-order p, the explosion as $t \to \infty$ may be too extreme.

In models (6.2) and (6.3) we have, for all $s > 0$, $\text{cov}(y_t, y_{t-s}) = \text{cov}(u_t, u_{t-s})$. In the case where u_t are i.i.d., this autocovariance is exactly zero at all lags, which is different from the unit root process discussed below. Although the theoretical covariance is zero for all lags, this assumes that the time-varying mean is used. Suppose we calculate the sample covariance in the usual way with the global sample mean. We have $\bar{y} = \sum_{t=1}^{T} t/T = (T+1)/2$. First, we divide through the observations by T, that is, replace t by t/T. Then we have

$$\hat{\gamma}(k) = \frac{1}{T} \sum_{t=1}^{T} (y_t - \bar{y})(y_{t-k} - \bar{y}) \to \int_0^1 (u - 0.5)^2 \, du > 0,$$

and the sample autocorrelation of y_t is approximately one for all finite lags k.

Estimation of the parameters β and inference about them is straightforward. The main difference from the standard regression setting is that although the CLT applies, the rate of convergence may be different from usual. The theory follows lines developed in Grenander (1954) that include even more generality regarding the regressors. Let X be the $T \times (p + 1)$ matrix containing a column of ones and columns containing the powers of t. We have

$$X^T X = \begin{pmatrix} T & \sum_{t=1}^{T} t & \cdots & \sum_{t=1}^{T} t^p \\ & \sum_{t=1}^{T} t^2 & & \vdots \\ & & \ddots & \\ & & & \sum_{t=1}^{T} t^{2p} \end{pmatrix}.$$

A typical element of this matrix is $\sum_{t=1}^{T} t^{i+j}$, which is of order (grows like) T^{i+j+1}; for example, $\sum_{t=1}^{T} t = T(T+1)/2$ and $\sum_{t=1}^{T} t^2 = T(T+1)(2T+1)/6$. Therefore, $X^T X/T$ does not converge to a positive-definite limit. Instead, we must normalize by a more general diagonal matrix. Let $\Delta = \text{diag}(T, T^3, \ldots, T^{p+1})$ be the $p+1 \times p+1$ matrix of normalizers. Then we have

$$\lim_{T \to \infty} \Delta^{-1/2} X^T X \Delta^{-1/2} = M, \tag{6.4}$$

where M is a positive-definite matrix. Let $\widehat{\beta} = (X^T X)^{-1} X^T y$, where $y = (y_1, \ldots, y_T)$, let $\widehat{T}_t = x_t^T \widehat{\beta} = (1, t, \ldots, t^p)\widehat{\beta}$ be the fitted trend, and let $\widehat{u}_t = y_t - \widehat{T}_t$ be the detrended data (aka OLS residuals).

We first treat the case where $u_t = \varepsilon_t$ in (6.2) is i.i.d. with mean zero and variance σ^2. In that case, $\Delta^{-1/2} X^T \varepsilon$ satisfies a CLT (Grenander, 1954). In particular, it follows that

$$\Delta^{1/2}(\widehat{\beta} - \beta) \Longrightarrow N(0, \sigma^2 M^{-1}), \tag{6.5}$$

where $\beta = (\beta_0, \beta_1, \ldots, \beta_p)^T$ and $\widehat{\beta} = (\widehat{\beta}_0, \widehat{\beta}_1, \ldots, \widehat{\beta}_p)^T$. We also have, for any fixed t,

$$\sigma^{-1/2}\left(x_t^T \left(X^T X\right)^{-1} x_t\right)^{-1/2}(\widehat{T}_t - T_t) \Longrightarrow N(0, 1);$$

although the trend error is dominated by the largest component, the intercept estimation and so $\widehat{T}_t - T_t$ is of order $T^{-1/2}$ in probability.

Inference procedures such as t-statistics and Wald statistics are exactly as in standard linear regression and do not usually need to take account of the rate of convergence. For example, under the null hypothesis that $R\beta = r$ we have

$$W = \widehat{\sigma}^{-2}(R\widehat{\beta} - r)^T X^T X(R\widehat{\beta} - r) \Longrightarrow \chi_q^2, \tag{6.6}$$

where $\widehat{\sigma}^2 = \sum_{t=1}^T \widehat{u}_t^2 / T$. We may test $\beta_1 = \cdots = \beta_p = 0$. Another application is to provide a model-based confidence interval for the trend realization. For example,

$$\widehat{T}_t \pm z_{\alpha/2} \widehat{\sigma}\left(x_t^T \left(X^T X\right)^{-1} x_t\right)^{1/2} \tag{6.7}$$

is an asymptotically valid $1 - \alpha$ pointwise confidence band for the trend function T_t. In the case where ε_t is serially correlated, we may replace the short-run variance estimator by a long-run variance.

For interpretation and further understanding we investigate the limiting variance in the quadratic special case.

Example 6.1 Suppose that $x_t^T = (1, t, t^2)$. Then

$$\lim_{T \to \infty} \begin{pmatrix} T^{-1/2} & 0 & 0 \\ 0 & T^{-3/2} & 0 \\ 0 & 0 & T^{-5/2} \end{pmatrix} X^T X \begin{pmatrix} T^{-1/2} & 0 & 0 \\ 0 & T^{-3/2} & 0 \\ 0 & 0 & T^{-5/2} \end{pmatrix}$$

$$= \begin{pmatrix} 1 & 1/2 & 1/3 \\ 1/2 & 1/3 & 1/4 \\ 1/3 & 1/4 & 1/5 \end{pmatrix} = M,$$

which has inverse

$$M^{-1} = \begin{pmatrix} 9 & -36 & 30 \\ -36 & 192 & -180 \\ 30 & -180 & 180 \end{pmatrix}.$$

The parameter estimates are mutually correlated and the inverse matrix has quite large elements, although these are offset by the large sample size scaling. In this case, the standard errors for the parameters β are

$$\widehat{\sigma}\left(\sqrt{\frac{9}{T}}, \sqrt{\frac{192}{T^3}}, \sqrt{\frac{180}{T^5}}\right),$$

where $\widehat{\sigma}^2$ is the usual residual-based variance estimator. We may use this to construct confidence intervals for the individual parameter. We may want to test the null hypothesis that there is no trend, that is, $\beta_1 = \beta_2 = 0$. The Wald statistic is then equivalent to

$$\left(\sqrt{T^3}\widehat{\beta}_1, \sqrt{T^5}\widehat{\beta}_2\right)\widehat{\sigma}^{-2}\begin{pmatrix} 1/3 & 1/4 \\ 1/4 & 1/5 \end{pmatrix}\left(\sqrt{T^3}\widehat{\beta}_1, \sqrt{T^5}\widehat{\beta}_2\right)^{\mathsf{T}}$$

$$= \widehat{\sigma}^{-2}\left(\frac{1}{3}T^3\widehat{\beta}_1^2 + \frac{1}{2}T^4\widehat{\beta}_1\widehat{\beta}_2 + \frac{1}{5}T^5\widehat{\beta}_2^2\right).$$

This should be compared with the critical value from a χ_2^2 distribution.

We now consider the full model (6.2) with the stationary error process, in which case something remarkable happens. We note that

$$\mathrm{var}(\widehat{\beta}) = \left(X^{\mathsf{T}}X\right)^{-1}\left(X^{\mathsf{T}}\Gamma_T X\right)\left(X^{\mathsf{T}}X\right)^{-1},$$

where Γ_T is the $T \times T$ covariance matrix of the errors u. By Amemiya (1985, Theorem 6.1.1),

$$\left(X^{\mathsf{T}}X\right)^{-1}\left(X^{\mathsf{T}}\Gamma_T X\right)\left(X^{\mathsf{T}}X\right)^{-1} \simeq \left(X^{\mathsf{T}}\Gamma_T^{-1}X\right)^{-1}, \tag{6.8}$$

that is, for this class of models OLS and GLS share the same asymptotic distribution. This follows because for any Toeplitz matrix Γ_T we have $\Gamma_T X \simeq XB$ for a nonsingular matrix B. The rate of convergence is the same as in the i.i.d. error case, provided

$$\lim_{T\to\infty}\Delta^{-1/2}X^{\mathsf{T}}\Gamma_T^{-1}X\Delta^{-1/2} = M_*$$

for some positive-definite matrix M_*. Under the conditions of Herrndorf, we have $\Delta\left(\widehat{\beta} - \beta\right) \Longrightarrow N(0, M_*^{-1})$.

To carry out inference we need to consistently estimate the asymptotic variance. There are two approaches to this. If one has an ARMA model for u_t, then one can estimate the parameters thereof and substitute in the estimated value of Γ_T^{-1}. Alternatively, one can use Newey–West standard errors that approximate $\left(X^{\mathsf{T}}\Gamma_T X\right)$ nonparametrically. How does trend affect long-run variance calculations? Suppose that u_t is a stationary mixing process. Then

$$\mathrm{var}\left(\sum_{t=1}^{T} t^p u_t\right)$$

$$= T^{2p+1}\mathrm{var}\left(\frac{1}{\sqrt{T}}\sum_{t=1}^{T}\left(\frac{t}{T}\right)^p u_t\right)$$

$$= T^{2p+1}\left(\frac{1}{T}\sum_{t=1}^{T}\left(\frac{t}{T}\right)^{2p}\mathrm{var}(u_t) + \frac{1}{T}\sum\sum_{t\neq s}\left(\frac{t}{T}\right)^p\left(\frac{s}{T}\right)^p\mathrm{cov}(u_t, u_s)\right)$$

$$\simeq T^{2p+1}\left(\gamma_u(0)\int_0^1 u^{2p}\,\mathrm{d}u + \frac{1}{T}\sum_{t=1}^{T-1}\sum_k\left(\frac{t}{T}\right)^p\left(\frac{t+k}{T}\right)^p\gamma_u(k)\right)$$

$$\simeq T^{2p+1} \left(\gamma_u(0) \int_0^1 u^{2p} \, du + \frac{1}{T} \sum_t \left(\frac{t}{T} \right)^{2p} \sum_k \gamma_u(k) \right)$$

$$\simeq T^{2p+1} \int_0^1 u^{2p} \, du \left(\gamma_u(0) + 2 \sum_{k=1}^{\infty} \gamma_u(k) \right).$$

More generally, if the error process possesses both heteroskedasticity and autocorrelation (with weak dependence), then we are still able to justify inference procedures based on estimating the matrix $X^{\mathsf{T}} \Gamma_T X$.

In the presence of trending heteroskedasticity, some of the above theory may break down. Specifically, suppose that $\text{var}(y_t) = \gamma_0 + \gamma_1 t + \cdots + \gamma_p t^p$, that is, the variance trends at the same rate as the mean. In this case, we have consistency and asymptotic normality for the highest-order polynomial coefficient but at a slower rate, that is, the variance of $\widehat{\beta}_p$ is of order $T^{3p+1}/T^{4p+2} = T^{-(p+1)}$. For example, with a linear trend in mean and linear variance trend, we have rate of convergence T rather than $T^{3/2}$, which is exactly as in the unit root case. On the other hand, the intercept and more generally the slopes on lower-order mean terms are not consistently estimable.

6.2.1.1 Filtering

Consider the filtered series $x_t = \sum_{j=-n}^n w_j y_{t+j}$ for some $n \geq 1$ and some weighting sequence $\{w_j\}$. Provided

$$\sum_{j=-n}^n w_j = 1, \ \sum_{j=-n}^n w_j j = 0, \ldots, \ \sum_{j=-n}^n w_j j^p = 0,$$

the filtered series satisfies

$$x_t = \beta_0 + \beta_1 t + \cdots + \beta_p t^p + \sum_{j=-n}^n w_j u_{t+j}$$

for any values of the parameters $\beta_0, \beta_1, \ldots, \beta_p$. If u_t were i.i.d., then $\text{var}(x_t) = \sigma_u^2 \sum_{j=-n}^n w_j^2$. For example, if $w_j = 1/(2n+1)$, then $\sum_{j=-n}^n w_j = 1$, $\sum_{j=-n}^n w_j j = 0$, and $\text{var}(x_t) = \sigma_u^2/(2n+1)$. The SMA filter returns the exact linear trend with less noise, which sounds a bit like estimation! The detrended series can be constructed as $y_t - x_t = \sum_{j=-n}^n \widetilde{w}_j u_{t+j}$ with $\widetilde{w}_0 = 1 - w_0$ and $\widetilde{w}_j = -w_j$ otherwise. An alternative way of detrending is to use the differencing filter $\Delta^p y_t$. In the trend-stationary $p = 1$ case we have $\Delta y_t = \beta_1 + u_t - u_{t-1}$, and the error term has a unit root MA structure, assuming it was i.i.d. in the first place. So although differencing apparently eliminates the nonstationarity in the mean, it induces noninvertibility in the error term. We may estimate β_1 by the sample mean of the differenced series; this will converge at rate T to the true value but with a nonstandard limit distribution.

6.2.1.2 More General Parametric Trends

The polynomial trend is strong, and some authors have suggested alternative, weaker, trends. Phillips and Sun (2003) considered trend regressions with nonstandard terms such as $\log(t)$ and $t^{-1/2}$ (evaporating trends), for which the distribution theory may become

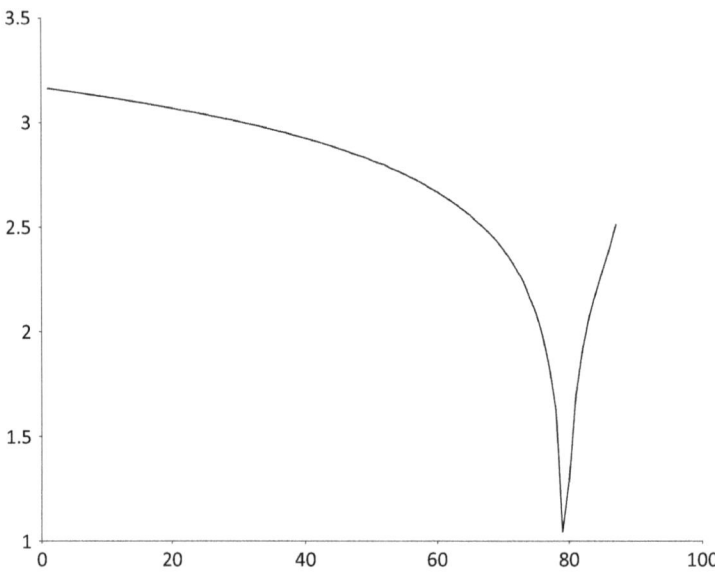

Figure 6.2 Sornette's nonlinear crash model.

more complicated. Sornette (2017) suggested the class of nonlinear "crash" models with

$$g(t) = a + b(t_* - t)^\theta + (t_* - t)^\theta \left(\gamma_1 \cos \left(\omega \log \left(t_* - t \right) \right) + \gamma_2 \sin \left(\omega \log \left(t_* - t \right) \right) \right)$$

for $t \leq t_*$, where t_* is a critical time point representing a market crash, θ is a parameter that describes the shape of the crash, and the term involving $\gamma_1, \gamma_2, \omega$ builds in a periodic cycle around the crash, "aftershocks" as he called it. Typically, $a > 0$, $b < 0$, and $0 < \theta < 1$. In the special case with $\gamma_1 = \gamma_2 = 0$ we just have a nonlinear trend model. For given t_*, θ we have a linear regression and can find the parameters a, b by linear regression using data up to time t_*. The parameter θ is then found by grid search of the profiled least squares objective function using the sample of data $\{1, \ldots, t_*\}$. The quantity t_* is found by comparing the fits over different such choices. In Figure 6.2 we show an example of a trajectory from such a model showing the acceleration into the catastrophe and the recovery period without log periodic oscillations.

6.2.2 Nonparametric Trend Fitting

A general method for trend estimation is based on the linear filter (also known as the SMA),

$$\widehat{T}_t = \sum_{j=-n}^{n} w_j y_{t-j} = w(L)y_t, \tag{6.9}$$

where $w(L) = w_{-n}L^{-n} + \cdots + w_n L^n$, and w_j are weights that sum to one. For example, $w_j = 1/(2n+1)$ is two-sided equal weighting; $w_j = 1(j \leq 0)/(n+1)$ is one-sided equal

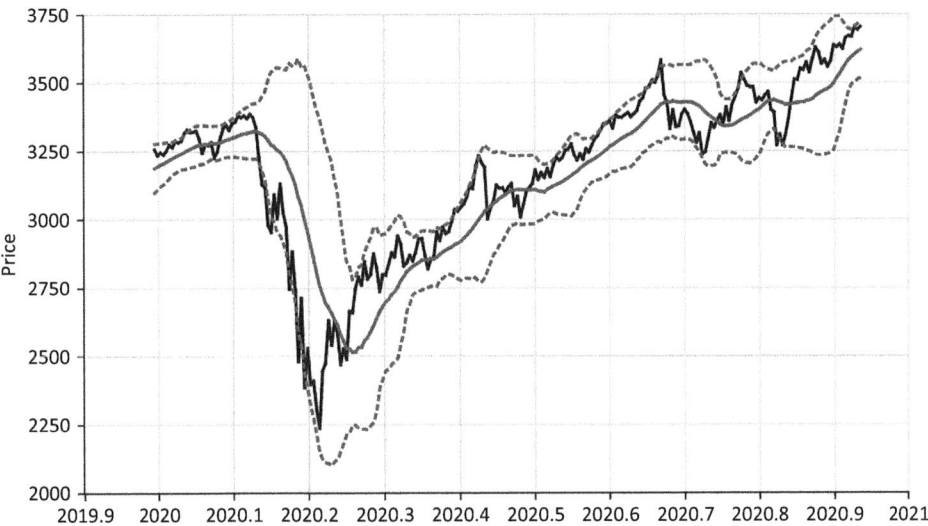

Figure 6.3 Bollinger bands for 2020.

weighting. This also includes polynomial trend fitting to a certain extent.[1] The thinking behind this is to eliminate short-run fluctuations that have more to do with noise. During the COVID-19 pandemic common practice was to report the seven-day one-sided moving average to eliminate the short-run variation in the new case numbers, and in particular eliminating the day-of-the-week effect. In trading, the so-called Bollinger bands involve an ($n = 20$)-day one-sided moving average of price level (combined with a pseudo-confidence band based on the standard deviation of the deviations of the fitted trend from the actual price within the 20-day period). The idea is that if the actual price escapes from the bands on the downside, this is a buy signal, whereas if the price escapes from the band on the upside, this is a sell signal. In Figure 6.3 we show how this works for the S&P500 during 2020. This idea is still in the vocabulary of traders and features in various "professional" syllabi; a trademark was granted in 2011. The properties of linear filters are well understood when the underlying process is stationary, as discussed in Chapter 4, and a lot of intuition is obtained from this analysis. We next analyze this type of trend estimator under a nonparametric trend model that captures some of the motivation for taking these weighted averages.

In the nonparametric literature the SMA can be interpreted as a linear regression smoother, in fact a very special case of a class of procedures designed to estimate a trend regression function under only smoothness conditions. Suppose that

$$y_t = g\left(\frac{t}{T^\varkappa}\right) + \sigma\left(\frac{t}{T^\varkappa}\right)\varepsilon_t, \quad t = 1, \ldots, T, \tag{6.10}$$

where $g(\cdot)$ and $\sigma(\cdot)$ are smooth but unknown functions. The parameter $\varkappa \in (0, 1]$ is usually set equal to one, in which case g, σ are defined on $[0, 1]$, but if $\varkappa < 1$ then these

---

[1] For example, suppose we fit a no-intercept linear trend: we have $\widehat{T}_t = \sum_{j=1}^T w_{tj}y_j$ with $w_{tj} = t \times j / \sum_{j=1}^T j^2$ (here the weighting varies with the time point).

functions can be defined on the positive real line. The rescaled time $(t/T^{\varkappa})$ here leads to a triangular array structure that is used to develop asymptotic approximations, and that is used elsewhere in the structural break and weak instruments literatures. The error process ε_t we may assume is a general stationary and mixing process and represents the short-term fluctuations of the series. This model allows for a general functional form for the trend but with a limitation that in the usual $\varkappa = 1$ case the smoothness property implies that the trend function $g(\cdot)$ (which is the "parameter of interest" here) is bounded, unlike, say, in the global polynomial trend model; we may call the trend a local trend or a weak trend in view of this. In practice, any estimated trend is bounded on the support of the data, and the difference arises in terms of the extrapolation outside of the data; a polynomial trend model will imply rapid growth to plus or minus infinity, whereas the nonparametric model only allows intermediate-term extrapolation and cannot say where the function g will go far outside of the data support. This is probably a more accurate reflection of the limitation of human knowledge in most cases. Nevertheless, if, say, $\varkappa = 1/2$, the function g can be defined on $\mathbb{R}_+$ and we have a combination of long-span (global trend) and infill (local trend) asymptotics so that the trend function can be unbounded; implicitly, this asymptotic framework was considered in Bandi and Phillips (2003). We mainly focus on the case $\varkappa = 1$ in the following.

The kernel smoother of $g(u)$, $u \in [0, 1]$, is defined as

$$\widehat{g}(u) = \frac{\sum_{t=1}^{T} K\left((u - t/T)/h\right) y_t}{\sum_{t=1}^{T} K\left((u - t/T)/h\right)}, \tag{6.11}$$

where $h = h(T)$ is a bandwidth sequence and K is a continuous function satisfying $\int K(s)\,ds = 1$, $\int sK(s)\,ds = 0$. Leading examples of kernels are:

Triangular (or Bartlett): $K(u) = 1 - |u|$ for $|u| \leq 1$ and $K(u) = 0$ otherwise.
Epanechnikov: $K(u) = 0.75(1 - u)^2$ for $|u| \leq 1$ and $K(u) = 0$ otherwise.
Gaussian: $K(u) = (1/\sqrt{2\pi}) \exp(-0.5u^2)$ for all $u \in \mathbb{R}$.
Double exponential: $K(u) = (1/2) \exp(-|u|)$ for all $u \in \mathbb{R}$.

These are all probability densities; the Epanechnikov kernel has compact support and has some optimality property. The Gaussian and exponential kernels have unbounded support and so give positive weight to all data observations, although given the rapid decay rate of the Gaussian and exponential densities the difference in practice relative to a compactly supported density is not great. This estimator was introduced by Nadaraya (1964) and Watson (1964) for some general covariate process. Because the covariate here is time and is therefore equally spaced, the denominator does not vary with u, at least for $u \in (0, 1)$; we may instead write

$$\widehat{g}(u) = \frac{1}{Th} \sum_{t=1}^{T} K\left(\frac{u - t/T}{h}\right) y_t = \sum_{t=1}^{T} w_{Tt}(u) y_t, \tag{6.12}$$

where the weights $w_{Tt}(u)$, $t = 1, \ldots, T$, are deterministic and satisfy $\sum_{t=1}^{T} w_{Tt}(u) = 1$.

There is a well-established theoretical understanding of $\widehat{g}(u)$ as an estimator of $g(u)$ at $u \in (0, 1)$.

Theorem 6.1   *Suppose that g is twice continuously differentiable at $u \in (0,1)$ and σ^2 is continuous at $u \in (0,1)$. Suppose that ε_t is stationary and mixing, satisfying the Herrndorf conditions. Then, provided $h \to 0$ and $Th^5 \to c > 0$ (i.e., $h \propto T^{-1/5}$),*

$$\sqrt{Th}\,(\widehat{g}(u) - g(u)) \Longrightarrow N(b(u), v(u)) \tag{6.13}$$

with $b(u) = c^{1/2}g''(u)\mu_2(K)$ and $v(u) = \sigma^2(u) \times \mathrm{lrvar}(\varepsilon) \times \|K\|_2^2$, where $\mu_2(K) = \int K(s)s^2\,ds$ and $\|K\|_2^2 = \int K(s)^2\,ds$.

The estimator is consistent and asymptotically normal at the rate $T^{2/5}$, which is slower than the usual $T^{1/2}$ consistency of parametric estimators, reflecting the more ambitious goal of estimating effectively an infinite number of parameters (which translates into estimating the single quantity $g(u)$ but using only locally relevant information). This is the optimal rate under the smoothness conditions and delivers a **mean squared error** of order $T^{-4/5}$ containing both a squared bias term and a variance term. The error autocorrelation affects the asymptotic variance here in the same way as it affects estimation of the mean of a stationary process. Note that if g is a function of $t/T^\varkappa$ with $0 < \varkappa < 1$, the estimator is defined exactly the same and we still have consistency and the same limit theorem, provided only that we reflect the more sparse information by taking $T^\varkappa h^5 \to c$, in which case the rate of convergence in the CLT is the slower rate $T^{2\varkappa/5}$. If $\varkappa = 1/2$, the MSE is of order $T^{-2/5}$.

An optimal bandwidth can be explicitly determined by minimizing the asymptotic MSE with respect to c. The limiting MSE depends only on the unknown quantities $g''(u)$, $\sigma^2(u)$, and $\mathrm{lrvar}(\varepsilon)$, as well as on the weighting function effects, $\mu_2(K)$ and $\|K\|_2^2$. For the uniform kernel, $\mu_2(K) = 1/3$ and $\|K\|_2^2 = 1/2$; for the Epanechnikov kernel, $\mu_2(K) = 0.200$ and $\|K\|_2^2 = 0.600$; for the Gaussian kernel, $\mu_2(K) = 1$ and $\|K\|_2^2 = 0.282$; for the double exponential kernel, $\mu_2(K) = 2$ and $\|K\|_2^2 = 0.25$. The optimal bandwidth depends on all these quantities and varies with them so that different kernels lead to different bandwidths. Having accounted for that, we can compare the kernels according to their implied optimal MSE. The relative efficiency of the kernel can be measured by $\mathrm{Eff}(K) = (\|K\|_2^2)^2 \times \mu_2(K)$ (Fan and Gijbels, 1996). For the Epanechnikov, $\mathrm{Eff}(K) = 0.072$; for the Gaussian, $\mathrm{Eff}(K) = 0.0795$; and for the exponential, $\mathrm{Eff}(K) = 0.125$, so that according to this criterion the exponential kernel is quite significantly suboptimal, whereas the Gaussian is quite close to the optimal Epanechnikov weighting. One advantage of the Gaussian and exponential kernels is that the resulting estimates are infinitely differentiable in u everywhere, whereas for kernels on compact support the estimator usually has a finite number of derivatives – in the uniform case the estimator is not even continuous as a function of u, and in practice yields rather jumpy-looking pictures.

Confidence intervals for the trend at a point u may be constructed from this result. Usual practice is to ignore the bias and to estimate the asymptotic variance consistently. We may estimate $\sigma^2(u)$ by $\widehat{\sigma}^2(u) = \sum_{t=1}^{T} w_{Tt}(u)(y_t - \widehat{g}(t/T))^2$ or by $\widehat{\sigma}^2(u) = \sum_{t=1}^{T} w_{Tt}(u)y_t^2 - \widehat{g}(u)^2$ (Fan and Yao, 1998). Then apply a standard procedure for long-run variance estimation to the residuals $\widehat{\varepsilon}_t = (y_t - \widehat{g}(t/T))/\widehat{\sigma}(t/T)$, and then multiply by the known constant $\|K\|_2^2$ to give $\widehat{v}(u)$. Alternatively, one can apply long-run variance estimation to the weighted residuals $w_{Tt}\widehat{u}_t$ without separating the contributions of the

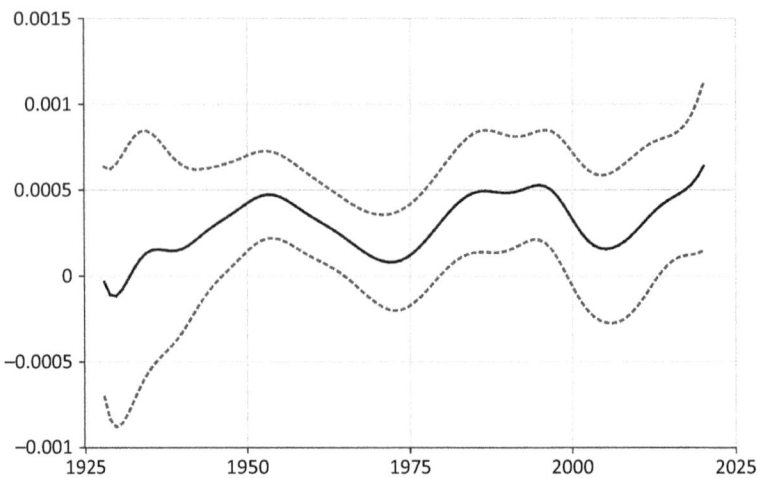

Figure 6.4 Conditional mean smooth of S&P500 daily returns on $x_t = t/T$.

time-varying variance and the autocorrelation. One can also apply self normalization, or resampling methods. Under some conditions we have that

$$I_\alpha(u) = \widehat{g}(u) \pm z_{\alpha/2} \sqrt{\frac{\widehat{v}(u)}{Th}} \qquad (6.14)$$

is a valid confidence interval for $g(u)$. In Figure 6.4 we show the trend of the S&P500 daily returns along with this pointwise 95% confidence interval. The Bollinger bands are usually constructed with a short-run variance rather than a long-run variance, which implicitly assumes that the faddy departures from the fundamental price are not serially correlated, which does not seem realistic. Li and Linton (2022) developed the ReMeDI method for estimating the autocorrelation function of serially correlated noise.

The equal-weighting two-sided linear filter (6.9) can be cast in this form with $K(s) = w(s) = 1/2$ for $s \in [-1, 1]$. This choice of weighting is optimal from the point of view of variance minimization but ignores the issue of bias. The optimal weighting on $[-1, 1]$ that minimizes the mean squared error is $w(s) = 0.75(1 - s^2)$ – the Epanechnikov kernel. The key assumption is smoothness of $g(\cdot)$, and with further smoothness we can improve the rate of convergence. The choice of bandwidth parameter h is key to implementation; various methods are available for this, such as plug-in or cross validation, although the time series dependence of the error term may complicate this.

The equal-weighting one-sided linear filter that is used in the Bollinger procedure can also be cast as a special case where the weighting function w is uniform on $[-1, 0]$. The EWMA smoother is equivalent to taking a one-sided exponential density $w(u) = \exp(-u)$, $u > 0$. From the point of view of estimation this would be suboptimal since the bias term is then of order h rather than h^2. However, from the point of view of prediction we do not have data on future outcomes so using one-sided weighting is inevitable. Nevertheless, one can obtain better theoretical properties for one-sided smoothers by using weights that are not uniform but take some negative values. Specifically, if w satisfies $\int_{-1}^{0} sw(s)\, du = 0$, then the estimator has a bias of order h^2 as for the two-sided smoother. For example, $w(s) = 4 + 6s$ and $w(s) = 3 - 6u^2$ both satisfy $\int w(s)\, ds = 1$

and $\int sw(s)\,ds = 0$. An alternative way of achieving "boundary bias" correction is to use the local linear fitting method (Fan and Gijbels, 1996).

Spline estimators are another popular methodology for trend fitting. The cubic spline estimator $\widehat{g}_\lambda$ is defined as the (unique) minimizer of

$$Q_\lambda(g) = \sum_{t=1}^{T}(y_t - g(t/T))^2 + \lambda \int \{g''(u)\}^2 \, du. \tag{6.15}$$

The spline $\widehat{g}_\lambda$ has the following properties: It is a cubic polynomial between two successive observations ordered by time; at the observation points, $\widehat{g}_\lambda(\cdot)$ and its first two derivatives are continuous; at the boundary of the observation interval the spline is linear. This characterization of the solution to (6.15) allows the integral term on the right-hand side to be replaced by a quadratic form, where the second derivative is replaced by the second difference operator $\Delta^2 = (1 - L)^2$, that is,

$$Q_\lambda(g) = \sum_{t=1}^{T}(y_t - g_t)^2 + \lambda \sum_{j=3}^{T}\{g_j - 2g_{j-1} + g_{j-2}\}^2 = (y - g)^\mathsf{T}(y - g) + \lambda g^\mathsf{T} D g,$$

where D is the $T \times T$ second difference matrix, which is tridiagonal (Eubank, 1988; Wahba, 1990). The objective function is in terms of the $T \times 1$ vector denoted $g = (g(1/T), \ldots, g(1))^\mathsf{T}$. Computation of the estimator proceeds by standard, although computationally intensive, matrix techniques, namely ridge regression. In particular, $\widehat{g} = (I + \lambda D)^{-1} y$. The smoothing parameter λ controls the degree of smoothness of the estimator $\widehat{g}_\lambda$. As $\lambda \to 0$, $\widehat{g}_\lambda$ interpolates the observations, while if $\lambda \to \infty$, $\widehat{g}_\lambda$ tends to a least squares regression line. Although $\widehat{g}_\lambda$ is linear in the y data (Härdle, 1990, 58–59), its dependency on the design and on the smoothing parameter is rather complicated. Spline estimation goes back to Whittaker (1922); he called it "graduation." Hodrick and Prescott (1997) applied this to macroeconomic data and since then, amongst macroeconomists, it has been called the HP filter.

The HP filter is currently widely used to detrend macro series. There are several issues with the common usage. First, using detrended and deseasonalized series may distort the relationship between them according to the "dynamic" view of time series, a point well made by Sims (1974). A second point is that the generated regressor nature of such series and the consequent effect on inference is not acknowledged sufficiently. If one interprets the detrending as fitting a nonparametric regression to the series first, any parametric fitting that is done on the residuals will generally be affected by the sampling variability associated with the nonparametric fitting. For example, suppose that $y_t = g(t/T) + \varepsilon_t$, where ε_t is a stationary and weakly dependent process with marginal CDF F and density function f. Let $\widehat{g}(u)$ be a linear smoother (for example, the kernel smoother) of $g(u)$, and let $\widehat{\varepsilon}_t = y_t - \widehat{g}(t/T)$. Define $\widehat{F}_T(e) = \frac{1}{T}\sum_{t=1}^{T} 1\,(\widehat{\varepsilon}_t \le e)$. Then it follows by complicated arguments that

$$\sqrt{T}(\widehat{F}_T(e) - F(e)) = \frac{1}{\sqrt{T}}\sum_{t=1}^{T}(1\,(\varepsilon_t \le e) - F(e)) + f(e)\frac{1}{\sqrt{T}}\sum_{t=1}^{T}\varepsilon_t + o_P(1).$$

If the errors ε_t were observed, then the second term on the right-hand side would not be present. This term represents the cost of the detrending; any inference procedure about

F that ignores this effect will be wrong. Of course, there are some parameters for which the effect of the initial estimation does not matter in large samples. For example, the estimation of the autocovariance function of ε_t is not affected in terms of the limiting distribution by preliminary estimation of the deterministic trend.

In some cases, one may be concerned about large values of the error terms that unduly influence the trend estimation. An alternative to mean smoothing is median or even quantile smoothing, where a running median is estimated. For example,

$$\widehat{\alpha} = \arg\min_{\alpha} \sum_{t=1}^{T} K\left(\frac{u - t/T}{h}\right) |y_t - \alpha|$$

is called the local median estimator. Under some conditions $\widehat{g}(u) = \widehat{\alpha}$ is consistent and asymptotically normal. The **Hampel filter** is a sort of compromise smoothing method that is designed to eliminate outliers. Let $\widehat{g}_k(t/T)$ denote the median value from the moving data window around the point t (formally, a local median estimator with uniform kernel containing k observations). Then let

$$x_t = \begin{cases} y_t & \text{if } |y_t - \widehat{g}_k(t/T)| < cs_k(t), \\ \widehat{g}_k(t/T) & \text{if } |y_t - \widehat{g}_k(t/T))| \geq cs_k(t), \end{cases}$$

where $s_k(t)$ is a robust scale measure from the moving data window around the point t, namely

$$s_k(t) = 1.4826 \times \text{median}\{|y_s - \widehat{g}_k(t/T)|, s \in [t - k, t + k]\}.$$

The factor 1.4826 makes the median absolute deviation scale estimate an unbiased estimate of the standard deviation for Gaussian data. The constant c is a personal choice; the larger c is, the more tolerant of outliers the procedure is.

6.2.2.1 Application

Li and Linton (2021) fitted global (and one local) quadratic regression models to the logarithm of new cases and new deaths from COVID-19 at the national level; that is, they considered the nonparametric and parametric models

$$\log(c_t) = m(t/T) + \varepsilon_t, \tag{6.16}$$

$$\log(c_t) = \alpha + \beta t + \gamma t^2 + \varepsilon_t, \tag{6.17}$$

where ε_t is a mean-zero error process and c_t is the number of new cases (plus one) or the number of new deaths (plus one). Provided $\gamma < 0$, the quadratic curve has a single peak at the point $t_{\max} = -\beta/2\gamma$, which was considered a quantity of interest. In the parametric case the entire sample $\{c_1, \ldots, c_T\}$ is used to estimate the parameters α, β, and γ, while in the nonparametric case a rolling window of observations $\{c_t, c_{t-1}, \ldots, c_{t-n}\}$, where n was 40, was used to estimate a quadratic approximation to $m(\cdot)$.

Note that $E(c_t) = \exp(\alpha + \beta t + \gamma t^2) E(\exp(\varepsilon_t))$, that is, unravelling the logarithmic transformation leads to a bias, albeit a bias that can easily be corrected for. Given estimates $\widehat{\alpha}$, $\widehat{\beta}$, and $\widehat{\gamma}$, we estimate $E(c_t)$ by

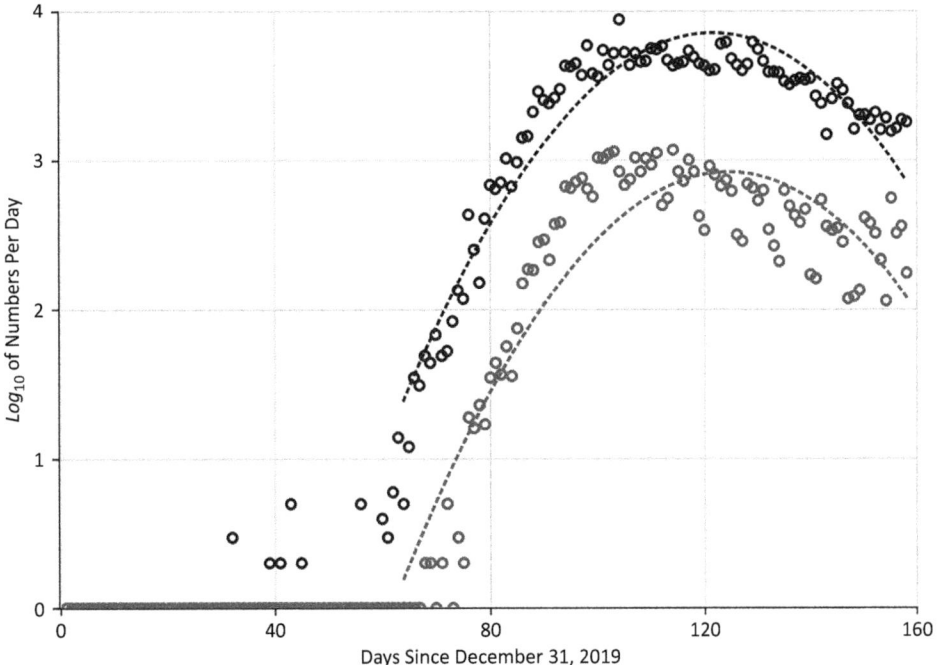

Figure 6.5 Daily logarithm of UK COVID-19 new cases (+ 1) and deaths (+ 1) along with the global quadratic trend.

$$\widehat{c}_t = \exp(\widehat{\alpha} + \widehat{\beta}t + \widehat{\gamma}t^2) \times \overbrace{\frac{1}{\#I} \sum_{s \in I} \exp(\widehat{\varepsilon}_s)}^{\text{bias adjustment}},$$

where the bias adjustment uses a sample average over either the full sample or the rolling window. In Figure 6.5 we show the results of this method applied to UK data in June 2020. We did a parallel analysis for the new daily deaths, which sits below the new daily cases in the figure.

6.2.3 Testing for Trend

We consider here how to test for a trend with the null hypothesis of no trend against the general alternative. The polynomial regression estimators considered above can be used to set up a Wald, LM, or LR test with the null hypothesis of $\beta_1 = \cdots = \beta_p = 0$ versus the general alternative. One can also use the nonparametric regression estimators to test whether $g(u)$ is constant with respect to u. Here, we mention some classic nonparametric approaches to testing for absence of trend.

The **Theil–Sen estimator** is based on computing the median of all pairwise slopes. Let $\widehat{b}_{ts} = (y_t - y_s)/(t - s)$ be the pairwise slopes for $t \neq s$. There are $T(T - 1)/2$ such pairwise slopes. Let $\widehat{b} = \text{median}\{\widehat{b}_{ts}\}$. This estimator is robust to a certain number of outliers in y_t. Peng, Wang, and Wang (2008) established the consistency and asymptotic

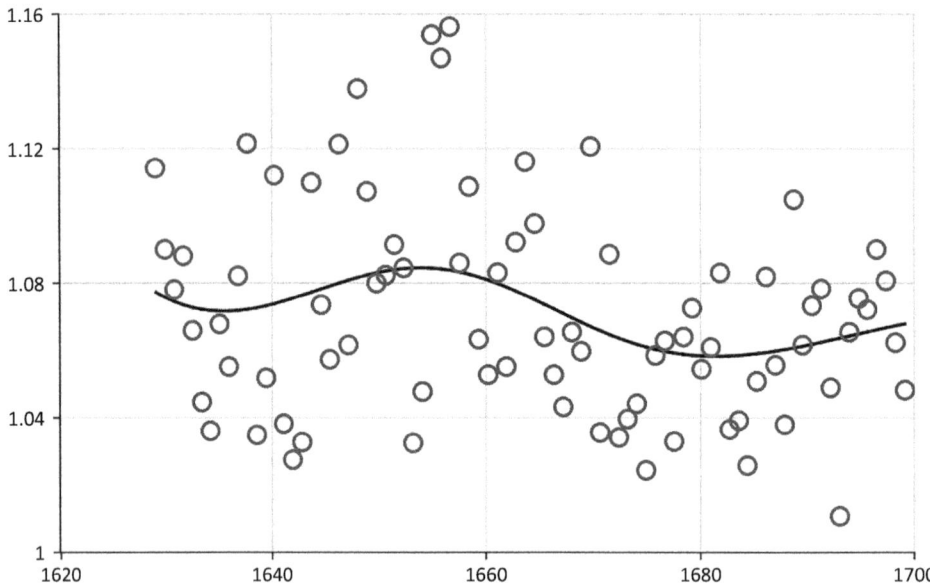

Figure 6.6 Local linear trend fitted with automatic bandwidth to Arbuthnot's sex ratio along with the raw data.

normality of the Theil–Sen (TS) estimator under linear regression with i.i.d. errors. They showed that

$$T^{3/2}\big(\widehat{b} - \beta\big) \Longrightarrow N\left(0, \frac{4}{\left(\int f^2(u)\,du\right)^2}\right),\tag{6.18}$$

where f is the density of the error (plus the intercept). In the normal case, $\int f^2(u)\,du = 1/2\sqrt{\pi}$, in which case the asymptotic variance of $\widehat{b}$ is approximately $16\pi/T^3$. For the Cauchy density, $\int f^2(u)\,du = 1/2\pi$, in which case the asymptotic variance of $\widehat{b}$ is approximately $16\pi^2/T^3$. The TS estimator converges at the usual $T^{3/2}$ rate in this case, unlike the OLS estimator, which converges at the rate T to a nonnormal distribution.

We apply this to the Arbuthnot sex ratio data and find $\widehat{b} = -0.00025$ with a 95% confidence interval of $[-0.01896, 0.01847]$. Some have argued that one can obtain a confidence interval from $\widehat{b}_{\alpha/2}, \widehat{b}_{1-\alpha/2}$, where $\widehat{b}_\alpha$ is the α-quantile of $\{\widehat{b}_{ts}\}$. This gives the interval $[-0.01398, 0.01157]$; the values of $\widehat{b}_{ts}$ vary from -0.087 to $+0.106$. By comparison, the OLS estimator of the ratio on a time trend is -0.000300, with a standard error of 0.000143. The OLS procedure seems to detect a downward trend with mild confidence, whereas the TS estimator says this is not significant even under an i.i.d. confidence interval. The TS estimator does not consistently detect slowly moving nonparametric trends. We plot the kernel smoother of the ratio in Figure 6.6; if there is a trend it is very weak.

We next look at the Toronto temperature data from 1840 to 2016 organized by month. We estimate the linear trend model using OLS estimation, quantile regression, and the Theil–Sen estimator – the results are shown in Table 6.2. The standard error for the TS estimator is 0.00301. From the OLS estimates, only January fails to yield a significant upward trend over the whole period. The point estimates vary from 0.0064 (January) to

Table 6.2 Toronto temperature trends by month.

Month	OLS Lower	OLS Estimate	OLS Upper	Quantile Lower	Quantile Estimate	Quantile Upper	TS Lower	TS Estimate	TS Upper
January	−0.0007	0.0064	0.0136	0.0035	0.0050	0.0097	−0.5400	0.0058	0.5667
February	0.0049	0.0112	0.0176	−0.0040	0.0118	0.0106	−0.5000	0.0115	0.4824
March	0.0124	0.0192	0.0260	0.0176	0.0200	0.0333	−0.4857	0.0191	0.5333
April	0.0112	0.0166	0.0220	0.0182	0.0185	0.0029	−0.4000	0.0167	0.4400
May	0.0119	0.0174	0.0230	0.0194	0.0152	0.0155	−0.4364	0.0174	0.4667
June	0.0101	0.0146	0.0191	0.0196	0.0153	0.0122	−0.3143	0.0143	0.3500
July	0.0071	0.0114	0.0158	0.0129	0.0106	0.0007	−0.3000	0.0116	0.3429
August	0.0080	0.0120	0.0161	0.0090	0.0148	0.0115	−0.3000	0.0120	0.3333
September	0.0085	0.0134	0.0182	0.0153	0.0115	0.0149	−0.3273	0.0133	0.3800
October	0.0108	0.0161	0.0215	0.0130	0.0145	0.0063	−0.3667	0.0162	0.4000
November	0.0146	0.0191	0.0236	0.0185	0.0167	0.0198	−0.3250	0.0184	0.3800
December	0.0097	0.0156	0.0215	0.0121	0.0151	0.0104	−0.4667	0.0158	0.5000

0.0191 (November). The parameter β measures the average annual change in temperature in degrees centigrade, which suggests that over 100 years the average annual temperature will have increased by 1.5 degrees.

6.3   Unit Root Processes and Stochastic Trends

This section is concerned with the class of ARMA(p, q) processes where the roots of the autoregressive polynomial lie on the unit circle. There are two cases: (i) the roots are real valued, that is, lie in $\{-1, 1\}$, or (ii) they are complex valued. We first deal with the well-known real-valued special case.

Suppose that

$$y_t = \mu + y_{t-1} + \varepsilon_t, \qquad (6.19)$$

where ε_t is i.i.d. with mean zero and finite variance. This is called the random walk plus drift (when $\mu = 0$, we have the plain vanilla random walk, which is one of the most studied processes in probability theory, and also termed a martingale). The process y_t is nonstationary (although its difference $\Delta y_t = y_t - y_{t-1} = \mu + \varepsilon_t$ is i.i.d. and hence stationary). In particular, we have $y_t = y_0 + t\mu + \sum_{s=1}^{t} \varepsilon_s$ for every t, where y_0 is the **initial condition**. We cannot now suppose that the process has been going on for an infinite amount of time, because $\sum_{s=0}^{\infty} \varepsilon_{-s}$ could not make sense as a random variable, and so the starting condition is of some significance. We suppose that y_0 is drawn from some random variable with mean m and variance v. By conditioning on y_0, it is as if this were a fixed number.

We may calculate the conditional mean and the variance of this process given the initial condition, that is,

$$E(y_t \mid y_0) = y_0 + t\mu, \qquad \text{var}(y_t \mid y_0) = \sigma^2 t.$$

We may also calculate the unconditional mean and variance, $E(y_t) = m + t\mu$ and $\text{var}(y_t) = \sigma^2 t + v$, by the law of iterated expectation. When $\mu > 0$, the conditional and unconditional means of the process tend to infinity and the processes tend to increase without bound. However, because of the increasing variance they wander far and wide around this trend.[2] We do have $E(y_t)/\text{var}(y_t) \to \mu/\sigma^2$, since the mean and the variance grow at the same rate. In the case where $\mu = 0$, the process has no particular tendency to increase or decrease and the main feature is its wandering far and wide due to the increasing variance. In this case $y_t/\sqrt{t}$ satisfies a CLT for large t, which we will exploit below.

We have, for any μ and any t, s,

$$\text{cov}(y_t, y_{t-s} \mid y_0) = E\left((y_t - E(y_t \mid y_0))(y_s - E(y_s \mid y_0))\right)$$

$$= E\left(\sum_{r=1}^{t} \varepsilon_r \times \sum_{r'=1}^{t-s} \varepsilon_{r'}\right) = \sigma^2 \times (t - s),$$

$$\text{corr}(y_t, y_{t-s} \mid y_0) = \frac{t-s}{\sqrt{t(t-s)}} = \sqrt{1 - \frac{s}{t}}.$$

For any fixed s, $\text{corr}(y_t, y_{t-s} \mid y_0) \to 1$ as $t \to \infty$. For $s = (1-\alpha)t$, $\text{corr}(y_t, y_{t-s} \mid y_0) \to \alpha$ as $t \to \infty$. The high values of the autocorrelation function make the trajectory of the random walk relatively smooth. What about the partial autocorrelation? It is zero, because y_t is a Markov process.

Note that if the shocks are heteroskedastic, we cannot assert that y_t is necessarily non-stationary in such an extreme way. Suppose that $y_0 = 0$ and $\mu = 0$, while $\varepsilon_t \sim N(0, \sigma_t^2)$. Then $E(y_t) = 0$ and $\text{var}(y_t) = \sum_{s=1}^{t} \sigma_s^2$. Furthermore, $\text{cov}(y_t, y_{t-s}) = \text{var}(y_{t-s})$ for $s > 0$. Therefore, if $\sum_{s=1}^{\infty} \sigma_s^2$ exists, then the process y_t is asymptotically second-order stationary, in fact $y_T \sim N(0, \sum_{s=1}^{T} \sigma_s^2) \to N(0, \sum_{s=1}^{\infty} \sigma_s^2)$ as $T \to \infty$. For example, $\sigma_s^2 = \rho^{s-1}$ for $\rho \in (0, 1)$, in which case $\sum_{s=1}^{\infty} \sigma_s^2 = 1/(1-\rho) < \infty$. However, the process y_t is not mixing because $\text{cov}(y_t, y_{t-s}) \to \sum_{j=1}^{\infty} \sigma_j^2$ as $t \to \infty$ for any fixed s, that is, $\text{corr}(y_t, y_{t-s}) \to 1$ as $t \to \infty$ for all s. We have

$$\lim_{t \to \infty} \text{corr}(y_t, y_j) = \frac{\sum_{s=1}^{j} \sigma_s^2}{\sqrt{\sum_{s=1}^{\infty} \sigma_s^2 \sum_{s=1}^{j} \sigma_s^2}};$$

for example, with $j = 1$ this is $\sigma_1/\sqrt{\sum_{s=1}^{\infty} \sigma_s^2}$. This phenomenon is related to what Conley et al. (1997) called volatility-induced stationarity, although their setting was a continuous-time process with dynamic volatility.

The anti-random walk (with $\phi = -1$), $y_t = \mu - y_{t-1} + \varepsilon_t$, is also nonstationary and can be analyzed along similar lines. Note that

$$y_t = y_0 + \mu \sum_{s=1}^{t} (-1)^s + \sum_{s=1}^{t} (-1)^s \varepsilon_s,$$

---

[2] We may also suppose that the process operates backwards in time given the initial condition y_0. In that case, we have $E(y_{-t} \mid y_0) = y_0 - t\mu$, $\text{var}(y_{-t} \mid y_0) = \sigma^2 t$. The uncertainty about the past should equally grow the further back we look.

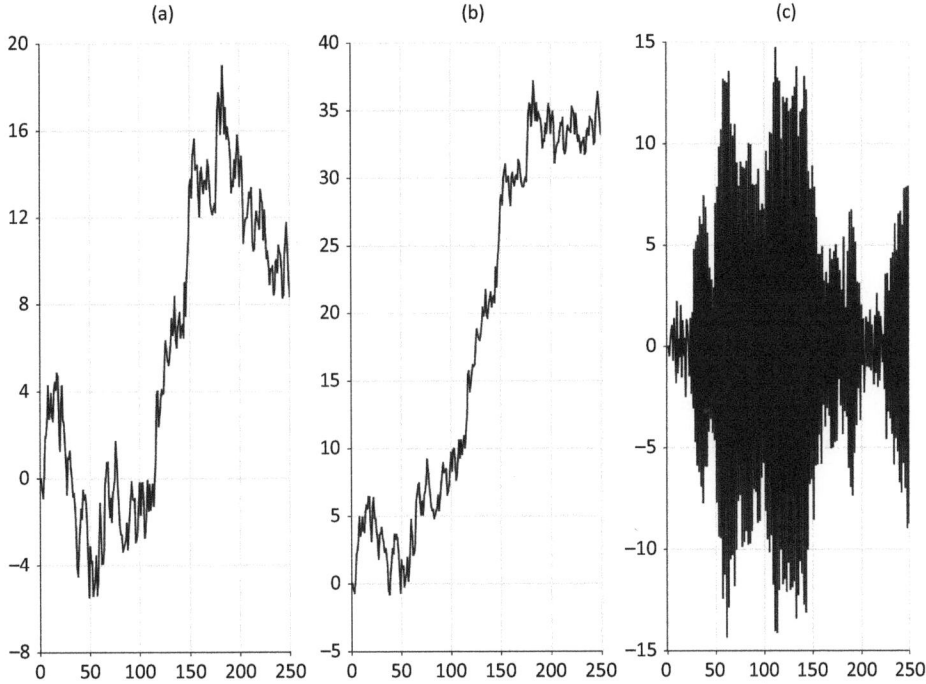

Figure 6.7 Random walks with $y_0 = 0$ and standard normal innovations. (a) $\mu = 0$; (b) $\mu = 0.1$; (c) anti-random walk with $\mu = 0.1$.

which has $E(y_t \mid y_0) = y_0 + \mu \sum_{s=1}^{t}(-1)^s$ (either $y_0 + \mu$ or y_0 depending on whether t is even or odd), whereas $\text{var}(y_t \mid y_0) = \sigma^2 t$ in agreement with the standard random walk, and $\text{cov}(y_t, y_{t-s} \mid y_0) = (-1)^s \sigma^2 \times (t - s)$. We compare in Figure 6.7 sample paths from the three types of random walks.

In practice we are mostly interested in the standard random walk; however, we may wish to allow for more general shocks than i.i.d. ones. Suppose that

$$y_t = \mu + y_{t-1} + u_t, \tag{6.20}$$

where u_t is a stationary mean-zero process. In this case, $\Delta y_t = y_t - y_{t-1} = \mu + u_t$ is stationary, and we say that y_t is **difference stationary**. It is also called an $I(1)$ (integrated of order one) process. Suppose that, in particular, $u_t = \omega(L)\varepsilon_t$, where $\omega(L) = \omega_0 + \omega_1 L + \cdots$ is square summable at least and ε_t are i.i.d., that is, u_t is a weakly dependent stationary linear process. If u_t takes the form of an ARMA(p, q) process then we say that y_t is autoregressive integrated moving average ARIMA(p,d,q), with in this case the differencing order $d = 1$.

In the pure random walk model any shocks have permanent effects because $y_t = y_0 + t\mu + \sum_{s=1}^{t} \varepsilon_s$, that is, the impulse response function satisfies $\partial y_t / \partial \varepsilon_s = 1$ for all $t \geq s$. The same is true for the more general difference stationary process, but tracing through the effects of shocks ε_s on y_t is more complicated.

We next show an important representation that any difference stationary process possesses, namely the **Beveridge–Nelson decomposition**.

Theorem 6.2 *Suppose that y_t satisfies (6.20). Then we can write, for any such difference stationary process,*

$$y_t = x_t + z_t, \tag{6.21}$$

where x_t is a pure random walk with

$$x_t = \mu + x_{t-1} + \omega(1)\varepsilon_t, \tag{6.22}$$

while z_t is a linear process with $z_t = \omega^*(L)\varepsilon_t$, $\omega_j^* = -\sum_{i=j+1}^{\infty} \omega_i$.

This just follows from the fact that $\omega(L) = \omega(1) + (1-L)\omega^*(L)$. Here, $\omega(1) = \sum_{j=0}^{\infty} \omega_j$. This decomposition gives a unique definition of the trend component of an $I(1)$ process. There are other decompositions, or rather models, for trend and stationary components. Suppose that

$$y_t = x_t + z_t, \tag{6.23}$$

with $x_t = \mu + x_{t-1} + u_t$ and $z_t = \omega(L)\varepsilon_t$, where ω is a lag polynomial and ε_t, u_t are i.i.d. shocks that may be contemporaneously correlated, that is, $E(u_t\varepsilon_t) = \sigma_{u\varepsilon}$. The local-level model, treated below, assumes that $\sigma_{u\varepsilon} = 0$ and $\omega_j = 0, j \geq 1$, so that z_t is i.i.d.

A random walk is often called a stochastic trend. We may compare the stochastic trend with the deterministic nonparametric trend we considered in the previous section. Specifically, for a continuously differentiable function g we have

$$g(t/T) = g((t-1)/T) + \frac{1}{T}g'((t-1)/T) + R_{t,T},$$

where $T\max_{t,T}|R_{t,T}| \to 0$, so that we can write $g_t \simeq g_{t-1} + e_t$, where $g_t = g(t/T)$ and $e_t = g'((t-1)/T)/T$. In this case the increment is nonrandom but it is also small, whereas the increment to the stochastic trend model is stochastic, mean zero, and, unless scaled, of $O_P(1)$. This means that, depending on the realization, the actual stochastic trend can go anywhere. A hybrid model is $y_t = g(t/T) + y_{t-1} + u_t$, where u_t is i.i.d. with mean zero and finite variance.

6.3.1 Explosive Process

The process $y_t = \mu + \phi y_{t-1} + \varepsilon_t$ with $\phi > 1$ is explosive.[3] That is, the process y_t increases rapidly over time – there is a very strong positive feedback from the shock to future values of y_t. This model with a sequence of $\phi_T > 1$ has been proposed to capture asset market "bubbles" or hyperinflations (Phillips, Shi, and Yu, 2015). By recursive substitution we have

$$y_t = y_0 + \mu \sum_{s=1}^{t} \phi^{t-s} + \sum_{s=1}^{t} \phi^{t-s}\varepsilon_s.$$

In this case both mean and variance grow rapidly to infinity because $\sum_{s=1}^{t} \phi^t$ grows faster than any polynomial in t. Furthermore, y_t is not difference stationary (although the quasi-difference $y_t - \phi y_{t-1}$ is stationary, for what it is worth).

---

[3] There is a stationary solution to the difference equation, as we discussed in Chapter 3, but this is defined in terms of future values of the process.

6.3.2   Higher-Order Unit Roots

Nonstationarity in higher-order processes can be quite complex, literally. Consider an AR(p) process whose roots are $z_1^*, \ldots, z_p^*$, some of which lie on the unit circle, say $z_1^*, \ldots, z_q^*$, corresponding to locations $\exp(i\omega_1), \ldots, \exp(i\omega_q)$, whereas the roots $z_{q+1}^*, \ldots, z_p^*$ lie inside the unit circle. Note that if $\omega_j \in \{-\pi, 0, \pi\}$, then the root is real and equal to plus or minus one; if $\omega_j \notin \{-\pi, 0, \pi\}$, then the root is complex and has a conjugate root with opposite angle $-\omega_j$. Therefore, pairing the complex conjugates, we obtain

$$\Delta_{\omega_j} = (1 - \exp(i\omega_j)L)\,(1 - \exp(-i\omega_j)L)$$
$$= 1 - (\exp(i\omega_j) + \exp(-i\omega_j))\,L + L^2 = 1 - 2\cos(\omega_j)L + L^2,$$

because the cosine function is even and the sine function is odd. Note that if $\omega_j = \pi/m$, we have $(\exp(i\omega_j)z)^m = \exp(im\omega_j)z^m = z^m$. In other words, ω_j is a solution of the equation $z^m = 1$; this is called a seasonal unit root with season/period m. If π/ω_j is real valued, then no such interpretation abounds.

Example 6.2   Consider the AR(2) process

$$y_t = 2\cos(\omega)y_{t-1} - y_{t-2} + \varepsilon_t$$
$$= 2\cos(\omega)\,(2\cos(\omega)y_{t-2} - y_{t-3} + \varepsilon_{t-1}) - (2\cos(\omega)y_{t-3} - y_{t-4} + \varepsilon_{t-2}) + \varepsilon_t$$
$$= \varepsilon_t + 2\cos(\omega)\varepsilon_{t-1} + \left(4\cos^2(\omega) - 1\right)\varepsilon_{t-2} + \cdots$$

The process can be continued to some initial values y_0, y_{-1}. The sample autocorrelations of this process can be negative, depending on ω.

Example 6.3   Consider the AR(2) process $y_{t+1} = y_t + y_{t-1} + \varepsilon_{t+1}$, where ε_t is i.i.d. with mean zero and variance σ^2. We have $E(y_{t+1}) = \mu_{t+1} = \mu_t + \mu_{t-1}$, which is a Fibonacci sequence (if $\mu_0 = 0$ and $\mu_1 = 1$). It follows that

$$\mu_t = \frac{\varphi^t - \psi^t}{\sqrt{5}},$$

where $\varphi = (1 + \sqrt{5})/2$ is the golden ratio and $\psi = (1 - \sqrt{5})/2$. As $t \to \infty$, $\mu_{t+1}/\mu_t \to \varphi = 1.618\ldots$ and the process has an explosive mean. On the other hand, if $\mu_0 = 0$ and $\mu_1 = 0$, then $\mu_t = 0$ for all t. The characteristic polynomial $1 - z - z^2$ has real roots φ, ψ; one is explosive and one is stable. Therefore, we can write $(1 - \varphi L)\,y_t = x_t$ and $(1 - \psi L)\,x_t = \varepsilon_t$. We have

$$y_{t+1} = \varepsilon_{t+1} + \varepsilon_t + 2y_{t-1} + y_{t-2} = \sum_{j=0}^{t} f_j \varepsilon_{t+1-j},$$

where f_j are the Fibonacci numbers, so the variance is $\sigma^2 \sum_{j=0}^{t} f_j^2$, which grows like the sum of squared Fibonacci numbers, which is exponentially fast. Differencing the process does not eliminate the nonstationarity.

6.3.3   Recurrence

A unit root process with a drift increases to infinity (or decreases to minus infinity) without ever returning to its starting point, or to any given point for that matter. A homoskedastic deterministic trend process possesses exactly the same property (in that case with or without an intercept). This is in contrast with a stationary process which, it can be shown, crosses any given point an infinite number of times: it visits home a positive fraction of the sample on average, which allows for conventional statistical inference. This property is called recurrence. There is a further classification of recurrence into **null recurrent** and **positive recurrent**. Positive recurrence essentially means that the expected time until a process returns to any given set is finite. A stationary process is positive recurrent. A unit root process is null recurrent, meaning that the expected time until a process returns to any given set is infinite. For a unit root process or Brownian motion, the rate of return is $T^{1/2}$, which means that the frequency of visitation divided by T goes to zero.

6.3.4   Estimation in a Unit Root Setting

We consider here the estimation question in the presence of unit roots. That is, we consider the properties of our usual estimates of (ARMA) parameters when the process itself is nonstationary, that is, the autoregressive polynomial has roots on the unit circle. In this case, one gets superconsistent estimates of some parameters, but with nonstandard distributions, so we will spend some time on developing this theory.

Suppose that $y_t = \phi y_{t-1} + u_t$, where $u_t \sim \text{WN}(0, \sigma^2)$. Then,

$$\widehat{\phi}_{\text{OLS}} = \frac{\sum_{t=2}^{T} y_t y_{t-1}}{\sum_{t=2}^{T} y_{t-1}^2} \xrightarrow{P} \phi \quad \text{for all } \phi.$$

Furthermore, if $|\phi| < 1$, we have $\sqrt{T}(\widehat{\phi} - \phi) \Longrightarrow N(0, 1 - \phi^2)$. If $\phi = 1$, $1 - \phi^2 = 0$, so the implied variance above is zero and the CLT fails. So what happens in this case? If $\phi = 1$, we can show that $T(\widehat{\phi} - \phi) \Longrightarrow X$, where X is a random variable that is not Gaussian; in fact its distribution is not symmetric around zero, and indeed $E(X) < 0$. The rate of convergence is faster than usual but the asymptotic distribution is nonstandard. Many interpretation issues hinge on this question, or rather on whether $\phi = 1$ or $\phi < 1$. The issue here for estimation arises if we want to consider the parameter space $\phi \in [-1, 1]$ rather than imposing $\phi \in (-1, 1)$. Before discussing the random variable X and its distribution we need to cover the functional central limit theorem, which is the main technical tool needed to deliver this result.

6.3.5   Functional Central Limit Theorem

The **empirical process** is defined as

$$F_T(u) = \frac{1}{T} \sum_{t=1}^{T} 1(y_t \leq u).$$

This defines a continuous-time stochastic process, that is, $\{F_T(u): u \in \mathbb{R}\}$. It has been extensively studied since Glivenko (1933) and Cantelli (1933) established the uniform convergence of $F_T(\cdot)$ to the population distribution function $F(\cdot)$, when y_t are i.i.d. These results have been extended to allow y_t to be stationary and mixing. Define the (normalized) partial sum process for a zero-mean random sequence ε_t,

$$S_T(0:u) = \frac{1}{\sqrt{T}} \sum_{s=1}^{\lfloor uT \rfloor} \varepsilon_s,$$

where $\lfloor \cdot \rfloor$ denotes the largest integer smaller than $\cdot$, and $u \in [0,1]$. This also defines a continuous-time stochastic process, that is, $\{S_T(0:u): u \in [0,1]\}$. The sample path of this process is discontinuous and so it lies in the so-called $D([0,1])$ space. We can replace it by a continuous approximation,

$$S_T^*(0:u) = S_T(0:u) + \frac{Tu - \lfloor Tu \rfloor}{\sqrt{T}} \varepsilon_{\lfloor Tu \rfloor + 1},$$

which just interpolates linearly between the jumps; note that $(Tu - \lfloor Tu \rfloor)/\sqrt{T} \leq C/\sqrt{n}$. The process $S_T^*(0:u)$ lies in $C([0,1])$, the space of continuous functions on $[0,1]$. The simplest example of a continuous-time process is Brownian motion or a Wiener process, $B(\cdot)$. We will treat this process in more detail in Chapter 12.

By the Herrndorf CLT, for any fixed $u \in [0,1]$,

$$S_T(0:u) \implies N(0, u \times \text{lrvar}(\varepsilon_t)).$$

This subsumes the full-sample case where $u = 1$. Furthermore, for any u, u' with $u < u'$,

$$E\left[S_T(0:u)S_T(0:u')\right] = E\left[\left(\frac{1}{\sqrt{T}}\sum_{s=1}^{\lfloor uT \rfloor} \varepsilon_s\right)\left(\frac{1}{\sqrt{T}}\sum_{s=1}^{\lfloor uT \rfloor} \varepsilon_s + \frac{1}{\sqrt{T}}\sum_{s=\lfloor uT \rfloor+1}^{\lfloor u'T \rfloor} \varepsilon_s\right)\right]$$
$$= E\left[S_T(0:u)^2\right] + E\left[S_T(0:u)S_T(u:u')\right]$$
$$= E\left[S_T(0:u)^2\right],$$

because

$$E\left[S_T(0:u')^2\right] = E\left[(S_T(0:u) + S_T(u:u'))^2\right]$$
$$= E\left[S_T(0:u)^2\right] + E\left[S_T(u:u')^2\right] + 2E\left[S_T(0:u)S_T(u:u')\right]$$
$$\simeq u\,\text{lrvar}(\varepsilon_t) + (u' - u)\text{lrvar}(\varepsilon_t) + 2E\left[S_T(0:u)S_T(u:u')\right]$$
$$= u'\text{lrvar}(\varepsilon_t) + 2E\left[S_T(0:u)S_T(u:u')\right].$$

Therefore, we must have $E\left[S_T(0:u)S_T(u:u')\right] \to 0$ as $T \to \infty$. This says that $S_T(0:u)$, $S_T(u:u')$ are jointly asymptotically normal and independent of each other in large samples.

They are not perfectly independent, though, and it is worthwhile calculating the exact covariances. We have

$$E\left[\left(\frac{1}{\sqrt{T}}\sum_{s=1}^{\lfloor uT\rfloor}\varepsilon_s\right)\left(\frac{1}{\sqrt{T}}\sum_{s=\lfloor uT\rfloor+1}^{\lfloor u'T\rfloor}\varepsilon_s\right)\right]$$

$$=\frac{1}{T}\sum_{s=1}^{\lfloor uT\rfloor}\sum_{s'=\lfloor uT\rfloor+1}^{\lfloor u'T\rfloor}E\left(\varepsilon_s\varepsilon_{s'}\right)$$

$$=\frac{1}{T}\left[\sum_{j=1}^{\lfloor uT\rfloor}j\gamma_\varepsilon(j)+\sum_{j'=\lfloor uT\rfloor+1}^{\lfloor u'T\rfloor}(\lfloor u'T\rfloor-j)\,\gamma_\varepsilon(j+\lfloor u'T\rfloor)\right]\simeq\frac{1}{T}\sum_{j=1}^{\lfloor uT\rfloor}j\gamma_\varepsilon(j)\to 0$$

as $T\to\infty$ for any $u\in[0,1]$, provided $\sum_{j=1}^\infty j^\alpha|\gamma_\varepsilon(j)|<\infty$ for any $\alpha>0$.

The functional central limit theorem (FCLT) is about the process $S_T(0:\cdot)$ as a whole. We need one additional condition to establish this result, called either **tightness** or **stochastic equicontinuity**. The idea is that if u and u' are close, the values of $S_T(0:u)$ and $S_T(0:u')$ should be close in some sense. We next give two equivalent definitions; see Andrews (1994) for a full treatment.

Definition 6.1 (Stochastic equicontinuity 1)   For all $\epsilon,\eta>0$ there exists $\delta>0$ such that

$$\limsup_{T\to\infty}\Pr\left[\sup_{\{u,u':\|u-u'\|\le\delta\}}\|S_T(0:u)-S_T(0:u')\|>\eta\right]<\epsilon.$$

Definition 6.2 (Stochastic equicontinuity 2)   For all deterministic sequences $\{\delta_T\}$ with $\delta_T\downarrow 0$ we have

$$\sup_{\{u,u':\|u-u'\|\le\delta_T\}}\|S_T(0:u)-S_T(0:u')\|\xrightarrow{P}0.$$

For the empirical distribution this condition is easily satisfied because the empirical distribution itself is flat except at the sample points where it makes small jumps with height $1/T$. For the partial sum process this condition is also easily verified. When this condition is satisfied we say that $S_T(0:\cdot)$ converges weakly to a limiting stochastic process (the FCLT), that is,

$$S_T(0:\cdot)\Longrightarrow\text{lrvar}(\varepsilon_t)\times B(\cdot).\tag{6.24}$$

See Appendix C for sufficient conditions in the case of a strong mixing process.

The stochastic equicontinuity condition is not always satisfied. For example, the centered and scaled kernel trend estimator

$$S_T(u)=\sqrt{Th}\frac{1}{Th}\sum_{t=1}^T w(u-t/T)/h)\,(y_t-g(t/T))$$

satisfies a CLT (under standard conditions on the process y_t) for any u in $[0,1]$, but it does not satisfy an FCLT. This can be understood by considering the fact that for any distinct u,u' the two random variables $S_T(u),S_T(u')$ are asymptotically independent.

6.3.6   Testing for Unit Roots

We next discuss the standard methods for testing the unit root hypothesis, which is a vast, vast literature that I will not be able to do justice to. We first consider the simplest case, the OLS estimator in the no-intercept autoregression $y_t = \phi y_{t-1} + \varepsilon_t$, in which case the null hypothesis is that $\phi = 1$ and the alternative hypothesis is that $\phi \in (-1, 1)$. We can write the autoregression in error correction form (as an error correction model, or ECM),

$$\Delta y_t = \gamma y_{t-1} + \varepsilon_t, \tag{6.25}$$

where $\gamma = \phi - 1$. The OLS estimator satisfies

$$\widehat{\phi}_{\text{OLS}} - 1 = \frac{\sum_{t=2}^{T} y_t y_{t-1}}{\sum_{t=2}^{T} y_{t-1}^2} - 1 = \frac{\sum_{t=2}^{T} \Delta y_t y_{t-1}}{\sum_{t=2}^{T} y_{t-1}^2} = \frac{\sum_{t=2}^{T} \varepsilon_t y_{t-1}}{\sum_{t=2}^{T} y_{t-1}^2}.$$

We suppose first that ε_t is i.i.d. Then we have that $\varepsilon_t y_{t-1}$ is an MDS, so that the numerator has mean zero and

$$\text{var}\left(\sum_{t=2}^{T} \varepsilon_t y_{t-1} \mid y_0 \right) = \sum_{t=2}^{T} \text{var}\left(\varepsilon_t y_{t-1} \mid y_0 \right) = \sigma^2 \sum_{t=2}^{T} E\left(y_{t-1}^2 \mid y_0 \right)$$

$$= \sigma^2 \sum_{t=2}^{T} \left(y_0^2 + t\sigma^2 \right) = O(T^2)$$

as $T \to \infty$, which is a nonstandard rate.

The usual OLS t-statistic for $\phi = 1$ is

$$t_\phi = \frac{\sum_{t=2}^{T} \Delta y_t y_{t-1}}{s\left(\sum_{t=2}^{T} y_{t-1}^2 \right)^{1/2}}, \qquad s^2 = \frac{1}{T} \sum_{t=2}^{T} \left(y_t - \widehat{\phi} y_{t-1} \right)^2,$$

and note that, regardless of the true value of ϕ, $s^2 \xrightarrow{P} \sigma^2$.

We use the identity

$$y_T^2 - y_1^2 = \sum_{t=2}^{T} \left(y_t - y_{t-1} \right)\left(y_t + y_{t-1} \right) = 2 \sum_{t=2}^{T} \Delta y_t y_{t-1} + \sum_{t=2}^{T} (\Delta y_t)^2$$

and, rescaling by T, we obtain

$$T\left(\widehat{\phi}_{\text{OLS}} - 1 \right) = \frac{\frac{1}{2}\left((1/T)\left(y_T^2 - y_1^2 \right) - (1/T) \sum_{t=2}^{T} (\Delta y_t)^2 \right)}{(1/T^2) \sum_{t=2}^{T} y_{t-1}^2}.$$

We have $y_1^2/T \xrightarrow{P} 0$, and

$$\frac{1}{\sqrt{T}} y_T \Longrightarrow \sigma B(1), \qquad \frac{1}{T} y_T^2 \Longrightarrow \sigma^2 B(1)^2, \qquad \frac{1}{T} \sum_{t=2}^{T} (\Delta y_t)^2 \xrightarrow{P} \sigma^2.$$

Furthermore, replacing sums by integrals,

$$\frac{1}{T^2} \sum_{t=2}^{T} y_{t-1}^2 = \frac{1}{T} \sum_{t=2}^{T} \left(\frac{1}{\sqrt{T}} y_{t-1} \right)^2 \Longrightarrow \sigma^2 \int_0^1 B(u)^2 \, du.$$

Therefore, we obtain the limiting results

$$T\left(\widehat{\phi}_{\mathrm{OLS}} - 1\right) \implies \frac{\frac{1}{2}\left(B(1)^2 - 1\right)}{\int B(u)^2\,\mathrm{d}u}, \qquad t_\phi \implies \frac{\frac{1}{2}\left(B(1)^2 - 1\right)}{\left(\int B(u)^2\,\mathrm{d}u\right)^{1/2}}.$$

These distributions are often called Dickey–Fuller (DF) distributions, and both are ratios of two random variables (Fuller, 1995). Large negative values of the test statistic are evidence against the null hypothesis of a unit root and in favor of the stationary alternative. The critical values for this test are given below. With these values the test has correct null rejection frequency, that is, a Type I error of α. The test will reject the null hypothesis with probability tending to one when it is false in the sense that $\phi \neq 1$, that is, the Type II error goes to zero with sample size for any $\phi \neq 1$.

A lot of work has gone into evaluating the properties of the test under sequences of local alternatives of the form $\phi = 1 - c/T$; these are called roots local to unity. In that case, the test statistics converge to a limiting distribution that depends on c; the power of the test is positive for all $c > 0$ and increases with the value of c.

We have so far described the methodology for the case where the null hypothesis is the driftless random walk. There are also versions of this that allow an intercept or an intercept and linear trend. In general, we may define

$$\widehat{\gamma} = \widehat{\phi} - 1 = \frac{\sum_{t=2}^{T} \Delta y_t \widehat{e}_{t-1}}{\sum_{t=2}^{T} \widehat{e}_{t-1}^2},$$

where $\widehat{e}_t$ is

$$\widehat{e}_t = \begin{cases} y_t, & \text{no intercept,} \\ y_t - \widehat{\mu}, & \text{intercept,} \\ y_t - \widehat{\mu} - \widehat{\beta}t, & \text{intercept and trend,} \end{cases}$$

where $\widehat{\mu}, \widehat{\beta}$ are the intercept and slope OLS estimators. The limiting distributions in the i.i.d. error case are of the form

$$T\widehat{\gamma} \implies \frac{\frac{1}{2}\left(B^e(1)^2 - 1\right)}{\int B^e(s)^2\,\mathrm{d}s},$$

where $B^e(s) = B(s) - \int B(s)\,\mathrm{d}s$ in the intercept case and $B^e(s) = B(s) - (4 - 6s) \int B(s)\,\mathrm{d}s - (12s - 6) \int sB(s)\,\mathrm{d}s$ in the intercept plus trend case. The asymptotic critical values for the DF tests of $\phi = 1$ versus $\phi < 1$ under i.i.d. errors are given in Table 6.3.

One rejects the corresponding null hypothesis if the test statistic is less than the corresponding critical value. For example, consider the Shiller stock price and dividend data

Table 6.3 Dickey–Fuller critical values.

Model	$T(\widehat{\phi} - 1)$		$T(\widehat{\phi} - 1)/se$	
	1%	5%	1%	5%
No intercept	−13.8	−8.1	−2.58	−1.95
Intercept	−20.7	−14.1	−3.43	−2.86
Intercept and trend	−29.5	−21.8	−3.96	−3.41

available monthly from 1871 to 2022 (see Appendix D). We find that for log prices allowing for an intercept the DF test statistic is 1.360 033 6, which cannot reject the unit root hypothesis even at the 5% level. Similarly, for the log dividend price ratio the DF test statistic is $-6.572\,060\,7$, which cannot reject the unit root null at the 5% level. As Dybvig and Zhang (2018) argued, this calls into question the Campbell–Shiller framework. Both these series, however, contain autocorrelation in the residuals.

6.3.6.1 Serial Correlation

The DF test is only valid if the error term u_t is i.i.d. This may be rather restrictive for some data series, that is, we may wish to allow for additional weak dynamics in the error term representing cyclical or other behavior. Suppose that u_t is a stationary mixing and weakly dependent series. Then,

$$T\widehat{\gamma} \Longrightarrow \frac{\frac{1}{2}\left(B(1)^2 - \kappa\right)}{\int B(s)^2\,\mathrm{d}s} = \frac{\int B\,\mathrm{d}B - \frac{1}{2}(\kappa - 1)}{\int B(s)^2\,\mathrm{d}s}, \qquad \kappa = \frac{\gamma_u(0)}{\mathrm{lrvar}(u)},$$

so that the distribution is affected by an asymptotic bias.

There are several ways of adjusting for the serial correlation in the error terms to get a valid test. The augmented Dickey–Fuller test (ADF) allows the error term to be correlated over time up to a certain order. This test is based on estimating the regression (or special cases $\beta = 0$ and/or $\mu = 0$),

$$\Delta y_t = \mu + \beta t + \gamma y_{t-1} + \sum_{j=1}^{p-1} \phi_j \Delta y_{t-j} + \eta_t, \tag{6.26}$$

by least squares and using the DF critical values (as given in Table 6.3) for the estimated γ or t-ratio. EViews (see Appendix E) allows you to specify the value of p yourself or to use some model selection algorithm to choose it for you. It also allows you to choose no intercept, intercept, or intercept and trend as the baseline. For the log dividend price ratio the ADF test statistic (based on $\beta = 0$ but intercept included and $p = 3$) is $-8.719\,501\,0$, but this still cannot reject the unit root null at the 5% level.

The Phillips–Perron test (PP; Phillips and Perron, 1988) is an alternative way of correcting for serial correlation in u_t. This involves explicit estimation of the variance and long-run variance of the error term and using that to bias-correct the original DF test procedure. Most computer packages perform the ADF and PP tests.

6.3.6.2 The KPSS Test

The so-called KPSS (Kwiatkowski–Phillips–Schmidt–Shin; Kwiatkowski *et al.*, 1992) test is widely used. This starts from a different null hypothesis. Suppose that

$$y_t = \alpha + \beta t + r_t + \varepsilon_t, \qquad r_t = r_{t-1} + u_t, \tag{6.27}$$

where u_t is i.i.d. with mean zero and variance σ_u^2, while ε_t is a stationary weakly dependent process. The null hypothesis is that $\sigma_u^2 = 0$ versus the alternative that $\sigma_u^2 > 0$. The null hypothesis is $y_t = \alpha + \beta t + \varepsilon_t$, or $y_t = \alpha + \varepsilon_t$ in the case where $\beta = 0$; that is, the null hypothesis is either a linear trend or a stationary process against the alternative that the process contains a stochastic trend as well.

The estimation of the model under the alternative can be done using the state space approach, see Chapter 8, but this is demanding. The test is based on estimation of the model under the null hypothesis, that is, running the regression of y_t on a constant and the deterministic trend (or just a constant, or just a trend) and obtaining the residuals $\widehat{\varepsilon}_t = y_t - \widehat{\alpha} - \widehat{\beta}t$. Then let

$$\text{KPSS} = \frac{1}{T^2} \sum_{t=1}^{T} \left(\frac{S_t}{\widehat{\omega}} \right)^2, \tag{6.28}$$

where $S_t = \sum_{s=1}^{t} \widehat{\varepsilon}_t$ and $\widehat{\omega}^2$ is an estimate of the long-run variance of $\widehat{\varepsilon}_t$. Under the null hypothesis,

$$\text{KPSS} \implies B(r) + r(2 - 4r)B(1) + 6r(r^2 - 1) \int_0^1 B(r)\, dr, \tag{6.29}$$

where B is the standard Brownian motion. The limiting distribution is nonstandard but has been tabulated. One rejects the null hypothesis if KPSS is larger than the corresponding critical value. Note also, as in the case of the Dickey–Fuller tests, that the precise form of the trending null hypothesis affects the limiting distribution so that if we drop t in the regression the limit is $B(r) - rB(1)$. These tests are all consistent against a general class of alternatives measured by the size of σ_u^2. There are also modifications of these tests to allow for stationary short-run dynamics in ε_t. EViews allows you to choose no intercept, intercept, or intercept and trend as the baseline, and it also allows you to specify the length of the autoregressive dynamics in ε_t yourself or to use some model selection algorithm to choose it for you. For some series such as (the logarithm of) INDPRO it does not matter much which of these choices you make, but for some series it can change the answer you get.

These tests are all consistent against a general class of alternatives. For stationary time series, tests of hypotheses like lack of correlation have power against local alternatives of the form $c/\sqrt{T}$. The unit root tests have power against local alternatives of the form c/T. That is, suppose that $y_t = \phi_T y_{t-1} + u_t$, where $\phi_T = 1 - c/T$ with $c > 0$. This is called a local-to-unity process.

6.3.7   Long-Memory or Fractional Processes

We next consider an alternative nesting of the unit root and stationary ARMA class of processes.

Definition 6.3   A stationary short-memory process y with finite variance satisfies $\sum_{j=-\infty}^{\infty} |\gamma_y(j)| < \infty$, where $\gamma_y(\cdot)$ is its autocovariance function. A long-memory process is one for which this condition is violated, and in particular $\sum_{j=-\infty}^{\infty} |\gamma_y(j)| = \infty$.

For example, a stationary AR(p) process $y_t = \mu + \phi_1 y_{t-1} + \cdots + \phi_p y_{t-p} + \varepsilon_t$, where ε_t is i.i.d. with mean zero and finite variance, has $|\gamma_y(j)| \leq c\rho^j$ for some ρ with $0 < \rho < 1$, which is clearly summable. It is usual to be more specific about the way the summability condition is violated. Suppose that, for some $C > 0$ and $d \in \mathbb{R}$,

$$\gamma_y(k) \sim C|k|^{2d-1} \quad \text{as } k \to \infty. \tag{6.30}$$

There are several cases of interest:

- If $d \geq 0$, the process is long memory. If $d < 0$, the process is short memory.
- If $d \in (-1/2, 1/2)$, then y_t is stationary and invertible.
- If $d > 1/2$, then y_t is nonstationary.

This class of models nests the random walk or unit root case, which corresponds to the $d = 1$ case, but it does so in a more subtle way than the AR(1) process, because it allows for a whole range of nonstationary behavior when $d \in [1/2, 1]$. Define the fractional differencing operator $(1 - L)^d$. For $d < 1$, one can define the binomial expansion of $(1 - L)^d$ (think of L as a small number) and its inverse,

$$(1 - L)^d = \sum_{j=0}^{\infty} \frac{\Gamma(j-d)}{\Gamma(j+1)\Gamma(-d)} L^j, \qquad (1 - L)^{-d} = \sum_{j=0}^{\infty} \frac{\Gamma(j+d)}{\Gamma(j+1)\Gamma(d)} L^j,$$

where $\Gamma(x) = \int_0^\infty t^{x-1} \exp(-t)\, dt$ is the Gamma function, which satisfies $\Gamma(x+1) = x\Gamma(x)$ for any real x.

Definition 6.4   For any d, let $(1 - L)^d \widetilde{y}_t = \varepsilon_t$, where ε_t is an i.i.d. mean-zero series. Provided $d < 1/2$, we can write $\widetilde{y}_t = (1 - L)^{-d} \varepsilon_t = \sum_{j=0}^{\infty} \psi_j \varepsilon_{t-j}$, where $\psi_j = \Gamma(j + d)/\Gamma(j+1)\Gamma(d)$.

It follows that y_t satisfies (6.30). The autocorrelation and partial autocorrelation functions are (provided $d < 1/2$)

$$\rho(j) = \prod_{i=1}^{j} \frac{d+i-1}{i-d}, \qquad \pi(j) = \frac{d}{j-d}. \tag{6.31}$$

We may define long memory directly using the spectral density.

Definition 6.5   A stationary process y with spectral density $f_y(\cdot)$ exhibits short memory if the spectral density satisfies $f_y(\lambda) \leq C < \infty$ for all $\lambda \in [-\pi, \pi]$ and is continuous at the frequency $\lambda = 0$. The process is long memory if there exists a $d \in (0, 1/2)$ and a C such that $f_y(\lambda) \sim C_f |\lambda|^{-2d}$ as $\lambda \to 0$.

The function $f_y(\lambda)$ has a pole at the origin; nevertheless, provided $d \in (0, 1/2)$, it is still integrable and we have $\int_{-\pi}^{\pi} f_y(\lambda)\, d\lambda = \gamma_y(0)$. The spectral density satisfies $\log f_y(\lambda) \sim \log C_f - 2d \log(\lambda)$ as $\lambda \to 0$, that is, it is a line with a negative slope of $-2d$; on the other hand, for short-memory series the logarithm of the spectral density has no slope and is approximately constant near the origin. The asymptotic behavior of the autocovariance function at long lags is determined by the asymptotic behavior of the spectral density at the origin. There is a relation between the constants C and C_f that can be established under further conditions, namely, $C = 2C_f \Gamma(1-d) \sin(\pi d)$ for $d \in (0, 1/2)$.

In practice, we may also wish to allow for some short-range dependence, and so consider the more general model

$$(1 - L)^d \widetilde{y}_t = u_t, \qquad A(L) u_t = B(L) \varepsilon_t, \tag{6.32}$$

which is called the autoregressive fractionally integrated moving average (ARFIMA) process; in fact, this process is commonly written ARMA(p, d, q), which includes the ARIMA process when d takes positive integer values, but also the fractional case when d is not integer.

The spectral density of this process is

$$f_y(\lambda) = \frac{\sigma^2}{2\pi} |1 - \exp(i\lambda)|^{-2d} \left| \frac{B(\exp(i\lambda))}{A(\exp(i\lambda))} \right|, \quad -\pi \le \lambda \le \pi.$$

The presence of $d > 0$ induces a pole in the spectrum at the origin.

6.3.7.1 Estimation and Inference of a Long-Memory Process

We now discuss estimation and inference issues in this class of models. Clearly, the key question is about estimation of the differencing parameter d. We first comment on the behavior of the sample mean in this case.

Suppose that y_t is stationary and satisfies (6.30) for $d \in [0, 1/2]$. Then it follows that

$$\text{var}(\bar{y}) = \frac{1}{T} \sum_{j=-T}^{T} \left(1 - \frac{|j|}{T} \right) \gamma_y(j)$$

$$\sim C \frac{1}{T} \sum_{j=-T}^{T} \left(1 - \frac{|j|}{T} \right) |j|^{2d-1}$$

$$\sim T^{2d-1} \times \int_0^1 (1-x)x^{2d-1}\, dx \sim T^{2d-1} \times \frac{C}{d(1+2d)}.$$

Provided $d < 1/2$, this goes to zero so that the sample mean is consistent, but the rate of convergence is affected by the quantity d, specifically, $\bar{y} - \mu = O_P(T^{-1/(2+d)})$. Note that if y_t is a Gaussian process, then $\bar{y}$ is Gaussian with mean μ and variance as given above. If d, C were known, then we could construct consistent confidence intervals for μ based on

$$\bar{y} \pm z_{\alpha/2} T^{-1/(2+d)} \sqrt{\frac{d(1+2d)}{C}}.$$

If the sequence is not Gaussian but a linear process, then a CLT is satisfied under the above conditions so the confidence interval is asymptotically valid in this case. However, generally we must learn both C and d from the data. One graphical way of getting some idea of d is to plot the log variance against sample size (by computing the sample variance for different subsample sizes), since $\log \text{var}(\bar{y}) = a + (2d - 1)\log(T)$. We discuss estimation below, but first note the unusual feature that d is the power of the sample size. Suppose that $\widehat{d}$ is a consistent estimator of d, then we need to show that $T^{\widehat{d}}/T^d \overset{P}{\longrightarrow} 1$; taking logs, we have to show that $(\widehat{d} - d)\log(T) \overset{P}{\longrightarrow} 0$, which is slightly stronger than $\widehat{d} - d = o_P(1)$.

The log periodogram regression is perhaps the simplest procedure for estimation of d For the harmonic frequencies λ_j close to zero ($j = 1, \ldots, m$), we have $\log I_y(\lambda_j) \simeq c - 2d \log \lambda_j + u_j$, where c is a constant and u_j are mean-zero random variables. We let

$\widehat{d}$ be the OLS estimator from this regression. Robinson (1994) proved that for the case $|d| < 1/2$ and $m = m(T) \to \infty$ but $m/T \to 0$,

$$\sqrt{m}(\widehat{d} - d) \Longrightarrow N\left(0, \frac{\pi^2}{24}\right).$$

The rate of convergence is slower than the square root of the sample size and depends on the choice of m. The confidence interval for d is

$$\widehat{d} \pm z_{\alpha/2}\sqrt{\frac{\pi^2}{24m}}.$$

6.3.7.2 A Test for Long Memory

Suppose that $(1 - L)^d y_t = \varepsilon_t$, where ε_t is a stationary short-memory process (with summable autocovariance function). We test the hypothesis $d = 0$ versus $d > 0$. Harris, McCabe, and Leybourne (2008) considered the following test statistic:

$$\tau = \frac{S_T}{\sqrt{\omega_T}}, \quad S_T = \frac{1}{(T - m)^{1/2}} \sum_{j=m}^{T-1} \frac{\widetilde{\gamma}_j}{j - m + 1}, \quad \omega_T = \sum_{j=-L}^{L} h_j \sum_{i=-L}^{L} \widetilde{\gamma}_i \widetilde{\gamma}_{i+j},$$

where $\widetilde{\gamma}_j$ is the estimated autocovariance function of y_t and $h_0 = \pi^2/6$, $h_j = \sum_{i=1}^{|j|} i^{-1}/|j|$, $j = \pm 1, \pm 2, \ldots$ Here, $m = (cT)^{1/2} \to \infty$ for some $c > 0$ and $l = l(T) \to \infty$. Under the null hypothesis, τ is asymptotically standard normal; under the alternative the statistic diverges.

6.4   Seasonality

We now turn to the issue of seasonality, that is, regular or periodic variation in a time series related to the seasons or higher-frequency variation.

6.4.1   General Framework

There are several ways of handling seasonality. It is very common practice to assume the additive decomposition

$$y_t = T_t + S_t + R_t, \tag{6.33}$$

where T_t is the trend component, S_t is the seasonal component, and R_t is the remainder term, where y_t is some transformation of the raw data such as the logarithm (which is equivalent to the multiplicative decomposition $y_t = T_t S_t R_t$ for the raw data). Seasonal adjustment basically estimates the seasonal component S_t then defines the seasonally adjusted data as $y_t - \widehat{S}_t$. This is widely done in macroeconomics using a variety of technologies, with the current best practice being called X-13ARIMA-SEATS, which aims to leave the trend intact but takes out the seasonal variation. In detrending, one estimates the trend T_t and constructs the detrended data $y_t - \widehat{T}_t$. In academic research one often works with data $y_t - \widehat{T}_t - \widehat{S}_t$ that has both been detrended and deseasonalized, which is a bit like taking alcohol and hops out of beer. Before we get there we have to define what makes T

a trend and what makes S a seasonal component, that is, how to separately identify these components.

We first define the seasonal component to be such that $S_t = S_{t-J}$ for some known integer J, called the period, or rather

$$\Delta_J S_t = 0, \tag{6.34}$$

where $\Delta_J = 1 - L^J$ is the seasonal differencing operator. This is the case of an exact or deterministic seasonality. This still does not provide identification because we may always take $S_t \to S_t + w$ and $T_t \to T_t - w$ without changing their sum and still preserving the periodicity. One approach is to normalize the seasonal component so that $\sum_{j=1}^{J} S_{t-j} = 0$, that is,

$$\Psi_J(L)S_t = 0, \tag{6.35}$$

where $\Psi_J(L) = (1 + L + \cdots + L^{J-1})$. Note that $(1-L)\Psi_J(L) = \Delta_J$. Under this restriction, the aggregated data $\Psi_J(L)y_t$ reflect only the trend and not the seasonal component. That is, we have

$$\sum_{j=1}^{J} y_{t+j} = \sum_{j=1}^{J} T_{t+j} + \sum_{j=1}^{J} S_{t+j} + \sum_{j=1}^{J} R_{t+j} = \sum_{j=1}^{J} T_{t+j} + \sum_{j=1}^{J} R_{t+j}.$$

Of course, this filter also affects both the trend and the remainder term, but in some cases the effect is manageable. If T_t is a deterministic polynomial of order p, then $\sum_{j=1}^{J} T_{t+j}$ is a deterministic polynomial of order p, albeit with transformed coefficients. If T_t is a pure random walk, then so will $\sum_{j=1}^{J} T_{t+j}$ be.

We discuss below specific methods for determining the trend and seasonal components, where the seasonal obeys the above restrictions. Before we do that we discuss some ways of measuring the magnitude of the different components given some specific estimates.

6.4.1.1 Strength of Effect

One proposal to measure the strength of the seasonal component (in a model without trend) is the peak-to-trough measure,

$$s = \max_{j=1,\dots,J} \sum_{t=0}^{T-J} S_{t+jJ} - \min_{j=1,\dots,J} \sum_{t=0}^{T-J} S_{t+jJ}.$$

If seasonality is measured by dummy variables, then $s = \max_{1 \le j \le J} \widehat{\gamma}_j - \min_{1 \le j \le J} \widehat{\gamma}_j$. One may normalize by the standard deviation of the data to compare across very different time series. For example, Feinstein (2002) showed that the seasonality in mortality rates varies by age and cause of death using US data. In particular, death by respiratory illness has a high seasonality and is very high in the 0–4 age group and also in the over-50 age group, in fact it increases monotonically with age after 50. On the other hand, death by neoplasm is much less seasonal for all ages. Climates usually have pronounced seasonality. In Figure 6.8 we show all the annual curves of monthly maximum temperature at Oxford over the period 1850–2022, that is, we plot 172 curves by month. The last 10

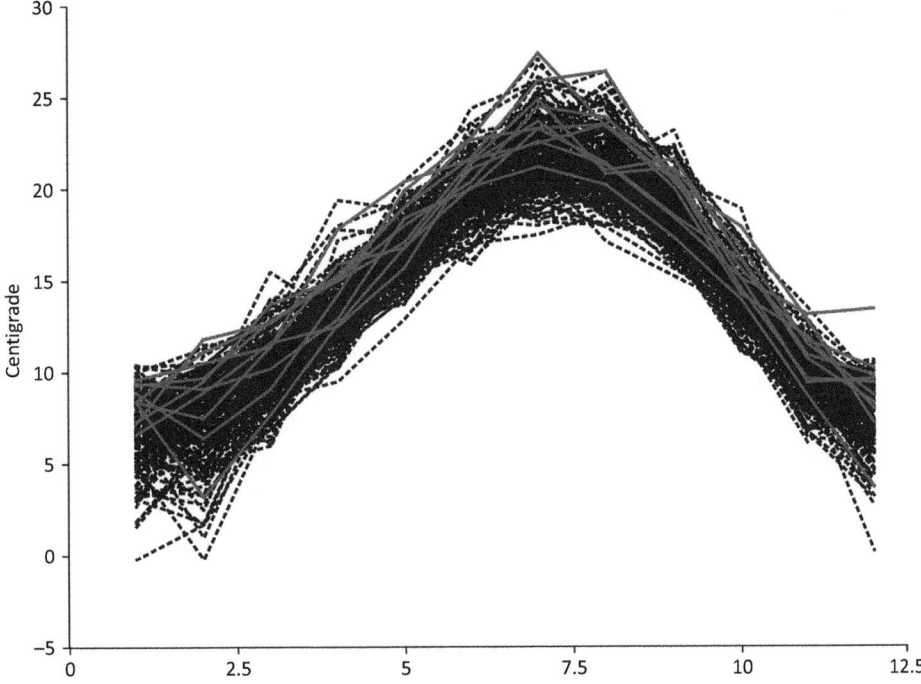

Figure 6.8 Maximum temperature in Oxford by year, plotted against month of the year.

years are shown in solid. From this, one can see the magnitude of the seasonal variation and the variability over years. The seasonal variation dominates the trend in this case.

An alternative measure of the strength of seasonality is

$$R_S^2 = 1 - \frac{\sum_{t=1}^{T}(R_t - \overline{R})^2}{\sum_{t=1}^{T}(S_t + R_t - \overline{S+R})^2},$$

which for uncorrelated components would lie between zero and one like a standard R-squared measure, but in general this may be negative. We may likewise measure the strength of the trend by

$$R_T^2 = 1 - \frac{\sum_{t=1}^{T}(R_t - \overline{R})^2}{\sum_{t=1}^{T}(T_t + R_t - \overline{T+R})^2}.$$

6.4.2 Deterministic Trend and Seasonal Model

One approach is based on a parametric model for both components. Suppose that there are J types of observations that are mutually exclusive and exhaustive. We use J dummy variables, one for each type, that is, $D_{1t} = 1$ if observation day t is type 1 and $D_{1t} = 0$ otherwise. Likewise $D_{2t} = 1$ if day t is type 2 and $D_{2t} = 0$ otherwise, and so on. If these represent seasonality then $S_t = S_{t-J}$. With daily stock market data, Monday to Friday, there would be five categories and the seasonal part repeats every week.

We suppose that the model for the response variable y is of the form

$$y_t = \beta_0 + \beta_1 t + \cdots + \beta_p t^p + \sum_{j=1}^{J} D_{jt}\delta_j + u_t, \tag{6.36}$$

where $T_t = \beta_0 + \beta_1 t + \cdots + \beta_p t^p$ is the trend and $S_t = \sum_{j=1}^{J} D_{jt}\delta_j$ is the seasonal component, while u_t is a mean-zero stationary process. The coefficients δ_j represent the effect of category j on the outcome. In the absence of seasonality, we might expect that $\delta_j = 0$ for $j = 1, \ldots, J$.

Because the categories are exclusive we have $\sum_{t=1}^{T} D_{jt}D_{kt} = 0$, while because they are exhaustive $D_{1t} + \cdots + D_{Jt} = 1$ for each t. This means that unrestricted estimation of the regression is not well defined and we need to impose at least one linear restriction to make progress. One possibility is to impose the restriction that $\sum_{j=1}^{J} \delta_j = 0$, which implies that the seasonal effect obeys the restriction (6.35). It follows that

$$y_t = \beta_0 + \beta_1 t + \cdots + \beta_p t^p + \sum_{j=1}^{J-1} D_{jt}^* \delta_j + \varepsilon_t,$$

where $D_{jt}^* = D_{jt} - D_{Jt}$ (goodbye December). This equation can be estimated by OLS. We can write this in matrix form,

$$y = Z\beta + D\delta + \varepsilon = X\theta + \varepsilon,$$

where $Z = (1, t, \ldots, t^p)_{t=1}^{T}$ is $T \times (p+1)$ and $D = (D_{1t}^*, \ldots, D_{J-1,t}^*)_{t=1}^{T}$ is $T \times (J-1)$, and $\beta = (\beta_0, \beta_1, \ldots, \beta_p)^{\mathsf{T}} \in \mathbb{R}^{p+1}$ and $\delta \in \mathbb{R}^{J-1}$. The OLS estimator is $\widehat{\theta} = (X^{\mathsf{T}}X)^{-1}X^{\mathsf{T}}y$, where $X = (Z, D)$. We may use the partial least squares formula, so that

$$\widehat{\delta} = \left(D^{\mathsf{T}}M_Z D\right)^{-1} D^{\mathsf{T}}M_Z y, \qquad \widehat{\beta} = \left(Z^{\mathsf{T}}M_D Z\right)^{-1} Z^{\mathsf{T}}M_D y,$$

where for a matrix A, $M_A = I - A(A^{\mathsf{T}}A)^{-1}A^{\mathsf{T}}$ denotes the projection matrix.

We first treat the case where $u_t = \varepsilon_t$ in (6.36) is i.i.d. with mean zero and variance σ^2. In this case we have

$$\sqrt{T}\left(\widehat{\delta} - \delta\right) \Longrightarrow N(0, V_D), \quad V_D = \sigma^2 \lim_{T \to \infty} \left(\frac{D^{\mathsf{T}}M_Z D}{T}\right)^{-1},$$

$$\Delta_T\left(\widehat{\beta} - \beta\right) \Longrightarrow N(0, V_T), \quad V_T = \sigma^2 \lim_{T \to \infty} \left(\Delta_T^{-1/2} Z^{\mathsf{T}}M_D Z \Delta_T^{-1/2}\right)^{-1}. \tag{6.37}$$

The differenced dummy variables are mutually correlated; the intercept column is orthogonal to all the dummy variable columns, but the trend variables are correlated with the dummy variables. The trend and seasonal component parameters are asymptotically uncorrelated, and so one can make inferences about them separately. Furthermore, regarding the trend part (the coefficients on $t, t^2, \ldots$ etc.), one can effectively ignore the seasonal component. On the other hand, regarding the seasonal component, if one ignores the trend one will have inconsistent estimates. This is a feature of a strong trend model; in the local trend model, the situation is similar but different.

We may test for the absence of seasonality by the Wald statistic that takes the form

$$\widehat{\delta}^{\mathsf{T}} D^{\mathsf{T}} M_Z D \widehat{\delta} / \sigma^2. \tag{6.38}$$

This is asymptotically chi-squared with $J - 1$ degrees of freedom under the null hypothesis. We may also want to evaluate the individual t-statistics. An alternative approach to testing for seasonality is to use an LM-type approach that estimates the trend component without seasonal effects and then fits the full seasonal dummy variable (no intercept) regression to the residuals.

We now consider the general case where u_t is a stationary process, which allows short-term and seasonal fluctuations around the trend. We may wish to model this process by, for example, an ARMA(p, q) process, and to estimate the parameters of that process, jointly with the trend and seasonal parameters, by, for example, the ML method. Alternatively, we may just wish to make inference statements about the trend and the seasonal components, in which case u is treated as a nuisance; in that case we may simply consider the effects of serial correlation in the error process on the limiting distribution of the regression parameters. In this case, although the trend variables satisfy $\Gamma_T Z = ZB$ for a nonsingular matrix B, the dummy variables do not necessarily satisfy this condition. The consequence is that OLS $\neq$ GLS. Nevertheless, we can obtain a CLT at the usual rate for the OLS estimators of the seasonal parameters and at the trend rate for the trend parameters:

$$\sqrt{T}\left(\widehat{\delta} - \delta\right) \Longrightarrow N\left(0, V_D\right), \qquad \Delta_T\left(\widehat{\beta} - \beta\right) \Longrightarrow N\left(0, V_T\right),$$

$$V_D = \lim_{T \to \infty} \left(\frac{D^{\mathsf{T}} M_Z D}{T}\right)^{-1} \lim_{T \to \infty} \left(\frac{D^{\mathsf{T}} M_Z \Gamma_T M_Z D}{T}\right) \lim_{T \to \infty} \left(\frac{D^{\mathsf{T}} M_Z D}{T}\right)^{-1},$$

$$V_T = \lim_{T \to \infty} \left(\Delta_T^{-1/2} Z^{\mathsf{T}} M_D Z \Delta_T^{-1/2}\right)^{-1} \lim_{T \to \infty} \left(\Delta_T^{-1/2} Z^{\mathsf{T}} M_D \Gamma_T M_D Z \Delta_T^{-1/2}\right)$$

$$\times \lim_{T \to \infty} \left(\Delta_T^{-1/2} Z^{\mathsf{T}} M_D Z \Delta_T^{-1/2}\right)^{-1}.$$

We may conduct inference about β and δ using standard linear regression techniques combined with long-run variance estimation. Alternatively, if we have a model for u_t we may use that. In fact, our primary interest may be in the short-run dynamics of the error process, so suppose that u_t is an ARMA(p, q) process $A(L)u_t = B(L)\varepsilon_t$, where ε_t is i.i.d. with mean zero and variance σ^2. A nice feature of the trend and seasonal model is that estimation of the parameters of A and B can be carried out on the deseasonalized data,

$$\widehat{u}_t = y_t - \sum_{k=0}^{p} \widehat{\beta}_k t^k - \sum_{j=1}^{J-1} D_{jt}^* \widehat{\delta}_j.$$

In fact, the large-sample behavior of the estimates of these ARMA parameters is the same as if one was working with u_t itself, so that, theoretically at least, deseasonalizing data does not affect the short-run dynamic relationships captured by A and B.

We may want to combine different levels of seasonality, for example daily seasonality and monthly seasonality. In this case we define two levels of dummy variables $D_{j_k t}^k$, where $k = 1, 2$ and $j_k = 1, \ldots, J_k$. In this case, we generally have $\sum_{t=1}^{T} D_{jt}^1 D_{kt}^2 / T \nrightarrow 0$. Nevertheless, we end up with a linear regression and the theory is essentially as above. One issue is how many terms to drop in the regression.

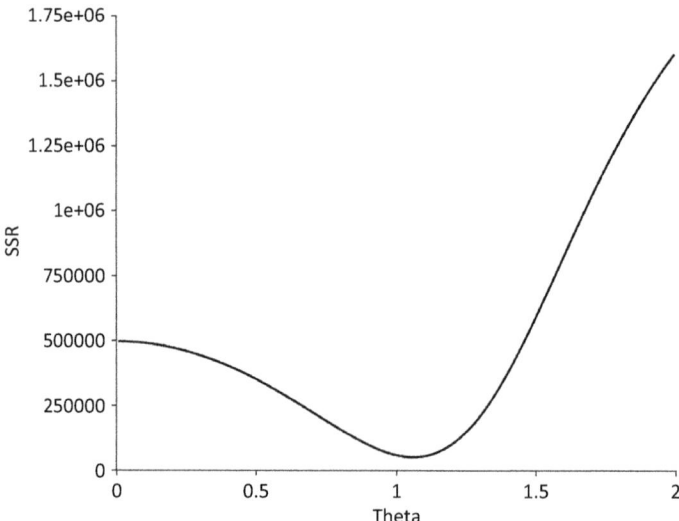

Figure 6.9 Profiled sum of squared regression residuals.

A second deterministic model for seasonality is based on trigonometric polynomials. Specifically, let

$$S_t = \sum_{j=1}^{k} \alpha_j \sin(\pi\theta_j t) + \gamma_j \cos(\pi\theta_j t), \qquad (6.39)$$

where θ_j^{-1} is the period of the jth component, and α_j, γ_j are parameters that define the magnitude of each component. For example, with $k = 1$ and $\theta_j = 1/J$, the properties of sines and cosines guarantee that $S_t = S_{t-J}$ for all t. This approach is suited to cases where the seasonality is regular, such as climate data. This approach can be extended to allow for multiple known periods. This approach has the advantage of being parsimonious, because only $2k$ parameters have to be estimated whereas for monthly seasonality, say, 11 dummy parameters would have to be estimated. For the Scottish mortality data one would have to use 51 dummy variables to describe the seasonality (but on the other hand they are mutually orthogonal regressors), and perhaps it would be sufficient to use a smaller number of trigonometric functions. Below we show how the method works on the Scottish mortality data. In this case we take the 51 estimated seasonal coefficients $\widehat{\beta}_j$ and fit the regression $\alpha \sin(\pi\theta j/52) + \gamma \cos(\pi\theta j/52)$ (we find $\widehat{\theta} = 1.05$ minimizes the profiled least squares objective functions shown in Figure 6.9) and then plot the fitted approximation along with the original coefficients in Figure 6.10.[4] In this case there does seem to be a single strong seasonal pattern: Scots are less likely to die in the summer and more likely to die in the winter.

One issue is holidays, which can be somewhat irregular. These can be handled by another category of dummy variables. For example, Figure 6.11 shows, for the US and

---

[4] The dummy variable model nests this as a special case, so we first obtain consistent estimates of the dummy coefficients and then fit them to a curve. The alternative method is to replace the dummy variables by the trignometric terms in the original time series regression.

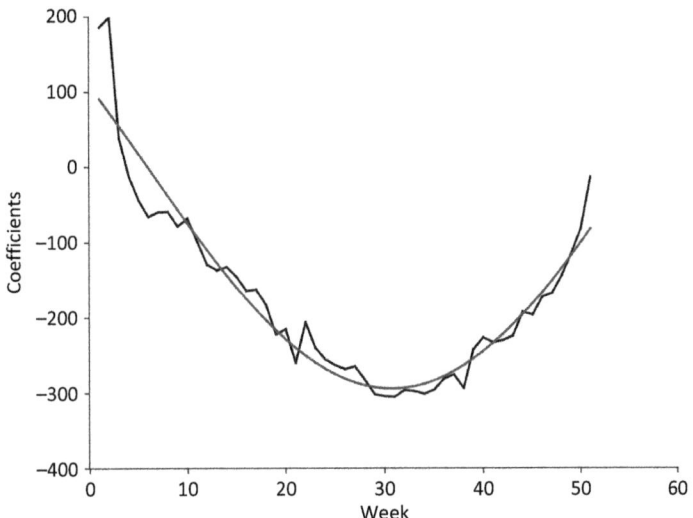

Figure 6.10 Original unrestricted seasonal coefficients along with a trigonometric fit.

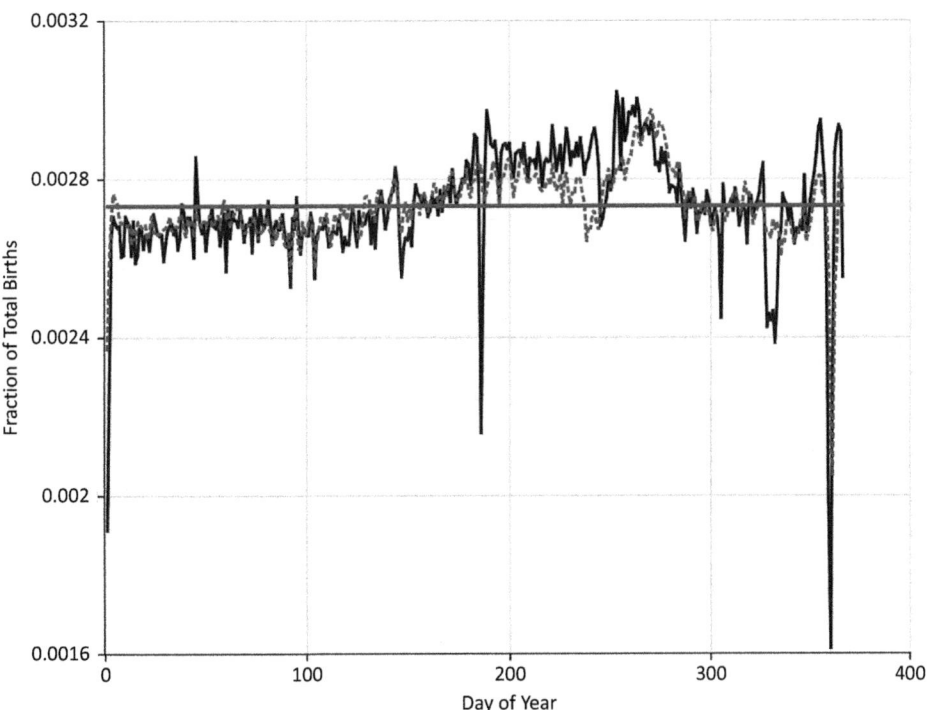

Figure 6.11 Frequency of birth by day of the year, US (solid) and UK (dashed).

UK, the frequency of births by day of the year plotted with the equally distributed line. There is a seasonal pattern to this series but there are big dips in both countries on December 25 and January 1, and in the US on July 4. Evidently, baby-delivering is either brought forward or delayed to avoid these important holidays. In this case, one might add dummy variables for these key dates and fit the rest of the curve with a couple of trigonometrics.

6.4.3 Nonparametric Trend and Seasonal Model

We consider the nonparametric analysis of seasonal time series. Suppose that we have a periodic or slowly varying periodic time series with period J and data $y_{1,t}, \ldots, y_{J,t}$ for "year" t. We suppose that J is fixed and $t = 1, \ldots, n$, with $T = nJ$ and n large but J fixed. The model is

$$
\begin{pmatrix} y_{t_1} \\ \vdots \\ y_{t_J} \end{pmatrix} = \begin{pmatrix} m_1(t_1/T) \\ \vdots \\ m_J(t_J/T) \end{pmatrix} + \begin{pmatrix} \varepsilon_{t_1} \\ \vdots \\ \varepsilon_{t_J} \end{pmatrix},
$$

where $m(\cdot) = (m_1(\cdot), \ldots, m_J(\cdot))^{\mathsf{T}}$ is a $J \times 1$ vector of smooth functions. We assume that m_j are smooth functions and that the errors are i.i.d. or weakly dependent. We can estimate $m_j(\cdot)$ using the dataset $\{y_{t_j}, t = 1, \ldots, n\}$. This is the starting point of the Cleveland *et al.* (1990) STL smoothing procedure that is embedded in R, for example. We can rewrite this model as

$$
y_t = \sum_{j=1}^{J} D_{jt} m_j(t/T) + \varepsilon_t, \tag{6.40}
$$

where $D_{jt} = 1$ if t is in period j. Here, the time index runs over $t = 1, \ldots, T$. We define the global trend as $f(u) = \sum_{j=1}^{J} m_j(u)/J$, and rewrite the model in an STL decomposition,

$$
y_t = f(t/T) + \sum_{j=1}^{J} D_{jt} \left[m_j(t/T) - f(t/T) \right] + \varepsilon_t,
$$

where $T_t = f(t/T)$ and $S_t = \sum_{j=1}^{J} D_{jt}(m_j(t/T) - f(t/T))$. We may estimate the global trend by averaging the period-specific trends and then interpret $m_j(u) - f(u)$ as the period-j-specific trend relative to this global trend. This model allows the seasonal effect to vary over time in a smooth (in time) way.

In some applications, say the stock market, we have observations more frequent than the periodicity, for example daily observations but only a monthly period. Or we may have multiple subcategories, for example day of the week effect and month of the year effect. In that case we may have $I_1, \ldots, I_J$ with $I_j \cap I_k = \varnothing$ and $\cup_{j=1}^{J} I_j = I = \{1, \ldots, T\}$, while $L_1, \ldots, L_M$ with $L_j \cap L_k = \varnothing$ and $\cup_{j=1}^{M} L_j = I$, but $I_j \cap L_k$ is not necessarily empty. The model is

$$
y_t = \sum_{j=1}^{J} D_{jt} m_j(t/T) + \sum_{k=1}^{M} D_{kt} g_k(t/T) + \varepsilon_t.
$$

In this case, for example, we may take January, Mondays as our first series $y_{t_{j_k}}$ with $t = 1, \ldots, n$, say. We have 60 different categories. We may define the January seasonal as the average of the January, Monday, ..., January, Friday, and so on.

6.4.4 Stochastic Seasonal Model

A seasonal AR(p) process is

$$
y_t = \phi_1 y_{t-J} + \phi_2 y_{t-2J} + \cdots + \phi_p y_{t-pJ} + \varepsilon_t,
$$

where J is the length of the seasonal effect. For example, with monthly data we may take $J = 12$. This is a special case of the AR(pJ) process that behaves similarly to the AR(p) process on multiples of J. For the $p = 1$ case, if $|\phi_1| < 1$ the process is stationary by the same arguments as for the AR(1) process. The MA representation is then $y_t = \sum_{k=0}^{\infty} \phi^{k-1} \varepsilon_{t-kJ}$, and the autocorrelation function is

$$\rho(j) = \text{corr}(y_t, y_{t-j}) = \begin{cases} \phi^k & \text{if } j = kJ \text{ for some integer } k, \\ 0 & \text{otherwise.} \end{cases}$$

This function is like the autocorrelation of the AR(1) process but with $J - 1$ zero values in between the decaying nonzero values. The autocorrelation function is maximized over $k = 1, 2, \ldots$ at $k = J$, which is one way of identifying the value J, were this to be unknown.

A seasonal MA(q) process is $y_t = \varepsilon_t - \theta_1 \varepsilon_{t-J} - \cdots - \theta_q \varepsilon_{t-qJ}$, where J is the length of the seasonal effect. This behaves similarly to the MA(q) process except that its horizon is longer and there are gaps between the seasonally aligned observations.

Hillmer and Tiao (1982) built a general approach for capturing seasonal effects along with trends. They assumed that deterministic effects have been removed from y_t. They supposed that (6.33) holds for some trend T, some seasonal S, and some "noise" R. They further assumed that T, S, and R all follow the stochastic processes

$$A_T(L)T_t = B_T(L)w_t, \quad A_S(L)S_t = B_S(L)\eta_t, \quad A_R(L)R_t = B_R(L)u_t, \tag{6.41}$$

where w_t, u_t, and η_t are i.i.d. mean-zero shocks and are mutually uncorrelated, that is, the processes are ARIMA(p_j, d_j, q_j). They assume that the autoregressive polynomials A_j have no common zeros, and have roots on or outside the unit circle (i.e., unit roots). The stochastic trend is assumed to be of the form

$$A_T(L) = 1 - L^d \tag{6.42}$$

for some known integer d, and $B_T(L)$ is a polynomial of degree at most d, while the seasonal process satisfies

$$A_S(L) = 1 + L + \cdots + L^{J-1} \tag{6.43}$$

and $B_S(L)$ is a polynomial of degree at most $J - 1$. This seasonal operator is such that $A_S(L)S_t = \sum_{t=0}^{J-1} S_t$. In the stochastic model we consider here, this quantity is not zero but a stationary moving average process, which is a natural generalization of the deterministic model in which $\sum_{t=0}^{J-1} S_t = 0$. The remainder process is assumed to be a stationary ARMA process. These stochastic processes seem to capture the notion of what a trend is and what a seasonal component is. The spectral density of T_t has an infinite peak at the origin (the pseudo-spectrum, that is), whereas the spectral density of S_t is infinite at the seasonal frequencies $\lambda = 2k\pi/J$ for $k = 1, \ldots, \lfloor J/2 \rfloor$, and achieves a minimum at $\lambda = 0$. The model for S, T, and R implies that the observed series y_t is an ARIMA process,

$$A(L)y_t = B(L)\varepsilon_t, \tag{6.44}$$

where $A(L)$ is the highest common factor of $A_S(L)$, $A_T(L)$, and $A_R(R)$. The question is whether the model components (T, S, R) are identified under this structure. Because of the additivity of the autocovariance function and the spectrum we have $\gamma_y(j) = \gamma_T(j) +$

$\gamma_S(j) + \gamma_R(j)$ and $f_y(\lambda) = f_T(\lambda) + f_S(\lambda) + f_R(\lambda)$, which gives restrictions on the set of allowable parameters in the trend, seasonal, and remainder processes, but it is not sufficient for identification of the whole model.

We can see that (Findley et $al.$, 1998) $A(L) = A_T(L)A_S(L)A_R(L)$, and once d is specified, we may identify $A_R(L) = A(L)/A_T(L)A_S(L)$. It is more difficult to identify the moving average polynomials. Suppose we have determined the autoregressive part, so we essentially have the model

$$B(L)\varepsilon_t = B_T(L)w_t + B_S(L)\eta_t + B_R(L)u_t, \tag{6.45}$$

where B is known and the right-hand side components are mutually uncorrelated processes. Clearly, there are many choices of B_T, B_S, and B_R compatible with B. The order of B is the maximum order of B_T, B_S, and B_R. One solution is to make $B_T(L) = 1$ and $B_S(L) = 1$, and place no restrictions on $B_R(L)$. In that case we may identify all model components from the ARIMA model for y. Bell and Hilmer (1984) proposed an alternative restriction to identify the model.

The X-13 procedure is based on the decomposition

$$\phi(L)\Phi(L^J)\left(1 - L\right)^d\left(1 - L^J\right)^D y_t = \theta(L)\Theta(L^J)\varepsilon_t,$$

where $\phi(L) = 1 - \phi_1 L - \cdots - \phi_p L^p$, $\Phi(L^J) = 1 - \Phi_1 L^J - \cdots - \Phi_P L^{JP}$, $\theta(L) = 1 - \theta_1 L - \cdots - \theta_q L^q$, and $\Theta(L^J) = 1 - \Theta_1 L^J - \cdots - \Theta_Q L^{JQ}$, which allows for general ARMA p, P, q, Q and differencing orders d, D.

The seasonal long-memory process can be defined as $f_y(\lambda) \sim C_f|\lambda - \lambda_0|^{-2d}$ as $\lambda \to \lambda_0 \in [-\pi, \pi]$, where $d \in (0, 1/2)$. A process that satisfies this is

$$\left(1 - 2\cos(\lambda_0)L + L^2\right)^d y_t = \varepsilon_t,$$

where ε_t is i.i.d. with mean zero and variance σ^2. This is often called the Gegenbauer process. It can be written as a moving average with coefficients that decay like $d - 1$. In this case,

$$C_f = \frac{\sigma^2}{2\pi}\sin(\lambda_0).$$

The autocovariance function is of the form $\gamma_y(k) \sim Ck^{2d-1}\cos(2\pi k\lambda_0)$ as $k \to \infty$; this oscillates about zero but the decay is the same as in a standard long-memory process.

There seem to be several methods of seasonal adjustment used by central banks and other agencies, and it is not often easy to find out which method has been used with which particular tuning parameters for a given series. The X11, X12, and X13 methods with various versions (developed by the US census bureau) are dominant, although STL also features. In fact, the practical issues raised by seasonal adjustment are considerable.

6.5   Application

In Figures 6.12–6.15 we show some STL decompositions. We first consider the US unemployment monthly series, seasonally adjusted and seasonally unadjusted from January 1948 to April 2021. We consider models for the level of unemployment and the

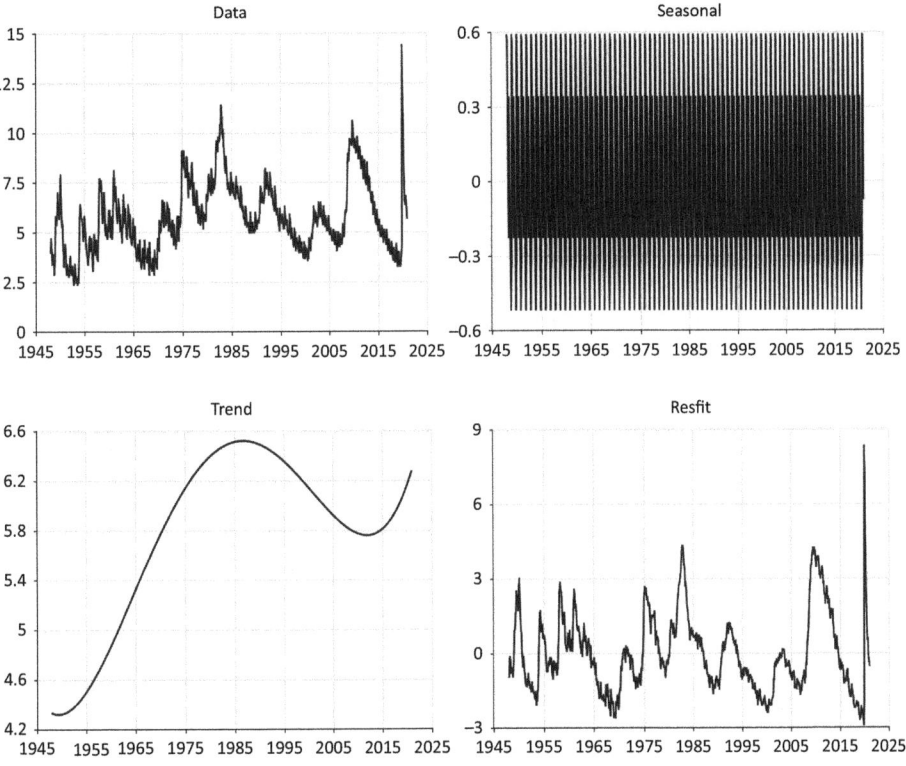

Figure 6.12 STL of log of monthly unemployment with quartic trend.

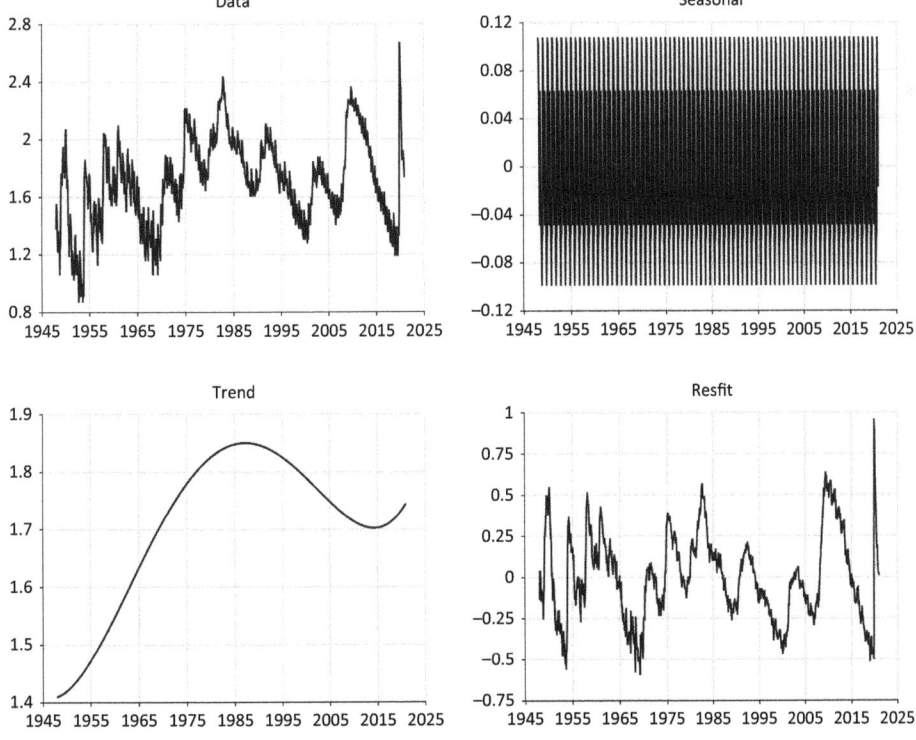

Figure 6.13 STL of the level of monthly unemployment (not seasonally adjusted).

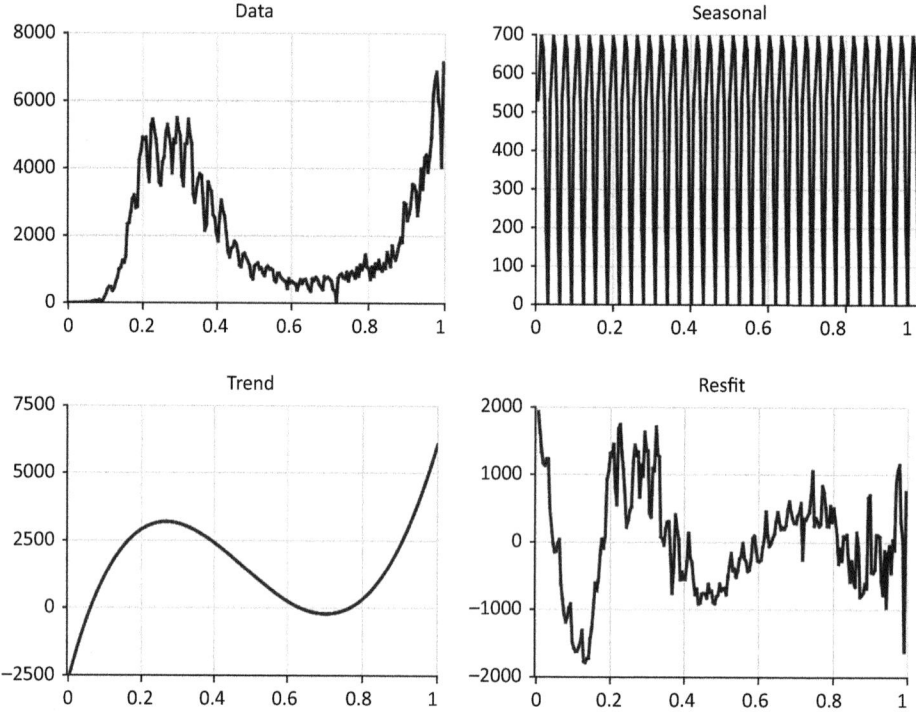

Figure 6.14 STL decomposition of daily UK COVID data using a quartic polynomial and day of the week dummies.

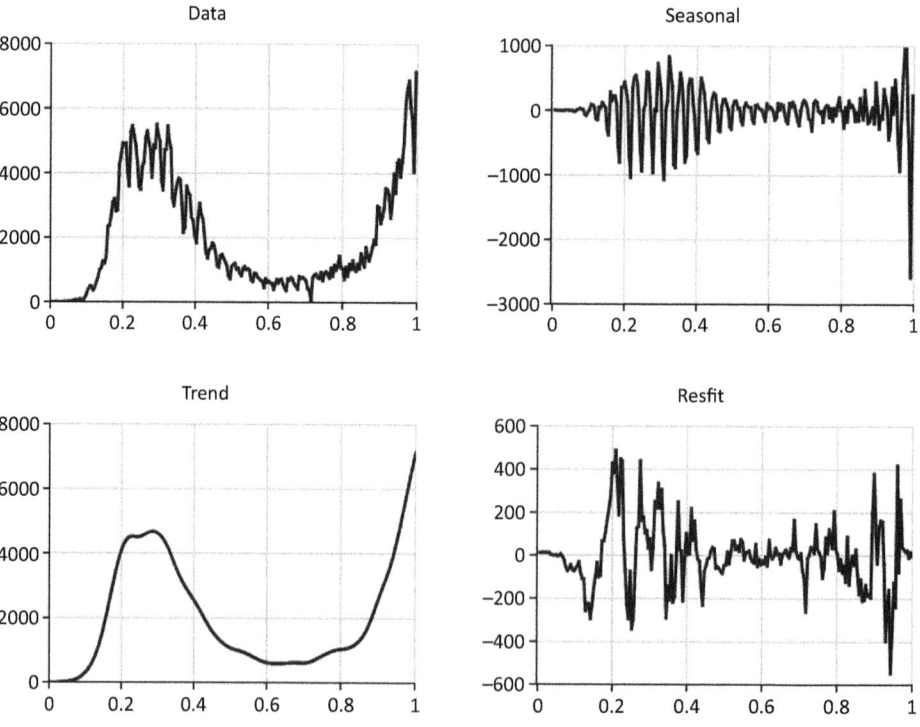

Figure 6.15 STL based on kernel smoothing.

logarithm of unemployment, and we consider a quartic trend along with differences of monthly dummy variables to the January dummy variable. We first consider the seasonally unadjusted series. The regression of the logarithm on the quartic trend alone produces an adjusted R^2 of 0.179 (with significant t-statistics on the quadratic, cubic, and quartic polynomial). Adding in the 11 dummy variables increases the adjusted R^2 to 0.220, which is a statistically significant improvement; 5 of the 11 seasonal dummy variables are significant. A similar result is obtained for the level regressions, with the adjusted R^2 increasing from 0.146 to 0.19 as we add the seasonal dummies. We show the STL decompositions in Figures 6.12 and 6.13. The seasonal component is statistically significant but it is not large, in the level formulation the coefficients are respectively 0.563 74, 0.299 34, −0.071 82, −0.223 26, 0.338 97, 0.180 63, −0.142 11, −0.337 46, −0.515 02, −0.362 45, and −0.319 49; the max-min measure of seasonal variation is around 1.10%. The trend is quite pronounced. The residuals are still heavily serially correlated. The seasonally adjusted series would add the trend back to the residual. By comparison, applying the same procedures to the officially seasonally adjusted series we find the trend is significant as before in either formulation but the seasonal dummies are not significant either individually or jointly in either formulation. They did a good job.

We next show, in Figures 6.14 and 6.15, an application of deterministic STL decomposition using polynomial trend and kernel smoothing applied to the daily UK COVID-19 case series.

6.6   Summary

We considered different types of nonstationarity and their implications for modelling, estimation, and inference. We considered both trend and seasonal components. We considered deterministic parametric approaches as well as nonparametric smoothing methods. We also considered stochastic trend approaches based on random walks and their generalizations. In each case we provided the tools to also conduct inference.

The R language has a function stl that decomposes a time series into trend, seasonal, and residual. Hastie and Tibshirani (1990) gave a good description of this method. The package seasonal is a powerful interface between R and X-13ARIMA-SEATS, the seasonal adjustment software developed by the United States Census Bureau. Stock (1994) is a great survey of the unit root literature.

6.7   Exercises

6.1 Suppose that $y_t = \alpha + \beta t^{-\gamma} + u_t$, where u_t is i.i.d. normally distributed with mean zero and variance σ^2. Suppose that $\gamma > 0$ is an unknown parameter; this is called the evaporating trend model. Let $\widehat{\sigma}^2 = (1/T) \sum_{t=1}^{T} (y_t - \bar{y})^2$. Show that $\widehat{\sigma}^2$ is a consistent estimator of σ^2. Suggest a confidence interval for the parameter α.

6.2 Suppose that $y_{1t} = \beta y_{2t} + u_{1t}$, $y_{2t} = \gamma t + u_{2t}$, where $(u_{1t}, u_{2t})^{\mathsf{T}}$ is i.i.d. normally distributed with mean zero and a covariance matrix

$$\Sigma = \begin{pmatrix} 2 & 1 \\ 1 & 1 \end{pmatrix}$$

that is known to the econometrician. Suggest three different ways of estimating the structural parameter β and compare their large-sample efficiency.

6.3 Suppose that $x_t = x_{t-1} + w_t \varepsilon_t$, $y_t = \sum_{s=0}^{t} x_s$, where $x_0 = 0$ and ε_t are i.i.d. shocks with mean zero and variance σ^2, while $\{w_t\}$ are deterministic weights. What are the properties of x_t, y_t in the following two cases?

(a) $w_t = 1$ for all $t \geq 1$

(b) $w_t = 1/t$ for all $t \geq 1$

6.4 Suppose that $x_t = x_{t-1} + u_t$, where u_t are independent shocks with $u_t \sim U[-x_{t-1}, 1 - x_{t-1}]$, and let $x_0 \in [0, 1]$. Explain why $x_t \in [0, 1]$. Prove that if $x_0 \sim U[0, 1]$, then $x_1 \sim U[0, 1]$ and so on, that is, x_t is a stationary process with standard uniform marginal distribution. Let $y_t = \Phi^{-1}(x_t)$, where Φ is the CDF of a standard normal random variable. Generate a sample path and comment on the properties of the process y_t. Show that its autocorrelations are very small and not different from zero.

6.5 Suppose we have daily data y_t over many years and we suppose that

$$y_t = \beta_1 D_{1t} + \cdots + \beta_m D_{mt} + \varepsilon_t,$$

where ε_t is i.i.d. with mean zero and variance σ_ε^2, while D_{jt} are annual dummies with $D_{jt} = 1$ if observation t is in year t.

(a) Show that the OLS estimator of β_j is just the average value of y in year j.

(b) We wish to test whether there is an upward trend in y, that is,

$$H_0: \beta_1 \leq \beta_2 \leq \cdots \leq \beta_m,$$

against the null hypothesis that is the violation of this. Provide a test of this hypothesis.

6.6 You are working with the Covid19 daily data of new cases and new deaths for the USA from December 31, 2019 to December 14, 2020. Let c_t, d_t be the natural logarithms of the new cases and new deaths plus one. Let D_{jt} be day of the week dummy variables with $D_{1t} = 1$ if day t is Monday and $D_{1t} = 0$ otherwise. Estimate the following models, and discuss the results.

(a) For $y_t = c_t$ or d_t,

$$y_t = \beta_0 + \beta_1 t + \beta_2 t^2 + \beta_3 t^3 + \beta_4 t^4 + D_{1,t} \gamma_1 + \cdots + D_{7,t} \gamma_7 + \varepsilon_t.$$

(b) For $y_t = c_t$ or d_t,

$$x_t = (1 - L)^2 \left(1 + L + \cdots + L^6\right) y_t,$$
$$x_t = \phi x_{t-1} + \varepsilon_t - \theta \varepsilon_{t-1}.$$

6.7 Consider the two monthly unemployment time series UNRATENSA and UNRATE. Run the regressions

$$y_t = \mu + \sum_{j=1}^{11} \gamma_j D_{jt} + \varepsilon_t,$$

where D_{jt} are monthly regressions and y_t is unemployment (either seasonally adjusted or seasonally unadjusted) and comment on the different results.

6.8 Consider the two monthly unemployment time series UNRATENSA and UNRATE. Run the regressions

$$y_t - \bar{y} = \sum_{j=1}^{12} \gamma_j D_{jt} + \varepsilon_t,$$

where D_{jt} are monthly regressions and y_t is unemployment with sample mean $\bar{y}$ (either seasonally adjusted or seasonally unadjusted). Compare the approaches of the two questions.

6.9 Consider the two monthly unemployment time series UNRATENSA and UNRATE. Fit an AR(12) model to both series and comment on the difference in fit between the two series.

6.10 Carry out some unit root tests on both UNRATENSA and UNRATE. Specifically, do the DF test with intercept and with intercept and trend, and likewise the ADF tests with $p = 5$. Comment on the difference.

6.11 Using the Covid19 dataset, extract the time series of cases and deaths from COVID-19 for Sweden over the period 20200101–20201214. Let $y_t = \log(c_t + 1)$, where c_t is the number of new daily cases. Fit the model

$$y_t = \alpha + \sum_{j=1}^{p} \beta_j t^j + u_t$$

for different values of p and choose the best p. Then let $\hat{u}_t = y_t - \hat{\alpha} + \sum_{j=1}^{p} \hat{\beta}_j t^j$ for each day. Run the regression

$$\hat{u}_t = \sum_{j=1}^{7} \gamma_j D_{jt} + e_t,$$

where D_{jt} are day of the week dummies. Test the hypothesis that $\gamma_1 = \cdots = \gamma_7 = 0$ under the assumption that u_t is i.i.d. Now reestimate the model

$$y_t = \alpha + \sum_{j=1}^{p} \beta_j t^j + \sum_{j=1}^{7} \gamma_j D_{jt} + u_t$$

and compare the results. If you are feeling lucky, do the same for Norway and compare the results.

7 Multivariate Linear Time Series

So far we have focused on univariate time series, which is often a starting point for analysis. However, most economic models involve the interaction between different series, such as quantity and price. We discuss here the vector time series case. First we examine stationarity and dependence considerations, then we define multivariate autocovariances, and then we consider some linear time series models for vector processes. Many concepts generalize naturally, but there are some new issues to consider in the multivariate case. There are also some new mathematical requirements in terms of matrix algebra.

7.1 Second-Order Properties: Autocovariance and Autocorrelation

The concepts of stationarity and weak dependence carry over directly to the vector case with some additional complications. For a vector $y_t = (y_{1t}, \ldots, y_{nt})^\mathsf{T} \in \mathbb{R}^n$ define the mean vector $m_t = E(y_t)$ and autocovariance matrix

$$\Gamma_{yy}(t, s) = E((y_t - \mu)(y_s - \mu)^\mathsf{T})$$

for each t, s, assuming that these quantities are well defined. For some arguments we will further require that $C \leq E((y_t - \mu)(y_t - \mu)^\mathsf{T}) \leq C^{-1}$ for some finite positive-definite matrix C, where the ordering is in the sense of matrix partial order. Provided m_t does not depend on t and $\Gamma_{yy}(t, s) = \Gamma_{yy}(t - s)$ for all integer t, s, we say that the process y_t is weakly stationary. We may equivalently say that the vector y_t is weakly stationary provided the scalar process $c^\mathsf{T} y_t$ is weakly stationary for every vector $c \in \mathbb{R}^n$, perforce for each element of the vector. One issue is how to label the case where some components of a vector are stationary and others are nonstationary, in which case the above definition would say the vector process is not stationary. We discuss this case later. It is also possible that each individual series is weakly stationary but the vector itself is not.[1]

Example 7.1 Suppose that

$$y_{1t} = \rho_t u_t + \sqrt{1 - \rho_t^2} w_t, \qquad y_{2t} = u_t,$$

---

[1] A vector process may not be white noise even if all its components are. For example, suppose that $y_t = (\varepsilon_t, \varepsilon_{t-1}, \ldots, \varepsilon_{t-n})^\mathsf{T}$, where ε_t are i.i.d. and so each component is white noise; however, the vector y_t is autocorrelated with $E(y_{1t} y_{2,t+1}) = \sigma^2$. Furthermore, a vector process may not be mixing even if all its components are marginally mixing.

where u_t, w_t are i.i.d. standard normal random variables and mutually independent, while ρ_t is a deterministic sequence. The correlation between y_{1t} and y_{2t} is ρ_t and varies over time, while the marginal means and variances are zero and one respectively for all t, and the marginal autocovariance functions are zero for all lags. In this case, the vector (y_{1t}, y_{2t}) is nonstationary and $c_1 y_{1t} + c_2 y_{2t}$ is nonstationary unless $c_1 \times c_2 = 0$.

Suppose that $y_t \in \mathbb{R}^n$ is a vector (weakly) stationary series; then the autocovariance matrix is defined as

$$\Gamma_{yy}(k) = E\big((y_t - \mu) (y_{t+k} - \mu)^\top \big) \tag{7.1}$$

for $k = 0, \pm 1, \ldots$ The usual definition of the cross-autocorrelation matrix is

$$R_{yy}(k) = D^{-1/2} \Gamma(k) D^{-1/2}, \tag{7.2}$$

where D is the diagonal matrix containing the diagonal elements of $\Gamma(0)$; $R_{yy}(0)$ is the contemporaneous correlation matrix of the vector y_t that has unit diagonals and off-diagonals bounded by one in magnitude. There is an analogous multivariate partial autocorrelation matrix, but it seems not much used. Replacing the subscript y by i, j to denote individual components, $R_{ij}(k) \in [-1, 1]$ for any pair i, j, and any k. An alternative multivariate association measure is $R_{yy}^{\&}(k) = \Gamma(0)^{-1/2} \Gamma(k) \Gamma(0)^{-1/2}$, where $A^{1/2}$ denotes the unique square root of the symmetric positive-definite matrix A, which has the property $R_{yy}^{\&}(0) = I_n$; we mostly concentrate on $R_{yy}(k)$. For any $i = 1, \ldots, n$,

$$\Gamma_{ii}(k) = \mathrm{cov}(y_{it}, y_{i,t+k}), \qquad R_{ii}(k) = \mathrm{corr}(y_{it}, y_{i,t+k}), \quad k = 0, 1, 2, \ldots,$$

are the marginal autocovariance and autocorrelation functions. The new thing here is the so-called cross-autocovariance and cross-autocorrelation

$$\Gamma_{ij}(k) = \mathrm{cov}(y_{it}, y_{j,t+k}), \qquad R_{ij}(k) = \mathrm{corr}(y_{it}, y_{j,t+k}) = \frac{\Gamma_{ij}(k)}{\Gamma_{ii}^{1/2}(0) \Gamma_{jj}^{1/2}(0)},$$

which measure the predictability of future $y_{j,t+k}$ (in the case $k > 0$) by current y_{it}. Note that it can be the case that $\Gamma_{ij}(k) \geq \Gamma_{ii}(k), \Gamma_{jj}(k)$ and $R_{ij}(k) \geq R_{ii}(k), R_{jj}(k)$, and we see an example of this below. We may interpret $R_{ij}(k)$ as the slope coefficient β_{ijk} in the linear regression of the standardized variables (they may have different means and variances), that is, we have

$$\frac{y_{j,t+k} - \mu_j}{\sigma_j} = \beta_{ijk} \frac{y_{i,t} - \mu_i}{\sigma_i} + e_{ijk,t},$$

where e_{ijk} is an error term uncorrelated with y_{it}, while μ_i, σ_i are the means and standard deviations of the time series y_{it}, and $\beta_{ijk} = R_{ij}(k)$. Analogously to the univariate case we may define the $nT \times nT$ autocovariance matrix

$$\Gamma_Y = \begin{pmatrix} \Gamma_{11} & \cdots & \Gamma_{1n} \\ \vdots & \ddots & \vdots \\ \Gamma_{n1} & \cdots & \Gamma_{nn} \end{pmatrix}$$

$$= E\big[(\mathrm{vec}(Y) - E(\mathrm{vec}(Y))) (\mathrm{vec}(Y) - E(\mathrm{vec}(Y)))^\top \big], \tag{7.3}$$

where the $n \times T$ matrix $Y = (y_{it})_{i,t}$ and $\mathrm{vec}(Y)$ is the row-wise vectorization operator (Magnus and Neudecker, 1988). The matrix Γ_Y is symmetric, involving the $T \times T$ matrices Γ_{ij}.

Hong, Linton, and Zhang (2017) defined the multivariate variance ratio as

$$\mathrm{VR}(K) = \frac{\mathrm{var}(y_t)^{-1/2} \times \mathrm{var}(y_t(K)) \times \mathrm{var}(y_t)^{-1/2}}{K},$$

where $y_t(K) = y_t + \cdots + y_{t+K-1}$ is the K-period sum of y_t. It follows that

$$\mathrm{VR}(K) = I_n + 2\sum_{k=1}^{K-1} \left(1 - \frac{k}{K}\right)\left(R_{yy}^{\&}(k) + R_{yy}^{\&}(-k)\right),$$

that is, the variance ratio is a weighted combination of the forward and backward autoassociation matrices $R_{yy}^{\&}(k)$.

In the univariate case we have $\gamma(k) = \gamma(-k)$, but the multivariate analogue of this is not necessarily true. In particular, we have $\Gamma_{ij}(k) \neq \Gamma_{ji}(k)$, and the differences may have interpretation. In fact, $\Gamma_{ij}(k) = \Gamma_{ji}(-k)$ and, in matrix terms, $\Gamma_{yy}(k) = \Gamma_{yy}(-k)^{\mathsf{T}}$ and $R_{yy}(k) = R_{yy}(-k)^{\mathsf{T}}$. Suppose that $\Gamma_{ij}(k) \neq 0$ and $\Gamma_{ji}(k) = 0$ for some k. Then we interpret this as meaning that i is predicting future j but not vice versa (although see the discussion under Granger causality). This is an important property that is possessed by many models. Patterns of lead–lag behavior are likely to be complicated and we may need to check over multiple lags. Hong, Linton, and Zhang (2017) proposed computing the difference of a forward variance ratio and a backward variance ratio as a measure of the degree to which unit i precedes unit j up to horizon K.

As in the univariate case we may distinguish between the case where $\sum_{k=0}^{\infty} \Gamma_{yy}(k)$ exists or it does not. Here, we talk element by element and it is sufficient that all the diagonal elements of the matrix $\Gamma_{yy}(k)$ are summable as this implies that the off-diagonal ones are summable too by the Cauchy–Schwarz inequality. We define the long-run variance of the stationary vector process as

$$\mathrm{lrvar}(y_t) = \sum_{k=-\infty}^{\infty} \Gamma_{yy}(k) = \Gamma_{yy}(0) + \sum_{k=1}^{\infty}\left(\Gamma_{yy}(k) + \Gamma_{yy}(k)^{\mathsf{T}}\right), \tag{7.4}$$

when this limit exists.

The spectral density matrix is defined (when it exists) as the Fourier transform of the autocovariance matrix, element by element, thus

$$f_{yy}(\lambda) = \frac{1}{2\pi}\sum_{k=-\infty}^{\infty} \Gamma_{yy}(k)\exp\left(-\mathrm{i}\lambda k\right), \tag{7.5}$$

which has diagonal elements given by the marginal spectral density of the ith process that we discussed earlier. As in the univariate case, the long-run variance matrix can be expressed as $\mathrm{lrvar}(y_t) = 2\pi f_{yy}(0)$. The off-diagonal elements, denoted $f_{ij}(\lambda)$, are complex valued in general, and they also have interpretations. The quantity

$$\mathcal{H}_{jk}^2(\lambda) = \frac{|f_{jk}(\lambda)|^2}{f_{jj}(\lambda)f_{kk}(\lambda)} \tag{7.6}$$

is called the squared **coherency** function; it is a real-valued function that lies between zero and one. It measures the strength of the linear relationship between y_{jt} and y_{kt} at frequency λ, a frequency-domain counterpart of the cross-autocorrelation. The counterpart of the slope of the best linear predictor coefficient $\beta = \mathrm{cov}(y_{jt}, y_{kt})/\mathrm{var}(y_{jt})$ is $\widetilde{\beta}(\lambda) = f_{jk}(\lambda)f_{jj}(\lambda)^{-1}$, which is frequency specific and complex valued. A linearly filtered series $x_t = \sum_{k=-\infty}^{\infty} \psi_k y_{t-k}$ (for $n \times n$ matrices ψ_k with $\sum_{k=-\infty}^{\infty} |\psi_{k;i,j}| < \infty$) has spectral density

$$f_{xx}(\lambda) = B_\psi(\lambda)^* f_{yy}(\lambda) B_\psi(\lambda),$$

where $*$ denotes the complex conjugate transpose of the matrix, while $B_\psi(\lambda) = \sum_{k=-\infty}^{\infty} \psi_k \exp(-\mathrm{i}\lambda k)$ is the multivariate transfer function. The multivariate filters change not just the properties of the individual series but also the relationships between them.

Example 7.2   Suppose that $y_{jt} = \alpha + \beta y_{kt} + \varepsilon_t$, where ε_t is i.i.d. with mean zero, variance σ^2, and is independent of the process y_{kt}. Suppose that we observe the filtered series $y_{jt}^* = \sum_{l=0}^{\infty} \psi_l y_{j,t-l}$ and $y_{kt}^* = \sum_{l=0}^{\infty} \phi_l y_{k,t-l}$, which may arise from seasonal adjustment. Let $\widetilde{\beta}(\lambda) = f_{j,k}(\lambda)/f_{j,j}(\lambda)$ and $\widetilde{\beta}^*(\lambda) = f_{j,k}^*(\lambda)/f_{j,j}^*(\lambda)$ denote the band spectrum regression parameters from the regressions with (y_{jt}, y_{kt}) and (y_{jt}^*, y_{kt}^*) respectively (Engle, 1974). Then

$$\widetilde{\beta}^*(\lambda) = \frac{\widetilde{\psi}(\lambda)}{\widetilde{\phi}(\lambda)} \widetilde{\beta}(\lambda). \tag{7.7}$$

For any stationary vector process y_t with finite variance there exists a Wold representation

$$y_t = \sum_{k=0}^{\infty} W_k \varepsilon_{t-k} + v_t, \tag{7.8}$$

where $\{\varepsilon_t\}$ is a white noise process, that is, mean zero and uncorrelated with its own past, while v_t is a linearly deterministic process, and $\sum_{k=0}^{\infty} |W_{k;i,j}| < \infty$ for all i,j. There is a further uniqueness issue in the vector case related to the contemporaneous relationship between the shocks ε_t. Specifically, we can replace $W_j \mapsto W_j\Omega$ and $\varepsilon_s \mapsto \Omega^{-1}\varepsilon_s$ for any nonsingular matrix Ω. One approach to resolve this is to suppose that ε_t satisfies $E(\varepsilon_t \varepsilon_t^\mathsf{T}) = I_n$, so that the shocks are identical in magnitude and mutually orthogonal. This kind of resolves the question, although note that if $\varepsilon_t \mapsto Q\varepsilon_t = \varepsilon_t^*$, where Q is an orthonormal matrix (i.e., $QQ^\mathsf{T} = Q^\mathsf{T}Q = I$), then $E(\varepsilon_t^*) = 0$ and $E(\varepsilon_t^* \varepsilon_t^{*\mathsf{T}}) = I_n$. Shocks that are perfectly mutually uncorrelated are appealing for modelling purposes since they can be labelled in terms of economic concepts and one can talk about their unique effect. Under some conditions one may invert the moving average representation to obtain $y_t - v_t = \sum_{j=0}^{\infty} C_j(y_{t-j} - v_{t-j}) + \varepsilon_t$ for some matrices C_j.

7.1.1   Estimation and Inference about Means, Autocovariances and Autocorrelations

We next discuss estimation based on the data $\{y_1, \ldots, y_T\}$. We estimate the population mean by the sample mean, and the population autocovariance and autocorrelation matrix functions by the sample equivalents,

$$\bar{y} = \frac{1}{T} \sum_{t=1}^{T} y_t,$$

$$\widehat{\Gamma}_{yy}(k) = \frac{1}{T} \sum_{t=1}^{T-k} (y_t - \bar{y})(y_{t+k} - \bar{y})^{\mathsf{T}},$$

$$\widehat{R}_{yy}(k) = \widehat{D}^{-1/2} \widehat{\Gamma}_{yy}(k) \widehat{D}^{-1/2},$$

where $\widehat{D} = \text{diag}(\widehat{\Gamma}(0))$. The matrices $\widehat{\Gamma}_{yy}(k), \widehat{R}_{yy}(k)$ are positive definite and symmetric for $k = 0$ but not necessarily so for $k \neq 0$.

The properties of the vector sample mean follow as for the univariate case. Specifically, under the Herrndorf (1984) conditions, $\sqrt{T}(\bar{y} - \mu) \implies N(0, V)$, where $V = \text{lrvar}(y_t)$. The inference methods we discussed in Chapter 5 are all available here to conduct hypothesis tests about μ or construct confidence regions.

We next consider the statistical properties of the sample autocovariance and autocorrelation matrices. By the same arguments as for the univariate case we have

$$\widehat{\Gamma}_{yy}(k) - \Gamma_{yy}(k) = \frac{1}{T} \sum_{t=1}^{T-k} (y_t - \bar{y})(y_{t+k} - \bar{y})^{\mathsf{T}} - E\big((y_t - \mu)(y_{t+k} - \bar{y})^{\mathsf{T}}\big)$$

$$= \frac{1}{T} \sum_{t=1}^{T-k} (y_t - \mu)(y_{t+k} - \mu)^{\mathsf{T}} - E\big((y_t - \mu)(y_{t+k} - \bar{y})^{\mathsf{T}}\big)$$

$$+ \frac{1}{T} \sum_{t=1}^{T-k} (\bar{y} - \mu)(y_{t+k} - \bar{y})^{\mathsf{T}} + \frac{1}{T} \sum_{t=1}^{T-k} (y_t - \mu)(\bar{y} - \mu)^{\mathsf{T}}$$

$$+ (\bar{y} - \mu)(\bar{y} - \mu)^{\mathsf{T}}$$

$$= \frac{1}{T} \sum_{t=1}^{T-k} V_{t;k} + o_P(T^{-1/2}),$$

where $V_{t;k} = (y_t - \mu)(y_{t+k} - \mu)^{\mathsf{T}} - E((y_t - \mu)(y_{t+k} - \mu)^{\mathsf{T}})$, which is an $n \times n$ matrix with mean zero. We let $v_{t;0} = \text{vech}(V_{t;0})$, and $v_{t;k} = \text{vec}(V_{t;k})$ for $k \neq 0$ be the $(n(n+1)/2) \times 1$ and $n^2 \times 1$ vectors containing the unique elements of $V_{t;0}, V_{t;k}$, respectively. Then, applying the CLT for vector stationary mixing vector processes, we have

$$\sqrt{T}\big(\text{vech}(\widehat{\Gamma}_{yy}(0)) - \text{vech}(\Gamma_{yy}(0))\big) \implies N(0, V_\Gamma(0)),$$

$$V_\Gamma(0) = \text{lrvar}(v_{t;0}) = \Gamma_{v_0 v_0}(0) + \sum_{s=1}^{\infty} \big(\Gamma_{v_0 v_0}(s) + \Gamma_{v_0 v_0}(s)^{\mathsf{T}}\big), \tag{7.9}$$

and, for $k \geq 1$,

$$\sqrt{T}\big(\text{vec}(\widehat{\Gamma}_{yy}(k)) - \text{vec}(\Gamma_{yy}(k))\big) \implies N(0, V_\Gamma(k)),$$

$$V_\Gamma(k) = \text{lrvar}(v_{t;k}) = \Gamma_{v_k v_k}(0) + \sum_{s=1}^{\infty} \big(\Gamma_{v_k v_k}(s) + \Gamma_{v_k v_k}(s)^{\mathsf{T}}\big), \tag{7.10}$$

where $\Gamma_{v_k v_k}(s) = E\big(v_{t;k} v_{t+s;k}^{\mathsf{T}}\big)$ for $k = 0, \pm 1, \ldots$ The matrices $\Gamma_{v_k v_k}(k)$ can be related to $\Gamma_{yy}(\cdot)$ and certain other cumulants in special cases, but the formulas are messy and too detailed to repeat here. We can equivalently say that $\widehat{\Gamma}_{yy}(k)$ is asymptotically matrix normal; see Appendix B.

Regarding the sample autocorrelation matrix, we have

$$\sqrt{T}\big(\widehat{R}_{yy}(k) - R_{yy}(k)\big) = D^{-1/2}\sqrt{T}\big[\widehat{\Gamma}_{yy}(k) - \Gamma_{yy}(k)\big]D^{-1/2}$$
$$- D^{-1/2}\Gamma_{yy}(k)D^{-1/2}D^{-1/2}\big[\widehat{D} - D\big]D^{-1/2}$$
$$- D^{-1/2}\sqrt{T}\big[\widehat{D} - D\big]D^{-1/2}D^{-1/2}\Gamma_{yy}(k)D^{-1/2}$$
$$+ o_P(1),$$

by Taylor expansion. The leading term in the expansion is

$$\sqrt{T}\big(\widehat{R}_{yy}(k) - R_{yy}(k)\big) = \frac{1}{\sqrt{T}}\sum_{t=1}^{T-k} W_{t;k} + o_P(1),$$
$$W_{t;k} = D^{-1/2}V_{t;k}D^{-1/2} - D^{-1/2}\Gamma_{yy}(k)D^{-1/2}D^{-1/2}\mathrm{diag}(V_{t;0})D^{-1/2}$$
$$- D^{-1/2}\mathrm{diag}(Z_{t;0})D^{-1/2}D^{-1/2}\Gamma_{yy}(k)D^{-1/2}.$$

Let $w_{t;k} = \mathrm{vec}(W_{t;k})$, $k \neq 0$; then $w_{t;k}$ is stationary and mixing with $E(w_{t;k}) = 0$. Therefore, for each k with $\widehat{\rho}_{yy}(k) = \mathrm{vec}(\widehat{R}_{yy}(k))$ and $\rho_{yy}(k) = \mathrm{vec}(R_{yy}(k))$ we have, as $T \to \infty$,

$$\sqrt{T}\,(\widehat{\rho}(k) - \rho(k)) \Longrightarrow N(0, V_R(k)), \qquad V_R(k) = \mathrm{lrvar}(w_{t;k}). \tag{7.11}$$

We can estimate the asymptotic variance matrix in the general case just as in the univariate case with some truncation and weighting applied to the estimated residual vectors $\widehat{v}_{t;k}, \widehat{w}_{t;k}$. We may also work with standard errors delivered from special cases.

In the special case that y_t is i.i.d. we have $\Gamma_{ij}(k) = 0$ for all $k \neq 0$ and the limiting variance $V_\Gamma(k)$ simplifies to $\Gamma_{v_k v_k}(0)$; under Gaussianity this is, for $k \geq 1$, $V_\Gamma(k) = \Gamma_{v_k v_k}(0) = \mathcal{D}_+ (\Gamma_{yy}(0) \otimes \Gamma_{yy}(0))\mathcal{D}_+^{\mathsf{T}}$, where $\mathcal{D}_+$ is the so-called duplication matrix of Magnus and Neudecker (1988) that is selecting the appropriate elements of the $n^2 \times n^2$ matrix $\Gamma_{yy}(0) \otimes \Gamma_{yy}(0)$. Furthermore, we have, for every i, j and $k \neq 0$, $V_{R_{i,j}}(k) = 1$, that is, the asymptotic distribution of the cross-autocorrelations are all standard normal under the i.i.d. assumption. The case $k = 0$ is different as this is the contemporaneous correlation and $R_{ij}(0)$ can be nonzero even under the i.i.d. assumption. In this case, $V_{R_{i,j}}(0) = E(z_{it}^2 z_{jt}^2) - E^2(z_{it} z_{jt})$. If y_t is Gaussian, $V_{R_{i,j}}(0) = 1 + 2R_{i,j}(0)$.

In the special case that $y_t - \mu$ is an MDS, then $W_{t;k} = D^{-1/2}V_{t;k}D^{-1/2}$, where $V_{t;k} = (y_t - \mu)(y_{t+k} - \mu)^{\mathsf{T}}$ for $k \geq 1$. In this case the following provides a consistent estimator of $V_R(k)$:

$$\widehat{V}_R(k)$$
$$= \big(\widehat{D}^{-1/2} \otimes \widehat{D}^{-1/2}\big)\frac{1}{T}\sum_{t=1}^{T-k} \widehat{v}_{t;k}\widehat{v}_{t;k}^{\mathsf{T}}\big(\widehat{D}^{-1/2} \otimes \widehat{D}^{-1/2}\big)$$
$$= \frac{1}{T}\sum_{t=1}^{T-k}\big(\widehat{D}^{-1/2}(y_{t+k} - \bar{y})(y_t - \bar{y})^{\mathsf{T}}\widehat{D}^{-1/2} \otimes \widehat{D}^{-1/2}(y_t - \bar{y})(y_{t+k} - \bar{y})\widehat{D}^{-1/2}\big),$$

where $\widehat{v}_{t;k} = \mathrm{vec}\,((y_t - \bar{y})(y_{t+k} - \bar{y})^{\mathsf{T}}) = (y_{t+k} - \bar{y}) \otimes (y_t - \bar{y})$. The diagonal elements of this $(n(n+1)/2) \times (n(n+1)/2)$ matrix are used in the standard error construction and are robust to heteroskedasticity.

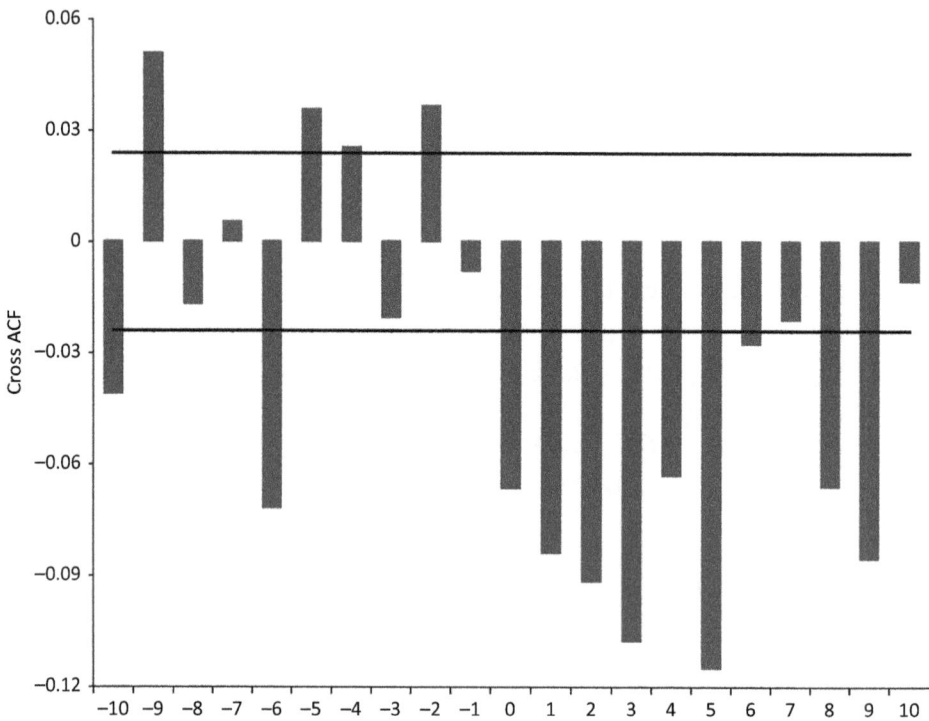

Figure 7.1 For S&P500 daily returns, $\text{cov}(r_t, r^2_{t+i})$.

Regarding univariate confidence intervals, for any element $\widehat{R}_{ij}(k)$ we may define the univariate confidence interval based on its corresponding asymptotic distribution, or use the Fisher z-transform to ensure that the confidence interval is contained in $[-1, 1]$, as already discussed.

7.1.2   Applications

We first consider the daily S&P500 returns series r_t and squared stock returns r^2_t (which measure the so-called leverage or volatility feedback effects), so $y_t = (r_t, r^2_t)^\top$; the results are shown in Figure 7.1. There is significance in both directions, but stronger significance in the effect of returns on future squared returns, although the absolute level of the autocorrelations is small. The direction of this effect is negative, whereas from past squared returns to future returns the effects are both positive and negative, and less significant.

We next consider the relationship between daily US stock returns (S&P500) and Chinese stock returns (SSEC) in Figure 7.2. There are significant effects in both directions. The strongest effect is from today's US returns to tomorrow's Chinese returns, perhaps reflecting the time zone fact that the Chinese market has already closed before the US market opens. There is also a significant negative effect in the other direction at lag 5.

We next consider the asymmetry of cross-autocorrelation matrices. We work with five Fama–French size-sorted (from smallest to largest) portfolios' daily returns, dataset

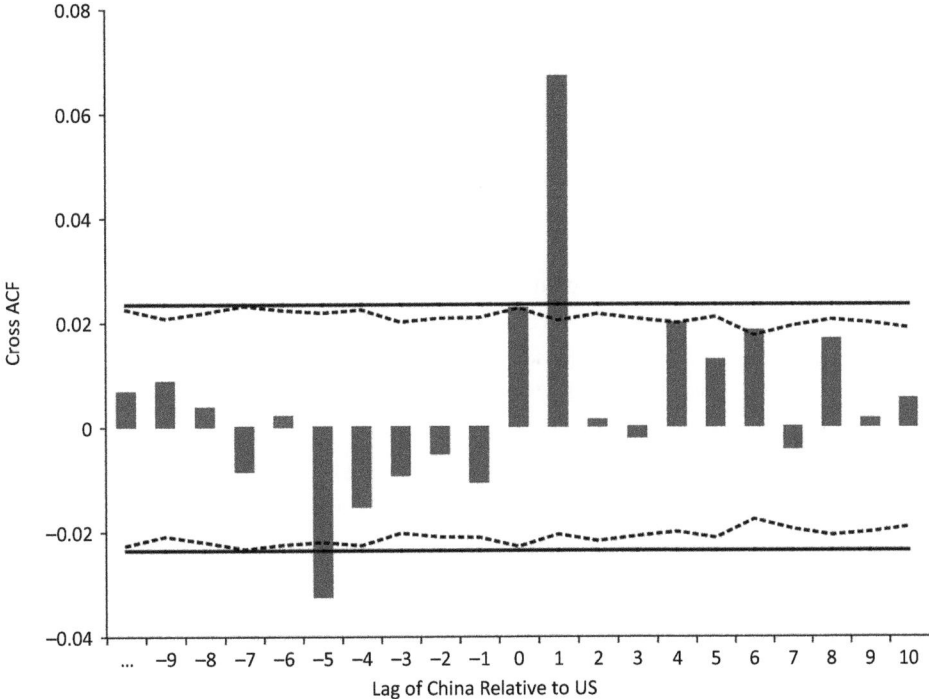

Figure 7.2 For S&P500 and SSEC daily returns, $\text{cov}\left(r_t^{\text{US}}, r_{t+i}^{\text{China}}\right)$.

`ffsizedaily`. Below we show the cross-autocorrelation matrices. The standard errors under the i.i.d. assumption are 0.0063.

$$
\widehat{R}(0) = \begin{array}{c} R_{1,t} \\ R_{2,t} \\ R_{3,t} \\ R_{4,t} \\ R_{5,t} \end{array} \left(\begin{array}{ccccc} 1.0000 & 0.9236 & 0.8896 & 0.8467 & 0.7322 \\ 0.9236 & 1.0000 & 0.9590 & 0.9268 & 0.8256 \\ 0.8896 & 0.9590 & 1.0000 & 0.9642 & 0.8841 \\ 0.8467 & 0.9268 & 0.9642 & 1.0000 & 0.9292 \\ 0.7322 & 0.8256 & 0.8841 & 0.9292 & 1.0000 \end{array} \right),
$$

$$
\widehat{R}(1) = \begin{array}{c} R_{1,t-1} \\ R_{2,t-1} \\ R_{3,t-1} \\ R_{4,t-1} \\ R_{5,t-1} \end{array} \left(\begin{array}{ccccc} 0.1591 & 0.1198 & 0.0912 & 0.0573 & -0.0074 \\ 0.1962 & 0.1406 & 0.1161 & 0.0808 & 0.0021 \\ 0.2102 & 0.1650 & 0.1322 & 0.0970 & 0.0112 \\ 0.2168 & 0.1793 & 0.1513 & 0.1078 & 0.0171 \\ 0.2082 & 0.1797 & 0.1587 & 0.1217 & 0.0246 \end{array} \right).
$$

This shows that cross-autocorrelations between larger stocks and future smaller stocks are larger than the other way around. We can see this by looking at the difference of the ACF matrix and its transpose:

$$
\widehat{R}(1) - \widehat{R}(1)^{\mathsf{T}} = \left(\begin{array}{ccccc} 0.0000 & -0.0764 & -0.1190 & -0.1595 & -0.2156 \\ 0.0764 & 0.0000 & -0.0489 & -0.0985 & -0.1775 \\ 0.1190 & 0.0489 & 0.0000 & -0.0543 & -0.1475 \\ 0.1595 & 0.0985 & 0.0543 & 0.0000 & -0.1046 \\ 0.2156 & 0.1775 & 0.1475 & 0.1046 & 0.0000 \end{array} \right).
$$

7.1.3   The Signal Plus Noise Model

Suppose that we observe a vector series y_t generated by

$$y_t = y_t^* + u_t, \tag{7.12}$$

where y_t^*, u_t are two unobserved stochastic processes. This model has been studied under a variety of assumptions; the whole field of signal processing is concerned with variants of this. Silver (2012) wrote a best-selling book about the prediction of elections, trying to extract the so-called signal from the so-called noise. In the classical setting of Kolmogorov and Wiener the two unobserved process are stationary, Gaussian, and mutually independent with known autocovariance functions γ_{y^*}, γ_u. The question is to define the best estimate of the signal y_t^* in the presence of the noise u_t based on these functions and the series y_t. There are different versions of this problem. The so-called smoothing problem, where the target is $E(y_t^* \mid y_t, y_{t\pm1}, y_{t\pm2}, \ldots)$; the filtering problem, where the target is $E(y_t^* \mid y_t, y_{t-1}, y_{t-2}, \ldots)$; and the prediction problem, $E(y_{t+1}^* \mid y_t, y_{t-1}, y_{t-2}, \ldots)$ (Pollock, 2007).

Suppose instead that y_t^* is a random walk plus drift,

$$y_t^* = \mu + y_{t-1}^* + \varepsilon_t, \tag{7.13}$$

where ε_t is i.i.d. with mean zero and covariance matrix Ω_ε, while u_t is a stationary mixing series with autocovariance matrix $\Gamma_{uu}(j)$, $j = 0, \pm1, \ldots$, that satisfies $\sum_{j=-\infty}^{\infty} |\Gamma_{uu}(j)_{i,k}| < \infty$ for every element i, k. This model is widely used in many fields. In economics it is called the **permanent–temporary** decomposition (Muth, 1960). In finance this model is used to represent the behavior of stock prices, where y_t^* is the so-called efficient price and u_t is a noise process reflecting fads or bubbles (Poterba and Summers, 1988), or other departures from market efficiency induced by microstructure (Hasbrouck, 2007). In the long run the efficient price dominates since the random walk with drift grows rapidly, whereas the fad process, being assumed stationary, stays tethered to its ergodic distribution. Here, the objective may be to obtain the best estimate of the efficient price, or to estimate the covariance matrix of the efficient price or the autocorrelation properties of the noise.

Taking first differences, we have

$$\Delta y_t = y_t - y_{t-1} = \mu + \varepsilon_t + u_t - u_{t-1}.$$

Therefore, $\mu = E(\Delta y_t)$ and

$$\Gamma_{\Delta y, \Delta y}(0) = \text{var}\,(\Delta y_t) = \Omega_\varepsilon + 2\Gamma_{uu}(0) - \Gamma_{uu}(1) - \Gamma_{uu}(1)^\mathsf{T},$$
$$\Gamma_{\Delta y, \Delta y}(j) = \text{cov}\,(\Delta y_t, \Delta y_{t-j}) = 2\Gamma_{uu}(j) - \Gamma_{uu}(j-1) - \Gamma_{uu}(j+1).$$

It can be shown by cancellation that

$$\sum_{j=-\infty}^{\infty} \Gamma_{\Delta y, \Delta y}(j) = \Omega_\varepsilon, \tag{7.14}$$

that is, the long-run variance of the observed differenced series equals the contemporaneous covariance matrix of the shock ε_t. If u_t is i.i.d., then Δy_t is an MA(1) process and the result simplifies to $\text{var}\,(\Delta y_t) + \text{cov}\,(\Delta y_t, \Delta y_{t-1}) + \text{cov}\,(\Delta y_t, \Delta y_{t+1}) = \Omega_\varepsilon$, while, in this case, $\Gamma_{uu}(0) = -\Gamma_{\Delta y, \Delta y}(1)$. This case can also be treated as a state space model, see

Chapter 8, and one can obtain filtered estimates of $E(y_t^* \mid y_{t-1}, \ldots, y_1)$. In the case where u_t is MA(q) then $\Gamma_{uu}(q) = -\Gamma_{\Delta y, \Delta y}(q+1)$, and then we can work backwards to obtain an expression for $\Gamma_{uu}(j), j = 0, \ldots, q-1$, in terms of $\Gamma_{\Delta y, \Delta y}(j), j = 0, \ldots, q$. In the case where the autocovariance of the u_t process is not specified parametrically, that is, it is MA(∞), Li and Linton (2022) proposed the ReMeDI method to estimate $\Gamma_{uu}(j)$ based on long forward and backward differencing.

An alternative approach can be based on taking second differences, whence we obtain

$$\Delta^2 y_t = y_t - 2y_{t-1} + y_{t-2} = \varepsilon_t - \varepsilon_{t-1} + u_t - 2u_{t-1} + u_{t-2},$$

which eliminates μ, that is, one does not have to estimate the mean. In this case, we have

$$\sum_{j=-\infty}^{\infty} E\left(\Delta^2 y_t \Delta^2 y_{t-j}^{\mathsf{T}}\right) = 2\Omega_\varepsilon.$$

If u_t is i.i.d., then $\Delta^2 y_t$ is an MA(2) process with zero mean and $\Gamma_{uu}(0) = -E\left(\Delta^2 y_t \Delta^2 y_{t-1}^{\mathsf{T}}\right)/4$.

This model is often used to describe stock prices. Let y_t denote (log) stock prices and $r_t = \Delta y_t$ denote stock returns, and in particular $r_t = (r_{it}, r_{mt})^{\mathsf{T}}$, where r_{mt} are market returns and r_{it} are returns on stock i. Furthermore, let $r^* = \Delta y^*$, and in particular $r_t^* = (r_{it}^*, r_{mt}^*)^{\mathsf{T}}$, where $y_{it} = y_{it}^* + u_{it}$ and $y_{mt} = y_{mt}^* + u_{mt}$ follow the signal plus noise model. We suppose that the market model holds between the fundamental returns, that is, for each firm i, $r_{it}^* = \alpha_i^* + \beta_i^* r_{mt}^* + e_{it}$, where e_{it} is i.i.d. over t with variance σ_i^2. If the noise process u_t is autocorrelated, then the usual market model regressions of r_{it} on a constant and r_{mt} will give biased estimates of β_i^*, that is,

$$\beta_i = \frac{\mathrm{cov}(r_{it}, r_{mt})}{\mathrm{var}(r_{mt})} \neq \beta_i^* = \frac{\mathrm{cov}(r_{it}^*, r_{mt}^*)}{\mathrm{var}(r_{mt}^*)},$$

and $\alpha_i = E(r_{it}) - \beta_i E(r_{mt}) = E(r_{it}^*) - \beta_i E(r_{mt}^*) \neq \alpha_i^*$. In fact, the true market beta is, in general,

$$\beta_i^* = \frac{\mathrm{lrcov}(r_{it}, r_{mt})}{\mathrm{lrvar}(r_{mt})}, \tag{7.15}$$

that is, it is a function of the long-run variance matrix of the vector series r_t. One can estimate the long-run covariance matrix of the vector of returns and market returns and take the corresponding function of its elements. An alternative approach is based on the frequency-domain representation of $\beta_i^* = f_{i,m}(0)/f_{mm}(0)$, where $f_{ij}(\lambda)$ is the cross-spectrum of the two asset returns at frequency λ. Specifically, the band spectral regression (using frequency zero) proposed in Engle (1974) can be used explicitly to estimate the underlying β_i^*. This effectively amounts to using low-frequency data, which is a common way of mitigating the effect of the microstructure noise component of returns.

In the special case of i.i.d. u_t one can show that

$$\beta_i^* = \frac{\mathrm{cov}(r_{it}, r_{mt}) + \mathrm{cov}(r_{it}, r_{m,t-1}) + \mathrm{cov}(r_{it}, r_{m,t+1})}{\mathrm{var}(r_{mt}) + 2\mathrm{cov}(r_{mt}, r_{mt-1})} = \frac{\beta_i + \beta_i^+ + \beta_i^-}{1 + 2\rho_m(1)},$$

where $\rho_m(1) = \mathrm{cov}(r_{mt}, r_{mt-1})/\mathrm{var}(r_{mt})$ is the autocorrelation of the market return. In that case one needs to do three different regressions of returns on market returns, returns on future market returns, and returns on past market returns, and then add the three betas and correct for the market autocorrelation. If in fact $\rho_m(1) = 0$, then one may simply regress r_{it} on a constant, $r_{m,t}$, $r_{m,t-1}$, $r_{m,t+1}$, and the market beta is measured by the sum of the corresponding coefficients (Dimson, 1979).

7.2   Dynamic Regression Models

We have looked at pure time series models with dynamic response and static regression models. In practice, we may want to consider models that have both features.

7.2.1   Distributed Lag Model

Suppose that

$$y_t = \alpha + \sum_{j=0}^{\infty} \beta_j x_{t-j} + \varepsilon_t, \tag{7.16}$$

where for now ε_t is assumed to be i.i.d. with mean zero and variance σ^2. This captures the idea of dynamic response: the affect on y of a change in x may take several periods to work through. Evidently, we require that $\sum_{j=0}^{\infty} |\beta_j| < \infty$ for the sum to be well defined. This model allows for a wide range of dynamic responses of y to changes in x. The impulse response function of y_{t+k} with respect to x_t is $\mathbb{I}_{y:x}(k) = \beta_k$, the cumulative impulse response function is $\mathcal{I}_{y:x}(j) = \sum_{k=0}^{j} \mathbb{I}_{y:x}(k)$, and the long-run effect is $\mathcal{I}_{y:x}(\infty) = \sum_{s=0}^{\infty} \beta_s$.

This model is very flexible, but there are too many free parameters β_j, which makes estimation difficult and imprecise. To reduce the dimensionality it is appropriate to make restrictions on β_j, and we consider some popular approaches to parameterizing the βs.

Example 7.3   The polynomial lag model is to suppose that

$$\beta_j = \begin{cases} a_0 + a_1 j + \cdots + a_d j^d & \text{if } j \leq n-1, \\ 0 & \text{if } j \geq n, \end{cases}$$

where the coefficients a_j, $j = 0, \ldots, d$, are free parameters and d is some given integer with $d < n$ (Almon, 1965). We have, by substitution,

$$y_t = a_0 \sum_{j=0}^{n-1} x_{t-j} + a_1 \sum_{j=0}^{n-1} j x_{t-j} + \cdots + a_1 \sum_{j=0}^{n-1} j^d x_{t-j} + \varepsilon_t,$$

which is a linear regression of y_t on the $d+1$ variables $\sum_{j=0}^{n-1} x_{t-j}$, $\sum_{j=0}^{n-1} j x_{t-j}$, ..., $\sum_{j=0}^{n-1} j^d x_{t-j}$. Alternatively, we may view y_t as a linear regression on $x_t, \ldots, x_{t-n+1}$ subject to $n-d-1$ linear restrictions. Specifically, we note that $\Delta^{d+1} \beta_j = 0$, $j = 0, 1, \ldots, n-1$, where Δ^j is the jth-order differencing operation. Let R_d denote the $(n-d-1) \times n$ matrix that represents $(d+1)$th-order differencing, that is,

$$R_0 = \begin{pmatrix} 1 & -1 & & \\ & \ddots & \ddots & \\ & & 1 & -1 \end{pmatrix}, \quad R_1 = \begin{pmatrix} 1 & -2 & 1 & \\ & \ddots & \ddots & \\ & & 1 & -2 & 1 \end{pmatrix}, \quad \cdots$$

Then we have $R_d\beta = 0$, where $\beta = (\beta_0, \beta_1, \ldots, \beta_{n-1})^\mathsf{T}$. Therefore, we may estimate β by least squares of y_t on $x_t, \ldots, x_{t-n}$ subject to the $n - d - 1$ linear restrictions.

Example 7.4   Shiller (1973) extended this model to allow $\Delta^{d+1}\beta_j$ to satisfy stochastic linear restrictions, namely $\Delta^{d+1}\beta_j = v_j, j = 0, \ldots, n - 1$, where v_j are normally distributed with mean zero and variance σ^2/k^2 for some k (this can have a frequentist interpretation or a Bayesian one, see below).

Example 7.5   The geometric lag model sets $\beta_j = \beta\lambda^j, j = 0, 1, \ldots$, for some $0 < \lambda < 1$, where β, λ are free parameters. This model implies monotonic and rapid decay, often called exponential decay. We can rewrite the model as

$$y_t = \alpha + \beta \sum_{j=0}^{\infty} \lambda^j x_{t-j} + \varepsilon_t = \alpha + \beta \left[\sum_{j=0}^{\infty} (\lambda^j L^j) \right] x_t + \varepsilon_t = \alpha + \beta \frac{1}{1 - \lambda L} x_t + \varepsilon_t.$$

Therefore, $(1 - \lambda L)y_t = \alpha(1 - \lambda L) + \beta x_t + (1 - \lambda L)\varepsilon_t$, which is the same as

$$y_t = \alpha(1 - \lambda) + \lambda y_{t-1} + \beta x_t + \varepsilon_t - \lambda\varepsilon_{t-1}.$$

The last equation is called the lagged dependent variable representation, which from an estimation point of view is convenient.

We next consider three important examples arising from economic reasoning.

Example 7.6 (Adaptive expectations)   Suppose that demand, y_t, is related to expected future price, x_{t+1}^*, by $y_t = \alpha + \beta x_{t+1}^* + \varepsilon_t$, where the expected price is made at time t and is unobserved by the econometrician. We observe the actual price sequence x_t. We further suppose that expectations are revised according to the rule

$$\underbrace{x_{t+1}^* - x_t^*}_{\text{revised expectations}} = (1 - \lambda) \underbrace{(x_t - x_t^*)}_{\text{forecast error}},$$

$$x_{t+1}^* = \underbrace{\lambda x_t^*}_{\text{old forecast}} + \underbrace{(1 - \lambda)x_t}_{\text{news}}.$$

This model seems to capture reasonable updating heuristics. We write $(1 - \lambda L)x_{t+1}^* = (1 - \lambda)x_t$, which implies that

$$x_{t+1}^* = \frac{(1 - \lambda)}{1 - \lambda L} x_t = (1 - \lambda) \left[x_t + \lambda x_{t-1} + \lambda^2 x_{t-2} + \cdots \right].$$

It follows that y_t is in the distributed lag form with geometric decay, that is,

$$y_t = \alpha + \frac{\beta(1 - \lambda)}{1 - \lambda L} x_t + \varepsilon_t.$$

Example 7.7 (Partial adjustment)   Suppose that $y_t^* = \alpha + \beta x_t$, where y_t^* is the desired level. However, because of costs of adjustment, the actual change of the variable y follows

$$y_t - y_{t-1} = (1 - \lambda)(y_t^* - y_{t-1}) + \varepsilon_t.$$

Substituting in, we get

$$y_t = (1 - \lambda)y_t^* + \lambda y_{t-1} + \varepsilon_t = \alpha(1 - \lambda) + \lambda y_{t-1} + \beta(1 - \lambda)x_t + \varepsilon_t.$$

Example 7.8 (Error correction)   Suppose that the long-run equilibrium relationship is $y = \lambda x$. Disequilibria are corrected according to the dynamic equation

$$\Delta y_t = \beta \left(y_{t-1} - \lambda x_{t-1}\right) + \lambda \Delta x_{t-1} + \varepsilon_t,$$

where $\beta < 0$. This implies that

$$y_t = y_{t-1}(1 + \beta) + \lambda(1 - \beta)x_{t-1} - \lambda x_{t-2} + \varepsilon_t, \tag{7.17}$$

$$y_t = \frac{\lambda(1 - \beta) - \lambda L}{1 - (1 + \beta)L}x_{t-1} + \frac{1}{1 - (1 + \beta)L}\varepsilon_t. \tag{7.18}$$

In epidemiological models it is typical to allow for a different decay structure that may not be monotonic.

Example 7.9   For example, suppose that y_t is the number of new deaths for a disease and x_t is the number of new cases on day t. In this case we might expect the lag polynomial to have a peak maybe 10–20 days in the past; in fact, this peak time is one of the main parameters of interest. This structure can be focused on by setting

$$\beta_j = \frac{1}{\sigma}f\left(\frac{j - \mu}{\sigma}\right), \quad j = 1, 2, \ldots,$$

where f is a symmetric unimodal density with mode at zero, while μ, σ are location and scale parameters respectively, for example Gaussian. In this case, the peak value of β_j occurs when $j = \mu$, in which case $\beta_{\max} = f(0)/\sigma$. For $j < \mu$ the weights increase, while for $j > \mu$ the weights decrease towards zero. The parameters μ, σ have to be estimated by nonlinear methods.

Example 7.10   The HAR model is now quite popular in empirical finance for dealing with long lag structures. Suppose that integers $p_1 < p_2 < \cdots < p_q$ for some integer q, and let

$$y_t = \beta_1 x_{t-1} + \cdots + \beta_1 x_{t-p_1} + \beta_2 x_{t-p_1-1} + \cdots + \beta_2 x_{t-p_2} + \cdots$$
$$+ \beta_q x_{t-p_{q-1}-1} + \cdots + \beta_q x_{t-p_q} + \varepsilon_t$$
$$= \beta_1 \left(x_{t-1} + \cdots + x_{t-p_1}\right) + \cdots + \beta_q \left(x_{t-p_{q-1}-1} + \cdots + x_{t-p_q}\right) + \varepsilon_t. \tag{7.19}$$

The lag coefficients follow a step function with step points determined by the grouping, which is prespecified. For example, with daily data: $p_1 = 5$, and the first week has the same coefficients; $p_2 = 5 + 22$, and the next month has the same coefficients; $p_3 = 5 + 22 + 255$, and the year after that has the same coefficients. This allows for a long number of lags with a relatively small number of parameters to estimate. The HAR structure can be tested easily by a classical Wald statistic.

Example 7.11   Suppose that we take the EWMA filter $(1 - \theta) \sum_{j=0}^{\infty} \theta^j x_{t-j}$, apply it using different known values of θ, and then allow the data to determine which filters matter. This corresponds to the regression model

$$y_t = \sum_{l=1}^{L} \omega_l \left((1 - \theta_l) \sum_{j=0}^{\infty} \theta_l^j x_{t-j} \right) + \varepsilon_t,$$

where ω_l, $l = 1, \ldots, L$, are unknown parameters and $\theta_1, \ldots, \theta_L$ are given parameters reflecting different dynamic adjustments of x. Note that mixtures of exponential distributions can deliver Pareto tails (long memory). Specifically, suppose that θ is Gamma with parameters α, β; then the distribution of the mixture, by substituting $\theta \rightarrow y = \theta(\beta x + 1)/\beta$, is

$$\begin{aligned}
f(x \mid \alpha, \beta) &= \int_0^{\infty} \theta \exp(-\theta x) \frac{1}{\Gamma(\alpha)\beta^\alpha} \theta^{\alpha-1} \exp(-\theta/\beta)\, d\theta \\
&= \frac{1}{\Gamma(\alpha)\beta^\alpha} \int_0^{\infty} \exp(-\theta((\beta x + 1)/\beta)\theta^\alpha\, d\theta \\
&= \frac{1}{\Gamma(\alpha)\beta^\alpha} \left(\frac{\beta}{\beta x + 1} \right)^{\alpha-1} \int_0^{\infty} \exp(-y)y^\alpha\, dy \\
&= \frac{\Gamma(\alpha+1)}{\Gamma(\alpha)\beta^\alpha} \left(\frac{\beta}{\beta x + 1} \right)^{\alpha+1}.
\end{aligned}$$

This density is like a Pareto density with tails like $x^{-(\alpha+1)}$ as $x \rightarrow \infty$ (Chicheportiche and Bouchaud, 2014).

7.2.2 Estimation of ADL Models

We consider the general ADL model

$$A(L)y_t = B(L)x_t + u_t, \tag{7.20}$$

with A, B polynomials of order p, q (possibly infinite), where the error term satisfies $E(u_t \mid X) = 0$. In the case where u_t is i.i.d., the parameters of A, B can be estimated by OLS of y_t on $y_{t-1}, \ldots, y_{t-p}, x_t, \ldots, x_{t-q}$. However, we may have reason to expect, or to arrive at by a process of modelling, that u_t is autocorrelated. In that case, that OLS estimator is generally inconsistent. Suppose that the error process is autocorrelated, for example

$$u_t = C(L)\varepsilon_t, \quad \varepsilon_t \text{ i.i.d. } 0, \sigma^2. \tag{7.21}$$

That is, in (7.16) we allow the error terms to be autocorrelated. In this case a general estimation method involves maximizing the Gaussian likelihood (assuming that $\varepsilon_t \sim N(0, \sigma^2)$) for $y_1, \ldots, y_T \mid x_1, \ldots, x_T$ with respect to the parameters of A, B, C. An alternative approach is to use instrumental-variable methods, which avoid the specification and estimation of a process for u_t. For example, if A is of order p, we may choose $z_t = (x_t, x_{t-1}, \ldots, y_{t-p-1}, y_{t-p-2}, \ldots)$ as instruments. There are many instruments; efficiency considerations require that one has a good way of combining them such as in our GMM discussion. Instrumental variables are not generally as efficient as ML when the error terms are normally distributed.

The structural parameters of interest are some vector θ such that the coefficients of A, B, C all depend on θ, possibly in a nonlinear way. For example, in the error correction example, the parameters of interest are λ, β and the corresponding representations in (7.17) and (7.18) show how these parameters enter in a complicated way into the two representations. The structural parameters may be estimated by minimum distance (Rothenberg, 1973) from the parameters of A, B, C.

7.2.3   Granger Causality

When is it justified to say that a variable X causes a variable Y? There are various approaches to this question in different scientific areas (Imbens and Rubin, 2015; Pearl, 2000). We focus on the approach of Granger causality (Granger, 1969; Sims, 1972). There are two fundamental principles: (i) the cause precedes its effect in time; (ii) the causal series contains special information about the series being caused that is not available otherwise. In fact, we expect that there are many factors that contribute to the outcome Y in a causal sense and so identifying whether a single variable causes another is not sufficient for understanding. For example, it is reasonable to believe that environment, genetic inheritance, and luck contribute in a causal way to our fortune, but perhaps the question is, what is the relative contribution of these factors?

Let Y and X be stationary time series, possibly vectors. The concept of **Granger causality** is widely used to describe the temporal relationship between two series in terms of a notion of causality or forecastability. One version of this is to say that X does not cause Y if Y_{t+1} is independent of $X_t, X_{t-1}, \ldots$ given $Y_t, Y_{t-1}, \ldots$ That is, future Y is independent of current and past X given current and past Y. This definition is quite hard to work with in the full generality and rather strong in terms of its implications, so we consider a more restricted definition based around mean independence. Suppose that

$$Y_t = a_0 + a_1 Y_{t-1} + \cdots + a_p Y_{t-p} + b_1 X_{t-1} + \cdots + b_p X_{t-p} + \varepsilon_{yt},$$
$$X_t = c_0 + c_1 X_{t-1} + \cdots + c_p X_{t-p} + d_1 Y_{t-1} + \cdots + d_p Y_{t-p} + \varepsilon_{xt},$$

where ε_{yt} and ε_{xt} are taken to be two uncorrelated white-noise series, with $E(\varepsilon_{yt}\varepsilon_{ys}) = 0 = E(\varepsilon_{xt}\varepsilon_{xs})$ for all $t \neq s$. In theory p can equal infinity, but in practice, of course, due to the finite length of the available data, p will be assumed finite and shorter than the given time series. We may say that X is Granger causing Y provided some b_j is not zero. Similarly, we may say that Y is causing X if some d_j is not zero. If both of these events occur, there is said to be a mutually respectful feedback relationship between X and Y. One may test for the absence of causality by applying an F-test on the coefficients. This is automatically done in EViews. This line of analysis can be seen as a special case of vector autoregression, to which we now turn.

7.3   Vector Autoregressive and Moving Average Models

Suppose that $y_t = (y_{1t}, \ldots, y_{nt})^\mathsf{T}$ is a vector time series.

Definition 7.1 (Vector autoregression)   Suppose that

$$y_t = \alpha + A_1 y_{t-1} + \cdots + A_p y_{t-p} + \varepsilon_t,$$

where $\varepsilon_t = (\varepsilon_{1t}, \ldots, \varepsilon_{nt})^\mathsf{T}$ is i.i.d., mean zero, and has variance matrix Ω_ε, which is assumed to be nonsingular. Then y_t is a VAR(p) process.

If initial conditions $y_0, y_{-1}, \ldots, y_{1-p}$ are given, this is a well-defined process for all $t = 1, 2, \ldots$ We assume in this section that the model holds for $t = 0, \pm 1, \ldots$, that is, the process is stationary, and check what conditions are required to make this self-consistent. This model embodies two sorts of interactions: contemporaneous correlation between shocks ε_{it} and ε_{jt}, and dynamic interaction between y_{it} and past values of y_{jt} (and vice versa). Note that if y_t is a stationary VAR(p) with mean μ and covariance matrix Σ, then the standardized random variable $y_t^* = \Sigma^{-1/2}(y_t - \mu)$ is also a VAR(p) process with zero intercept and coefficient matrices $A_j^* = \Sigma^{-1/2} A_j \Sigma^{1/2}$ and error process ε_t^* with mean zero and covariance matrix $\Omega_\varepsilon^* = \Sigma^{-1/2} \Omega_\varepsilon \Sigma^{-1/2}$. It is convenient to write the general model using lag polynomial notation, $A(L)y_t = \alpha + \varepsilon_t$, where the matrix lag polynomial $A(L) = I_p - A_1 L - \cdots - A_p L^p$ for square matrices $A_j, j = 0, \ldots, p$.

For the first series y_{1t} we have

$$y_{1t} = \alpha_1 + \sum_{j=1}^{n} A_{1;1j} y_{j,t-1} + \cdots + \sum_{j=2}^{n} A_{p;1j} y_{j,t-p} + \varepsilon_{1t},$$

which shows how this process depends on the p history of all of the ys. In the special case where $A_{k;1j} = 0$ for $k = 1, \ldots, p$ and $j = 2, \ldots, n$, this reverts to the univariate autoregression of order p. In general, this is a regression model for y_{1t} explained by an intercept and the np covariates $y_{1,t-1}, \ldots, y_{1,t-p}, y_{2,t-1}, \ldots, y_{n,t-p}$. However, the covariates in this regression model are not strongly exogenous (although they are weakly so) and there is dynamic feedback, which itself is of interest.

We focus on the VAR(1) case for now where $A(L) = I_n - AL$, dropping the subscript on A. This can be justified by writing the VAR(p) process as a VAR(1) process in an expanded state variable, which is left as an exercise. By substitution we have

$$y_t = \alpha + \varepsilon_t + A(\alpha + \varepsilon_{t-1}) + A^2(\alpha + \varepsilon_{t-2}) + A^3 y_{t-3} + \cdots$$
$$= \sum_{j=0}^{\infty} A^j (\alpha + \varepsilon_{t-j}) = \alpha \sum_{j=0}^{\infty} A^j + \sum_{j=0}^{\infty} A^j \varepsilon_{t-j} = \mu + \sum_{j=0}^{\infty} A^j \varepsilon_{t-j},$$

where $\mu = E(y_t)$, provided the sum $\sum_{j=0}^{\infty} A^j$ is well defined, which depends on the properties of the matrix A, and in particular on its eigenvalues. This matrix is $n \times n$ and is not necessarily symmetric, so may have real or complex eigenvalues, and they may be repeated. Nevertheless, provided all eigenvalues of the matrix A are less than one in modulus, the system is stable and the infinite sum is well defined, and indeed $\sum_{j=0}^{\infty} A^j = (I_n - A)^{-1}$. It further follows that the process $\sum_{j=0}^{\infty} A^j \varepsilon_{t-j}$ is well defined in mean square, as we discussed for the univariate case, and the process y_t is weakly stationary. In general, y_{1t} depends on all lags of all ε_{jt}.

The autocovariance matrix of the stationary process y_t satisfies

$$\Gamma(0) = E\left[(y_t - \mu)(y_t - \mu)^\mathsf{T} \right]$$
$$= A E\left[(y_{t-1} - \mu)(y_{t-1} - \mu)^\mathsf{T} \right] A^\mathsf{T} + \Omega_\varepsilon = A\Gamma(0)A^\mathsf{T} + \Omega_\varepsilon, \tag{7.22}$$

which is a linear equation in the symmetric square matrix $\Gamma(0)$; it is called a Sylvester equation. We can substitute for $A\Gamma(0)A^\mathsf{T}$ using the equation $A\Gamma(0)A^\mathsf{T} = A^2\Gamma(0)(A^\mathsf{T})^2 + A\Omega_\varepsilon A^\mathsf{T}$, and continuing this process one obtains

$$\Gamma(0) = \sum_{s=0}^{\infty} A^s \Omega_\varepsilon (A^s)^\mathsf{T}. \tag{7.23}$$

This can also be seen from the MA(∞) representation $y_t - \mu = \sum_{j=0}^{\infty} A^j \varepsilon_{t-j}$. An alternative way of representing this information is by vectorizing (7.22) to obtain

$$\text{vec}(\Gamma(0)) = (A \otimes A)\text{vec}(\Gamma(0)) + \text{vec}(\Omega_\varepsilon) = (I_{n^2} - (A \otimes A))^{-1} \text{vec}(\Omega_\varepsilon), \tag{7.24}$$

where the inversion is valid provided all the eigenvalues of the matrix A are less than one (which implies that all the eigenvalues of the Kronecker product matrix $A \otimes A$ are less than one and hence that $I_{n^2} - (A \otimes A)$ is invertible). Furthermore, we have

$$\Gamma(k) = E\left[(y_t - \mu)(y_{t+k} - \mu)^\mathsf{T} \right] = \Gamma(0)(A^k)^\mathsf{T} = \sum_{s=0}^{\infty} A^s \Omega_\varepsilon (A^{s+k})^\mathsf{T} \tag{7.25}$$

for $k = 1, 2, \ldots$, and $\Gamma(-k) = A^k \Gamma(0)$, which is not necessarily equal to $\Gamma(k)$.

The spectral density matrix for the VAR(1) process is

$$f(\lambda) = \frac{1}{2\pi} \left((I_n - A \exp{(i\lambda)})^* \right)^{-1} \Omega_\varepsilon \left(I_n - A \exp{(i\lambda)} \right)^{-1}, \quad \lambda \in [-\pi, \pi], \tag{7.26}$$

where $*$ denotes the complex conjugate transpose of a complex matrix. Hence, the long-run variance is $2\pi f(0) = \left((I_n - A)^\mathsf{T} \right)^{-1} \Omega_\varepsilon (I_n - A)^{-1}$.

The autocorrelation matrix does not have a simple form in general, except in some special cases such as when A is diagonal or if Ω_ε has the same diagonal elements.

Example 7.12   Suppose that $A = \phi I_n + \delta i_n i_n^\mathsf{T}$ for scalars $\phi, \delta \in (-1, 1)$. The eigenvalues of this symmetric matrix are $n\delta + \phi$ and ϕ (repeated $n - 1$ times). Therefore, provided $|n\delta + \phi| < 1$ and $|\phi| < 1$, the system is stable, that is, y_t is stationary. The case where $\delta = 0$ is obvious. In the case where $\phi = 0$, the matrix A is of rank one and so singular, but never mind – this is not ruled out by our conditions so far. In this case, $A^k = (\delta^k n^k) i_n i_n^\mathsf{T}$ and

$$\Gamma(k) = i_n^\mathsf{T} \Omega_\varepsilon i_n \sum_{s=0}^{\infty} \delta^{2s+k} n^{2s+k} \times i_n i_n^\mathsf{T}, \qquad R(k) = (\delta n)^k \times i_n i_n^\mathsf{T},$$

where the sums exist provided $|\delta|n < 1$. In this case $R_{ij}(k)$ is the same for all i, j; the decay rate is like that of a univariate autoregression with coefficient δn when $|\delta|n < 1$.

We may ask what is the marginal autocovariance function $\gamma_{ii}(\cdot)$ implied by the general VAR model? Recall that the autocovariance function of the univariate AR(1) process is quite restrictive, involving only monotonic decay (when $\phi > 0$). The VAR(1) process allows much more general decay and oscillation, as we now show. Note that we can write a univariate AR(p) process $y_t = \phi_1 y_{t-1} + \cdots + \phi_p y_{t-p} + \varepsilon_t$ as a VAR(1) process $x_t = A x_{t-1} + u_t$ with

$$x_t = \begin{pmatrix} y_t \\ \vdots \\ y_{t+1-p} \end{pmatrix}, \qquad u_t = \begin{pmatrix} \varepsilon_t \\ 0 \\ \vdots \end{pmatrix}, \qquad A = \begin{pmatrix} \phi_1 & \phi_2 & \cdots & \phi_p \\ 1 & 0 & \cdots & \\ 0 & 1 & & \\ 0 & & \cdots & \ddots \end{pmatrix}.$$

This shows that, for this particular choice of A matrix and state variables, the autocovariance function for the first element, say y_t, can take any of the forms implied by the univariate AR(p) process, and indeed more than that. In particular, the marginal process derived from a general VAR(1) may be very complicated, so that $E(y_{1t} \mid y_{1,t-1}, y_{1,t-2}, \ldots)$ may depend on all lags, that is, y_{1t} may not be Markov of any finite order. This suggests that the value of the VAR process is in reducing the number of parameters needed to describe the process. However, it can be shown that the marginal processes from a vector VAR(p) process are univariate ARMA(p^*, q^*) in general, where $p^* = np$ and $q^* = (n-1)p$, although the order can be less in special cases (it can be just an AR(p) in the case where all A_j are diagonal; Zellner and Palm, 1974). The bivariate VAR(1) process in particular is a pair of ARMA(2,1) processes, albeit with some restrictions on the parameters. The number of parameters in the univariate representations is exactly the same as in the VAR representation, $np + n(n-1)p + n(n+1)/2$ compared to the $n^2p + n(n+1)/2$ of the VAR process, because the parameters of the autoregressive polynomial are identical across equations (although if we fit unrestricted ARMA(p^*, q^*) models we have to estimate more parameters). The advantage of the VAR is to understand the joint dynamic relationship, and to avoid the estimation of moving average parameters, which require nonlinear estimation.

We next consider pure moving average models.

Definition 7.2 (Vector moving average (VMA) models)   Suppose that

$$y_t = \mu + \varepsilon_t - \Theta_1 \varepsilon_{t-1} - \cdots - \Theta_q \varepsilon_{t-q},$$

where ε_t is i.i.d., mean zero, and has variance matrix Ω_ε. Then y_t is a VMA(q) process.

It is convenient to write this model using the lag polynomial notation $y_t = \mu + B(L)\varepsilon_t$, where $B(L) = I - \Theta_1 L - \cdots - \Theta_q L^q$. The process is weakly stationary for any values of Θ_j, and invertible provided $\det(B(z)) \neq 0$ for any z with $|z| \leq 1$. In that case we have the autoregressive representation $(I_n - B(L))^{-1}(y_t - \mu) = \varepsilon_t$.

For the VMA(1) process, $B(L) = I_n - \Theta L$, the process is invertible provided the eigenvalues of Θ are less than one in modulus. In this case, we have

$$\Gamma(j) = \begin{cases} \Omega_\varepsilon + \Theta\Omega_\varepsilon\Theta^\mathsf{T} & \text{if } j = 0, \\ -\Theta\Omega_\varepsilon & \text{if } j = +1, \\ -\Omega_\varepsilon\Theta^\mathsf{T} & \text{if } j = -1, \\ 0 & \text{if } j \notin \{-1, 0, 1\}. \end{cases} \tag{7.27}$$

The autocorrelation matrix does not have a simple form unless there are restrictions on Θ and Ω_ε. The spectral density matrix of the VMA(1) process is

$$f(\lambda) = \frac{1}{2\pi} \left(I - \Theta \exp\left(2\pi i\lambda\right) \right)^* \Omega_\varepsilon \left(I - \Theta \exp\left(2\pi i\lambda\right) \right),$$

where $*$ denotes complex conjugate transpose.

Example 7.13   Suppose that, for some $n \times n$ matrix A,

$$y_t = Ax_t, \qquad x_{it} = \varepsilon_{it} - \theta\varepsilon_{i,t-1},$$

where $x_t, \varepsilon_t \in \mathbb{R}^n$ and ε_{it} are mutually independent with identical variance σ_ε^2. This is a VMA(1) with a special structure; in particular, $\Gamma(0) = \sigma_\varepsilon^2 (1 + \theta^2) A A^\mathsf{T}$ and $\Gamma(1) = -\theta \sigma_\varepsilon^2 A A^\mathsf{T}$, so that $R(k) = 0$ for $k \geq 2$ and

$$R(1) = \frac{-\theta}{(1 + \theta^2)} \times \text{diag}(AA^\mathsf{T})^{-1/2} AA^\mathsf{T} \text{diag}(AA^\mathsf{T})^{-1/2}.$$

Example 7.14   Suppose that

$$y_{1t} = \varepsilon_{1t} + \varepsilon_{2,t-1}, \qquad y_{2t} = \varepsilon_{2t} + \theta \varepsilon_{2,t-1},$$

where ε_{jt} are i.i.d. with mean zero and variance one, while $|\theta| < 1$. The process y_{1t} is i.i.d., while y_{2t} is an MA(1) process. In fact, $\Gamma_{11}(1) = 0$, $R_{11}(1) = 0$, while

$$\Gamma_{21}(1) = 1, \quad \Gamma_{22}(1) = \theta, \quad R_{21}(1) = \frac{1}{\sqrt{2(1 + \theta^2)}}, \quad R_{22}(1) = \frac{\theta}{1 + \theta^2},$$

so that the cross-autocovariance can be larger than either marginal autocovariance, as stated above.

The mixed VARMA(p, q) process can be written in the form $A(L)y_t = \alpha + B(L)\varepsilon_t$ as in the univariate case, where A, B are lag polynomial matrices. Under some conditions we can express y_t in VAR(∞) form, $C(L)y_t = \alpha' + \varepsilon_t$, or in MA($\infty$) form, $y_t = \alpha'' + D(L)\varepsilon_t$.

The **impulse response function** is a common way of measuring the dynamic effects of shocks (ε_t) on outcomes. This is defined as a matrix of functions with, specifically,

$$\mathbb{I}_{ij}(k) = \frac{\partial y_{i;t+k}}{\partial \varepsilon_{jt}}. \tag{7.28}$$

In the scalar case, when $y_t = \sum_{j=0}^\infty \psi_j \varepsilon_{t-j}$, $\mathbb{I}(k) = \psi_k$ and is nonstochastic. In the multivariate case, if there is an MA(∞) representation $y_t = \sum_{l=0}^\infty \Psi_l \varepsilon_{t-l}$, then $\mathbb{I}_{ij}(k) = \Psi_{k;i,j}$ and is also nonstochastic. The impulse response function is a nonlinear function of the matrices $A_1, \ldots, A_p, \Omega_\varepsilon$. For a VAR(1) process, we have $\Psi_k = A^k$, which is straightforward to compute. For a VAR(p), it is a bit more complicated. In this case, we have the recursive definitions

$$\Psi_k = \sum_{i=0}^k \Psi_{k-i} A_i, \quad k = 1, 2, \ldots, \tag{7.29}$$

where $A_i = 0$ for $i > p$ and $\Psi_0 = I_n$. Therefore, $\Psi_1 = A_1$, $\Psi_2 = A_1^2 + A_2$, and so on. A second way of computing the impulse response is to write the VAR(p) as a VAR(1) with an expanded state vector and $np \times np$ coefficient matrix F, then Ψ_k can be read off from F^k.

The error process in the VAR model ε_t is usually assumed to have a nondiagonal covariance matrix Ω_ε, and for interpretation purposes one may wish to rewrite the error in terms of standardized shocks (that have variance one), or indeed that are both standardized and mutually uncorrelated (Sims, 1980). Specifically, we may write $\varepsilon_t = Dz_t$, where D is the diagonal matrix containing the square root of the diagonal elements of Ω_ε, in which case $E(z_{it}) = 0$ and $E(z_{it}^2) = 1$ for all $i = 1, \ldots, n$. Alternatively, we may write $\varepsilon_t = Pw_t$, where P is the **Cholesky factor**, that is, $\Omega_\varepsilon = PP^\mathsf{T}$, where P is a lower triangular matrix and P^{T} is upper triangular. In that case $E(w_{it}) = 0$ and $E(w_{it}^2) = 1$, but also $E(w_{it}w_{jt}) = 0$ for all $i, j = 1, \ldots, n$. We have

$$\frac{\partial y_{i;t+k}}{\partial z_{jt}} = (\Psi_k D)_{i,j}, \qquad \frac{\partial y_{i;t+k}}{\partial w_{jt}} = (\Psi_k P)_{i,j}, \tag{7.30}$$

which in both cases involve elements of the original error process's covariance matrix.

A number of quantities of interest are derived from the impulse response function. We may be interested in the entire trajectory $\Psi_{i,j;k}$, $k = 1, 2, \ldots, K$, for some chosen maximum horizon. Sometimes we care about the location of the maximum value of $\Psi_{ij;k}$, that is, $k_{\max} = \arg\max_{k=1,\ldots,K} |\Psi_{ij;k}|$, which is an integer-valued parameter. Diebold and Yılmaz (2014) proposed measuring the connectedness between different units at horizon h from the impulse response function, calculating the **generalized spillover index**

$$d_{ij}^K = \frac{\sigma_{jj}^{-1} \sum_{k=0}^{K-1} \left(e_i^{\mathsf{T}} \Psi_k \Omega_\varepsilon e_j\right)^2}{\sum_{k=0}^{K-1} \left(e_i^{\mathsf{T}} \Psi_k \Omega_\varepsilon \Psi_k^{\mathsf{T}} e_j\right)} \tag{7.31}$$

for each i, j, where e_i is the vector with 1 at the ith position and zero elsewhere. They showed how this quantity can capture spillovers across financial markets in a quantitative way.

7.3.1 Estimation and Inference

The estimation and inference discussion about VAR processes is similar to the univariate autoregressive case except for the matrix algebra.

7.3.1.1 Yule–Walker

We suppose that $E(y_t) = 0$. We first define the Yule–Walker equations for the vector case:

$$\Gamma(k) = A_1 \Gamma(k-1) + A_2 \Gamma(k-2) + \cdots + A_p \Gamma(k-p)$$

for $k = 1, \ldots, p$, where $\Gamma(-k) = \Gamma(k)^{\mathsf{T}}$ and $\Gamma(k) = E(y_t y_{t-k}^{\mathsf{T}})$. In vector form,

$$\gamma(k) = \left(\Gamma(k-1)^{\mathsf{T}} \otimes I_n\right) a_1 + \cdots + \left(\Gamma(k-p)^{\mathsf{T}} \otimes I_n\right) a_p,$$

where $\gamma(k) = \mathrm{vec}(\Gamma(k))$ and $a_k = \mathrm{vec}(A_k)$. Therefore, one has the pn^2 system

$$\begin{pmatrix} \gamma(1) \\ \vdots \\ \gamma(p) \end{pmatrix} = \begin{pmatrix} \Gamma(0) \otimes I_n & \Gamma(1)^{\mathsf{T}} \otimes I_n & \cdots & \Gamma(p-1)^{\mathsf{T}} \otimes I_n \\ & \ddots & & \vdots \\ & & \ddots & \\ & & & \Gamma(0) \otimes I_n \end{pmatrix} \begin{pmatrix} a_1 \\ \vdots \\ a_p \end{pmatrix},$$

and we may proceed to estimation by replacing the matrices $\Gamma(k)$ by the sample estimates $\widehat{\Gamma}(k)$, and then solving the empirical system. In practice this system can be quite large, and one may resort to algorithms such as Gauss–Seidel, which is a standard numerical technique for solving large systems of equations.

7.3.1.2 Regression

We may also pursue the regression formulation as for the univariate case. Collect the data as follows:

$$\widetilde{X} = \begin{pmatrix} y_{11} & & y_{n,1} \\ \vdots & \cdots & \vdots \\ y_{1,T-1} & & y_{n,T-1} \end{pmatrix}, \quad X = (i_{T-1}, \widetilde{X}), \quad Y_i = (y_{i2}, \ldots, y_{iT})^\mathsf{T},$$

where i_{T-1} is a $T-1$ column vector of ones. Then we can write the equation for the ith variable as

$$Y_i = \alpha_i i_{T-1} + \widetilde{X} a_i + e_i = Y_i = X\beta_i + e_i,$$

where $e_i = (\varepsilon_{i2}, \ldots, \varepsilon_{iT})^\mathsf{T}$, while $a_i = (A_{i1}, \ldots, A_{in})^\mathsf{T}$ and $\beta_i = (\alpha_i, a_i^\mathsf{T})^\mathsf{T}$. In this regression model we have $E(\varepsilon_{it} \mid y_{t-1}) = 0$, which is sufficient for OLS, but we cannot assume here that $E(e_i \mid X) = 0$. We may write the standard OLS formulas in this case using the FWL theorem,

$$\widehat{\beta}_i = (X^\mathsf{T}X)^{-1}X^\mathsf{T}Y_i, \qquad \widehat{a}_i = (\widetilde{X}^\mathsf{T}M\widetilde{X})^{-1}\widetilde{X}^\mathsf{T}MY_i, \qquad \widehat{\alpha}_i = \bar{y}_i - \bar{y}\,\widehat{a}_i,$$

where $\bar{y}$ is the $n \times 1$ vector with typical element $\bar{y}_j = \sum_{t=2}^{T} y_{j,t-1}/(T-1)$, while $M = I_{T-1} - i_{T-1}i_{T-1}^\mathsf{T}/(T-1)$ is the demeaning projection matrix.

We may apply the usual OLS theory for $\widehat{\beta}_i$ (allowing for the dependence of the elements of the X matrix). Specifically, under the i.i.d. shock assumption we have, for example,

$$\sqrt{T}\,(\widehat{a}_i - a_i) \Longrightarrow N(0, V_{ii}), \qquad V_{ii} = \sigma_i^2 \times \Gamma(0)^{-1},$$

where the probability limit of the $n \times n$ matrix $\widetilde{X}^\mathsf{T}M\widetilde{X}/(T-1)$ is in this case the variance matrix $\Gamma(0)$, and σ_i^2 is the ith diagonal element of the matrix Ω_ε. One can obtain standard errors in the usual OLS way, and if one wishes to conduct inference about a_i or β_i then these standard methods apply. However, in many cases one is interested in the system as a whole and in making inferences about all the parameters of the system $(\alpha, A, \Omega_\varepsilon)$, and for this we need the joint distributions for $\widehat{a}_i, \widehat{a}_j$, and so on; in the general case where ε_{it} is correlated with ε_{jt} we need to use a system analysis, which brings in some new notation.

From a system point of view the outcome variables all have linear regression equations but with errors that are mutually contemporaneously correlated, so this can be interpreted as a "seemingly unrelated regression" system (Zellner, 1962). Specifically, by horizontal stacking we obtain

$$Y = i_{T-1}\alpha^\mathsf{T} + \widetilde{X}A^\mathsf{T} + E = XB + E$$

for the $(T-1) \times n$ matrices $Y = (Y_1, \ldots, Y_n)$ and $E = (e_1, \ldots, e_n)$ and the $(n+1) \times n$ matrix $B = (\beta_1, \ldots, \beta_n)$. Since the equations all have the same np covariates, algebraically we have GLS = OLS. We may write $\widehat{B} = (\widehat{\beta}_1, \ldots, \widehat{\beta}_n)$.

We may equivalently write the OLS estimators of all the parameters α, A as

$$\widehat{A} = \left(\sum_{t=2}^{T} (y_t - \bar{y})(y_{t-1} - \bar{y})^\mathsf{T} \right) \left(\sum_{t=2}^{T} (y_{t-1} - \bar{y})(y_{t-1} - \bar{y})^\mathsf{T} \right)^{-1},$$

$$\widehat{\alpha} = \frac{1}{T} \sum_{t=2}^{T} (y_t - \widehat{A}y_{t-1}).$$

We next consider the large-sample properties of these estimators. By substitution, we have

$$\sqrt{T}(\widehat{A} - A) = \left(\sum_{t=2}^{T} \varepsilon_t \, (y_{t-1} - \bar{y})^{\mathsf{T}} \right) \left(\sum_{t=2}^{T} (y_{t-1} - \bar{y}) \, (y_{t-1} - \bar{y})^{\mathsf{T}} \right)^{-1}$$

$$\simeq \left(\frac{1}{\sqrt{T}} \sum_{t=2}^{T} \varepsilon_t \, (y_{t-1} - \mu)^{\mathsf{T}} \right) \left(\frac{1}{T} \sum_{t=2}^{T} (y_{t-1} - \mu) \, (y_{t-1} - \mu)^{\mathsf{T}} \right)^{-1},$$

where the replacement of $\bar{y}$ by μ follows by arguments we have already seen for the sample autocovariance matrix. We have

$$\frac{1}{T} \sum_{t=2}^{T} (y_{t-1} - \mu) \, (y_{t-1} - \mu)^{\mathsf{T}} \xrightarrow{P} \Gamma(0)$$

by the LLN (element by element). Since $A, \widehat{A}$ are matrices we vectorize them to provide a CLT. For notational ease, we let $\widetilde{y}_t = y_t - \mu$, and write

$$z_t = \text{vec}\big(\varepsilon_t \widetilde{y}_t^{\mathsf{T}}\big) = (\widetilde{y}_{t-1} \otimes I_n)\varepsilon_t, \tag{7.32}$$

which is now an $n^2 \times 1$ vector of martingale differences. We have

$$E\big(\text{vec}\big(\varepsilon_t \widetilde{y}_{t-1}^{\mathsf{T}}\big) \text{vec}\big(\varepsilon_t \widetilde{y}_{t-1}^{\mathsf{T}}\big)^{\mathsf{T}}\big) = E\big((\widetilde{y}_{t-1} \otimes I_n)\varepsilon_t \varepsilon_t^{\mathsf{T}} \big(\widetilde{y}_{t-1}^{\mathsf{T}} \otimes I_n\big)\big)$$

$$= E\big((\widetilde{y}_{t-1} \otimes I_n)\Omega_\varepsilon \big(\widetilde{y}_{t-1}^{\mathsf{T}} \otimes I_n\big)\big)$$

$$= E\big((\widetilde{y}_{t-1} \otimes I_n) (1 \otimes \Omega_\varepsilon) \big(\widetilde{y}_{t-1}^{\mathsf{T}} \otimes I_n\big)\big)$$

$$= E\big(\widetilde{y}_{t-1}\widetilde{y}_{t-1}^{\mathsf{T}}\big) \otimes \Omega_\varepsilon = \Gamma(0) \otimes \Omega_\varepsilon.$$

It follows that, with $a = \text{vec}(A)$ and $\widehat{a} = \text{vec}(\widehat{A})$, $\sqrt{T}(\widehat{a} - a) \Longrightarrow N(0, \Upsilon)$, where

$$\Upsilon = (\Gamma(0) \otimes I_n)^{-1} (\Gamma(0) \otimes \Omega_\varepsilon) (\Gamma(0) \otimes I_n)^{-1} = \Gamma^{-1}(0) \otimes \Omega_\varepsilon.$$

Note that as in the univariate case Ω_ε figures in both the numerator and the denominator (since $\Gamma(0)$ and hence $\Gamma^{-1}(0)$ depend on Ω_ε as shown above), but unlike in the univariate case the two terms do not necessarily cancel. However, there is a univariate scale invariance in the sense that if $\Omega_\varepsilon \to c\Omega_\varepsilon$ for scalar c, then $\Gamma(0) \to c\Gamma(0)$ and the asymptotic variance of $\widehat{a}$ does not depend on c. In the i.i.d. case, $\Gamma(0) = \Omega_\varepsilon$ and $\Upsilon = \Gamma^{-1}(0) \otimes \Gamma(0)$, which is not equal to the identity in general except when $\Gamma(0)$ is diagonal. In the VAR(p) case the limiting distribution is block diagonal with blocks $\Gamma^{-1}(0) \otimes \Gamma(0)$, that is, it is $(\Gamma^{-1}(0) \otimes \Gamma(0)) \otimes I_p$. We can equivalently say that $\sqrt{T}(\widehat{A} - A)$ is asymptotically **matrix normal**, MN$(0, \Omega_\varepsilon, \Gamma^{-1}(0))$; see Appendix B.

The intercept vector satisfies

$$\sqrt{T}(\widehat{\alpha} - \alpha) = \frac{1}{\sqrt{T}} \sum_{t=2}^{T} \varepsilon_t - \sqrt{T}(\widehat{A} - A) \frac{1}{T} \sum_{t=2}^{T} y_{t-1}$$

$$= \frac{1}{\sqrt{T}} \sum_{t=2}^{T} \varepsilon_t \big(1 - \widetilde{y}_{t-1}^{\mathsf{T}} \Gamma^{-1}(0)\mu\big) + o_P(1),$$

so that $\sqrt{T}(\widehat{\alpha} - \alpha) \Longrightarrow N(0, \tau\Omega_\varepsilon)$, with

$$\tau = E\big(1 - \widetilde{y}_{t-1}^{\mathsf{T}} \Gamma^{-1}(0)\mu\big)^2 = 1 + \mu^{\mathsf{T}}\Gamma^{-1}(0)\mu.$$

Furthermore, $\widehat{\alpha}$ and $\widehat{A}$ are asymptotically correlated as from standard OLS theory.

The error covariance matrix may be estimated by the residual sample covariance matrix,

$$\widehat{\Omega}_\varepsilon = \frac{1}{T}\sum_{t=2}^{T}\widehat{\varepsilon}_t\widehat{\varepsilon}_t^{\mathsf{T}}, \qquad \widehat{\varepsilon}_t = y_t - \widehat{\alpha} - \widehat{A}y_{t-1}. \tag{7.33}$$

Under the assumption that the shocks are i.i.d., this is a consistent estimator of Ω_ε.

7.3.1.3 Gaussian Likelihood

The conditional log likelihood for the VAR model under the assumption that $\varepsilon_t \sim N(0, \Omega_\varepsilon)$ is

$$\mathcal{L}_C(\theta) = -\frac{Tn}{2}\log 2\pi - \frac{T}{2}\log\det(\Omega_\varepsilon)$$
$$- \frac{1}{2}\sum_{t=2}^{T}(y_t - \alpha - Ay_{t-1})^{\mathsf{T}}\Omega_\varepsilon^{-1}(y_t - \alpha - Ay_{t-1}), \tag{7.34}$$

where $\theta \in \mathbb{R}^{3n(n+1)/2}$ contains all the parameters in $\alpha, A, \Omega_\varepsilon$. The conditional MLEs are exactly the same as the OLS estimators. The full likelihood involves adding a term for the initial observation, $y_1 \sim N(0, \Sigma)$, where $\text{vec}(\Sigma) = (I_{n^2} - (A \otimes A))^{-1}\text{vec}(\Omega_\varepsilon)$. The log likelihood in terms of the parameters $\mu, A, \Omega_\varepsilon$ just involves replacing the terms $y_t - \alpha - Ay_{t-1}$ by $y_t - \mu - A(y_{t-1} - \mu)$.

7.3.1.4 Goodness of Fit

How well does the VAR model explain the sample data? What are the relative contributions of the different variables (and their lags) to the explanation? We consider the VAR(p) case.

For a given variable y_{it}, we may calculate the usual regression R_i^2 and adjusted R_i^{*2} as

$$R_i^2 = 1 - \frac{\sum_{t=2}^{T}\widehat{\varepsilon}_{it}^2}{\sum_{t=2}^{T}(y_{it} - \bar{y}_i)^2}, \qquad R_i^{*2} = 1 - (1 - R_i^2)\frac{T-1}{T-np-1},$$

where $\bar{y}_i = \sum_{t=1}^{T} y_{it}/T$. This is the traditional regression measure of goodness of fit, where R_i^2 lies between zero and one, with one indicating a very strong fit and zero indicating the opposite. The adjusted measure takes account of how many variables are working on the fit and discounts the fit for large models. An alternative is to work with the log likelihood or the likelihood-related AIC and BIC measures we discuss below.

The semi-partial R^2 of variable k affecting variable i is defined as

$$R_{\text{spartial};i,-k}^2 = R_i^2 - R_{i;-k}^2, \tag{7.35}$$

where $R_{i;-k}^2$ is calculated as R_i^2 except that variable k (and all of its lags) is dropped from the system. This measures the incremental contribution of variable k, how much extra the variable k brings to the fitting purpose. The partial R^2 of variable k affecting variable i is defined as

$$R_{\text{partial};i,-k}^2 = \frac{R_i^2 - R_{i;-k}^2}{1 - R_{i;-k}^2}, \tag{7.36}$$

which is an alternative measure. These are examples of what nowadays are called **variable importance measures**.

One can define a system goodness-of-fit measure / R^2 in various ways. For example,

$$R_{\text{system}}^2 = \frac{\sum_{i=1}^n \sum_{t=2}^T \widehat{\varepsilon}_{it}^2}{\sum_{i=1}^n \sum_{t=2}^T (y_{it} - \bar{y}_i)^2}.$$

Likewise, one can adjust R_{system}^2 for the number of explanatory variables in each regression equation and use AIC or BIC, which we turn to next.

7.3.1.5 Model Selection

Suppose that we wish to determine the order of the VAR, that is, how many lags p should be included. This involves a trade-off between goodness of fit and parsimony. The most-used model selection criteria are

$$\text{AIC}(p) = -2\widehat{\mathcal{L}} + 2d(p,n), \qquad \text{BIC}(p) = -2\widehat{\mathcal{L}} + d(p,n)\log T,$$

where $\widehat{\mathcal{L}}$ is the log likelihood function at the estimated parameters,

$$\widehat{\mathcal{L}} = \mathcal{L}(\widehat{\alpha}, \widehat{A}_1, \ldots, \widehat{A}_p, \widehat{\Omega}_\varepsilon \mid y) = -\frac{Tn}{2}\log 2\pi - \frac{T}{2}\log\det(\widehat{\Omega}_\varepsilon) - \frac{Tn}{2}, \qquad (7.37)$$

while $d(p,n)$ is the total number of (relevant) parameters $n^2 p$ and the constants in the likelihood can be ignored, so for example we can work with

$$\text{AIC}(p) = \log\det(\widehat{\Omega}_\varepsilon) + \frac{2n^2 p}{T}.$$

We should choose $\widehat{p} \in \{0, 1, \ldots, p_{\max}\}$ to minimize the criteria. We may also wish to choose which variables to include in the system and the model selection methods can be adapted to that question in that case, also taking account of the $n(n+1)/2$ parameters in the error covariance matrix.

7.3.1.6 Inference under I.I.D. Shocks

We may want to construct confidence intervals about the individual elements of the matrix A or to test various hypotheses about the whole matrix. One may have single-equation hypotheses, that is, hypotheses that only concern the regression parameters of a single equation such as $R_i \beta_i = r_i$, where R_i is a known $q \times (n+1)$ matrix and r_i is a known $q \times 1$ vector. For example, the hypothesis that lagged values of variable j do not affect variable i. We consider the general system hypothesis case.

A general class of linear hypotheses of interest about the matrix A are $Ra = r$, where R is a known $q \times n^2$ matrix and r is a known $q \times 1$ vector. For example, the Granger causality test is of this form; specifically, writing

$$A = \begin{pmatrix} A_{11} & A_{12} \\ A_{21} & A_{22} \end{pmatrix},$$

in this case the null hypothesis is that $A_{12} = 0$. The Wald statistic is

$$W = T(R\widehat{a} - r)^{\mathsf{T}} \left(R\big(\widehat{\Gamma}^{-1}(0) \otimes \widehat{\Omega}_\varepsilon\big)R^{\mathsf{T}}\right)(R\widehat{a} - r), \qquad (7.38)$$

which is asymptotically $(T \to \infty)$ $\chi^2(q)$ under the null hypothesis and grows without bound whenever $Ra \neq r$. Alternatively, one can use bootstrap procedures, either parametric (i.e., Gaussian distribution) or nonparametric, resampling from the centered residuals directly.

The likelihood ratio and score tests are also available in this case based on the working assumption than ε_t is Gaussian. The log likelihood function at the estimated parameters is

$$\mathcal{L}(\widehat{\alpha}, \widehat{A}, \widehat{\Omega}_\varepsilon) = -\frac{Tn}{2} \log 2\pi - \frac{T}{2} \log \det(\widehat{\Omega}_\varepsilon) - \frac{Tn}{2}. \tag{7.39}$$

This formula is also true for the MLE computed under the linear restrictions provided $\widehat{\Omega}_\varepsilon$ is replaced by $\widetilde{\Omega}_\varepsilon$, the MLE of Ω_ε under the constraints (restricted model). Suppose we wish to test a general hypothesis about $\theta = (\alpha^\mathsf{T}, a^\mathsf{T})^\mathsf{T}$, this could be a linear restriction on A but it could also involve restrictions on the other parameters. The likelihood ratio statistic is

$$\mathrm{LR} = T\big(\log \det(\widetilde{\Omega}_\varepsilon) - \log \det(\widehat{\Omega}_\varepsilon)\big), \tag{7.40}$$

where $\widetilde{\Omega}_\varepsilon$ is the MLE of Ω_ε under the constraints (restricted model). Under the null hypothesis this is asymptotically distributed as χ_q^2. Of course, the computation of the restricted estimators $\widetilde{\alpha}, \widetilde{A}, \widetilde{\Omega}_\varepsilon$ can be quite tricksy even in this linear case. Furthermore, the LR tests are not robust to heteroskedasticity, which we discuss next.

7.3.1.7 Inference under MDS Shocks

Suppose that ε_t is a stationary MDS but is not necessarily i.i.d., how do we conduct inference about the parameters? In this case we essentially apply White's system standard errors to the linear regression estimators. Under some conditions, we have $\sqrt{T}\,(\widehat{a} - a) \Longrightarrow N(0, \Upsilon)$, with

$$\Upsilon = (\Gamma(0) \otimes I_n)^{-1} \Lambda (\Gamma(0) \otimes I_n)^{-1},$$

where, with z_t defined in (7.32),

$$\Lambda = \lim_{T \to \infty} \frac{1}{T} \sum_{t=1}^{T} E(z_t z_t^\mathsf{T}) = E\big((y_{t-1} - \mu)(y_{t-1} - \mu)^\mathsf{T} \otimes E(\varepsilon_t \varepsilon_t^\mathsf{T} \mid \mathcal{F}_{t-1})\big),$$

assuming the limit exists, where $\mathcal{F}_{t-1}$ is generated by all the past values $y_{t-1}, y_{t-2}, \ldots$ There is no cancellation of terms unless $E(\varepsilon_t \varepsilon_t^\mathsf{T} \mid \mathcal{F}_{t-1})$ does not vary with past values $\mathcal{F}_{t-1}$. Nevertheless, it is straightforward to estimate Λ and construct robust standard errors from

$$\widehat{\Upsilon} = \big(\widehat{\Gamma}(0) \otimes I_n\big)^{-1} \frac{1}{T} \sum_{t=1}^{T} \big((y_{t-1} - \bar{y})(y_{t-1} - \bar{y})^\mathsf{T} \otimes \widehat{\varepsilon}_t \widehat{\varepsilon}_t^\mathsf{T}\big)\big(\widehat{\Gamma}(0) \otimes I_n\big)^{-1}. \tag{7.41}$$

Alternatively, one can use bootstrap procedures based on the wild bootstrap (Mammen, 1993).

7.3.1.8 Impulse Responses

The analogue estimator of the impulse response function satisfies a CLT. Let $\widehat{\iota} = (\widehat{\iota}(1)^\mathsf{T}, \ldots, \widehat{\iota}(K)^\mathsf{T})^\mathsf{T}$ and $\iota = (\iota(1)^\mathsf{T}, \ldots, \iota(K)^\mathsf{T})^\mathsf{T}$, where $\iota(k) = \mathrm{vec}(\mathbb{I}(k))$ and $\widehat{\iota}(k) = \mathrm{vec}(\widehat{I}(k))$. Since $\iota = f(\theta)$, where θ is the vector of parameters $\alpha, A_1, \ldots, A_p, \Omega_\varepsilon$, while f is a smooth function, we may apply the delta method to obtain $\sqrt{T}(\widehat{\iota} - \iota) \Longrightarrow N(0, V_{\mathbb{I}}(\theta))$ for some $Kn^2 \times Kn^2$ matrix $V_{\mathbb{I}}(\theta)$. This result is easy to state in this abstract way, but the matrix $V_I(\theta)$ is complicated and requires a deep respect for matrix algebra to understand. We may estimate $V_I(\theta)$ by $V_I(\widehat{\theta})$ and derive standard errors from the diagonal elements in the usual way. Conventional practice is to report the impulse response curves along with pointwise standard error bands,

$$\left[\widehat{\mathbb{I}}_{ij}(k) - z_{\alpha/2} \times \text{stderr}_{ij;k}, \widehat{\mathbb{I}}_{ij}(k) + z_{\alpha/2} \times \text{stderr}_{ij;k}\right], \quad k = 1, 2, \ldots, K.$$

This ignores the joint distribution over k and over other i, j pairs as it just relies on the CLT for $Z_{ijk} = \sqrt{T}(\widehat{\mathbb{I}}_{ij}(k) - \mathbb{I}_{ij}(k))/\sigma_{ijk}$ for each separate i, j, k, where σ_{ijk}^2 is the asymptotic variance. A simple way to deal with this is to use uniform confidence intervals based on an assumption that Z_{ijk} are i.i.d. across i, j, k. By the **continuous mapping theorem**,

$$\max_{\substack{1 \le i,j \le n \\ 1 \le k \le K}} Z_{ijk} \Longrightarrow W,$$

where Z_i are i.i.d. standard normal random variables. The distribution of W is $\Pr(W \le x) = \Phi(x)^q$, where $q = n^2 K$. Therefore, the uniform confidence intervals are of the form

$$\left[\widehat{\mathbb{I}}_{ij}(k) - w_{\alpha/2} \times \text{stderr}_{ij;k}, \widehat{\mathbb{I}}_{ij}(k) + w_{\alpha/2} \times \text{stderr}_{ij;k}\right], \tag{7.42}$$

where $w_{\alpha/2}$ satisfies $(1 - 2\Phi(-w_{\alpha/2}))^q = 1 - \alpha$. For $\alpha = 0.05$ and $q = 250$, $w_{\alpha/2} = 3.712$. This says that to construct a 95% interval for $q = 250$ we need to consider intervals proportional to ± 3.712 instead of the usual ± 1.96. These intervals are wider.

An alternative way of conducting inference without delving into algebra is to use the bootstrap. For example, consider the impulse responses.

1. Let $\widehat{A}_1, \ldots, \widehat{A}_p, \widehat{\Sigma}$ be the estimates of the reduced-form parameters and $\widehat{\Psi}_l = \sum_{i=0}^{l} \widehat{\Psi}_{l-i} \widehat{A}_i$ be the estimated impulse response matrix, and let $\widehat{\varepsilon}_t$ be the VAR residuals.
2. Let $\{\varepsilon_t^*\}$ be drawn with replacement from the centered empirical distribution of $\{\widehat{\varepsilon}_t\}$, and define recursively, for $t = p + 1, \ldots, T$,

$$y_t^* = \widehat{A}_1 y_{t-1}^* + \cdots + \widehat{A}_p y_{t-p}^* + \varepsilon_t^*,$$

where the initial values $y_1^*, \ldots, y_p^*$ can be drawn from the sample $\{y_t\}$ distribution.
3. Then define the bootstrap estimates $\widehat{A}_1^*, \ldots, \widehat{A}_p^*, \widehat{\Sigma}^*$ from the sample $\{y_t^*\}$ and define $\widehat{\Psi}_l^* = \sum_{i=0}^{l} \widehat{\Psi}_{l-i}^* \widehat{A}_i^*$.
4. Compute critical values from the distribution of $\widehat{\Psi}_l^*$ across bootstrap draws.

Alternatively, one can draw ε_t^* from the $N(0, \widehat{\Sigma})$ distribution instead of the empirical distribution. One can allow for time series heteroskedasticity by drawing z_{it}^* from any scalar distribution with mean zero and variance one and taking $\varepsilon_{it}^* = z_{it}^* \times \widehat{\varepsilon}_{it}$ for $i = 1, \ldots, n$.

Here is an alternative simulation procedure for the case that $p = 1$ so that $\mathbb{I}(k) = A^k$. In this case we have

$$\widehat{A}^k - A^k = \left(A + \frac{1}{\sqrt{T}}\sqrt{T}(\widehat{A} - A)\right)^k - A^k$$

$$\simeq \left(A + \frac{1}{\sqrt{T}}\text{MN}(0, \Omega_\varepsilon, \Gamma^{-1}(0))\right)^k - A^k, \tag{7.43}$$

where the approximation is valid from the CLT. Specifically, we can obtain

$$\widehat{A}^2 - A^2 \simeq A \times \frac{1}{\sqrt{T}} \mathrm{MN}(0, \Omega_\varepsilon, \Gamma^{-1}(0)) + \frac{1}{\sqrt{T}} \mathrm{MN}(0, \Omega_\varepsilon, \Gamma^{-1}(0)) A$$

$$= \frac{1}{\sqrt{T}} \mathrm{MN}(0, (I + A)\Omega_\varepsilon, \Gamma^{-1}(0)(I + A)),$$

and so on. One may conduct inference by simulating many instances of $\mathrm{MN}(0, \widehat{\Omega}_\varepsilon, \widehat{\Gamma}^{-1}(0))$ and hence W_k, where

$$W_k = \left(\widehat{A} + \frac{1}{\sqrt{T}} \mathrm{MN}(0, \widehat{\Omega}_\varepsilon, \widehat{\Gamma}^{-1}(0)) \right)^k - \widehat{A}^k.$$

This is a sort of parametric bootstrap.

One could care about the multiple testing aspect here, which is potentially quite extreme since many different estimates are involved. One approach to this is to work with uniform confidence bands by taking the maximum over $k = 1, \ldots, K$ and $i, j = 1, \ldots, n$, and conducting inference using subsampling or some other resampling method (Whang and Kim, 2003).

An alternative approach to computing impulse responses is based on the so-called **local projection** method of Jordà (2005). In this case, for horizon k we fit a linear multivariate regression of y_{t+k} on $y_{t-1}, \ldots, y_{t-p}$. The kth impulse response is the corresponding coefficient matrix on the first lag, denoted $B_{1;k}$. Under the original VAR with i.i.d. shocks assumption, this regression will have moving average errors and this needs to be accounted for in inference methods. Standard errors for the elements of this matrix can be constructed using the methods discussed in Chapter 5. This is the same idea as in **predictive regression** (Stambaugh, 1999).

7.3.2   Estimation of a VMA Model

Estimation of vector MA processes is complicated, even more so than in the univariate case. Specifically, it is hard to find closed-form estimators even for the very simplest case. For example, in the VMA(1) case we have, by substitution of $\Theta = -\Gamma(1)\Omega_\varepsilon^{-1}$,

$$\Gamma(1)P_\varepsilon\Gamma(1)^\mathsf{T}P_\varepsilon - \Gamma(0)P_\varepsilon + I_n = 0,$$

which is a matrix quadratic equation in the precision matrix $P_\varepsilon = \Omega_\varepsilon^{-1}$. Unfortunately, there does not exist a formula for the solution(s) of the matrix quadratic equation, unlike in the scalar case. One can, of course, use numerical methods to solve these equations, or do the Gaussian QMLE. Methods based on estimating long VARs are not attractive when the dimensionality is even modest.

7.3.3   Structural VAR

Econometricians of an earlier generation focused a lot on the simultaneous equations model, where, for example, supply and demand curves are specified in terms of endogenously determined prices and quantities, and exogenously determined variables that affect either or both curves. A lot of the methodology was developed at the Cowles

Foundation (Malinvaud, 1983). This literature in a time series context has been absorbed into the structural VAR (SVAR) literature, which includes contemporaneous interactions amongst the variables as in the classic simultaneous equations literature, as well as dynamic responses. A common question in empirical macroeconomics: What is the effect of a policy intervention (interest rate increase, fiscal stimulus) on macroeconomic aggregates of interest – output, inflation, and so on? Let y_t be a vector of macro time series, and let ε_t^r denote an unanticipated monetary policy intervention or shock. We want to know the dynamic causal effect of ε_t^r on y_t, which is defined as

$$\frac{\partial y_{t+h}}{\partial \varepsilon_t^r}, \quad h = 0, 1, 2, \ldots, \tag{7.44}$$

where the partial derivative holds all other variables constant. This dynamic causal effect is the impulse response function of y_t to the "shock" (unexpected intervention). The definition of what are the relevant shocks is at the heart of this question.

The following is a very general class of models called structural VAR(p):

$$\Phi_0 y_t = \alpha^* + \Phi_1 y_{t-1} + \cdots + \Phi_p y_{t-p} + \varepsilon_t, \tag{7.45}$$

where ε_t is i.i.d., mean zero, and with variance matrix Ω_ε. We can write this in shorthand as $\Phi(L)y_t = \alpha^* + \varepsilon_t$. We do not assume that $\Phi_0 = I_n$, and this allows for contemporaneous effects of one variable on another as in the classic simultaneous equation. The parameters of this model are $\{\alpha^*, \Phi_0, \Phi_1, \ldots, \Phi_p, \Omega_\varepsilon\}$. Assuming that Φ_0 is a nonsingular square matrix, we can define the associated reduced form,

$$y_t = \alpha + A_1 y_{t-1} + \cdots + A_p y_{t-p} + u_t,$$

where $A_j = \Phi_0^{-1}\Phi_j$, $j = 1, \ldots, p$, and $u_t = \Phi_0^{-1}\varepsilon_t$, where u_t is mean zero with covariance matrix $\Sigma_u = \Phi_0^{-1}\Omega_\varepsilon(\Phi_0^{-1})^\mathsf{T}$, that is, $A(L)y_t = \alpha + u_t$. The parameters of the reduced form are $(\alpha, A_1, \ldots, A_p, \Sigma_u)$, and as we have seen these are identifiable by OLS estimation with the observed data. The key question here is how to recover the structural parameters $(\alpha^*, \Phi_0, \Phi_1, \ldots, \Phi_p, \Omega_\varepsilon)$. This is nontrivial: the model is not identified without restrictions on the coefficient matrices because the structural form contains in principle $n + (p+1)n^2 + n(n+1)/2$ parameters whereas the reduced form contains $n + pn^2 + n(n+1)/2$, so in terms of paying the bar bill, we are short n^2 parameters.

Suppose that we normalize the covariance matrix of the structural errors to be the identity matrix, that is, $\Omega_\varepsilon = I_n$, in which case the structural shocks are of equal scale and mutually uncorrelated. This imposes a total of $n(n+1)/2$ restrictions, but, even in the case $n = 2$, this is insufficient. In this case $\Sigma_u = \Phi_0^{-1}(\Phi_0^{-1})^\mathsf{T}$n and we are effectively trying to obtain the unrestricted matrix Φ_0 from the covariance matrix Σ_u. Essentially, we have $n(n+1)/2$ equations in n^2 unknowns, the elements of Φ_0. There is a shortfall of the number of available "observations" from Σ_u to infer the values of Φ_0 because Σ_u has to be symmetric, whereas Φ_0 need not be. Note that an alternative but equivalent set of restrictions is to normalize the diagonal elements of Φ_0 to be equal to one and to take $\Omega_\varepsilon = \mathrm{diag}\{\sigma_1, \ldots, \sigma_n\}$, which likewise fails the count.

There are a number of ways of proceeding: (i) identification by short-run restrictions; (ii) identification by long-run restrictions; (iii) identification by sign restrictions; (iv) identification from heteroskedasticity.

7.3.3.1 Triangular Systems

One solution is to assume that Φ_0 is lower or upper triangular, that is,

$$
\Phi_0 = \begin{pmatrix}
\phi_{11} & 0 & & & 0 \\
\phi_{21} & \ddots & & & \vdots \\
& \phi_{32} & \ddots & & \\
& & \ddots & \ddots & 0 \\
\phi_{n1} & \cdots & & \phi_{n,n-1} & \phi_{nn}
\end{pmatrix},
$$

which imposes exactly the required number of restrictions, that is, it satisfies the so-called order condition, which is necessary for identification but not sufficient. The system also needs to satisfy an additional rank condition to avoid redundancy. This structure is called triangular or recursive. The first variable does not depend contemporaneously on any others, the second variable only depends on the first, and so on. Let $y_t = (p_t, \mathrm{gdp}_t, m_t, i_t)^\mathsf{T}$, where p is the log of the price level, gdp is the log of the real GDP, m is the log of the monetary aggregate such as $M1$, and i is the Federal Funds rate. One version of the triangular assumption is that

$$
\begin{pmatrix}
u_t^p \\
u_t^{\mathrm{gdp}} \\
u_t^m \\
u_t^i
\end{pmatrix} =
\begin{pmatrix}
\Phi_0^{11} & 0 & 0 & 0 \\
\Phi_0^{21} & \Phi_0^{22} & 0 & 0 \\
\Phi_0^{31} & \Phi_0^{32} & \Phi_0^{33} & 0 \\
\Phi_0^{41} & \Phi_0^{42} & \Phi_0^{43} & \Phi_0^{44}
\end{pmatrix}
\begin{pmatrix}
\varepsilon_t^p \\
\varepsilon_t^{\mathrm{gdp}} \\
\varepsilon_t^m \\
\varepsilon_t^i
\end{pmatrix},
$$

where Φ_0^{ij}, $i \geq j$, are free parameters. This says that the price level does not respond to shocks to real income, money supply, or interest rates contemporaneously, only with a lag. Real GDP does not respond to shocks to the money supply or interest rates contemporaneously, only with a lag. Some economists might find these restrictive assumptions. One might instead choose a different ordering of variables that imposes other recursive restrictions, but any such ordering has a similar weakness. There are some examples where this structure is plausible (Kilian and Lütkepohl, 2017, p. 224).

7.3.3.2 Long-Run Restrictions

The MA representation of y_t can be expressed in terms of the structural errors or the reduced-form errors. Specifically, (setting $\alpha = \alpha^* = 0$ for simplicity) we have the moving average representation $y_t = D(L)\varepsilon_t$, where $D(L) = \sum_{j=0}^\infty D_j L^j$. Then $D(1) = \sum_{j=0}^\infty D_j$ is the long-run effect of the structural shock ε_t on y_t. Suppose that we assume $D_{ij}(1) = 0$ for certain i, j, which says that the long-run effect of structural shock j on outcome i is zero. These conditions imply restrictions on Φ_0, which permit identification provided the counting is right. Blanchard and Quah (1989) had two variables (unemployment and output), with the restriction that the demand shock has no long-run effect on the unemployment rate. This imposed a single zero restriction, which is all that is needed for system identification in this case. This approach has been at the center of a debate about whether technology shocks lead to a short-run decline in hours, based on long-run restrictions (Kilian and Lütkepohl, 2017).

7.3.4   Nonstationary VAR and Cointegration

We now consider the case where some or all of the variables $y_t \in \mathbb{R}^n$ are nonstationary. Suppose that $y_t = y_{t-1} + \varepsilon_t$, where ε_t is i.i.d. with mean zero and variance matrix Ω_ε. The theory of multivariate random walks is complex: For $n = 2$ the process is recurrent, albeit at a much slower rate than when $n = 1$, while if $n \geq 3$ the process is not recurrent, that is, it is called **transient**. As the saying goes, the drunken man will return to his home, but the drunken bird will never get back to its nest, which may be why birds don't drink. This has to do with how the sample paths evolve in n-dimensional space. Of course, we can calculate, as before, $y_t = \sum_{s=1}^{t} \varepsilon_s + y_0$, so that $E(y_t \mid y_0) = y_0$ and $E\big((y_t - y_0) (y_t - y_0)^\mathsf{T} \mid y_0 \big) = t \times \Omega_\varepsilon$. If Ω_ε is nonsingular, then all linear combinations $c^\mathsf{T} y_t$ satisfy the properties of a scalar unit root process.

One issue in applications is the so-called **spurious regression** problem, namely, two random walks with uncorrelated shocks will appear to be correlated in sample. That is, the linear regression slope coefficient (of one random walk on the other) converges to a random variable rather than zero. The same is true, by the way, of deterministic trend models, that is, suppose that $y_t = \alpha + \beta t + \varepsilon_t$ and $x_t = \alpha' + \beta' t + \varepsilon_t'$, where ε_t and ε_t' are uncorrelated processes; then $y_t = \delta + \gamma x_t + u_t$ for $\gamma = \beta/\beta'$, that is, the regression of y_t on x_t will give a nonzero coefficient. This suggests one should be cautious in interpreting correlations between trending series. Doing the regressions in differences will clarify the relationship between y and x.

We consider the more general case of the VAR(1)

$$y_t = A y_{t-1} + \varepsilon_t \tag{7.46}$$

with a matrix A for which not all the eigenvalues are less than one in absolute value, which includes the case $A = I_n$ considered above but also many other cases. Suppose that A is a symmetric matrix. Then we may write $A = Q \Lambda Q^\mathsf{T}$, where Λ is the diagonal matrix containing the ordered (largest to smallest) eigenvalues of A, while Q is an orthonormal matrix satisfying $Q Q^\mathsf{T} = Q^\mathsf{T} Q = I_n$. In this case, premultiplying by Q^T we can write $x_t = \Lambda x_{t-1} + \varepsilon_t^*$, where $x_t = Q^\mathsf{T} y_t$, while $\varepsilon_t^* = Q^\mathsf{T} \varepsilon_t$ is mean zero and has covariance matrix $Q^\mathsf{T} \Omega Q$. The component x_{jt} is stationary if and only if $|\lambda_j| < 1$. Note that $y_t = Q x_t$ so that y_t is stationary only if all the x_t are. In general, the matrix A need not be symmetric. In that case, we have the **Jordan decomposition** (Sims, 2015).

The general VAR model (7.46) may be rewritten as $\Delta y_t = \Pi y_{t-1} + \varepsilon_t$, where $\Pi = -I_n + A$. We have the following result.

Theorem 7.1 (Granger representation theorem)   *Let $A(z) = Az - I$, where $z \in \mathbb{C}$. Suppose that:*

(i) *The roots of the characteristic polynomial (defined from $\det(A(z)) = 0$) are either outside the unit circle or equal to one.*
(ii) *The matrix $A(1) = \Pi = -I_n + A$ has reduced rank $r < n$, that is, $\Pi = \alpha \beta^\mathsf{T}$, where α and β are $n \times r$ matrices of full column rank r.*
(iii) *The matrix $\alpha_\perp^\mathsf{T} \beta_\perp$ has full rank r, where $\alpha_\perp$ and $\beta_\perp$ are the orthogonal complements to α and β with $\alpha_\perp^\mathsf{T} \alpha = 0$, $\beta_\perp^\mathsf{T} \beta = 0$.*

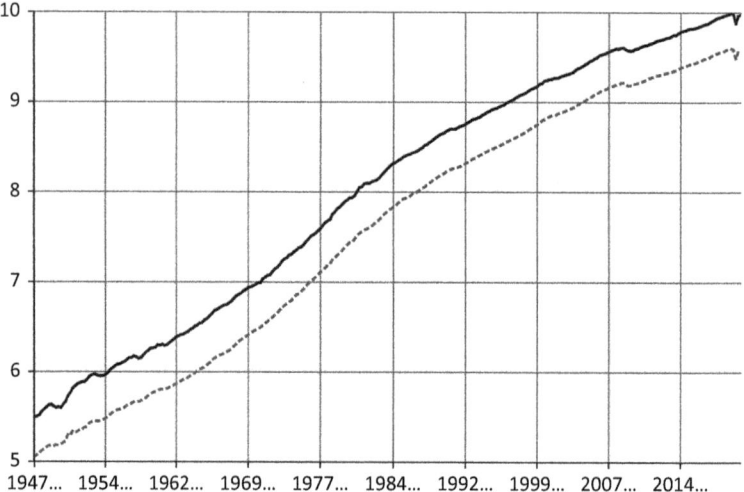

Figure 7.3 Log of GDP (solid) and log of PCE (dashed).

Then we can write

$$y_t = C \sum_{s=1}^{t} \varepsilon_s + (I - C) \sum_{i=0}^{\infty} (I + \alpha\beta^{\mathsf{T}})^i \varepsilon_{t-i} + Cy_0,$$

where $C = \beta_\perp (\alpha_\perp^{\mathsf{T}} \beta_\perp)^{-1} \alpha_\perp^{\mathsf{T}}$ is of rank r.

This represents the general process in terms of three components: a nonstationary component, a stationary component, and an initial condition.

We next consider the concept of **cointegration**, which is a special property that is not possessed by all unit root processes, but it is suggested by some economics arguments, that is, that there should be stable long-run relationships between some variables.

Definition 7.3   Suppose $y_t \in \mathbb{R}^n$ is a vector of unit root or $I(1)$ processes. Now suppose that there is an $\alpha \in \mathbb{R}^n$ such that $\alpha^{\mathsf{T}} y_t$ is stationary or $I(0)$. Then we say that y_t are cointegrated with cointegrating vector α.

We next discuss some examples. Aggregate (log) consumption and (log) income appear to be nonstationary processes, but there should exist a long-run equilibrium relationship between these variables relative to which there are only stationary deviations, see Figure 7.3. The quantity theory of money specifies $M \times V = P \times T$ (money, real income, and prices are in long-run balance), which can be phrased in terms of cointegration. The present value model of stock prices P and earnings or dividends D is of the form

$$P_t = \sum_{i=1}^{\infty} \left(\frac{1}{1+R} \right)^i E_t D_{t+i},$$

where both variables P_t, D_t are I(1) and R is the interest or discount rate. It follows that

$$P_t - \frac{D_t}{R} = \frac{1}{R} \sum_{i=0}^{\infty} \left(\frac{1}{1+R} \right)^i E_t \Delta D_{t+i}$$

is I(0). Gatev, Goetzmann, and Rouwenhorst (2006) used the cointegration model to design the pairs trading strategy under the assumption that the log price of certain stock pairs are cointegrated. Other examples include the term structure of interest rates and purchasing power parity.

The cointegrating vector is not unique, so without loss of generality we may normalize on one component. Suppose that $y_t = (y_{1t}, y_{2t}^\mathsf{T})^\mathsf{T}$ and let $\alpha = (1, -\beta^\mathsf{T})^\mathsf{T}$, in which case $u_{1t} = y_{1t} - \beta^\mathsf{T} y_{2t}$ is stationary. We may write this as a regression equation, $y_{1t} = \beta^\mathsf{T} y_{2t} + u_{1t}$. We can estimate the cointegrating parameter β by the OLS regression of y_{1t} on y_{2t}, so that

$$\widehat{\beta} = \left(\sum_{t=1}^{T} y_{2t} y_{2t}^\mathsf{T} \right)^{-1} \sum_{t=1}^{T} y_{2t} y_{1t}.$$

Suppose that $u_{1t} = y_{1t} - \beta^\mathsf{T} y_{2t}$ is a stationary mean-zero process for a particular value of β. One neat thing here is that even if there is contemporaneous correlation between y_{2t} and u_{1t}, that is, endogeneity, the estimator $\widehat{\beta}$ is consistent and even superconsistent. The distribution theory is again nonstandard, but has been tabulated. Suppose that $n = 2$ and that $y_{2t} = y_{2,t-1} + \varepsilon_t$, where both u_t and ε_t are i.i.d. with zero mean and finite variance, and are mutually independent. Then

$$\frac{1}{T^2} \sum_{t=1}^{T} y_{2t}^2 \Longrightarrow \int B_\varepsilon(s)^2 \, ds,$$

$$\frac{1}{T} \sum_{t=1}^{T} y_{2t} u_t \Longrightarrow \int B_\varepsilon(s) \, dB_u(s), \qquad (7.47)$$

$$T(\widehat{\beta} - \beta) \Longrightarrow \frac{\int B_\varepsilon(s) \, dB_u(s)}{\int B_\varepsilon(s)^2 \, ds},$$

where $B_\varepsilon(\cdot), B_u(\cdot)$ are independent Brownian motions. This limiting distribution is nonstandard, and testing hypotheses about β requires some work to get suitable critical values.

On the other hand, if we suppose only that u_t, ε_t are stationary linear processes, then the problem is even worse. We have

$$T(\widehat{\beta} - \beta) \Longrightarrow \frac{\int B_\varepsilon(s) \, dB_u(s) + \lambda}{\int B_\varepsilon(s)^2 \, ds}, \qquad \lambda = \sum_{k=0}^{\infty} E(u_t \varepsilon_{t+k}). \qquad (7.48)$$

This estimator is consistent but its limiting distribution is not centered at zero and depends on the long-run covariance type parameter λ. One can correct for the bias by estimating λ using the methods described in Chapter 5.

Phillips (1991a) formulated the more general triangular system. Suppose that $y_t = (y_{1t}^\mathsf{T}, y_{2t}^\mathsf{T})^\mathsf{T} \in \mathbb{R}^{n_1+n_2}$ are unit root processes, and that

$$y_{1t} = B y_{2t} + u_{1t}, \qquad y_{2t} = y_{2t-1} + u_{2t}, \qquad (7.49)$$

where $u_t = (u_{1t}^\mathsf{T}, u_{2t}^\mathsf{T})^\mathsf{T}$ are stationary and weakly dependent with mean zero. There are n_1 cointegrating relations $y_{1t} - B y_{2t}$. Special results apply in this case. This model assumes knowledge about the number of cointegrating relations, that is, n_1, and it makes a particular normalization on the variable y_1.

There are two alternative representations of this model. Taking first differences we have the error correction form (ECM)

$$\Delta y_t = - \begin{pmatrix} I_{n_1} & B \\ 0 & I_{n_2} \end{pmatrix} y_{t-1} + v_t = -EA y_{t-1} + v_t,$$

$$E = \begin{pmatrix} I_{n_1} \\ 0 \end{pmatrix}, \qquad A = (I, -B), \qquad v_t = \begin{pmatrix} I_{n_1} & B \\ 0 & I_{n_2} \end{pmatrix} u_t.$$

Further, suppose that v_t is i.i.d. with covariance matrix Ω, then the conditional mean equation of y_{1t} given $\{y_{2,t}\}$ is

$$y_{1t} = B y_{2,t-1} + C \Delta y_{2,t} + v_{1 \cdot 2, t}, \tag{7.50}$$

where $C = \Omega_{12} \Omega_{22}^{-1}$ and $v_{1 \cdot 2, t} = v_{1,t} - \Omega_{12} \Omega_{22}^{-1} v_{2,t}$. Under Gaussianity of the shock process, the distribution of y_{1t} given $\{y_{2,t}\}$ is Gaussian and depends on the parameter B, whereas the marginal distribution of the process $\{y_{2,t}\}$ is also Gaussian but does not depend on B. The maximum likelihood estimator of B under normal errors is the OLS estimator from the regression equation (7.50).

Under general conditions the FCLT holds for v_t,

$$\frac{1}{\sqrt{T}} \sum_{t=1}^{\lfloor \cdot T \rfloor} v_t \Longrightarrow \Omega^{1/2} B(\cdot) \equiv S(\cdot),$$

where B is a vector of independent Brownian motions. Phillips (1991a) showed that the OLS estimator $\widehat{B}$ from the equation with $y_{2,t-1}$ and $\Delta y_{2,t}$ satisfies

$$T(\widehat{B} - B) \Longrightarrow \int_0^1 dS_{1 \cdot 2} S_2^{\mathsf{T}} \left(\int_0^1 S_2 S_2^{\mathsf{T}} \right)^{-1}, \tag{7.51}$$

where $S = (S_1^{\mathsf{T}}, S_2^{\mathsf{T}})^{\mathsf{T}}$ and $S_{1 \cdot 2} = S_1 - \Omega_{12} \Omega_{22}^{-1} S_2$. The distribution is actually mixed normal (because $S_{1 \cdot 2}$ and S_2 are independent), that is, it is of the form $N(0, V)$ for some random covariance matrix V. This means that Wald tests about the elements of B can be constructed with the usual chi-squared limiting distribution. If u_t are stationary linear processes, then the limiting distribution is affected and one can apply a bias correction method.

7.3.5   Testing for Cointegration

If the cointegrating vector α is known a priori, then one can test the null hypothesis of cointegration by carrying out ADF tests on the residuals $\alpha^{\mathsf{T}} y_t$. If the null hypothesis of a unit root in that regression cannot be rejected, then the null hypothesis of cointegration is rejected and vice versa. Engle and Granger (1987) considered the case where α is unknown. They proposed testing for the null hypothesis of cointegration by carrying out ADF tests on the residuals from this regression (with some modification to the critical values that they outlined).

Johansen (1988, 1991) developed a test for the presence of cointegration and the number of cointegrating relations without imposing any particular normalization or ordering of the data and extending the classical multivariate analysis literature. If we have an n-vector unit root series y_t, there can be no cointegrating relations, one cointegrating relation, two cointegrating relations, ..., or $n-1$ cointegrating relations. Johansen tests these restrictions sequentially to find the right number of cointegrating relations in the data.

Suppose that $y_t = A_1 y_{t-1} + \cdots + A_p y_{t-p} + \varepsilon_t$, with given initial conditions $y_0, y_{-1}, \ldots, y_{1-p} \in \mathbb{R}^n$. Here, ε_t are i.i.d. with mean zero and covariance matrix Ω_ε. The null hypothesis is that the matrix polynomial $A(L) = I_n - A_1 L - \cdots - A_p L^p$ has unit roots, that is, $\det(A(z)) = 0$ at $z = 1$. We can rewrite this model in ECM,

$$\Delta y_t = \Gamma_1 \Delta y_{t-1} + \cdots + \Gamma_{p-1} \Delta y_{t-p+1} + \Pi y_{t-p} + \varepsilon_t,$$

with $\Gamma_i = A_1 + \cdots + A_i - I_n$, $i = 1, \ldots, p-1$, and $\Pi = A_1 + \cdots + A_p - I_n$. The null hypothesis is

$$H_0 : \Pi = \alpha \beta^{\mathsf{T}} \tag{7.52}$$

for some $n \times r$ full-rank matrices α, β, that is, y_t is nonstationary but $\beta^{\mathsf{T}} y_t$ is stationary. The parameters α, β cannot be uniquely determined since they form an overparameterization of the model, but one can estimate the space spanned by β.

Let R_{0t} denote the residuals from the linear regression of Δy_t on $\Delta y_{t-1}, \ldots, \Delta y_{t-p+1}$, and let R_{pt} denote the residuals from the linear regression of Δy_{t-p} on $\Delta y_{t-1}, \ldots, \Delta y_{t-p+1}$. The Johansen trace test is the likelihood ratio

$$\text{LR} = -T \sum_{i=r+1}^{n} \log\left(1 - \widehat{\lambda}_i\right), \tag{7.53}$$

where $\widehat{\lambda}_{r+1}, \ldots, \widehat{\lambda}_n$ are the $n-r$ smallest canonical correlations, $\widehat{\lambda}_1 \geq \cdots \geq \widehat{\lambda}_n$, which are the ordered solutions of the equations $\det\left(\lambda S_{kk} - S_{0k} S_{00}^{-1} S_{k0}\right) = 0$ with respect to λ, where the S matrices are defined as

$$S_{00} = \frac{1}{T} \sum_{t=1}^{T} R_{0t} R_{0t}^{\mathsf{T}}, \qquad S_{0k} = \frac{1}{T} \sum_{t=1}^{T} R_{0t} R_{kt}^{\mathsf{T}},$$

$$S_{k0} = \frac{1}{T} \sum_{t=1}^{T} R_{kt} R_{0t}^{\mathsf{T}}, \qquad S_{kk} = \frac{1}{T} \sum_{t=1}^{T} R_{kt} R_{kt}^{\mathsf{T}}.$$

Johansen (1988) showed that under the null hypothesis LR converges in distribution to the random variable

$$\mathcal{J} = \text{tr}\left(\left(\int_0^1 dB B^{\mathsf{T}} \right) \left(\int_0^1 B B^{\mathsf{T}} \, du \right) \int_0^1 B \, dB^{\mathsf{T}} \right), \tag{7.54}$$

where B is an $n-r$ dimensional vector of standard Brownian motions with covariance matrix I_{n-r}. The $\mathcal{J}$-distribution is not Gaussian but its distribution does not depend on any unknown quantities and is tabulated. Johansen (1991) extended this to include intercept and trends, and seasonal dummies. The null hypothesis for the "maximum eigenvalue" test is as for the trace test, but the alternative is $r = r_0 + 1$. Testing proceeds sequentially for $r_0 = 1, 2, \ldots$

MacKinnon, Haug, and Michelis (1999) suggested improved critical values for both tests, which are widely used, for example by EViews. Onatski and Wang (2018) showed that the quality of the asymptotic approximations deteriorates with n and suggested alternative limiting distributions that provide better approximations in this case.

7.3.6   Large-Dimensional Case

Suppose that n is large, the so-called big data case; then what? The issue is that the VAR model is then too general, with too many parameters compared to the information available to estimate them.

One approach is to impose restrictions on the A_j matrices. For example, that A_j be diagonal. This reverts to a set of univariate models and has already been treated as univariate AR(p), although if the errors are contemporarily correlated this model can allow for contemporaneous correlation between the outcome variables but rules out any cross-autocorrelation, which is somewhat restrictive. More generally, we may impose **sparsity** on the coefficient and covariance matrices, that is, $A_{ij} = 0$ for many $i \neq j$ combinations and/or $\Sigma_{ij} = 0$ for many $i \neq j$ combinations. Modern treatments allow the location of the zeros to be determined empirically, so it is not necessarily known a priori where the zeros lie; specifically, methods like the LASSO can be used, which we take up in more detail in Chapter 11. An alternative approach is to set $A_j = a_j I_n + b_j i_n i_n^\mathsf{T}$, where a_j, b_j are scalars; in this case A_j is not sparse but it is highly structured. This model allows for cross-autocorrelation, but it imposes strong restrictions on the diagonal elements. More generally, we may write $A_j = \mathrm{diag}(a_j) - a_j a_j^\mathsf{T}$, in which $a_j = (a_{j1}, \ldots, a_{jn})^\mathsf{T}$ is a vector of free parameters.

Another approach is through factor analysis. Suppose that $y_t = Bf_t + \varepsilon_t$, where $f_t \in \mathbb{R}^K, \varepsilon_t \in \mathbb{R}^n$ are latent (unobserved vectors), while B is an $n \times K$ matrix of unknown parameters. The right-hand side is full of unknowns. The key thing here is to allow $K < n$, in which case the outcome variable y is driven by a small number of common factors. In observable factor models, f_t is observed, in which case this is a multivariate linear regression, but when f_t is unobserved the standard regression techniques cannot be applied. This model generalizes the signal plus noise model for a univariate time series where $B = 1$. Bai (2003) developed an inferential theory; Bai and Ng (2002) developed a model selection and test for the number of factors; Onatski (2009) developed an alternative test of the number of factors K. We may further suppose that the factors themselves follow a VAR,

$$f_t = \Phi_1 f_{t-1} + \cdots + \Phi_p f_{t-p} + \eta_t,$$

where η_t are i.i.d. with mean zero and $K \times K$ covariance matrix Ω_η, while ε_t are usually assumed to be i.i.d. with a diagonal covariance matrix, which reflects the modelling aspiration that the latent factors capture all the comovements. The matrices Φ_j are of dimension $K \times K$ and contain many fewer parameters than n^2. The dynamic factors generate autocovariances in the observed y_t. An alternative approach here is to suppose that $y_t = B(L)f_t + \varepsilon_t$, where $B(L) = \sum_{j=1}^p B_j L^j$ is a lag polynomial and B_j are $n \times K$ matrices. This is called a dynamic factor model (Forni *et al.*, 2000).

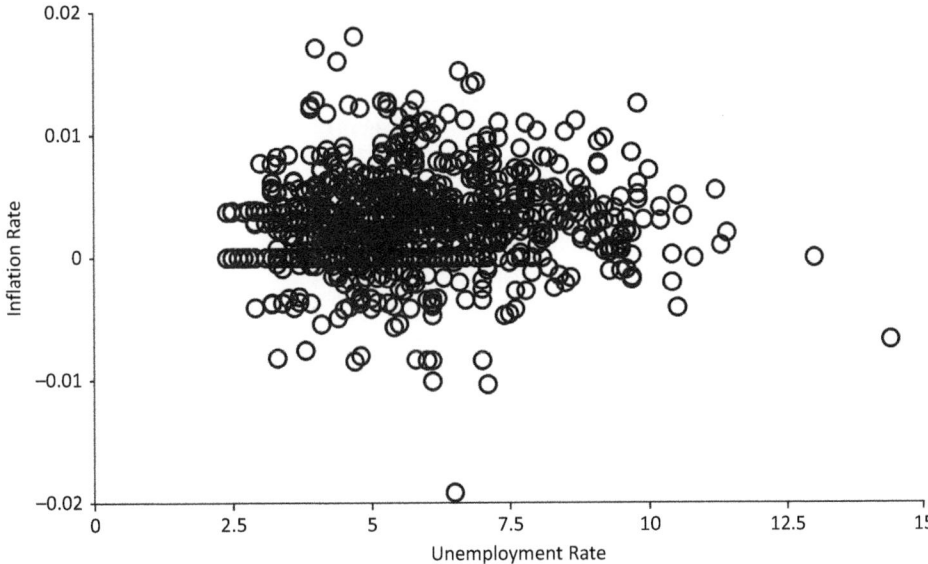

Figure 7.4 Contemporaneous relationship between inflation and unemployment.

A special case of the factor model approach is associated with the name independent component analysis (ICA). That is, suppose that $\varepsilon_t \equiv 0$ so that

$$y_t = Bf_t, \qquad f_t = \Phi_1 f_{t-1} + \cdots + \Phi_p f_{t-p} + \eta_t,$$

where $\Phi_k = \text{diag}\{\phi_{1k}, \ldots, \phi_{nk}\}$. Then we may substitute to obtain

$$y_t = A_1 y_{t-1} + \cdots + A_p y_{t-p} + \varepsilon_t,$$

where $A_k = B\Phi_k(B^\mathsf{T} B)^{-1} B^\mathsf{T}$ and $\varepsilon_t = B\eta_t$. The coefficient matrices A_j are no longer diagonal but they are all driven by the same nondiagonal matrix B. The matrix B can be identified as the square root of the covariance matrix of y_t, and after rotation of the system we have a diagonal representation. In this case, the raw variables may be cross-autocorrelated.

7.4   Application

The Phillips curve suggests that there should be a negative relationship between inflation (or expected inflation) and unemployment. Clearly, this is hard to detect from the scatter plot of contemporaneous values of these quantities in Figure 7.4. A dynamic model is needed to detect the relationship. We consider the bivariate relationship between realized inflation and the logarithm of unemployment. We work with the non-seasonally adjusted monthly data from March 1948 to July 2020, a total of $T = 869$ observations; the model and errors are shown in Table 7.1. The first lag of inflation has a significant negative effect on unemployment, although the first lag of unemployment has a much stronger effect. We show two versions of the impulse response function in Figures 7.5 and 7.6.

Table 7.1 VAR(2) for unemployment and inflation.

	INFLATION	log(UNRATENSA)
INFLATION(−1)	0.446 412	−3.240 580
	(0.033 19)	(0.992 26)
	[13.4509]	[−3.265 87]
INFLATION(−2)	0.138 152	0.706 304
	(0.033 11)	(0.989 92)
	[4.172 52]	[0.713 50]
log(UNRATENSA(−1))	0.002 251	1.018 862
	(0.001 13)	(0.033 87)
	[1.986 31]	[30.0776]
log(UNRATENSA(−2))	−0.001 616	−0.069 411
	(0.001 14)	(0.034 03)
	[−1.419 68]	[−2.039 49]
C	7.15×10^{-5}	0.094 003
	(0.000 63)	(0.018 85)
	[0.113 37]	[4.986 13]
R^2	0.287 192	0.901 613
Adjusted R^2	0.283 892	0.901 157

Note: Standard errors are shown in (parentheses) and the *t*-statistic in [brackets].

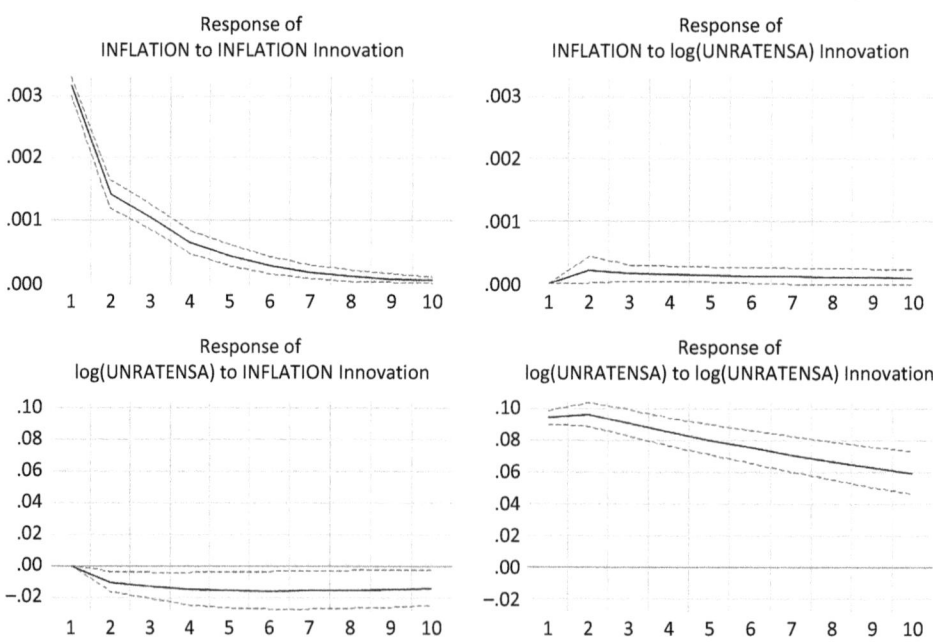

Figure 7.5 Impulse response function from bivariate VAR of inflation and unemployment.

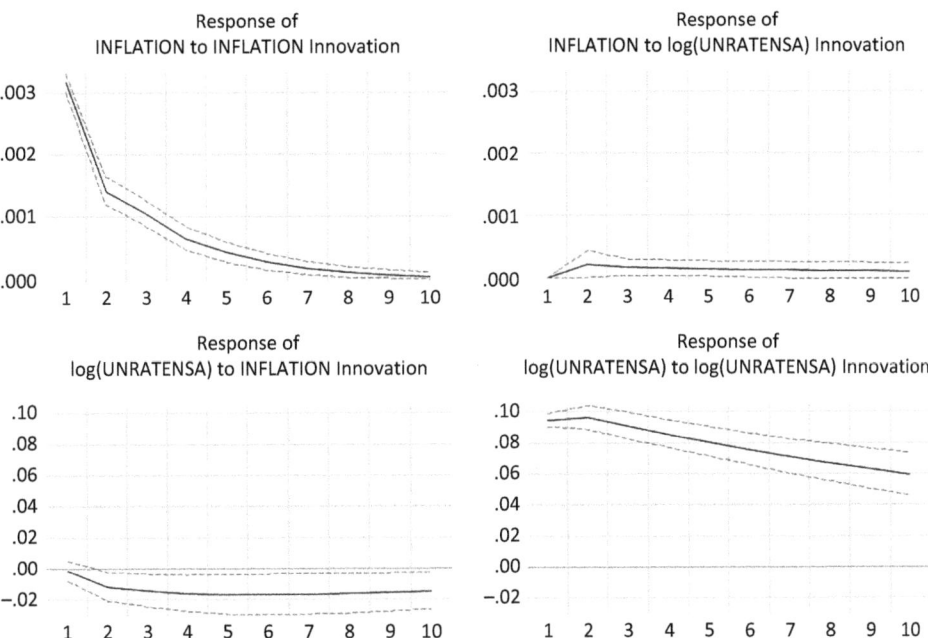

Figure 7.6 Impulse response function from bivariate VAR of inflation and unemployment, Cholesky factor.

We next work with $y_t = (\log(V_t), \log(P_t))^{\mathsf{T}}$, where V is daily trading volume and P is the daily closing price on the S&P500 from sp500. First, we carried out ADF tests on both series in EViews with lag length determined by the BIC (which chooses over 43 lags; for prices lag length was determined at 2, while for volume lag the length was chosen as 33). In both cases the unit root null hypothesis cannot be rejected, with p-values around 0.8. We next carried out the Johansen tests for cointegration between the two series allowing for $p = 4$. Both the trace and rank statistics strongly reject the null hypothesis of no cointegrating relations in favor of one relationship. Normalizing on price we obtain $\log(P_t) - 0.532 \log(V_t)$ as the cointegrated vector. This is quite close to the so-called square root law of price impact of trading.

7.5   Summary

We generalized the univariate setting to the multivariate setting, considering the relationship between different time series. We considered the dependence measurement issue and the modelling issue. Distributed lag models and vector autoregression are the key models that are widely used in economic applications. We considered both stationary and nonstationary contexts, as well as reduced-form and structural representation.

The R language has several packages devoted to the estimation and analysis of VARs, including vars, which does frequentist estimation and inference. Kilian and Lütkepohl (2017) is an excellent in-depth treatment of vector autoregressions; see also Watson (1994) for an earlier treatment.

7.6   Exercises

7.1 For the dataset `ffdaily` let $y_t = (\text{MKT}, \text{SMB}, \text{HML})^\mathsf{T}$ be the daily returns on the three market factors. Calculate the sample mean vector and cross-autocovariance matrix for each (roughly) decade of data and compare across decades. Use the confidence interval based on the assumption of i.i.d. data (within decade).

7.2 For the dataset `ffdaily` let $y_t = (\text{MKT}, \text{SMB}, \text{HML})^\mathsf{T}$ be the daily returns on the three market factors. For each decade of data fit a VAR of order 5. Compare the parameter estimates across decades.

7.3 For the dataset `ffdaily` let $y_t = (\text{MKT}, \text{SMB}, \text{HML})^\mathsf{T}$ be the daily returns on the three market factors. Test the hypothesis that MKT does not Granger cause SMB.

7.4 For the dataset `sp500stocks` let y_{it} denote the return on stock i on day t. Compute the sample cross-autocorrelation matrix (441×441) $\widehat{R}(k)$ and use this to compute the diagonalized variance ratio matrix

$$\text{VRd}(K) = \widehat{R}(0) + 2\sum_{k=1}^{K}\left(1 - \frac{k}{K}\right)\left(\widehat{R}(k) + \widehat{R}(-k)\right)$$

for $K = 5$ and $K = 22$. Order $\text{VRd}_{ij}(K)$ from largest to smallest across all pairs i, j with $i \neq j$. Which pairs of stocks are most highly copersistent? Now do the same thing with $\text{VRd}_{ij}(K) - \widehat{R}_{ij}(0)$.

7.5 Suppose that the vector time series y_t is stationary and mixing with mean vector $\mu = (\mu_1^\mathsf{T}, \mu_2^\mathsf{T})^\mathsf{T}$. Explain how you can carry out a test of the hypothesis that $\mu_1 = \mu_2$ versus the general alternative. For the dataset `ffdaily` let $y_t = (\text{MKT}, \text{SMB}, \text{HML})^\mathsf{T}$ be the daily returns on the three market factors. Test whether the mean of the three components is the same.

7.6 Suppose that we observe a scalar series y_t generated by $y_t = y_t^* + u_t$, where u_t is i.i.d. $N(0, \sigma_u^2)$ and $y_t^* = y_{t-1}^* + \varepsilon_t$, where ε_t is i.i.d. $N(0, \sigma_\varepsilon^2)$ and ε, u are mutually independent processes. Define $r_t^* = y_t^* - y_{t-1}^* = \varepsilon_t$. Calculate $E(r_t^* \mid r_t)$, $E(r_t^* \mid r_t, r_{t-1})$, and $E(r_t^* \mid r_t, r_{t-1}, r_{t-2})$.

7.7 The autocorrelation matrix in the VAR case does not have a simple form in general except in some special cases such as when A is diagonal (which is the univariate case) or if Ω_ε has the same diagonal elements. In the following cases, state the conditions for stationarity and derive the autocorrelation matrix $R_{yy}(j)$.

(a) Suppose that $y_t = Ay_{t-1} + \varepsilon_t$, where $A = \phi i_n i_n^\mathsf{T}$ for scalar $\phi \in (-1, 1)$.

(b) Suppose that, for a scalar variable z_t, $y_t = i_n z_t$, $z_t = \phi z_{t-1} + e_t$. Write y_t as a VAR(1) process and give the precise form of A and $\Omega_\varepsilon = \phi I_n$.

7.8 Suppose that $y_t = (y_{1t}, \ldots, y_{nt})^\mathsf{T} \in \mathbb{R}^n$ satisfies $y_t = \mu i_n + \varepsilon_t$, where i_n is the unit n-vector, while $\varepsilon_t \in \mathbb{R}^n$ is a stationary mixing process with autocovariance function $\Gamma_{\varepsilon\varepsilon}(\cdot)$. Let

$$\widehat{\mu} = \frac{1}{nT}\sum_{t=1}^{T}\sum_{i=1}^{n} y_{it}.$$

(a) Derive the limiting distribution of $\widehat{\mu}$, making clear what additional assumptions you need, in each of the following cases:

  (i) $T \to \infty$ and n is fixed
 (ii) $n \to \infty$ and T is fixed
(iii) $n, T \to \infty$.
(b) Obtain a test of the hypothesis that $\mu = 0$ versus $\mu \neq 0$.

7.9 Suppose that we observe y_t generated by $y_t = y_t^* + u_t$, where y_t^*, u_t are two unobserved mutually independent Gaussian stochastic processes with autocovariance functions γ_{y^*}, γ_u. Define the objective function

$$Q_T(w) = E\left[\left(y_t^* - \sum_{j=-n}^{n} w_j y_{t-j}\right)^2\right].$$

(a) Calculate the first-order conditions $\partial Q_T(w)/\partial w_j = 0$ for each j (you may interchange expectation and differentiation).
(b) Suppose that $\gamma_u(k) = 0$ for all $k \neq 0$ and $\gamma_{y^*}(k) = 0$ for $k > n$. Solve for the optimal weighting.
(c) Now suppose that y_t is a vector. How would the argument change in this case?

7.10 Suppose that $y_t = Ay_{t-p} + \varepsilon_t$, where ε_t is i.i.d. with mean zero and covariance matrix Ω_ε, and A has roots less than one in magnitude, while $p > 1$. Calculate the autocovariance function of y_t.

7.11 Suppose that $y_t \in \mathbb{R}^n$ satisfies $\Phi y_t = Ay_{t-4} + \varepsilon_t$, where ε_t is i.i.d. with distribution $N(0, I_n)$.
(a) Under what conditions on Φ, A is the process y_t stationary?
(b) Given a sample $\{y_1, \ldots, y_T\}$ and knowledge of the nonsingular matrices A, Φ, provide the impulse response function.
(c) Now suppose that A, Φ are unknown. Discuss identification of this model.

7.12 Suppose that

$$y_t = \left(\begin{array}{c} y_{1t} \\ y_{2t} \end{array}\right) = \left(\begin{array}{c} a\sin(\theta t) \\ b\cos(\theta t) \end{array}\right),$$

where a, b are mutually independent random variables with $a, b = \pm 1$ with equal probability. Determine whether the process y_t is stationary or not. Does there exist a linear combination of y_{1t}, y_{2t} that is stationary? What about nonlinear combinations?

7.13 Suppose that $y_t = A_1 y_{t-1} + \cdots + A_p y_{t-p} + \varepsilon_t$, where ε_t is i.i.d. with mean zero and $n \times n$ covariance matrix Σ. Suppose further that $A_j = \theta^{j-1}A_0, j = 1, \ldots, p$, where A_0 is a fixed $n \times n$ matrix and $\theta \in (-1, 1)$. Discuss stationarity conditions.
(a) Discuss estimation in this model in the case where θ is known but A_0, Σ are not.
(b) Discuss estimation in this model in the case where A_0 is known but θ, Σ are not.
(c) Discuss estimation in this model in the case where θ, A_0, Σ are unknown.

7.14 Suppose that (y_t, x_t) is a stationary mean-zero process with autocovariance matrix $\Gamma_{y,x}(\cdot)$. Let $\tilde{y}_t = A(L)y_t$ and $\tilde{x}_t = B(L)x_t$, where $A(L) = \sum_{j=0}^{\infty} a_j L^j$ and $B(L) = \sum_{j=0}^{\infty} b_j L^j$. Derive the autocovariance matrix $\Gamma_{\tilde{y},\tilde{x}}(\cdot)$ of the process $(\tilde{y}_t, \tilde{x}_t)$.

7.15 Suppose that $y_t = \varepsilon_t - \Theta\varepsilon_{t-1}$, where $\varepsilon_t \sim N(0, \Omega_\varepsilon)$ for some positive-definite covariance matrix Ω_ε. Show that

$$\Gamma(0) = P_\varepsilon^{-1} + \Gamma(1)P_\varepsilon\Gamma(1)^\mathsf{T},$$

where $\Gamma(j)$ is the population autocovariance matrix and $P_\varepsilon = \Omega_\varepsilon^{-1}$. Suppose that $n = 2$. Derive three equations for the unknowns (p_{11}, p_{12}, p_{22}) of the precision matrix P_ε, where

$$P_\varepsilon = \begin{pmatrix} p_{11} & p_{12} \\ p_{12} & p_{22} \end{pmatrix}, \qquad \Omega_\varepsilon = \begin{pmatrix} \omega_{11} & \omega_{12} \\ \omega_{12} & \omega_{22} \end{pmatrix},$$

and rewrite them as cubic equations.

7.16 Suppose that $y_t = Ay_{t-1} + \varepsilon_t - \Theta\varepsilon_{t-1}$, where ε_t is i.i.d. with mean zero and $n \times n$ covariance matrix Ω_ε, and that y_t is stationary. Calculate $\Gamma_y(1)$ and $\Gamma_y(-1)$ in terms of the parameter matrices, taking $\Gamma_y(0)$ as given. Define a recursive equation for $\Gamma_y(k)$ for $k \geq 2$ in terms of $\Gamma_y(1), \Gamma_y(0)$.

7.17 Suppose that

$$y_{1t} = \phi_1 y_{1,t-1} + \varepsilon_{1t} - \theta_1\varepsilon_{1,t-1},$$
$$y_{2t} = \phi_2 y_{2,t-1} + \varepsilon_{2t} - \theta_2\varepsilon_{2,t-1},$$

where ε_{jt} are i.i.d. with mean zero and variance σ_j^2, and mutually independent. Write

$$y_t = \begin{pmatrix} y_{1t} \\ y_{2t} \end{pmatrix} = Ay_{t-1} + u_t,$$

where $u_t = (u_{1t}, u_{2t})^\mathsf{T}$ are i.i.d. with mean zero and covariance matrix Σ; in other words, try to find expressions for the 2×2 matrices A, Σ in terms of $\phi_1, \theta_1, \sigma_1^2, \phi_2, \theta_2$, and σ_2^2.

7.18 Suppose that

$$y_t = \alpha + \beta\left(x_t - E(x_t \mid \mathcal{F}_{t-1})\right) + \gamma y_{t-1} + u_t,$$
$$x_t = \mu + \phi x_{t-1} + \varepsilon_t,$$

where y_t is the log of real GNP, x_t is the log of the price level, and $\mathcal{F}_{t-1}$ contains all past information $y_{t-1}, x_{t-1}, \ldots$ Suppose that $-1 < \gamma < 1$ and $\beta > 0$. You may assume that ε_t, u_t are bivariate Gaussian with a diagonal covariance matrix. Write this model as a structural VAR and discuss identification.

7.19 Consider the structural VAR

$$\begin{pmatrix} 1 & \gamma_{12} \\ \gamma_{21} & 1 \end{pmatrix}\begin{pmatrix} y_{1t} \\ y_{2t} \end{pmatrix} = \begin{pmatrix} b_{11} & b_{12} \\ b_{21} & b_{22} \end{pmatrix}\begin{pmatrix} y_{1,t-1} \\ y_{2,t-1} \end{pmatrix} + \begin{pmatrix} \sigma_{11} & 0 \\ 0 & \sigma_{22} \end{pmatrix}\begin{pmatrix} \varepsilon_{1t} \\ \varepsilon_{2t} \end{pmatrix},$$

with $\theta = (\gamma_{12}, \gamma_{21}, b_{11}, b_{12}, b_{21}, b_{22}, \sigma_{11}, \sigma_{22})^\mathsf{T}$ and where ε_{jt} are i.i.d. standard normal, and the reduced form

$$\begin{pmatrix} y_{1t} \\ y_{2t} \end{pmatrix} = \begin{pmatrix} a_{11} & a_{12} \\ a_{21} & a_{22} \end{pmatrix}\begin{pmatrix} y_{1,t-1} \\ y_{2,t-1} \end{pmatrix} + \begin{pmatrix} c_{11} & c_{12} \\ c_{12} & c_{22} \end{pmatrix}\begin{pmatrix} \varepsilon_{1t} \\ \varepsilon_{2t} \end{pmatrix},$$

with parameters $\pi = (a_{11}, a_{12}, a_{21}, a_{22}, c_{11}, c_{12}, c_{22})^\mathsf{T}$. Discuss the following identifying assumptions and their plausibility or interpretability:

(a) $\gamma_{12} = \gamma_{21} = \gamma$
(b) $\gamma_{12} = 0$
(c) $b_{12} = b_{21}$
(d) $b_{12} = 0$
(e) $\sigma_{11} = \sigma_{22}$
(f) $\sigma_{11} = 1$,

$$
\begin{pmatrix} 1 & \gamma_{12} \\ \gamma_{21} & 1 \end{pmatrix}^{-1} \begin{pmatrix} b_{11} & b_{12} \\ b_{21} & b_{22} \end{pmatrix}
$$

$$
= \frac{1}{1 - \gamma_{12}\gamma_{21}} \begin{pmatrix} b_{11} - \gamma_{12}b_{21} & b_{12} - \gamma_{12}b_{22} \\ b_{21} - \gamma_{21}b_{11} & b_{22} - \gamma_{21}b_{12} \end{pmatrix}.
$$

7.20 Suppose that $y_t = Ay_{t-1} + \varepsilon_t$, where $\varepsilon_t \sim N(0, \Omega_\varepsilon)$, and suppose it is known that y_t is stationary with distribution $N(0, I_n)$.

(a) What does this imply about the covariance matrix Ω_ε?
(b) How could you use this information to improve your estimates of A?
(c) How would you test whether this restriction is true in a given dataset?

8 State Space Models and the Kalman Filter

The state space framework represents a general class of linear time series models that can be written in terms of unobservable quantities that are assumed to possess certain laws of motion. The driving force of the state space model arises from its Markovian representation. We discuss the class of state space models and some special cases in detail. We define the Kalman filter and show how it can be used to construct the likelihood function of the state space model, which defines an estimation procedure for the unknown parameters.

8.1 State Space Models

We consider the classical setup where $\alpha_t \in \mathbb{R}^m$ is the state variable , perhaps unobserved, whose evolution is governed by the linear dynamic equation

$$\alpha_t = F_t \alpha_{t-1} + v_t, \tag{8.1}$$

while the observed outcome $y_t \in \mathbb{R}^n$ is related to the state variable by the observation equation

$$y_t = H_t \alpha_t + w_t. \tag{8.2}$$

Here, F_t, H_t are matrices containing perhaps unknown parameters and observable variables, while v_t, w_t are mutually uncorrelated shock vectors with mean zero and covariance matrices Q_t, R_t respectively, which may also contain unknown parameters and observable variables. There are generalizations to allow for correlation between the shocks v_t, w_t, but we concentrate on the case given above as it is already general enough to include many of the time series models we have considered so far as special cases. The key property of α_t is that it is a Markov process, so that it only depends on α_{t-1}; the state vector contains all the dynamic action, whereas the observation equation is purely static. The representation is not unique and there may be many ways of writing a given process in state space form; generally, we will seek the lowest-dimensional representation. In the following we drop the explicit dependency of F, H, Q, and R on time for simplicity.

The process α_t may be stationary or nonstationary, depending on the matrix F. It is a first-order VAR and so the condition for stationarity is that the largest eigenvalue of F be less than one. If that is satisfied we see that the mean of α_t is zero and its unconditional variance V satisfies the equation $V = FVF^{\mathsf{T}} + Q$, which can be solved to express V in terms of the matrices F, Q. On the other hand, α_t may not be stationary by design (a vector of unit root processes). If α_t is stationary, then y_t is stationary by construction, but if α_t is nonstationary, then all, some, or none of the components of y_t are nonstationary, depending on the matrix H.

One objective is to estimate the unknown parts of F, H, Q, and R, which can be done by Gaussian ML as we see below. A second objective is to estimate the state vectors $\{\alpha_1, \ldots, \alpha_T\}$ and to predict their future values; in fact, this was the original rocket science motivation for the model. In most cases α_t cannot be consistently estimated but one can obtain optimal estimates under the assumption of Gaussianity; one can also provide confidence intervals for the state vector based on this assumption.

We next consider some examples. The so-called **local-level model** (also known as the random walk plus noise model, see (7.13)) for the scalar series y_t is

$$y_t = \alpha_t + \varepsilon_t, \qquad \alpha_t = \alpha_{t-1} + \eta_t, \tag{8.3}$$

where $\varepsilon_t \sim N(0, \sigma_\varepsilon^2)$ and $\eta_t \sim N(0, \sigma_\eta^2)$ are mutually independent shocks. The state variable α_t is unobserved. It is a pure random walk, that is, it is nonstationary. Since α_t is nonstationary, we must initialize it. We suppose that $\alpha_0 \sim N(\mu, \sigma^2)$, where μ, σ^2 are known. In this case, the unknown parameters are σ_ε^2 and σ_η^2, and these determine the relative magnitude of the signal (μ) from the noise (ε). There are variations of this model where $\sigma_\varepsilon^2 \to 0$ and/or $\sigma_\eta^2 \to 0$, and you are asked to explore these in the exercises. We note that the distributional assumption (Gaussian shocks) is made partially for convenience, since in that case the best linear predictor is equal to the best predictor, and it is appropriate for linear models. For some purposes we may just replace the normality assumption by the weaker white noise assumption.

This model is used in macroeconomics and finance to represent decomposition into a slowly moving trend process and a random component, and is called structural by Harvey (1989) and Hasbrouck (2007). For example, it is used to capture departures from the EMH, in which case the true (log) efficient price is designated as α_t, which behaves like a martingale, and the observed price is equal to the efficient price plus some noise ε_t. In some interpretations, ε_t represents market microstructure noise (Roll, 1984; Hasbrouck, 2007). In other interpretations, ε_t represent fads or irrational departures from the EMH pricing over a longer term (although the assumption that the noise is i.i.d. is a bit hard to justify, as we discussed).

Taking first differences of y_t we obtain $\Delta y_t = \eta_t + \varepsilon_t - \varepsilon_{t-1}$, which eliminates the state variable α_t. This is an MA(1) process to second order because

$$\text{cov}(\Delta y_t, \Delta y_{t-j}) = \begin{cases} \sigma_\eta^2 + 2\sigma_\varepsilon^2 & \text{if } j = 0, \\ -\sigma_\varepsilon^2 & \text{if } j = 1, \\ 0 & \text{if } j > 1. \end{cases}$$

We mean that there exists a series of i.i.d. shocks u_t with variance σ_u^2 such that $\Delta y_t = u_t - \theta u_{t-1}$ for some θ. We have already discussed how to estimate the parameters of a moving average process by ML or by MoM. For example, one can estimate $\sigma_\eta^2, \sigma_\varepsilon^2$ from the equations $\sigma_\varepsilon^2 = -\text{cov}(\Delta y_t, \Delta y_{t-1})$ and $\sigma_\eta^2 = \text{var}(\Delta y_t) + 2\text{cov}(\Delta y_t, \Delta y_{t-1})$, although these will not be efficient estimates under Gaussianity. The implied moving average parameter θ and shock variance σ_u^2 can be obtained from $\sigma_\varepsilon^2, \sigma_\eta^2$ or by direct estimation of the likelihood for the observed data.

The original process y_t is an ARIMA(0,1,1) process under this model assumption. Collecting all observations into a vector $y = (y_1, \ldots, y_T)^\top$, we have, in particular,

$$y \sim N(m, \Omega), \qquad m = \mu i_T, \qquad \Omega = \sigma^2 i_T i_T^\top + \Sigma, \qquad (8.4)$$

$$\Sigma_{st} = \begin{cases} s\sigma_\eta^2 & \text{if } 1 \le s < t, \\ \sigma_\varepsilon^2 + s\sigma_\eta^2 & \text{if } s = t, \\ t\sigma_\eta^2 & \text{if } s > t \ge 1. \end{cases} \qquad (8.5)$$

We could use this description to calculate the likelihood function of the observed data and thereby to estimate the structural parameters σ_ε^2 and σ_η^2, but when T is large the covariance matrix Ω is hard to invert and the computations become difficult/time consuming. Instead, the Kalman filter is used to solve the computations recursively and exploit the specific structure here more effectively.

We can extend the local-level model in a number of ways. One can allow for components that are themselves random walks. Random walks are built on random walks, which are built on further random walks. You soon get dizzy with all the random walks. We next consider a general class of regression models with time-varying parameters,

$$y_t = x_t^\top \beta_t + \varepsilon_t, \qquad \beta_t = \beta_{t-1} + u_t,$$

where u_t is a vector of innovations. This is one way of allowing parameters to vary over time. The local-level model is a special case of this with $x_t = 1$. Another special case of this is the model

$$\pi_t = -r_t + \beta i_t + \varepsilon_t, \qquad r_t = r_{t-1} + u_t,$$

where π_t is realized inflation, i_t is the nominal interest rate (known at time $t - 1$), and r_t is the (expected) real interest rate. The Fisher equation ($i = \pi + r$) says that $i_t = E(\pi_t \mid \mathcal{F}_{t-1}) + r_t$, which implies that $\beta = 1$. In this case, we can write this in the form of the local-level model for $i_t - \pi_t$. Another example is the time-varying market model

$$R_{it} - R_{ft} = \alpha_{it} + \beta_{it}(R_{mt} - R_{ft}) + \varepsilon_{it},$$

$$\alpha_t = \alpha_{t-1} + u_t, \qquad \beta_t = \beta_{t-1} + \eta_t,$$

where R_{it} is the observed return on stock i at time t, R_{mt} is the return on the market, and R_{ft} is the risk-free rate. Here, $\alpha_t = (\alpha_{1t}, \ldots, \alpha_{nt})^\top$ and $\beta_t = (\beta_{1t}, \ldots, \beta_{nt})^\top$ are unobserved time-varying parameters. The state vector here is of dimension $2n \times 1$. The static capital asset pricing model (CAPM) says that $\alpha_t = 0$ and $\beta_t = \beta$ for some vector. We allow both parameter vectors to evolve as random walks, and it is natural to set $\alpha_1 = 0$ and $\beta_1 = i_n$.

8.1.1 State Space Representation of an ARMA Process

Suppose that y_t is an ARMA(p, q) process with $A(L)y_t = B(L)\varepsilon_t$, where ε_t are i.i.d. shocks. The process y_t can be written as an ARMA(d,d) process with some coefficients zero, where $d = \max\{p, q + 1\}$. In this case we can write y_t in state space form with a state vector of dimension d. There are a number of ways of representing the general process in state space form, none of them easy!

The main issue is with the MA part. Consider the MA(1) process $y_t = \varepsilon_t - \theta_1\varepsilon_{t-1}$. In this case we may take $\alpha_t = (\varepsilon_t, \varepsilon_{t-1})^\top$ and $H = (1, -\theta)$ for a suitable choice of F

(see Exercise 8.8). That is, the MA(1) process can be written as a Markov process in the two-dimensional state variable.

We next consider the stationary and invertible ARMA(2,1) process

$$y_t = \phi_1 y_{t-1} + \phi_2 y_{t-2} + \varepsilon_t - \theta_1 \varepsilon_{t-1},$$

and write down in full the three standard state space representations. These three approaches are equally valid and mostly deliver similar answers.

The Harvey Approach   (Harvey, 1989) The specification is as follows:

$$\alpha_t = \begin{pmatrix} y_t \\ \phi_2 y_{t-1} - \theta \varepsilon_t \end{pmatrix}, \quad F = \begin{pmatrix} \phi_1 & 1 \\ \phi_2 & 0 \end{pmatrix}, \quad v_t = \begin{pmatrix} \varepsilon_t \\ -\theta \varepsilon_t \end{pmatrix}, \quad H = (1,0).$$

The Hamilton Approach   (Hamilton, 1994) Write

$$(1 - \phi_1 L - \phi_2 L^2) y_t = (1 - \theta_1 L)\varepsilon_t,$$

and so $(1 - \phi_1 L - \phi_2 L^2)(y_t/(1 - \theta_1 L)) = \varepsilon_t$. It follows that $x_t = y_t/(1 - \theta L)$ is an AR(2) process and so we take our state vector to include x_t, x_{t-1}. Specifically, let

$$\alpha_t = \begin{pmatrix} x_t \\ x_{t-1} \end{pmatrix}, \quad F = \begin{pmatrix} \phi_1 & \phi_2 \\ 1 & 0 \end{pmatrix}, \quad v_t = \begin{pmatrix} \varepsilon_t \\ 0 \end{pmatrix}, \quad H = (1, \theta_1).$$

The Akaike Approach   This involves using the conditional expectation of the outcome, given the past in the state vector. For the ARMA(2,1) process letting $\widehat{y}_{t+j|t} = E(y_{t+j} \mid y_t, \ldots, y_1), j = 1, 2, \ldots$, we have

$$\widehat{y}_{t+2|t} = \phi_1 \widehat{y}_{t+1|t} + \phi_2 y_t,$$

because $E(\varepsilon_{t+1} \mid y_t, \ldots, y_1) = 0$. This is a linear difference equation. We have the AR(∞) representation $y_t = \sum_{j=1}^{\infty} \psi_j y_{t-j} + \varepsilon_t$, where $\psi_j(\phi_1, \phi_2, \theta_1)$. It follows that $y_t = \widehat{y}_{t|t-1} + \varepsilon_t$. Therefore, we may take

$$\alpha_t = \begin{pmatrix} y_t \\ \widehat{y}_{t+1|t} \end{pmatrix}, \quad F = \begin{pmatrix} 0 & 1 \\ \phi_2 & \phi_1 \end{pmatrix}, \quad v_t = \begin{pmatrix} \varepsilon_t \\ \psi_1 \varepsilon_t \end{pmatrix}, \quad H = (1,0).$$

8.2   Kalman Filter for a Local-Level Model

The Kalman filter is a useful algorithm for computing best estimates of the state vector. It is essentially the recursive application of the BLP calculation. Recall that for two random variables Y, X,

$$E_L(Y \mid X) = \alpha + \beta X, \qquad \beta = \frac{\text{cov}(Y, X)}{\text{var}(X)}, \qquad \alpha = E(Y) - \beta E(X).$$

If Y, X are jointly normal, then $E(Y \mid X) = E_L(Y \mid X)$. Furthermore, $Y \mid X$ is normal with mean $E(Y \mid X)$ and variance $\text{var}(Y \mid X) = \text{var}(Y) - \beta^2 \text{var}(X)$.

We next work through the calculations for the local-level model. Since the state variable is unobserved we seek to estimate it, specifically to calculate $E(\alpha_t \mid y_t, y_{t-1}, \ldots, y_1)$, as this is the best guess of the state vector using all the available information up to time t. We suppose for now that the parameters $\sigma_\eta^2, \sigma_\varepsilon^2$ are known. We may define, for each t, the vectors $\boldsymbol{\alpha}_{1:t} = (\alpha_1, \ldots, \alpha_t)^\mathsf{T}$, $\mathbf{y}_{1:t} = (y_1, \ldots, y_t)^\mathsf{T}$, and $\boldsymbol{\varepsilon}_{1:t} = (\varepsilon_1, \ldots, \varepsilon_t)^\mathsf{T}$, in which case $\mathbf{y}_{1:t} = \boldsymbol{\alpha}_{1:t} + \boldsymbol{\varepsilon}_{1:t}$, where the vectors $\boldsymbol{\alpha}_{1:t}, \boldsymbol{\varepsilon}_{1:t}$ are mutually independent. Therefore, we have

$$E\left(\boldsymbol{\alpha}_{1:t} \mid \mathbf{y}_{1:t}\right) = E\left(\boldsymbol{\alpha}_{1:t}\mathbf{y}_{1:t}^\mathsf{T}\right)E\left(\mathbf{y}_{1:t}\mathbf{y}_{1:t}^\mathsf{T}\right)^{-1}\mathbf{y}_{1:t}$$
$$= E\left(\boldsymbol{\alpha}_{1:t}\boldsymbol{\alpha}_{1:t}^\mathsf{T}\right)\left(E\left(\boldsymbol{\alpha}_{1:t}\boldsymbol{\alpha}_{1:t}^\mathsf{T}\right) + \sigma_\varepsilon^2 I_t\right)^{-1}\mathbf{y}_{1:t} = W_t\mathbf{y}_{1:t},$$

where W_t is a $t \times t$ matrix of nonrandom values determined from the distribution of $\boldsymbol{\alpha}_{1:t}$. Likewise,

$$\mathrm{var}\left(\boldsymbol{\alpha}_{1:t} \mid \mathbf{y}_{1:t}\right) = E\left(\boldsymbol{\alpha}_{1:t}\boldsymbol{\alpha}_{1:t}^\mathsf{T}\right) - E\left(\boldsymbol{\alpha}_{1:t}\mathbf{y}_{1:t}^\mathsf{T}\right)E\left(\mathbf{y}_{1:t}\mathbf{y}_{1:t}^\mathsf{T}\right)^{-1}E\left(\mathbf{y}_{1:t}\boldsymbol{\alpha}_{1:t}^\mathsf{T}\right)$$

is a $t \times t$ matrix of nonrandom values.

The difficulty is that for large t this is too computationally burdensome; we seek a recursive way of doing this. We design a recursive procedure that has an initialization and at each step an update that only works with low-dimensional quantities. Suppose we have

$$\alpha_{t|t-1} = E\left(\alpha_t \mid \mathbf{y}_{1:t-1}\right), \qquad V_{t|t-1} = \mathrm{var}\left(\alpha_t \mid \mathbf{y}_{1:t-1}\right). \tag{8.6}$$

Indeed, we may assume that $\alpha_t \mid \mathbf{y}_{1:t-1} \sim N(\alpha_{t|t-1}, V_{t|t-1})$. Suppose we observe new information y_t. How do we update our estimates to $\alpha_{t|t}$ and $V_{t|t}$? How do we update our estimate of α_{t+1} given $\mathbf{y}_{1:t}$, and what is the conditional variance of that prediction, denoted $V_{t+1|t}$?

We note from the model structure that $E\left(\alpha_t \mid \mathbf{y}_{1:t-1}\right) = E\left(y_t \mid \mathbf{y}_{1:t-1}\right)$, and this quantity is uncorrelated with $y_t - E\left(\alpha_t \mid \mathbf{y}_{1:t-1}\right)$ by construction. Because the vectors $\boldsymbol{\alpha}_{1:T}, \mathbf{y}_{1:T}$ and all conditional distributions are normal, all conditional expectations are linear. In particular, for some nonrandom (known at time $t - 1$) vector $c_t \in \mathbb{R}^{t-1}$ and nonrandom scalar K_t we have

$$E\left(\alpha_t \mid \mathbf{y}_{1:t}\right) = c_t^\mathsf{T}\mathbf{y}_{1:t-1} + K_t y_t. \tag{8.7}$$

Taking expectations of both sides of the equation conditional on $\mathbf{y}_{1:t-1}$, we obtain

$$E\left(\alpha_t \mid \mathbf{y}_{1:t-1}\right) = c_t^\mathsf{T}\mathbf{y}_{1:t-1} + K_t E\left(y_t \mid \mathbf{y}_{1:t-1}\right),$$

and using the law of iterated expectations,

$$E\left(y_t \mid \mathbf{y}_{1:t-1}\right) = E\left(\alpha_t \mid \mathbf{y}_{1:t-1}\right) = E\left(E\left(\alpha_t \mid \mathbf{y}_{1:t}\right) \mid \mathbf{y}_{1:t-1}\right),$$

we obtain the linear equation for $E\left(\alpha_t \mid \mathbf{y}_{1:t-1}\right)$,

$$E\left(\alpha_t \mid \mathbf{y}_{1:t-1}\right) = c_t^\mathsf{T}\mathbf{y}_{1:t-1} + K_t E\left(\alpha_t \mid \mathbf{y}_{1:t-1}\right),$$

which can be solved to obtain

$$E\left(\alpha_t \mid \mathbf{y}_{1:t-1}\right) = \frac{c_t^\mathsf{T}\mathbf{y}_{1:t-1}}{1 - K_t}$$

provided $K_t \neq 1$. Substituting this back into (8.7), we find

$$E(\alpha_t \mid \mathbf{y}_{1:t}) = c_t^\mathsf{T}\mathbf{y}_{1:t-1} + K_t y_t = (1 - K_t)\frac{c_t^\mathsf{T}\mathbf{y}_{1:t-1}}{1 - K_t} + K_t y_t$$
$$= (1 - K_t)E(\alpha_t \mid \mathbf{y}_{1:t-1}) + K_t y_t$$
$$= E(\alpha_t \mid \mathbf{y}_{1:t-1}) + K_t(y_t - E(\alpha_t \mid \mathbf{y}_{1:t-1})).$$

We have eliminated the vector c_t. This can be rewritten as $\alpha_{t|t} = \alpha_{t|t-1} + K_t(y_t - \alpha_{t|t-1})$, and it remains to find K_t.

By the formula for the best linear predictor, we have (where everything is conditional on $\mathbf{y}_{1:t-1}$)

$$K_t = \frac{\mathrm{cov}(\alpha_t, y_t - \alpha_{t|t-1})}{\mathrm{var}(y_t - \alpha_{t|t-1})}, \tag{8.8}$$

because in the linear regression of α_t on $\alpha_{t|t-1}, y_t - \alpha_{t|t-1}$, the two predictors are mutually orthogonal. We write $y_t - \alpha_{t|t-1} = \alpha_t - \alpha_{t|t-1} + \varepsilon_t$, and so

$$\mathrm{var}(y_t - \alpha_{t|t-1}) = \mathrm{var}(\alpha_t \mid \mathbf{y}_{1:t-1}) + \sigma_\varepsilon^2.$$

Furthermore,

$$\mathrm{cov}(\alpha_t, y_t - \alpha_{t|t-1}) = E(\alpha_t(\varepsilon_t + \alpha_t - \alpha_{t|t-1})) = \mathrm{var}(\alpha_t \mid \mathbf{y}_{1:t-1}) = V_{t|t-1}.$$

It follows that

$$K_t = \frac{V_{t|t-1}}{V_{t|t-1} + \sigma_\varepsilon^2}. \tag{8.9}$$

Finally, by the properties of Gaussian distributions,

$$V_{t|t} = \mathrm{var}(\alpha_t \mid \mathbf{y}_{1:t})$$
$$= \mathrm{var}(\alpha_t \mid \mathbf{y}_{1:t-1}, y_t - \alpha_{t|t-1})$$
$$= \mathrm{var}(\alpha_t \mid \mathbf{y}_{1:t-1}) - \frac{\mathrm{cov}(\alpha_t, y_t - \alpha_{t|t-1})^2}{\mathrm{var}(y_t - \alpha_{t|t-1})} = V_{t|t-1} - \frac{V_{t|t-1}^2}{V_{t|t-1} + \sigma_\varepsilon^2}.$$

To conclude, the Kalman filter update equations for the local-level model are:

$$\alpha_{t|t} = \alpha_{t|t-1} + K_t(y_t - \alpha_{t|t-1}), \tag{8.10}$$

$$K_t = \frac{V_{t|t-1}}{V_{t|t-1} + \sigma_\varepsilon^2}, \tag{8.11}$$

$$V_{t|t} = V_{t|t-1} - \frac{V_{t|t-1}^2}{V_{t|t-1} + \sigma_\varepsilon^2}, \tag{8.12}$$

where K_t is called the **Kalman gain**. The prediction steps here are

$$\alpha_{t+1|t} = \alpha_{t|t}, \qquad V_{t+1|t} = V_{t|t} + \sigma_\eta^2. \tag{8.13}$$

We take initial values $\alpha_{0|0} = \mu$ and $V_{0|0} = \sigma^2$ for some μ, σ^2.

Let us explore the gain sequence, or equivalently the conditional variance sequence. We have

$$V_{t+1|t} = \phi_t V_{t|t-1} + \sigma_\eta^2, \qquad \phi_t = \frac{\sigma_\varepsilon^2}{V_{t|t-1} + \sigma_\varepsilon^2},$$

which is a nonlinear deterministic equation with a given initialization; note that $\phi_t \in (0, 1)$, so the sequence contracts. Suppose that V_t, ϕ_t converge to limits, $\overline{V}, \phi$; then the limit must satisfy

$$\overline{V} = \phi\overline{V} + \sigma_\eta^2, \qquad \phi = \frac{\sigma_\varepsilon^2}{\overline{V} + \sigma_\varepsilon^2}.$$

We can rewrite this as a quadratic equation in $\overline{V}$, that is, $\overline{V}^2 + b\overline{V} + c = 0$, where $b = -\sigma_\eta^2$ and $c = -\sigma_\eta^2\sigma_\varepsilon^2$. It follows that

$$\overline{V} = \frac{\sigma_\eta^2 + \sqrt{\sigma_\eta^4 + 4\sigma_\eta^2\sigma_\varepsilon^2}}{2} = \frac{\sigma_\eta^2}{2}\sqrt{1 + 4\frac{\sigma_\varepsilon^2}{\sigma_\eta^2}},$$

since we know that the value of $\overline{V}$ must be nonnegative.

Note that the steady-state value does not depend on the initialization μ, σ^2 so long as $\sigma^2 < \infty$. In this case we obtain the simpler recursions for the estimated state vector

$$\alpha_{t+1|t} = \omega\alpha_{t|t-1} + (1 - \omega)y_t, \qquad \omega = \frac{\overline{V}}{\overline{V} + \sigma_\varepsilon^2},$$

that is, $\alpha_{t+1|t} = (1 - \omega)\sum_{j=0}^{t} \omega^j y_{t-j}$; in other words, it is an EWMA, or a linear filter of past observations. Often people just pick some value for ω like $\omega = 0.97$, and then there is no need for parameter estimation.

8.3   Likelihood Estimation

In practice, the parameters are not known and have to be estimated. The likelihood function is composed of terms like $\log f(y_{t+1} \mid \mathbf{y}_{1:t})$, which in the Gaussian case is

$$\log f(y_{t+1} \mid \mathbf{y}_{1:t}) = -\frac{1}{2}\log\sigma_{t+1|t}^2 - \frac{1}{2\sigma_{t+1|t}^2}(y_{t+1} - \mu_{t+1|t})^2,$$

$$E(y_{t+1} \mid \mathbf{y}_{1:t}) = \mu_{t+1|t} = E(\alpha_{t+1} \mid \mathbf{y}_{1:t}),$$

$$\text{var}(y_{t+1} \mid \mathbf{y}_{1:t}) = \sigma_{t+1|t}^2 = \text{var}(\alpha_{t+1} \mid \mathbf{y}_{1:t}) + \sigma_\varepsilon^2.$$

The log likelihood then is $\mathcal{L}(\vartheta \mid y) = \sum_t \log f(y_{t+1} \mid \mathbf{y}_{1:t})$, where the unknown parameters ϑ enter both $\mu_{t+1|t}$ and $\sigma_{t+1|t}^2$. In the local-level model the structural parameters are $\sigma_\varepsilon^2, \sigma_\eta^2$. We use the Kalman filter to compute the likelihood for given parameter values and then optimize over the parameter space to deliver the estimated values. In the local-level case, $\mu_{t+1|t} = \alpha_{t+1|t}$ and $\sigma_{t+1|t}^2 = V_{t+1|t} + \sigma_\varepsilon^2$.

8.3.1   Kalman Filter for Estimation of ARMA(p, q)

We can write $y_t = c^\mathsf{T}\alpha_t$, $\alpha_t = A\alpha_{t-1} + bu_t$, where $\alpha_t \in \mathbb{R}^m$, with $m = \max\{p, q+1\}$ and $\alpha_t \sim N(0, V)$ while $u_t \sim N(0, 1)$, where c, A, b, and V depend on the ARMA parameters. The matrix V is uniquely determined by the equation $V = AVA^\mathsf{T} + bb^\mathsf{T}$. The log likelihood, apart from a constant, is

$$\mathcal{L}(\theta \mid y) = -\frac{1}{2} \sum_{t=1}^{T} \log\left(c^{\mathsf{T}} V_{t|t-1} c\right) + \frac{\left(y_t - c^{\mathsf{T}} \alpha_{t|t-1}\right)^2}{c^{\mathsf{T}} V_{t|t-1} c}.$$

In particular, with $\alpha_{1|0} = 0$ and $V_{1|0} = V$, we have

$$\alpha_{t+1|t} = A\alpha_{t|t-1} + \frac{AV_{t|t-1} c\left(y_t - c^{\mathsf{T}} \alpha_{t|t-1}\right)^2}{c^{\mathsf{T}} V_{t|t-1} c},$$

$$V_{t+1|t} = bb^{\mathsf{T}} + AV_{t|t-1} A^{\mathsf{T}} - \frac{AV_{t|t-1} cc^{\mathsf{T}} V_{t|t-1} A^{\mathsf{T}}}{c^{\mathsf{T}} V_{t|t-1} c}.$$

8.4 Missing Data

Suppose that there are some missing observations, what do we do? We assume that the reason for missingness is unrelated to the dynamic process governing the data; in standard parlance, the data is missing at random. In a static framework, one approach is to just delete the observation and work with the remaining dataset, but this is more problematic in a time series setting because if the observation that is missing occurs right in the middle of the sample, we might have to also delete the observations before that one, or the observations afterwards. Let us consider some examples.

Suppose that $y_t = \phi y_{t-1} + \varepsilon_t$, where $|\phi| < 1$. Suppose that observation y_{t_0} is missing, that is, the sample is $\{y_1, \ldots, y_{t_0-1}, y_{t_0+1}, \ldots, y_T\}$. The conditional (on y_0) log density is

$$\sum_{t=t_0+2}^{T} \log f(y_t \mid y_{t-1}) + \log f(y_{t_0+1} \mid y_{t_0-1}) + \sum_{t=2}^{t_0-1} \log f(y_t \mid y_{t-1}) + \log f(y_1),$$

which makes use of the Markovian structure, that is, $f(y_{t_0+1} \mid y_{t_0-1}, \ldots, y_1) = f(y_{t_0+1} \mid y_{t_0-1})$. Note that $y_{t_0+1} \mid y_{t_0-1} \sim N\left(\phi^2 y_{t_0-1}, \sigma_\varepsilon^2(1 + \phi^2)\right)$. Of course, omitting the term $\log f(y_{t_0+1} \mid y_{t_0-1})$ in this case would not affect consistency or even the limiting distribution, but in cases with many missing terms there can be efficiency loss or even lack of identification (for example, suppose that only $y_1, y_3, y_5, \ldots$ are observed – then one can only identify ϕ^2, not ϕ itself).

Suppose that $y_t = \varepsilon_t - \theta \varepsilon_{t-1}$. We have, in this case, that $(y_1, \ldots, y_{t_0-1})^{\mathsf{T}}$ and $(y_{t_0+1}, \ldots, y_T)^{\mathsf{T}}$ are mutually independent vectors and so the log likelihood of $\{y_1, \ldots, y_{t_0-1}, y_{t_0+1}, \ldots, y_T\}$ is just the sum of the log likelihood of $\{y_1, \ldots, y_{t_0-1}\}$ and the log likelihood of $\{y_{t_0+1}, \ldots, y_T\}$. We may impute the missing observation by $E(y_{t_0} \mid y_1, \ldots, y_{t_0-1})$ or $E(y_{t_0} \mid y_1, \ldots, y_{t_0-1}, y_{t_0+1}, \ldots, y_T)$. However, in the general ARMA(p, q) case with multiple missing observations it is not so simple and the Kalman filter provides a way of dealing with missing observations in an automatic way.

When there are missing observations, the Kalman filter still wants to compute $\alpha_{t+1|t}$ and $V_{t+1|t}$ in the best possible way. Since y_t is unavailable, it cannot make use of the measurement equation, but it can still use the transition equation. Thus, when y_t is missing, the Kalman filter instead computes

$$\alpha_{t+1|t} = F\alpha_{t|t-1}, \qquad V_{t+1|t} = FV_{t|t-1} F^{\mathsf{T}} + Q.$$

This says that given α_{t_0-1}, the best guess as to α_{t_0} without observing y_{t_0} is just the evolution specified in the transition equation. This can be performed for any number of time periods with missing data.

8.5   General State Space and the Kalman Filter

Suppose that $\alpha_t = F_t\alpha_{t-1} + B_tx_t + v_t$, $y_t = H_t\alpha_t + w_t$, where $v_t \sim N(0, Q_t)$ and $w_t \sim N(0, R_t)$ are mutually independent shocks, with $\alpha_t, v_t \in \mathbb{R}^n$, $x_t \in \mathbb{R}^p$, and $y_t, w_t \in \mathbb{R}^m$, while F_t, Q_t are $n \times n$ matrices, H_t is $m \times n$, B_t is $n \times p$, and R_t is $m \times m$. This includes VARMAX models (VARMA plus additional exogenous regressors), for example, and time-varying coefficient models. The Kalman filter equations are as follows.

Algorithm   Let $\alpha_{0|0}, V_{0|0}$ be starting values. For $t = 1, 2, \ldots, T$, calculate:

1. Prediction equations:

$$\alpha_{t|t-1} = F_t\alpha_{t-1|t-1} + B_tx_t,$$
$$V_{t|t-1} = F_tV_{t-1|t-1}F_t^{\mathsf{T}} + Q_t.$$

2. Update equations:

$$\alpha_{t|t} = \alpha_{t|t-1} + K_t(y_t - H_t\alpha_{t|t-1}),$$
$$V_{t|t} = V_{t|t-1} - K_tH_tV_{t|t-1},$$
$$K_t = V_{t|t-1}H_t^{\mathsf{T}}\left(H_tV_{t|t-1}H_t^{\mathsf{T}} + R_t\right)^{-1}.$$

The forecast error at each step is $e_{t|t-1} = y_t - y_{t|t-1} = y_t - H_t\alpha_{t|t-1}$, which is mean zero given the past with conditional covariance matrix $V_{t|t-1} = H_tV_{t|t-1}H_t^{\mathsf{T}} + R_t$.

We may also be interested in $E(\alpha_t \mid \mathbf{y}_{1:T}) = E(\alpha_t \mid y_T, \ldots, y_t, \ldots, y_1)$, which is the best guess of the state vector using all the available information. Because of Gaussianity, these conditional expectations are linear, and these can also be calculated recursively (using the estimated parameters). The **Kalman smoother** can be implemented by a recursive procedure with starting values $\widehat{\alpha}_T = \alpha_{T|T}$ and $\widehat{V}_T = V_{T|T}$. For $t = T - 1, \ldots, 1$,

$$\widehat{\alpha}_t = \alpha_{t|t} + G_t\left(\widehat{\alpha}_{t+1} - F_t\alpha_{t|t}\right),$$
$$\widehat{V}_t = V_{t|t} + G_t\left(\widehat{V}_{t+1} - \left(F_tV_{t|t}F_t^{\mathsf{T}} + Q_t\right)\right)G_t^{\mathsf{T}},$$
$$G_t = V_{t|t}F_t^{\mathsf{T}}\left(F_tV_{t|t}F_t^{\mathsf{T}} + Q_t\right)^{-1}.$$

Note that $\alpha_{t|T}$ is not a consistent estimator of α_t.

8.6   Application

We consider some data examples of local-level models. First, in Figure 8.1 we show quarterly US GDP along with the filtered random walk trend, and then the prediction error in Figure 8.2. It seems to do an excellent job of tracking GDP, at least until the COVID-19 pandemic.

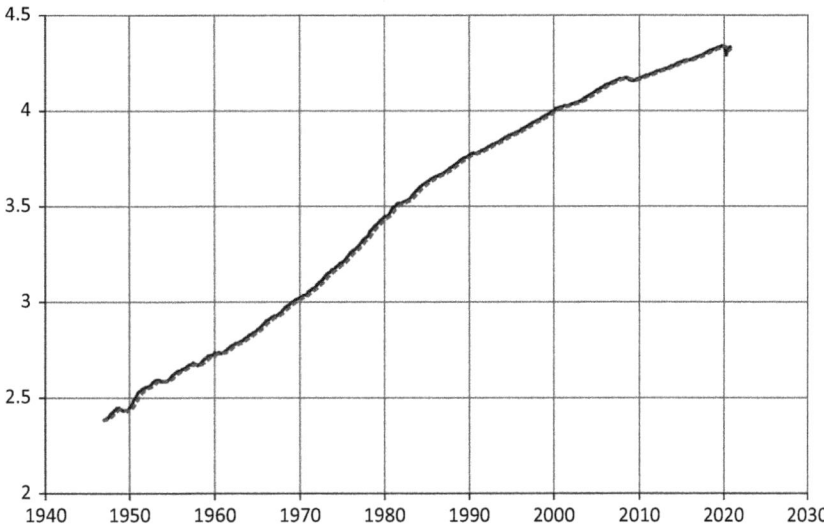

Figure 8.1 Quarterly log of GDP with local-level fitting.

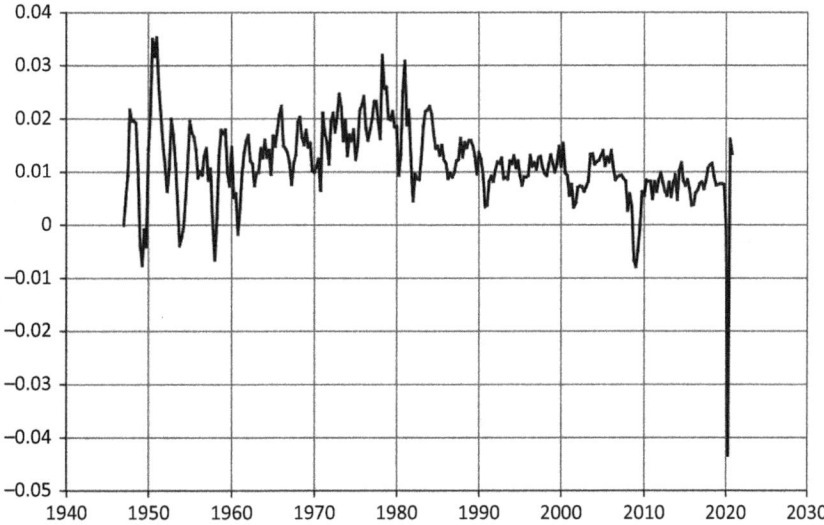

Figure 8.2 Prediction error of US quarterly GDP, $y_t - \alpha_{t|t-1}$.

We next consider the daily Gamestop stock closing price from the GME dataset over the whole period up until "the events of early 2021," where the stock price experienced a massive rise over a short period of time, apparently fuelled by excited retail traders. In Figure 8.3 the random walk fits pretty well the log price, and the differenced log price (the daily return) is also tracked fairly well up to the big movements, as shown in Figures 8.4 and 8.5.

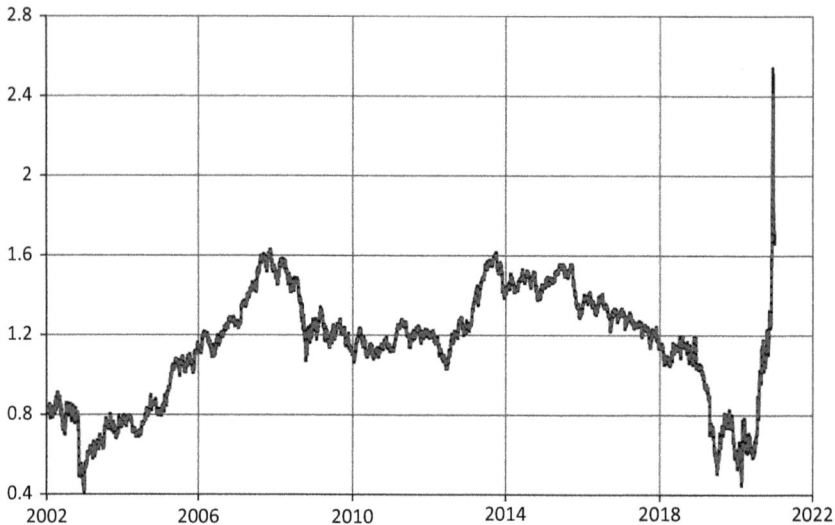

Figure 8.3 Gamestop log stock price with local level.

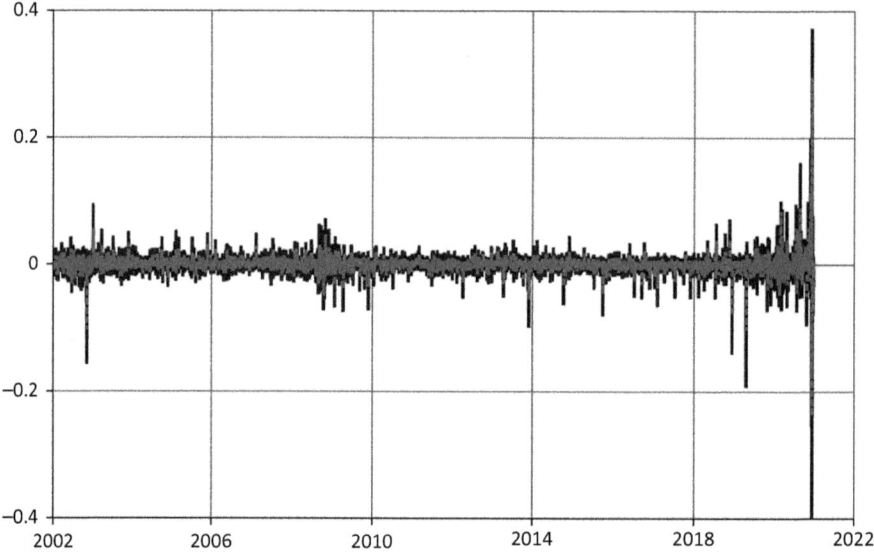

Figure 8.4 Gamestop returns.

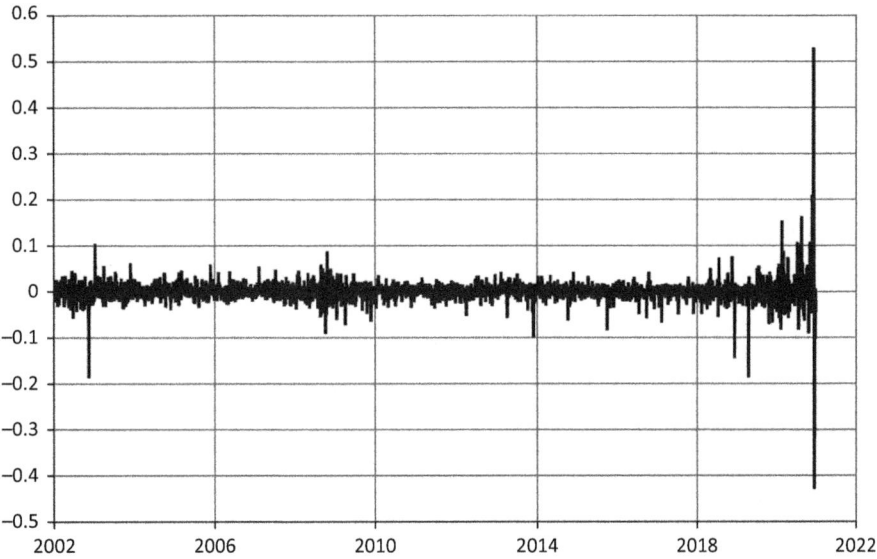

Figure 8.5 Gamestop prediction error.

8.7   Summary

We considered the state space model and its use in modelling different economic time series. We defined the Kalman filter, a recursive algorithm that is widely used in practice, and showed the steps in its construction for the local-level model. The R language has several packages for state space modelling and forecasting, including `statespacer`. Harvey (1989) is the classic reference for state space modelling and its applications in economics.

8.8   Exercises

8.1 For the PCE and INDPRO datasets fit the local-level model using the recursions (8.10)–(8.13).

8.2 Suppose that

$$y_t = \alpha_t + u_t, \qquad u_t = \phi u_{t-1} + \varepsilon_t, \qquad \alpha_t = \alpha_{t-1} + \eta_t,$$

where $\varepsilon_t \sim N(0, \sigma_\varepsilon^2)$ and $\eta_t \sim N(0, \sigma_\eta^2)$ are mutually independent shocks and $|\phi| < 1$. Put this model in state space form and explain how you would estimate the parameters $\phi, \sigma_\varepsilon^2, \sigma_\eta^2$.

8.3 Consider the linear regression with constant parameters $y_t = \beta^\mathsf{T} x_t + \varepsilon_t$, where ε_t is i.i.d. with mean zero and finite variance σ_ε^2. The OLS estimator of β based on all the data is well known. We consider the recursive least squares or real-time estimation. The OLS estimator using data up to time t is

$$\widehat{\beta}_t = \left(\sum_{s=1}^{t} x_s x_s^\mathsf{T} \right)^{-1} \sum_{s=1}^{t} x_s y_s, \qquad \widehat{\sigma}_{\varepsilon t}^2 = \frac{1}{t} \sum_{s=1}^{t} \left(y_s - x_s^\mathsf{T} \widehat{\beta}_t \right)^2,$$

which is the sample analogue of the BLP formula above . We have the decomposition $y_t = x_t^\mathsf{T} \widehat{\beta}_t + \widehat{u}_t$. Now suppose that we observe new information y_{t+1}, x_{t+1}. How do we update $\widehat{\beta}_t$ and $\widehat{\sigma}_{\varepsilon t}^2$?

8.4 For the local-level model, collect all observations into a vector $y = (y_1, \dots, y_T)^\mathsf{T}$ and show that $\alpha \sim N(m_\alpha, \Omega_\alpha)$, $y \sim N(m_y, \Omega_y)$ for some vectors m_α, m_y and covariance matrices Ω_α, Ω_y, and give an expression for them.

8.5 Consider the multivariate local-level model for $y_t \in \mathbb{R}^n$

$$y_t = \alpha_t + \varepsilon_t, \qquad \alpha_t = \alpha_{t-1} + \eta_t,$$

where $\varepsilon_t \sim N(0, \Omega_\varepsilon)$ and $\eta_t \sim N(0, \Omega_\eta)$ are mutually independent processes. Show that the Kalman recursion $a_{t+1} = a_t + K_t(y_t - a_t)$ holds for some $n \times n$ matrix K_t and find an expression for K_t in terms of the covariance matrix Ω_ε and the matrix $\text{var}(\alpha_t \mid \mathbf{y}_{1:t-1})$.

8.6 Suppose $\alpha_1 \sim N(0, \sigma_\eta^2)$ and $Y_1 = \alpha_1 + \varepsilon_1$. Show that

$$\alpha_1 \mid Y_1 \sim N(m(Y_1), v_1),$$

$$m(y) = \frac{\sigma_\eta^2}{\sigma_\varepsilon^2 + \sigma_\eta^2} y,$$

$$v_1 = \sigma_\eta^2 - \frac{\left(\sigma_\eta^2\right)^2}{\sigma_\eta^2 + \sigma_\varepsilon^2} = \frac{\sigma_\eta^2 \sigma_\varepsilon^2}{\sigma_\varepsilon^2 + \sigma_\eta^2} = \left(\frac{1}{\sigma_\varepsilon^2} + \frac{1}{\sigma_\eta^2}\right)^{-1}.$$

Then, suppose $\alpha_2 \mid \alpha_1 \sim N(\alpha_1, \sigma_\eta^2)$ and $Y_2 = \alpha_2 + \varepsilon_2$. Show that

$$E(\alpha_2 \mid Y_1) = E(\alpha_1 \mid Y_1) = m(Y_1),$$

$$\text{var}(\alpha_2 \mid Y_1) = \sigma_\eta^2 + \left(\frac{1}{\sigma_\varepsilon^2} + \frac{1}{\sigma_\eta^2}\right)^{-1}.$$

8.7 Suppose that the observed log of an exchange-traded fund (ETF) secondary market price p_t is equal to a fundamental value p_t^* plus a transitory premium u_t, where $p_t^* = p_{t-1}^* + \eta_t$ and $u_t = \phi u_{t-1} + \varepsilon_t$, where $|\phi| < 1$ and $\eta_t \sim N(0, \sigma_\eta^2)$, $\varepsilon_t \sim N(0, \sigma_\varepsilon^2)$. Furthermore, we observe the net asset value of underlying holdings of the ETF (possibly slightly stale), called q_t, and

$$q_t = (1 - \varphi)p_t^* + \varphi q_t + u_t,$$

where $|\varphi| < 1$ and $u_t \sim N(0, \sigma_u^2)$. Write this model for p_t, q_t in state space form and suggest how to estimate the parameters ϕ, φ, σ_ε^2, σ_η^2, and σ_u^2.

8.8 Consider that a time series y_t is generated from an ARIMA(1,1,1) model, so that

$$y_t - y_{t-1} = \phi\left(y_{t-1} - y_{t-2}\right) + \varepsilon_t - \theta\varepsilon_{t-1},$$

where ε_t is i.i.d. $N(0, 1)$. Define the state vector

$$\alpha_t = \begin{pmatrix} y_t \\ y_{t-1} \\ \varepsilon_t \end{pmatrix}.$$

Write down a state space representation for y_t, that is, express y_t as a state space model $\alpha_t = F\alpha_{t-1} + v_t$, $y_t = H\alpha_t + w_t$. In your answer you should:

(a) specify the components H, F, v_t, and w_t;

(b) write down the distributions of v_t and w_t.

8.9 Suppose that

$$\alpha_t = \begin{pmatrix} 1 & 0 \\ 0 & \varphi \end{pmatrix} \alpha_{t-1} + v_t, \qquad v_t \sim N(0, \Sigma),$$

where Σ is a given covariance matrix and $|\varphi| < 1$.

(a) Suppose that $\Sigma = \text{diag}\{\sigma_{v1}^2, \sigma_{v2}^2\}$ and $y_t = (\ 0 \ \ 1\ ) \alpha_t + w_t$; write down the Kalman filter equations for α_t and discuss initialization.

(b) Suppose that Σ is not diagonal. How does your answer to part (a) change?

(c) Suppose that Σ is not diagonal, and $y_t = \frac{1}{2}(\ 1 \ \ 1\ ) \alpha_t + w_t$. How does your answer to part (a) change?

9   Bayesian Methods

The purpose of this chapter is to briefly present the general Bayesian approach to estimation, inference, forecasting, and model selection, and to contrast it with the frequentist approach, which is the main framework we have adopted in this book. The Bayesian approach has some advantages in some settings and has many adherents in certain parts of the world. The key input to this method is the choice of prior distribution, and a major issue in this field is how to compute the derived posterior distributions.

9.1   The Classical Setting

Bayesianists have a comprehensive approach to inference that is different from the frequentist approach. In the Bayesian approach, parameters θ (or at least some of them) are treated as random variables. There is a prior density function, denoted by $\pi(\theta)$, which reflects our knowledge about θ before seeing the sample. The objective is to update the prior using the sample data as represented by the likelihood and obtain the posterior distribution of θ by Bayes' theorem. There is only one result in Bayesian statistics: Bayes' theorem. For densities, this says that

$$f_{X|Y}(x \mid y) = \frac{f_{Y|X}(y \mid x)f_X(x)}{f_Y(y)} = \frac{f_{Y|X}(y \mid x)f_X(x)}{\int f_{Y,X}(y,x)\,\mathrm{d}x},$$

where f generically denotes densities here, either conditional, joint, or marginal. Bayesians use this formula repeatedly but with a different notation.

Suppose we have a sample of data generically denoted by $\mathcal{X}^T$. Let $\pi(\theta \mid \mathcal{X}^T)$ denote the posterior density of the parameter given the data; then

$$\underbrace{\pi(\theta \mid \mathcal{X}^T)}_{\text{posterior}} \propto \underbrace{L(\theta \mid \mathcal{X}^T)}_{\text{likelihood}} \times \underbrace{\pi(\theta)}_{\text{prior}}, \tag{9.1}$$

where the likelihood function is denoted by $L(\theta \mid \mathcal{X}^T)$, as usual emphasizing the argument θ. To make it clearer how this is just a rewrite of Bayes' theorem, we also use $f(\mathcal{X}^T \mid \theta)$ for the conditional density of the data given θ, so that $f(\mathcal{X}^T \mid \theta) = L(\theta \mid \mathcal{X}^T)$. Here, the proportional sign means that the right-hand side does not necessarily integrate to one, and one should normalize the function so obtained to satisfy this requirement, that is, divide by the marginal density, which we may denote by $f(\mathcal{X}^T) = \int f(\mathcal{X}^T \mid \theta)\pi(\theta)\,\mathrm{d}\theta$. That is,

$$\pi(\theta \mid \mathcal{X}^T) = \frac{L(\theta \mid \mathcal{X}^T) \times \pi(\theta)}{\int L(\theta \mid \mathcal{X}^T)\pi(\theta)\,\mathrm{d}\theta} = \frac{f(\mathcal{X}^T \mid \theta) \times \pi(\theta)}{f(\mathcal{X}^T)}.$$

The normalization step can in many cases be done mechanically, and in any case as far as the shape of the posterior, that is, the relative importance of different θ values, the numerator is all that matters.

To summarize: What you know about θ after the data arrive is what you knew before (the prior) and what the data told you (likelihood). Once one has the posterior density the plan is to report various features of it like its mean, its median, or its mode as "the estimator of θ," and intervals containing θ with prespecified probability as the counterpart to frequentist confidence intervals. The mode of the posterior is the natural analogue of the MLE since it maximizes the posterior.

Example 9.1 Suppose that X is the outcome of a coin toss whose bias is unknown, that is, $X = 1$ with probability $p \in (0, 1)$ and $X = 0$ with probability $1 - p$. Suppose that one tosses the coin T times and finds k heads and $T - k$ tails. The likelihood of the sample (distribution of the data) is

$$f(\mathcal{X}^T \mid p) = \binom{T}{k} p^k (1 - p)^{T-k}.$$

Suppose that the prior distribution on p, $\pi(p)$, is uniform over $[0, 1]$, that is, it places equal probability on different values of p within this interval. In this case, the posterior density of p is

$$
\begin{aligned}
\pi(p \mid \mathcal{X}^T) &= \frac{f(\mathcal{X}^T \mid p) \pi(p)}{\int f(\mathcal{X}^T \mid p) \pi(p) \, dp} \\
&= \frac{p^k (1 - p)^{T-k}}{\int_0^1 p^k (1 - p)^{T-k} \, dp} = \frac{(T+1)!}{k! \, (T-k)!} p^k (1 - p)^{T-k}.
\end{aligned}
$$

In fact, this is the distribution of a Beta$(k + 1, T - k + 1)$ random variable. The posterior mean is $(k + 1)/(T + 2)$ and the posterior mode is k/T (which is the MLE).

Example 9.2 Suppose that the population probability in favor of a particular outcome in an election is $p \in [0, 1]$; we sample $T = 100$ individuals, and find that $k = 55$ of them are in favor of the outcome. What is the probability that $p > 1/2$? We suppose again the ignorance prior, whence

$$\Pr\left(p > 0.5 \mid \mathcal{X}^T\right) = \frac{101!}{55! 45!} \int_{0.5}^1 p^{55} (1 - p)^{45} \, dp = 0.840 \, 14.$$

Example 9.3 Suppose that $x = (x_1, \ldots, x_k)$, with $x_i \in \{0, 1\}$ with probabilities $p_i \in (0, 1)$ such that $\sum_{i=1}^k x_i = n$ for some given n. The commonly used prior here is the Dirichlet (with given parameters $\alpha_1, \ldots, \alpha_k$). Then

$$f(p \mid \alpha) = \frac{\Gamma\left(\sum_{i=1}^k \alpha_i\right)}{\prod_{i=1}^k \Gamma(\alpha_i)} p_1^{\alpha_1 - 1} \cdots p_k^{\alpha_k - 1}.$$

Example 9.4 Suppose that we observe a single data point $X \sim N(\mu_x, \sigma_x^2)$, where σ_x^2 is assumed to be known and not of interest. The prior for the parameter μ_x is the density of

$\mu_x \sim N(\mu, \sigma^2)$, where μ and σ^2 are known and fixed; they are called hyperparameters. Then the posterior density of μ_x is given by $\mu_x \mid X \sim N(m, v)$, with

$$m = \mu + \frac{\sigma^2}{\sigma^2 + \sigma_x^2}(X - \mu) = \overbrace{\frac{\sigma_x^2}{\sigma^2 + \sigma_x^2}\mu}^{\text{contribution of prior}} + \overbrace{\frac{\sigma^2}{\sigma^2 + \sigma_x^2}X}^{\text{contribution of data}} \,,$$

$$v = \sigma^2 - \frac{\sigma^4}{\sigma^2 + \sigma_x^2} = \frac{\sigma_x^2 \sigma^2}{\sigma^2 + \sigma_x^2} = \left(\frac{1}{\sigma^2} + \frac{1}{\sigma_x^2}\right)^{-1}.$$

The posterior mean is a weighted average of the prior mean and the data mean, while the posterior variance is the harmonic average of the variance of the prior and the data. In this case the mean is equal to the mode.

Example 9.5   Suppose now that we observe T observations $\mathcal{X}^T$. In this case we have $\overline{X} \sim N(\mu_x, \sigma_x^2/T)$. We can show that the posterior density becomes $\mu_x \mid \mathcal{X}^T \sim N(m_T, v_T)$, with m_T, v_T as defined above except that $\sigma_x^2 \mapsto \sigma_x^2/T$. That is, the posterior mean and variance are

$$m_T = \frac{\sigma_x^2/T}{\sigma^2 + \sigma_x^2/T}\mu + \frac{\sigma^2}{\sigma^2 + \sigma_x^2/T}\overline{X}, \qquad v_T = \left(\frac{1}{\sigma^2} + \frac{T}{\sigma_x^2}\right)^{-1}.$$

We have, as $T \to \infty$, $m_T \xrightarrow{P} \mu_x$: the data dominates. Bayesians also have a **law of small numbers**, that is, when $T \to 0$, $m_T \xrightarrow{P} \mu$.

It is as if we had two independent measurements of μ_x, one from the distribution $N(\mu_x, \sigma_x^2/T)$ and the other from the distribution $N(\mu, \sigma^2)$, and we combined the two measurements in an equal fashion. The analysis of normal mean can be extended to regression.

Example 9.6   Consider the multivariate linear regression $y_t = Bx_t + \varepsilon_t$, where $\varepsilon_t \sim N(0, \Omega_\varepsilon)$. The prior can be factorized as $\pi(B, \Omega_\varepsilon) = \pi(\Omega_\varepsilon)\pi(B \mid \Omega_\varepsilon)$. Suppose that $\beta \mid \Omega_\varepsilon \sim N(\beta_0, \Omega_\varepsilon \otimes \Lambda^{-1})$ and that Ω_ε is treated as fixed. The OLS/MLE of B is $\widehat{B} = Y^\mathsf{T} X(X^\mathsf{T} X)^{-1}$. The posterior mean of B is

$$B^* = \left(X^\mathsf{T} X + \Lambda\right)^{-1}\left(X^\mathsf{T} X\widehat{B} + \Lambda\right).$$

The prior in the above example is **conjugate** (normal + normal = normal) and **informative** – it puts most weight close to the point μ, with a degree of certainty expressed by σ^2. When σ^2 is very small, the prior information is very precise. An alternative class of prior distributions are called **ignorance priors**, in which effectively $\sigma^2 \to \infty$. Formally, we take the prior measure to be the Lebesgue measure on $\mathbb{R}$ (note that this is not a probability measure), that is, μ is essentially equally likely to be in any interval of the real line. This is also called an **improper prior**, because it is not a probability measure. Nevertheless, Bayes' theorem works in this case, since the normalization enforces that the posterior is a proper density (integrates to one). In that case, the posterior density of $\mu_y \mid y$ is $N(y, \sigma_y^2)$, consistent with the above arguments, and the posterior density of $\mu_y \mid \mathbf{y}_{1:T}$ is $N(\overline{y}, \sigma_y^2/T)$. In general, calculating posterior densities analytically can be too difficult.

However, it is easy to do it by simulation methods such as **Markov chain Monte Carlo** (MCMC), which we discuss below.

Do we need a prior for the prior? In the above example, how come μ and σ^2 are known? This is the guilty secret of Bayesian analysis: they complain that in the frequentist version of inference, parameters are treated as fixed quantities with no use of prior information, but then hidden inside their priors lie quantities that are treated in exactly the same way. They just go to one further station on the train. There are also hierarchical approaches in which one further specifies priors for the priors, which takes you even further up the line.

We consider how to construct a Bayesian confidence interval, sometimes called a **credible interval**. We will work with the specific binomial case for simplicity. Suppose that one observes k values of $X = 1$ and $T - k$ values of $X = 0$, and suppose that the prior distribution on p, $\pi(p)$, is uniform over $[0, 1]$. In this case, we have seen that the posterior density $\pi(p \mid \mathcal{X}^T)$ of p is a Beta$(k + 1, T - k + 1)$ random variable. A Bayesian credible interval $[L, U]$ satisfies

$$\int_L^U \pi(p \mid \mathcal{X}^T)\,\mathrm{d}p = 1 - \alpha. \tag{9.2}$$

In general there are many solutions to this equation. The simplest approach is to take equal tail probabilities, that is,

$$\int_0^L \pi(p \mid \mathcal{X}^T)\,\mathrm{d}p = \int_U^1 \pi(p \mid \mathcal{X}^T)\,\mathrm{d}p = \frac{\alpha}{2}.$$

An alternative approach is called the **highest posterior density** (HPD) region I_α, which is chosen such that the posterior density for every point in this set is higher than the posterior density for any point outside of this set, that is, for all $p \in I_\alpha$, $\pi(p \mid \mathcal{X}^T) \geq \pi(p' \mid \mathcal{X}^T)$ for all $p' \notin I_\alpha$. That is, we find L, U such that $\pi(p \mid \mathcal{X}^T)$ is maximized on $[L, U]$. We may find simulation methods convenient to calculate the integral.

Consider the special case that $k = 0$, so that $\widehat{p} = 0$, in which case we have to solve

$$(T + 1) \int_0^U (1 - p)^T\,\mathrm{d}p = 1 - \alpha = \left(1 - (1 - U)^{T+1}\right).$$

Therefore, $U = 1 - \alpha^{1/(T+1)}$. When taking the significance level $\alpha = 0.05$ and $T = 10$, one obtains $U = 0.238$, which means that with 95% confidence we may assert that the random set $[0, 0.238]$ contains p. When $T = 100$ we obtain $[0, 0.029]$. This is also the HPD interval.

9.2   Time Series

We next consider the Bayesian approach in time series. The same principles apply, but the models are somewhat more complex.

9.2.1   ARMA Processes

We start with the simplest example of a Gaussian autoregression with no drift. We consider different priors.

Example 9.7   Suppose that $y_t = \phi y_{t-1} + \varepsilon_t$, where $\varepsilon_t \sim N(0, 1)$ and $y_0 = 0$. In this case the likelihood is

$$L = (2\pi)^{-T/2} \exp\left(-\frac{1}{2}\sum_{t=1}^{T}(y_t - \phi y_{t-1})^2\right),$$

and can be rewritten as

$$L = \frac{1}{(2\pi)^{T/2}} \exp\left(-\frac{1}{2}\sum_{t=1}^{T}(y_t - \widehat{\phi} y_{t-1})^2 - \frac{1}{2}(\widehat{\phi} - \phi)^2 \sum_{t=1}^{T} y_{t-1}^2\right),$$

where $\widehat{\phi}$ is the MLE. Suppose that the prior is that ϕ is uniform on $[-1, 1]$; then the posterior is

$$\pi_T(\phi \mid y_1, \ldots, y_T) \propto \exp\left(-\frac{1}{2}(\widehat{\phi} - \phi)^2 \sum_{t=1}^{T} y_{t-1}^2\right),$$

where the constant of proportionality is obtained by integration of the right-hand side expression over $\phi \in (-1, 1)$. The shape of the posterior is then like a Gaussian with mean $\widehat{\phi}$ and variance $\widehat{v}^2 = 1/\sum_{t=1}^{T} y_{t-1}^2$ that is truncated to $(-1, 1)$. The mode of the posterior is $\widehat{\phi}$, but the mean of the posterior is

$$E(\phi \mid y_1, \ldots, y_T) = \widehat{\phi} - \frac{\phi\big((1 - \widehat{\phi})/\widehat{v}\big) - \phi\big((-1 - \widehat{\phi})/\widehat{v}\big)}{\Phi\big((1 - \widehat{\phi})/\widehat{v}\big) - \Phi\big((-1 - \widehat{\phi})/\widehat{v}\big)} \widehat{v},$$

where ϕ is the standard normal density and Φ is the standard normal CDF. Here, $E(\phi \mid y_1, \ldots, y_T)$ could be larger or smaller than $\widehat{\phi}$.

Example 9.8   Suppose instead that we take as prior the normal distribution $\phi \sim N(\alpha, \omega^2)$. Then

$$\pi_T(\phi \mid y_1, \ldots, y_T) \propto \exp\left(-\frac{1}{2}(\widehat{\phi} - \phi)^2 \sum_{t=1}^{T} y_{t-1}^2\right) \exp\left(-\frac{(\phi - \alpha)^2}{2\omega^2}\right)$$

$$\propto \exp\left(-\frac{1}{2\delta_T^2}(\mu_T - \phi)^2\right),$$

$$\mu_T = \frac{1/\omega^2}{(1/\omega^2) + \sum_{t=1}^{T} y_{t-1}^2}\alpha + \frac{\sum_{t=1}^{T} y_{t-1}^2}{(1/\omega^2) + \sum_{t=1}^{T} y_{t-1}^2},$$

$$\delta_T^2 = \sum_{t=1}^{T} y_{t-1}^2 + \frac{1}{\omega^2}.$$

The shape of the posterior is Gaussian with mean μ_T and variance δ_T^2.

The two priors yield quite different posteriors. There has been a considerable debate about which prior is appropriate, especially in the context of unit roots. In the second example, the posterior mean is shrunk towards α; if $\alpha = 0$, then the posterior mean is closer to zero. In principle one could take $\alpha = 1$, in which case the posterior mean is closer to one. From the Bayesian point of view there is nothing special about the point $\phi = 1$. Phillips (1991b) discussed the **Jeffrey's prior**, which is proportional to the square root of the determinant of the information matrix I_θ. This has the advantage of being invariant to transformations, unlike the other two priors we considered above. In our special case, the Jeffrey's prior is

$$\pi(\phi) \propto -E\left(\frac{\partial^2 \mathcal{L}}{\partial \phi^2}(\phi)\right) \propto \begin{cases} T/(1-\phi^2) & \text{if } \phi \in (-1,1), \\ T(T-1)/2 & \text{if } \phi \in \{-1,1\}. \end{cases}$$

This prior puts a lot of density near the unit root case.

Example 9.9   Suppose that $y_t = \varepsilon_t - \theta \varepsilon_{t-1}$, where ε_t is i.i.d. $N(0,1)$. Then $y \sim N(0, \Sigma(\theta, \sigma_\varepsilon^2))$ and the likelihood is

$$L(y \mid \sigma_\varepsilon^2, \theta) = \frac{1}{(2\pi\sigma_\varepsilon^2)^{T/2} (\det(R(\theta)))^{1/2}} \exp\left(-\frac{1}{2\sigma_\varepsilon^2} y^\mathsf{T} R(\theta)^{-1} y\right).$$

We assume a prior $\pi(\sigma_\varepsilon^2, \theta) = \pi(\theta \mid \sigma_\varepsilon^2)\pi(\sigma_\varepsilon^2)$; usually these are assumed to be independent, in which case we just need a prior for θ and a prior for σ_ε^2. For example, $\theta \sim U[-1,1]$ or a Beta prior with support $[-1,1]$, while σ_ε^2 follows a Gamma distribution on $[0,\infty)$. It follows that

$$\pi(\theta, \sigma_\varepsilon^2 \mid y) = \frac{L(\theta, \sigma_\varepsilon^2 \mid y)\pi(\theta, \sigma_\varepsilon^2)}{\int_0^\infty \int_{-1}^1 L(\theta, \sigma_\varepsilon^2 \mid y)\pi(\theta, \sigma_\varepsilon^2)\, d\theta\, d\sigma_\varepsilon^2}, \quad \theta \in [-1,1],\ \sigma_\varepsilon^2 > 0.$$

The posterior is complicated to calculate analytically. However, one can calculate it by simulation methods, see the discussion below.

In the general $ARMA(p,q)$ case, one has to specify a prior distribution for all the parameters. If the process is assumed to be stationary and invertible, then the parameter space is subject to a number of inequality restrictions. When specifying the prior, and indeed integrating the product of likelihood with prior, we need to take account of these restrictions, which makes this a nontrivial task.

9.2.2   General Time Series Models

We consider a general time series framework where $\mathbf{x}_{0:T} = \{x_0, \ldots, x_T\}$ contains hidden states and possibly unknown parameters θ, suppressed for now, while $\mathbf{y}_{1:T} = \{y_1, \ldots, y_T\}$ is the observed data. Bayes' theorem says that the density of $\mathbf{x}_{0:T}$ given the data $\mathbf{y}_{1:T}$ satisfies

$$f(\mathbf{x}_{0:T} \mid \mathbf{y}_{1:T}) = \frac{f(\mathbf{y}_{1:T} \mid \mathbf{x}_{0:T})f(\mathbf{x}_{0:T})}{f(\mathbf{y}_{1:T})},$$

where $f(\mathbf{x}_{0:T})$ is the prior density, and $f(\mathbf{y}_{1:T} \mid \mathbf{x}_{0:T})$ is the likelihood model for the observed data, while $f(\mathbf{y}_{1:T})$ is the normalization constant defined by

$$f(\mathbf{y}_{1:T}) = \int f(\mathbf{y}_{1:T} \mid \mathbf{x}_{0:T})f(\mathbf{x}_{0:T})\, d\mathbf{x}_{0:T}.$$

The problem is that the full conditional distribution is hard to work with when T is large for the sort of dynamic models of interest, and one has to approach this computation in a sequential or recursive fashion similar to the Kalman filter.

We start by specifying an initial prior distribution $f(x_0)$ of the state at time 0. Then we specify a dynamic model for the transition of the state, $f(x_t \mid \mathbf{x}_{0:t-1})$, and a measurement model, $f(y_t \mid \mathbf{x}_{0:t})$, where usually $\mathbf{x}_{0:t-1}$ is replaced by x_{t-1} (justified under the Markov assumption) and $\mathbf{x}_{0:t}$ is replaced by x_t. The difference between the frequentist and Bayesian approach here is only with regards to whether the parameter vector θ is included in the state vector or not. The above computations are very time consuming, especially when the time series is long. For this reason it is helpful to break the problem down into subproblems where this is possible. We proceed as follows.

Algorithm For $t = 1, 2, \ldots, T$, calculate:

1. Filtering distribution:

$$f(x_t \mid \mathbf{y}_{1:t}) = \frac{f(y_t \mid x_t)f(x_t \mid \mathbf{y}_{1:t-1})}{\int f(y_t \mid x_t)f(x_t \mid \mathbf{y}_{1:t-1})\, \mathrm{d}x_t}.$$

2. State prediction distribution:

$$f(x_{t+1} \mid \mathbf{y}_{1:t}) = \int f(x_{t+1} \mid x_t)f(x_t \mid \mathbf{y}_{1:t})\, \mathrm{d}x_t.$$

We may at each step calculate the data predictive distribution

$$f(y_{t+1} \mid \mathbf{y}_{1:t}) = \int f(y_{t+1} \mid \mathbf{x}_{0:t})f(\mathbf{x}_{0:t} \mid \mathbf{y}_{1:t})\, \mathrm{d}\mathbf{x}_{0:t},$$

which in the frequentist world is used to construct the likelihood. This density also has uses in out-of-sample prediction when $t = T$.

Example 9.10 In the local-level model the filtering distribution is $N(\alpha_{t|t}, V_{t|t})$, the state prediction distribution is $N(\alpha_{t+1|t}, V_{t+1|t})$, and the data predictive distribution is $N(\mu_{t+1|t}, \sigma^2_{t+1|t})$, where the means and variances $\alpha_{t|t}, V_{t|t}$ and $\alpha_{t+1|t}, V_{t+1|t}$ are given in expressions (8.10)–(8.13), and $\mu_{t+1|t} = \alpha_{t+1|t}$, $\sigma^2_{t+1|t} = V_{t+1|t} + \sigma^2_\varepsilon$.

In the Bayesian framework we include parameters in the vector $\mathbf{x}_{0:T}$, but to emphasize this we include them separately. Of interest is the posterior distribution of the parameter vector and state vector given all the data,

$$f(\theta, \mathbf{x}_{0:T} \mid \mathbf{y}_{1:T}) = \frac{f(\mathbf{y}_{1:T} \mid \theta, \mathbf{x}_{0:T})f(\theta, \mathbf{x}_{0:T})}{f(\mathbf{y}_{1:T})},$$

and its marginal distribution, $f(\theta \mid \mathbf{y}_{1:T}) = \int f(\theta, \mathbf{x}_{0:T} \mid \mathbf{y}_{1:T})\, \mathrm{d}\mathbf{x}_{0:T}$, which is the source of all truth to a Bayesianista, that is, this can be used to construct credible intervals about θ and so on. It can be hard to calculate $f(\mathbf{y}_{1:T})$ analytically, and we usually use simulation methods; see below to do this.

Example 9.11 For the local-level model, let $\theta = (\sigma^2_\varepsilon, \sigma^2_\eta, \alpha_0)^\top$ be the parameter vector. The most general Bayesian analysis assumes the prior distribution

$$\alpha_0 \sim N(\mu, \sigma^2), \qquad \sigma^2_\varepsilon \sim \mathrm{IG}(m_\varepsilon, v_\varepsilon), \qquad \sigma^2_\eta \sim \mathrm{IG}(m_\eta, v_\eta),$$

where IG denotes the inverse Gaussian distribution, and $\tau = (\mu, \sigma^2, m_\varepsilon, v_\varepsilon, m_\eta, v_\eta)^{\mathsf{T}}$ is the hyperparameter vector. The inverse Gaussian density is

$$f(x; \mu, \lambda) = \sqrt{\frac{\lambda}{2\pi x^3}} \exp\left(-\frac{\lambda(x-\mu)^2}{2\mu^2 x}\right), \quad x > 0. \tag{9.3}$$

In this case, analytic formulas for the distributions $\sigma_\varepsilon^2 \mid \mathbf{y}_{1:T}, \boldsymbol{\alpha}_{1:T}$ and $\sigma_\eta^2 \mid \mathbf{y}_{1:T}, \boldsymbol{\alpha}_{1:T}, \alpha_0$, and $\boldsymbol{\alpha}_{1:T} \mid \mathbf{y}_{1:T}, \theta$ are available (inverse Gaussians and normal). But to find $f(\theta \mid \mathbf{y}_{1:T})$ requires the calculation of complicated high-dimensional integrals arising from integrating out over the state vector.

9.3 Markov Chain Monte Carlo

Bayesianistas end up calculating expectations of functions of parameter vectors. For example, to compute the posterior we have to calculate the normalizing integral $E = \int f(\mathbf{y}_{1:T} \mid \theta)\pi(\theta)\, d\theta$. This can be very hard analytically, except in special cases that are called conjugate. One solution is to use simulation methods. Suppose we can draw a random sample $\theta_1^*, \ldots, \theta_R^*$ from π, then let

$$\widehat{E} = \frac{1}{R} \sum_{r=1}^{R} f(\mathbf{y}_{1:T} \mid \theta_r^*).$$

This is a consistent estimator of E as $R \to \infty$. In the case where θ is a vector, it can be hard to draw from the full joint distribution for θ and so we next consider an iterative or sequential approach that works in a wide range of cases, which we consider next.

9.3.1 Gibbs Sampling

We want to estimate or sample from the joint density $f(\theta_1, \theta_2)$, which is hard to do. However, suppose the conditional densities $f(\theta_1 \mid \theta_2)$ and $f(\theta_2 \mid \theta_1)$, ..., are easily computable. Then we proceed as follows.

Let $\left(\theta_1^{(1)}, \theta_2^{(1)}\right)$ be some initial sample.

1. Given $\left(\theta_1^{(i)}, \theta_2^{(i)}\right)$, we sample
   (a) $\theta_1^{(i+1)}$ from $f(\theta_1 \mid \theta_2^{(i)})$,
   (b) $\theta_2^{(i+1)}$ from $f(\theta_2 \mid \theta_1^{(i+1)})$,
   ...
2. Repeat until convergence.

We compute the sequences $\theta^{(1)} = \left(\theta_1^{(1)}, \theta_2^{(1)}\right)$, $\theta^{(2)} = \left(\theta_1^{(2)}, \theta_2^{(2)}\right)$, ... There are results guaranteeing convergence of this algorithm such that essentially $\theta^{(\infty)}$ is a random draw from the joint density f. In practice, one stops the algorithm based on some threshold that measures convergence.

9.3.2 The Metropolis–Hastings Algorithm

1. Draw the starting point $\theta^{(0)}$ from an arbitrary initial distribution.

2. For $i = 1, \ldots, N$:
   (a) Sample a candidate point θ^* from the proposal distribution $q(\theta^* \mid \theta^{(i-1)})$.
   (b) Evaluate the acceptance probability

$$\alpha_i = \min \left\{ 1, \exp\left(\varphi_T(\theta^{(i-1)}) - \varphi_T(\theta^*)\right) \frac{q(\theta^{(i-1)}) \mid q(\theta^{(i-1)} \mid \theta^*)}{q(\theta^* \mid \theta^{(i-1)})} \right\}.$$

   (c) Generate a uniform random variable $U \sim U(0,1)$ and set

$$\theta^{(i)} = \begin{cases} \theta^* & \text{if } U \le \alpha_i, \\ \theta^{(i-1)} & \text{otherwise.} \end{cases}$$

One common choice of proposal distribution is the Gaussian distribution $q(\theta^* \mid \theta^{(i-1)}) = N(\theta^* \mid \mu^{(i-1)}, \Sigma^{(i-1)})$. The algorithm is named in part for Nicholas Metropolis, the first coauthor of a 1953 paper that also included Edward Teller and others. Hastings extended it to the more general case.

9.4   Bayesian VAR

We next consider Bayesian vector autoregression, which is a major area of application, and which has seen many impressive developments. The Bayesian approach effectively introduces further structure that allows one to obtain plausible results even with the small samples of macroeconomics.

9.4.1   General Setup

Suppose that $y_t \in \mathbb{R}^n$, where

$$y_t = \mu + A_1 y_{t-1} + \cdots + A_p y_{t-p} + \varepsilon_t,$$

with $\varepsilon_t \sim N(0, \Sigma)$. We can write the model in vector form,

$$y = (I_n \otimes X)\alpha + \varepsilon, \tag{9.4}$$

where y, ε are $nT \times 1$ vectors with $\varepsilon \sim N(0, \Sigma \otimes I_T)$, while $\alpha = (\mu^{\mathsf{T}}, \text{vec}(A_1)^{\mathsf{T}}, \ldots, \text{vec}(A_p)^{\mathsf{T}})^{\mathsf{T}}$ is the $n^2 p$ vector of mean parameters. If the time series dimension T is not large relative to n, as is often the case with macroeconomics datasets, then it can be very difficult to obtain precise estimates of all the parameters in α, and a Bayesian approach is one way of imposing structure on the problem.

9.4.2   Priors

A variety of priors can be used with the VAR. They differ in relation to three issues. First, what type of prior information is taken account of. Second, the priors may differ in whether they lead to analytical results for the posterior and predictive densities or whether simulation methods like MCMC are required to carry out Bayesian inference. Natural conjugate priors lead to analytical results, which can greatly reduce the computational burden. Nonconjugate priors that require MCMC methods can be very computationally demanding, particularly if one is carrying out a recursive forecasting exercise, which requires repeated calculation of posterior and predictive distributions. Third, the priors differ in how easily they can handle departures from the unrestricted VAR such as allowing different equations to have different explanatory variables (zero restrictions), allowing for VAR coefficients to change over time, allowing for heteroskedastic structures for the errors of various sorts, and so on. Natural conjugate priors typically do not lend themselves to such extensions.

9.4.2.1 The Minnesota Prior

Early work with Bayesian VARs (BVARs) with shrinkage priors was done by researchers at the University of Minnesota or the Federal Reserve Bank of Minneapolis (Doan, Litterman, and Sims, 1984; Litterman, 1986). The priors they used have come to be known as **Minnesota priors**. In their framework the prior for α is $N(\alpha_0, V_0)$, where the hyperparameters α_0, V_0 are chosen as follows:

- In the stationary case, the α_0 are equal to zero; if there are nonstationary variables then the coefficient on the own lagged dependent variable is set equal to one and all the others are set equal to zero.
- In either case the $n^2 p \times n^2 p$ covariance matrix V_0 is assumed to be diagonal with downweighting by lag structure of the form $r^{-\kappa}$, where r is the corresponding lag and $\kappa \geq 1$ is given. The constant associated with the own effects is larger than the constant associated with cross effects.

For example, suppose that $n = 2$ and $p = 2$, so that when $\alpha = (A_{1,11}, A_{1,12}, A_{2,11}, A_{2,12}, A_{1,21}, A_{1,21}, A_{2,21}, A_{2,22})^\mathsf{T}$ we have the 8×8 diagonal covariance matrix

$$
V_0 = \begin{pmatrix}
\phi_0 & 0 & 0 & 0 & 0 & 0 & 0 & 0 \\
0 & \phi_0\phi_1\omega_{1:2} & 0 & 0 & 0 & 0 & 0 & 0 \\
0 & 0 & \frac{\phi_0}{2^\kappa} & 0 & 0 & 0 & 0 & 0 \\
0 & 0 & 0 & \frac{\phi_0\phi_1\omega_{1:2}}{2^\kappa} & 0 & 0 & 0 & 0 \\
0 & 0 & 0 & 0 & \phi_0\phi_1\omega_{1:2} & 0 & 0 & 0 \\
0 & 0 & 0 & 0 & 0 & \phi_0 & 0 & 0 \\
0 & 0 & 0 & 0 & 0 & 0 & \frac{\phi_0\phi_1\omega_{1:2}}{2^\kappa} & 0 \\
0 & 0 & 0 & 0 & 0 & 0 & 0 & \frac{\phi_0}{2^\kappa}
\end{pmatrix},
$$

where ϕ_0, ϕ_1 are hyperparameters, while $\omega_{1:2} = \sigma_2^2/\sigma_1^2$ is the relative standard errors of the two variables. In practice, this is replaced by a sample estimate. For short lags $\kappa = 1$ is quite common, but for longer lags higher discounting may be used. The error covariance matrix Σ is treated outside the Bayesian paradigm, and replaced by an estimate, typically the sample residual covariance matrix $\widehat{\Sigma}$. This could be called a hybrid or Frankenbrid approach. In this case, the posterior for α follows by standard analysis for normal distributions, and is $\alpha \mid y \sim N\left(\overline{\alpha}, \overline{V}\right)$, with

$$
\overline{V} = \left(V_0^{-1} + \left(\widehat{\Sigma}^{-1} \otimes (X^\mathsf{T}X)\right)\right)^{-1}, \qquad \overline{\alpha} = \overline{V}\left(V_0^{-1}\alpha_0 + \left(\widehat{\Sigma}^{-1} \otimes X\right)^\mathsf{T}y\right).
$$

Durbin (1953) and Theil and Goldberger (1961) showed how to implement stochastic prior information in a linear model within a frequentist framework. Suppose that (9.4) holds, and that $R\alpha = \alpha_0 + \eta$, where $\eta \sim N(0, V_0)$. That is, we have a vector of linear restrictions $R\alpha$ that are not exactly equal to the known quantity α_0 but are equal up to the normal variation. One can think of $\alpha_0 = R\alpha + \eta$ as additional observations on α and write the system as

$$\begin{pmatrix} y \\ \alpha_0 \end{pmatrix} = \begin{pmatrix} I_n \otimes X \\ R \end{pmatrix} \alpha + \begin{pmatrix} \varepsilon \\ \eta \end{pmatrix}.$$

This interpretation gives another way of understanding the posterior form. In the frequentist world, restrictions can improve efficiency and reduce effective dimensionality. The Bayesian approach uses imprecise restrictions and obtains similar benefits.

9.4.2.2 Fully Conjugate Priors

Suppose that α, Σ are random variables with a prior $\pi(\alpha, \Sigma) = \pi(\alpha \mid \Sigma)\pi(\Sigma)$ that can be expressed as

$$\alpha \mid \Sigma \sim N(\alpha_0, \Sigma \otimes V_0), \qquad \Sigma^{-1} \sim W(\Psi_0^{-1}, v_0),$$

where α_0, V_0, Ψ_0, and v_0 are user-specified parameters of the prior matrix. Here, W is the Wishart distribution. This leads to quite complicated expressions for the posterior mean and variance matrix, although they lie in the same Normal/Wishart family.

9.5   Bayesian versus Frequentist

Some Bayesians talk a lot about coherence and rationality. Others talk about flexibility and applicability. They often say words to the effect "Let me through, I am a Bayesian, I have the solution to the problem that you frequentists have messed up." Efron (1986) and Cox (2006) compared the frequentist and Bayesian approaches. Cox argued that

A very major difficulty with this as a basis for the public discussion of scientific evidence is that it treats personal intuition as on the same basis as evidence from hard data. More explicitly it treats all probabilities of, say, 0.5 as on an equal footing, whether they are based on careful stable measurements of frequency or on the most transitory of personal judgements. In some situations prior distributions based on a careful summary of expert judgement may be used quantitatively, but then scrutiny of their evidence base is crucial.

The Bayesian approach generically imposes much more structure, such as the prior distribution, which may not be warranted. However, it can deliver reasonable answers in some complex cases where the frequentist approach fails. One question is whether the priors advocated by old-fashioned Bayesianistas are meaningful priors, that is, in what sense could this represent someone's (everyone's) opinion about the parameters of the model. How could someone really form an opinion about a 1000×1000 covariance matrix, and if they could, why would it look like a Wishart distribution? In practice, the priors are chosen for mathematical convenience, not as the expression of a real opinion carefully thought out. Furthermore, the prior is personal. My prior could be quite different from your prior, and again different from the presenter of the research paper. How do I go from your prior to my prior and back again? Is the prior chosen by some data-dependent process to make the results appear reasonable? In any event, specification of priors usually involves fixing certain hyperparameters in the same way as a frequentist does, except without the possibility of learning the true value of such hyperparameters. They are "kicked into the long grass." Finally, there is the Black Swan problem (Taleb, 2010). According to some researchers,[1]

This is the Black Swan paradox. The takeaway from this story is that we cannot rule out some hypothesis because we have never witnessed it before. This is why Bayesian statistics (in contrast to frequentism) has become so vital in machine learning today.

The idea here seems to be that the prior could be chosen to allow for the possibility that some swans are black even if one had not seen one so far, with the interpretation that the frequentist would blow up once a black swan observation occurs, whereas a Bayesian would just update their prior. This seems to be a stretch – my interpretation is exactly the opposite. If Europeans of the sixteenth century could write down a prior it would have put zero probability on a swan being black, and if that were the case the whole framework fails, in the same way as if a coin were to land on its rim when the prior was located only on heads or tails. According to the Bayesian setup, if the prior puts zero probability on such an event then so will the posterior; the prior defines what possible values the parameters can take. The frequentist would simply adjust their sample calculations; they are always seeing observations they have never seen before, in fact this occurs with probability one for a continuous distribution.

Both approaches have merit, and ultimately it may be a matter of taste as to which approach you prefer. There is even a term that signifies possession of both tastes simultaneously, **empirical Bayes**, where the prior is replaced by estimated distributions from previous samples.

9.6 Summary

We introduced the Bayesian framework for inference and distinguished it from the frequentist approach. We considered several standard examples and looked at its role in time series. We specifically considered Bayesian vector autoregression and some of the main ways that this methodology is implemented. We compared the Bayesian and frequentist approaches. The R language has several packages devoted to the estimation and analysis of Bayesian VARs, including BVAR and Bayesian structural time series, bsts. West and Harrison (1997) is the main source for Bayesian state space models. Koop and Korobilis (2010) is a recent reference on Bayesian methods for time series. Sims and Zha (1999) proposed constructing Bayesian error bands for impulse responses.

9.7 Exercises

9.1 For the dataset SP500, calculate the daily return in annualized percentages, that is, $r_t = 25\,000 \times \log(P_t/P_{t-1})$, where P_t is the daily closing price. Suppose that $r_t \sim N(\mu_r, \sigma_r^2)$, where the prior for the parameter μ_r is $N(\mu, \sigma^2)$, with μ and σ

[1] See https://deepai.org/machine-learning-glossary-and-terms/black-swan-paradox

known (use 8% and 20%). Also, set $\sigma_r = 20\%$. Derive the posterior distribution of μ_r given the full time series.

9.2 For the dataset SP500, calculate the daily return $r_t = \log(P_t/P_{t-1})$, where P_t is the daily closing price, for the full sample $t = 1, \ldots, T$. Let $X_t = 1(r_t > 0)$ and suppose that $X_t = 1$ with probability $p \in (0, 1)$ and $X_t = 0$ with probability $1 - p$. Suppose that the prior distribution on p is $\pi(p)$. Calculate the posterior for p given each year of data $\{r_{250(k-1)+1}, \ldots, r_{250k}\}$ for each available k, for the case where

(a) $\pi(p)$ is uniform on $[0, 1]$

(b) $\pi(p)$ is uniform on $[0.4, 0.6]$

(c) $\pi(p)$ is Beta on $[0, 1]$ with density $\Gamma(\alpha + \beta)p^{\alpha-1}(1 - p)^{\beta-1}/\Gamma(\alpha)\Gamma(\beta)$, where α, β are chosen to match the mean and variance of X_t over the full sample.

9.3 Suppose that $X \sim N(\mu, \sigma^2)$ with density denoted $\phi(x \mid \mu, \sigma^2)$. Prove that, for any $\mu, \sigma^2, \mu', \sigma'^2$, we have, for some c, m, v,

$$\phi(x \mid \mu, \sigma^2)\phi(x \mid \mu', \sigma'^2) = c\phi(x \mid m, v).$$

Find c, m, v.

9.4 Suppose that y_{1t}, y_{2t} are i.i.d. standard normal random variables with correlation ρ. Write down the likelihood function $L(\rho \mid y_{11}, y_{21}, \ldots, y_{1T}, y_{2T})$ based on the sample $\{y_{11}, y_{21}, \ldots, y_{1T}, y_{2T}\}$. What is the MLE of ρ? Suppose that the prior distribution on ρ, $\pi(\rho)$, is uniform on $[-1, 1]$. Calculate the posterior for ρ. Now suppose that the prior distribution for

$$\tau = \log\left(\frac{1+\rho}{1-\rho}\right)$$

is $N(0, 1)$. Calculate the posterior for ρ.

9.5 Suppose that $y_t \in \mathbb{R}^n$ is i.i.d. $N(\mu, I_n)$. Suppose that the prior for the vector μ is $N(\mu_0 i_n, \sigma_0^2 I_n)$, where μ_0, σ_0^2 are known scalars. Show that

$$\begin{pmatrix} y_t \\ \mu \end{pmatrix} \sim N(m, V), \qquad m = \mu_0 i_{2n}, \qquad V = \begin{pmatrix} (\sigma_0^2 + 1)I_n & \sigma_0^2 I_n \\ \sigma_0^2 I_n & \sigma_0^2 I_n \end{pmatrix},$$

and therefore that, with $\bar{\mu} = \sum_{i=1}^n \mu_i/n$ and $\bar{y}_t = \sum_{i=1}^n y_{it}/n$,

$$\bar{\mu} \mid y_t \sim N\left(\mu_0 + \frac{\sigma_0^2}{\sigma_0^2 + 1}(\bar{y}_t - \mu_0), \frac{\sigma_0^2}{n(\sigma_0^2 + 1)}\right).$$

9.6 A random sample of n students is drawn from a large population, and their weights are measured. The average weight of the n sampled students is $y = 150$ pounds. Assume the weights in the population are normally distributed with unknown mean θ and known standard deviation 20 pounds. Suppose your prior distribution for θ is normal with mean 180 and standard deviation 40.

(a) Give your posterior distribution for θ. (Your answer will be a function of n.)

(b) A new student is sampled at random from the same population and has a weight of $\tilde{y}$ pounds. Give a posterior predictive distribution for $\tilde{y}$.

(c) For $n = 10$, give a 95% posterior interval for θ and a 95% posterior predictive interval for $\tilde{y}$.

(d) Do the same for $n = 100$.

9.7 Suppose that the series y_t is a stationary first-order autoregression with mean level 0, autocorrelation 0.8, and error variance 1.

(a) Show that $y_t \mid y_{t-1}, y_{t-2}, \ldots \sim N(0.8y_{t-1}, 1)$ for all t.

(b) Prove that the distribution of y_t, given the observations at all other time points t, depends only on y_{t-1}, y_{t+1}.

(c) What is the distribution of y_t given y_{t-1} and y_{t+1}?

9.8 Suppose that $y_t = \phi y_{t-1} + \varepsilon_t$, where $\varepsilon_t \sim N(0, \sigma^2)$. Suppose that the prior is that ϕ is uniform on $[0, 1]$; obtain an expression for the posterior of ϕ, $\pi_T(\phi \mid y_1, \ldots, y_T)$. You may assume here that σ^2 is known. Devise a Bayesian credible interval for ϕ.

9.9 Suppose that $y_t = \phi y_{t-1} + \varepsilon_t$, where $\varepsilon_t \sim N(0, \sigma^2)$ as in the previous question. Suppose that the prior is that $\phi \sim N(0, \epsilon)$ for some $\epsilon > 0$. Obtain the predictive distribution $f(y_{T+1} \mid y_{1:T})$ from the Bayesian point of view and compare it with the frequentist version.

9.10 Suppose that $y_t = \varepsilon_t - \theta \varepsilon_{t-1}$, where $\varepsilon_t \sim N(0, 1)$ and $T = 2$. Suppose that the prior for θ is uniform on $[-1, 1]$. Obtain an expression for the posterior of θ, $\pi_T(\theta \mid y_1, y_2)$.

9.11 Suppose that $y_t = \varepsilon_t - \theta \varepsilon_{t-1}$, where $\varepsilon_t \sim N(0, 1)$ and $T = 2$. Suppose that the prior for θ is $N(0, \epsilon)$ for some $\epsilon > 0$. Obtain an expression for the posterior of θ, $\pi_T(\theta \mid y_1, y_2)$.

9.12 Suppose that $y_t = (y_{1t}, y_{2t})^\mathsf{T}$ and that $y_t = Ay_{t-1} + \varepsilon_t$, where $\varepsilon_t \sim N(0, I_2)$ and $y_0 = 0$; suppose also that $a = (A_{11}, A_{12}, A_{21}, A_{22})^\mathsf{T}$ has prior distribution with independent components $N(0, \tau I_4)$. Derive the posterior distribution of a given the sample $y_1, \ldots, y_T$.

9.13 Suppose that $y_t = (y_{1t}, y_{2t})^\mathsf{T}$ and that $y_t = Ay_{t-1} + \varepsilon_t$, where $\varepsilon_t \sim N(0, I_2)$ and $y_0 = 0$; suppose also that $a = (A_{11}, A_{12}, A_{21}, A_{22})^\mathsf{T}$ has prior distribution with independent components $U(-1, 1)$. Derive the posterior distribution of a given the sample $y_1, \ldots, y_T$.

10   Nonlinear Time Series Models

We have spent a lot of time discussing linear models, about which a lot is known. It is now time to consider **nonlinear models**, which is also a vast subject. It is a bit ironic perhaps to define a class of models by what they are not, but this reflects the focus on simplicity favored by practitioners. The class of nonlinear models is very large and research on them is ongoing. We consider a selection of models that are widely used in applications, including threshold models, switching models, and GARCH models. Many of these models are of the form

$$y_t = \mu_t(\theta) + \sigma_t(\theta)\varepsilon_t, \tag{10.1}$$

where ε_t is i.i.d. with mean zero and variance one, or possesses some more general property, while $\mu_t(\theta), \sigma_t(\theta) \in \mathcal{F}_{t-1}$ (past information $y_{t-1}, y_{t-2}, \ldots$). This is a generalization of the location–scale class from classical statistics. An important class of nonlinear models allows for nonadditive noise such as $y_t = f(y_{t-1}, y_{t-2}, \ldots, \varepsilon_t; \theta)$ for some function f. One motivation for nonlinearity comes from limited dependent variables such as binary outcomes, count data, and so on, and we consider some approaches to dealing with such data.

10.1   Threshold Models and Structural Change

We consider several different models that allow for different regimes to operate. These can capture structure change and regime switching, issues that some applications seem to call for.

10.1.1   Exogenous Regime Switching

Suppose that

$$y_t = \begin{cases} \alpha_1 + \beta_1 t + \varepsilon_{1t} & \text{if } t \in I_1, \\ \alpha_2 + \beta_2 t + \varepsilon_{2t} & \text{if } t \in I_2, \end{cases}$$

where I_1 is the set of time points where the first regime holds and I_2 is the set of time points where the second regime holds, while (α_1, β_1) and (α_2, β_2) are different parameter values. The shocks $\varepsilon_{1t}, \varepsilon_{2t}$ are i.i.d. with mean zero and variance σ_1^2 and σ_2^2 respectively. This is called a broken-trend or segmented-trend model, or piecewise linear, or a structural break, and in general the regression function is discontinuous. This model is firmly in the deterministic camp, since the trend itself does not interact with the shock process (although the model generally does allow for breaks in error variances). Chow (1960) and

Quandt (1960) developed tests of the null hypothesis of equality of the intercept and slope parameters in the case where the regime classification I_1 and I_2 is known. Their tests are based on what are standard regression F-statistics, and are equivalent to the likelihood ratio test under the assumption of normality on ε_t. A special case of this is the so-called hockey-stick model for global temperature popularized by Albert Gore Jr. In that case,

$$y_t = \begin{cases} \alpha + \varepsilon_{1t} & \text{if } t \le t_0, \\ \alpha + \beta(t - t_0) + \varepsilon_{2t} & \text{if } t > t_0, \end{cases}$$

where t_0 is the beginning of the warming period. This model corresponds to a continuous change rather than a discontinuous change. As an exercise you might develop and apply standard likelihood-based tests of the absence of a hockey stick.

Suppose instead that

$$\begin{cases} A_1(L)(y_t - \mu_1) = B_1(L)\varepsilon_{1t} & \text{if } t \in I_1, \\ A_2(L)(y_t - \mu_2) = B_2(L)\varepsilon_{2t} & \text{if } t \in I_2, \end{cases}$$

where ε_{jt} are i.i.d. with mean zero and variance σ_j^2, while $A_j(L)$ and $B_j(L)$ are lag polynomials of orders p_j, q_j. This is called the **threshold ARMA** model, or rather the special case of it with two regimes. This model is designed to capture changing dynamics according to specific time periods. Blanchard and Watson (1982), and the literature it inspired, allow for switching between stationary dynamics and short-lived explosive behavior with a view to catching bubbles.

In some cases it is reasonable to assume knowledge of the regimes; for example, we may assume that there is a process during recessions and a process during the rest of the time, where the timing of the recessions could be taken as the NBER scheme and assumed exogenous. More common, however, is the case where the regimes are to be estimated from the data. We next consider the case where the regime classification is unknown. The simplest model has $I_1 = \{1, \ldots, T_1\}$ and $I_2 = \{T_1 + 1, \ldots, T\}$, in which case the main difficulty is in estimating the point T_1. To make a formal analysis one usually assumes a triangular array structure such that the number of observations in regime 1, T_1, represents a fraction of the sample, that is, $T_1/T \to \pi$ for some $\pi \in (0, 1)$. In this case the process lives a positive fraction of time in each regime.

Suppose that the full parameter vector is θ and the log likelihood function of the full sample (assuming no break) is $\mathcal{L}(\theta \mid y)$, and let $\widehat{\theta}$ be the MLE. For each $\pi \in [0, 1]$, let $\mathcal{L}_1$ be the log likelihood based on data $y_{1:T_1}$, where $T_1 = \lfloor \pi T \rfloor$, and let $\widehat{\theta}_1$ be the MLE; let $\mathcal{L}_2$ be the log likelihood based on data $y_{T_1+1:T}$ and let $\widehat{\theta}_2$ be the MLE based on that data. These are recursive forward and backward windows. Then define

$$\widehat{\pi} = \arg \max_{\pi \in [0,1]} Q_T(\pi),$$

where $Q_T(\pi) = \mathcal{L}_1(\widehat{\theta}_1) + \mathcal{L}_2(\widehat{\theta}_2)$, and let $\widehat{\theta}_1 = \widehat{\theta}_1(\widehat{\pi}), \widehat{\theta}_2 = \widehat{\theta}_2(\widehat{\pi})$. Figure 10.1 shows the partition scheme.

It turns out that, provided there is a $\pi \in (0, 1)$ with $\theta_1(\pi) \neq \theta_2(\pi)$, $\widehat{\pi}$ converges to π in probability very fast. Therefore, we can assume that π is perfectly known in analyzing

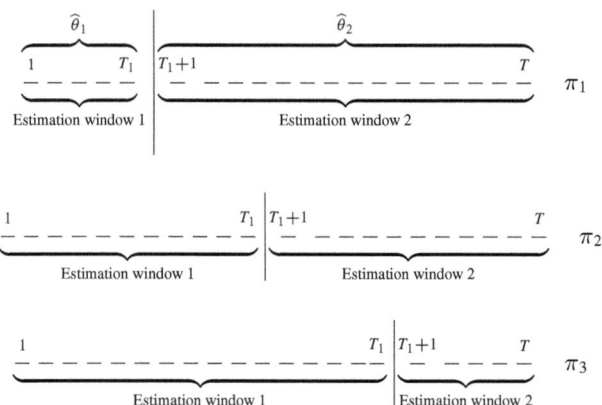

Figure 10.1 Forward and backward estimation windows.

$\theta_1(\widehat{\pi}), \theta_2(\widehat{\pi})$, that is, the usual standard errors can be used. To test the hypothesis of no structural break, one can proceed to construct the supremum Wald, LR, or LM tests

$$\sup_{\pi \in \Pi} W(\pi), \qquad \sup_{\pi \in \Pi} \mathrm{LR}(\pi), \qquad \sup_{\pi \in \Pi} \mathrm{LM}(\pi), \tag{10.2}$$

where $\mathrm{LR}(\pi)$, for example, is the (Gaussian) likelihood ratio for the test of no break versus a break at πT; here, Π is a strict compact subset of $[0, 1]$. Andrews (1993) derived the limiting distribution of these test statistics under weak conditions on the error terms. He provided tables of critical values that can be used. Subsequent work by Andrews and Ploberger (1994) provided further discussion, and Hansen (1997) provided a method to calculate p-values. Hidalgo and Seo (2013) considered the case where Π_T is a sequence of compact sets that approaches $[0, 1]$, which allows the possibility that breaks occur towards the end of the sample (or towards the beginning of the sample).

Perron (1989) considered the null hypothesis that a time series has a unit root with possibly nonzero drift against the alternative that the process is "trend-stationary." He allowed for the presence of a one-time change in the level or in the slope of the trend function, and showed that standard tests of the unit root hypothesis against trend-stationary alternatives cannot reject the unit root hypothesis if the true data-generating mechanism is that of stationary fluctuations around a trend function which contains a one-time break. He derived test statistics that distinguish between the two hypotheses when a break is present and its temporal location is known. He applied these tests to the Nelson and Plosser (1982) dataset, and to the postwar quarterly real GNP series. In the former series, the break is due to the 1929 crash and takes the form of a sudden change in the level of the series. For 11 out of the 14 series analyzed by Nelson and Plosser he rejected at a high confidence level the unit root hypothesis. In the case of the postwar quarterly real GNP series, the break in the trend function occurs at the time of the oil price shock (1973) and takes the form of a change in the slope. Here again one can reject the null hypothesis of a unit root. If one is ready to postulate that the 1929 crash and the slowdown in growth after 1973 are not realizations of an underlying time-invariant stochastic process but can be modeled as exogenous, then the conclusion is that most macroeconomic time series are not characterized by the presence of a unit root. Fluctuations are indeed stationary around a deterministic trend function. The only "shocks" that have had persistent effects are the 1929 crash and the 1973 oil price shock.

More generally, we may have a model

$$y_t = \alpha + \phi y_{t-1} + (\gamma + \delta D_t) z_t + \beta^\mathsf{T} x_t + \varepsilon_t, \qquad D_t = 1(\theta_t > \theta^*),$$

where z_t, x_t, θ_t are observed variables, while α, ϕ, γ, δ, and β are unknown parameters. If θ^* is unknown, then one can estimate it by profiled least squares provided the error terms are serially uncorrelated. Otherwise, an instrumental-variable procedure may be used to estimate α, ϕ, γ, δ, and β conditional on θ^* and then search over this parameter.

10.1.2 Markov Switching and SETAR Models

Suppose that

$$y_t = \begin{cases} \alpha_1 + \phi_1 y_{t-1} + \varepsilon_t & \text{if } y_{t-1} > c, \\ \alpha_2 + \phi_2 y_{t-1} + \varepsilon_t & \text{if } y_{t-1} < c \end{cases}$$
$$= s_t(\alpha_1 + \phi_1 y_{t-1}) + (1 - s_t)(\alpha_2 + \phi_2 y_{t-1}) + \varepsilon_t,$$

where the threshold point c is unknown and $s_t = 1(y_{t-1} > c)$. One question here is whether the process y_t is stationary. Provided $|\phi_j| < 1$, $j = 1, 2$, each regime-specific process is stationary and so it seems reasonable to expect that y_t may be stationary. In fact, Petruccelli and Woolford (1984) showed, in the case where $\alpha_1 = \alpha_2 = c = 0$, that the process y_t is stationary provided $\phi_1 < 1$, $\phi_2 < 1$, and $\phi_1 \phi_2 < 1$. For example, the point $\phi_1 = 0.99$ and $\phi_2 = -3$ is in the stationarity region of the threshold process even though the second regime is explosive.

Let $\theta = (\alpha_1, \phi_1, \alpha_2, \phi_2)^\mathsf{T}$ denote the unknown regime-specific parameters. One can estimate the threshold parameter c by profiling. That is, for a given c, regress y_t on $x_t(c) = s_t(c), s_t(c)y_{t-1}, 1 - s_t(c), (1 - s_t(c))y_{t-1}$, and let $\widehat{\theta}(c)$ be the 4×1 vector of parameter estimates. Then let $\widehat{c}$ satisfy

$$\widehat{c} = \arg\min_c \sum_{t=2}^{T} \left(y_t - \widehat{\theta}(c)^\mathsf{T} x_t(c)\right)^2,$$

and let $\widehat{\theta} = \widehat{\theta}(\widehat{c})$. This latter minimization is over a scalar parameter and can be accomplished by grid search; note that the objective function here is not continuous in c so that grid search is strongly advised over gradient-based methods.

An alternative class of processes makes the regime switching stochastic and possibly endogenous. Specifically, suppose there is an unobserved binary stochastic process s_t such that if $s_t = 1$ then regime 1 operates, and suppose that $y_t \sim N(\mu_\mathrm{H}, \sigma_\mathrm{H}^2)$, whereas if $s_t = 0$ then regime 2 operates and $y_t \sim N(\mu_\mathrm{L}, \sigma_\mathrm{L}^2)$. For example, suppose that s_t is i.i.d. with probability π associated with regime 1. Then

$$\Pr(y_t \leq y \mid y_{t-1})$$
$$= \Pr(s_t = 1) \Pr(y_t \leq y \mid y_{t-1}, s_t = 1) + \Pr(s_t = 0) \Pr(y_t \leq y \mid y_{t-1}, s_t = 0)$$
$$= \pi \Pr(y_t \leq y \mid y_{t-1}, s_t = 1) + (1 - \pi) \Pr(y_t \leq y \mid y_{t-1}, s_t = 0).$$

Furthermore,

$$f_y(y_t) = \pi \frac{1}{\sqrt{2\pi\sigma_H^2}} \exp\left(-\frac{1}{2\sigma_H^2}(y_t - \mu_H)^2\right)$$
$$+ (1 - \pi)\frac{1}{\sqrt{2\pi\sigma_L^2}} \exp\left(-\frac{1}{2\sigma_L^2}(y_t - \mu_L)^2\right),$$

which is a normal mixture distribution. Meijer and Ypma (2008) proved that the parameter vector $\theta = (\pi, \mu_H, \sigma_H^2, \mu_L, \sigma_L^2)^\mathsf{T}$ is locally identified provided π is strictly between 0 and 1, and either $\mu_H \neq \mu_L$ or $\sigma_H^2 \neq \sigma_L^2$.

Hamilton (1989) considered the more general class of Markov switching models where s_t is a Markov process such that

$$\pi_{ij} = \Pr(s_t = i \mid s_{t-i} = j), \quad i, j \in \{0, 1\}.$$

Since $s_1, \ldots, s_T$ is not observed, we have to average over the joint distribution of $s_1, \ldots, s_T$, which is supported on $\{0, 1\}^T$. We use the Markov property to write

$$p(s_1, \ldots, s_T) = p(s_T \mid s_{T-1}, \ldots, s_1) \times p(s_{T-1} \mid s_{T-2}, \ldots, s_1) \times \cdots \times p(s_1)$$
$$= p(s_T \mid s_{T-1}) \times p(s_{T-1} \mid s_{T-2}) \times \cdots \times p(s_1) = \prod_{t=2}^{T} \pi_{t|t-1} \times \pi_1,$$

which is just a function of $\pi = (\pi_{00}, \pi_{01}, \pi_{10})^\mathsf{T}$, since $\pi_{11} = 1 - \pi_{00} - \pi_{01} - \pi_{10}$. It is of the form $\pi_{00}^{n_{00}} \times \pi_{01}^{n_{01}} \times \pi_{10}^{n_{10}} \times \pi_{11}^{n_{11}}$, where n_{ij} is the number of observations in the corresponding category. Since we do not observe $s_1, \ldots, s_T$ we have to average over all possible configurations to give the likelihood of the observed data $\{y_1, \ldots, y_T\}$ as

$$f(y_1, \ldots, y_T) = \sum_{s_1, \ldots, s_T \in \{0,1\}} f(y_1, \ldots, y_T \mid s_1, \ldots, s_T) p(s_1, \ldots, s_T),$$

where $f(y_1, \ldots, y_T \mid s_1, \ldots, s_T)$ is the conditional density of $\{y_1, \ldots, y_T\}$ given $\{s_1, \ldots, s_T\}$. This could be a quite general likelihood depending on the unknown parameters θ; in the special case we consider above, $f(y_T, \ldots, y_1 \mid s_T, \ldots, s_1)$ is a product of independent normal random variables with means and variances given by whether the state $s_t = 1$ or $s_t = 0$. In general, $f(y_1, \ldots, y_T)$ depends on parameters θ and π, which can be obtained by maximizing f or $\log f$. However, this is computationally impossible in general because the number of atoms in distribution p is 2^T, which is just too large for any typical T encountered in practice. Instead, a set of recursive Kalman filter type equations are built up that allow the estimation of unknown parameters by MLE.

10.1.3 Application

We investigate a simple trend break model for the quarterly log of US GDP 1947–2023 (with four quarters offset at beginning and end). We first show the log likelihood as a function of breakpoint in Figure 10.2, which shows this increases to a peak around 1980 and stays flat until 2000 when it declines; the maximum of this objective function occurs at 1980Q1. The backward slope at this point is 0.017 46 and the forward slope is 0.012 01. The forward and backward slopes in Figure 10.3 show some variation, especially at the

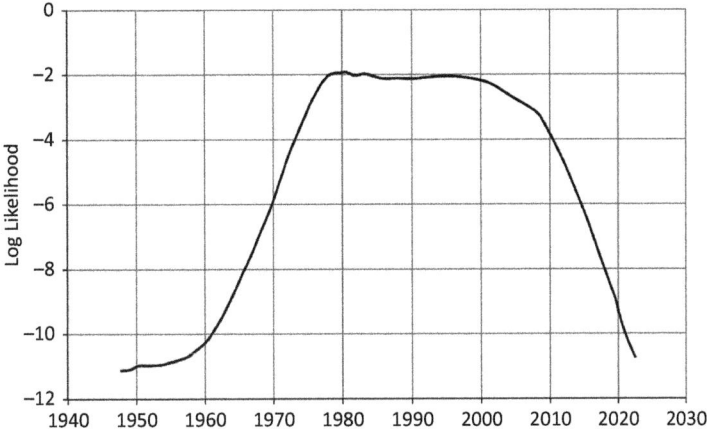

Figure 10.2 Log likelihood of trend break model for quarterly log of US GDP, 1947–2023/3.

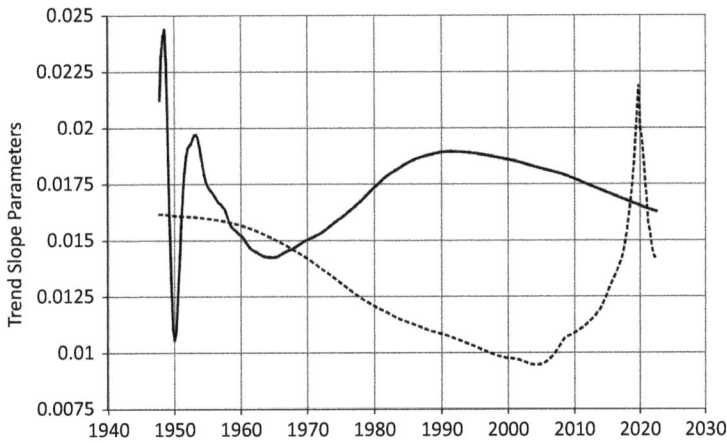

Figure 10.3 Forward and backward trend slope estimates. The solid line is estimated based on sample $y_{1:T_1}$ and the dashed line on sample $y_{T_1+1:T}$.

beginnings of the corresponding samples, due to the low effective sample size. The an alysis concludes that trend growth has declined and 1980Q1 is the most likely point of change of this sort. Figure 10.4 shows the final trend break model along with the data. Similar results have been found for other Western countries, with big falls in growth rates following the oil shocks of the 1970s and 1980s.

The next example is UK daily FTSE stock prices from 1984 to 2021. We fit AR(1) and MA(1) processes to the stock returns and test for a break in the dynamic parameters. In both cases, the strongest evidence of a break occurs at the end of the 1990s, although there appear to be multiple other local peaks; see Figures 10.5 and 10.7. Looking backward from this time there appeared to be strong momentum in the stock return series, whereas looking forward there appeared to be reversal features. The forward and backward parameter estimates are shown in Figures 10.6 and 10.8.

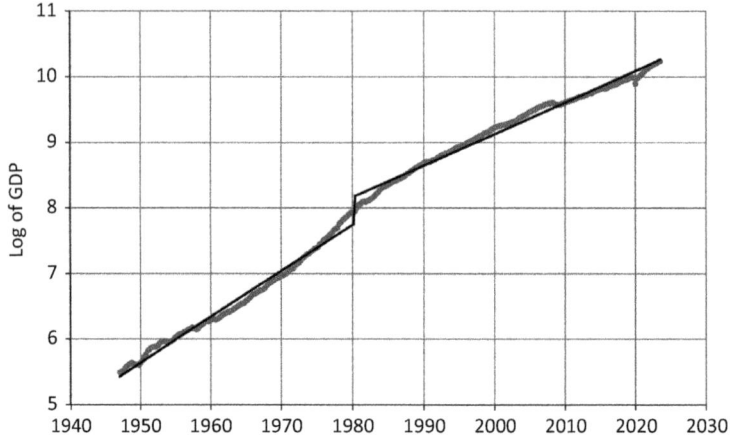

Figure 10.4 Time series plot of GDP along with broken trend model, with break in 1980Q1.

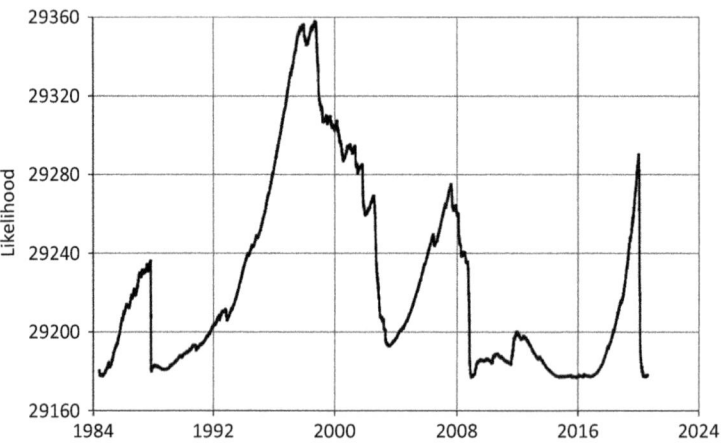

Figure 10.5 FTSE 100 daily stock returns, threshold AR(1) process. Likelihood of break point.

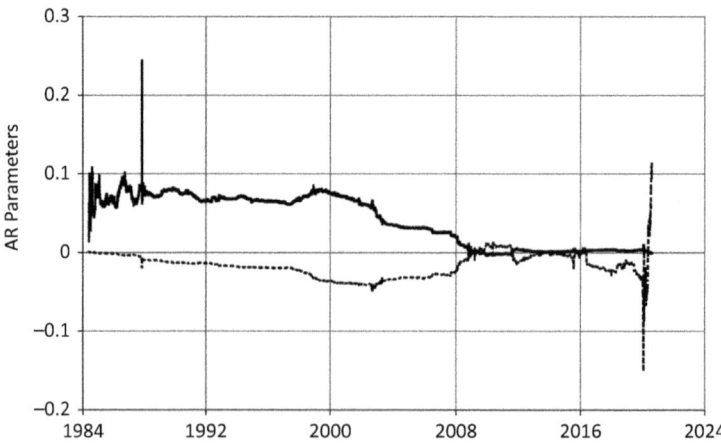

Figure 10.6 Forward and backward AR(1) fits to stock return. The solid line is sample $y_{1:T_1}$ and the dashed line is sample $y_{T_1+1:T}$.

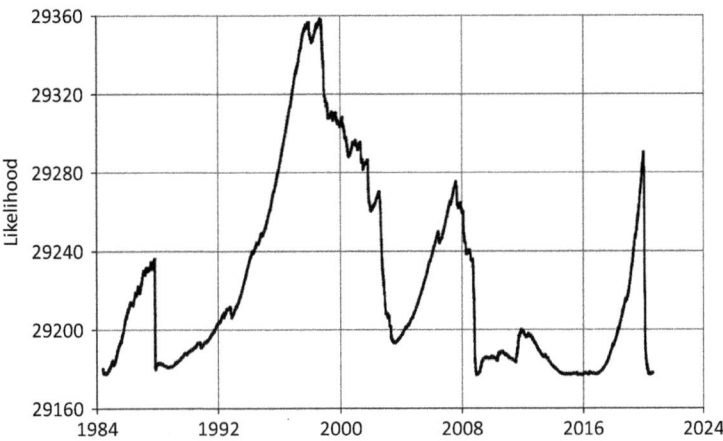

Figure 10.7 FTSE 100 daily stock returns, switching MA process. Likelihood of break point.

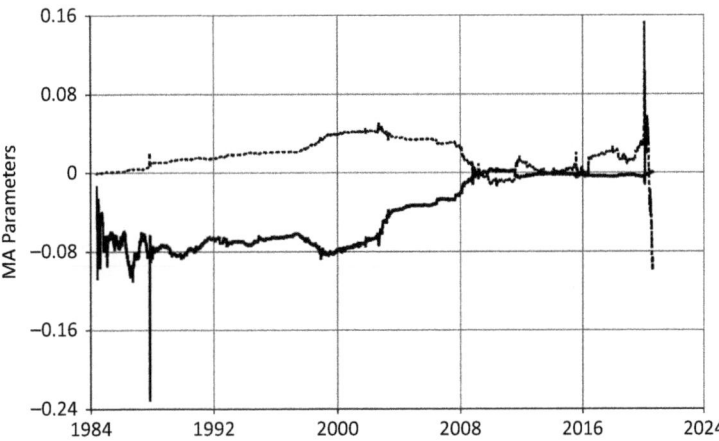

Figure 10.8 Forward and backward sample MA(1) fits to stock return. The solid line is sample $y_{1:T_1}$ and the dashed line is sample $y_{T_1+1:T}$.

10.2   Nonlinear Chaotic Processes

Suppose that $y_{t+1} = f(y_t), f(y) = \theta y(1-y)$, with $y_0 \in (0,1)$ and $\theta \in (0,4]$. This process is nonstochastic, there is no error term! However, it can behave in a way that makes it hard to distinguish from a stochastic process. For some values of θ, the sequence y_t converges to a fixed point. For other values of θ, the sequence y_t is periodic. And for other values of θ, the sequence y_t is crazy or chaotic; see the movie *Jurassic Park* for an introduction to chaos theory. We show the time series plot of $\Phi^{-1}(y_t)$ (adjusted to have mean zero and variance one in sample) against time in Figure 10.9, when y_0 was a randomly chosen number on $[0,1]$ and $\theta = 4$. This can be compared with Gaussian white noise in Figure 10.10.

The Lyapunov exponent is defined as the following limit, if it exists:

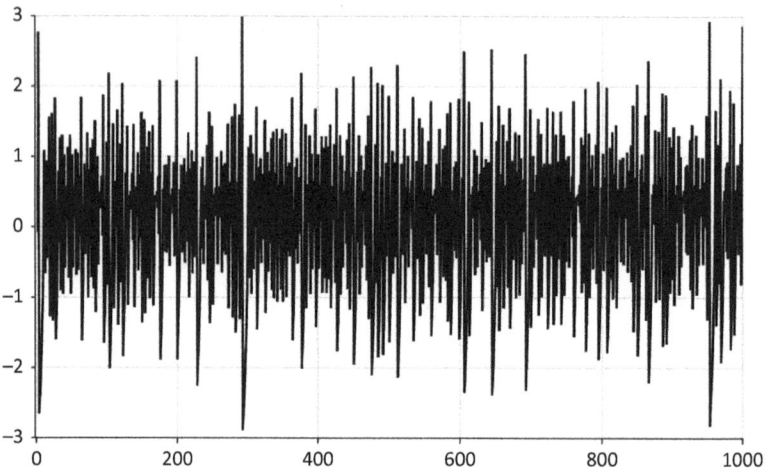

Figure 10.9 Time series of transformed chaotic map.

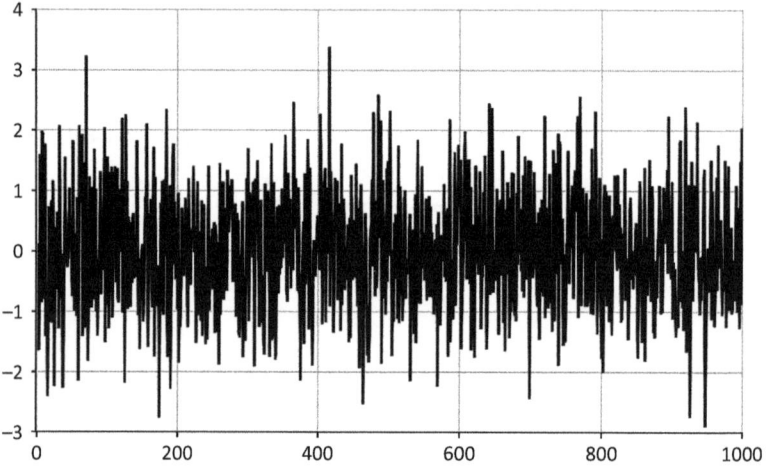

Figure 10.10 Time series of Gaussian white noise.

$$\lambda(y_0) = \lim_{T \to \infty} \frac{1}{T} \sum_{t=1}^{T} \log\left(|f'(y_t)|\right). \tag{10.3}$$

If $\lambda > 0$, the process is said to be globally stable but locally explosive. Specifically, the logistic map has sensitivity to initial conditions for some values of θ, for example $\theta = 4$. This is called the butterfly effect, which is derived from the metaphorical example of the details of a tornado (the exact time of formation, the exact path taken) being influenced by minor perturbations such as a distant butterfly flapping its wings several weeks earlier. Formally, there exists a $\delta > 0$ such that, for all $y_0 \in (0,1)$ and any set $J \subset (0,1)$ containing y_0, there exists $y_0' \in J$ and $n > 0$ such that $|f^n(y_0) - f^n(y_0')| > \delta$. There are many applications of chaotic dynamic processes in weather modelling and in economics (Baumol and Benhabib, 1989; Brock and Hommes, 1997).

It can be shown that (for $\theta = 4$) the process is ergodic, that is, for any integrable function $g(\cdot)$, the time average and space average exist and are equal. In particular, the ergodic density takes the form

$$h(x) = \frac{1}{\pi\sqrt{x(1-x)}}.$$

This means that if the initial condition y_0 is chosen from the density h, then y_t will have that density too for all t. If y_0 is randomly chosen from some other density, eventually, for large enough t, y_t will approximately follow the density h. This density is positive throughout $(0, 1)$ and infinite at both boundary points 0 and 1. Plots of the series on $[0, 1]$ show it hitting the boundary often, which is clear from the form of the density. This process is also mixing in the sense that for each pair of open sets $A, B \subset (0, 1)$ there exists an n_0 such that, for $n > n_0, f^n(A) \cap B \neq \varnothing$. For example, if we take disjoint sets like $A = (0, 1/2)$ and $B = (1/2, 1)$, this means that eventually the image of A under the mapping f intersects with B. This class of models is discussed further in Tong (1990).

We may embed this model into a wider class of models. Specifically, suppose that

$$y_t = \theta y_{t-1}(1 - y_{t-1}) + \varepsilon_t,$$

where ε_t is an independent sequence of random variables that are superimposed on the so-called skeleton $\theta y_{t-1}(1 - y_{t-1})$. Provided ε_t is supported on $S_t = [-\theta y_{t-1}(1 - y_{t-1}), 1 - \theta y_{t-1}(1 - y_{t-1})]$, the process y_t is confined to live on $[0, 1]$ provided $y_0 \in [0, 1]$. Whang and Linton (1999) developed some econometric methodology for estimating Lyapunov exponents for stochastic systems with potentially chaotic skeletons.

10.3   GARCH Models

We next consider a class of discrete time series models developed primarily to capture the notion of time-varying volatility for financial asset returns. The key properties of stock returns and asset returns generally are that:

- Marginal distributions of stock returns are leptokurtic.
- The scale of stock returns does not appear to be constant over time.
- Stock returns are almost uncorrelated but dependent. Highly volatile periods tend to cluster together.

In Figure 10.11 we show the correlogram of the S&P500 stock index daily return series from 1950 to 2017, along with the correlogram of the absolute value of this return. This shows the strong positive dependence in the absolute values of returns.

Linear models cannot capture all these phenomena well. Specifically, suppose, for summable weights ($\sum_{i=0}^{\infty} |a_i| < \infty$), $y_t = \sum_{i=0}^{\infty} a_i \varepsilon_{t-i}$, where ε_s is i.i.d. with mean zero and finite variance σ_ε^2. The linear process has conditional mean $E(y_t \mid y_{t-1}, y_{t-2}, \ldots) = \sum_{i=1}^{\infty} b_i y_{t-i}$ for some coefficients b_i (under an invertibility condition, see Chapter 3). However, the model implies constant conditional variance $\text{var}(y_t \mid y_{t-1}, y_{t-2}, \ldots) = \sigma_\varepsilon^2 a_0^2$, which is restrictive and does not capture salient features of many financial data. Furthermore, if ε_t is Gaussian, then y_t is a Gaussian process.

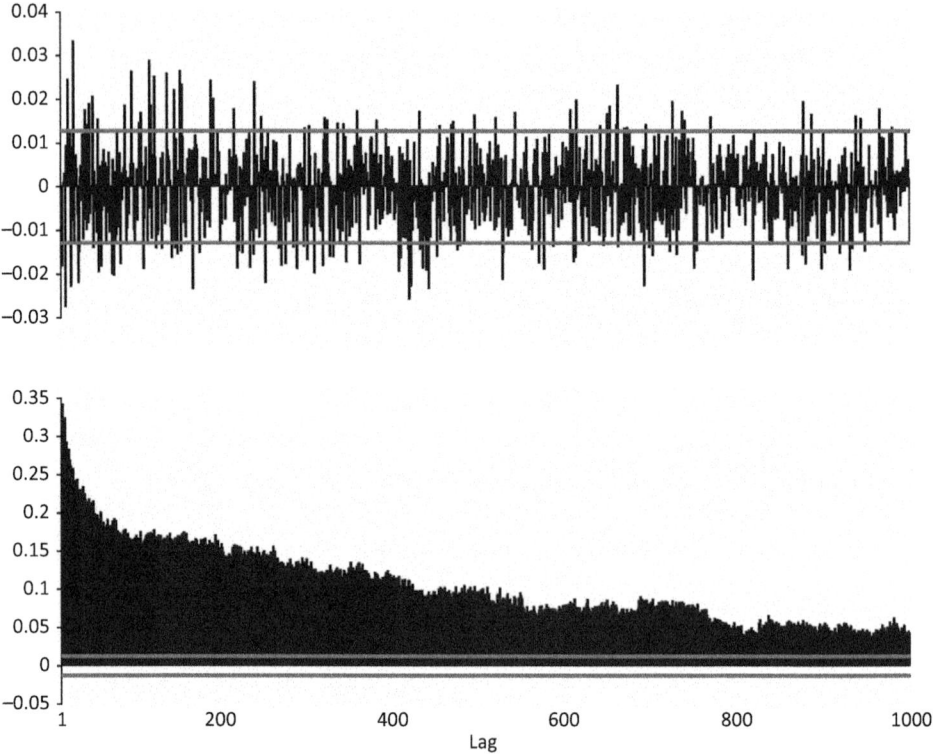

Figure 10.11 ACF of the daily S&P500 returns and of the absolute value of returns out to 1000 lags.

10.3.1 The GARCH Model

The breakthrough model for financial volatility was Engle's (1982) autoregressive conditional heteroskedasticity (ARCH) model, subsequently generalized by Bollerslev (1986) to the generalized autoregressive conditional heteroskedasticity (GARCH) model. Let $\mathcal{F}_t = \{y_t, y_{t-1}, \ldots\}$ be currently available information, and let

$$\mu_t = E(y_t \mid \mathcal{F}_{t-1}), \qquad \sigma_t^2 = \mathrm{var}(y_t \mid \mathcal{F}_{t-1}). \tag{10.4}$$

We first assume for simplicity that $\mu_t = 0$, so the question is only about modelling the conditional variance σ_t^2. The GARCH model specifies this as a dynamic equation.

Definition 10.1 (GARCH(p, q))   For all t,

$$\sigma_t^2 = \omega + \beta(L)\sigma_t^2 + \gamma(L)y_t^2, \tag{10.5}$$

where $\beta(L) = \sum_{k=1}^{p} \beta_k L^k$ and $\gamma(L) = \sum_{j=1}^{q} \gamma_j L^j$. The special case with $\beta_1, \ldots, \beta_p = 0$ is called the ARCH(q) process.

The conditional variance depends linearly on past squared values of observed variables and on past values of σ_t^2. The parameters $\omega, \beta_1, \ldots, \beta_p, \gamma_1, \ldots, \gamma_q$ determine the properties of the process. Provided $\omega > 0$ and $\gamma_j, \beta_k \geq 0$, then $\sigma_t^2 > 0$ with probability one (this seems like a minimal requirement for a model of volatility); these are sufficient but not necessary conditions. Nelson and Cao (1992) worked out the necessary and sufficient conditions for the general GARCH(p, q) model. For example, in the GARCH(1,2) model they showed that the sufficient conditions are $\beta, \gamma_1 \geq 0$ and $\beta\gamma_1 + \gamma_2 \geq 0$. This allows $\gamma_2 < 0$ provided the other parameters compensate. To some extent this just makes life more complicated because writing down these inequalities that characterize the positivity region is very tedious; to impose this in estimation is challenging, to say the least.

As usual with dynamic processes, there is a question about the initial condition. There are two general approaches to this. A convenient mathematical approach is to assume that the process started in the infinite past, that is, $t = 0, \pm 1, \ldots$, in which case we do not need to specify the initial condition. This approach requires stationarity. With this assumption many calculations are easy and simple to state. An alternative approach is to specify some initial condition $\sigma_1^2 > 0$, and then to define the process from this starting point. This approach is well suited to the case where the process is nonstationary.

Suppose also that

$$y_t = \varepsilon_t \sigma_t \tag{10.6}$$

with ε_t i.i.d. with mean zero and variance one. Then (10.5) and (10.6), along with the initial condition, provide a complete specification of the GARCH(p, q) process.

10.3.2 Weak Stationarity

We next consider the question of stationarity, that is, whether under this definition y_t is a stationary process and if so, what its stationary variance is. The process y_t is an MDS since σ_t only depends on the past, so its mean and autocovariances are identically zero. Suppose that $\mathrm{var}(y_t) < \infty$, and this does not change with time so is denoted by σ^2. Then it must satisfy

$$\sigma^2 = E(\sigma_t^2) = \omega + \sum_{k=1}^{p} \beta_k \sigma^2 + \sum_{j=1}^{q} \gamma_j E(y_{t-j}^2) = \omega + \sigma^2 \left(\sum_{k=1}^{p} \beta_k + \sum_{j=1}^{q} \gamma_j \right),$$

and we have that the process y_t is weakly stationary and has finite unconditional variance

$$\sigma^2 = \mathrm{var}(y_t) = E(\sigma_t^2) = \frac{\omega}{1 - \sum_{k=1}^{p} \beta_k - \sum_{j=1}^{q} \gamma_j},$$

provided $\sum_{k=1}^{p} \beta_k + \sum_{j=1}^{q} \gamma_j < 1$.

We consider below the distinction between weak and strong stationarity, which is a key issue for this class of models.

10.3.3 Marginal Distribution of y_t

We next ask about the marginal distribution of the series y_t. The general finding is that y_t will be **heavy tailed** even if the innovation ε_t in (10.6) is standard normal. Suppose that ε_t is standard normal, then its excess kurtosis $\kappa_4(\varepsilon) = E\left(\varepsilon_t^4\right)/3E^2\left(\varepsilon_t^2\right) - 3 = 0$. Note that for any random variable $\kappa_4 \geq -3$.

Theorem 10.1 *Suppose that the process y_t is a GARCH(1,1) process that is weakly stationary and possesses finite (time-invariant) fourth moments, and let $\kappa_4(\varepsilon)$ be the excess kurtosis of the shock process. Then, provided $1 - (3 + \kappa_4(\varepsilon))\gamma^2 > 0$, the excess kurtosis of y_t is finite and*

$$\kappa_4(y) = \frac{6\gamma^2 + \kappa_4(\varepsilon)(1 - \beta^2 + 2\gamma^2 - 2\beta\gamma)}{1 - 2\gamma^2 - (\beta + \gamma)^2 - \gamma^2\kappa_4(\varepsilon)}. \tag{10.7}$$

In the Gaussian shock case $\kappa_4(\varepsilon) = 0$ and the formula simplifies somewhat; in that case, $\kappa_4(y) = 6\gamma^2/(1 - 2\gamma^2 - (\beta + \gamma)^2) \geq 0$ and increases with γ; for $\gamma = 1/2$ and $\beta = 0$ we have $\kappa_4(y) = 6$. Even for quite modest values of γ, the implied distribution of y_t is quite leptokurtic, which is consistent with a lot of evidence about daily stock returns, for example. In the Gaussian shock case, if $\beta = 0$ and $\gamma \geq 1/3^{1/2}$, then $E(y_t^4) = \infty$. The existence of moments is important for the interpretation of the sample correlogram of y_t and y_t^2, and inference about these quantities. Some authors have argued that this restriction on γ is too strong, since we expect $E(y_t^4) < \infty$ more or less and we might expect γ to be large. See He and Teräsvirta (1999) for more general results.

10.3.4 Dependence Property

The next task is to understand the dependence embodied in the ARCH process. We write

$$\sigma_t^2 = \omega + \beta(L)\sigma_t^2 + \gamma(L)\sigma_t^2\varepsilon_t^2 = \omega + (\beta(L) + \gamma(L))\,\sigma_t^2 + \gamma(L)\eta_t,$$

where $\eta_t = y_t^2 - \sigma_t^2 = \sigma_t^2(\varepsilon_t^2 - 1)$ is a mean-zero innovation uncorrelated with its past, albeit heteroskedastic, that is, η_t is an MDS. In the GARCH(1,1) special case σ_t^2 is an AR(1) process with dynamic parameter $\beta + \gamma$. More generally, it is an ARMA process. We also have $\sigma_t^2 = y_t^2 - \eta_t$, and so

$$\begin{aligned}
y_t^2 = \sigma_t^2\varepsilon_t^2 = \sigma_t^2 + \eta_t &= (\beta(L) + \gamma(L))\,\sigma_t^2 + \gamma(L)\eta_t + \eta_t \\
&= (\beta(L) + \gamma(L))\,y_t^2 - (\beta(L) + \gamma(L))\,\eta_t + \gamma(L)\eta_t + \eta_t \\
&= (\beta(L) + \gamma(L))\,y_t^2 - \beta(L)\eta_t + \eta_t.
\end{aligned}$$

Therefore, in terms of its second-order properties y_t^2 is an ARMA process; it will have an MA(∞) representation in terms of the not-i.i.d. shocks η_t. We have $\mathrm{cov}(y_t^2, y_{t-k}^2) \leq c\,(\beta + \gamma)^{k-1}$. Therefore, provided $\beta + \gamma < 1$ (plus the restrictions needed for the fourth moments to be bounded), the covariance function of y_t^2 decays exponentially fast. Both y_t^2 and σ_t^2 are positively dependent in this case at all lags. This model generates **volatility clustering**, whereby volatile periods tend to be followed by volatile periods and quiet periods tend to be followed by quiet periods. The process y_t itself is nonlinear because we cannot write it as a weighted sum of i.i.d. shocks.

Mikosch and Stărică (2000) argued that the covariance function (of y_t) is not so useful for the GARCH type of processes, because the theory for sample autocovariance functions typically requires moments of fourth order to exist. Instead, one may consider mixing measures of dependence such as strong mixing or β-mixing.

Theorem 10.2 (Carrasco and Chen, 2002, Corollary 6)   *Suppose that ε_t is a sequence of i.i.d. real-valued random variables with mean zero and variance one. Suppose that ε_t has a continuous density (with respect to the Lebesgue measure on the real line), and its density is positive on $\mathbb{R}$. Then, a sufficient condition for the GARCH(1,1) process y_t to be β-mixing with exponential decay, that is, for some $\phi < 1$, $\beta(k) \leq c\rho^k$ for all k, is that the process is weakly stationary, that is, $\beta + \gamma < 1$.*

Actually, it has been shown that the IGARCH process (see Definition 10.3) is also mixing with exponential decay under some mild additional conditions (Meitz and Saikonnen, 2008), so that the dependence property is not coupled with the moment existence (i.e., the weak stationarity condition).

For the purposes of understanding and for the derivation of properties like stationarity it is convenient to assume that ε_t is i.i.d. But for other purposes, such as for estimation, one often only requires conditional moment specifications, that is, we might not require the innovation to be i.i.d. Drost and Nijman (1993) proposed a classification of GARCH models according to the properties of the innovation ε_t. The so-called strong GARCH is where ε_t is i.i.d. with $E(\varepsilon_t) = 0$ and $E(\varepsilon_t^2) = 1$. This is a full model specification and useful for deriving properties like stationarity and mixing. It restricts all conditional cumulants of y_t given past information $\mathcal{F}_{t-1}$ to be constant, and indeed to be the cumulants of ε_t. That is, $\kappa_j(y_t \mid \mathcal{F}_{t-1}) = \kappa_j(\varepsilon_t)$ for all j for which this is well defined. The so-called semi-strong GARCH is where ε_t satisfies $E(\varepsilon_t \mid \mathcal{F}_{t-1}) = 0$ and $E(\varepsilon_t^2 \mid \mathcal{F}_{t-1}) = 1$. This is not a full model specification. Under this condition it follows that $E(y_t \mid \mathcal{F}_{t-1}) = 0$ and $E(y_t^2 \mid \mathcal{F}_{t-1}) = \sigma_t^2$, that is, the quantity σ_t^2 is truly the conditional variance. However, this specification does not restrict, for example, the third and fourth conditional cumulants of the y_t process; the process y_t could have an asymmetric and heavy-tailed distribution, which could vary over time. For example, $E\left(y_t^4 \mid \mathcal{F}_{t-1}\right) = E\left(\varepsilon_t^4 \mid \mathcal{F}_{t-1}\right)\sigma_t^4$, and so the excess conditional kurtosis satisfies $\kappa_4(y_t \mid \mathcal{F}_{t-1}) = E\left(\varepsilon_t^4 \mid \mathcal{F}_{t-1}\right) - 3 = \kappa_4(\varepsilon_t \mid \mathcal{F}_{t-1})$, which may vary over time. In practice, this can be important.

Under some conditions we can represent GARCH(p, q) processes as an infinite sum.

Definition 10.2 (ARCH(∞) model)   Suppose that

$$y_t = \sigma_t\varepsilon_t, \qquad \sigma_t^2 = \psi_0 + \sum_{j=1}^{\infty} \psi_j y_{t-j}^2, \tag{10.8}$$

where ψ_j satisfy $\sum_{j=1}^{\infty} |\psi_j| < \infty$, while ε_t is i.i.d. with mean zero and variance one.

The GARCH(p, q) model is the special case of (10.8) where ψ_j depend only on the β, γ, and ω parameters. In the GARCH(1,1) process it is easy to see (assuming an infinite past) that (10.8) holds with $\psi_0 = \omega/(1 - \beta)$ and $\psi_j = \gamma\beta^{j-1}, j = 1, 2, \ldots$, where the sum is well defined provided that $0 \leq \beta < 1$.

In practice, estimated parameters often lie close to the boundary of the weakly stationary region. In Table 10.1 we show estimates of the GARCH(1,1) model for daily S&P500 stock index return series from 1950–2018. The computations were carried out in EViews.

We show in Figure 10.12 the conditional standard deviation for the daily series, which shows the peak value in October 1987. In Figure 10.13 we show the standardized residuals

Table 10.1 GARCH(1,1) parameter estimates.

	Daily	Weekly	Monthly
ϕ_1	0.0893 (0.008 07)	0.002 871 (0.021 709)	0.020 311 (0.049 513)
ϕ_2	−0.0253 (0.007 84)	0.032 247 (0.022 462)	−0.058 747 (0.045 839)
ω	8.55×10^{-7} (6.57×10^{-8})	1.14×10^{-5} (2.50×10^{-6})	0.000 103 (4.63×10^{-5})
β	0.9094 (0.002 37)	0.845 708 (0.014 920)	0.870 139 (0.040 540)
γ	0.082 93 (0.001 86)	0.131 007 (0.012 950)	0.074 298 (0.027 528)

Note: Standard errors in parentheses. These estimates are for the raw data series and refer to the AR(2)-GARCH(1,1) model

$$y_t = c + \phi_1 y_{t-1} + \phi_2 y_{t-2} + \underbrace{\varepsilon_t \sigma_t}_{u_t}, \qquad \sigma_t^2 = \omega + \beta \sigma_{t-1}^2 + \gamma u_{t-1}^2.$$

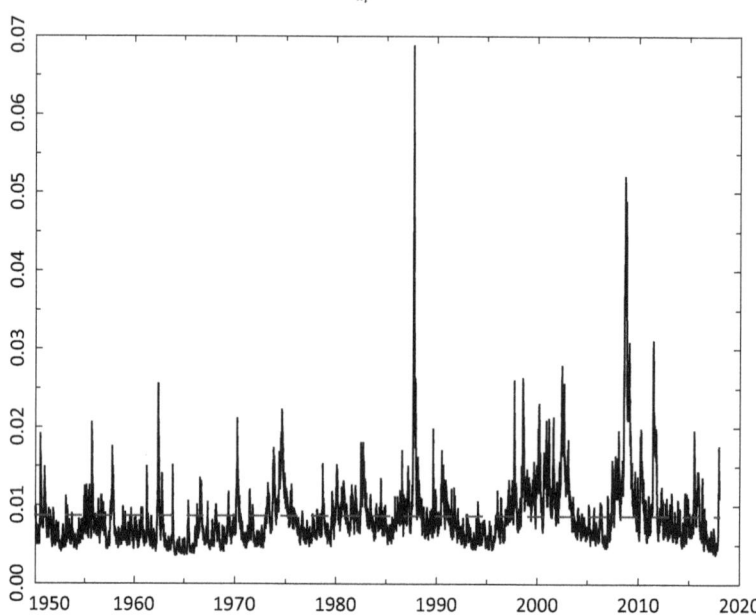

Figure 10.12 Conditional standard deviation of daily returns of S&P500 daily returns.

$\widehat{\varepsilon}_t$ from the estimated model. This shows that the model has reduced the maximum achieved negative value from −21 to around −11. Although this is a big reduction, it is still hard to rationalize within a normal distribution, since such values would be extremely unlikely to occur.

Bampinas, Ladopoulos, and Panagiotidis (2018) estimated a constant-mean GARCH (1,1) using daily data from January 2008 to December 2011 for all the constituents of the S&P1500. They found mean values for $\beta = 0.878$ and $\gamma = 0.114$ with cross-sectional standard deviations of 0.079 and 0.056 respectively, suggesting that there is quite a variation across smaller stocks in the values taken by these two key parameters, but nevertheless $\beta + \gamma$ is often quite close to one.

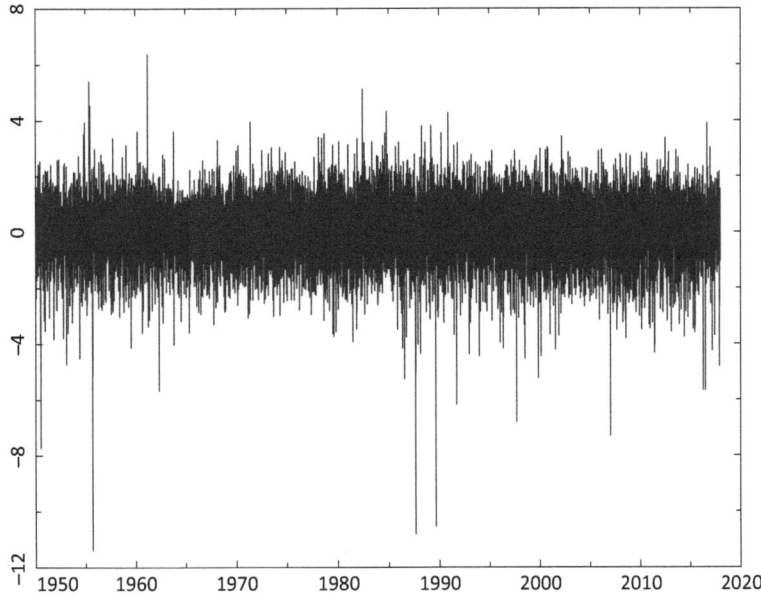

Figure 10.13 Standardized residuals of S&P500 daily returns.

We next discuss a special case of the GARCH process where the weak stationarity condition fails.

Definition 10.3   The IGARCH(1,1) model satisfies $\beta + \gamma = 1$, that is, for $\beta \in (0,1)$ with arbitrary initialization,

$$\sigma_t^2 = \omega + \beta\sigma_{t-1}^2 + (1 - \beta)y_{t-1}^2.$$

This violates the conditions for weak stationarity, and it is not asymptotically weakly stationary either. In this case the unconditional variance of y_t is infinite and the conditional variance converges to infinity with the time horizon. However, the process y_t itself can still be a strongly stationary process as we discuss more formally below. We can also show that y_t is weakly dependent (mixing) in this case (in contrast to the unit root case for linear time series). Note the difference between conditional variance and unconditional variance. One implication of the lack of an unconditional variance is that

$$\frac{1}{\sqrt{T}} \sum_{t=1}^{T} (y_t - E(y_t)) \tag{10.9}$$

does not obey a CLT, and so many standard tests based on the sample mean or correlogram are not valid. However, for any function λ such that $E(\lambda(y_t)^2) \leq C < \infty$ we have the CLT

$$\frac{1}{\sqrt{T}} \sum_{t=1}^{T} (\lambda(y_t) - E(\lambda(y_t))) \implies N(0, V), \tag{10.10}$$

where V is some finite variance (under Herrndorf's conditions). There are many robust statistics such as the quantilogram that work with bounded functions of the data and so obey CLTs under these conditions. We close with a special case of the IGARCH model (with no intercept) that has some special properties.

Example 10.1   A special case of the IGARCH model is called the **RiskMetrics** model (also known as the EWMA for variance). Suppose that $y_t = \sigma_t \varepsilon_t$, $\sigma_t^2 = \beta \sigma_{t-1}^2 + (1-\beta) y_{t-1}^2$, which is an IGARCH process but with no intercept. We can also write this as

$$\sigma_t^2 = \sigma_{t-1}^2 \left(\beta + (1-\beta) \varepsilon_{t-1}^2 \right),$$

so that $\log(\sigma_t^2)$ is a random walk with i.i.d. innovations, that is,

$$\log(\sigma_t^2) = \log(\sigma_{t-1}^2) + \eta_{t-1}, \qquad \eta_{t-1} = \log(\beta + (1-\beta)\varepsilon_{t-1}^2).$$

The properties of this process depend on the expectation of η_{t-1}. Specifically:

(i) If $E(\eta_{t-1}) > 0$, then $\log(\sigma_t^2)$ is a random walk with positive drift and so $\sigma_t^2 \to \infty$ with probability one.

(ii) If $E(\eta_{t-1}) < 0$, then $\log(\sigma_t^2)$ is a random walk with negative drift and so $\sigma_t^2 \to 0$ with probability one.

(iii) If $E(\eta_{t-1}) = 0$, then $\log(\sigma_t^2)$ is a driftless random walk (and so recurrent, see Chapter 6).

In any of these cases, $\log(\sigma_t^2)$ and hence σ_t^2 are nonstationary. If we assume that $E(\varepsilon_t^2) = 1$ then, by Jensen's inequality,

$$
\begin{aligned}
E(\eta_{t-1}) &= E\left[\log(\beta + (1-\beta)\varepsilon_{t-1}^2) \right] \\
&< \log(\beta + (1-\beta)E(\varepsilon_{t-1}^2)) \\
&= \log(\beta + (1-\beta)) = 0,
\end{aligned}
$$

so that $\log(\sigma_t^2)$ is a random walk with negative drift and so $\sigma_t^2 \to 0$ with probability one. However, the process y_t is weakly stationary since, for all t,

$$E(\sigma_t^2) = \prod_{s=1}^{t} E\left(\beta + (1-\beta)\varepsilon_s^2 \right) E\left(\sigma_0^2 \right) = E\left(\sigma_0^2 \right).$$

This example shows some of the strange things that can happen with nonlinear processes.

10.3.5 Strong Stationarity

We now formally consider the issue of strong stationarity. Consider the GARCH(1,1) process

$$y_t = \sigma_t \varepsilon_t, \qquad \sigma_t^2 = \omega + \beta \sigma_{t-1}^2 + \gamma y_{t-1}^2, \qquad (10.11)$$

with ε_t i.i.d. nondegenerate, $\beta \geq 0$, and $\omega, \gamma > 0$. We usually assume that $E(\varepsilon_t) = 0$ and $\mathrm{var}(\varepsilon_t) = 1$ so that σ_t^2 is interpreted as a conditional variance. In that case, as we have seen, a necessary and sufficient condition for weak stationarity is that $\beta + \gamma < 1$. We next provide the conditions for strong stationarity.

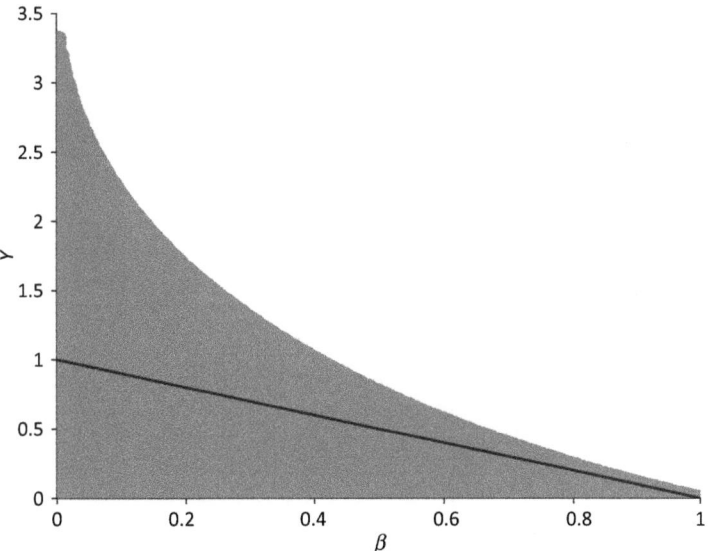

Figure 10.14 Stationary region for the Gaussian GARCH(1,1) model.

Theorem 10.3 (Nelson, 1990a)   *Suppose that ε_t is i.i.d., and that $\omega, \beta, \gamma > 0$. Then y_t has a strictly stationary solution if and only if $E[\log(\beta + \gamma\varepsilon_t^2)] < 0$. The solution is unique, and*

$$\sigma_t^2 = \omega\left(1 + \sum_{j=1}^{\infty}\prod_{i=1}^{j}\left(\gamma\varepsilon_{t-i}^2 + \beta\right)\right).$$

When $E(\varepsilon_t^2) = 1$ we have, by Jensen's inequality,

$$E\left(\log(\beta + \gamma\varepsilon_t^2)\right) < \log\left(E(\beta + \gamma\varepsilon_t^2)\right) = \log(\beta + \gamma).$$

Therefore, it can be that $E(\log(\beta + \gamma\varepsilon_t^2)) < 0$ even when $\beta + \gamma \geq 1$. In the ARCH(1) Gaussian case, we have strong stationarity provided only that $\gamma < 3.5$. That is, in the region $1 \leq \gamma < 3.5$, the process y_t is strongly stationary but not weakly stationary. We show the stationary region for the general GARCH(1,1) case with Gaussian shocks in Figure 10.14, which for $\beta = 0$ coincides with the ARCH(1) solution.

Suppose that (10.11) holds and that ε_t has the standard Cauchy distribution (in which case $E(\varepsilon_t^2) = \infty$). Then we have

$$E\left(\log(\beta + \gamma\varepsilon_t^2)\right) = 2\log(\beta^{1/2} + \gamma^{1/2}).$$

In this case, the necessary and sufficient condition for stationarity is $\beta^{1/2} + \gamma^{1/2} < 1$, which restricts the parameter space more than the condition $\beta + \gamma < 1$ (that is required for weak stationarity when the shock variance exists). Figure 10.15 shows this region. In this case, not even the conditional variance is defined, but the process σ_t^2 is well defined

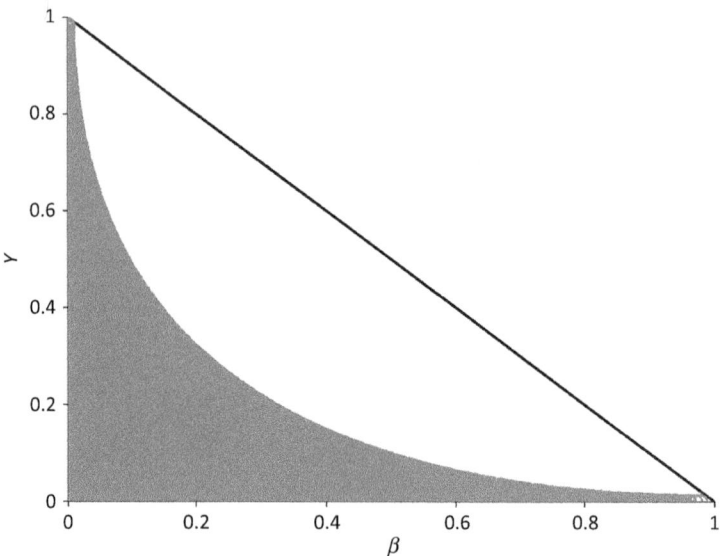

Figure 10.15 The stationary region for a GARCH(1,1) process with Cauchy errors, $\beta^{1/2} + \gamma^{1/2} < 1$.

and is strongly stationary under these conditions. In that case we might interpret σ_t^2 as a dynamic scale process and ignore the variance terminology altogether.

The distribution of $_u\sigma_t^2$ is not known in closed form, but one can simulate the random variable given parameter values. The marginal distribution of y_t is mixed normal, with mean zero and random variance with the distribution of $_u\sigma_t^2$. The representation of $_u\sigma_t^2$ in terms of $\varepsilon_{t-1}, \varepsilon_{t-2}, \ldots$ brings out the nonlinearity inherent in this process.

10.3.6   Other Variations on the GARCH Model

The GARCH class of models has imposed a very specific functional form in terms of how past values of y_t affect σ_t^2. In particular, it does not allow asymmetric news impact curves $(\partial \sigma_t^2 / \partial y_{t-1})$: good news and bad news have the same effect on volatility. The martingale hypothesis says that $\text{cov}(y_t, y_{t-j}^2) = 0$ for $j = 1, 2, \ldots$ The standard GARCH model with symmetrically distributed errors (such as standard normal) implies that $\text{cov}(\sigma_t^2, y_{t-j}) = 0$ and $\text{cov}(y_t^2, y_{t-j}) = 0$ for $j = 1, 2, \ldots$ However, there is strong empirical evidence for a negative correlation between y_t^2 and y_{t-j}, and a positive correlation between y_t^2 and y_{t+j} in some financial time series. Nelson (1991) introduced the exponential GARCH model to address this issue. An alternative model that allows for asymmetric effects is the so-called GJR model (Glosten, Jagannathan, and Runkle, 1993).

Definition 10.4 (GJR GARCH(1,1))   For all t,

$$\sigma_t^2 = \omega + \beta_1 \sigma_{t-1}^2 + \gamma y_{t-1}^2 + \delta y_{t-1}^2 1(y_{t-1} < 0). \tag{10.12}$$

This model is similar to the GARCH process, except that the news impact curve is allowed to be asymmetric when $\delta \neq 0$. Table 10.2 shows estimates of this model. In

Table 10.2 Estimation of asymmetric GJR GARCH model.

	Daily	Weekly	Monthly
ρ_1	0.138 788 (0.009 524)	0.007 065 (0.022 000)	0.014 661 (0.045 131)
ρ_2	−0.019 06 (0.009 449)	0.051 815 (0.022 044)	−0.018 694 (0.045 083)
ω (×1000)	0.000 072 1 (0.000 006 4)	0.001 30 (0.000 242)	0.862 000 (0.249 000)
β	0.920 489 (0.002 243)	0.850 348 (0.015 580)	0.442 481 (0.176 365)
γ	0.034 018 (0.002 613)	0.047 885 (0.013 504)	−0.076 662 (0.042 047)
δ	0.078 782 (0.003 302)	0.140 013 (0.020 349)	0.266 916 (0.094 669)

Note: Standard errors in parentheses. These estimates are for the S&P500 data series and refer to the AR(2)-GJR GARCH(1,1) model

$$y_t = c + \rho_1 y_{t-1} + \rho_2 y_{t-2} + \varepsilon_t \sigma_t,$$
$$\sigma_t^2 = \omega + \beta \sigma_{t-1}^2 + \gamma u_{t-1}^2 + \delta u_{t-1}^2 1(u_{t-1} < 0).$$

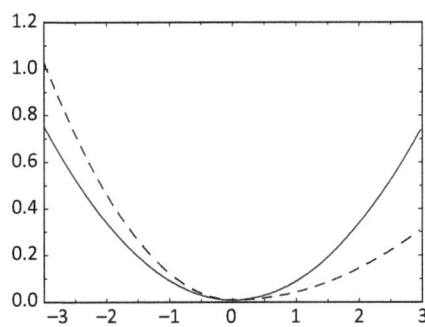

Figure 10.16 Comparison of the estimated news impact curves from GARCH(1,1) and GJR(1,1) for daily S&P500 returns.

Figure 10.16 we compare the estimated news impact curves of the GARCH model (solid line) and the GJR asymmetric GARCH (dashed line) model.

There has been a proliferation of different models since the original papers, too many to list here. Hansen and Lunde (2005) compared the GARCH(1,1) model with some of these other models according to forecast performance. The comparison was made using realized volatility as the target. They looked at daily IBM stock returns and exchange rates. They found that for exchange rates the GARCH(1,1) model is the best, whereas for IBM stock returns, models that account for leverage such as the GJR do better.

10.3.7 Estimation of Parameters

We next turn to estimation and consider a general class of models. The large-sample results can be adapted to a range of different models within the GARCH family.

10.3.7.1 Gaussian Likelihood

The usual method of parameter estimation is based on the Gaussian likelihood. Suppose that $y_t = \mu_t(\theta) + \sigma_t(\theta)\varepsilon_t$, where $\varepsilon_t \sim N(0, 1)$ and $\mu_t(\theta), \sigma_t(\theta)$ depend only on past observations $\mathcal{F}_{t-1} = \{y_{t-1}, y_{t-2}, \ldots\}$, and $\theta \in \Theta \subset \mathbb{R}^p$ is a vector of unknown parameters. Then the conditional distribution of y_t is normal, $y_t \mid \mathcal{F}_{t-1} \sim N(\mu_t, \sigma_t^2)$. Therefore, the sample log likelihood (conditional on the first observation) is (up to a constant that does not depend on parameter values)

$$\mathcal{L}(\theta) = \sum_{t=2}^{T} \mathcal{L}_t(\theta), \qquad \mathcal{L}_t(\theta) = -\frac{1}{2}\log \sigma_t^2(\theta) - \frac{1}{2}\left(\frac{y_t - \mu_t(\theta)}{\sigma_t(\theta)}\right)^2, \qquad (10.13)$$

where $\sigma_t^2(\theta)$ and $\mu_t(\theta)$ are built up by recursions from some starting values, which we discuss below. We define $\widehat{\theta}$ as the value of θ that maximizes $\mathcal{L}(\theta)$ over the parameter space Θ. The marginal density of y_1 is mixed normal with stochastic variance whose distribution is not given in a closed form.

We next discuss the recursions needed to compute $\sigma_t^2(\theta)$. Specifically, in the pure GARCH(1,1) case we have $\theta = (\omega, \beta, \gamma)^\mathsf{T}$ and

$$\sigma_t^2(\theta) = \omega + \beta\sigma_{t-1}^2(\theta) + \gamma y_{t-1}^2, \quad t = 2, \ldots, T.$$

We can compute these recursions for all parameter values θ, given some starting values. There are several approaches to starting values for the GARCH(1,1) model: (i) $\sigma_1^2(\theta) = \omega/(1-\beta-\gamma)$; (ii) $\sigma_1^2 = T^{-1}\sum_{t=1}^{T} y_t^2$; (iii) $\sigma_1^2 = y_1^2$; (iv) treat σ_1^2 as an unknown parameter to estimate along with θ. The first approach imposes weak stationarity in the sense that the initial value is taken from the implied mean of the volatility. The second approach does not impose anything, except that in the absence of weak stationarity the random variable σ_1^2 may diverge with sample size. The third approach is arbitrary but does not impose anything with regard to stationarity or otherwise. Likewise, the final approach does not impose anything with regard to stationarity, but on the other hand requires finding another parameter in the optimization.

We have seen that there are some restrictions on the values of the parameters in order that $\sigma_t^2(\theta) \geq 0$, in which case the parameter space Θ is restricted by the inequality restrictions. Also, in some cases one might want to impose weak or strong stationarity, which yields additional inequality restrictions. The usual algorithms for doing the optimization ignore the inequality restrictions. Some use analytic expression for the first and/or second derivatives of the log likelihood, and some use numerical derivatives in some places. Software exists on the web to compute the estimates in a number of languages. EViews uses the **Marquadt algorithm** by default. Brooks, Burke, and Persand (2001) discussed different software and how they implement the maximization, with some surprising conclusions![1]

In the pure GARCH case the likelihood derivatives are defined in a recursive fashion:

$$\frac{\partial \mathcal{L}_t}{\partial \theta}(\theta) = -\frac{1}{2}\left(\varepsilon_t^2(\theta) - 1\right)\frac{\partial \log \sigma_t^2(\theta)}{\partial \theta}, \qquad \varepsilon_t^2(\theta) = \frac{y_t^2}{\sigma_t^2(\theta)},$$

---

[1] Kristensen and Linton (2006) proposed a method for estimation of the GARCH(1,1) model based on the autocovariance function of $(y_t - \mu_t)^2$ that obviates the need to do numerical maximization.

$$\frac{\partial^2 \mathcal{L}_t}{\partial \theta \partial \theta^{\mathsf{T}}}(\theta) = -\frac{1}{2}\left(\varepsilon_t^2(\theta) - 1\right)\frac{\partial^2 \log \sigma_t^2(\theta)}{\partial \theta \partial \theta^{\mathsf{T}}} + \frac{1}{2}\varepsilon_t^2(\theta)\frac{\partial \log \sigma_t^2(\theta)}{\partial \theta}\frac{\partial \log \sigma_t^2(\theta)}{\partial \theta^{\mathsf{T}}},$$

$$\frac{\partial \log \sigma_t^2(\theta)}{\partial \theta} = \frac{1}{\sigma_t^2(\theta)}\frac{\partial \sigma_t^2(\theta)}{\partial \theta},$$

where for $t = 2, \ldots, T$ we define recursively (from some starting values):

$$\frac{\partial \sigma_t^2(\theta)}{\partial \omega} = 1 + \beta\frac{\partial \sigma_{t-1}^2(\theta)}{\partial \omega},$$

$$\frac{\partial \sigma_t^2(\theta)}{\partial \beta} = \sigma_{t-1}^2(\theta) + \beta\frac{\partial \sigma_{t-1}^2(\theta)}{\partial \beta},$$

$$\frac{\partial \sigma_t^2(\theta)}{\partial \gamma} = y_{t-1}^2 + \beta\frac{\partial \sigma_{t-1}^2(\theta)}{\partial \gamma}.$$

One can expect the MLE to be consistent, asymptotically normal, and even efficient under the full specification. In fact, this estimator is also consistent and asymptotically normal under weaker conditions, specifically that the conditional mean and the conditional variance are correctly specified (i.e., semi-strong GARCH), but the conditional normality of the error distribution is not required. In this more general setting the estimation procedure is sometimes referred to as the QMLE. The large-sample results for the QMLE are stated in quite general terms in Bollerslev and Wooldridge (1992).

Theorem 10.4   *Under the conditions of Bollerslev and Wooldridge (1992),*

$$T^{1/2}\big(\hat{\theta} - \theta_0\big) \Longrightarrow N(0, \mathcal{J}^{-1}\mathcal{I}\mathcal{J}^{-1}),$$

$$\mathcal{J} = E\left(\frac{1}{T}\frac{\partial \mathcal{L}_T^2(\theta_0)}{\partial \theta \partial \theta^{\mathsf{T}}}\right), \qquad \mathcal{I} = E\left(\frac{\partial \mathcal{L}_t}{\partial \theta}\frac{\partial \mathcal{L}_t}{\partial \theta^{\mathsf{T}}}(\theta_0)\right).$$

If ε_t is i.i.d., $\mathcal{I} \propto \mathcal{J}$. In particular,

$$\mathcal{I} = \frac{1}{4}E((\varepsilon_t^2 - 1)^2)E\left(\frac{\partial \log \sigma_t^2(\theta_0)}{\partial \theta}\frac{\partial \log \sigma_t^2(\theta_0)}{\partial \theta^{\mathsf{T}}}\right),$$

$$\mathcal{J} = \frac{1}{2}E\left(\frac{\partial \log \sigma_t^2(\theta_0)}{\partial \theta}\frac{\partial \log \sigma_t^2(\theta_0)}{\partial \theta^{\mathsf{T}}}\right),$$

$$\mathcal{J}^{-1}\mathcal{I}\mathcal{J}^{-1} = E((\varepsilon_t^2 - 1)^2)\left[E\left(\frac{\partial \log \sigma_t^2(\theta_0)}{\partial \theta}\frac{\partial \log \sigma_t^2(\theta_0)}{\partial \theta^{\mathsf{T}}}\right)\right]^{-1}.$$

When $\varepsilon_t \sim N(0, 1)$, $E\left((\varepsilon_t^2 - 1)^2\right) = E\left(\varepsilon_t^4\right) - 1 = 2$.

The theory is based on Taylor series expansion and the CLT for martingale difference sequences to the standardized score function and the law of large numbers for the standardized Hessian matrix. The particular form of the asymptotic variance is valid because the score function is a martingale difference sequence, that is, with probability one,

$$E\left(\frac{\partial \mathcal{L}_t}{\partial \theta}(\theta_0) \mid \mathcal{F}_{t-1}\right) = 0 \tag{10.14}$$

under the correct conditional mean and conditional variance (semi-strong specification). In this case, the correlation between $\partial \mathcal{L}_t(\theta_0)/\partial \theta$ and $\partial \mathcal{L}_s(\theta_0)/\partial \theta$ is zero for any $t \neq s$.

The large-sample theory is difficult to work out from primitive conditions even for simple models. Some notable contributions include:

- Lumsdaine (1996) included the IGARCH case but assumed strong stationarity and symmetric unimodal i.i.d. ε_t with $E(\varepsilon_t^{32}) < \infty$.
- Lee and Hansen (1994) proved consistency and asymptotic normality for the GARCH(1,1) model under weaker conditional moment conditions and allowed for semi-strong processes with some higher-level assumptions.
- Hall and Yao (2003) assumed weak stationarity and showed that if $E(\varepsilon_t^4) < \infty$ then asymptotic normality holds, but also established limiting behavior (nonnormal) under weaker moment conditions.
- Jensen and Rahbek (2004) established consistency and asymptotic normality of the QMLE in a strong GARCH model without strict stationarity (actually for only a subset of the parameters when the process is nonstationary).

10.3.7.2 Standard Errors

We next turn to the question of standard errors and inference. There are three different sorts of estimates of the asymptotic covariance matrix of $\widehat{\theta}$. Define

$$\widehat{\mathcal{J}} = \frac{1}{T}\frac{\partial^2 \mathcal{L}(\widehat{\theta})}{\partial\theta\partial\theta^{\mathsf{T}}}, \qquad \widehat{\mathcal{I}} = \frac{1}{T}\sum_{t=1}^{T}\frac{\partial \mathcal{L}_t}{\partial\theta}\frac{\partial \mathcal{L}_t}{\partial\theta^{\mathsf{T}}}(\widehat{\theta}). \tag{10.15}$$

These are consistent estimates of $\mathcal{J}$ and $\mathcal{I}$ under some conditions.

Gaussian Errors The simplest estimate of the asymptotic variance matrix takes the i.i.d. Gaussian structure used in the estimation seriously and uses either $\widehat{\mathcal{J}}^{-1}$ or $\widehat{\mathcal{I}}^{-1}$, which are only consistent under the strong Gaussian GARCH model, that is, Gaussian i.i.d. errors. These are how the default standard errors are obtained in EViews, for example.

I.I.D. Errors In the second case we may assume that the errors ε_t are i.i.d. but not necessarily Gaussian. In that case, the asymptotic variance of $\widehat{\theta}$ is $E((\varepsilon_t^2 - 1)^2)\mathcal{J}^{-1}$, where $E((\varepsilon_t^2 - 1)^2)$ may not be equal to two. In this case, we may estimate the asymptotic variance consistently by

$$\frac{1}{T}\sum_{t=1}^{T}(\widehat{\varepsilon}_t^2 - 1)^2\widehat{\mathcal{J}}^{-1}, \tag{10.16}$$

where $\widehat{\varepsilon}_t = y_t/\sigma_t(\widehat{\theta})$.

Martingale Difference Sequence Errors Finally, if we are only willing to assume a semi-strong GARCH model such as that ε_t and $\varepsilon_t^2 - 1$ are martingale difference sequences, then we should take the full sandwich estimator

$$\widehat{\mathcal{J}}^{-1}\widehat{\mathcal{I}}\widehat{\mathcal{J}}^{-1}, \tag{10.17}$$

which will be consistent under general conditions, since $\widehat{\mathcal{J}} \xrightarrow{P} \mathcal{J}, \widehat{\mathcal{I}} \xrightarrow{P} \mathcal{I}$. This can be used to provide confidence intervals about the parameters or to test hypotheses about

Table 10.3 Daily GARCH in mean *t*-error.

	α	ρ_1	ρ_2	ν	ω	β	γ
Parameter estimate	2.503	0.0845	−0.0366	6.663	6.33×10^{-7}	0.9170	0.0781
Standard error	1.040	0.0079	0.0078	0.2951	8.69×10^{-8}	0.0042	0.0042

$y_t = c + \alpha\sigma_t^2 + \rho_1 y_{t-1} + \rho_2 y_{t-2} + \varepsilon_t \sigma_t, \; \varepsilon_t \sim t_\nu$, and $\sigma_t^2 = \omega + \beta\sigma_{t-1}^2 + \gamma u_{t-1}^2$.

them, for example the absence of heteroskedasticity would correspond to the null hypothesis that $\beta = \gamma = 0$. The general restriction $R\theta = r$ with R a $q \times p$ matrix with $q < p$ and r a $q \times 1$ vector may be tested using the Wald statistic

$$W = T(R\widehat{\theta} - r)^{\mathsf{T}} (R\widehat{\mathcal{J}}^{-1}\widehat{\mathcal{I}}\widehat{\mathcal{J}}^{-1}R^{\mathsf{T}})^{-1}(R\widehat{\theta} - r),\tag{10.18}$$

which is distributed as chi-squared with q degrees of freedom in large samples.

10.3.7.3 Estimation Based on Alternative Methods

In practice one often finds that the rescaled residuals $\widehat{\varepsilon}_t$ are leptokurtic and incompatible with the normal distribution, and one often rejects formal tests of this hypothesis. Some authors advocate using alternative likelihood criteria. The most popular alternative to the normal distribution is the *t*-distribution with known or unknown degrees of freedom ν. In this case, the likelihood function is (apart from constants) $\mathcal{L}(\theta, \nu) = \sum_{t=1}^{T} \mathcal{L}_t(\theta, \nu)$, where

$$\mathcal{L}_t(\theta, \nu) = -\sigma_t(\theta) - \frac{\nu + 1}{2} \log \left(1 + \frac{y_t^2}{(\nu - 2)\sigma_t^2(\theta)}\right)$$
$$+ \log \Gamma \left(\frac{\nu + 1}{2}\right) - \frac{1}{2} \log(\nu - 2) - \log \Gamma \left(\frac{\nu}{2}\right).\tag{10.19}$$

This is implemented in EViews. In Table 10.3 we show parameter estimates for daily data obtained by this method.

Note that the estimated degrees of freedom are around 6.66 with quite a tight standard error. For this distribution, the value -11 or less obtained in Figure 10.13 is still unlikely but occurs with a probability in the region of 7.8×10^{-6} rather than 2×10^{-28} as for the normal distribution. The GARCH in mean effect is positive and significant, although not strongly so. The unconditional standard deviation is around 0.011. The standard errors in this case are calculated as if the *t*-distribution were correctly specified, that is, from the information matrix.

The estimators $\widehat{\theta}$ and $\widehat{\nu}$ are consistent and asymptotically normal provided the model is correct. In fact, $\widehat{\theta}$ remains consistent under some departures from the *t*-distribution. Newey and Steigerwald (1997) investigated the consistency of estimated GARCH parameters using non-Gaussian QMLE objective functions. They showed that if the assumed error and true error are symmetric then the QMLE is still consistent, but otherwise it may not be. This is in contrast with the Gaussian QMLE, which is consistent regardless of the shape of the error distribution (provided only that $E(\varepsilon_t^4) < \infty$).

10.3.8   Long-Memory Processes

The GARCH(1,1) process $\sigma_t^2 = \omega + \beta\sigma_{t-1}^2 + \gamma y_{t-1}^2$ is of the ARCH(∞) form (provided the process is weakly stationary, which requires $\gamma + \beta < 1$), that is, we can write

$$\sigma_t^2 = \psi_0(\theta) + \sum_{j=1}^{\infty} \psi_j(\theta) y_{t-j}^2 \tag{10.20}$$

for constants $\psi_j(\theta)$ satisfying $\psi_j(\theta) = \gamma\beta^{j-1}$. These coefficients decay very rapidly to zero, which implies that the actual amount of memory in the process is quite limited. It implies the same rate of decay in the autocorrelation function of y_t^2. The empirical evidence on the autocorrelation function of y_t^2 suggests rather slower decay. Therefore, we consider time series processes that are consistent with such slow decay.

We now turn to long-memory GARCH-type volatility models. Suppose that

$$\sigma_t^2 = \psi_0(\theta) + \sum_{j=1}^{\infty} \psi_j(\theta) y_{t-j}^2 \tag{10.21}$$

for some parameter vector θ. Specifically, suppose that $\psi_j = Cj^{-\theta}$ for some $\theta > 0$, as in (6.30). The coefficients satisfy $\sum_{j=1}^{\infty} \psi_j^2(\theta) < \infty$ provided $\theta > 1/2$, and $\sum_{j=1}^{\infty} |\psi_j(\theta)| < \infty$ provided $\theta > 1$.

Definition 10.5   Baillie, Bollerslev, and Mikkelsen (1996) defined the fractional integrated GARCH process (FIGARCH) where

$$(1 - L)^d \sigma_t^2 = \omega + \gamma\eta_{t-1} = \omega + \gamma\sigma_{t-1}^2(\varepsilon_{t-1}^2 - 1),$$

with ε_t an i.i.d. mean-zero and variance-one series; $\eta_{t-1} = \sigma_{t-1}^2(\varepsilon_{t-1}^2 - 1)$ is therefore MDS.

When $d = 1$ we have the IGARCH process. When $d < 1$ we apply the binomial expansion to express σ_t^2 in the form (10.21) with slowly decaying coefficients. By substitution we also obtain the expression

$$(1 - L)^d y_t^2 = \omega + \eta_t - (1 - \gamma)\eta_{t-1},$$

which can be written in the form given above. One can extend this class of processes to also allow short-memory filters $A(L), B(L)$ so that, for example, $A(L)(1 - L)^d\sigma_t^2 = B(L)(\omega + \gamma\eta_{t-1})$. Estimation of the parameter d can be carried out by a variety of methods (Robinson, 1994).

Evidence for Long Memory in Stock Returns   Breidt, Crato, and de Lima (1998) considered the daily CRSP value-weighted index. They found that some series have d larger than 1/2 in squared returns and log-squared returns. Lo (1991) found little evidence of long memory in stock returns y_t using the rescaled range statistic. In Table 10.4 we give estimates of d for daily stock return data. The estimated values are quite low in this case, and the standard errors are small. The estimated values of d reduce further if a short-range model is fitted first. Evidence for long memory in daily stock returns based

Table 10.4 Estimated d by frequency.

	Daily	Weekly	Monthly
y_t	−0.0181	−0.0026	0.0079
y_t^2	0.1484	0.2862	0.0986
$\log y_t^2$	0.2638	0.2453	0.1782

Note: Estimation of d is by Whittle likelihood for the returns on the S&P500 index for the period 1955–2002 for three different data frequencies. Replace $y_t = 0$ by ε in $\log y_t^2$.

on correlograms may be questionable due to the issues raised by Mikosch and Stărică (2000).

In practice the following class of processes are widely used in place of long-memory processes.

Definition 10.6   The heterogeneous autoregressive conditional heteroskedasticity model (HARCH) satisfies

$$\sigma_t^2 = \omega + \theta_1 \left(\frac{1}{K_1} \sum_{j=N_1+1}^{N_1+K_1} y_{t-j}^2 \right) + \cdots + \theta_r \left(\frac{1}{K_r} \sum_{j=N_r+1}^{N_r+K_r} y_{t-j}^2 \right),$$

where $K_1, \ldots, K_r$ and $N_1, \ldots, N_r$ are specified, such as $K_1 = 5$, $K_2 = 22$, and so on (Corsi, 2009).

It has been fashionable recently to work with this process, which is a kind of poor man's long-memory process. It is a special case of the ARCH(∞) class of processes with free parameters $\omega, \theta_1, \ldots, \theta_r$, so there is little more to say about this process in terms of its properties or estimation. In practice, however, these processes can approximate long-memory processes well.

10.3.9 Multivariate Models

We now consider models for a vector of time series. We focus on zero-mean series, which could be the residuals from a VAR equation.

Definition 10.7   The conditional covariance matrix of some $n \times 1$ vector of the conditional mean-zero series y_t is

$$\Sigma_t = E(y_t y_t^{\mathsf{T}} \mid \mathcal{F}_{t-1}), \tag{10.22}$$

where $\mathcal{F}_{t-1}$ is the information set consisting of the past return history of all the series.

The conditional covariance matrix contains on the diagonals the conditional variance of each series, but on the off-diagonals it contains the conditional covariance between the two series. This matrix is important for asset pricing and portfolio choice considerations alongside the conditional mean (which we have assumed is zero here). In particular, we may define the conditional $\beta_{im,t}$ of asset i with respect to the market portfolio as the ratio of the conditional covariance to the conditional variance of the market return,

$$\beta_{im,t} = \frac{\text{cov}(r_{it}, r_{mt} \mid \mathcal{F}_{t-1})}{\text{var}(r_{mt} \mid \mathcal{F}_{t-1})},$$

and the conditional CAPM says that $E(r_{it} - r_{ft} \mid \mathcal{F}_{t-1}) = \beta_{it}\gamma_t$, where γ_t is the time-varying risk premium and r_{ft} is the risk-free rate.

Definition 10.8   Let $h_t = \text{vech}(\Sigma_t)$ denote the unique elements. Here, $\text{vech}(\cdot)$ denotes the unique upper (or lower) triangle of the square matrix (including diagonal elements). Bollerslev, Engle, and Wooldridge (1988) defined a general dynamic model for the conditional covariance matrix of the form

$$h_t = a + Bh_{t-1} + C\text{vech}(y_{t-1}y_{t-1}^\mathsf{T}), \tag{10.23}$$

where a is an $n(n+1)/2 \times 1$ parameter vector, while B and C are $n(n+1)/2 \times n(n+1)/2$ matrices.

This naive GARCH extension has $n^2(n+1)^2/2 + n(n+1)/2$ parameters, so with a modest $n = 1000$ this requires estimating five hundred billion (5×10^{11}) parameters! There are simply too many parameters for estimation and too many for interpretation. In particular, the conditional variance of asset i depends on all the lagged values $y_{j,t-s}y_{k,t-s}$ for $j, k = 1, \ldots, n$ and $s = 1, 2, \ldots$; each one of these terms has a parameter associated with it, and sorting out their meaning is an impossible task. In addition, one usually wants to ensure that the conditional covariance matrix is positive definite, but this model makes it very difficult to do so in estimation as this involves a complicated system of inequality restrictions across the many parameter values. In practice, therefore, this model is only feasible for at most $n = 3$.

The main properties of the univariate GARCH process can be extended to this general multivariate model. Specifically, we can write the outer product of y_t, $x_t = \text{vech}(y_t y_t^\mathsf{T})$, as a VARMA process. Specifically,

$$x_t = h_t + \text{vech}\left(\Sigma_t^{1/2}(\varepsilon_t\varepsilon_t^\mathsf{T} - I_n)\Sigma_t^{1/2}\right) = a + Bh_{t-1} + Cx_{t-1} + \eta_t$$
$$= a + (B + C)x_{t-1} + \eta_t - B\eta_{t-1},$$

where $\eta_t = \text{vech}\left(\Sigma_t^{1/2}(\varepsilon_t\varepsilon_t^\mathsf{T} - I_n)\Sigma_t^{1/2}\right)$ satisfies $E(\eta_t \mid \mathcal{F}_{t-1}) = 0$. This shows that the generalization of squared y follows a VARMA process. Note, however, that the matrices $y_t y_t^\mathsf{T}$ and $\varepsilon_t\varepsilon_t^\mathsf{T}$ are of rank one so that the process x_t has a lot of cross-sectional dependence in its shock process. We can obtain conditions for strong and weak stationarity and mixing from the parameters and error distribution. For example, provided $I - B - C$ is invertible we have weak stationarity of returns and the unconditional variance matrix has unique elements $E(x_t) = [I - (B + C)]^{-1} a$.

Estimation can in principle be done through the (quasi-)likelihood function of $y_T, \ldots, y_2$ given y_1,

$$\mathcal{L}(\theta; y_T, \ldots, y_2, y_1) = \text{const} - \frac{1}{2}\sum_{t=1}^{T} \log \det(\Sigma_t(\theta)) - \frac{1}{2}\sum_{t=1}^{T} y_t^\mathsf{T}\Sigma_t(\theta)^{-1}y_t, \tag{10.24}$$

where θ is the full set of parameters in a, B, C. However, in practice the log likelihood function can be relatively flat unless the sample size is very big because the number of parameters is large. Indeed, computing $\Sigma_t(\theta)^{-1}$ can be challenging without further restrictions.

There are many approaches to reducing the number of parameters needed to describe the conditional covariance matrix. An early extension is the so-called BEKK model (Baba *et al.*, 1990).

Definition 10.9   In the BEKK model,

$$\Sigma_t = AA^{\mathsf{T}} + B\Sigma_{t-1}B^{\mathsf{T}} + Cy_{t-1}y_{t-1}^{\mathsf{T}}C^{\mathsf{T}}, \tag{10.25}$$

where A, B, C are $n \times n$ unrestricted parameter matrices, in which case

$$h_t = D_+(A \otimes A)D_- \mathrm{vech}(I_n) + D_+(B \otimes B)D_- h_{t-1}$$
$$+ D_+(C \otimes C)D_- \mathrm{vech}(y_{t-1}y_{t-1}^{\mathsf{T}}),$$

where D_+, D_- are so-called duplication matrices of zeros and ones such that $\mathrm{vech}(A) = D_+ \mathrm{vec}(A)$ and $D_- \mathrm{vech}(A) = \mathrm{vec}(A)$ for any matrix A.

This gives a big reduction in the number of parameters and imposes symmetry and positive definiteness on Σ_t automatically. The discussion around stationarity and dependence is the same for this process: provided $I - D_+(B \otimes B)D_- h_{t-1} - D_+(C \otimes C)D_+$ is invertible we have weak stationarity of y_t. However, there are still a lot of parameters to estimate for large n, and the meaning of the individual parameters is not so clear. In practice these first-generation models are not widely used outside the bivariate or trivariate case. We next consider a number of approaches to reducing the dimensionality of the parameter space further.

One approach is to replace the parameter matrices by scalars, that is, let $A = ai_m$, $B = bI_m$, and $C = cI_m$, where a, b, c are scalars and $m = n(n+1)/2$. This approach can be weakened by just doing this for the dynamic parameters b and c, and taking $A = (1 - b - c)\mathrm{vech}(\Sigma_0)$, where Σ_0 is the unconditional covariance matrix. In the variance targeting approach, one replaces the unconditional variance by the sample variance, which eliminates the need to estimate this large matrix inside a nonlinear optimization problem (but this, alas, has consequences for standard errors that are often not accounted for). We next consider some second-generation models.

10.3.9.1 Constant Conditional Correlation

The **constant conditional correlation** model is due to Bollerslev (1990).

Definition 10.10   The constant conditional correlation model is

$$E(y_t y_t^{\mathsf{T}} \mid \mathcal{F}_{t-1}) = \Sigma_t = D_t R D_t, \qquad D_t = \mathrm{diag}\{\sigma_{1t}, \dots, \sigma_{nt}\},$$
$$\sigma_{it}^2 = \omega_i + \beta_i \sigma_{i,t-1}^2 + \gamma_i y_{i,t-1}^2,$$

where R is a time-invariant correlation matrix

$$R_{ij} = \frac{E(\varepsilon_{it}\varepsilon_{jt})}{\left(E(\varepsilon_{it}^2)E(\varepsilon_{jt}^2)\right)^{1/2}} = E(\varepsilon_{it}\varepsilon_{jt}).$$

Provided $\beta_i, \gamma_i \geq 0$ and $\omega_i > 0$, the matrix Σ_t is automatically symmetric and positive definite. The unconditional variances are $\sigma_i^2 = \omega_i/(1 - \beta_i - \gamma_i)$ provided the process is weakly stationary. The conditional covariance is $R_{ij}\sigma_{it}\sigma_{jt}$, which varies over time. The unconditional covariance is more complicated to derive because σ_{it} is a function of $\varepsilon_{i,t-1}, \varepsilon_{i,t-2}, \ldots$ and σ_{jt} is a function of $\varepsilon_{j,t-1}, \varepsilon_{j,t-2}, \ldots$, which are contemporaneously correlated shocks. For example, in the case where ε_t is Gaussian and $\beta_i = \beta_j = 0$, we have (assuming that this expectation exists)

$$
\begin{aligned}
E\left(\sigma_{it}^2\sigma_{jt}^2\right) &= E\left(\left(\omega_i + \gamma_i y_{i,t-1}^2\right)\left(\omega_j + \gamma_j y_{j,t-1}^2\right)\right) \\
&= \omega_i\omega_j + \omega_i\gamma_j\sigma_j^2 + \omega_j\gamma_i\sigma_i^2 + \gamma_i\gamma_j E\left(\sigma_{i,t-1}^2\sigma_{j,t-1}^2\right)E\left(\varepsilon_{it}^2\varepsilon_{jt}^2\right) \\
&= \frac{\omega_i\omega_j + \omega_i\gamma_j\sigma_j^2 + \omega_j\gamma_i\sigma_i^2}{1 - \gamma_i\gamma_j\left(1 + 2\rho_{ij}^2\right)}.
\end{aligned}
$$

Estimation of the parameters of this model is straightforward. First, estimate univariate GARCH processes by, for example, Gaussian QMLE. Then estimate R by the sample correlation matrix of the standardized residuals ($\widehat{\varepsilon}_{it} = y_{it}/\widehat{\sigma}_{it}$),

$$\widehat{R}_{ij} = \frac{(1/T)\sum_{t=1}^{T}\widehat{\varepsilon}_{it}\widehat{\varepsilon}_{jt}}{\left((1/T)\sum_{t=1}^{T}\widehat{\varepsilon}_{it}^2 (1/T)\sum_{t=1}^{T}\widehat{\varepsilon}_{jt}^2\right)^{1/2}}.$$

The estimated conditional covariance matrix is then given by

$$\widehat{\Sigma}_t = \widehat{D}_t\widehat{R}\widehat{D}_t, \qquad \widehat{D}_t = \mathrm{diag}\{\widehat{\sigma}_{it}\}.$$

This allows for time variation in the conditional covariance matrix, though of a rather restrictive sort, but imposes that the conditional correlation matrix R is not time varying.

An alternative model is the independent component model whereby $y_t = \Omega^{1/2}u_t$, where Ω is a symmetric and positive-definite matrix, while $u_t = (u_{1t}, \ldots, u_{nt})^{\mathsf{T}}$ are mean-zero and independent components with unit-conditional variance. That is, $E(u_{jt} \mid \mathcal{F}_{t-1}) = 0$ and

$$\sigma_{jt}^2 = \mathrm{var}(u_{jt} \mid \mathcal{F}_{t-1}) = 1 - \beta_j - \gamma_j + \beta_j\sigma_{j,t}^2 + \gamma_j u_{j,t-1}^2.$$

In this case,

$$E(y_t y_t^{\mathsf{T}} \mid \mathcal{F}_{t-1}) = \Sigma_t = \Omega^{1/2}D_t\Omega^{1/2}, \qquad D_t = \mathrm{diag}\{\sigma_{1t}^2, \ldots, \sigma_{nt}^2\}.$$

We have $E(y_t y_t^{\mathsf{T}}) = \Omega$, so the unconditional covariance matrix is simple in this case. Furthermore, we can estimate Ω by

$$\widehat{\Omega} = \frac{1}{T}\sum_{t=1}^{T}y_t y_t^{\mathsf{T}}$$

and let $\widehat{u}_t = \widehat{\Omega}^{-1/2}y_t$. Then estimate the parameters β_j, γ_j for series j using the series $\widehat{u}_{jt}$.

10.3.9.2 Dynamic Conditional Correlation

The **dynamic conditional correlation** model of Engle and Sheppard (2001) generalizes the CCC model to allow for time variation in the conditional correlation.

Definition 10.11   The dynamic conditional correlation model is $\Sigma_t = D_t R_t D_t$, $D_t = \mathrm{diag}\{\sigma_{it}\}$, where, for each $i = 1, \ldots, n$,

$$\sigma_{it}^2 = \omega_i + \beta_i \sigma_{it}^2 + \gamma_i y_{i,t-1}^2.$$

The matrix R_t has the typical element

$$R_{ij,t} = \frac{q_{ij,t}}{\left(q_{ii,t} q_{jj,t}\right)^{1/2}}, \qquad q_{ij,t} = c_{ij} + b_{ij} q_{ij,t-1} + a_{ij} \varepsilon_{i,t-1} \varepsilon_{j,t-1}$$

for coefficients a_{ij}, b_{ij}, c_{ij}.

The model innovation is the dynamic equation for $q_{ij,t} = \mathrm{cov}(\varepsilon_{it}, \varepsilon_{jt} \mid \mathcal{F}_{t-1})$, which is not bounded, whereas $R_{ij,t} \in [-1, 1]$. If we restrict the parameters to be homogeneous ($c_{ij} = c$, $b_{ij} = b$, and $a_{ij} = a$) then Σ_t is guaranteed to be positive semidefinite (provided also the individual GARCH processes are).

Estimation of this model is a little more involved than for the CCC model, but the first step is the same: estimate the univariate GARCH processes and standardize y_t by the fitted value $\hat{\sigma}_{it}$. In the second step one maximizes the derived likelihood $\mathcal{L}(a, b, c)$ with respect to parameters a, b, c.

See Bauwens, Laurent, and Rombouts (2006) for a review of multivariate GARCH models.

10.4 Copula Models

Suppose that X_1 and X_2 are two continuously distributed random variables. Letting $Y_1 = F_{X_1}(X_1)$ and $Y_2 = F_{X_2}(X_2)$, then Y_1 and Y_2 are uniformly distributed on $[0, 1]$. The function

$$C(u_1, u_2) = \Pr\left(Y_1 \leq u_1, Y_2 \leq u_2\right)$$

is called the **copula** of X_1, X_2; it is a bivariate distribution function on $[0, 1] \times [0, 1]$. The joint distribution of X_1, X_2 is equivalently described by the copula $C(u_1, u_2)$ and the two marginal distribution functions F_{X_1} and F_{X_2}.

Theorem 10.5 (Sklar, 1959)   *Suppose that X_1, X_2 are continuously distributed. Then the joint distribution of X_1, X_2 can be written uniquely as*

$$\Pr\left(X_1 \leq x, X_2 \leq x_2\right) = C\left(F_{X_1}(x_1), F_{X_2}(x_2)\right)$$

for some distribution function $C \colon [0, 1]^2 \longrightarrow [0, 1]$.

This approach converts marginal distributions into a standard scale, which allows modelling of the dependence through the function $C(\cdot, \cdot)$ in a common framework, while not restricting the marginal distributions in any way.

The case where $C(u_1, u_2) = u_1 u_2$ corresponds to X_1 and X_2 being mutually independent; other choices of C allow for dependence between the two random variables.

Example 10.2   The Gaussian copula is

$$C(u_1, u_2; \rho) = \Phi_2\left(\Phi^{-1}(u_1), \Phi^{-1}(u_2); \rho\right), \tag{10.26}$$

where Φ is the standard univariate normal CDF, while $\Phi_2(s, t; \rho)$ is the CDF of the standard bivariate normal distribution (with mean vector zero and variances equal to one) with correlation parameter ρ. This implies the following model for the bivariate CDF and density function of X_1, X_2:

$$F(x_1, x_2) = \frac{1}{2\pi\sqrt{1 - \rho^2}} \int_{-\infty}^{\Phi^{-1}(F_1(x_1))} \int_{-\infty}^{\Phi^{-1}(F_2(x_2))} \exp\left(-\frac{s^2 + t^2 - 2\rho st}{2(1 - \rho^2)}\right) ds\, dt, \tag{10.27}$$

$$f(x_1, x_2) = \frac{1}{\sqrt{1 - \rho^2}} \exp\left(-\frac{\rho\Phi^{-1}(F_1(x_1))\Phi^{-1}(F_2(x_2))}{2(1 - \rho^2)}\right) \times f_1(x_1)f_2(x_2). \tag{10.28}$$

This has been called "the formula that killed Wall Street," and not because it is too complicated;[2] it is because it was widely used in credit risk modelling, because it is very flexible with regard to the marginal distributions not being Gaussian, and so had the veneer of respectable generality. The weakness was that not only are extreme events likely but when they happen for one risk they tend to happen to all risks.

A time series version of this model can be represented as

$$\Phi^{-1}(F(y_t)) = \phi\Phi^{-1}(F(y_{t-1})) + \varepsilon_t, \tag{10.29}$$

where ε_t is i.i.d. $N(0, 1 - \phi^2)$ and $\phi \in (-1, 1)$ (Chen and Fan, 2006). This defines a stationary Gaussian process for $y_t^\dagger = \Phi^{-1}(F(y_t))$. The motivation for this model could be that the series y_t has heavy tails, for example a Cauchy marginal distribution, but the dependence is of this simple autoregressive type after transformation. One can more generally allow $y_t^\dagger$ to be ARMA(p, q). The missing step for estimation is the CDF F, which we discuss in Chapter 11, and the fact that the error variance is restricted. We may also define a multivariate version of this process. Suppose that X_t, Y_t follow a Gaussian copula VAR. That is, the marginal distributions F, G could be anything (even the Cauchy distribution), but the dependence structure is driven by a VAR on the transformed variables. Specifically, we suppose that

$$\begin{pmatrix} X_t^\dagger \\ Y_t^\dagger \end{pmatrix} = A \begin{pmatrix} X_{t-1}^\dagger \\ Y_{t-1}^\dagger \end{pmatrix} + \varepsilon_t,$$

where $X_t^\dagger = \Phi^{-1}(F(X_t))$ and $Y_t^\dagger = \Phi^{-1}(G(Y_t))$ are marginally standard normal with mutual correlation ρ and $\varepsilon_t \sim N(0, \Omega_\varepsilon)$, where

$$\Omega_\varepsilon = \begin{pmatrix} 1 & \rho \\ \rho & 1 \end{pmatrix} - A \begin{pmatrix} 1 & \rho \\ \rho & 1 \end{pmatrix} A^\mathsf{T}.$$

---

[2] Needless to say, the rumors of Wall Street's death were greatly exaggerated.

The free parameters of this model are A and ρ, which can be estimated by ML (Chen and Fan, 2006).

It is known that the Gaussian copula is symmetric and has no tail dependence, and hence cannot be used to model economic and financial time series exhibiting complicated nonlinear asymmetric dependence and clusters of large and/or small values. Joe (1997) and Nelson (1990a) provided many non-Gaussian copulas that might be used for this purpose. Patton (2006) used the symmetrized Joe–Clayton copula

$$C_{\text{SJC}}(u, v) = \frac{1}{2}(C_{\text{JC}}(u, v \mid \tau^{\text{U}}, \tau^{\text{L}}) + C_{\text{JC}}(1 - u, 1 - v \mid \tau^{\text{L}}, \tau^{\text{U}}) + u + v - 1),$$

$$1 - C_{\text{JC}}(u, v \mid \tau^{\text{U}}, \tau^{\text{L}}) = (1 - ((1 - (1 - u)^{\kappa})^{-\gamma} + (1 - (1 - v)^{\kappa})^{-\gamma} - 1)^{-1/\gamma})^{1/\kappa},$$

where $\kappa = 1/\log_2(2 - \tau^{\text{U}})$ and $\gamma = -1/\log_2(\tau^{\text{L}})$, where

$$\tau^{\text{L}} = \lim_{\varepsilon \to 0} \frac{C(\varepsilon, \varepsilon)}{\varepsilon}, \qquad \tau^{\text{U}} = \lim_{\varepsilon \to 1} \frac{C(\varepsilon, \varepsilon)}{\varepsilon}$$

are measures of dependence known as tail dependence. Tail dependence captures the behavior of the random variables during extreme events. For a Gaussian copula $\tau^{\text{L}} = \tau^{\text{U}} = 0$, but this is not necessary in the Joe–Clayton copula. Patton tested for asymmetry in a model of the dependence between the Deutsche mark and the yen, and found evidence that the mark–dollar and yen–dollar exchange rates are more correlated when they are depreciating against the dollar than when they are appreciating. Chen and Fan (2006) provided a theory for estimation of copula-based models; see Patton (2012) for a review.

10.5 Models for Limited Dependent Variables

In many situations the time series of interest is not real valued. For example, it may be binary, $\{0, 1\}$, or counts, $\{0, 1, 2, \ldots\}$. For example, the sequence of buy and sell limit orders on the London Stock Exchange can be viewed as a binary time series. The number of goals scored by Arsenal and their opponents in the Premier League during the 2023 season is shown in Figure 10.17 as a time series with $T = 38$ observations; this is a pair of count-valued variables that takes values in $\{0, 1, 2, \ldots\}$. One can use linear techniques such as the autocorrelation function and ARMA(p, q) models to capture the dynamic effects, but they are not likely to be well suited to the integer-valued nature of the series. If one is interested in prediction, for example, then it is not going to be helpful to predict a scoreline of 2.37–1.92 as bookmakers do not allow this is a possible outcome.

There are special time series models that take account of this structure, and which are generally nonlinear. We first consider the binary case. Suppose that $y_t \in \{0, 1\}$ and that y_t is not i.i.d., and in particular

$$\Pr(y_t = 1 \mid \mathcal{F}_{t-1}) = \pi_{t-1}$$

varies over time. For example, we may take

$$\pi_{t-1} = F\left(\alpha + \phi_1 y_{t-1} + \cdots + \phi_p y_{t-p}\right),$$

where the "link function" F is some given CDF such as the logistic, the standard normal, or the standard Cauchy. The model for y_t is nonlinear, unless F is linear. Cox and Snell

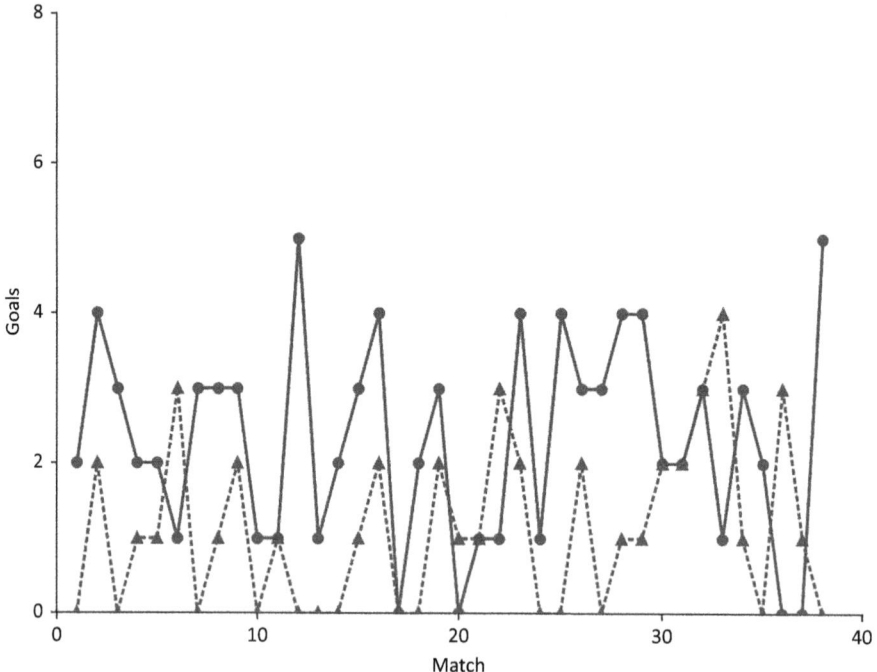

Figure 10.17 Goals scored by Arsenal (circles) and opponents (triangles) during 38 Premier League matches in the 2022/23 season.

(1989) considered this model with the logistic link function. The outcome y_t depends on the values of $y_{t-1}, \ldots, y_{t-p}$ unless $\phi_1 = \cdots = \phi_p = 0$. Under some conditions on $\phi_1, \ldots, \phi_p$, the process y_t is stationary and weakly dependent. Estimation of the parameters can easily be carried out by maximum likelihood. The conditional likelihood given $y_1, \ldots, y_p$ is

$$
\mathcal{L}(\alpha, \phi_1, \ldots, \phi_p \mid y_1, \ldots, y_T)
$$
$$
= \sum_{t=p+1}^{T} y_t \log \left(F \left(\alpha + \phi_1 y_{t-1} + \cdots + \phi_p y_{t-p} \right) \right)
$$
$$
+ (1 - y_t) \log \left(1 - F \left(\alpha + \phi_1 y_{t-1} + \cdots + \phi_p y_{t-p} \right) \right),
$$

which can be maximized with respect to $\alpha, \phi_1, \ldots, \phi_p$. One may add additional explanatory variables into the equation for π_{t-1}.

This specification is purely in terms of observed binary variables; an alternative approach is to work with latent state variables and imbue them with a dynamic structure. Suppose that

$$
\Pr(y_t = 1 \mid \alpha_t, \beta) = F\left(\beta^{\mathsf{T}} x_t + \alpha_t\right), \qquad \alpha_t = \phi \alpha_{t-1} + \eta_t,
$$

with η_t i.i.d. $N(0, \sigma^2)$ and $|\phi| < 1$, where x_t are observed exogenous covariates and α_t is a latent state variable. The parameters here are β, ϕ, σ^2, and the exact likelihood is

$$L(\beta, \phi, \sigma^2 \mid y_1, \ldots, y_T) = \int \left(\prod_{t=1}^{T} F(\beta^{\mathsf{T}} x_t + \alpha_t) \right) f_{\phi, \sigma^2}(\alpha_1, \ldots, \alpha_T) \, d\alpha_1 \cdots d\alpha_T,$$

where $f_{\phi, \sigma^2}(\alpha_1, \ldots, \alpha_T)$ is the joint distribution of the latent variables, which is multivariate Gaussian. This requires T-dimensional integration to compute, and there is no general simple recursive lower-dimensional approach like the Kalman filter. In practice the likelihood may be approximated by simulation methods, but it is still not an attractive procedure to carry out. Davis and Yau (2011) recommended a pairwise likelihood method that is computationally feasible.

An alternative approach is to suppose that there is some latent y_t^* such that

$$y_t^* = \alpha + \phi_1 y_{t-1}^* + \cdots + \phi_p y_{t-p}^* + \varepsilon_t,$$

where ε_t is i.i.d. $N(0, \sigma_\varepsilon^2)$, but we only observe $y_t = 1(y_t^* > 0)$. In this case, the stationarity conditions for y_t are implied by the stationarity of y_t^*. We have

$$\Pr\left(y_t = 1 \mid y_{t-1}^*, \ldots, y_{t-p}^*\right) = \Phi\left(\frac{\alpha + \phi_1 y_{t-1}^* + \cdots + \phi_p y_{t-p}^*}{\sigma_\varepsilon}\right),$$

but of course we do not observe $y_{t-1}^*, \ldots, y_{t-p}^*$ either. The observable regression is

$$\Pr\left(y_t = 1 \mid y_{t-1}, \ldots, y_{t-p}\right)$$
$$= E\left(\Phi\left(\frac{\alpha + \phi_1 y_{t-1}^* + \cdots + \phi_p y_{t-p}^*}{\sigma_\varepsilon}\right) \mid y_{t-1}, \ldots, y_{t-p}\right),$$

which does not depend on time but is a difficult computation. A special case is $E(h(y^*) \mid y = 1) = E(h(y^*) \mid y^* > 0) = \int_0^\infty h(y^*) \, dF_*(y^*)$, which is already quite a painful calculation to carry out. Let $\pi(\alpha, \phi, \sigma_\varepsilon^2 \mid y_{t-1}, \ldots, y_{t-p})$ denote this probability. We can estimate this quantity by simulation for given parameter values. First note that, without loss of generality, we may take $\sigma_\varepsilon = 1$. Let $\{\varepsilon_t^{*(r)}\}_{t=1}^{T}$ be standard normal random variables, let

$$y_t^{*(r)} = \alpha + \phi_1 y_{t-1}^{*(r)} + \cdots + \phi_p y_{t-p}^{*(r)} + \varepsilon_t^{*(r)}$$

for $r = 1, \ldots, R$ be simulated data for given parameter values α, ϕ, and define $\{y_t^{(r)}\}_{t=1}^{T}$, where $y_t^{(r)} = 1(y_t^{*(r)} > 0)$. We can determine whether $y_t^{(r)} = 1$ or 0 for each time period in each trajectory. We then estimate $\pi(\alpha, \phi \mid y_{t-1} = i_1, \ldots, y_{t-p} = i_p)$, where $i_j \in \{0, 1\}$, by

$$\widehat{\pi}(\alpha, \phi \mid y_{t-1} = i_1, \ldots, y_{t-p} = i_p)$$
$$= \frac{1}{R} \sum_{r=1}^{R} \frac{\sum_{t=1}^{T} 1\left(y_t^{(r)} = 1, y_{t-1}^{(r)} = i_1, \ldots, y_{t-p}^{(r)} = i_p\right)}{\sum_{t=1}^{T} 1\left(y_{t-1}^{(r)} = i_1, \ldots, y_{t-p}^{(r)} = i_p\right)}.$$

This can be put into a likelihood function, which can be maximized over the parameter values α, ϕ, setting $i_j = y_{t-j}$.

Hausman, Lo, and MacKinlay (1992) considered the ordered probit model for stock prices defined on a one-eighth of a dollar grid. Given the difficulty with parametric models, an alternative is to work with nonparametric methods, which is the subject of Chapter 11.

10.6 Summary

We have considered several nonlinear time series models such as threshold models and models for structural change. We also considered chaotic processes that rose to prominence from several other fields, and GARCH models that were developed to understand and explain financial time series and the dynamic risk–return relationship. We also considered copula models and models for binary and other limited dependent outcomes, and discussed some tools for testing for the presence of nonlinearity. The R language has several packages to fit GARCH models, including `rugarch`. Teräsvirta (2018) reviewed a broad class of nonlinear models, and Tong (1990) is a classic reference. Shephard (2005) contains many of the key papers in one place.

10.7 Exercises

10.1 Suppose that for some known $u_0 = t_0/T \in (0,1)$,

$$y_t = \begin{cases} \alpha + \varepsilon_t & \text{if } t \leq t_0, \\ \alpha + \beta(t - t_0) + \varepsilon_t & \text{if } t > t_0, \end{cases}$$

where ε_t is a zero-mean Gaussian process. Derive the Wald, Lagrange multiplier, and likelihood ratio tests of the null hypothesis that $\beta = 0$ versus the alternative that $\beta > 0$.

10.2 Suppose that

$$y_t = \begin{cases} \phi_1 y_{t-1} + \varepsilon_{1t} & \text{if } t \in I_1, \\ \phi_2 y_{t-1} + \varepsilon_{2t} & \text{if } t \in I_2, \end{cases}$$

where the regimes I_1, I_2 are known, and in particular $I_1 = \{1, \ldots, T/2\}$ and $I_2 = \{1 + T/2, \ldots, T\}$. You may assume that T is large. How would you:
(a) test whether $\phi_1 = \phi_2$ when $\sigma_1^2 = E(\varepsilon_{1t}^2) = \sigma_2^2 = E(\varepsilon_{2t}^2) = \sigma^2$?
(b) test whether $\phi_1 = \phi_2 = 0$ when $\sigma_1^2 = E(\varepsilon_{1t}^2) = \sigma_2^2 = E(\varepsilon_{2t}^2) = \sigma^2$?
(c) test whether $\phi_1 = \phi_2$ when $\sigma_1^2 = E(\varepsilon_{1t}^2)$ and $\sigma_2^2 = E(\varepsilon_{2t}^2)$ may not be equal?
(d) test whether $\phi_1 = \phi_2 = 0$ when $\sigma_1^2 = E(\varepsilon_{1t}^2)$ and $\sigma_2^2 = E(\varepsilon_{2t}^2)$ may not be equal?

10.3 Consider the deterministic process

$$y_{t+1} = \begin{cases} 2y_t & \text{if } 0 \leq y_t < 1/2, \\ 2y_t - 1 & \text{if } 1/2 \leq y_t \leq 1. \end{cases}$$

What values will y_{3002} take if $y_0 = 13/28$ and if $y_0 = (13/28) \times (1 - 8^{-1000})$?

10.4 Suppose that z_t is a stationary mixing process with mean μ and autocovariance $\gamma_z(\cdot)$, and that x_t is a binary sequence that is ± 1 with equal probability and independent of the process z. Let $y_t = x_t z_t$. Derive the autocovariance function of y_t.

10.5 Suppose that, for $i = 1, \ldots, n$, $y_{it} = \beta_i x_t + u_{it} = \beta_i x_t + \sigma_{it} \varepsilon_{it}$, where x_t is an observed macro time series, while ε_{it} is i.i.d. standard normal and independent of x_t and of ε_{js} for any i, j, t, s, whereas

$$\sigma_{it}^2 = \omega_i + \beta_i \sigma_{i,t-1}^2 + \gamma_i u_{i,t-1}^2,$$

where $\beta_i + \gamma_i < 1$. Let $y_t = (y_{1t}, \ldots, y_{nt})^\top$.

(a) What is the conditional covariance matrix of y_t, that is, $\text{var}(y_t \mid x_t, x_{t-1}, \ldots y_{t-1}, y_{t-2}, \ldots)$.

(b) Suppose that x_t is i.i.d. with mean μ_x and variance σ_x^2. What is the covariance matrix of y_t conditional only on past y, $\text{var}(y_t \mid y_{t-1}, y_{t-2}, \ldots)$?

(c) What is the unconditional covariance matrix of y_t, $\text{var}(y_t)$?

10.6 Suppose there is an unobserved binary stochastic process s_t such that if $s_t = 1$ then regime 1 operates, and suppose that $y_t \sim N(\mu_H, \sigma_H^2)$, whereas if $s_t = 0$ then regime 2 operates and $y_t \sim N(\mu_L, \sigma_L^2)$. Suppose that s_t is a stationary Markov process with $\pi_{ij} = \Pr(s_t = i \mid s_{t-1} = j)$ and $\pi = \Pr(s_t = 1)$.

(a) Calculate $E(y_t)$, $\text{var}(y_t)$.

(b) Calculate $\text{cov}(y_t, y_{t-1})$, and hence the best linear predictor of y_t given y_{t-1}.

(c) Calculate $\Pr(s_t = 1 \mid y_t)$.

10.7 Consider the process $y_{t+1} = (1/2 + \varepsilon_{t+1}) y_t$, where ε_t is i.i.d. with mean zero and variance $1/2$. Assuming that y_t is stationary, calculate expressions for $E(y_t)$ and $E(y_t^2)$, and show that these both go to zero as $t \to \infty$.

10.8 Consider the process $y_t = \varepsilon_t \varepsilon_{t-1}$, where ε_t is standard normal.

(a) Calculate its mean, variance, and autocovariance function. Is this process weakly stationary? Is it strongly stationary? Is it α-mixing?

(b) Try and think about whether it is a Markov process and a martingale difference sequence. What are the difficulties in answering this question?

(c) Simulate a time series y_t from this model.

10.9 Suppose that $y_t = \cos(2\pi\theta t + \varepsilon_t)$, where ε_t is an i.i.d. uniform random variable on $[-\pi, \pi]$. Calculate the autocovariance function of y_t. Now suppose that ε_t is a Gaussian autoregression with mean zero, variance one, and parameter ϕ. Calculate the autocovariance function of y_t.

10.10 Suppose that $y_t = \mu + \sigma_t \varepsilon_t$, where ε_t is i.i.d. $N(0, 1)$ and μ is an unknown parameter. Compare the following two specifications for σ_t^2 in terms of their stationarity, their dependence, and their higher-order moments.

(a) $\sigma_t^2 = \omega + \beta\sigma_{t-1}^2 + \gamma y_{t-1}^2$

(b) $\sigma_t^2 = \omega + \beta\sigma_{t-1}^2 + \gamma(y_{t-1} - \mu)^2$

10.11 Suppose that $y_t = \beta^\mathsf{T} x_t + \sigma_t \varepsilon_t$, where ε_t and $\varepsilon_t^2 - 1$ are martingale difference sequences, while

$$\sigma_t^2 = \omega + \beta\sigma_{t-1}^2 + \gamma(y_{t-1} - \beta^\mathsf{T} x_{t-1})^2,$$

where $\beta + \gamma < 1$. Here, $x_t \in \mathbb{R}^K$ are observed covariates. Discuss several ways of constructing a confidence interval for the parameter β_i for some $i \in \{1, 2, \ldots, K\}$, commenting on the properties of x_t that are assumed.

10.12 Suppose that $y_t = \beta^\mathsf{T} x_t + \sigma_t \varepsilon_t$, where ε_t and $\varepsilon_t^2 - 1$ are martingale difference sequences, while

$$\sigma_t^2 = \omega + \gamma(y_{t-1} - \beta^\mathsf{T} x_{t-1})^2,$$

where $x_t \in \mathbb{R}^K$ are observed covariates. Discuss how to test the hypothesis that $\gamma = 0$ versus the hypothesis that $\gamma > 0$.

10.13 Suppose that $y_t = \sigma_t \varepsilon_t$, where ε_t is i.i.d. $N(0, 1)$ and $\sigma_t^2 = \omega + \gamma y_{t-1}^2$. Suppose that y_t is weakly stationary with variance σ^2. Show that $\omega = \sigma^2(1 - \gamma)$. The target variance estimator involves replacing σ^2 by $\hat{\sigma}^2 = \sum_{t=1}^{T} y_t^2 / T$ and then doing the no-intercept regression

$$\hat{\gamma} = \frac{\sum_{t=2}^{T} (y_{t-1}^2 - \hat{\sigma}^2)(y_t^2 - \hat{\sigma}^2)}{\sum_{t=2}^{T} (y_{t-1}^2 - \hat{\sigma}^2)^2}.$$

Compare this estimator with the Gaussian MLE.

10.14 Consider the IGARCH(1,1) process $y_t = \sigma_t \varepsilon_t$ with

$$\sigma_t^2 = \omega + \beta \sigma_{t-1}^2 + (1 - \beta) y_{t-1}^2,$$

where $y_0 = 0$ is given and ε_t is i.i.d. with distribution $N(0, 1)$.
(a) Show that the process y_t is not weakly stationary when $\beta \in (0, 1)$.
(b) Let $x_t = y_t^2$. Write x_t as an ARMA(1,1) process of the form

$$x_t = \mu + \phi x_{t-1} + \eta_t - \theta \eta_{t-1},$$

where η_t is a martingale difference sequence; give explicit expressions for μ, ϕ, θ. Hence show that y_t^2 is not weakly stationary.
(c) Now consider the differenced process $\Delta x_t = x_t - x_{t-1}$. Is this weakly stationary?

10.15 For the sp500 dataset calculate the daily stock return $r_t = (P_t - P_{t-1})/P_{t-1}$, where P_t is the closing price. Fit the GARCH(1,1) model to the data for the whole period. Now work with each decade separately and fit the GARCH(1,1) model to each subperiod. Compare the results.

10.16 Suppose that $y_t = (y_{1t}, y_{2t})$ satisfies $y_t = \Sigma_t^{1/2} \varepsilon_t$, where ε_t is i.i.d. with mean zero and covariance vector I_2, while

$$\text{vech}(\Sigma_t) = \begin{pmatrix} \sigma_{11,t} \\ \sigma_{12,t} \\ \sigma_{22,t} \end{pmatrix} = \begin{pmatrix} a_{11} \\ a_{12} \\ a_{22} \end{pmatrix} + \begin{pmatrix} b_{11} & 0 & b_{13} \\ 0 & b_{22} & 0 \\ b_{31} & 0 & b_{33} \end{pmatrix} \begin{pmatrix} y_{1,t-1}^2 \\ y_{1,t-1} y_{2,t-1} \\ y_{2,t-1}^2 \end{pmatrix}.$$

Discuss the justification behind such a specification. Under what conditions is the process y_t weakly stationary? Consider the regression equations

$$y_{1t}^2 = \alpha_1 + \beta_{11} y_{1,t-1}^2 + \beta_{12} y_{2,t-1}^2 + e_{1t},$$
$$y_{2t}^2 = \alpha_2 + \beta_{21} y_{1,t-1}^2 + \beta_{22} y_{2,t-1}^2 + e_{2t},$$
$$y_{1t} y_{2t} = \alpha_3 + \beta_3 y_{1,t-1} y_{2,t-1} + e_{3t}.$$

Do the OLS estimators here provide consistent estimators of the parameters a_{ij}, b_{ij}?

11 Nonparametric Methods and Machine Learning

So far we have emphasized parametric models to take account of potential nonlinearity in which we allow for a small number of unknowns whose meaning is specified. We next turn to nonparametric methods that allow for nonlinearity in a flexible way, without specifying a particular form, that is, without specifying the unknowns. There is a range of settings where these methods are useful, and there is a range of different nonparametric methods designed to learn functional form.

11.1 Nonparametric CDF and Quantile Estimation

Suppose that y_t is a stationary and mixing process with stationary distribution (CDF) F. The distribution function features in theories about stochastic dominance and measuring inequality. In this estimation problem we impose no additional conditions on F other than what is implied by its definition as a probability, $F(y) = \Pr(y_t \leq y)$. Specifically, F lies between zero and one and is weakly increasing in y so that $F(y) \geq F(y')$ for any y, y' with $y \geq y'$. It can also be shown that F is continuous except at possibly a countable number of such points, but it need not have any other properties. In that sense the set of distributions is very large; it includes continuous and discrete distributions, and distributions that contain both components. One could assume further that F is a smooth function with a density f, but this is not necessary here as we shall see. Define the α-quantile of y_t by the number q_α that satisfies $F(q_\alpha) = \alpha$ for any $\alpha \in [0, 1]$, which is uniquely defined when the CDF is strictly increasing, and in which case q_α is a strictly increasing function of α.

We estimate $F(y)$ by the empirical CDF

$$F_T(y) = \frac{1}{T} \sum_{t=1}^{T} 1 (y_t \leq y), \quad y \in \mathbb{R}. \tag{11.1}$$

This estimator obeys $0 \leq F_T(y) \leq 1$ and is weakly increasing; it is a step function with jumps of height $1/T$ (assuming no ties, which happens with probability zero for continuously distributed data). This is a **càdlàg** (*continue à droite, limite à gauche*) function but is not continuous regardless of whether the population CDF F is continuous or not. We estimate the quantile function by the sample quantity $\widehat{q}_\alpha$ for any $\alpha \in [0, 1]$, that is, $\widehat{q}_\alpha$ is any number such that

$$F_T(\widehat{q}_\alpha) = \alpha. \tag{11.2}$$

Clearly, $\widehat{q}_\alpha$ may not be unique even when q_α is, and some further rule is used to enforce uniqueness. We have the property that $\widehat{q}_\alpha$ is weakly increasing in α. The multivariate extension of the CDF and its estimation is straightforward, based on the coordinatewise definition $y_{1t} \leq y_1, \ldots, y_{nt} \leq y_n$, but the multivariate quantile is a topic of some subtlety that is not addressed here.

The empirical CDF is consistent (uniformly over $\mathbb{R}$) and satisfies an FCLT under some regularity conditions, that is,

$$\sqrt{T}\left(F_T(\cdot) - F(\cdot)\right) \Longrightarrow G(\cdot), \tag{11.3}$$

where the limit is a Gaussian process with a complicated covariance function (Davidson, 1994). Specifically, the asymptotic variance of $F_T(y)$ is the long-run variance of the indicator series $x_t = 1(y_t \leq y)$, that is, $\sum_{j=-\infty}^{\infty}(F_j(y, y) - F^2(y))$, where $F_j(y, y) = \Pr(y_t \leq y, y_{t-j} \leq y)$. Inference about F requires long-run variance estimation, or block bootstrap, or similar. Note that this is true even if y_t itself is an MDS, since this generally does not imply that $1(y_t \leq y) - F(y)$ is an MDS. For this theory, the target function F has to be weakly increasing and be almost everywhere continuous but otherwise is not restricted, and despite that the empirical CDF is consistent at the rate of $\sqrt{T}$. This is not the case for density or regression estimation, as we shall see. The sample quantile function is also consistent and satisfies an FCLT at a rate of the square root of the sample size under some conditions (Shorack and Wellner, 1986).

Durbin (1973) extended the classic results in the i.i.d. setting to allow for the case where F may depend on parameters. For example, if y_t is a stationary Gaussian process with mean μ and variance σ^2, we may estimate the CDF of $x_t = (y_t - \mu)/\sigma$ by

$$\widetilde{F}_T(x) = \frac{1}{T}\sum_{t=1}^{T}\left(\frac{y_t - \bar{y}}{s} \leq x\right),$$

where $\bar{y}, s^2$ are the sample mean and variance of y_t.

A concrete application of CDF estimation is in the testing of stochastic dominance (Levy, 2006). Suppose that $\{(x_t, y_t), t = 1, \ldots, T\}$ is a stationary sequence, where $F(x) = \Pr(x_t \leq x)$ and $G(y) = \Pr(y_t \leq y)$ are the marginal CDFs. For example, they could be stock returns that are mutually dependent and dependent over time. The null hypothesis of interest is that F dominates G, that is, $F(x) \leq G(x)$ for all x. In this case any rational, as yet unsatisfied, investor should prefer x over y. The test statistic is

$$\tau_T = \sqrt{T}\sup_{x \in \mathbb{R}}\left(F_T(x) - G_T(x)\right),$$

which under the null hypothesis either tends to minus infinity (if $F \neq G$) or, if $F = G$, converges in distribution to a complicated limiting random variable. Under the alternative, $\tau_T \to \infty$. In the time series case, Linton, Maasoumi, and Whang (2008) proposed a subsampling method for inference. That is, calculate

$$\tau_b^*(t) = \sqrt{b}\sup_{y \in \mathbb{R}}\left(\frac{1}{b}\sum_{j=0}^{b-1}1\left(y_{t+j} \leq y\right) - \frac{1}{T}\sum_{t=1}^{T}1\left(y_t \leq y\right)\right)$$

for $t = 1, \ldots, T + 1 - b$. Figure 11.1 shows a comparison of the CDFs and integrated CDFs of the daily stock returns of five tech stocks.

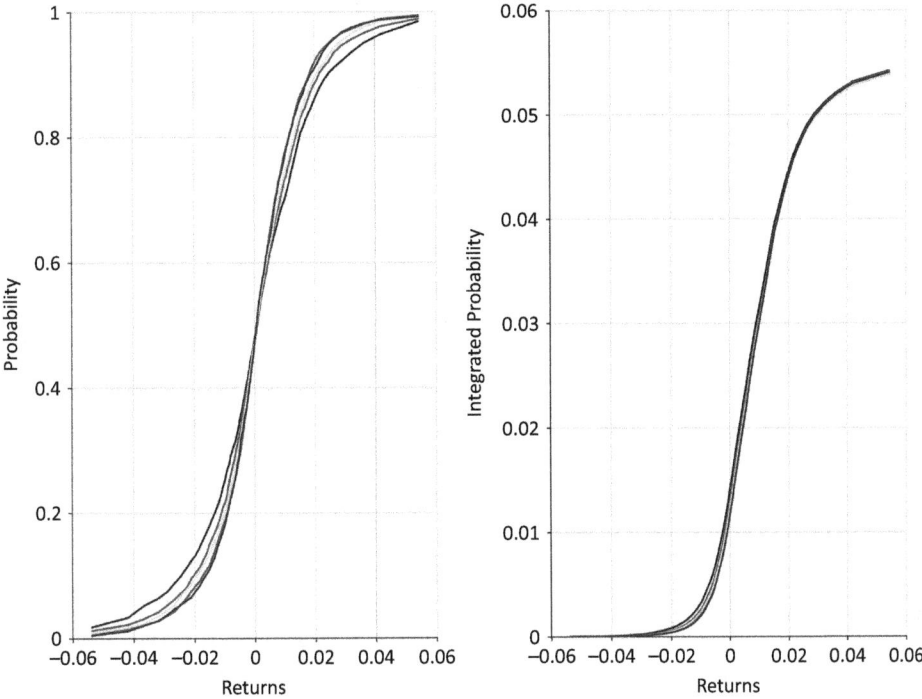

Figure 11.1 Estimated and integrated CDFs of daily stock returns for Facebook, Google, Amazon, Apple, and Microsoft.

Related to this, the Mann–Whitney test is a classic statistic (formulated for i.i.d. bivariate data) that tests whether $\Pr(x_t > y_t) = \Pr(x_t < y_t) = 1/2$. Suppose that we have samples $\{x_1, \ldots, x_T\}$ and $\{y_1, \ldots, y_T\}$, then

$$U_T = \frac{1}{T^2} \sum_{t=1}^{T} \sum_{s=1}^{T} 1(x_t > y_s).$$

Under the null hypothesis that $\Pr(x_t > y_t) = 1/2$ and that x_t, y_t are mutually independent and weakly dependent, Dedecker and Saulière (2017) showed that

$$\sqrt{T}\left(U_T - \frac{1}{2}\right) \Longrightarrow N(0, V), \qquad V = \text{lrvar}(F(x_t)) + \text{lrvar}(G(y_t)).$$

One can apply the methods of Chapter 5 to carry out this test.

Suppose that y_t follows a Gaussian copula autoregression (10.29). That is, the marginal distribution F could be anything (even the Cauchy distribution), but the dependence structure is driven by an autoregression on the transformed variables. We compute

$$F_T(x) = \frac{1}{T} \sum_{t=1}^{T} 1\left(y_t \leq x\right),$$

and let $u_t = F_T(y_t)$ and $z_t = \Phi^{-1}(F_T(y_t))$, and then fit an AR($p$) model to z_t. We applied this to the S&P500 daily return series and obtained $\phi_1 = 0.026\,435$ (0.006\,557),

$\phi_2 = -0.021\,862$ (0.006 559), $\phi_3 = -0.001\,753$ (0.006 560), $\phi_4 = 0.003\,435$ (0.006 559), and $\phi_5 = 0.001\,447$ (0.006 556).

11.1.1 A Semiparametric Model of Tail Thickness

The CDF estimator has the limitation that $F_T(y) = 0$ for all $y < \min\{y_1, \ldots, y_T\}$ and $F_T(y) = 1$ for all $y > \max\{y_1, \ldots, y_T\}$, and so there is no way to extrapolate beyond what has already been seen in the sample. In many applications we would like to have some way of assessing the likelihood of extreme values that have not yet been seen. How likely is it that we have a catastrophic flood in the next 10 years?

We consider some models for the tail thickness of a distribution that allow us to extrapolate beyond the sample data. One model, for example, is the normal distribution. This has light tails, meaning that $\Pr(y_t > x)$ decays to zero very fast as $x \to \infty$ such that all moments exist. For daily stock returns this is a little restrictive. Alternative distributions like the t-distribution allow more general tail behavior. The Pareto distribution has been widely used, following Mandelbrot (1963), to model stock returns and income distributions, and is quite flexible with regard to the tail behavior. Since our focus here is really on the tails of the distribution we consider a semiparametric model that specifies what happens in the tails but does not specify what happens in the center of the distribution.

Definition 11.1   We suppose that y_t has CDF F on $\mathbb{R}$, which is unknown, and satisfies

$$F(y) \simeq 1 - L(y)y^{-\kappa} \tag{11.4}$$

as $y \to \infty$. Here, $\kappa > 0$ is called the tail index and $L(y)$ is a constant or a **slowly varying function** for which $\lim_{y\to\infty} L(ay)/L(y) = 1$ for all $a > 0$. If $F(y)$ has a density $f(y)$, then $f(y) \simeq \kappa L(y)y^{-(\kappa+1)}$ as $y \to \infty$. The quantile function satisfies $q_{1-\alpha} = L^*(1/\alpha)\alpha^{-1/\kappa}$ as $\alpha \to 0$, where $L^*(1/\alpha)$ is a constant or slowly varying function.

This is a kind of smoothness condition, but only operating in the tails of the distribution. One can separately model left and right tails, but usually the focus is just on the downside area. The Cauchy distribution falls into this class for both upper and lower tails with $\kappa = 1$, and more generally the t-distribution with degrees of freedom κ follows this law. Suppose that $L(y) = c \log y$ (which is the leading example of a slowly varying function). The function $L(y)$, although not explicitly specified, plays a less important role than κ. Under the model assumption, $E(|y_t|^\gamma) = \infty$ for all $\gamma \geq \kappa$ but $E(|y_t|^\gamma) < \infty$ for all $\gamma < \kappa$. Thus, the parameter κ is the key quantity that measures the frequency of large events and the existence of moments. This model is semiparametric, since it only concerns large values of y and says nothing specific about how F behaves when y is close to zero, for example. The large-y case behavior is what we need to understand how sample extremes would behave. The model imposes heavy tails on the distribution F; distributions such as the normal with a thin tail are ruled out of this ecology. The model also rules out super heavy-tailed distributions such as the **log Cauchy**, whose distribution tails decay slower than $y^{-\kappa}$ for any κ (logarithmically, in fact).

This Pareto tail model is used in many contexts in physical and social sciences (**Zipf's law, Gibrat's law**). It describes city sizes quite well. It seems to describe high-frequency stock returns (and trading volume) better than the Gaussian model. In fact, the GARCH model with i.i.d. Gaussian innovations implies that observed returns satisfy this model. We next discuss how to estimate the parameters of this model.

11.1.2 Estimation of Tail Thickness

The model depends on the quantities κ and $L(y)$, which are generally unknown. We next consider how to estimate them. We first order the data $y_{(1)} > \cdots > y_{(T)}$, where the notation indicates that the index of the typical **order statistic** $y_{(t)}$, say, is some other t' that is suppressed here. The integers (t) are known as the **ranks** of the corresponding t' and satisfy $\Pr(y_t > y_{(j)}) \simeq j/T$. Let M be a large integer but smaller than T. For large-order statistics $y_{(j)}$ with $j \leq M + 1$, we have

$$\log \Pr(y_t > y_{(j)}) \simeq -\kappa \log(y_{(j)}) + \log L(y_{(j)}),$$

so that, subtracting $\log \Pr(y_t > y_{(M+1)})$ from both sides, we obtain approximately

$$\log(j/(M+1)) = -\kappa \log(y_{(j)}/y_{(M+1)}) + \log L(y_{(j)})/L(y_{(M+1)})$$
$$\simeq -\kappa \log(y_{(j)}/y_{(M+1)}), \tag{11.5}$$

because $L(y_{(j)})/L(y_{(M+1)}) \to 1$ as $T \to \infty$. Furthermore, since $\int_1^t \log(x)\,dx = t \log t - t + 1$ we have $\log(M+1) - \sum_{j=1}^{M} \log(j)/M \to 1$. Therefore,

$$\frac{1}{M} \sum_{j=1}^{M} \log \frac{y_{(j)}}{y_{(M+1)}} = \frac{1}{\kappa} \frac{1}{M} \sum_{j=1}^{M} (\log(M+1) - \log j)$$

$$= \frac{1}{\kappa} \left(\log(M+1) - \frac{1}{M} \sum_{j=1}^{M} \log j \right) \simeq \frac{1}{\kappa},$$

which suggests how to estimate κ. We next formally define an estimator of κ, and use this to define an estimator of extreme quantiles, that is, quantiles q_α with $\alpha \to 1$ (and $\alpha \to 1$ at any rate, thereby allowing extrapolation outside of the sample range).

Definition 11.2 (Hill (1975) estimator) Let $M = M(T)$ be some threshold value. Compute

$$\frac{1}{\widehat{\kappa}} = \frac{1}{M} \sum_{j=1}^{M} \log \left(\frac{y_{(j)}}{y_{(M+1)}} \right), \tag{11.6}$$

$$\widehat{q}_{1-\alpha} = \widehat{L}_T \alpha^{-1/\widehat{\kappa}}, \quad \widehat{L}_T = y_{(M+1)} \left(\frac{M}{T} \right)^{1/\widehat{\kappa}}, \quad \text{for } \alpha < M/T. \tag{11.7}$$

For the quantile estimator one can extrapolate in other ways. For example, we may take $\widehat{L}_T = y_{(1)}/T^{1/\widehat{\kappa}}$, in which case this estimator coincides with the sample maximum when $\alpha = 1/T$. The estimated tail thickness parameter is consistent and asymptotically normal at rate $M^{1/2}$ provided $M \to \infty$ and $M/T \to 0$.

Theorem 11.1   *Suppose, for i.i.d. data, that the von Mises condition*

$$\lim_{y \to \infty} \frac{y f(y)}{1 - F(y)} = \kappa > 0 \tag{11.8}$$

holds, where F has a density $f = F'$. Then

$$M^{1/2} (\widehat{\kappa} - \kappa) \Longrightarrow N(0, \kappa^2). \tag{11.9}$$

The quantity M has to be chosen not too big and not too small. There is a theory for determination of optimal M under additional conditions, but this is beyond the scope of our work here. We explore below the practical consequences of different choices of M.

There are several alternative estimators of κ in popular use. Gabaix and Ibragimov (2011) proposed the log rank estimator, which is based on fitting the linear regression

$$\log (i - \delta) = a - b \log \left(y_{(i)} \right), \quad i = 1, \dots, M, \tag{11.10}$$

for given $\delta \in [0, 1)$ to find the estimates $\widehat{a}_\delta, \widehat{b}_\delta$. They showed that $\widehat{b}_\delta \to \kappa$ as $M \to \infty$, and indeed (11.9) holds. They recommended taking $\delta = 1/2$ as this most improves the finite-sample performance of the estimator. This estimator is quite popular in practice and equally easy to apply.

The distribution theory for these estimators has been extended to a general time series context. Under very weak conditions on the amount of dependence, the consistency result for the Hill estimator generalizes to stationary time series data (Resnick and Stărică, 1998). Hill (2010) showed under some conditions that

$$M^{1/2} (\widehat{\kappa} - \kappa) \Longrightarrow N(0, \Phi) \tag{11.11}$$

for some variance Φ. In general $\Phi \geq \kappa^2$, and Φ depends on the dependence structure. For some special cases, including strong GARCH models, $\Phi = \kappa^2$. The result holds because although the strong GARCH process has dependent extremes, a crucial stochastic array has linearly independent extremes. This property is found in many similar strong GARCH-type processes. However, this property is not guaranteed to hold, for example, in a semi-strong GARCH process, and in this case Φ is not necessarily equal to κ^2. Hill (2010) proposed an estimator of Φ that is consistent under general conditions.

We apply the Hill method to the S&P500 daily returns. In Figure 11.2 we show the estimated tail indexes (upper and lower) against the threshold value M. The estimates depend on the threshold chosen but seem to stabilize to somewhere between three and four. The standard errors from (11.9) with $M = 100$ are of the order 0.3–0.4 and so these quantities seem to be quite well measured. This is broadly consistent with the empirical results presented in Gabaix *et al.* (2006), which argued that returns follow a cubic power law ($\kappa = 3$) consistently over time and internationally. They worked with high-frequency data on around 1000 stocks over 1994–1997, aggregating to 15 minutes, 1 hour, 1 day, and 1 week. They also argued that trading volume follows a half-cubic law ($\kappa = 3/2$) and presented a theory that explains these empirical regularities. They also argued that, based on the power-law distribution, the 1929 and 1987 crashes are not "outliers," meaning that these values are broadly consistent with the extreme value theory associated with the cubic law.

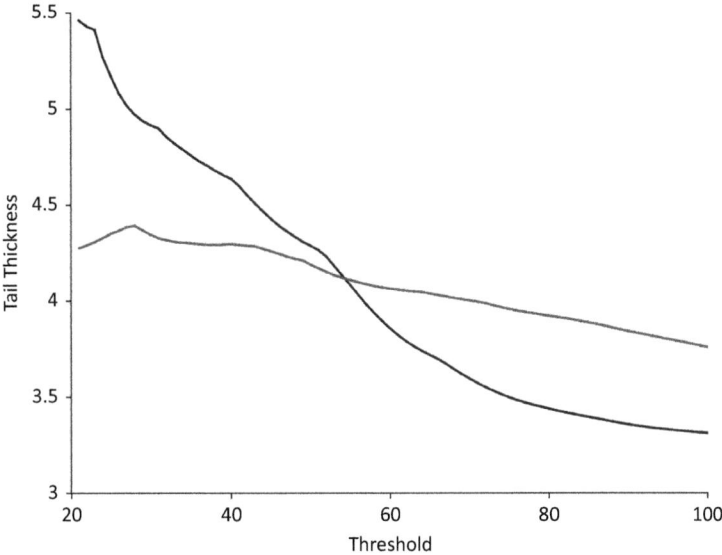

Figure 11.2 Estimation of tail thickness parameters of daily S&P500 stock returns by threshold level.

11.1.3 Nonparametric Dependence Testing

One approach is to work with the autocorrelations of transforms of the raw series like ranks or signs. The Spearman rank correlation is well known to high school students and is easily computed in terms of the empirical distribution function. Suppose that y_t is a stationary series and let $x_t = TF_T(y_t) \in \{1, 2, \ldots, T\}$, where F_T is the empirical CDF defined in (11.1). Then the rank autocorrelation is the sample autocorrelation of the series x_t. Likewise, we may take $x_t = \text{sign}(y_t)$ and compute its sample autocorrelations. Under the null hypothesis of i.i.d. data, the rank and sign autocorrelations are approximately $N(0, 1/T)$ and so Bartlett bounds may be used. In fact, for the sign transformation this continues to be true provided only that the conditional distribution of y_t given the past is symmetric about its median. One can also calculate cross-autocorrelations of a bivariate time series in this way. These methods are sometimes called nonparametric or robust, because they do not implicitly or explicitly assume a target or benchmark distribution and retain validity under extreme conditions such as Pareto tails.

The **quantilogram** (Linton and Whang, 2007; Han *et al.*, 2016) is a more general way for testing dependence in a time series. Suppose that y_t is a stationary process whose marginal distribution has quantiles q_α for $0 < \alpha < 1$. Define the quantilogram

$$\rho_\alpha(k) = \frac{E\left(\psi_\alpha(y_t - q_\alpha)\psi_\alpha(y_{t+k} - q_\alpha)\right)}{E\left(\psi_\alpha^2(y_t - q_\alpha)\right)}, \quad k = 1, 2, \ldots, \tag{11.12}$$

where $\psi_\alpha(x) = \text{sign}(x) - (1 - 2\alpha)$ is the check function. By definition, we have $E(\psi_\alpha(y_t - q_\alpha)) = 0$ for all α. For a series that is i.i.d., $\rho_\alpha(k) = 0$ for all α and all $k \neq 1$. This can be (partially) true for some non-i.i.d. series, that is, $\rho_\alpha(k) = 0$ for some α and all $k \neq 1$.

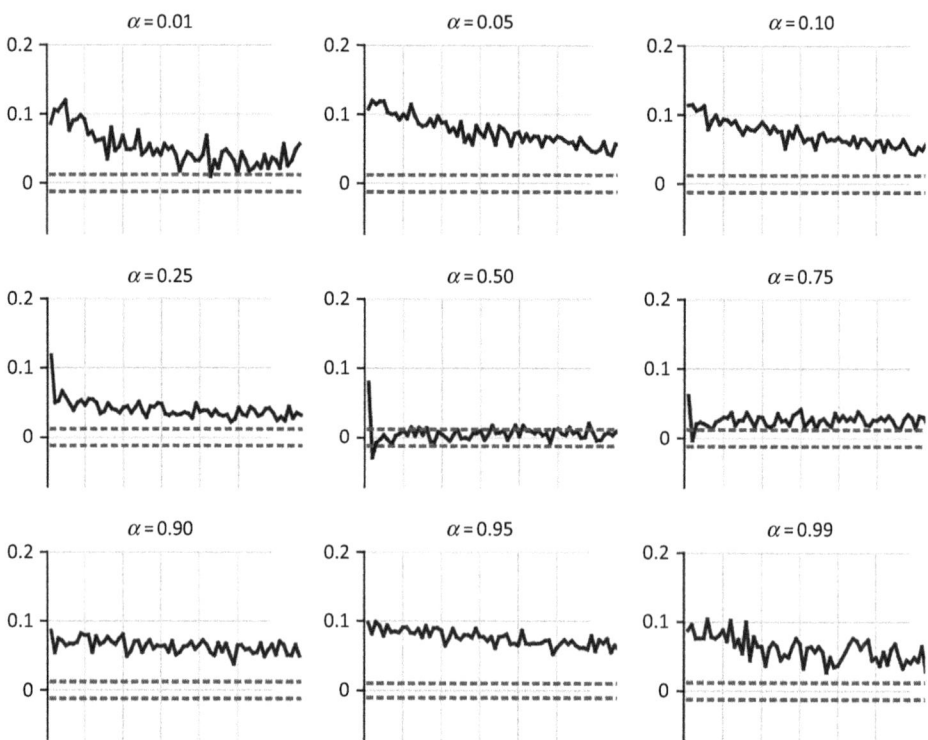

Figure 11.3 Quantilogram of daily Fama–French market returns out to 66 lags, for different α values.

We compute the empirical counterpart of $\rho_\alpha(\cdot)$. We first estimate q_α by the sample quantile $\widehat{q}_\alpha$. Then let

$$\widehat{\rho}_\alpha(k) = \frac{\sum_{t=1}^{T-k} \psi_\alpha(y_t - \widehat{q}_\alpha)\psi_\alpha(y_{t+k} - \widehat{q}_\alpha)}{\sqrt{\sum_{t=1}^{T-k} \psi_\alpha^2(y_t - \widehat{q}_\alpha)}\sqrt{\sum_{t=1}^{T-k} \psi_\alpha^2(y_{t+k} - \widehat{q}_\alpha)}},$$

$k = 1, 2, \ldots, T-1$, for any $\alpha \in (0, 1)$. Note that $-1 \leq \widehat{\rho}_\alpha(k) \leq 1$ for any α, k because this is just a sample correlation based on the data $\psi_\alpha(y_t - \widehat{q}_\alpha)$. Under the assumption of i.i.d., these can be compared with the Bartlett bounds. Han *et al.* (2016) developed a more general theory and provided tools for inference based on bootstrap and other methods. The R package `quantilogram` offers a range of options for implementing this. The quantilogram of S&P500 daily returns in Figure 11.3 shows strong dependence in the lower quantiles, $\alpha = 0.01, 0.05$, whereas at the median, $\alpha = 0.5$, the dependence is as mild as for the usual autocorrelations.

11.2   Nonparametric Smoothing

We next turn to settings where we need to use **smoothing methods**, which are designed to exploit smoothness in the function being estimated, so we take some time to introduce a class of smoothness measures. For ease of reference we call them the **Stone class** after

Stone (1980, 1982). For a function $f \colon \mathbb{R}^d \to \mathbb{R}$ and integer vector $v = (v_1, \ldots, v_d)^\mathsf{T}$, write $D^v f(x) = \partial^{\sum_{j=1}^d v_j} f(x_1, \ldots, x_d)/\partial^{v_1} \cdots \partial^{v_d}$, when this exists. Then define

$$\mathfrak{F}^{r,\alpha,C,d} = \left\{ f \colon \mathbb{R}^d \to \mathbb{R} \text{ such that, } \forall v \in \mathbb{R}^d \text{ with } \sum_{j=1}^d v_j \leq r, \right.$$

$$\left. |D^v f(x) - D^v f(y)| \leq C \, \|x - y\|^\alpha \right\}. \quad (11.13)$$

This is the set of functions that are i.e. 'r times' differentiable in each coordinate whose rth derivatives obey the **Hölder condition** (given in the second inequality) for some $\alpha \in (0, 1]$ and some $C < \infty$. The key parameters here are $r + \alpha$ and d, the smoothness and the dimensionality, which determine how well a given function $f \in \mathfrak{F}^{r,\alpha,C,d}$ can be estimated in terms of MSE. The higher the smoothness, the better, whereas the higher the dimensionality, the worse: the curse of dimensionality and the blessing of smoothness (Stone, 1980, 1982). Spectral density estimation (discussed in Chapter 4) is a special case of this in which $d = 1$; in that case, the smoothness of the spectral density relates to the memory/persistence of the time series process itself.

11.2.1 Density Estimation

Suppose that the population random variable is continuously distributed with a density $f(y)$, $y \in \mathbb{R}$, and it is of interest to estimate that density. Note that the density function can be interpreted as the (almost everywhere) derivative of the CDF,

$$f(y) = \lim_{h \to 0} \frac{1}{2h} \Pr(y - h \leq y_t \leq y + h) = \lim_{h \to 0} \frac{1}{2h} E\left(1(y - h \leq y_t \leq y + h)\right),$$

but the density function cannot be estimated by the derivative of $F_T(y)$, since this is a discontinuous function at the sample points and zero elsewhere. However, a numerical derivative with small h (but not too small) would be

$$\widehat{f}(y) = \frac{1}{2h} \left[F_T(y + h) - F_T(y - h) \right].$$

This can be written in the form

$$\widehat{f}(y) = \frac{1}{2Th} \sum_{t=1}^T 1 \left(|y_t - y| \leq h \right).$$

We now define a more general class of kernel estimators of the density. Let h be a scalar bandwidth and $K(\cdot)$ a kernel satisfying $\int K(u) \, du = 1$ and $K_h(\cdot) = h^{-1} K(h^{-1} \cdot)$. Then define the kernel density estimator,

$$\widehat{f}(y) = \frac{1}{T} \sum_{t=1}^T K_h(y - y_t). \quad (11.14)$$

This estimator was introduced by Rosenblatt (1956). The bandwidth and kernel determine the properties of $\widehat{f}(y)$.

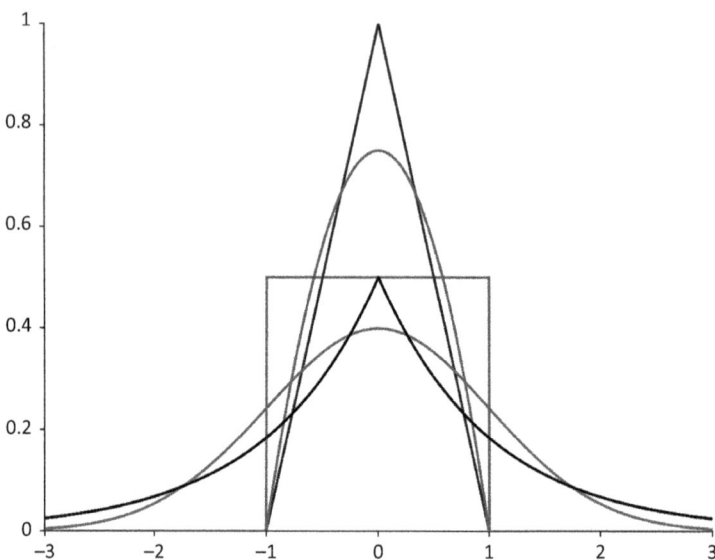

Figure 11.4 Different kernels: uniform, triangular, quadratic, Gaussian, and exponential.

Definition 11.3   Define, for any kernel K, $\mu_{i,j}(K) = \int u^i K(u)^j \, du$ for i, j integers, where the integrals here are over the support of the kernel, which in general is some compact interval or the real line. Note that $\mu_{0,2}(K) = \|K\|_2^2$. A kernel K is said to be of order q if K is a bounded continuous function that satisfies $\mu_{0,1}(K) = 1$, $\mu_{i,1}(K) = 0$, $i = 1, \ldots, q-1$, and $\mu_{q,1}(K) < \infty$.

Frequently, attention is restricted to K being a probability density function symmetric about zero for which $q = 2$. In this case, $\widehat{f}_h(y) \geq 0$ for all y. In the special case where the support of y is the entire real line, we also have $\int_{-\infty}^{\infty} \widehat{f}_h(y) \, dy = 1$ and so the density estimator is a proper density itself. The tails of the kernel density estimator (i.e., beyond the sample range) are like the tails of the kernel K. So, for example, if K were standard normal, then the tails of $\widehat{f}(y)$ as $y \to \pm\infty$ behave like the tails of the normal density function. If K has a compact support then $\widehat{f}(y) = 0$ for all y more than a small distance from the realized sample range. Figure 11.4 shows some leading kernels.

If there are restrictions on the support of y (such as it is compact or bounded below by zero) it may be advisable to use a more complicated kernel that has two or more parameters (Chen, 1999). So-called boundary kernels are functions of two arguments, $K(u, t)$, where the parameter t controls the support of the kernel; thus, $K(u, t)$ has support $[-1, t]$ and satisfies $\int_{-1}^{t} K(u, t) \, du = 1$, $\int_{-1}^{t} u^j K(u, t) \, du = 0$, $j = 1, \ldots, q - 1$, and $\int_{-1}^{t} u^q K(u, t) \, du < \infty$, as for regular kernels.

Sometimes we might be interested in the derivatives of the density, such as, for example, when determining the mode of a distribution. Density derivatives can be estimated by differentiating the estimate of f the required number of times. This works provided the estimate of f is itself smooth enough, which can be achieved, for example, by taking K to be smooth like the Gaussian density function, in which case the estimator is infinitely differentiable everywhere (even if the true density function is not).

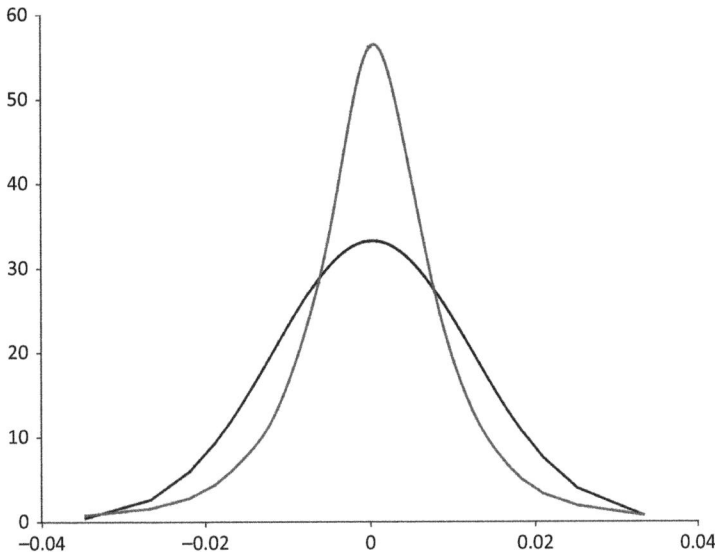

Figure 11.5 S&P500 daily return kernel density estimate along with a normal distribution.

Suppose that $y_t \in \mathbb{R}^d$. Then we replace the univariate K and h by a multivariate kernel $\mathcal{K}$ that integrates to one over $\mathbb{R}^d$ and a symmetric and positive definite bandwidth matrix H; specifically, we replace $K((y - y_t)/h)/h$ in (11.14) by $\mathcal{K}(H^{-1/2}(y - y_t))/\sqrt{\det(H)}$. A special case of this is where $\mathcal{K}$ is elliptically symmetric so that $\mathcal{K}(H^{-1/2}(y - y_t)) = K(\|y - y_t\|_H)$, where $\|A\|_H = [\text{tr}(A^\mathsf{T} H^{-1} A)]^{1/2}$. In practice one does not want to choose an entire matrix of bandwidths without some structure. There are several simplifying approaches. First, let $H = h\Sigma$, where Σ is some known symmetric positive-definite matrix (such as the sample covariance matrix of x) and h is a scalar bandwidth sequence. A second approach is based on "product kernels," where $\mathcal{K}(y) = K(y_1) \times \cdots \times K(y_d)$ and $H = \text{diag}\{h_1, \ldots, h_d\}$, where again h_j may reflect the scale of the jth covariate. In this case,

$$\widehat{f}(y) = \frac{1}{T} \sum_{t=1}^{T} K_{h_1}(y_1 - y_{1t}) \times \cdots \times K_{h_d}(y_d - y_{dt}).$$

The main issue in the multivariate case is the so-called curse of dimensionality: the sparsity of data increases with dimensions, which implies deterioration of performance.

We next show some density estimates based on the Gaussian kernel. In Figure 11.5 we show the kernel density estimate of the daily S&P500 stock returns over the period 1927 to 2020 along with a normal density with the same mean and variance. The estimated density is close to symmetric around its mean. The key difference visible from this figure is the peakedness of the estimated density at zero, which is the counterpart of the heavy-tailed behavior (which is harder to see from the density plot). In Figure 11.6 we show the estimated density of the daily VIX time series along with a normal density with the same mean and variance. This density is strongly asymmetric with a long right tail and some apparent hard lower bound. In Figure 11.7 we show the estimated density of the log of the daily VIX time series along with a normal density with the same mean and

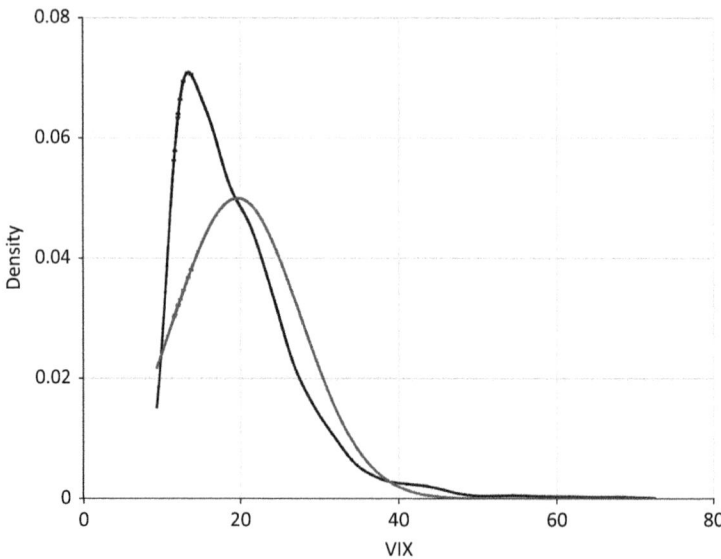

Figure 11.6 Density plot of daily VIX closing prices along with normal density with the same mean and variance. The bandwidth is Silverman rule of thumb, sample size $T = 8328$.

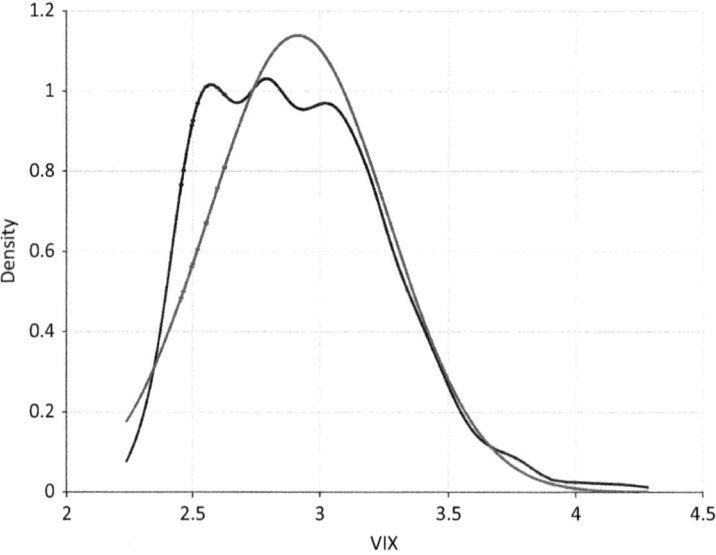

Figure 11.7 Density plot of daily log(VIX) along with normal density with the same mean and variance. The bandwidth is Silverman rule of thumb, $h = 0.061$.

variance. This density is closer to symmetric but has a rather flat top and still a longer right tail.

In Figure 11.8 we show the estimated density of marathon times from the dataset `marathon`; this density seems to have a fairly flat single peak between four and five hours, has a clear lower bound at about two hours, and a rather longer right tail.

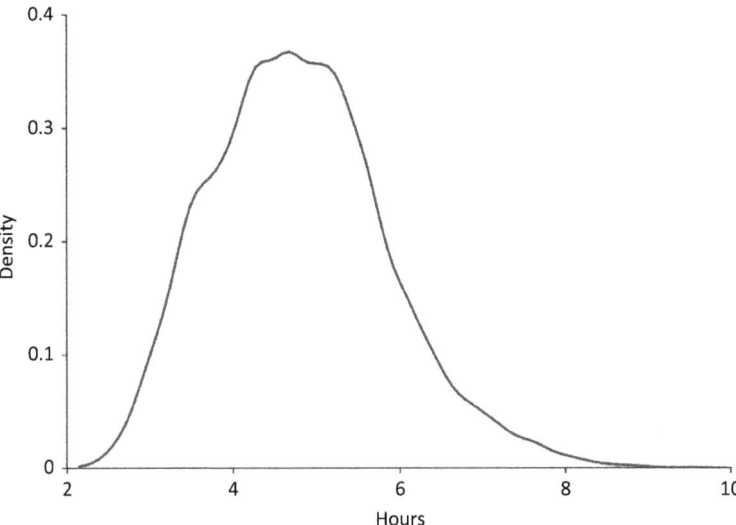

Figure 11.8 Marathon time kernel density estimate.

11.2.2 Regression and Autoregression

Suppose that (X, Y) are random variables, where $X \in \mathbb{R}^d$ and $Y \in \mathbb{R}$. We seek to estimate the conditional expectation at the point $x \in \mathbb{R}^d$, $m(x) = E(Y \mid X = x)$. The function $m(\cdot)$ is unknown but obeys some smoothness properties. A formal definition of conditional expectation is rather abstract and can be found in probability texts. If $E(Y^2) < \infty$, then we can interpret the regression function $m(\cdot)$ as the function of X that minimizes $E[\{Y - g(X)\}^2]$ with respect to (measurable) functions g.

Suppose that one observes a sample $\{(x_t, y_t), t = 1, \ldots, T\}$, where (x_t, y_t) is a stationary and mixing process with the same distribution as (X, Y). Then we can write this in regression model format,

$$y_t = m(x_t) + \varepsilon_t, \quad t = 1, \ldots, T, \tag{11.15}$$

where ε_t is a random error that satisfies $E(\varepsilon_t \mid x_t = x) = 0$ with probability one. We shall also assume that $\mathrm{var}(y_t \mid x_t = x) = \sigma^2(x) < \infty$. The dimensionality of X and the smoothness of m determine how well this function can be estimated, but also the dependence of the error process matters. Note that the derived process $\{\varepsilon_t, t = 1, \ldots, T\}$, is stationary and mixing by construction. The covariates x_t may include lagged values of the output y_t, in which case there may be implied restrictions on $\mathrm{cov}(\varepsilon_t, \varepsilon_s)$, but in general we may have $\mathrm{cov}(\varepsilon_t, \varepsilon_s) \neq 0$. We are also interested in the trend case where x_t, or some components of x_t, are the deterministic trend t/T, which was already treated above. We shall suppose here that x_t is continuously distributed; the case where x_t is discrete is somewhat easier and more akin to CDF estimation, since one would observe repeated values at the same covariate support point.

For some time series, especially financial time series, it is also of interest to model the conditional variance, thus we may consider nonparametric autoregressive variance with exogenous variables models (NARVAX(p, p', q, q')) of the form

$$y_t = m(y_{t-1}, \ldots, y_{t-p}, x_t, \ldots, x_{t-p'}) + \sigma(y_{t-1}, \ldots, y_{t-q}, x_t, \ldots, x_{t-q'}) \varepsilon_t, \quad (11.16)$$

where $E(\varepsilon_t \mid \mathcal{F}_{t-1}) = 0$ and $E(\varepsilon_t^2 - 1 \mid \mathcal{F}_{t-1}) = 0$. Here, $\mathcal{F}_{t-1}$ is the sigma field generated by the past history of y_t, x_t while $m(\cdot), \sigma(\cdot)$ are unknown functions such that

$$m(y_{t-1}, \ldots, y_{t-p}, x_t, \ldots, x_{t-p'}) = E(y_t \mid \mathcal{F}_{t-1}),$$
$$\sigma(y_{t-1}, \ldots, y_{t-q}, x_t, \ldots, x_{t-q'}) = \text{var}(y_t \mid \mathcal{F}_{t-1}).$$

Under some conditions on m, σ, ε the dynamic process y_t is stationary and mixing, and these restrict the functions m, σ and in particular their growth at infinity. Masry and Tjøstheim (1995) treated this general case, discussing stationarity and mixing properties as well as estimation and inference methods. The nonparametric ARCH literature apparently begins with Pagan and Schwert (1990) and Pagan and Hong (1991). They considered the case where $\sigma_t^2 = \sigma^2(y_{t-1})$, where $\sigma(\cdot)$ is a smooth but unknown function, and the multilag version $\sigma_t^2 = \sigma^2(y_{t-1}, y_{t-2}, \ldots, y_{t-q})$; see also Gao (2007).

In what follows we just consider explicitly the case where x is univariate and can be past y_t or a separate covariate. We discuss a number of estimators of $m(x)$; many of these are linear "smoothers" of the form $\sum_{t=1}^{T} w_{Tt}(x) y_t$ for some weighting sequence $\{w_{Tt}(x)\}_{t=1}^{T}$ depending only on $x_1, \ldots, x_T$, but arise from different motivations and possess different statistical properties.

11.2.2.1 Kernel Estimation Methods in Detail

Suppose that (X, Y) has a joint density with $X \sim f_X$, $(X, Y) \sim f_{X,Y}$; then

$$m(x) = \int y f_{Y|X}(y \mid x) \, \mathrm{d}y = \int y \frac{f_{X,Y}(x, y)}{f_X(x)} \, \mathrm{d}x = \frac{\int y f_{X,Y}(x, y) \, \mathrm{d}y}{\int f_{X,Y}(x, y) \, \mathrm{d}y}. \quad (11.17)$$

If y was discrete or contained discrete components, we could define the conditional expectation more generally in terms of the conditional CDF of y given X so that $m(x) = \int y \, \mathrm{d}F(y \mid X = x)$, where the integral is defined appropriately. One approach to estimation of the regression function is to estimate the joint density and then integrate, which throws everything back to density estimation. Instead, we shall pursue a direct justification.

The basic idea for kernel regression smoothing comes from the Taylor expansion of the function m in a neighborhood of x. For a p times differentiable function (with continuous pth derivative) we have, for any X_t,

$$m(x_t) = m(x) + (x_t - x)m'(x) + \frac{1}{2}(x_t - x)^2 m''(x) + \cdots + \frac{(x_t - x)^p}{p!} m^{(p)}(x)$$
$$+ R_p(x_t, x),$$

where $R_p(x_t, x)$ is a remainder term that is small when x_t is close to x. Suppose that $|x_t - x| \leq h$, that is, x_t is close to x; then $m(x_t) = m(x) + O(h)$, that is, the function m is locally constant in a small neighborhood ($h \to 0$). Furthermore, $m(x_t) - m(x) - (x_t - x) m'(x) = O(h^2)$, that is, to a higher degree of accuracy, the function m is locally linear in a small neighborhood. According to this logic, we can treat y_t observations where x_t is a neighborhood of x as taking similar values of the target, and in view of this it is natural to average them. Define

$$\widehat{m}(x) = \frac{\sum_{t=1}^{T} K_h(x_t - x) y_t}{\sum_{t=1}^{T} K_h(x_t - x)}. \tag{11.18}$$

This is the Nadaraya–Watson estimator with kernel K and bandwidth h. The estimator is a weighted local average of the response variables according to the distance of the covariate x_t from x as determined by the kernel. For example, for the kernel $K(u) = 1(|u| \leq 1/2)$ and $d = 1$, it is the equal average of the y_t values with $|x_t - x| \leq 1/2$, but if the kernel is the Epanechnikov kernel, say, then observations further from x will receive lower weighting. The bandwidth h determines how wide the smoothing window is. The Nadaraya–Watson estimator is linear in y_t, that is,

$$\widehat{m}(x) = \sum_{t=1}^{T} w_{Tt}(x) y_t, \tag{11.19}$$

where $w_{Tt}(x) = K_h(x_t - x)/\sum_{t=1}^{T} K_h(x_t - x)$ depends only on the covariates $x_1, \ldots, x_T$. The weights satisfy $\sum_{t=1}^{T} w_{Tt}(x) = 1$, so that if $y_t \mapsto a + by_t$, $\widehat{m}(x) \mapsto a + b\widehat{m}(x)$. When $K \geq 0$, the weights are probability weights since they also satisfy $w_{Tt}(x) \in [0, 1]$. This estimator is always defined at the sample points x_t, and if the kernel K has infinite support then it is also well defined at all $x \in \mathbb{R}$ (including values outside the support of X); on the other hand, if the kernel has compact support, as is commonly the case, then there is a positive (but vanishing very rapidly) probability at any other point x that the denominator $w_{Tt}(x) = 0$ for all t (depending on the bandwidth). Note that as $h \to \infty$, $\widehat{m}(x) \to \bar{y}$ for all x, while as $h \to 0$, $\widehat{m}(x_t) \to y_t$ for all t. In neither of these extreme cases is the estimator necessarily consistent, although recent interest has focused on certain interpolating kernels for which the latter property holds but for which $\widehat{m}(\cdot)$ is consistent. In fact, this definition makes sense also when $x \in \mathbb{R}^d$, in which case K is understood to be defined on a subset of $\mathbb{R}^d$ and $K_h(\cdot) = h^{-d}K(h^{-1}\cdot)$. Derivatives can be estimated by differentiating the estimate of m the required number of times. This works provided the estimate of m is itself smooth enough, which can be achieved, for example, by taking K to be smooth like the Gaussian density function.

In practice, one often estimates at a grid of points $x_1, \ldots, x_J$. If the sample size is moderate one usually takes $J = T$ and $x = x_t$ for each covariate value x_t. In that case one obtains $\widehat{m} = \mathbf{S}y$, where $\widehat{m}$ and y are the $T \times 1$ estimator and dependent variable vectors respectively, while $\mathbf{S}$ is the $T \times T$ smoother matrix with typical element $S_{ts} = w_{Ts}(x_t)$. Let $\mathbf{K} = [K_h(x_t, x_s)]_{t,s}$, then $\mathbf{S} = \mathbf{K}./\mathbf{K}i$, where $./$ is the matrix division operation. We will talk more later about the properties of the matrix $\mathbf{S}$, but note that by construction $\mathbf{S}i = i$, where i is the $T \times 1$ vector of ones.

Figure 11.9 shows the kernel estimate on simulated data with an image of the kernel weighting imposed to show how the kernel downweights the observations within the window. Figure 11.10 shows how the kernel estimate varies with bandwidth in the no-noise case, and Figure 11.11 shows how the kernel estimate varies with bandwidth in the case where there is noise.

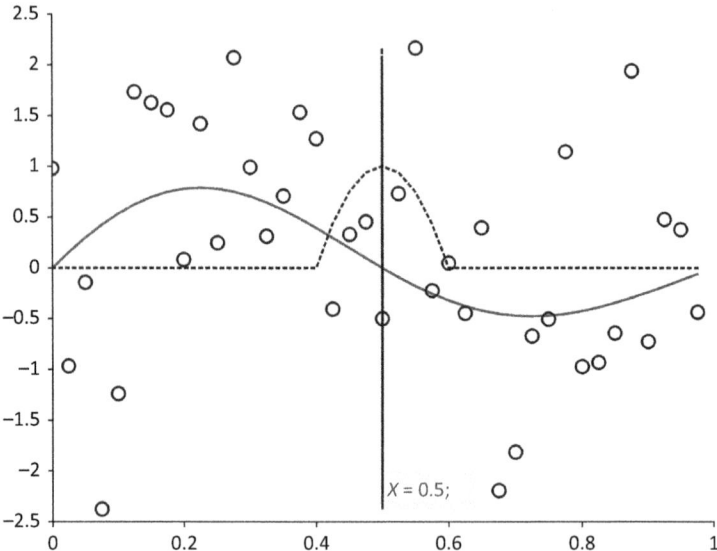

Figure 11.9 Simulated data and kernel estimate.

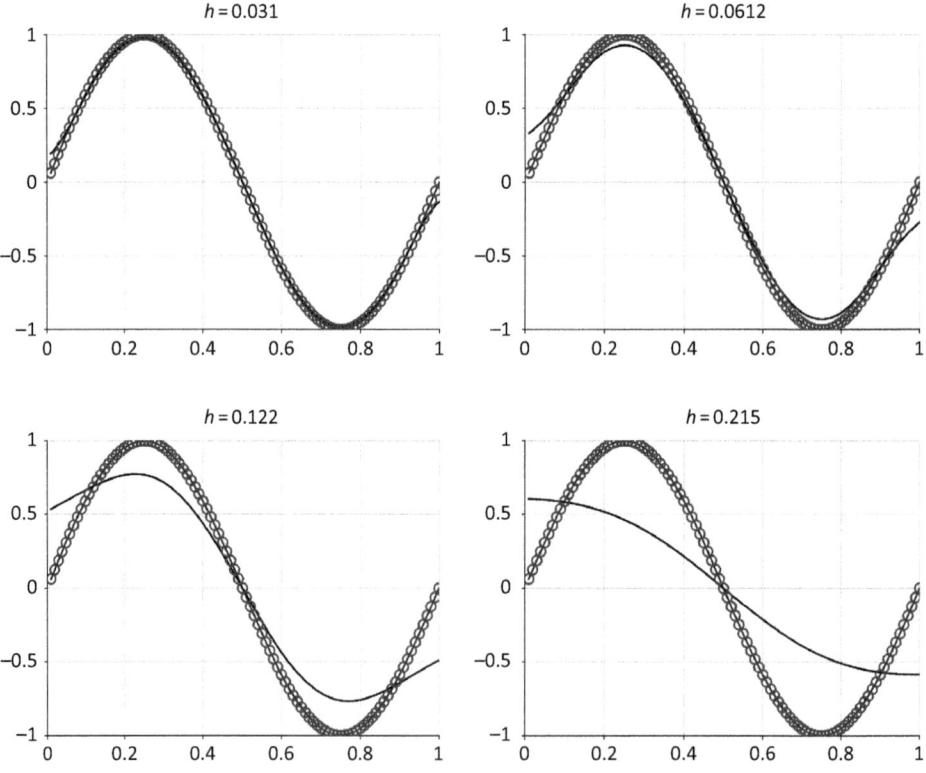

Figure 11.10 Data, true regression, and estimated regression for different bandwidths. No noise case. $y = \sin(2\pi x)$, $x_i = i/n$, $n = 100$.

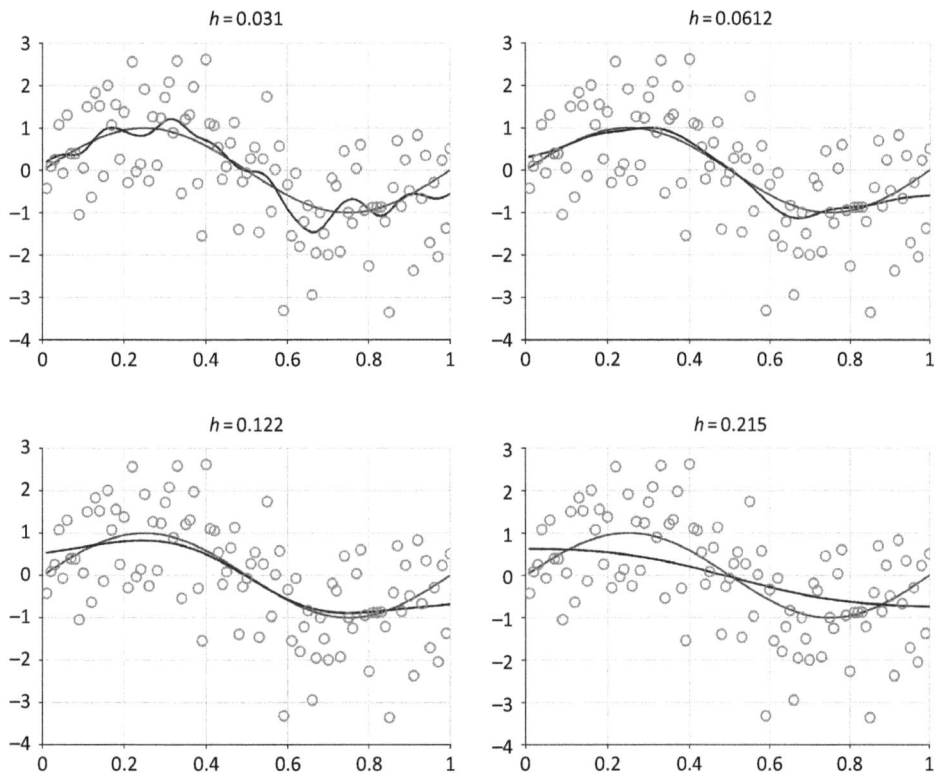

Figure 11.11 Unit noise case. $y = \sin(2\pi x) + \varepsilon, \varepsilon \sim N(0,1), x_i = i/n, n = 100$.

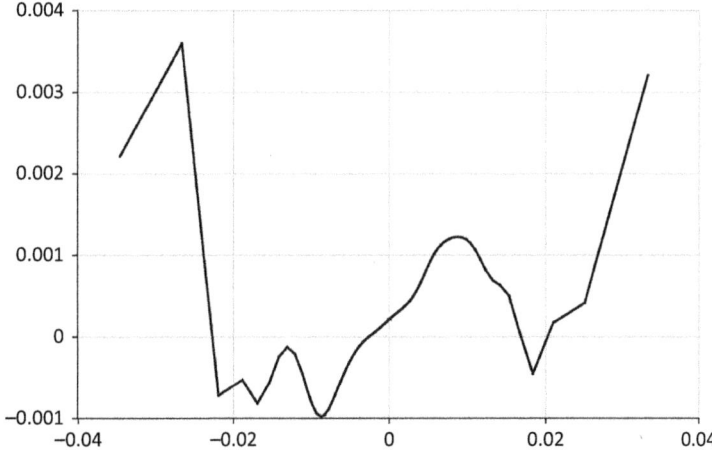

Figure 11.12 Conditional mean smooth of daily S&P500 stock returns on own lags, that is, $x_t = y_{t-1}$.

We next show some estimated regression curves. In Figure 11.12 we show the conditional mean smooth of daily S&P500 stock returns on its own first lag, that is, $x_t = y_{t-1}$. This shows no clear structure. In Figure 11.13 we show the conditional standard deviation on $x_t = y_{t-1}$, which seems to show a quadratic-type shape similar to that implied by

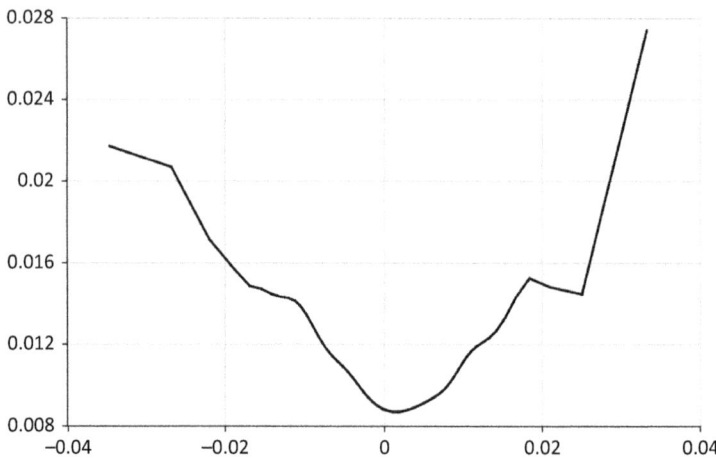

Figure 11.13 Conditional standard deviation smooth of daily S&P500 stock returns on own lags, that is, $x_t = y_{t-1}$.

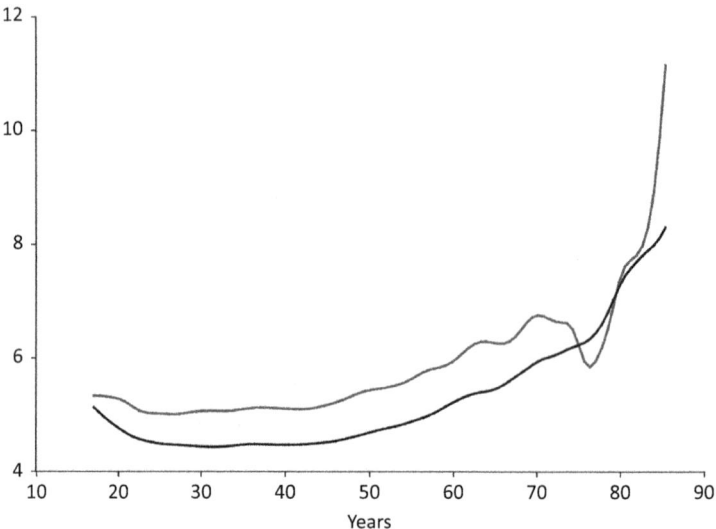

Figure 11.14 Male and female marathon times regression smoother against age.

the ARCH/GARCH models considered in Chapter 10. Finally, in Figure 11.14 we show the regression smoother of race time against age separately for males and females.

11.2.2.2 Local Linear Smoothing

We can interpret the kernel estimator as the minimizer of the local least squares criterion function

$$Q_T(\alpha) = \sum_{t=1}^{T} K_h(x_t - x) (y_t - \alpha)^2, \tag{11.20}$$

that is, $\widehat{\alpha}(x) = \arg\min_{\alpha \in \mathbb{R}} Q_T(\alpha) = \widehat{m}(x)$. The kernel here is localizing and we are finding the best constant value in the window. We now modify the characterization (11.20) by fitting a line instead of a constant in the support of $K_h(\cdot - x)$. More precisely, put

$$\begin{pmatrix} \widehat{\alpha} \\ \widehat{\beta} \end{pmatrix} = \operatorname*{argmin}_{\alpha, \beta} \sum_{t=1}^{T} (y_t - \alpha - \beta(x_t - x))^2 K_h(x_t - x)$$

and define $\widehat{m}_{\text{LL}}(x) = \widehat{\alpha}$. The estimator $\widehat{m}_{\text{LL}}$ is called the local linear estimator of $m(x)$. The quantity $\widehat{\beta}$ is an estimator of the first derivative of m, $m'(x)$. Provided there is a unique solution, we may write it as

$$\begin{pmatrix} \widehat{\alpha} \\ \widehat{\beta} \end{pmatrix} = \begin{bmatrix} S_{T,0,0}(x) & S_{T,0,1}(x) \\ S_{T,1,0}(x) & S_{T,1,1}(x) \end{bmatrix}^{-1} \begin{bmatrix} \tau_{T,0}(x) \\ \tau_{T,1}(x) \end{bmatrix},$$

where

$$S_{T,0,0}(x) = \sum_{t=1}^{T} K_h(x_t - x)/T,$$

$$S_{T,0,1}(x) = S_{T,1,0}(x) = \sum_{t=1}^{T} K_h(x_t - x)(x_t - x)/T,$$

$$S_{T,1,1}(x) = \sum_{t=1}^{T} K_h(x_t - x)(x_t - x)^2/T,$$

$$\tau_{T,0}(x) = \sum_{t=1}^{T} K_h(x_t - x)y_t/T,$$

$$\tau_{T,1}(x) = \sum_{t=1}^{T} K_h(x_t - x)(x_t - x)y_t/T.$$

We can write explicitly

$$\widehat{\alpha} = \frac{S_{T,1,1}(x)\tau_{T,0}(x) - S_{T,0,1}(x)\tau_{T,1}(x)}{S_{T,1,1}(x)S_{T,0,0}(x) - S_{T,0,1}^2(x)},$$

$$\widehat{\beta} = \frac{S_{T,1,0}(x)\tau_{T,0}(x) - S_{T,0,0}(x)\tau_{T,1}(x)}{S_{T,1,1}(x)S_{T,0,0}(x) - S_{T,0,1}^2(x)}.$$

The necessary and sufficient condition for uniqueness is that $S_{T,1,1}(x)S_{T,0,0}(x) - S_{T,0,1}^2(x) \neq 0$. This requires at least two observations inside the estimation window, so that the invertibility is not guaranteed at $x = x_t$.

Let $P_\theta(u) = \theta_0 + \theta_1 u + \cdots + \theta_p u^p/p!$ denote a polynomial for $p = 1, 2, \ldots$ Let $\widehat{\theta}_0, \ldots, \widehat{\theta}_p$ minimize

$$\sum_{t=1}^{T} K_h(x - x_t) \{y_t - P_\theta(x_t - x)\}^2$$

with respect to $\theta = (\theta_0, \theta_1, \ldots, \theta_p) \in \mathbb{R}^{p+1}$. Then $\widehat{\theta}_0$ serves as an estimator of $m(x)$, while $\widehat{\theta}_j$ estimates the jth derivative of m. These definitions can be easily extended to the case $d > 1$. The local polynomial method explicitly estimates the derivatives – the parameter estimate $\widehat{\theta}_j(x)$ estimates $m^{(j)}(x)$. The problem with this method is just that in high dimensions the number of local parameters to be estimated is very large. For d dimensions and order-p polynomial we have a total of $N = \sum_{l=0}^{p} N_l$ parameters, where $N_l = (l + d - 1)!/(d - 1)!l!$.

11.2.2.3 *k*-Nearest Neighbor Estimators

The k-nearest neighbor (k-NN) estimate is defined as a weighted average of the response variables in a varying neighborhood. This neighborhood is defined through those X-variables which are among the k-nearest neighbors of a point x, where neighborliness is defined through the distance $d(x, y) = |x - y|$ for $x, y \in \mathbb{R}$. That is, calculate $\varrho_t(x) = d(x, x_t)$, $t = 1, \ldots, T$, and order these from smallest to largest so that $\varrho_{(1)}(x) \leq \cdots \leq \varrho_{(T)}(x)$. In the case of ties, that is, $\varrho_t(x) = \varrho_s(x)$, one usually breaks that by taking the smaller of t, s. Let $\mathcal{N}(x) = \{t: \varrho_t(x) \leq \varrho_{(k)}(x)\}$ be the set of indices of the k-nearest neighbors of x. The classic k-NN estimate is the average of ys with index in $\mathcal{N}(x)$,

$$\widehat{m}_k(x) = \frac{1}{k} \sum_{t \in \mathcal{N}(x)} y_t. \tag{11.21}$$

The main difference from the standard kernel is that here the local averaging always picks out k observations to average, whereas the kernel estimator picks out a variable number of observations to average, so that in densely populated areas of the covariate space the kernel estimator carries out a lot of averaging, whereas out in the tails it carries out little averaging. We can think of this as like a kernel smoother (without denominator normalization) with a uniform kernel $K(u) = 0.5 \times 1(|u| \leq 1)$ and a variable bandwidth $h = \varrho_{(k)}(x)$, the distance between x and its furthest k-NN. If $x_t = t/T$ with $k/2 < t < T - k/2$, then there is a t_1 such that $t_1/T \leq x \leq (t_1 + 1)/T$; suppose that x is closer to t_1/T than $(t_1 + 1)/T$ and that k is even, then $\widehat{m}_k(x) = (y_{t_1} + y_{t_1-1} + \cdots + y_{t_1+1-k/2} + y_{t_1+1} + \cdots + y_{t_1+k/2})/k$, which is identical to a two-sided SMA and identical to a kernel estimator with a uniform kernel.

More generally, weighted nearest neighbors are defined in terms of some weighting scheme that depends on the neighbor priority as

$$\widehat{m}_k(x) = \frac{1}{k} \sum_{t \in \mathcal{N}(x)} w_t y_t,$$

where $\sum_{t \in \mathcal{N}(x)} w_t/k = 1$. For example, the declining weight structure $w_t = 2j/(k \times (k + 1))$ if $t = (j)$ and $w_t = 0$ otherwise. Nearest neighbors can be interpreted roughly speaking as kernel smoothing in "rank space." Let $F_T(\cdot)$ denote the empirical distribution of the covariate x_t. If the covariates were ordered with $x_{(1)} < \cdots < x_{(T)}$, then $F_T(x_{(t)}) = t/T$ are equally spaced observations and $F_T(x) \in [0, 1]$. Then $\widehat{m}_k(x)$ is just the kernel estimator with bandwidth $h = 2k$ applied to $F_T(x_{(t)})$. Mack (1981) and Stute (1984) developed the theory of k-NN estimators in an i.i.d. setting; Yakowitz (1987) extended this to time series. Nearest neighbors are popular with the new machine learning communities, and Biau and Devroye (2015) gave an excellent updated review of their properties.

11.2.2.4 Sieve Estimators

For simplicity, in this section we assume that x_t takes values in $[0, 1]^d$. We assume that $m \in L_2([0, 1]^d)$ where, as above, $m(x) = \mathbb{E}(y_t \mid x_t = x)$ is the regression function. Suppose that $(\psi_j)_{j=1}^{\infty}$ is a complete orthonormal basis of $L_2([0, 1]^d)$. Suitable basis systems include the *Legendre* polynomials described in Härdle (1990) or the *Fourier* series used in Gallant and Souza (1991). The (least squares) sieve estimator $\widehat{m}_J$ is defined as

$$\widehat{m}_J(x) = \sum_{j=1}^{J} \widehat{\mu}_j \psi_j(x),$$

where $(\widehat{\mu}_1, \ldots, \widehat{\mu}_J)$ minimizes the criterion

$$Q_T(\mu_1, \ldots \mu_J) = \sum_{t=1}^{T} \left(y_t - \sum_{j=1}^{J} \mu_j \psi_j(x_t) \right)^2.$$

Series estimators have received considerable attention in the econometrics literature, following Elbadawi, Gallant, and Souza (1983). This theory is very much tied to the structure of Hilbert space. These estimators are typically very easy to compute since they are OLS estimators, and they also have some other useful properties due to their interpretations as ordinary projections. Chen and Shen (1998) derived some large-sample properties of sieve estimators in time series settings. In addition, the extension to additive structures and semiparametric models is convenient (Andrews, 1991a; Andrews and Whang, 1990), and accommodation of shape restrictions and endogeneity is also quite simple. Chen (2007) gave an excellent account of these methods for a variety of models, including additive nonparametric regression in both cross-sectional and time series settings. On the downside, although it is possible to obtain pointwise normality for the centered and scaled estimators, it is not possible to obtain simple expressions for bias and variance as it is for kernel estimators.

11.2.2.5 Spline Estimators

Spline methods involve trading off the fit of the data with the smoothness of the estimated curve. The accuracy of the fit to the data is measured for example by the residual sum of squares,

$$\text{RSS}(\widehat{m}) = \frac{1}{T} \sum_{t=1}^{T} (y_t - \widehat{m}(x_t))^2.$$

We say that a function m is smooth if the kth derivative $m^{(k)}$ is small. This can be measured by $J_k(m) = \int m^{(k)}(x)^2 \, dx$. Functions m that have the same amount of smoothness can be described as functions m with $J_k(m) \leq C$, where C is some constant. Smoothing splines are now defined as functions that minimize the goodness-of-fit to the data (i.e., RSS) among all functions with the same amount of smoothness. More formally,

$$\widehat{m}(\cdot) = \arg \min_{m} \{\text{RSS}(m) : J_k(m) \leq C\}.$$

The smoothing spline $\widehat{m}$ depends on k and C. The quantity C is a smoothing parameter. For small C we get a smooth function $\widehat{m}$, for large C we get a rougher function $\widehat{m}$. On the other side, the goodness-of-fit $\text{RSS}(\widehat{m})$ decreases for increasing C. One can show that there is a one-to-one correspondence between the above optimization problem and

$$\min_{m(\cdot)} \text{RSS}(m) + \lambda J_k(m), \tag{11.22}$$

where λ is a tuning parameter related to C. The solution to this problem is a **natural spline** (Eubank, 1988). In the following we focus on the case $k = 2$, in which case the solution is a natural cubic spline.

Definition 11.4   A cubic spline function β on the interval $[a, b]$ with knot points $a = x_0 < x_1 < \cdots < x_n < x_{n+1} = b$ is

$$\beta(x) = d_i(x - x_i)^3 + c_i(x - x_i)^2 + b_i(x - x_i) + a_i, \quad x_i \le x \le x_{i+1},$$

for some constants $a_i, b_i, c_i, d_i, i = 0, 1, \ldots, n$. To preserve continuity it must be that $\beta^{(j)}(x_{i+1}) = \lim_{x \uparrow x_{i+1}} \beta^{(j)}(x)$ for $j = 0, 1, 2$. For example, $d_i(x_{i+1} - x_i)^3 + c_i(x_{i+1} - x_i)^2 + b_i(x_{i+1} - x_i) + a_i = a_{i+1}$. This implies linear restrictions on the parameters. A cubic spline on $[a, b]$ is a natural cubic spline if its second and third derivatives are zero at the end points a, b, which is fulfilled if $d_0 = c_0 = d_n = c_n = 0$.

The objective function (11.22) can be rewritten in terms of the cubic spline basis,

$$Q_T(\gamma) = (y - B\gamma)^{\mathsf{T}} (y - B\gamma) + \lambda \gamma^{\mathsf{T}} \Omega \gamma, \tag{11.23}$$

$$B_{T \times T} = \left(\beta_j(x)_i \right), \qquad \Omega_{T \times T} = \left(\int \beta_i''(x) \beta_j''(x) \, dx \right),$$

and the parameters γ can be found computationally efficiently using matrix routines. The estimator $\widehat{m} = (\widehat{m}(x_1), \ldots, \widehat{m}(x_T))^{\mathsf{T}}$ takes the explicit form

$$\widehat{m} = B\widehat{\gamma} = B(B^{\mathsf{T}}B + \lambda\Omega)^{-1} B^{\mathsf{T}} y,$$

which involves inversion of the $T \times T$ matrix $B^{\mathsf{T}}B + \lambda\Omega$. Splines are linear in the response variable. They can be considered as global estimators since $\widehat{\gamma}$ are found once and for all. Nevertheless, Silverman (1984) showed that they are asymptotically equivalent to local kernel smoothers with equivalent kernel $K(u) = \exp(-|u|/\sqrt{2}) \sin(|u|/\sqrt{2} + \pi/4)/2$, which is of fourth order, since its first three moments are zero, and with equivalent bandwidth $h = h(\lambda; x_t) = \lambda^{1/4} T^{-1/4} f(x_t)^{-1/4}$.

Silverman (1985) discussed a Bayesian interpretation of the spline procedure. Suppose that the $T \times 1$ vector y can be written as $y = m + \varepsilon$, where $\varepsilon \sim N(0, \sigma^2 I_T)$. Suppose that $\gamma \in \mathbb{R}^T$ has prior density $N(0, (\sigma^2/\lambda)\Omega^-)$, where the generalized inverse of Ω (see next section) is used because this matrix has two zero eigenvalues. The posterior distribution of γ is $N(\Psi^{-1}B^{\mathsf{T}}y, \sigma^2\Psi^{-1})$ with $\Psi = B^{\mathsf{T}}B + \lambda\Omega$. Hence, the posterior density of m is $N(B\Psi^{-1}B^{\mathsf{T}}y, \sigma^2 B\Psi^{-1}B^{\mathsf{T}})$, the mean of which corresponds to the spline estimator for a particular λ. The Bayesian interpretation links the prior with the tuning parameter λ via a scaling factor, so that a very tight prior is equivalent in this smoothing paradigm to a very large penalty on roughness. One can think of Bayesian methods to be smoothing methods but with a tuning parameter an essential feature of the prior.

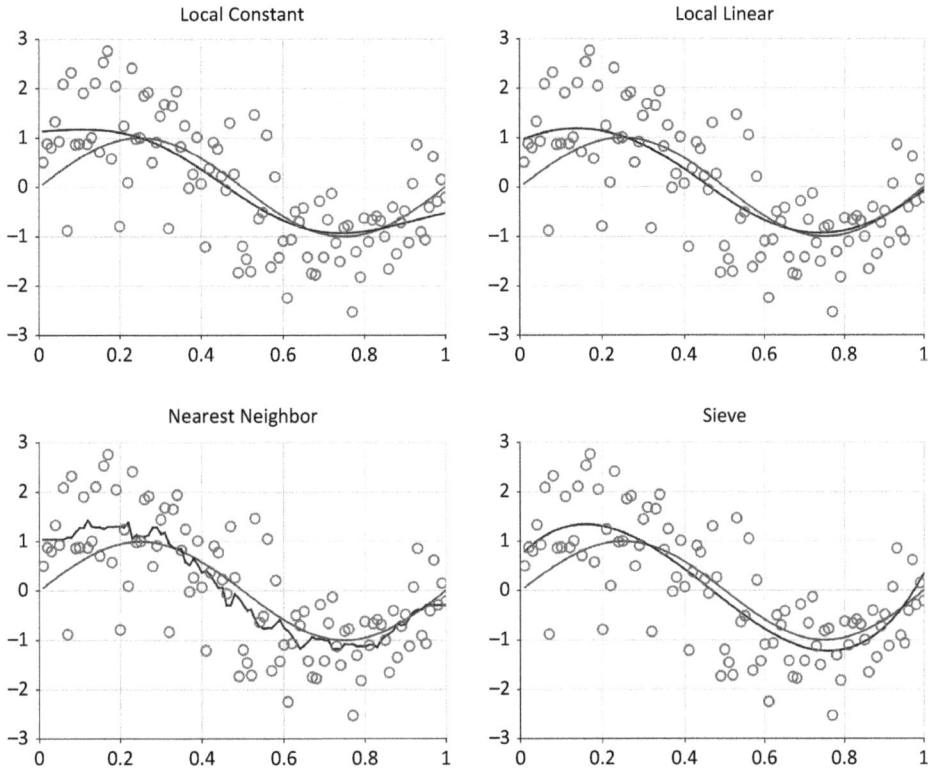

Figure 11.15 Kernel, local linear, nearest neighbor, and sieve estimators of a regression function.

For kernels, series, and spline estimators we can write $\widehat{y} = Sy$, where y is the $T \times 1$ data vector and $\widehat{y}$ is the $T \times 1$ estimator, so that S is a $T \times T$ smoothing matrix depending only on the smoothing parameter and weighting choice, and on the covariates. Hastie and Tibshirani (1990) discussed the properties of the smoothing matrix for several methods. Projection smoothers such as the least squares sieve estimator and the spline method produce an exactly symmetric matrix S (and S is idempotent), although other methods produce approximately symmetric matrices. The importance of symmetry is that (i) the estimator is **admissible** (it is not dominated by any other estimator according to MSE uniformly over the parameter space; Cohen, 1966), and (ii) has a Bayesian interpretation. One can easily symmetrize an asymmetric smoothing matrix if this is desired by $S \rightarrow (S + S^{\mathsf{T}})/2$.

Figure 11.15 compares four different smoothers, along with the data and the true regression. In practice the main differences occur at the ends of the sample.

11.2.2.6 Some Nonlinear Regression Estimators

The above estimators are all linear in the sense that $\widehat{m}(x) = \sum_{t=1}^{T} w_{Tt}(x)y_t$, where $\{w_{Tt}(x)\}$ only depend on the covariate $X_1, \ldots, X_T$. In the dynamic setting where x_t can include past y_t, this structure is less relevant. We now turn to some nonlinear smoothing methods.

Local Likelihood   The principle underlying the local polynomial estimator can be generalized in a number of ways. Tibshirani (1984) introduced the local likelihood procedure in which an arbitrary parametric regression function $g(x, \theta)$ substitutes the polynomial. Suppose that $f(y \mid G(x))$ is the density function (or frequency function) of $y \mid X$, where f is known and G is an unknown function related to the mean through a known function, that is, for known F, $G(x) = F(m(x))$. Then let $\widehat{\theta}_0, \ldots, \widehat{\theta}_p$ minimize

$$\mathcal{L}_T(\theta) = \sum_{t=1}^{T} K_h(x - x_t) \log f(y_t \mid P_\theta(x_t - x))$$

with respect to $\theta \in \mathbb{R}^{p+1}$. Then, $\widehat{\theta}_0$ serves as an estimator of $G(x)$, while $\widehat{\theta}_j$ estimates the jth derivative of G. This includes the standard local polynomial estimator as a special case when f is the normal density function. Suppose that y is binary, then

$$f(y \mid G(x)) = \Phi(G(x))^y [1 - \Phi(G(x))]^{1-y}, \qquad m(x) = \Phi(G(x)).$$

The advantage of this method is that it imposes the restrictions implied by the data (Fan, Heckman, and Wand, 1992). See also Gozalo and Linton (2000). Local GMM can be similarly defined (Lewbel, 2007).

Quantile Regression   To estimate conditional quantiles we use a version of local likelihood. The main difference is that $m(x)$ is not interpreted as the conditional mean any more but some other location parameter. Also, the criterion function need not be smooth. Let $\widehat{m}(x) = \widehat{\theta}_0$, where $\widehat{\theta}$ is any minimizer of the criterion function

$$\sum_{t=1}^{T} K_h(x - x_t) \rho_\alpha(y_t - P_\theta(x_t - x)),$$

with $\rho_\alpha(u) = u(\alpha - 1(u < 0))$. In general the solution is easy to compute but is not unique, so some additional restriction has to be imposed to obtain a well-defined solution. See Chaudhuri (1991) for a treatment under i.i.d. sampling, and Cai (2002) for an extension to time series.

Neural Network Estimation   We next consider neural network estimation, which has become very popular in machine learning triangles. To understand this we first present a well-known result by the famous mathematician Kolmogorov (Coppejans, 2004).

Theorem 11.2 (Kolmogorov, 1957)   *There exist d constants $\lambda_j > 0$, $j = 1, \ldots, d$, $\sum_{j=1}^{d} \lambda_j \leq 1$, and $2d+1$ continuous, strictly increasing functions g, ϕ_k, $k = 1, \ldots, 2d+1$, which map $[0, 1]$ to $[0, 1]$ and have the property that for each continuous function m from $[0, 1]^d$ to $\mathbb{R}$,*

$$m(x_1, \ldots, x_d) = \sum_{k=1}^{2d+1} g\left(\sum_{j=1}^{d} \lambda_j \phi_k(x_j)\right).$$

This interesting result says that every continuous function has an additive-like representation in terms of univariate functions. Recall that the curse of dimensionality says that the optimal rate for estimating multivariate functions is slower than the optimal rate for estimating one-dimensional functions or additive functions that are sums of univariate functions. Therefore, the Kolmogorov representation suggests we might be able to achieve the faster rates of univariate estimation. However, this turns out not to be true. Specifically, if the function m is smooth of a certain order, the above representation does not guarantee that the functions g, ϕ_k are smooth of the same order. This shows in some sense that smoothness and dimensionality are linked together. Nevertheless, this structure is at the heart of neural network estimation.

Suppose that we define, for $x \in \mathbb{R}^d$,

$$m_\theta(x) = \sum_{k=1}^{n_1} \alpha_k \sigma \left(\sum_{j=1}^{n_2} \lambda_{kj} \sigma(\omega_j^\mathsf{T} x + \delta_j) + c_k \right),$$

where the parameter vector θ includes $\omega_j \in \mathbb{R}^d$ and $\alpha_k, \delta_j, c_k, \lambda_{kj} \in \mathbb{R}$ for $j = 1, \ldots, n_2$ and $k = 1, \ldots, n_1$. Here, $\sigma \colon \mathbb{R} \to \mathbb{R}$ is a given so-called activation function or squishing function. This is called a two-hidden-layer feedforward neural network with layers of width n_1 and n_2.

Example 11.1   Often-used examples of activation functions include linear activation ($\sigma(t) = t$), ReLU activation ($\sigma(t) = \max(0, t)$), Heaviside activation ($\sigma(t) = 1_{t>0}$), and logistic activation ($\sigma(t) = (1 + \exp(-t))^{-1}$).

Estimation proceeds by minimizing the least squares objective function with respect to the free parameters θ; this is generally a high-dimensional optimization, but there are lots of well-studied algorithms for carrying this out. Sometimes a penalty function is included.

Barron (1994) considered the class of target functions m on $\mathbb{R}^d$ that have a Fourier representation $m(x) = \int_{\mathbb{R}^d} \exp(i\omega^\mathsf{T} x) \widetilde{f}(\omega) \, d\omega$, where

$$C_m = \int \left(\sum_{j=1}^{d} |\omega_j| \right) |\widetilde{m}(\omega)| \, d\omega < \infty.$$

He showed under some technical condition that a common class of neural networks can achieve integrated MSE of order $\sqrt{d \log T / / T}$ as sample size $T \to \infty$. That is, over this class of functions and for this estimation method the curse of dimensionality is vanquished. This class of functions is not the same as the Stone class, and this is why the results are different. In particular, as d increases, the class of functions effectively shrinks.

11.2.3 Large-Sample Properties of Kernel Estimators

We suppose throughout this section that y_t, x_t is stationary and α-mixing with, for some finite constant c and $\theta > 1$, $\alpha(j) = cj^{-\theta}$. The larger the value of θ, the weaker the dependence.

The following theorem describes the asymptotic behavior of the kernel density estimators $\widehat{f}(y)$.

Theorem 11.3   *Suppose that*

(i) *f is twice continuously differentiable at the point y;*
(ii) *the joint density of x_t, x_{t+k}, denoted $f_{0,k}(\cdot, \cdot)$, satisfies $|f_{0,k}(x, x') - f_0(x)f_0(x')| \leq C < \infty$ for all x, x';*
(iii) *the bandwidth $h = c_0 T^{-a}$ for some $1/5 \leq a < 1$;*
(iv) *K is symmetric, positive, and bounded, and it has a bounded support $[-1, 1]$.*

Then, provided $\theta > \max\{2, (1+a)/(1-a)\}$, as $T \to \infty$,

$$\sqrt{Th}\big(\widehat{f}(y) - f(y)\big) \Longrightarrow N\left(B_0(y), V_0(y)\right),$$

$$B_0(y) = \frac{c_0}{2}\mu_{2,1}(K)f''(y), \qquad V_0(y) = f(y) \times \mu_{0,2}(K).$$

In this case, the kernel smoothing in the state domain (sorting on the value of X) induces a scrambling that undoes the correlation structure so that the asymptotic variance only depends on the instantaneous variance; it is as if the process were i.i.d.

To show this result we use the following decomposition:

$$\widehat{f}(y) - f(y) = \frac{1}{T}\sum_{t=1}^{T} K_h(y_t - y) - f(y)$$

$$= \underbrace{\frac{1}{T}\sum_{t=1}^{T} K_h(y_t - y) - E(K_h(y_t - y))}_{V_T(y)} + \underbrace{E\big(\widehat{f}(y)\big) - f(y)}_{B_T(y)},$$

where $V_T(y)$ denotes a mean-zero stochastic term, whereas $B_T(y)$ is purely deterministic. The proof follows from the two lemmas below.

Lemma 11.1   *Under the assumptions of Theorem 11.3,*

$$B_T(y) = \frac{1}{2}h^2\mu_{2,1}(K)f''(y) + o(h^2).$$

Proof.   We give a heuristic argument; more details can be found in Masry (1996b). We have, by stationarity,

$$E(\widehat{f}(y)) - f(y) = E[K_h(y_t - y)] - f(y) = \frac{1}{h}\int K\left(\frac{y' - y}{h}\right)f(y')\,\mathrm{d}y' - f(y).$$

We next employ a change of variable argument, and to simplify the presentation we just assume that the support of y_t is $\mathbb{R}$ and that K is supported on $[-1, 1]$. Let $y' \to v = (y' - x)/h$, then

$$\frac{1}{h}\int K\left(\frac{y' - y}{h}\right)f(y')\,\mathrm{d}y' = \int K(v)f(y + hv)\,\mathrm{d}v.$$

Next, by a Taylor expansion we have

$$\int K(v)f(y+hv)\,dv$$

$$= f(y)\int K(v)\,dv + hf'(y)\int K(v)\,v\,dv + \frac{h^2}{2}f''(y)\int K(v)\,v^2\,dv$$

$$+ \frac{h^2}{2}\int \left(f''(y(v)) - f''(y)\right)K(v)v^2\,dv$$

$$= f(y) + \frac{1}{2}h^2\int K(v)\,v^2\,dv + o\left(h^2\right),$$

where $y(v)$ satisfies $|y(v) - y| \le h$.

Lemma 11.2   *Under the assumptions of Theorem 11.3,*

$$\sqrt{Th}V_T(y) \Longrightarrow N(0, \mu_{0,2}(K)f(y)).$$

Proof.   We have to show that

$$\frac{1}{\sqrt{T}}\sum_{t=1}^{T} Z_{T,t} \Longrightarrow N\left(0, \int K^2(v)\,dv f(y)\right),$$

$$Z_{T,t} = \frac{1}{\sqrt{h}}\left(K\left(\frac{y_t - y}{h}\right) - E\left(K\left(\frac{y_t - y}{h}\right)\right)\right).$$

We have, by construction, $E(Z_{T,t}) = 0$. Furthermore, for each T, the process $\{Z_{T,t}, t = 0, \pm 1, \pm 2, \ldots\}$ is stationary with a mean and autocovariance function that do not depend on t (although they do depend on T). Specifically,

$$\gamma_T(0) = \mathrm{var}\,(Z_{T,t}) = \frac{1}{h}E\left(K\left(\frac{y_t - y}{h}\right)^2\right) - \frac{1}{h}\left(E\left(K\left(\frac{y_t - y}{h}\right)\right)\right)^2$$

$$= \int K^2(u)f(y+vh)\,dv - h\left(\int K(u)f(y+vh)\,dv\right)^2$$

$$\simeq f(y) \times \int K^2(v)\,dv$$

for large T. Define the joint density $f_{0,r}$ of y_t, y_{t+r}. Then, for any $k \ne 0$, by iterated expectation and change of both variables,

$$\gamma_T(k)$$
$$= E\left(Z_{T,t}Z_{T,t+k}\right)$$
$$= \frac{1}{h}\int K\left(\frac{y'-y}{h}\right)K\left(\frac{y''-y}{h}\right)f_{0,k}(y',y'')\,dy'\,dy'' - \frac{1}{h}\left(E\left(K\left(\frac{y_t-y}{h}\right)\right)\right)^2$$
$$= h\int K(u)K(v)f_{0,k}(y+uh, y+vh)\,du\,dv - h\left(\int K(u)f(y+vh)\,dv\right)^2$$
$$\simeq h \times \left(f_{0,k}(y,y) - f(y)^2\right),$$

where the last line follows by the continuity of $f_{0,k}(x, y)$. For this process $\gamma_T(k)/\gamma_T(0) \to 0$ as $T \to \infty$, since $h \to 0$. Furthermore, suppose that $\sum_{k=1}^{\infty} |f_{0,k}(y, y) - f(y)^2| < \infty$, then it follows that

$$\lim_{T \to \infty} \text{var}\left(\frac{1}{\sqrt{T}}\sum_{t=1}^{T} Z_{T,t}\right) = \lim_{T \to \infty} \left(\frac{1}{T}\sum_{t=1}^{T} \text{var}(Z_{T,t})\right) = f(y)\int K^2(v)\, dv,$$

that is, the covariances are of smaller order collectively. The CLT follows by applying Herrndorf.

We next consider the regression problem. Define

$$b_{LL}(x) = m''(x), \quad b_{NW}(x) = m''(x) + 2\frac{m'(x)f'(x)}{f(x)}, \quad V_0(x) = \mu_{0,2}(K)\frac{\sigma^2(x)}{f(x)}.$$

Theorem 11.4   *We make the assumptions that:*

  (i) *K is symmetric, positive, and bounded, and it has a bounded support;*
  (ii) *the covariate density $f(\cdot)$ is continuous in x, and $f(x) > 0$;*
  (iii) *the joint density of x_t, x_{t+k}, denoted $f_{0,k}(\cdot, \cdot)$, satisfies $|f_{0,k}(x, x') - f_0(x)f_0(x')| \le C < \infty$ for all x, x';*
  (iv) *the regression function $m(\cdot)$ is twice continuously differentiable at the point x;*
  (v) *the conditional variance $\sigma^2(\cdot)$ is continuous at the point x;*
  (vi) *there exist $\delta, \gamma, C > 0$ with $E\left(|\varepsilon_t|^{2+\gamma} \mid x_t = x'\right) \le C$ for all x' with $|x - x'| \le \delta$.*

Suppose also that $\lim_{T \to \infty} Th^5 = c_0 < \infty$. Then, for some $\theta(\gamma) > \max\{2, (1 + a)/(1 - a)\}$,

$$\sqrt{Th}\left(\widehat{m}_{LL}(x) - m(x)\right) \Longrightarrow N\left(B_{0,LL}(x), V_0(x)\right),$$

$$B_{0,LL}(x) = \frac{c_0}{2}\mu_{2,1}(K)b_{LL}(x).$$

If also f is continuously differentiable at x, then

$$\sqrt{Th}\left(\widehat{m}_{NW}(x) - m(x)\right) \Longrightarrow N\left(B_{0,NW}(x), V_0(x)\right),$$

$$B_{0,NW}(x) = \frac{c_0}{2}\mu_{2,1}(K)b_{NW}(x).$$

The asymptotic variance of the two estimators is the same, and does not depend on the time series dependence, that is, $V_0(x)$ is the same as if y_t were i.i.d. with the same marginal density. This feature of kernel smoothing estimators is rather surprising and is quite different from what happens in the linear/parametric case, where the autocorrelation issue is important and difficult for inference. This phenomenon is sometimes called whitening by smoothing.[1] Standard errors may be calculated from the asymptotic variance estimator

$$\widehat{v}(x) = \frac{\widehat{\sigma}^2(x)}{\widehat{f}(x)} \times \mu_{0,2}(K),$$

---

[1] The case $x_t = t/T$ was treated in Chapter 6. In this case, the sorting on time is exactly on the same line as the time series dependence, so in this case the correlation structure is preserved and the long-run variance features in the limiting distribution as shown above. This is really a rolling window estimation. In this case y_t is "locally stationary." If the error term is an MDS then of course the long-run variance simplifies.

where $\widehat{\sigma}^2(x) = \sum_{t=1}^{T} w_{Tt}(x)\widehat{\varepsilon}_t^2$ and the residuals $\widehat{\varepsilon}_t = y_t - \widehat{m}(x_t)$ (or $\widehat{\varepsilon}_t = y_t - \widehat{m}(x)$ also works here). Alternatively, one $\widehat{v}(x)/Th$ can be estimated directly by $\sum_{t=1}^{T} w_{Tt}^2(x)\widehat{\varepsilon}_t^2$. These are valid provided that the bandwidth is chosen such that $Th^5 \to 0$.

Actually, this prewhitening by smoothing feature suggests an alternative method for conducting inference in parametric models: just smooth unnecessarily to eliminate the serial correlation. For example, if y_t is a stationary series with mean μ, one can smooth y_t against randomly generated uniform random variables and obtain a CLT centered at μ with a variance that is proportional to $\gamma_y(0) \times \|K\|^2$ (although the rate of convergence of the estimator is slower than the square root of the sample size, of course).

We next turn to the bias comparison. The LL estimator has a bias that only depends on the curvature of m, whereas the NW estimator's bias also depends on the curvature and the level of the covariate density, which is a weakness. In cases where the support of the covariate is bounded, the estimators also differ in how they perform at or near the boundary. The boundary bias of the NW estimator is of larger order, whereas the local linear estimator preserves at least the magnitude of its interior bias. The LL estimator is said to be design adaptive, whereas the NW is not (Fan and Gijbels, 1996).

Masry (1996a,b) gave full theoretical treatments of the large-sample properties of local polynomials (including local constants) in the stationary and mixing cases. Wang and Phillips (2009a,b) derived the properties in the nonstationary unit root case.

11.2.4 Cross-Validation

So far we have taken the choice of bandwidth and kernel as fixed. Here, we discuss how to choose the tuning parameter in practice. We focus on the most widely used method nowadays, the cross-validation method.

For an estimator $\widehat{m}(x_t) = \sum_{s=1}^{T} w_{ts} Y_s$, define the leave-one-out version:

$$\widehat{m}_t(x_t) = \frac{\sum_{s=1,s\neq t}^{T} w_{ts} y_s}{\sum_{s=1,s\neq t}^{T} w_{ts}}.$$

Then define

$$\text{CV}(h) = \frac{1}{T}\sum_{t=1}^{T}\{y_t - \widehat{m}_t(x_t)\}^2 \pi(x_t). \tag{11.24}$$

Choose $\widehat{h}_{cv} \in H_T$ to minimize $\text{CV}(h)$ for some set H_T, and then take $\widehat{m}_{\widehat{h}_{cv}}(\cdot)$. An equivalent method, which has some advantages computationally, is to use the penalized least squares,

$$\text{PLS}(h) = \frac{1}{T}\sum_{t=1}^{T}\{y_t - \widehat{m}(x_t)\}^2 \pi(X_t)\Xi(h),$$

where $\Xi(h)$ increases as the bandwidth h decreases. For kernel estimators $\Xi(h) = 1 + 2K(0)/Th$ or $\Xi(h) = (1 - K(0)/Th)^{-2}$. This latter approach is similar in spirit to the model selection ideas of time series such as AIC and BIC. Härdle and Marron (1985) established that the bandwidth $\widehat{h}_{cv}$ is asymptotically optimal under quite weak conditions, albeit for i.i.d. data. Kim and Cox (1996) extended this result to the time series case.

We may define CV for any linear smoother $\widehat{m} = Sy$ as

$$\text{CV} = \frac{1}{T} y^\top (I_T - S)^\top \Delta_S^{-2} (I_T - S) y, \qquad \Delta_S = \text{diag}\{1 - S_{11}, \ldots, 1 - S_{TT}\},$$

where the diagonal elements of the smoother S_{tt} are available. The generalized cross-validation method (Craven and Wahba, 1978) is easier to compute and is applicable for any linear smoother $\widehat{m} = Sy$:

$$\text{GCV} = \frac{(1/T)y^\top (I_T - S)^2 y}{((1/T)\text{tr}(I_T - S))^2}. \tag{11.25}$$

For the kernel smoother, $\text{tr}(I_T - W)/T \simeq 1 - K(0)/Th$.

This is an instance of the training/testing paradigm that is now claimed by the machine learners. We divide our sample data into two parts:

$$\underbrace{\{(x_s, y_s), \ s = 1, \ldots, T, \ s \neq t\}}_{\text{training}}, \qquad \underbrace{\{(x_t, y_t)\}}_{\text{testing}}.$$

The first part is used to calculate an estimator $\widehat{m}_t(x)$ for any x. This estimator is tested on $\{(x_t, y_t)\}$; specifically, we compute $\{y_t - \widehat{m}_t(x_t)\}^2$ as a measure of its performance. Then we sum up over all the testing sets to get the CV score for a given bandwidth. A more general strategy is to divide the index set $I_T = \{1, \ldots, T\}$ into two parts S, S^c, where $S \subset I_T$ (Tong and Yao, 1998). Specifically, let $S = \{1, \ldots, n\}$ and $S^c = \{n+1, \ldots, T\}$. Define $\widehat{m}_S(\cdot)$ based on the observations in $I_T(S)$ and define

$$\text{CV}_S(h) = \frac{1}{T - n} \sum_{t \in S^c} \{y_t - \widehat{m}_S(x_t)\}^2 \, \pi(x_t).$$

Then let $\widehat{h}_n = \arg\min_{h \in H_n} \text{CV}_S(h)$, which would be an estimate of the optimal bandwidth for estimation based on the sample $\{y_t, x_t, t \in S\}$. We then let $\widehat{h}_T = \widehat{h}_n \times \tau(n/T)$ for some function $\tau(\cdot)$ that reflects an assumption about smoothness.

11.2.5 Conditional CDF and Conditional Quantile

Suppose that $\{(y_t, x_t)\}_{t=-\infty}^{\infty}$ is a stationary and weakly dependent series (for example, strong mixing), then

$$F(y \mid x) = \Pr(y_t \leq y \mid x_t = x) = E\left(1(y_t \leq y) \mid x_t = x\right).$$

One estimator of $F(y \mid x)$ is based on smoothing the indicators $1(y_t \leq y)$ against x_t,

$$\widehat{F}(y \mid x) = \frac{\sum_{t=1}^{T} K_h(x - x_t) 1(y_t \leq y)}{\sum_{t=1}^{T} K_h(x - x_t)}.$$

We may define the conditional quantile as $Q(\alpha \mid x) = F^{-1}(\alpha \mid x)$, which can be estimated by $\widehat{Q}(\alpha \mid x) = \widehat{F}^{-1}(\alpha \mid x)$. The conditional density function can be estimated by

$$\widehat{f}(y \mid x) = \frac{\sum_{t=1}^{T} K_h(x - x_t) K_h(y - y_t)}{\sum_{t=1}^{T} K_h(x - x_t)},$$

see Chen, Linton, and Robinson (2000).

If the process y_t is a Markov process, then the transition density (with $x_t = y_{t-1}$) is a key quantity. For example, suppose that $x_t = \phi x_{t-1} + \varepsilon_t$, where ε_t is i.i.d. but we observe $y_t = \Lambda(x_t)$, for some monotonic transformation Λ with inverse G. It follows that the transition CDF is

$$F_{y_t|y_{t-1}}(y \mid y') = \Pr(y_t \leq y \mid y_{t-1} = y') = F_\varepsilon(G(y) - \phi G(y')).$$

Therefore, for any y, y' we have

$$\frac{\partial F_{y_t|y_{t-1}}(y \mid y')/\partial y'}{\partial F_{y_t|y_{t-1}}(y \mid y')/\partial y} = \frac{\phi G'(y')}{G'(y)},$$

and, indeed, for $y = y'$ the right-hand side equals ϕ.

11.2.5.1 Value at Risk

The value at risk is a well-known measure of risk that quantifies the extent of potential losses on a given asset (Embrechts, Klüppelberg, and Mikosch, 1997). The conditional value at risk (in terms of a given variable x_t) can be defined without reference to a model in terms of the conditional quantile as

$$\text{VAR}_\alpha(y_t \mid x_t) = Q(\alpha \mid x_t),$$

usually for $\alpha = 0.01$. We can estimate the value at risk nonparametrically by

$$\widehat{\text{VAR}}_\alpha(y_t \mid x_t) = \widehat{Q}(\alpha \mid x_t).$$

Figure 11.16 shows the estimated conditional $\text{VAR}_{0.05}$ for S&P500 daily returns. The very big improvement after the 1950s relative to the 1930s is clear.

The pointwise distribution theory for the conditional CDF is, under some conditions,

$$\sqrt{Th}\big(\widehat{F}(y \mid x) - F(y \mid x) - h^2 b(y, x)\big) \Longrightarrow N\left(0, \frac{F(y \mid x)(1 - F(y \mid x))}{f(x)}\|K\|^2\right)$$

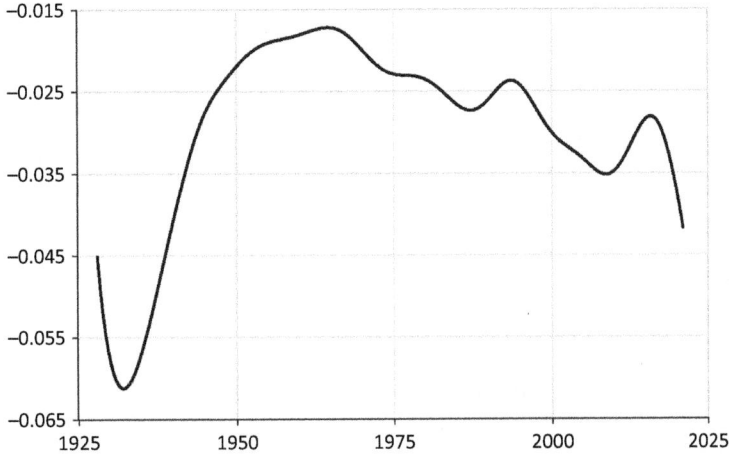

Figure 11.16 Conditional $\text{VAR}_{0.01}$ (lower quantile) smooth of daily S&P500 stock returns on $x_t = t/T$.

for given (y, x). Confidence intervals can be set from this. The pointwise distribution theory for the conditional quantile is

$$\sqrt{Th}\big(\widehat{Q}(\alpha \mid x) - Q(\alpha \mid x) - h^2 b(\alpha, x)\big) \Longrightarrow N\left(0, \frac{\alpha(1-\alpha)}{f(x)f(Q(\alpha \mid x) \mid x)^2} \|K\|^2\right)$$

for given α, x.

If we assume the location scale model with ε_t is i.i.d. with mean zero and variance one, then we can estimate the conditional value at risk by

$$\widehat{VAR}_\alpha(y_t \mid x_t) = \widehat{m}(x_t) + \widehat{\sigma}(x_t)\widehat{q}_\alpha, \quad \widehat{q}_\alpha = \widehat{F}_\varepsilon^{-1}(\alpha), \quad \widehat{F}_\varepsilon(e) = \frac{1}{T}\sum_{t=1}^{T} 1\,(\widehat{\varepsilon}_t \leq e),$$

where $\widehat{\varepsilon}_t = (y_t - \widehat{m}(x_t))/\widehat{\sigma}(x_t)$ and $\widehat{m}(\cdot), \widehat{\sigma}^2(\cdot)$ are the conditional mean and conditional variance smooths respectively. We may expect that using the i.i.d. structure should be more efficient, if it is correct.

11.2.6 Locally Stationary Processes

An alternative to stationarity is the concept of local stationarity, introduced by Dahlhaus (1997). The stochastic process $\{y_t\}$ is called locally stationary if there exists a family of stochastic processes $\{\widetilde{y}_{u,t}, t = 0, \pm 1, \pm 2, \ldots\}$ for $u \in [0, 1]$ such that

$$\Pr\left\{\max_{1 \leq t \leq T} |\widetilde{y}_{u,t} - y_t| \leq D_T T^{-1}\right\} = 1 \tag{11.26}$$

for all T, where $\{D_T\}$ is a positive process satisfying, for some $\eta > 0$, $\sup_{T \geq 1} E\left(|D_T|^{4+\eta}\right) < \infty$. For example, the process $y_t = \phi(t/T)y_{t-1} + \varepsilon_t$, where ε_t is i.i.d. with mean zero and variance σ^2, can be shown to satisfy this condition with $\widetilde{y}_{u,t} = \phi(u)\widetilde{y}_{u,t-1} + \varepsilon_t$, provided $\phi(\cdot)$ is smooth and satisfies $\sup_{u \in [0,1]} |\phi(u)| < 1$.

We estimate the local autocorrelation function for $j = 1, 2, \ldots$ and $u \in (0, 1)$ by $\widehat{\phi}_j(u)$, where

$$(\widehat{\alpha}_j(u), \widehat{\phi}_j(u)) = \arg\min_{\alpha, \beta} \sum_{t=j+1}^{T} K_h(u - t/T)\{y_t - \alpha - \phi y_{t-j}\}^2.$$

This uses the representation of the autocorrelation function as the slope of the best linear predictor. The solution to this has an explicit form just like the local linear kernel estimator. By including kernel downweighting one can ensure that the estimator $\widehat{\phi}_j(u)$ is smooth in (rescaled) time and reflects a better bias variance trade-off than the the equal weighting or rolling window approach. Dahlhaus and Subba Rao (2006) considered the extension to time-varying parameter ARCH models.

11.2.7 Regression Discontinuity / Structural Change

Suppose that the regression function $m(x) = E(y_t \mid x_t = x)$ has a point of discontinuity. Specifically, suppose that

$$m(x) = m^-(x)1[x < \zeta] + m^+(x)1[x \geq \zeta] = m^-(x) + \alpha 1[x \geq \zeta] \tag{11.27}$$

for some threshold value ζ in the interior of the support of the covariate, where the functions $m^-(\cdot)$ and $m^+(\cdot)$ are twice-differentiable functions. Note that we allow for a break in the level but not in the derivative, although this can also be accommodated. The parameter α measures the height of the jump. We can explicitly define $\alpha = m^+(x) - m^-(x)$, where $m^+(x) = \lim_{\delta \downarrow 0} m(x + \delta)$ and $m^-(x) = \lim_{\delta \downarrow 0} m(x - \delta)$. This is essentially the setting considered in the regression discontinuity literature (Imbens and Lemieux, 2008), where the location ζ is usually known. In many time series applications ζ is unknown and is one of the parameters of interest.

One setting where this framework is used is where x_t is a fixed design, for example, $x_t = t/T, t = 1, \ldots, T$. This can be useful in time series settings, where $m(t/T)$ represents a trend, in which case the interpretation is of structural change. In the regression discontinuity literature, the threshold location ζ is typically known, and the interest is in α. In the structural break literature, the location of ζ is also of interest.

We want to estimate the location of the breaks, the size of the breaks, and the smooth nonparametric components $m^-(\cdot)$ and $m^+(\cdot)$. The one-sided regression and density functions are estimated by

$$\widehat{m}^\pm(x) = \frac{\sum_{t=1}^T K^\pm \left(((x_t - x)/h) \right) y_t}{\sum_{t=1}^T K^\pm \left(((x_t - x)/h) \right)}, \qquad \widehat{f}^\pm(x) = \frac{1}{Th} \sum_{t=1}^T K^\pm \left(\frac{x_t - x}{h} \right),$$

where h is a bandwidth and $K^\pm : \mathbb{R}_+ \longrightarrow \mathbb{R}$ is a one-sided kernel. Specifically, K^+ is a kernel supported on $[-1, 0]$ with $\int_{-1}^0 K^+(u)\, du = 1$ and $\int_{-1}^0 K^+(u) u\, du = 0$, and K^- is a kernel supported on $[0, 1]$ with $\int_0^1 K^-(u)\, du = 1$ and $\int_0^1 K^-(u) u\, du = 0$. So $\widehat{m}^\pm(x)$ is an estimate of the conditional expectation $m(x)$ using data either to the left or to the right of x. In a similar sense, $\widehat{f}^\pm(x)$ is an estimate of the corresponding marginal densities (Müller, 1992).

Consider the quantity $\Psi(x)^2 = (m^+(x) - m^-(x))^2$. This is, by assumption, uniquely maximized at the point $x = \zeta$. We can then estimate this quantity nonparametrically with $\widehat{\Psi}(x)^2 = (\widehat{m}^+(x) - \widehat{m}^-(x))^2$. We then estimate the locations of the breaks by $\widehat{\zeta} = \arg \max_{x \in [h, 1-h]} \widehat{\Psi}(x)^2$. Essentially, at any given point on the curve in one dimension, we take one local average of the data to the left of that point and another local average of the data to the right of that point. The point on the unit interval where the squared difference in these local averages is maximized should be a good estimate of the break location. The size of the breaks can be estimated by $\widehat{\alpha} = \widehat{m}^+(x) - \widehat{m}^-(x)$.

Delgado and Hidalgo (2000) showed, under some conditions, that $\widehat{\zeta} - \zeta = O_p(h/T)^{1/2}$. Thus, the rate of convergence of the breakpoint estimator is faster than the regular univariate nonparametric rate. This means that the rate of convergence of the second-stage estimator for the backfitting components will not be affected. The next result shows that, unlike in most parametric settings, the breakpoint estimator has an asymptotically normal distribution. Furthermore, they are asymptotically uncorrelated. Define

$$s^+(x) = \lim_{\delta \downarrow 0} \text{var}(y \mid X = x + \delta), \qquad s^-(x) = \lim_{\delta \downarrow 0} \text{var}(y \mid X = x - \delta). \tag{11.28}$$

Delgado and Hidalgo (2000) also showed that, under some conditions,

$$\sqrt{\frac{T}{h}}(\widehat{\zeta} - \zeta_0) \Longrightarrow N(0, \sigma^2), \qquad \sigma^2 = \frac{s^-(\zeta_0) \|K^-\|^2}{f^-(\zeta_0)\alpha^2 K^-(0)^2} + \frac{s^+(\zeta_0) \|K^+\|^2}{f^+(\zeta_0)\alpha^2 K^+(0)^2}.$$

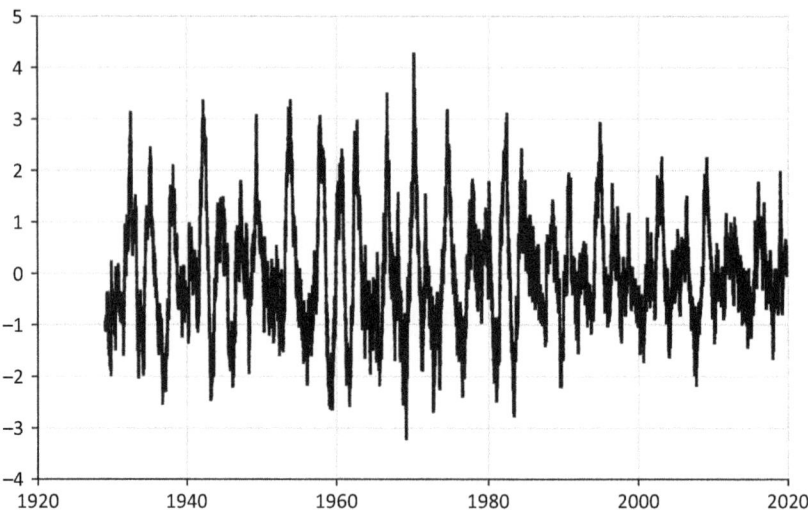

Figure 11.17 One-year rolling window structural break test; S&P500 daily stock returns.

Suppose that $x_t = t/T$, and that we think there may be a structural break in $m(\cdot)$. Let

$$m^+(u) = \frac{1}{T}\sum_{t=1}^{T} K_h^+(u - t/T)y_t, \qquad m^-(u) = \frac{1}{T}\sum_{t=1}^{T} K_h^-(u - t/T)y_t.$$

These estimates are asymptotically jointly normal and mutually uncorrelated, but the limiting variance depends on the autocorrelation of the error term. Under the null hypothesis of no break,

$$t(u) = \frac{\widehat{m}^+(u) - \widehat{m}^-(u)}{\sqrt{\widehat{\mathrm{lrvar}(\varepsilon)}}\sqrt{\widehat{\sigma}_+^2(x) \times \|K^+\|^2 + \widehat{\sigma}_-^2(x) \times \|K^-\|^2}} \implies N(0,1)$$

for any u. Here, $\widehat{\mathrm{lrvar}(\varepsilon)}$ is an estimate of $\mathrm{lrvar}(\varepsilon)$, the long-run variance of the errors.

We may make a formal test of the null hypothesis of no break by looking at, say, $\int_0^1 t(u)^2\,du$ or $\max_{u \in [\epsilon, 1-\epsilon]} |t(u)|$. In Figures 11.17 and 11.18 we show the pointwise test statistics for each time point for daily S&P500 stock returns for two different bandwidth choices, one year and five years. The strongest evidence for a structural break comes in the 1970s or early 1980s.

11.3   Large-Dimensional Models

We next consider recent developments in the analysis of large-dimensional models, or big data, or machine learning, depending on your choice of terminology. There are now many techniques available for analyzing such datasets, which are becoming more prevalent in economics and finance. The new techniques allow the user to throw in a large number of variables and obtain a representation involving only the most relevant as determined by

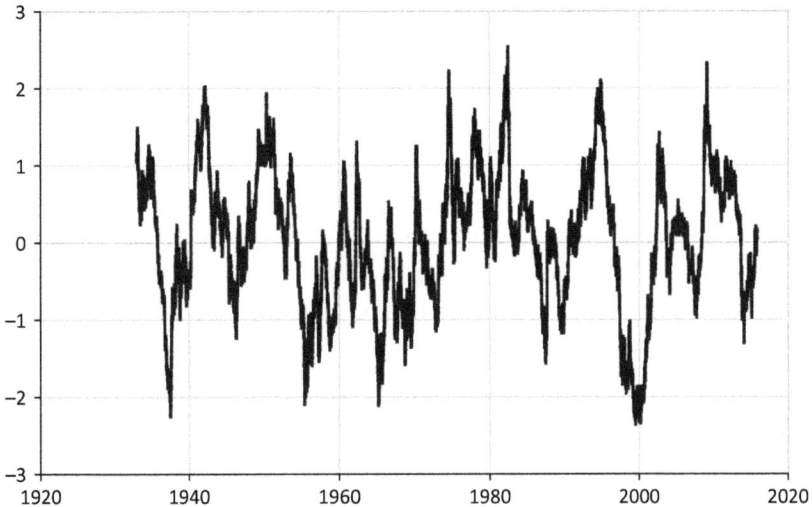

Figure 11.18 Five-year rolling window structural break test; S&P500 daily stock returns.

the data.[2] This is of great use in prediction problems but also increasingly these methods are applied in questions of causal inference where the role of some variables is not known. To some extent these methods compete with time series methods. Where the classical time series relies more on particular structures and models, machine learning relies on algorithms.

We present (some of) the main ideas in the framework of a classical linear regression model. Suppose that $y_t = \beta^\mathsf{T} x_t + \varepsilon_t$, where $y_1, \ldots, y_T$ are scalar-valued random variables, while $x_1, \ldots, x_T$ are elements of $\mathbb{R}^p$ and $\varepsilon_1, \ldots, \varepsilon_T$ are i.i.d. scalar-valued random variables independent of $x_1, \ldots, x_T$ with $E(\varepsilon_t) = 0$ and $\sigma^2 = E(\varepsilon_t^2) < \infty$. We can write this in matrix form:

$$y = X\beta + \varepsilon, \qquad y = \begin{pmatrix} y_1 \\ \vdots \\ y_T \end{pmatrix}, \quad \varepsilon = \begin{pmatrix} \varepsilon_1 \\ \vdots \\ \varepsilon_T \end{pmatrix}, \quad X = \begin{pmatrix} x_1^\mathsf{T} \\ \vdots \\ x_T^\mathsf{T} \end{pmatrix}.$$

We consider the high-dimensional case where p is large, that is, $p \to \infty$ as $T \to \infty$. We can distinguish several cases:

(i) The moderate high-dimensional case has $p/T \to 0$.

(ii) The knife-edge case has $p/T \to c$, $0 < c < \infty$.

(iii) The high-dimensional case has $p/T \to \infty$.

(iv) The ultra-high-dimensional case has $p \geq \exp(cT^\alpha) \to \infty$ for some $c, \alpha > 0$.

The least squares estimator is defined in general as

$$\widehat{\beta} \in \operatorname*{argmin}_{b \in \mathbb{R}^p} \sum_{t=1}^T (y_t - b^\mathsf{T} x_t)^2 = \operatorname*{argmin}_{b \in \mathbb{R}^p} \|y - Xb\|_2^2,$$

---

[2] This used to be given the perjorative term "data mining," and in the 1970s and 1980s much econometric ink was spilled trying to dissuade practitioners from doing this, but now it is celebrated as new-age wisdom.

and we estimate the regression function $E(y \mid X)$ by $\widehat{E}(y \mid X) = X\widehat{\beta}$. Define the column span of X, $\mathbb{L} = \{Xb\colon b \in \mathbb{R}^p\}$, which is a linear subspace of $\mathbb{R}^T$. For a linear subspace $\mathbb{L}$ of $\mathbb{R}^T$ and $y \in \mathbb{R}^T$ the point $z \in \mathbb{L}$ with $z = \arg\min_{z \in \mathbb{L}} \|y - z\|_2^2$ is called the (orthogonal) projection of y onto $\mathbb{L}$, and is uniquely defined. We write $z = P_{\mathbb{L}} y$. When X is of full rank, $P_{\mathbb{L}} = X(X^T X)^{-1} X^T$. In the case where $p > T$, $\mathrm{rank}(X) \leq T < p$ so that $X^T X$ is not invertible, and, although the projection is well defined, the OLS coefficients are not uniquely defined. Furthermore, the fit $X\widehat{\beta} = \Pi_{\mathbb{L}} y = y$, so that the least squares method does nothing, or rather interpolates the data.

We make some further model assumptions that will assist in interpretation and in reducing dimension.

Definition 11.5 (Sparsity assumption)   We suppose that

$$\|\beta\|_0 = s_0 = \#\{j\colon \beta_j \neq 0\} \ll T,$$

in the sense that $s_0(T)/T \to 0$. Here, S denotes the number of elements of a set S.

In this case, we may allow $p(T) \to \infty$ and possibly $p(T)/T \to \infty$, but the nonzero coefficients are less numerous than the sample size. The key issue is that we do not know which of the β_j coefficients are zero and which are not. This is the classic model selection problem, which we have already discussed. If the number of covariates under consideration is small, we can feasibly search over all the possible submodels, rank them according to some criteria, and then make our selection.

11.3.1   Moderate High-Dimensional Models

We review briefly the classical model selection methods. One chooses a model (indexed by k) to minimize the trade-off between fit and dimensionality given, for example, by the AIC,

$$\mathrm{AIC}(k) = \log(\mathrm{RSS}_k) + \frac{T + k}{T - k - 2}.$$

This penalty is related to the L_0 norm of the vector of parameters, that is, $\|\beta\|_0 = s_0 = \#\{j\colon \beta_j \neq 0\}$. Results in time series and regression allow the dimensionality of the largest model to grow logarithmically; Hannan and Quinn (1979) allow $\log k_{\max}/T \to 0$. In time series with ordered models the search is relatively easy because one typically just computes the models indexed by the longest lag rather than searching over all submodels of a given size, which would soon become impossible. If one has to consider all submodels, this forces big limits on $k_{\max}$ for computational reasons.

Portnoy (1984, 1985) considered the linear model with the number of parameters $p \to \infty$. He considered a general class of estimators (including nonlinear M estimators) and showed that $\|\widehat{\beta} - \beta\|_2^2 = O_P(p/T)$ provided $p \log p/T \to 0$, and further that $c^T \widehat{\beta}$ is asymptotically normal for any $c \neq 0$ provided the condition $(p \log p)^{3/2}/T \to 0$ is satisfied. Mammen (1993) proposed a wild bootstrap method for inference in large-dimensional linear regression with heteroskedastic errors. He considered the properties of linear contrasts, that is, the sequence of scalar random variables $\sqrt{T} c^T (\widehat{\beta} - \beta)$ and their distribution function, $H_T(x) = \Pr\left(\sqrt{T}c^\mathsf{T}(\widehat{\beta} - \beta) \le x\right)$. He proved that a wild bootstrap construction $H_T^*(x) = \Pr\left(\sqrt{T}c^\mathsf{T}(\widehat{\beta}^* - \widehat{\beta}) \le x \mid y, X\right)$ provides valid inference.

11.3.2 High-Dimensional Models

How do we accommodate large models where $p > T$? In this case the matrix $X^\mathsf{T}X$ is symmetric and positive semidefinite with eigendecomposition $Q\Lambda Q^\mathsf{T}$, where Q is an orthonormal matrix and Λ is a diagonal matrix with values $\lambda_1 \ge \cdots \ge \lambda_T > \lambda_{T+1} = \cdots = \lambda_p = 0$. One possibility is to use the **Moore–Penrose** inverse $(X^\mathsf{T}X)^- = Q\Lambda^- Q^\mathsf{T}$ in place of $(X^\mathsf{T}X)^{-1}$, where Λ^- is a diagonal matrix with entries $\lambda_1^{-1}, \ldots, \lambda_T^{-1}, 0, \ldots, 0$, in which case the set of minimizing coefficients is

$$\mathfrak{B} = \left\{ b \colon b = (X^\mathsf{T}X)^- X^\mathsf{T}y + (I_p - (X^\mathsf{T}X)^-(X^\mathsf{T}X))w, \ w \in \mathbb{R}^p \right\},$$

and $\widehat{\beta}_{\mathrm{MP}} = (X^\mathsf{T}X)^- X^\mathsf{T}y$ may be interpreted as the member of the minimizing space $\mathfrak{B}$ with smallest distance from the origin. Hastie *et al.* (2022) described some properties of this estimator in the high-dimensional case. We emphasize here the more established approaches.

We consider the following general two-step procedure:

1. Variable selection. Estimate the active set $S = \{j \colon \beta_j \ne 0\}$ and its complement S^c. Denote the set estimators by $\widehat{S}$ and $\widehat{S}^c$.
2. Put $\widetilde{\beta} = \widehat{\beta}_{\widehat{S}}$, where, with $b_I = (b_j 1(j \in I))_{j=1}^p$,

$$\widehat{\beta}_{\widehat{S}} = \operatorname*{argmin}_{b \in \mathbb{R}^p, b_{\widehat{S}^c} = 0} \|y - Xb\|_2^2.$$

There are many variable selectors $\widehat{S}$ such that $\widetilde{\beta} = \widehat{\beta}_{\widehat{S}}$ fulfills this in principle. On the other hand, finding $\widehat{S}$ is already too computationally complex for moderate sizes of p, because of the huge number of subsets of $\{1, \ldots, p\}$ (and hence models of a given size) over which one would have to search. We now consider the LASSO method that provides a computationally feasible solution to this question.

11.3.3 The LASSO Estimator

Our treatment follows Bühlmann and van de Geer (2011). For other discussions of this topic see also Bickel, Ritov, and Tsybakov (2009), van de Geer (2008), and the literature cited in these papers.

In practice it is convenient to standardize the covariates, so we assume that $T^{-1}\sum_{t=1}^T x_{tj}^2 = 1$, $j = 1, \ldots, p$. This can be easily achieved by replacing x_{tj} by $x_{tj}/\sqrt{T^{-1}\sum_{t=1}^T x_{tj}^2}$ and by replacing β_j by $\sqrt{T^{-1}\sum_{t=1}^T x_{tj}^2} \times \beta_j$. Then $x_{tj}\beta_j$ does not change and we have the same model equation as before. The point of this is that now, the values of $\beta_j, j = 1, \ldots, p$, are comparable in scale.

For a tuning parameter $\lambda \ge 0$, we define the LASSO estimator $\widehat{\beta}_\lambda$ as

$$\widehat{\beta}_\lambda \in \operatorname*{argmin}_{b \in \mathbb{R}^p} \left(\frac{1}{T}\|y - Xb\|_2^2 + \lambda\|b\|_1 \right), \tag{11.29}$$

where $\|b\|_q = \left(\sum_{j=1}^p |b_j|^q\right)^{1/q}$ for any $q > 0$. The second term, $\lambda\|b\|_1$, is a penalty factor and λ is called the penalty constant or tuning parameter. There are many fast numerical algorithms for the calculation of $\widehat{\beta}_\lambda$ because this is a convex problem. However, the estimator is nonlinear in y and it does not have a closed-form expression except in special cases (Tibshirani, 1996).

For comparison, the ridge regression estimator is defined as

$$\widehat{\beta}_\lambda^* \in \underset{b \in \mathbb{R}^p}{\operatorname{argmin}} \left(\frac{1}{T}\|y - Xb\|_2^2 + \lambda\|b\|_2^2\right). \tag{11.30}$$

This estimator is linear and has the closed-form expression

$$\widehat{\beta}_\lambda^* = (X^\mathsf{T} X + \lambda I_p)^{-1} X^\mathsf{T} y.$$

Here, λ is a tuning parameter. The Moore–Penrose estimator can be interpreted as $\widehat{\beta}_{\mathrm{MP}} = \lim_{\lambda\downarrow 0}\widehat{\beta}_\lambda^*$, and is sometimes called the ridgeless estimator.

11.3.3.1 Order of Convergence

Suppose that we know $S = \{j \colon \beta_j \neq 0\}$ and that we fit the **oracle model**,

$$y_t = \sum_{j \in S} x_{tj}\beta_j + \varepsilon_t,$$

by least squares. For the least squares estimator we get that

$$\widehat{\beta}_{\mathrm{ORACLE}} = \underset{b \in \mathbb{R}^p;\, b_j=0 \text{ for } j \in S^c}{\operatorname{argmin}} \frac{1}{T}\|y - Xb\|_2^2.$$

The column space $\mathbb{L}^*$ of the oracle model is given by $\mathbb{L}^* = \{Xb \colon b \in \mathbb{R}^p, b_j = 0 \text{ for } j \in S^c\}$. It holds that $E[\|X(\widehat{\beta}_{\mathrm{ORACLE}} - \beta)\|_2^2] = \sigma^2 s_0$, and so

$$\frac{1}{T}\left\|\widehat{E}_{\mathrm{ORACLE}}(y \mid X) - E(y \mid X)\right\|_2^2 = \frac{1}{T}\left\|X(\widehat{\beta}_{\mathrm{ORACLE}} - \beta)\right\|_2^2 = O_P\left(\frac{s_0}{T}\right).$$

We now formulate the main result of this section. For the theorem we need an assumption often called the **compatibility condition**.

Definition 11.6 (Compatibility condition)   There exists a $\phi > 0$ with

$$\|b_S\|_1^2 \leq \frac{b^\mathsf{T} X^\mathsf{T} X b}{T} \frac{s_0}{\phi^2}$$

for all $b \in \mathbb{R}^p$ with $3\|b_S\|_1 \geq \|b_{S^c}\|_1$. Equivalently, for any $L > 0$,

$$d(L, S_0) = \min\left\{\frac{b^\mathsf{T} X^\mathsf{T} X b}{T} \colon b \in \mathbb{R}^p, \|b_{S_0}\|_1 = 1, \|b_{S_0^c}\|_1 \leq L\right\} > 0.$$

If the matrix $X^\mathsf{T} X$ is nonsingular, then this condition automatically holds. In the high-dimensional case this condition restricts the dependence between the columns as the dimensionality increases. One can show that the compatibility condition holds for random predictor variables x_t with high probability, under suitable conditions. More explanation can be found in Bühlmann and van de Geer (2011).

Theorem 11.5 *We suppose that the compatibility condition holds with a constant $\phi >$ 0. For $t > 0$ we define $\widehat{\beta}_\lambda$ as the LASSO estimator with penalty constant*

$$\lambda = 4\widehat{\sigma}\sqrt{\frac{t^2 + 2\log p}{T}},$$

where $\widehat{\sigma}$ is an estimator for an upper bound of the standard deviation σ of the error process. Then

$$\|\widehat{\beta}_\lambda - \beta\|_1 = O_P\left(s_0\sqrt{\frac{\log p}{T}}\right),$$

$$\frac{1}{T}\left\|\widehat{E}(y \mid X) - E(y \mid X)\right\|_2^2 = \frac{1}{T}\|X(\widehat{\beta}_\lambda - \beta)\|_2^2 = O\left(\frac{s_0\log p}{T}\right).$$

This shows that, up to a factor $\log p$, the LASSO estimator has the same rate as the oracle estimator. One has to pay a price of order $\log p$ for not knowing S, at least if one uses the LASSO estimator. The larger the value of s_0 the bigger the penalty, and clearly we require s_0 to be of smaller order than T. One can also show that no estimator exists with a faster convergence rate than $(s_0\log p)/T$.

11.3.3.2 The Form of the LASSO and Ridge Estimators

Here, we consider the behavior of the LASSO estimator $\widehat{\beta}_\lambda$ and the ridge regression estimator $\widehat{\beta}_\lambda^*$ as a function of λ for fixed values $y_1, \ldots, y_T \in \mathbb{R}$, $x_1, \ldots, x_T \in \mathbb{R}^p$. One can see that increasing λ results in the absolute values of both $\widehat{\beta}_\lambda$ and $\widehat{\beta}_\lambda^*$ typically becoming smaller. But there is an important difference: For λ large enough, each element of $\widehat{\beta}_\lambda$ is equal to zero, where the value of λ differs for the elements of $\widehat{\beta}_\lambda$. This is not the case for ridge regression. Here, all coefficients typically decrease in absolute value, but without becoming exactly equal to zero. We next give two heuristic explanations for this.

In our first heuristic explanation we consider the model $y_t = \beta_t + \varepsilon_t$ with $t = 1, \ldots, T$. This is a linear model with $p = T$. For the LASSO estimator (we omit the factor $1/T$ that was used in the previous subsection because T is fixed in the discussion of this subsection), we get

$$\widehat{\beta}_\lambda \in \underset{b \in \mathbb{R}^p}{\text{argmin}} \left(\frac{1}{2}\|y - b\|_2^2 + \lambda\|b\|_1\right) = \underset{b \in \mathbb{R}^p}{\text{argmin}} \sum_{t=1}^T \left(\frac{1}{2}(y_t - b_t)^2 + \lambda|b_t|\right),$$

which in this case implies that

$$\widehat{\beta}_{\lambda,j} \in \underset{b_j \in \mathbb{R}}{\text{argmin}} \left(\frac{1}{2}(y_j - b_j)^2 + \lambda|b_j|\right).$$

A simple calculation gives the precise formula:

$$\widehat{\beta}_{\lambda,j} = \text{sign}(y_j)\,(|y_j| - \lambda)_+ = \begin{cases} y_j - \lambda & \text{if } y_j > \lambda, \\ y_j + \lambda & \text{if } y_j < -\lambda, \\ 0 & \text{if } |y_j| \leq \lambda, \end{cases}$$

where $(x)_+ = \max\{x, 0\}$. This operation is also called **soft thresholding**, that is, as the input y crosses the threshold $\pm\lambda$ it smoothly (linearly in fact) transitions into nonzero values rather than abruptly as in the **hard thresholding** procedure

$$\widehat{\beta}_{\lambda,j}^{**} = \begin{cases} y_j & \text{if } |y_j| > \lambda, \\ 0 & \text{if } |y_j| \leq \lambda. \end{cases}$$

Specifically, $\widehat{\beta}_{\lambda,j}$ is a continuous function of y_j, whereas $\widehat{\beta}_{\lambda,j}^{**}$ is not. For the ridge regression one finds that

$$\widehat{\beta}_{\lambda,j}^{*} = \frac{y_j}{1+\lambda}.$$

In this case the coefficients are also shrunk towards zero but they never reach zero exactly (unless $y_j = 0$). One can also in this case compare the LASSO and ridge regression estimators with a two-step estimator $\widehat{\beta}_{\lambda}^{**}$ that estimates the set $S = \{j: \beta_j \neq 0\}$. A natural estimate of S in this case would be $\widehat{S}_{\lambda} = \{j: |y_j| > \lambda\}$. Then we get the estimator $\widehat{\beta}_{\lambda,j}^{**}$.

Our second heuristic argumentation discusses the LASSO and ridge regression estimators for the simple case $p = 2$. For this discussion consider the contour lines of the functions

$$f_1(\beta) = |\beta_1| + |\beta_2|, \qquad f_2(\beta) = |\beta_1|^2 + |\beta_2|^2, \qquad g(\beta) = \sum_{t=1}^{T}(y_t - \beta^{\mathsf{T}}x_t)^2.$$

One sees that the contact points of f_1 and g are often points with $\beta_1 = 0$ or $\beta_2 = 0$. For an understanding of the argument note that $\widehat{\beta}_{\lambda}$ and $\widehat{\beta}_{\lambda}^{*}$ run through the solutions of $\min \sum(y_t - \beta^{\mathsf{T}}x_t)^2$ under the constraint that $|\beta_1| + |\beta_2| \leq C$ or $|\beta_1|^2 + |\beta_2|^2 \leq C$, respectively, with some C that runs through $\mathbb{R}_+$.

11.3.4 SCAD

The LASSO penalty term delivers model selection but because of the lack of smoothness it raises an issue with inference. An alternative approach, **smoothly clipped absolute deviation** (SCAD), developed by Fan and Li (2001), is to smooth over the penalty function in the tails. Let

$$Q_T(b) = \frac{1}{T}\|y - Xb\|_2^2 + \sum_{j=1}^{p} P_T(|b_j|),$$

where $P_T(\cdot)$ belongs to the class of **folded concave penalty functions**. This approach also gives lots of zeros but is somewhat more regular than LASSO under conditions on P_T. We just consider the following specific penalty function.

Definition 11.7   For some $a > 2$ and $t > 0$, let $P_T(\cdot)$ be such that

$$P_T'(u) = \lambda \left\{ 1(u \leq \lambda) + \frac{(a\lambda - u)_+}{(a-1)u}1(u > \lambda) \right\}.$$

This penalty function leaves large values of b not excessively penalized and makes the solution continuous, which the LASSO does not satisfy. In the special case $y_j = \beta_j + \varepsilon_j$, the SCAD estimator with this penalty is exactly

$$\widehat{\beta}_{P,j} = \begin{cases} \text{sign}(y_j)(|y_j| - \lambda)_+ & \text{if } |y_j| \leq 2\lambda, \\ \dfrac{(a-1)y_j - \text{sign}(y_j)a\lambda}{a-2} & \text{if } 2\lambda < |y_j| < a\lambda, \\ y_j & \text{if } |y_j| > a\lambda. \end{cases}$$

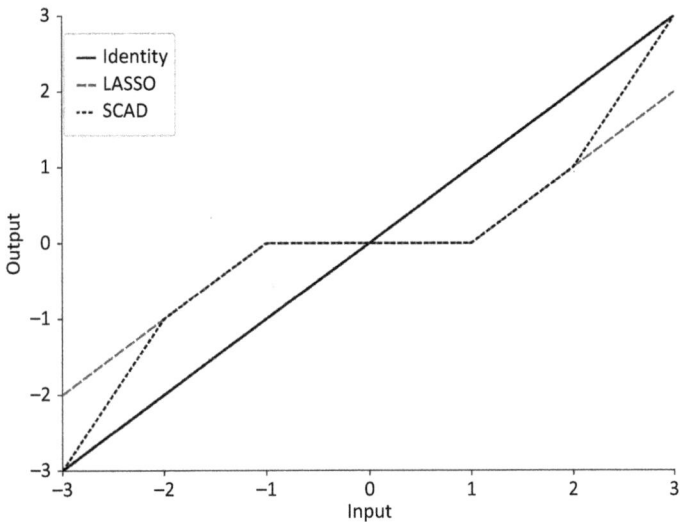

Figure 11.19 Comparison of LASSO and SCAD for $a = 3$ and $\lambda = 1$.

We compare the LASSO and SCAD thresholding functions in Figure 11.19. The SCAD estimator has a redescending penalty that disappears for large values, whereas the LASSO always applies some downward shrinkage.

For the true parameter β_0, let $d_T = \min\{|\beta_{0j}| : \beta_{0j} \neq 0, j = 1, \ldots, p\}/2$ represent the strength of the signal, or rather the separation of the nonzeros from the zeros.

Theorem 11.6 *Suppose that the regularity conditions of Dong, Gao, and Linton (2023) hold, which restrict d_T. Then, there exists a local minimizer $(\widehat{\beta}_{\widehat{S}}^{\mathsf{T}}, \widehat{\beta}_{\widehat{S^c}}^{\mathsf{T}})^{\mathsf{T}}$ for which*

$$\lim_{T \to \infty} \Pr(\widehat{\beta}_{\widehat{S^c}} = 0) = 1, \qquad \lim_{T \to \infty} \Pr(\widehat{S} = S) = 1.$$

Furthermore, letting $\Sigma_T^2 = (X_S^{\mathsf{T}} X_S)^{-1} X_S^{\mathsf{T}} D X_S (X_S^{\mathsf{T}} X_S)^{-1}$, we have, as $T \to \infty$,

$$\sqrt{T} c^{\mathsf{T}} \Sigma_T^{-1} (\widehat{\beta}_{\widehat{S}} - \beta_S) \Longrightarrow N(0, 1).$$

These methods all directly apply to autoregression where X contains lags of the dependent variable, say up to order $T - 1$. Belloni, Chernozhukov, and Hansen (2014) discussed inference methods after selection for the LASSO method.

11.3.5 OCMT

Chudik, Kapetanios, and Pesaran (2018) considered an alternative approach called one covariate at a time multiple testing (OCMT). In this approach one enters the selectable covariates one at a time into the regression and then does a t-test on whether the coefficient on the candidate variable is significant at a level α_T, where $\alpha_T \to 0$. A variable is selected if one rejects this t-test. This method guarantees correct selection under conditions on the rate at which α_T approaches zero. Although the individual estimators are biased, under some reasonable conditions, if a variable does matter it will lead to large values of the t-statistic with probability tending to one. After selecting the correct regressors, or a superset of the correct ones, one then does OLS on the selected regressors. This method can easily accommodate the case where some regressors are a priori known to belong and are therefore not tested – in that case one just includes those regressors in each of the candidate variable regressions. It seems that specific-to-general modelling is better than general-to-specific modelling after all.

11.3.6 Selection of Tuning Parameters

The LASSO and SCAD methods both require the choice of a tuning parameter λ, and the value of λ determines the performance of the procedure just like in kernel density and kernel regression estimation. The methodology for choosing an appropriate λ is similar to that in nonparametric regression. One typically splits the sample into three parts: the training set, the validation set, and the test set. The validation set is used to measure the performance in an unbiased way across different λ values leading to an optimal choice. The test set can then be used for further performance evaluation. This is quite natural in a stationary, weakly dependent time series setting but runs into problems in nonstationary environments.

11.4 Summary

We considered nonparametric approaches to modelling and estimation of densities, regression functions, CDFs, quantiles, and tail thickness parameters, all in the time series context. We considered different linear and nonlinear estimators and discussed the statistical properties of said estimators, exploiting smoothness assumptions. We considered bandwidth choice and some implementation issues. We also considered the setting where there are a large number of variables rather than a complex functional form. In this case the sparsity assumption replaced smoothness and we defined several methods, including the LASSO, to exploit the assumed sparsity. The R language has several packages to do density and regression smoothing, including ks. Neural networks are available in nnet; LASSO can be implemented in glmnet. For further reading, see Bühlmann and van de Geer (2011).

11.5 Exercises

11.1 For the dataset ffdaily, let y_t denote the SMB variable and x_t denote MKT. Estimate the nonparametric regressions of y_t on x_t ($E(y_t \mid x_t)$) and the conditional variance var$(y_t \mid x_t)$ using the following methods and compare the results.
(a) local linear smoother
(b) nearest neighbors
(c) sieve method

11.2 For the dataset sp500stocks let r_{it} denote the return on stock i on day t, and calculate all the sample cross-autocorrelations $\widehat{R}_{ij}(k)$. Letting $y_{k;l}$ denote the typical element $\widehat{R}_{ij}(k)$, calculate the kernel density across all instances l and plot the estimated density. How do these densities vary with k?

11.3 For the dataset `sp500stocks` let r_{it} denote the return on stock i on day t, and standardize returns by their mean and standard deviation, $y_{it} = (r_{it} - \bar{r}_i)/s_i$. Compute all the pairwise nonparametric regressions $E(y_{it} \mid y_{jt})$ ($i, j = 1, \ldots, 441$, $i < j$) using your method of choice. Identify those relationships with the greatest nonlinearity. Compare all the fits according to the value of $\sum_{t=1}^{T} \hat{\varepsilon}_{it}^2$, where $\hat{\varepsilon}_{it} = y_{it} - \hat{g}_{ij}(y_{jt})$ are the nonparametric residuals, and identify those relationships with the best fit.

11.4 Suppose that y_t is a stationary mixing process with marginal CDF F. Define the marginal empirical and joint empirical,

$$\widehat{F}_0(y) = \frac{1}{T}\sum_{t=1}^{T} 1\,(y_t \leq y), \qquad \widehat{F}_{0,k}(y, y') = \frac{1}{T}\sum_{t=k+1}^{T} 1\,(y_t \leq y, y_{t+k} \leq y'),$$

and let, for any $k \neq 0$, $\tau_{T,k}(y, y') = \sqrt{T}(\widehat{F}_{0,k}(y, y') - \widehat{F}_0(y)\widehat{F}_0(y'))$. What is the large-sample behavior of $\tau_{T,k}(y, y')$ under the null hypothesis that y_t is i.i.d.? How about under the general alternative? Discuss how you might combine across k, y, y'.

11.5 Suppose that y_t is a stationary mixing process with marginal CDF F, and let $I(y) = \int_{-\infty}^{y} F(x)\,dx$. Define the empirical distribution function $\widehat{F}(y) = T^{-1}\sum_{t=1}^{T} 1\,(y_t \leq y)$. Show that

$$\widehat{I}(y) = \int_{-\infty}^{y} \widehat{F}(x)\,dx = \frac{1}{T}\sum_{t=1}^{T}(y - y_t)\,1\,(y_t \leq y).$$

What are the properties of the estimator $\widehat{I}(y)$?

11.6 Suppose that $y_t = \varepsilon_t - \theta\varepsilon_{t-1}$, where ε_t is i.i.d. with density f_ε. Show that the density of y_t, f_y, satisfies

$$f_y(y) = \int_{-\infty}^{\infty} f_\varepsilon(y + \theta x)f_\varepsilon(x)\,dx.$$

Supposing that $\{\varepsilon_1, \ldots, \varepsilon_T\}$ is observed and θ is known, construct an estimate of $f_\varepsilon(\cdot)$ and hence construct an estimate of $f_y(y)$.

11.7 Consider the nonparametric regression $y_{t+1} = g(x_t) + u_{t+1}$, where g is an unknown but smooth function. Here, x_t is an observed predictor variable and y_t are one-period stock returns in period t, while u_{t+1} is an error term that satisfies $E(u_{t+1} \mid \mathcal{F}_t) = 0$, where $\mathcal{F}_t$ contains all the information available at time t, including x_t. Define the Nadaraya–Watson estimator

$$\hat{g}(x) = \frac{\sum_{t=1}^{T-1} K_h(x - x_t)y_{t+1}}{\sum_{t=1}^{T-1} K_h(x - x_t)},$$

where $K_h(\cdot) = K(\cdot/h)/h$ and K is a symmetric probability density. Suppose that $u_{t+1} = \sigma_t\varepsilon_t$ with ε_t i.i.d., while $\sigma_t^2 = v(x_t, z_t)$ for some function v where z_t is observed at time t. Also define $\sigma^2(x_t) = E(u_{t+1}^2 \mid x_t)$. Compare the asymptotic efficiency of the Nadaraya–Watson estimator with the following infeasible nonparametric "GLS estimators":

$$\hat{g}_{\sigma^2}(x) = \frac{\sum_{t=1}^{T-1} K_h(x - x_t)y_{t+1}\sigma^{-2}(x_t)}{\sum_{t=1}^{T-1} K_h(x - x_t)\sigma^{-2}(x_t)},$$

$$\widehat{g}_v(x) = \frac{\sum_{t=1}^{T-1} K_h(x - x_t)y_{t+1}v(x_t, z_t)^{-1}}{\sum_{t=1}^{T-1} K_h(x - x_t)v(x_t, z_t)^{-1}}.$$

You may do this analytically and numerically, that is, provide a simulation study.

11.8 Suppose that $y_t = \alpha_t + \varepsilon_t$, $\alpha_t = \alpha_{t-1} + \eta_t$, where $\varepsilon_t \sim N(0, \sigma_\varepsilon^2(t/T))$ and $\eta_t \sim N(0, \sigma_\eta^2(t/T))$ are mutually independent shocks, and $\sigma_\varepsilon^2(\cdot), \sigma_\eta^2(\cdot)$ are unknown smooth functions. We observe a sample $\{y_1, \ldots, y_T\}$, where T is large. Explain how to estimate $\sigma_\varepsilon^2(\cdot), \sigma_\eta^2(\cdot)$ from the differenced data Δy_t. Now, assuming that $\sigma_\varepsilon^2(\cdot), \sigma_\eta^2(\cdot)$ are known, write down the Kalman filter equations for α_t.

11.9 Suppose that $r_t, t = 1, \ldots, n$, are stock returns with population CDF F and standard deviation σ. The so-called bias ratio is estimated by

$$\widehat{\mathrm{BR}} = \frac{F_n(\widehat{\sigma}) - F_n(0)}{\epsilon_n + F_n(0) - F_n(-\widehat{\sigma})},$$

where $\widehat{\sigma}$ is the sample standard deviation and $F_n(\cdot)$ is the empirical distribution of the sample data. Here, ϵ_n is a small number, usually $1/n$, which is just there to guarantee the denominator is positive. The bias ratio of a pure equity index will usually be close to one. However, if a fund smooths its returns using subjective pricing of illiquid assets, the bias ratio will be higher (Lo, 2001). Derive a CLT for $\widehat{\mathrm{BR}}$ and thereby propose a confidence interval for the population quantity

$$\mathrm{BR} = \frac{F(\sigma) - F(0)}{F(0) - F(-\sigma)}.$$

Conduct a Monte Carlo study to investigate the properties of $\widehat{\mathrm{BR}}$ and the confidence interval you have proposed. In this case you may take $r_t \sim N(0, 1)$ and $\epsilon_n = 0$.

11.10 Suppose that $y_t = x_t + \varepsilon_t$, where x_t, ε_t are two mutually independent, stationary, continuously distributed stochastic processes. Show that

$$f_{x_t|y_t}(x \mid y) = \frac{f_{y_t|x_t}(y \mid x)f_{x_t}(x)}{f_{y_t}(y)},$$

$$f_{x_t,x_{t-1}|y_t,y_{t-1}}(x, x' \mid y, y') = \frac{f_{y_t,y_{t-1}|x_t,x_{t-1}}(y, y' \mid x, x')f_{x_t,x_{t-1}}(x, x')}{f_{y_t,y_{t-1}}(y, y')}.$$

Supposing that ε_t is i.i.d. with density function f_ε, and that x_t is a Gaussian autoregression $x_t = \phi x_{t-1} + \eta_t$, simplify the above expressions.

11.11 For the dataset $\texttt{sp500stocks}$ let r_{it} denote the return on stock i on day t. Consider the regression

$$r_{it} = \alpha + \sum_{k=1}^{255}\sum_{j=1}^{441} \beta_{ijk}r_{j,t-k} + \sum_{k=1}^{255}\sum_{j=1}^{441} \gamma_{ijk}r_{j,t-k}^2 + e_{it}.$$

How many parameters are there to estimate in total? Compute the ridge regression estimator and the Moore–Penrose estimator of α, β_{ijk}, and γ_{ijk}, and rank the parameter values by stocks. You may experiment with standardizing the variables.

12 Continuous-Time Processes

So far we have considered discrete-time series $\{y_t, t = 1, 2, \ldots, T\}$, where typically T is large, that is, the data cover a long span. In this chapter we look at continuous-time stochastic processes $\{y_t, t \in [0, T]\}$, where for each real-valued time t, y_t is a random variable defined on some sample space Ω. Continuous-time processes are important in mathematical finance, because they lead to simple pricing solutions, which are more complicated to implement in discrete-time settings. For example, the Black and Scholes (1973) option pricing theory exploits the continuousness of time to give a simple but nonlinear formula for the price of certain options. There is now a vast literature that extends their basic setting to more general problems such as interest rate models. There is currently a lot of interest in continuous-time processes due to high-frequency data in exchange rates, stock prices, and electricity data.

The strengths of continuous-time models include that they predict behavior at all sampling frequencies: second, minute, 10 minutes, hourly, daily, weekly, monthly, and irregular frequency. They tie in well with economic theory. Finally, some analysis is simple, as we shall see, for example, stationarity conditions. The weaknesses of continuous-time models include that estimation and some analysis can be difficult computationally. The predictions described in the previous paragraph can be too strong and not consistent with the data, especially for very high-frequency data. Finally, the statistical models are not as flexible as one can achieve with discrete-time models.

We start with the key building block of continuous-time processes, the Brownian motion or Wiener process.

12.1 Brownian Motion

Definition 12.1 The standard Brownian motion process B_t has the following defining properties:

- $B_t - B_s$ is independent of past information $\mathcal{F}_s = \sigma\{B_u : u \leq s\}$.
- $B_t - B_s \sim N(0, t - s)$.

It follows from this that for any set of distinct times $t_1, \ldots, t_n$, the vector $(B(t_1), \ldots, B(t_n))^\top$ is Gaussian. Wiener (1923) proved the existence of the Brownian motion stochastic process as a well-defined mathematical entity. The process B_t is nonstationary, with $\mathrm{cov}(B_s, B_t) = \min\{s, t\}$, but has stationary increments, since the distribution of $B_t - B_s$ only depends on $t - s$ and not on t. This process possesses the property of **infinite divisibility**, which is as follows. Let $B_0 = 0$. Then we can write, for any sequence/partition $0 = t_{n,0} \leq t_{n,1} \leq \cdots \leq t_{n,n} = t$,

$$B_t = \sum_{i=1}^{n} \left(B_{t_{n,i}} - B_{t_{n,i-1}} \right) = \sum_{i=1}^{n} Z_i$$

for independent random variables Z_i (in this case normal). This property is important for a number of applications.

Definition 12.2   Let B_t be standard Brownian motion with $B_0 = 0$ and define the Brownian bridge to time $T > 0$ as

$$\mathbb{B}_t = B_t - \frac{t}{T} B_T.$$

The process B_t is a martingale, meaning $E\left[\|B_t\| \right] < \infty$ for all t and $E\left[B_t \mid \mathcal{F}_s \right] = B_s$ for all $s < t$. In fact, it is the quintessential random walk with $B_t = B_{t-1} + Z_t$, where Z_t is a sequence of i.i.d. standard normal random variables. The process $\mathbb{B}_t$ is not a martingale because $E(\mathbb{B}_T \mid \mathcal{F}_s) = 0 \neq \mathbb{B}_s$.

Definition 12.3   The random variable B_t is just the mapping $\omega \mapsto B_t(\omega)$, $t \in [0, T]$. The **sample path** is just the mapping $t \mapsto B_t(\omega)$, $\omega \in \Omega$. For each realization of the stochastic process ω this is a function of time.

We next give some properties of the sample paths of Brownian motion. Brownian motion has continuous sample paths, and even sample paths that are locally Hölder continuous up to order $\gamma < 1/2$, that is, with probability one, $|B_t - B_s| \leq C |t - s|^{\gamma}$ for some finite constant C. However, the sample paths are nowhere locally Hölder continuous for any $\gamma > 1/2$, and in particular are nowhere differentiable.

Definition 12.4   A function $f\colon [0, T] \to \mathbb{R}$ is said to be of bounded p-variation ($p > 0$) if

$$\sup_{\text{Partitions } \{t_{n,i}: i=1,\ldots,n\} \text{ of } [0,T]} \sum_{i=1}^{n-1} |f(t_{n,i+1}) - f(t_{n,i})|^p < \infty.$$

Continuously differentiable functions have bounded 1-variation (or just bounded variation). The sample paths of Brownian motion are of **unbounded variation** on any compact interval (it roams around a lot). One consequence of this is that ordinary Riemann integration of a function f with respect to B is not well defined and one has to introduce the concept of **stochastic integration**.

12.2   Stochastic Integrals

We next introduce the concept of stochastic integration as it allows one to define a bigger class of stochastic processes and to analyze their properties. Heuristically, it is easy to see how we could make sense of defining linear combinations of Brownian motion when $f(\cdot)$ is a deterministic function, that is, we might expect that

$$y_t = \int_a^t f(s)\, \mathrm{d}B_s \sim N\left(0, \int_a^t f^2(s)\, \mathrm{d}s\right). \tag{12.1}$$

The more general integral $y_t = \int_a^t f(B_s, s)\, \mathrm{d}B_s$ is not so obvious in its meaning and needs the machinery of stochastic integration in order to define it.

Definition 12.5 (Stochastic integral)   Suppose that B is standard Brownian motion. Let $\{f_t, t \in [a,b]\}$ be some stochastic process adapted to the Brownian motion, that is, f_t is a function of $\{B_s,\ s \le t\}$ with $\int_a^b E(f_t^2)\, \mathrm{d}t < \infty$. Let

$$I(f) = \int_a^b f_t\, \mathrm{d}B_t = \lim_{n \to \infty} I_n(f), \qquad I_n(f) = \sum_{i=1}^n f_{t_{n,i}}(B_{t_{n,i+1}} - B_{t_{n,i}}), \tag{12.2}$$

where $t_{n,1} = a < t_{n,2} < \cdots < t_{n,n}$ is any partition of $[a,b]$ such that $\sup_i |t_{n,i+1} - t_{n,i}| \to 0$ as $n \to \infty$; the limit is defined in quadratic mean, that is,

$$\lim_{n \to \infty} E\big((I_n(f) - I(f))^2\big) = 0.$$

The limit can alternatively be defined in probability. Stochastic integration can also be defined for more general f, and for more general stochastic processes than B: the integral $\int H\, \mathrm{d}y$ is defined for a semimartingale y and locally bounded predictable process H (Protter, 2004).

Stochastic integration, like Riemann integration, is a linear operator, that is, for any functions f, g satisfying the above conditions and scalars α, β we have $I(\alpha f + \beta g) = \alpha I(f) + \beta I(g)$. The stochastic integral process is itself a martingale under some conditions on the integrand process f, that is, we have, with probability one,

$$E\left(\int_a^t f_u\, \mathrm{d}B_u \mid \mathcal{F}_s\right) = \int_a^s f_u\, \mathrm{d}B_u \tag{12.3}$$

for all $s < t$. The stochastic integral satisfies the **isometry property**

$$E\left(\left(\int_a^b f_t\, \mathrm{d}B_t\right)^2\right) = E\left(\int_a^b E(f_t^2)\, \mathrm{d}t\right), \tag{12.4}$$

which is already present in (12.1).

12.3   Diffusion Processes

We next introduce an important general class of processes that includes Brownian motion and many processes derived from it. We first recall the concept of a Markov process defined in Chapter 2 and now defined for continuous time. For example, AR and ARCH processes in discrete time and Brownian motion in continuous time are Markov processes. However, MA and GARCH processes are not Markov in the observed variables. A diffusion process can be defined as a continuous-time **strong Markov process** with continuous sample paths.[1] A more common way of introducing a diffusion process is through the stochastic differential equation representation.

Definition 12.6   Suppose that $y_0 = y$, and that

$$dy_t = \mu(y_t, t)\, dt + \sigma(y_t, t)\, dB_t, \tag{12.5}$$

where y is a given random variable and B_t is standard Brownian motion. The general diffusion process can equivalently be written as

$$y_t = y_0 + \int_0^t \mu(y_s, s)\, ds + \int_0^t \sigma(y_s, s)\, dB_s,$$

where the second integral is a stochastic integral but the first one is an ordinary Riemann integral.

The function $\mu(\cdot)$ is called the drift, while $\sigma^2(\cdot)$ is the volatility function or diffusion coefficient. Note that

$$\mu(y) = \lim_{\Delta \to 0} \frac{E\left(y_{t+\Delta} \mid y_t = y\right) - y}{\Delta} \tag{12.6}$$

whenever the expectation exists. Thus, $\mu(y)$ is really the time derivative of the conditional expectation. The volatility function or diffusion coefficient is similarly defined as

$$\sigma^2(y) = \lim_{\Delta \to 0} \frac{E\left((y_{t+\Delta} - y)^2 \mid y_t = y\right)}{\Delta}, \tag{12.7}$$

that is, it is the rate of change of the conditional variance. Because B_t is a Gaussian process with no unknown parameters, the entire distribution of the process $\{y_t\}$ is determined solely by $\mu(\cdot), \sigma(\cdot)$.

The process (12.5) generalizes discrete-time nonlinear stochastic difference equations $y_{t+1} - y_t = \mu(y_t, t) + \sigma(y_t, t)\varepsilon_{t+1}$, where $t = 1, 2, \ldots$ and $y_0 = y$. For a discrete-time stochastic difference equation given an initial condition we can always define a unique solution, y_{t+1}, provided $\mu(\cdot), \sigma(\cdot)$ are well defined on the domain. However, without some conditions there is no guarantee that there is a unique solution to the stochastic differential equation (12.5).

Theorem 12.1 (Lipster and Shiryaev, 2001, Chapter 4)   *The following conditions are sufficient to ensure that there is a unique solution $\{y_t, t \in [0, T]\}$ to (12.5) that is a Markov process with continuous sample paths and satisfies $\int E(y_t^2) < \infty$.*

(i) *$E(y^2) < \infty$.*
(ii) *Lipschitz condition: μ, σ are Borel-measurable functions, and there exists a finite K such that, for all $x, y \in \mathbb{R}$,*

$$|\mu(x, t) - \mu(y, t)| \le K|x - y|, \qquad |\sigma(x, t) - \sigma(y, t)| \le K|x - y|.$$

---

[1] The strong Markov property is the Markov property with time replaced by a stopping time τ, that is, if, for each stopping time τ, conditioned on the event $\{\tau < \infty\}$, we have that, for each $t \ge 0$, $y_{\tau + t}$ is independent of the past given y_τ.

(iii) *Growth condition: For some K and for all $x \in \mathbb{R}$,*

$$|\mu(x,t)| \leq K(1+x^2)^{1/2}, \qquad |\sigma(x,t)| \leq K(1+x^2)^{1/2}.$$

Conditions (ii) and (iii) do not guarantee that the solution process is stationary. Many reasonable and widely used processes are nonstationary. It depends on the application whether stationarity is a desirable property for y_t. Models for stock prices y_t are typically nonstationary.

12.3.1 Stationarity

We now provide conditions that ensure that a diffusion process is strictly stationary. We need an additional condition. Define the **scale density** associated with the process as

$$s(y) = \exp\left[-\int_{-\infty}^{y} \frac{2\mu(x)}{\sigma^2(x)} \, dx\right].$$

Theorem 12.2 *Suppose that the following condition is satisfied:*

$$\int_{-\infty}^{\infty} \frac{dy}{\sigma^2(y)s(y)} < \infty. \tag{12.8}$$

Then, the process y_t is strictly stationary with density p given by

$$p(y) \propto \frac{1}{\sigma^2(y)s(y)}. \tag{12.9}$$

Note that when $\mu(y) = 0$ for all y, the condition (12.8) becomes the simpler requirement that

$$\int_{-\infty}^{\infty} \frac{dy}{\sigma^2(y)} < \infty. \tag{12.10}$$

In this case the diffusion process is $dy_t = \sigma(y_t) \, dB_t$, which is a continuous-time version of the heteroskedastic unit root process $y_{t+1} - y_t = \sigma(y_t)\varepsilon_{t+1}$. Clearly, if $\sigma^2(y) = \sigma^2$ for all y, the condition (12.10) cannot be satisfied, but for other choices of $\sigma^2(y)$, such as $\sigma^2(y) = a + by^2$, it can. This means that we may have a random walk that is stationary, which may appear rather confusing given the standard assumptions in the literature. This was called **volatility-induced stationarity** by Conley *et al.* (1997).

We next rewrite the relations between p, μ, and σ^2 in a more useful way. Note that

$$\log(\sigma^2 \times p)(y) = 2\int_{-\infty}^{y} \frac{\mu(x)}{\sigma^2(x)} \, dy - I,$$

where I is the constant of integration. Differentiating with respect to y, we find

$$\frac{d}{dy}\log(\sigma^2 \times p)(y) = \frac{1}{(\sigma^2 \times p)(y)} \frac{d}{dy}(\sigma^2 \times p)(y) = 2\frac{\mu(y)}{\sigma^2(y)}.$$

It follows that $d(\sigma^2 \times p)(y)/dy = 2\mu(y)p(y)$, and therefore

$$\mu(y) = \frac{1}{2p(y)}\frac{d}{dy}(\sigma^2 \times p)(y), \tag{12.11}$$

$$\sigma^2(y) = \frac{2}{p(y)} \int_{-\infty}^{y} \mu(x)p(x)\,\mathrm{d}x. \tag{12.12}$$

The relations (12.9), (12.11), and (12.12) show that, given knowledge of any two of p, μ, σ^2, we may explicitly construct the third quantity. This property was exploited by Aït-Sahalia (1996), see Section 12.4.

12.3.2 Itô's Lemma, Rule, Formula, or Theorem

Suppose that we have some diffusion process y_t and transform it by some smooth function $f(y_t, t)$. What are the dynamics of $x_t = f(y_t, t)$? This question was answered by Itô. His result gives a very convenient algebra for manipulating diffusion processes.

Lemma 12.1   *Suppose that f has continuous second-order partial derivatives. Then, $x_t = f(y_t, t)$ is a diffusion process with law of motion*

$$\mathrm{d}x_t = \left(\frac{\partial f}{\partial y}(y_t, t)\mu(y_t, t) + \frac{\partial f}{\partial t}(y_t, t) + \frac{1}{2}\frac{\partial^2 f}{\partial y^2}(y_t, t)\sigma^2(y_t, t) \right) \mathrm{d}t$$
$$+ \frac{\partial f}{\partial y}(y_t, t)\sigma(y_t, t)\,\mathrm{d}B_t.$$

This follows heuristically by the fact that since $\mathrm{d}B_t \sim \sqrt{\mathrm{d}t}N(0, 1)$, we have $(\mathrm{d}B_t)^2 \sim \mathrm{d}t + \mathrm{d}t \times (N(0, 1)^2 - 1)$, and the stochastic part is mean zero but with variance of order $(\mathrm{d}t)^2$ and so is of smaller order in probability than the stochastic term $\mathrm{d}B_t$. Note the difference from the usual Taylor theorem due to the $(\mathrm{d}y_t)^2$ term. This is another manifestation of the difference between integration of ordinary deterministic functions and stochastic integration of random variables (see, for example, Mikosch, 1998). This result applies (with some modification) to more general functions f (not necessarily twice continuously differentiable) and processes y. If f is invertible in its first argument with inverse g so that $f(g(y, t), t) = y$, then we can express y_t as $\mathrm{d}x_t = m(x_t, t))\,\mathrm{d}t + v(x_t, t)\,\mathrm{d}B_t$ for functions m, v.

We can use Itô's lemma to calculate stochastic integrals, see Exercise 12.2 for an example.

12.3.3 Examples

For stock prices, geometric Brownian motion is a common model for prices y_t: $\mathrm{d}y_t = \mu y_t\,\mathrm{d}y + \sigma y_t\,\mathrm{d}B_t$. By Itô's lemma, this implies that $\mathrm{d}\log y_t = \mu\,\mathrm{d}t + \sigma\,\mathrm{d}B_t$, where $\mu' = \mu + \frac{1}{2}\sigma^2$ and $\sigma' = \sigma$. That is, returns are Brownian motion with drift. This formulation ensures the positivity of prices y_t. This model is used in Black–Scholes and other derivative pricing. The specification implies that stock prices are log normal, that is, $\log y_t - \log y_0 \sim N(\mu t, \sigma^2 t)$. This model is a bit restrictive because it implies time-invariant volatility, amongst other things; this is no longer accepted as a reasonable empirical model for stock returns. Credible models should allow the volatility to change with time and state.

We might expect that stock prices are nonstationary, although returns are stationary. For stock returns, interest is often on the diffusion coefficient $\sigma(\cdot)$, because the drift function is hard to identify. There is a connection between diffusion processes and discrete-time GARCH and stochastic volatility processes. Nelson (1990b) constructed a sequence of GARCH processes $_h y_t$ indexed by sampling frequency h such that, as $h \to 0$, $_h y_t$ converges in an appropriate sense to a diffusion process.

Definition 12.7   The Ornstein–Uhlenbeck or Vasicek process

$$dy_t = \beta(\alpha - y_t)\, dt + \pi\, dB_t.$$

The drift specification implies mean reversion, that is, the process tends towards the equilibrium value α with speed $\beta > 0$. The solution satisfies

$$y_t = y_0 e^{-\beta t} + \alpha\left(1 - e^{-\beta t}\right) + \pi \int_0^t e^{-\beta s}\, dB_s.$$

Thus, y_t is conditionally normal with

$$E\left(y_t \mid \mathcal{F}_s\right) = y_s e^{-\beta(t-s)} + \alpha\left(1 - e^{-\beta(t-s)}\right), \quad \text{var}\left(y_t \mid \mathcal{F}_s\right) = \frac{\pi^2}{2\beta}\left(1 - e^{-2\beta(t-s)}\right).$$

As $t \to \infty$, $E\left(y_t \mid \mathcal{F}_s\right) \to \alpha$ and $\text{var}\left(y_t \mid \mathcal{F}_s\right) \to \pi^2/(2\beta)$. One can find closed-form solutions to derivative pricing problems for this class of processes, which is why it is popular with practitioners. The likelihood function can be easily computed.

Definition 12.8   The Cox, Ingersoll, and Ross (1985) or square root process has $y_0 > 0$ and

$$dy_t = \beta(\alpha - y_t)\, dt + \pi y_t^{1/2}\, dB_t. \tag{12.13}$$

For this stochastic differential equation to have a unique solution it is necessary and sufficient that $2\beta\alpha > \pi^2$ (Feller, 1965).

Because of the square root in the volatility function, the process $\{y_t, t \in [0, T]\}$ never becomes negative, that is, the state space is $(0, \infty)$. One can show that y_t is conditionally (on y_0) distributed as a noncentral chi-squared. One can also get closed-form solutions to derivative pricing problems for this class of processes.

12.3.3.1 Multifactor Models

The class of multifactor models have additional state variables.

Example 12.1   Suppose that $dy_t = \mu_t\, dt + \sigma_t\, dB_{1t}$, $d\sigma_t = m_t\, dt + v_t\, dB_{2t}$, where B_{1t}, B_{2t} are Brownian motions. The process y_t is itself not Markovian, although it is **hidden Markov**, meaning that $(y_t, \sigma_t)^\top$ is jointly Markov. In the simplest case B_1 and B_2 are mutually independent. If we allow B_{1t}, B_{2t} to be correlated, then this is empirically more realistic as it permits leverage effects.

Example 12.2   The Heston (1993) model is

$$dy_t = \mu y_t\, dt + \sqrt{v_t} y_t\, dB_t, \qquad dv_t = \kappa(\theta - v_t)\, dt + \xi\sqrt{v_t}\, dW_t,$$

where B_t, W_t are standard Brownian motions with correlation $dB_t\, dW_t = \rho\, dt$. Here, μ is the rate of return of the asset, θ is the long variance or long-run average price variance (as t tends to infinity, the expected value of v_t tends to θ), κ is the rate at which v_t reverts to θ, and ξ is the volatility of the volatility, or vol of vol, and determines the variance of v_t. If the parameters obey the Feller condition $2\kappa\theta > \xi^2$, then the process ν_t is well defined. Heston found a semi-analytical formula for European option prices under this specification for stock prices.

12.4   Estimation of Diffusion Models

We next consider how to estimate diffusion models given an observation scheme, that is, a sample of data. We can broadly divide this into parametric, semiparametric, and nonparametric cases, and we consider all three here.

12.4.1   Parametric, Semiparametric, and Nonparametric Models

Definition 12.9   In the parametric case we have, for finite-dimensional unknown quantities θ_μ and θ_σ, $\mu(y; \theta_\mu)$ and $\sigma(y; \theta_\sigma)$. For example, geometric Brownian motion and the Cox–Ingersoll–Ross model are both parametric.

Definition 12.10   In the semiparametric case we may have either $\mu(y; \theta_\mu)$ and $\sigma(y)$, where $\sigma(\cdot)$ is an unknown function, or $\mu(y)$ and $\sigma(y; \theta_\sigma)$, where $\mu(\cdot)$ is an unknown function. That is, we specify one or other function parametrically and the other function is allowed to be of unknown functional form (Aït-Sahalia, 1996).

Definition 12.11   In the nonparametric case, both drift and diffusion, $\mu(y)$ and $\sigma(y)$, are of unknown functional form.

Estimation methods differ according to which specification is adopted. What kind of data are used is also key.

12.4.2   Data and Asymptotic Framework

There are several different types or levels of data. For example, in an electronic trading system, we may have a complete record of all messages sent by all traders to the matching engines of the trading system. These include the type of order, its price and quantity, as well as order cancellations and completed transactions. At a very fine level one may also observe the identities of the traders who submitted the messages. Associated with this data are the time stamp at various physical locations along the message pipeline. We are now discussing a very fine level of detail, whereas most datasets contain much less information. Most empirical work is conducted with transaction data, prices, and quantities along with the time at which the transaction was consummated. These occur at discrete intervals. The order book, on the other hand, is observed continuously, but one is often interested in particular time points when the best quotes change.

To put this in the context of the models we have been discussing, we typically do not observe the continuous sample path. We usually get observations, say prices and quantities, at times we label as $t_{n,0}, \ldots, t_{n,n}$. Typically, the data are not equally spaced, which may be treated in several ways:

- We may treat the observations as equally spaced. This is often called transaction time as opposed to calendar time (if the observations are transaction prices).
- We may take account of the time spacings between observations according to the calendar time hypothesis but assume that the time spacings are random and independent of the evolution of the process itself.
- We may instead allow that the time spacings themselves have information about the evolution of the price process. In this case, they must be jointly modelled with y; see, for example, Engle and Russell (1998).
- The data can be aggregated, or rather subsampled, to be approximately equally spaced, say five minutes, and then treated according to the calendar time hypothesis.

The analysis of estimation and inference procedures relies on large-sample approximations. There are three types of asymptotics regarding the observation schemes that are used:

- Infill/continuous record. We assume that the series y is observed inside a fixed interval, say $[0, T]$, and that as $n \to \infty$ the set $\{t_{n,1}, \ldots, t_{n,n}\}$ is becoming dense in $[0, T]$, that is, $\max_{1 \leq i \leq n}(t_{n,i} - t_{n,i-1}) \to 0$, typically at rate $1/n$. This is better suited to, say, intraday data than monthly data. In that case we may also consider the total number of observations n to be random, although this is seldom acknowledged (Cavaliere *et al.*, 2023).
- Long span. We assume that the largest time $t_{n,n} \to \infty$ and $\inf_i(t_{n,i} - t_{n,i-1}) > 0$. It is usually assumed that $t_{n,i} - t_{n,i-1} = 1$.
- Mixed case. This is where both long span and infill hold; see, for example, Bandi and Phillips (2003). In this case you have a triangular array of times $t_{n1}, \ldots, t_{nn}$ where $t_{n,n} \to \infty$ but $t_{n,i} - t_{n,i-1} \to 0$. For example, $t_{n,i} - t_{n,i-1} = 1/\sqrt{n}$ for $i = 1, \ldots, n$.

12.4.3 The Identification Issue

We first show that, based on the infill framework (that is, data are obtained within a fixed time interval), you cannot identify the drift μ of a diffusion process. Suppose that

$$\mathrm{d}\log y_t = \mu\,\mathrm{d}t + \sigma\,\mathrm{d}B_t. \tag{12.14}$$

Suppose that we observe prices at times $\{t_{n,0}, \ldots, t_{n,n}\}$, in which case

$$r_{t_{n,i}} = \log y_{t_{n,i}} - \log y_{t_{n,i-1}} \sim N(\mu(t_{n,i} - t_{n,i-1}), \sigma^2(t_{n,i} - t_{n,i-1})),$$

that is, stock returns are normally distributed. We can think of the model (12.14) as generating a regression for observed returns on the gap between price observations,

$$r_i = \mu\Delta_i + z_i\sigma\sqrt{\Delta_i},$$

for $i = 1, \dots, n$, where $z_i \sim N(0, 1)$. In the fixed-span case $\Delta_i = t_{n,i} - t_{n,i-1}$ is small, and the ratio of signal to noise goes to zero, whereas in the long-span case, Δ_i is fixed in magnitude and the signal-to-noise ratio stays bounded away from zero.

Therefore, the log likelihood function of the data $r_{t_{n,1}}, \dots, r_{t_{n,n}}$ is

$$\mathcal{L}(\mu, \sigma^2) = -\frac{n}{2} \log 2\pi - \frac{1}{2} \sum_{i=1}^{n} \log \left((t_{n,i} - t_{n,i-1}) \sigma^2 \right)$$

$$- \frac{1}{2} \sum_{i=1}^{n} \frac{\left(r_{t_{n,i}} - \mu(t_{n,i} - t_{n,i-1}) \right)^2}{\sigma^2 (t_{n,i} - t_{n,i-1})}.$$

Definition 12.12   The MLE of μ, σ is

$$\widehat{\mu} = \frac{\sum_{i=1}^{n} r_{t_{n,i}}}{\sum_{i=1}^{n} (t_{n,i} - t_{n,i-1})} = \frac{\log y_{t_n} - \log y_{t_1}}{t_n - t_1}, \tag{12.15}$$

$$\widehat{\sigma}^2 = \frac{1}{n} \sum_{i=1}^{n} \frac{\left(r_{t_{n,i}} - \widehat{\mu}(t_{n,i} - t_{n,i-1}) \right)^2}{(t_{n,i} - t_{n,i-1})}. \tag{12.16}$$

In the infill case, $t_n \to T$ and $t_1 \to 0$, so that

$$\widehat{\mu} = \frac{\log y_{t_{n,n}} - \log y_{t_{n,1}}}{t_{n,n} - t_{n,1}} \implies \frac{\log y_T - \log y_0}{T} \sim N(\mu, \sigma^2/T),$$

which does not concentrate at a point when $T < \infty$. That is, the variance of $\widehat{\mu}$ does not go to zero as the sample size increases. The estimator is unbiased but inconsistent. In this very special case one can construct a confidence interval for μ, since the estimator is normally distributed.

In the long-span case we may assume that $\sum_{i=1}^{n} (t_{n,i} - t_{n,i-1}) = t_{n,n} - t_{n,1} \to \infty$, in which case $\widehat{\mu} \xrightarrow{P} \mu$ and, further,

$$\sqrt{\frac{t_{n,n} - t_{n,1}}{\sigma^2}} \left(\widehat{\mu} - \mu \right) \implies N(0, 1)$$

as $n \to \infty$. In this case, the MLE is consistent, and we may construct confidence intervals for μ.

We have

$$\widehat{\sigma}^2 = \frac{1}{n} \sum_{i=1}^{n} \frac{\left(r_{t_{n,i}} - \mu(t_{n,i} - t_{n,i-1}) \right)^2}{(t_{n,i} - t_{n,i-1})} - (\widehat{\mu} - \mu)^2 \frac{t_{n,n} - t_{n,1}}{n},$$

$$E(\widehat{\sigma}^2) = \sigma^2 - E\left((\widehat{\mu} - \mu)^2 \right) \frac{t_{n,n} - t_{n,1}}{n} = \sigma^2 \left(1 - \frac{1}{n} \right),$$

and so the estimator with $n-1$ replacing n in the denominator is exactly unbiased as usual. In any case, $\widehat{\sigma}^2 \xrightarrow{P} \sigma^2$ and $\sqrt{n} \left(\widehat{\sigma}^2 - \sigma^2 \right) \implies N\left(0, 2\sigma^4\right)$. This is true for whatever sequence $\{t_{n,i}\}$, that is, for long span and infill.

Notice that in the infill case with $T = 1$, the estimator

$$\widehat{\sigma}^2 = \sum_{i=1}^{n} r_{t_{n,i}}^2 = \sigma^2 \sum_{i=1}^{n} \Delta_i z_i^2 + \mu^2 \sum_{i=1}^{n} \Delta_i^2 + 2\mu\sigma \sum_{i=1}^{n} z_i \Delta_i \sqrt{\Delta_i}$$

is also consistent, although it will be biased in small samples due to the presence of $\mu^2 \sum_{i=1}^n \Delta_i^2$, but this bias is of small order. Suppose that $t_{n,i} = i/n$, then $\sqrt{n}(\widehat{\sigma}^2 - \sigma^2) \Longrightarrow N(0, 2\sigma^4)$.

12.4.4 Maximum Likelihood Method for Parametric Diffusion Models in the Long-Span Case

We first consider the classic literature from the 1970s about estimating linear continuous-time models, that is, where $\sigma(\cdot)$ is constant or at least only a deterministic function of time (Bergstrom, 1984; Bergstrom and Nowman, 2007). We then consider the extension to nonlinear models.

12.4.4.1 Models Linear in Their Parameters

Specifically, suppose that $dy_t = (ay_t + b)\,dt + dB_t$, where a, b are unknown parameters, or equivalently, given initial condition y_0,

$$
y_t = \int_0^t e^{a(t-r)} B_r \, dr + \left(y_0 + \frac{b}{a} \right) e^{at} - \frac{b}{a}.
$$

Theorem 12.3 *Suppose that we observe the process $\{y_t, t \in [0, T]\}$ at times $t = 1, 2, \ldots$, and suppose that $y_0 = 0$. Then $y_t = \alpha + \phi y_{t-1} + \varepsilon_t$, where $\alpha = (e^a - 1)(b/a)$, $\phi = e^a$, and*

$$
\varepsilon_t = \int_{t-1}^t e^{a(t-r)} B_r \, dr \sim N\left(0, \frac{1}{2a} \left(e^{2a} - 1 \right) \right), \qquad E\left(\varepsilon_t \varepsilon_s \right) = 0 \, for \, s \neq t.
$$

The observed discrete-time process is a Gaussian AR(1), which can be estimated by MLE. The parameters of the continuous-time model enter the discrete-time process in a nonlinear way and can be obtained from the estimated α, ϕ by $a = \log \phi$ and $b = \alpha \log \phi / (\phi - 1)$.

The last 20 years has seen an explosion of work on high-frequency econometrics and this is best described in the exhaustive treatment of Aït-Sahalia and Jacod (2014). This has mostly concentrated on estimation of volatility quantities related to σ^2.

12.4.4.2 Nonlinear Models

The classic model for (short-term) interest rates is the Cox, Ingersoll, and Ross (1985) model specified in continuous time, that is,

$$
dy_t = \kappa(\mu - y_t)\,dt + \sigma \sqrt{y_t}\,dB_t,
$$

where B is a standard Brownian motion. The process $\{y_t, t \in [0, \infty)\}$ is a Markov process that is stationary provided $\kappa > 0$; furthermore, $y(t)$ is positive with probability one provided $\sigma > 0$.

Suppose that the data are observed at equally spaced time points $t = 1, 2, \ldots$ Then,

$$E(y_t \mid y_{t-1}, \ldots) = \mu + \exp(-\kappa)\,(y_{t-1} - \mu),$$

$$\operatorname{var}(y_t \mid y_{t-1}, \ldots) = \left(\frac{\sigma^2 \mu}{\kappa}\right)(1 - \exp(-\kappa))^2 + \left(\frac{\sigma^2}{\kappa}\right)(\exp(-\kappa) - \exp(-2\kappa))y_{t-1}.$$

That is, both the mean and the variance are affine (linear) in lagged outcomes. The steady-state mean and variance are μ and $\sigma^2 \mu / 2\kappa$. This process is not of the location scale form, that is, one cannot write $y_t = \mu_t + \sigma_t \varepsilon_t$ for i.i.d. ε_t with μ_t, σ_t depending only on past values. However, the transition density from y_{t-1} to y_t is known to be a noncentral chi-squared distribution with degrees of freedom $2q + 2$ and noncentrality $2cy_{t-1}\exp(-\kappa)$, that is,

$$f(y_t \mid y_{t-1}) = c \exp\left(c\,(y_t - y_{t-1}\exp(-\kappa))\right) \left(\frac{y_t}{y_{t-1}\exp(-\kappa)}\right)^{1/2}$$

$$\times \mathbb{B}_q(2c\sqrt{y_t y_{t-1}\exp(-\kappa)}),$$

$$c = \frac{2\kappa}{\sigma^2(1 - \exp(-\kappa))}, \qquad q = \frac{2\kappa\mu}{\sigma^2} - 1,$$

where $\mathbb{B}_q(\cdot)$ is the modified Bessel function of the first kind of order q. The parameters κ, μ, and σ^2 can be estimated from the sample data $\{y_1, \ldots, y_T\}$ by maximum likelihood, by least squares, or by weighted least squares.

When $\sigma(\cdot)$ is nonconstant and/or $\mu(\cdot)$ is nonlinear this argument typically cannot be applied, because the derived discrete-time process is much more complicated. The reason is that there is dependence of a complicated kind in the observed data. So how should one proceed?

One would like to use something like the prediction error decomposition to form the likelihood

$$\mathcal{L}(\theta \mid y_{t_{n,1}}, \ldots, y_{t_{n,n}}) = \prod_{i=1}^{n} p_{y_{t_{n,i+1}} \mid y_{t_{n,i}}}(y_{t_{n,i+1}} \mid y_{t_{n,i}}; \theta) p_{y_{t_{n,0}}}(y_{t_{n,0}}; \theta) \tag{12.17}$$

based on the observed data $\{y_{t_{n,1}}, \ldots, y_{t_{n,n}}\}$. Here, we use the Markov property that only the most recent past is needed to simplify the transition densities $p_{y_{t_{n,i+1}} \mid y_{t_{n,i}}, \ldots, y_{t_{n,1}}}(y_{t_{n,i+1}} \mid y_{t_{n,i}}, \ldots, y_{t_{n,1}}; \theta)$ (note that for stochastic volatility models, such as the Heston model, one needs further arguments to obtain the likelihood for the observed data since the Markov property does not hold). One may argue that for stationary processes the marginal term $p_{y_{t_{n,0}}}(y_{t_{n,0}}; \theta)$ only contributes a little to the total likelihood and may be ignored. The difficult part is to obtain the transition densities $p_{y_{t_{n,i+1}} \mid y_{t_{n,i}}}(y_{t_{n,i+1}} \mid y_{t_{n,i}}; \theta)$. These transition densities are not known in closed form except for very special cases. We consider several approaches to computing the likelihood or an approximation to it.

Partial Differential Equation Approach   It is known that the transition densities satisfy two sets of **partial differential equations** (PDEs), the Chapman–Kolmogorov so-called **forward and backwards equations**. Denote by $p(\Delta, y \mid x)$ the time-invariant transition density from $y_t = x$ to $y_{t+\Delta} = y$, for any $\Delta \geq 0$.

Definition 12.13 (Forward equation)

$$\frac{\partial p(\Delta, y \mid x)}{\partial \Delta} = -\frac{\partial}{\partial y}\left(\mu(y)p(\Delta, y \mid x)\right) + \frac{1}{2}\frac{\partial^2}{\partial y^2}\left(\sigma^2(y)p(\Delta, y \mid x)\right).$$

Definition 12.14 (Backward equation)

$$\frac{\partial p(\Delta, y \mid x)}{\partial \Delta} = -\mu(x)\frac{\partial p(\Delta, y \mid x)}{\partial x} + \frac{1}{2}\sigma^2(x)\frac{\partial^2 p(\Delta, y \mid x)}{\partial x^2}.$$

These equations specify laws of motion for the transition densities in terms of $\mu(\cdot)$ and $\sigma(\cdot)$. These equations each require boundary conditions, which we specify next.

Definition 12.15 (Boundary conditions) Let Ω denote the state space and $\partial\Omega$ its boundary. Then

$$\lim_{\Delta \to 0} p(\Delta, y \mid x) = \begin{cases} 1 & \text{if } x = y, \\ 0 & \text{otherwise}; \end{cases}$$

$$0 = \begin{cases} \lim_{y \to \partial\Omega} p(\Delta, y \mid x) = 0 & \text{(forward)}, \\ \lim_{x \to \partial\Omega} p(\Delta, y \mid x) = 0 & \text{(backward)}. \end{cases}$$

In most cases we consider $\Omega = \mathbb{R}$ so that $\partial\Omega = \{\pm\infty\}$. Likewise, the conditional expectations $V(x, \Delta) = E(y_{t+\Delta} \mid y_t = x)$ satisfy the PDE

$$\frac{1}{2}\sigma^2(x)\frac{\partial^2 V}{\partial x^2}(x, \Delta) + \mu(x)\frac{\partial V}{\partial x}(x, \Delta) + \frac{\partial V}{\partial \Delta}V(x, \Delta) = 0 \tag{12.18}$$

with $V(x, 0) = x$.

Lo (1988) showed how to construct an approximation to the MLE for parametric models based on solving the transition density PDE equations. The algorithm is:

1. For each θ, compute $\mu_\theta(y_{t_{n,i}})$ and $\sigma^2_\theta(y_{t_{n,i}})$.
2. Solve either the forward or backward equation for $p_{y_{t_{n,i+1}}|y_{t_{n,i}}}(y_{t_{n,i+1}} \mid y_{t_{n,i}}; \theta)$.
3. Compute the approximate likelihood function $\mathcal{L}(\theta)$.
4. Repeat to find the maximizing value of θ.

These equations must be solved for each parameter value θ, which makes this procedure computationally demanding and potentially inaccurate since the partial differential equations must be solved by numerical methods.

Simulation Methods We next consider an alternative way of approximating the likelihood function based on simulation, sometimes called **Euler discretization**.

Definition 12.16 In the interval $[t_{n,i}, t_{n,i+1})$ we can approximate the process by

$$y_{t_{n,i+(m+1)h}} = y_{t_{n,i+mh}} + \mu(y_{t_{n,i+mh}}; \theta)h + \sigma(y_{t_{n,i+mh}}; \theta)\varepsilon_{t_{n,i+(m+1)h}}h^{1/2} \tag{12.19}$$

for $m = 0, 1, \ldots, M-1$, where $h = (t_{n,i+1} - t_{n,i})/M$, and $\varepsilon_{t_{n,i+mh}}$ are i.i.d. standard normal random variables.

The approximation is valid as $h \to 0$ and $M \to \infty$. This says that on very small time intervals the process y can be approximated by a discrete-time process, with given mean and variance and normal conditional distribution. For this discrete-time process, the one-step-ahead transition densities are normal, $p_{y_{t_{n,i+(m+1)h}}|y_{t_{n,i+mh}}}(y \mid x; \theta) = \phi_{\mu_i(x), \sigma_i^2(x)}(y)$, where $\mu_i(x) = x + \mu(x; \theta)h$ and $\sigma_i^2(x) = \sigma^2(x; \theta)h$. However, we need the M-step-ahead densities, and to find them involves recursive integration. Thus,

$$p_{y_{t_n,i+(m+2)h} | y_{t_n,i+mh}}(y \mid x; \theta)$$

$$= \int p_{y_{t_n,i+(m+2)h} | y_{t_n,i+(m+1)h}}(y \mid z; \theta) p_{y_{t_n,i+(m+1)h} | y_{t_n,i+mh}}(z \mid x; \theta)\, \mathrm{d}z$$

$$= \int \phi_{\mu_i(z), \sigma_i^2(z)}(y) \phi_{\mu_i(x), \sigma_i^2(x)}(z)\, \mathrm{d}z.$$

There is no closed form for this transition density in general. To get the M-step-ahead densities you need to compute an $(M - 1)$-fold integral. One can do this by simulation methods, see Chapter 9.

12.4.5   Generalized Method of Moments Estimation for Long Span

We next consider the method of moments for estimating diffusion processes as it bypasses the technical complications around computing likelihood functions. When the process y_t is stationary we can obtain simple moment conditions that can be used to generate estimators of finite-dimensional parameters. Chen, Hansen, and Scheinkman (2009) presented some useful theory, which we describe next.

Definition 12.17   For any measurable function ϕ, define the shift operator $\mathcal{T}_t \phi(y) \equiv E(\phi(y_t) \mid y_0 = y)$ on the space of functions $L^2(P)$ that are square integrable with respect to P.

Definition 12.18   The **infinitesimal generator** $\mathcal{A}$ is an operator defined as (whenever the limit exists)

$$\lim_{t \to 0} \frac{\mathcal{T}_t \phi - \phi}{t} = \mathcal{A}\phi.$$

The operator $\mathcal{A}$ describes the local evolution of the process. Take $\phi \in L^2(P)$, a smooth test function. Then, by Itô's lemma we have

$$\mathrm{d}\phi_t = \phi'(y_t)\mathrm{d}y_t + \frac{1}{2}\phi''(y_t)(\mathrm{d}y_t)^2 = \left(\mu\phi' + \frac{\sigma^2}{2}\phi''\right)(y_t)\, \mathrm{d}t + (\sigma\phi')(y_t)\, \mathrm{d}W_t,$$

whence $\mathcal{A}\phi = \mu\phi' + (\sigma^2/2)\phi''$.

Theorem 12.4   *For all $\phi \in D$ the domain of $\mathcal{A}$, $E(\mathcal{A}\phi(y_t)) = 0$.*

Proof. $\{y_t\}$ stationary implies that $E(\phi(y_t))$ is independent of t. Therefore,

$$\frac{\mathrm{d}}{\mathrm{d}t}E(\phi(y_t)) \equiv 0$$

for all $\phi \in L^2(P)$. By the law of iterated expectation, for all $\phi \in L^2(P)$,

$$E(\phi(y_t)) = E(E(\phi(y_t) \mid y_0)) = E(\mathcal{T}_t \phi)$$

if and only if $E(\mathcal{T}_t \phi - \phi) = 0$. Now we restrict to $\phi \in D \subset L^2(P)$. Then

$$E\left(\lim_{t\to 0}\frac{1}{t}(\mathcal{T}_t\phi - \phi)\right) = E(\mathcal{A}\phi)$$

exists. It can be shown that, for suitable set of ϕ,

$$E(\mathcal{A}\phi) = E\left(\lim_{t\to 0}\frac{1}{t}(\mathcal{T}_t\phi - \phi)\right) = \lim_{t\to 0}\frac{1}{t}E(\mathcal{T}_t\phi - \phi) = 0.$$

This result can be used to deliver an estimation strategy as follows. Suppose that the drift and diffusion functions are parametric, denoted $\mu_\theta, \sigma_\theta^2$ for some unknown parameters $\theta \in \mathbb{R}^p$. Then compute a quadratic form in the vector of sample moments

$$G_{nk}(\theta) = \frac{1}{n}\sum_{i=1}^{n}\left(\phi_k'(y_{t_{n,i}})\mu_\theta(y_{t_{n,i}}) + \frac{1}{2}\phi_k''(y_{t_{n,i}})\sigma_\theta^2(y_{t_{n,i}})\right) \tag{12.20}$$

for some functions $\phi_1, \ldots, \phi_K$ chosen by the practitioner. We then define $\widehat{\theta}_{\text{GMM}}$ to minimize the objective function (5.16) with W_n a $K \times K$ symmetric positive-definite weighting matrix. If we take $W_{\text{opt}} = \Omega^{-1}$, then the resulting estimator is consistent and asymptotically normal, and optimal within this class of estimators. However, it is not as efficient as the MLE since it only uses the marginal distribution of the process. One can improve efficiency by using a second set of moment conditions that uses joint distribution information. For example, we know that $E(\phi(y_{t+1})\psi(y_t))$ and $E(\phi(y_t)\psi(y_{t+1}))$ do not depend on the calendar time t for all $\phi, \psi \in L^2(P)$. We can obtain restrictions from this second set of moment conditions, and these improve the efficiency of GMM.

12.4.6 Nonparametric and Semiparametric Approaches in Long Span

Aït-Sahalia (1996) considered a semiparametric model where the drift was parametric, $\mu(\cdot; \theta_\mu)$, but the volatility $\sigma(\cdot)$ was nonparametric. In particular, he considered a linear drift $\mu(r_t) = \beta(\alpha - r_t)$, where α, β are unknown parameters. The volatility function, which is crucial for a lot of derivative pricing, is unspecified. The framework he considered was one with equally spaced data (daily in application) and long-span asymptotics, that is, many weeks.

He proposed the following estimation strategy. Note that the conditional expectation of $r_{t+1} \mid r_t$ is linear, that is,

$$E(r_{t+1} \mid r_t) = \alpha + e^{-\beta}(r_t - \alpha) = \theta_0 + \theta_1 r_t \tag{12.21}$$

regardless of the volatility. Therefore, the parameters $\theta = (\theta_0, \theta_1)$ can be estimated by OLS, and used to obtain estimates of the more meaningful parameters (α, β). Second, estimate the marginal density of r_t by kernel smoothing methods, that is, let

$$\widehat{p}(r) = \frac{1}{nh}\sum_{i=1}^{n}K\left(\frac{r - r_{t_i}}{h}\right)$$

for some bandwidth h and kernel K. Under the stationarity condition and under weak dependence, this estimator is consistent as $n \to \infty$ (Bosq, 1996). Finally, one can estimate the volatility by the plug-in method:

$$\widehat{\sigma}^2(r) = \frac{2}{\widehat{p}(r)} \int_0^r \mu(r; \widehat{\theta}) \widehat{p}(r) \, dr. \tag{12.22}$$

This estimator is also consistent and asymptotically normal under some regularity conditions. He also developed estimators for derivatives prices and the sampling theory thereof. Aït-Sahalia (1996) applied his method to short-term interest rates and showed that the shape of $\sigma^2(r)$ is quite nonlinear. This methodology was extended by Kristensen (2010) to allow for nonlinear parametric drift.

12.4.7 Nonparametric and Semiparametric Approaches: Infill Asymptotics

Florens-Zmirou (1993) considered nonparametric estimation of the volatility function under infill asymptotics. The idea is that

$$\begin{aligned} (dy_t)^2 &= \sigma^2(y_t) \, dt + 2\mu(y_t)\sigma(y_t) \, dt \, dB_t + \mu^2(y_t)(dt)^2 \\ &= \sigma^2(y_t) \, dt + \text{noise} + \text{smaller}. \end{aligned}$$

Interpreting $(dy_t)^2$ as squared returns, one essentially has a nonparametric regression model over small time increments.

We follow the setup of Jiang and Knight (1997). Suppose that observations are equally spaced, infilling on $[0, T]$. Write $t_{n,i} = i\Delta_n$, $i = 1, \dots, n$, where $\Delta_n = T/n$ is the spacing of the data. Their estimator is

$$\widehat{\sigma}^2(y) = \frac{1}{\Delta_n} \frac{\sum_{i=1}^{n-1} K((y_{t_{n,i}} - y)/h) \left[y_{t_{n,i+1}} - y_{t_i} \right]^2}{\sum_{i=1}^{n-1} K((y_{t_{n,i}} - y)/h)}, \tag{12.23}$$

where K is a kernel and $h = h(n)$ is a bandwidth sequence. Florens-Zmirou is the special case with a uniform kernel. Jiang and Knight (1997) showed that $\widehat{\sigma}^2(x)$ is consistent and has asymptotically a **mixed normal** distribution. To discuss the limiting distribution we need the concept of **local time**.

Definition 12.19   The occupation measure counts the number of visitations of the Borel set B by the process y_s over the interval $[0, t]$,

$$\nu_t(B) = \int_0^t 1(y_s \in B) \, ds.$$

Definition 12.20   The local time of the process $\{y_t\}$ at point y over the time interval $[0, t]$ is defined as the random variable

$$L_t(y) = \lim_{\Delta \to 0} \frac{1}{2\Delta} \int_0^t 1(|y_s - y| < \Delta) \, ds.$$

The local time L_t can be interpreted as the Radon–Nikodym derivative of ν_t, that is, we have $\nu_t(B) = \int_B L_t(y) \, dy$. If y_t is stationary, $L_t(y) = tp(y)$. Local time is continuous in both arguments and is nondecreasing in t with probability one. The inverse local time is

$\tau_u(y) = \inf\{t > 0 : L_t(y) > u\}$, and is related to the **crossing time** for Brownian motion. A key property of local time is the following (we define the concept of a **semimartingale** in Definition 12.24).

Proposition 12.1   For semimartingale $\{y_t\}$ and for every Borel function f of (y_t),

$$\int_0^T f(y_t)\, dt = \int_{-\infty}^{+\infty} f(y) L_T(y)\, dy.$$

We next define the concept of recurrence, which is essential for any nonparametric estimation procedure.

Definition 12.21   The process $\{y_t\}$ is recurrent if, at every point y on its support, $L_T(y) \to \infty$ as $T \to \infty$.

This basically says that the process revisits the point y infinitely many times during the interval $[0, T]$ as time T goes to infinity. A stationary process is recurrent; indeed, the rate of convergence of $L_T(y)$ is of order T in this case, which means that it visits every point in its state space a positive fraction of T times. A large class of nonstationary processes are also recurrent but with lower rates of convergence. For a unit root process or Brownian motion the rate is $T^{1/2}$, which means that the frequency of visitation divided by T goes to zero. See Phillips and Park (1999) for a discussion of local time.

Jiang and Knight (1997) showed that

$$(nh_n)^{1/2}\left(\frac{\widehat{\sigma}^2(y)}{\sigma^2(y)} - 1\right) \Longrightarrow L_T^{-1/2}(y)Z \sim \mathrm{MN}(0, L_T^{-1}(y)), \qquad (12.24)$$

where Z is a standard normal independent of the random variable $L_T(y)$. Here, MN denotes mixed normal, that is, normal with a stochastic variance. The local time can be estimated by

$$\widehat{L}_T(y) = \frac{1}{\Delta_n nh} \sum_{i=1}^{n-1} K\left(\frac{y_{t_{n,i}} - y}{h}\right),$$

and they obtained that

$$(nh)^{1/2}\widehat{L}_T^{1/2}(y)\left(\frac{\widehat{\sigma}^2(y)}{\sigma^2(y)} - 1\right) \Longrightarrow Z, \qquad (12.25)$$

from which standard pointwise confidence intervals for $\sigma^2(y)$ can be produced.

Bandi and Phillips (2003) considered both infill and long-span asymptotics, and showed how to fully exploit the advantageous features of both informational accumulations. The time span is denoted T and the number of observations n. Let $\Delta_{n,T} = T/n$, where both $n, T \to \infty$ but $\Delta_{n,T} \to 0$. That is, the time span increases but the observations are becoming dense in the interval $[0, T]$. For example, if $T(n) = \sqrt{n}$, then this condition is fulfilled. They estimated both μ and σ^2 nonparametrically:

$$\widehat{\mu}(y) = \frac{1}{\Delta_{n,T}} \frac{\sum_{i=1}^{n-1} K((y_{t_{n,i}} - y)/h)\left(y_{t_{n,i+1}} - y_{t_{n,i}}\right)}{\sum_{i=1}^{n-1} K((y_{t_{n,i}} - y)/h)},$$

$$\widehat{\sigma}^2(y) = \frac{1}{\Delta_{n,T}} \frac{\sum_{i=1}^{n-1} K((y_{t_{n,i}} - y)/h) \left(y_{t_{n,i+1}} - y_{t_i}\right)^2}{\sum_{i=1}^{n-1} K((y_{t_{n,i}} - y)/h)},$$

where $h = h(n, T)$ is a bandwidth sequence. They actually worked with a slightly different estimator that updates the squared increment part by an estimator $\widetilde{\sigma}^2$,

$$\widehat{\sigma}^2(y) = \frac{\sum_{i=1}^{n-1} K((y_{t_{n,i}} - y)/h)\widetilde{\sigma}^2(y_{t_{n,i}})}{\sum_{i=1}^{n-1} K((y_{t_{n,i}} - y)/h)},$$

$$\widetilde{\sigma}^2(y_{t_{n,i}}) = \frac{1}{m_i \Delta_{n,T}} \sum_{j \in \mathcal{I}_i} \left(y_{t_{n,i_{j+1}}} - y_{t_{n,i_j}}\right)^2,$$

where I_i is the set of points for which y_{i_j} is close to y_i as measured by another bandwidth b_n, and m_i is the cardinality of I_i. They did not require stationarity, but did require a null recurrence property. They established the mixed asymptotic normality for both $\widehat{\mu}(y)$ and $\widehat{\sigma}^2(y)$, and gave explicit formulae for biases and so on.

12.5 Estimation of Quadratic Variation Volatility from High-Frequency Data

We continue our focus on estimation of volatility in high-frequency settings, but we consider a more general setting, not necessarily a diffusion process, and we change our target of estimation to accumulated volatility over an interval of time.

12.5.1 Quadratic Variation

Definition 12.22   The quadratic variation of a square-integrable process y_t is the process

$$\langle y, y \rangle_{0:t} = \text{plim}_{\max\{t_{n,k+1} - t_{n,k}\} \to 0} \sum_{t_{n,k} \le t} |y_{t_{n,k+1}} - y_{t_{n,k}}|^2, \qquad (12.26)$$

where $0 = t_{n,1} < t_{n,2} < \cdots < t_{n,n} = t$. We sometimes denote this just by $\text{QV}(t)$.

This is an ex-post measure of volatility over the interval $[0, t]$. For functions of bounded variation (Definition 12.4) the quadratic variation exists, and is zero. Furthermore, Andersen *et al.* (2003) showed that, under some quite general conditions, $E((y_{t+h} - y_t)^2 \mid \mathcal{F}_t) = E(\langle y, y \rangle_{t:t+h} \mid \mathcal{F}_t)$, that is, the conditional variance of returns is equal to the conditional expectation of the quadratic variation over the same interval. This justifies the current interest in this quantity as a parameter of interest.

Example 12.3   Suppose that y_t is the diffusion process $dy_t = \mu(y_t)\,dt + \sigma(y_t)\,dB_t$, where B_t is standard Brownian motion. Then

$$\text{QV}(t) = \langle y, y \rangle_{0:t} = \int_0^t \sigma^2(y_s)\,ds.$$

The quadratic variation is a stochastic process in general, but when $\sigma^2(y_t) = \sigma^2$ is constant it is just $t\sigma^2$, and when $t = 1$ this is just σ^2. However, the process $\langle y, y \rangle_t$ can be shown to exist for a much larger class of stochastic processes, namely, continuous square-integrable semimartingales. We now endeavor to define semimartingales.

Definition 12.23   A local martingale M is a stochastic process that satisfies the localized version of the martingale property. That is, there exists a sequence of stopping times τ_k with $\lim_{k \to \infty} \tau_k = \infty$ for which the stopped process $M_{\min\{t,\tau_k\}}$ is a martingale.

Every martingale is a local martingale; every bounded local martingale is a martingale, but not every local martingale is a martingale. In particular, a driftless diffusion process is a local martingale, but not necessarily a martingale.

Definition 12.24   A real-valued process y is called a semimartingale if it can be decomposed as $y_t = M_t + A_t$, where M is a local martingale and A is an adapted process (depends only on the past) of locally bounded variation with sample paths that are càdlàg.

The process A has zero quadratic covariation; essentially it is slower moving than M, and so its predictability does not help much. The class of semimartingales is basically the class of processes for which stochastic integration makes sense. The class of semi-martingales is large; it includes all martingales as special cases, as well as other processes. This includes Brownian-driven processes and processes with jumps. This class has economic meaning: there is an absence of arbitrage opportunities for this class of processes. The fundamental theorem of asset pricing states that no arbitrage means the existence of an equivalent martingale measure. **Girsanov's theorem** holds for semimartingales. **Fractional Brownian motion** is not a semimartingale (Rogers, 1997), and hence allows arbitrage opportunities.

12.5.2 Realized Volatility

We now consider a consistent estimator of the quadratic variation, called **realized volatil-ity**. Suppose that we have a sample of n log prices y_t observed at times $t_{n1}, \ldots, t_{nn}$ over the period $[0, 1]$. Define, for each $t \in [0, 1]$,

$$\mathrm{RV}_y^n(t) = \sum_{i=1}^{n-1} (y_{t_{n,i+1}} - y_{t_{n,i}})^2 \mathbf{1}\,(t_{n,i+1} \le t)\,. \tag{12.27}$$

This consistently estimates the quadratic variation of y over the interval $[0, 1]$. Jacod and Protter (1998) established the CLT of this quantity for Itô semimartingales. Andersen *et al.* (2003) established various useful properties. Barndorff-Nielsen and Shephard (2002) established consistency and the limiting distribution for the following class of Brownian semimartingales.

Definition 12.25   The process y_t is a Brownian semimartingale if

$$y_t = \int_0^t \mu_u \, \mathrm{d}u + \int_0^t \sigma_u \, \mathrm{d}B_u, \tag{12.28}$$

where the processes μ, σ are predictable (depend only on the past) and the process σ is càdlàg.

Barndorff-Nielsen and Shephard (2002) worked with the so-called no-leverage case, which corresponds to the process μ and σ being independent of the process B. They showed that, for the equispaced data case $t_{ni} = i/n$,

$$n^{1/2}\left(\mathrm{RV}_y^n(t) - \mathrm{QV}(t)\right) \Longrightarrow 2^{1/2}\int_0^t \sigma_u^2\, dB_u = \mathrm{MN}\left(0, 2\int_0^t \sigma_u^4\, du\right), \qquad (12.29)$$

that is, the limiting distribution is a mixed normal with random variance (that is, independent of the underlying normal). Note that the drift component is ignored in estimation and does not affect the limiting behavior. They also showed that one can estimate the **integrated quarticity** $\mathrm{IQ}(t) = \int_0^t \sigma_u^4\, du$ consistently by

$$\widehat{\mathrm{IQ}}(t) = \frac{n}{3}\sum_{i=1}^{n-1}(y_{t_{n,i+1}} - y_{t_{n,i}})^4 1(t_{n,i+1} \le t),$$

and they obtained a feasible CLT,

$$\frac{n^{1/2}\left(\mathrm{RV}_y^n(t) - \mathrm{QV}(t)\right)}{\sqrt{2\widehat{\mathrm{IQ}}(t)^{1/2}}} \Longrightarrow N(0,1). \qquad (12.30)$$

This can be used to set confidence intervals for the estimated volatility and to carry out hypothesis testing. Mykland and Zhang (2006) extended these results to the case with non-equally spaced data, in which case the limiting variance is $2\int_0^t \sigma_u^4\, dH_u$, where H_u is the quadratic variation of the observation time process, defined as

$$H_u = \mathrm{plim}_{n\to\infty} n \sum_{i=1}^{n}(t_{n,i+1} - t_{n,i})^2 1(t_{n,i+1} \le u).$$

Example 12.4   We can derive some intuition from the special case where $dy_t = \sigma_t\, dB_t$, where σ_t is a deterministic function, $\sigma_t = \sigma(t)$. In this case, returns are normally distributed with

$$y_{t_{n,i+1}} - y_{t_{n,i}} \sim N\left(0, \int_{t_{n,i}}^{t_{n,i+1}} \sigma^2(t)\, dt\right).$$

Suppose that $\sigma(t)$ is continuously differentiable. Then, by the mean value theorem, we can approximate the integral by $\int_{t_{n,i}}^{t_{n,i+1}} \sigma^2(t)\, dt \simeq (t_{n,i+1} - t_{n,i})\sigma_{t_{n,i}}^2$. Letting z_i be i.i.d. standard normal random variables, we have

$$n^{1/2}\left(\mathrm{RV}_y^n(t) - \mathrm{QV}(t)\right) = n^{1/2}\sum_{i=1}^{n-1}\left(\int_{t_{n,i}}^{t_{n,i+1}} \sigma^2(t)\, dt\right)(z_i^2 - 1)1(t_{n,i+1} \le t)$$

$$\simeq n^{1/2}\sum_{i=1}^{n-1}(t_{n,i+1} - t_{n,i})\sigma_{t_{n,i}}^2(z_i^2 - 1)1(t_{n,i+1} \le t)$$

$$\simeq N\left(0, 2n\sum_{i=1}^{n-1}(t_{n,i+1} - t_{n,i})^2\sigma_{t_{n,i}}^4 1(t_{n,i+1} \le t)\right).$$

Suppose that $t_{ni} = G(i/n)$ for some smooth, increasing function G with derivative g; then $t_{n,i+1} - t_{n,i} \simeq (1/n)g(i/n) = (1/n)g(G^{-1}(t_{n,i}))$ and

$$n \sum_{i=1}^{n-1} (t_{n,i+1} - t_{n,i})^2 \sigma_{t_{n,i}}^4 1(t_{n,i+1} \leq t)$$

$$\simeq \sum_{i=1}^{n-1} (t_{n,i+1} - t_{n,i}) g(G^{-1}(t_{n,i})) \sigma_{t_{n,i}}^4 1(t_{n,i+1} \leq t)$$

$$\simeq \int_0^t g(G^{-1}(u)) \sigma_u^4 \, du = \int_0^t \sigma_u^4 \, dH_u,$$

where the approximation of the sum by the integral follows by the definition of the integral, and $H_t = \int_0^t g(G^{-1}(u)) \, du$. In this case the limiting variance is nonstochastic, so the distribution is normal. The equally spaced data case corresponds to $g(u) = 1$.

12.5.3 Microstructure Error Model

These theoretical results are designed to work in a perfect continuous-time laboratory. In practice, quote and transaction prices take values in a discrete state space with a finite number of possible values and at discrete points in time. These market frictions mean that for very high-frequency data the above approximations can be poor, as has been evidenced in so-called **volatility signature plots**. Figure 12.1 shows the RV sampled at higher frequency plotted against frequency, which should show convergence to QV, but actually appears to show convergence to infinity.

To reflect the divergence between the predicted and actual behavior of RV, the literature has introduced a statistical model that tries to capture the effects of microstructure noise.

Definition 12.26   Suppose that we observe (log) prices $\{y_{t_{n,i}}, i = 1, \ldots, n\}$, where

$$y_{t_{n,i}} = x_{t_{n,i}} + \varepsilon_i, \tag{12.31}$$

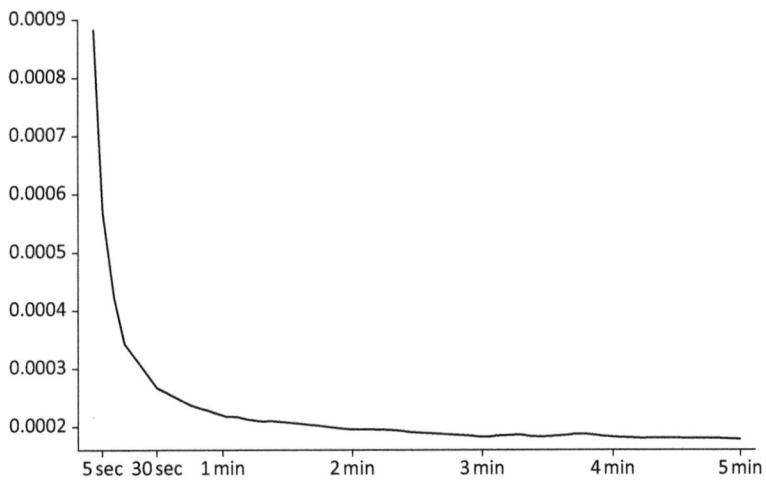

Figure 12.1 Volatility signature plot.

with $x_{t_{n,i}}$ realizations from a submartingale process x_t at times $t = t_{n,i}$, while ε_i are i.i.d. random variables with mean zero and variance σ_ε^2. The measurement error process ε is assumed to be independent of the process x.

This is a version of the signal plus noise model introduced in (7.12). The noise term is intended to represent market microstructure in a reduced-form sense (Zhang, Mykland, and Aït-Sahalia, 2005). In this model, the efficient price dominates the long run, but in the short run the measurement error may dominate in the RV calculation based on high-frequency returns.

Suppose that we calculate the realized variance based on this observed price sequence (at equally spaced time points). We just focus on the full days estimate, $\mathrm{RV}_y^n = \mathrm{RV}_y^n(1)$. We have

$$\mathrm{RV}_y^n = \sum_{i=1}^{n-1} \left(y_{t_{n,i+1}} - y_{t_{n,i}}\right)^2 = \sum_{i=1}^{n-1} \left(x_{t_{n,i+1}} - x_{t_{n,i}}\right)^2 + \sum_{i=1}^{n-1} \left(\varepsilon_{i+1} - \varepsilon_i\right)^2$$

$$+ 2\sum_{i=1}^{n-1} \left(\varepsilon_{i+1} - \varepsilon_i\right)\left(x_{t_{n,i+1}} - x_{t_{n,i}}\right).$$

The first term, $\sum_{i=1}^{n-1}(x_{t_{n,i+1}} - x_{t_{n,i}})^2$, is just the quadratic variation of the efficient price process, which converges in probability to $\mathrm{QV}(1)$. Then, note that, by the LLN for i.i.d. sequences,

$$\frac{1}{n}\sum_{i=1}^{n-1} \left(\varepsilon_{i+1} - \varepsilon_i\right)^2 \xrightarrow{P} 2\sigma_\varepsilon^2. \tag{12.32}$$

Furthermore, by the Cauchy–Schwarz inequality,

$$\left|\frac{1}{n}\sum_{i=1}^{n-1}(\varepsilon_{i+1} - \varepsilon_i)(x_{t_{n,i+1}} - x_{t_{n,i}})\right|$$

$$\leq \frac{1}{\sqrt{n}}\left(\frac{1}{n}\sum_{i=1}^{n-1}(\varepsilon_{i+1} - \varepsilon_i)^2\right)^{1/2}\left(\sum_{i=1}^{n-1}(x_{t_{n,i+1}} - x_{t_{n,i}})^2\right)^{1/2} \xrightarrow{P} 0.$$

It follows that, as $n \to \infty$, $\mathrm{RV}_y^n \xrightarrow{P} \infty$, that is, the RV estimator is inconsistent.

Some argue that one can improve matters by sampling at a lower frequency. Theoretically this just reduces the effect of measurement error, it does not eliminate it, but in practice it often appears to have eliminated the substantial consequences of market frictions.

Zhang, Mykland, and Aït-Sahalia (2005) introduced the **two scales realized volatility** (TSRV) estimator. This estimates the quadratic variation using a combination of realized variances computed on two different time scales or frequencies, thereby performing an additive bias correction to eliminate the bias from microstructure. It allows consistent estimation of the underlying quadratic variation in the presence of noise, albeit with a slower convergence rate than in the case without noise. Suppose that observations are equally spaced, $t_{ni} = i/n$.

Definition 12.27   Write $K \times (m+1) = n$ and let the first subsample be $\{y_0, y_{K/n}, \ldots,$ $y_{mK/n}\}$, the second $\{y_{1/n}, y_{(K+1)/n}, \ldots, y_{(mK+1)/n}\}$, and so on. In each subsample we have $m+1$ (log) prices and hence m returns. For $j = 1, \ldots, K$, let

$$\text{RVsub}_j = \sum_{i=1}^{m} \left(y_{(j+iK)/n} - y_{(j+(i-1)K)/n} \right)^2.$$

These are realized volatility computed on the lower frequency or slower time scale. This estimator would be consistent as $m \to \infty$ in the absence of microstructure noise. In the presence of noise we have

$$\frac{1}{m}\text{RVsub}_j = \frac{1}{m}\sum_{i=1}^{m} \left(y_{(j+iK)/n} - y_{(j+(i-1)K)/n} \right)^2$$

$$= \frac{1}{m}\sum_{i=1}^{m} \left(x_{(j+iK)/n} - x_{(j+(i-1)K)/n} \right)^2 + \frac{1}{m}\sum_{i=1}^{m} \left(\varepsilon_{j+iK} - \varepsilon_{j+(i-1)K} \right)^2$$

$$+ \frac{2}{m}\sum_{i=1}^{m} \left(x_{(j+iK)/n} - x_{(j+(i-1)K)/n} \right)\left(\varepsilon_{j+iK} - \varepsilon_{j+(i-1)K} \right) \xrightarrow{P} 2\sigma_\varepsilon^2$$

as $m \to \infty$. This estimator is inconsistent under (12.31), and indeed grows at the rate m. Consider the linear combination of the two scales, $\text{RVsub}_j - (m/n)\text{RV}$. The leading bias term is $2m\sigma_\varepsilon^2 - (m/n)2n\sigma_\varepsilon^2 = 0$, so that the leading bias term is knocked out by combining the full sample and the subsample estimator in this way. However, the dominant term is then

$$\sum_{i=1}^{m} \left\{ \left(\varepsilon_{j+iK} - \varepsilon_{j+(i-1)K} \right)^2 - 2\sigma_\varepsilon^2 \right\} = \sqrt{m} \times \frac{1}{\sqrt{m}}\sum_{i=1}^{m} \left\{ \left(\varepsilon_{j+iK} - \varepsilon_{j+(i-1)K} \right)^2 - 2\sigma_\varepsilon^2 \right\},$$

which is large and contains only noise. This term is eliminated by averaging over the subsamples. Specifically, consider the term

$$T = \frac{1}{K}\sum_{j=1}^{K}\sum_{i=1}^{m} \left(\left(\varepsilon_{j+iK} - \varepsilon_{j+(i-1)K} \right)^2 - 2\sigma_\varepsilon^2 \right)$$

$$= \frac{1}{K}\sum_{j=1}^{K}\sum_{i=1}^{m} \left(\varepsilon_{j+iK}^2 - \sigma_\varepsilon^2 \right) + \frac{1}{K}\sum_{j=1}^{K}\sum_{i=1}^{m} \left(\varepsilon_{j+(i-1)K}^2 - \sigma_\varepsilon^2 \right)$$

$$- 2\frac{1}{K}\sum_{j=1}^{K}\sum_{i=1}^{m} \varepsilon_{j+iK}\varepsilon_{j+(i-1)K}.$$

Each of these terms is mean zero. Furthermore, each term is like a sum of n independent random variables so that T is of order $\sqrt{m/K}$ in probability and satisfies a CLT after normalization. If $K/m \to \infty$, these terms are of smaller order in probability.

Definition 12.28   The TSRV estimator is

$$\widehat{\theta}_{\text{TSRV}} = \frac{1}{K}\sum_{j=1}^{K}\text{RVsub}_j - \frac{m}{n}\text{RV}_n. \tag{12.33}$$

The leading terms of $\widehat{\theta}_{\text{TSRV}} - \theta$, where $\theta = \langle x, x \rangle_1$, are T and

$$\sum_{i=1}^{m} \left(x_{(j+iK)/n} - x_{(j+(i-1)K)/n} \right)^2 - \theta$$

$$= \sqrt{m} \times \frac{1}{\sqrt{m}} \left(\sum_{i=1}^{m} \left(x_{(j+iK)/n} - x_{(j+(i-1)K)/n} \right)^2 - \theta \right).$$

If we choose m, K such that $1/m = m/K$, the two terms are balanced and this is the optimal configuration. In that case $m^2 = K$ so $m \simeq n^{1/3}$ and $K \simeq n^{2/3}$, so that the two leading terms are of order $n^{-1/6}$ in probability. In conclusion, we have the following result.

Theorem 12.5   *Suppose that $K = cn^{2/3}$ for some positive finite c. Then $\widehat{\theta}_{\text{TSRV}}$ is consistent and converges at rate $n^{1/6}$ to a mixed normal distribution,*

$$n^{1/6}(\widehat{\theta}_{\text{TSRV}} - \theta) \Longrightarrow \text{MN}(0, \omega), \qquad \omega = \frac{8}{c^2 \sigma_\varepsilon^4} + c \frac{4}{3} \int_0^1 \sigma_u^4 \, du.$$

The optimal choice of c can be determined from minimization of ω with respect to c. Zhang, Mykland, and Aït-Sahalia (2005) also gave a method for estimating ω from the data. The rate of convergence is slower than $\sqrt{n}$ because it is difficult to extract the signal from such large noise.

Zhang (2006) introduced the multiple scales realized volatility (MSRV) estimator that combines multiple ($\simeq n^{1/2}$) time scales. This is consistent and has a faster convergence rate of $n^{1/4}$. This has been shown to be the optimal rate, that is, the rate achieved by the Gaussian MLE for the special case of constant volatility. The class of estimators is

$$\widehat{\theta}_{\text{MSRV}} = \sum_{l=1}^{L} \alpha_l \frac{1}{K_l} \sum_{j=1}^{K_l} \text{RVsub}_j^{K_l},$$

where there are restrictions on $\alpha_1, \ldots, \alpha_L$, including $\sum_{l=1}^{L} \alpha_l \simeq 1$, and growth conditions on L, K. Zhang (2006) showed that, as $n \to \infty$,

$$n^{1/4}(\widehat{\theta}_{\text{MSRV}} - \theta) \Longrightarrow \text{MN}(0, \omega^*)$$

for some random ω^*. Aït-Sahalia, Mykland, and Zhang (2011) modified the TSRV and MSRV estimators and achieved consistency in the presence of serially correlated microstructure noise.

There are some other popular methods: preaveraging and realized kernels.

Definition 12.29   The **realized kernel** estimator is

$$\text{RK}_M = \sum_{|j| \leq M} k \left(\frac{j}{M} \right) \widehat{\gamma}_j(y), \qquad \widehat{\gamma}_j(y) := \sum_{i=j+1}^{n} y_{t_i} y_{t_{i-j}}, \ j = 0, \pm 1, \ldots,$$

where the kernel k satisfies $k(0) = 1$ and $k(s) \to 0$ as $s \to \infty$, and the bandwidth M controls the bias–variance trade-off.

Zhou (1996) was the first to consider the use of the kernel method to deal with the problem of microstructure noise in high-frequency data. For the case of independent noise, Zhou proposed this with $M = 1$. Hansen and Lunde (2006) examined the properties of Zhou's estimator and showed that, although unbiased under the presence of i.i.d. microstructure noise, the estimator is not consistent. However, they advocated that, while inconsistent, Zhou's kernel method is able to uncover several properties of the microstructure noise. Barndorff-Nielsen *et al.* (2008) developed some theory for this method.

Jacod *et al.* (2009) proposed the method of **preaveraging**, which involves averaging observed prices over a moderate number of time points to reduce the measurement error, and then applying RV to the preaveraged data. Aït-Sahalia and Jacod (2014) gave a comprehensive review of volatility estimation in a continuous-time framework.

Liu, Patton, and Sheppard (2015) compared some of these methods with "five-minute" RV.

12.6 Summary

We considered some continuous-time models built on Brownian motion, such as diffusion processes. We considered the properties of diffusion processes and their estimation based on long-span data and on short-span data. We considered recent methods for estimating volatility based on high-frequency data. The R language has several packages for estimating diffusion models, such as `mixedsde`. The `highfrequency` package contains useful utilities for handling high-frequency financial data. Aït-Sahalia and Jacod (2014) is an excellent further read.

12.7 Exercises

12.1 Suppose that δ_i, $i = 1, \ldots, n$, are i.i.d. Poisson distributed, that is, $\Pr(\delta_i = k) = \lambda^k \exp(-\lambda)/k!$ for $k = 0, 1, 2, \ldots$ Let $\tau_1 = \delta_1$, $\tau_2 = \tau_1 + \delta_2$, and so on. Now let $y_i = B(\tau_i)$, where $B(\cdot)$ is standard Brownian motion (independent of the Poisson sampling), and let $x_i = y_i - y_{i-1}$. This is called a subordinated stochastic process. What are the properties of the process $\{x_i, i = 1, \ldots, n\}$?

12.2 Suppose that the stock price P evolves according to geometric Brownian motion with volatility σ, that is, $dP_t = \mu P_t \, dt + \sigma P_t \, dB_t$, where B is standard Brownian motion. Show that, given initial value P_0,

$$P_t = P_0 \exp\left(\left(\mu - \frac{\sigma^2}{2}\right)t + \sigma B_t\right),$$

and hence calculate $E(P_t \mid P_0)$ and $\text{var}(P_t \mid P_0)$.

12.3 Black and Scholes (1973) showed that the option price $C(t)$ at time t with time to maturity τ and strike price X satisfies

$$C_t = P_t \Phi(d_1) - X e^{-r\tau} \Phi(d_2),$$

where r is the risk-free rate, and

$$d_1 = \frac{\log(P_t/X) + (r_t + \sigma^2/2)\tau}{\sigma\sqrt{\tau}}, \qquad d_2 = \frac{\log(P_t/X) + (r_t - \sigma^2/2)\tau}{\sigma\sqrt{\tau}},$$

where Φ is the standard normal CDF. Here, σ^2 is the variance per time unit of the underlying stock. Suppose that you have a time series of call option prices on options that have the same strike price and time to maturity, and you also observe the underlying prices and the interest rates for each day, that is, $\{C_t, P_t, r_t, t = 1, \ldots, T\}$. Explain how you might go about estimating σ^2.

12.4 Suppose that $dy_t = \mu(y_t)\,dt + \sigma(y_t)\,dB_t$ is a stationary diffusion process with marginal density standard normal. Discuss what restrictions this places on the functions $\mu(\cdot)$ and $\sigma(\cdot)$. You may start with the linear case, $\mu(y) = \alpha + \beta y$, and see which functions $\sigma(\cdot)$ are compatible with this restriction.

12.5 Suppose that $dy_t = \beta(\alpha - y_t)\,dt + \pi\,dB_t$. Explain how you might estimate the parameters α, β based on a sample of data $\{y_\Delta, y_{2\Delta}, \ldots, y_{n\Delta}\}$ for some fixed Δ and large n. What happens if Δ is small, that is, $\Delta = 1/\sqrt{n}$?

12.6 For the dataset `flash`, let P_t denote the price at the tth trade, and define the logarithmic return between consecutive trades as $r_t = \log(P_t) - \log(P_{t-1})$. Calculate the realized volatility for each five-minute interval and plot the results.

12.7 For the dataset `flash`, let P_t denote the price at the tth trade, and define the logarithmic return between consecutive trades as $r_t = \log(P_t) - \log(P_{t-1})$. Calculate the two-stage realized volatility for each five-minute interval and plot the results. Compare the results according to the parameter K.

12.8 From the dataset `ffdaily`, obtain the daily interest rate series. Estimate the parameters α, β from the relationship

$$r_{t+1} = \alpha + \exp(-\beta)\,(r_t - \alpha) + \varepsilon_t$$

using the sample $\{r_1, \ldots, r_T\}$. Calculate standard errors for β under the assumption that ε_t is an MDS. Calculate the kernel density

$$\widehat{p}(r) = \frac{1}{Th}\sum_{t=1}^{T} K\left(\frac{r - r_t}{h}\right)$$

for some bandwidth h and kernel K, and plot the result. Finally, estimate the volatility function $\sigma^2(r)$ at a grid of values $r_1, \ldots, r_K$ by the plug-in method,

$$\widehat{\sigma}^2(r) = \frac{2}{\widehat{p}(r)}\frac{1}{T}\sum_{t=1}^{T}\left(\widehat{\alpha} + \exp(-\widehat{\beta})\,(r_t - \widehat{\alpha})\right)1(r_t \le r).$$

12.9 Suppose that $dy_t = \mu(t)\,dt + (\sigma/\sqrt{n})\,dB_t$, where $B(0) = 0$ and $t \in [0, 1]$, while $\mu(\cdot)$ is a smooth unknown function on $[0, 1]$. This is confusingly called the white noise model. Suppose that $\mu(t) = \mu$, and we have a sample $y_i = y_{i/n}, i = 1, \ldots, n$, where n is large. Discuss the estimation of μ, σ^2. Now suppose that $\mu(t) = \sum_{j=0}^{p}\beta^j t^j$ for some given p. Discuss the properties of β and σ.

12.10 Suppose that we observe prices at times $t_{n,i} = i/n$, such that returns satisfy $r_i = \mu\Delta_i + z_i\sigma\sqrt{\Delta_i}$ for $i = 1, \ldots, n$, where $z_i \sim N(0, 1)$ and $\Delta_i = 1/n$. Compare the two estimators

$$\widehat{\sigma}^2 = \sum_{i=1}^n (r_i - \bar{r})^2, \qquad \widetilde{\sigma}^2 = \sum_{i=1}^n r_i^2$$

according to mean squared error, where $\bar{r} = \sum_{i=1}^n r_i/n$.

12.11 Suppose that $B(t)$ is standard Brownian motion, and let $y_{t_1}, \ldots, y_{t_n}$ be observed at time points $t_0, \ldots, t_n$, where $y_{t_i} = \mu + \sigma B(t_i) + \varepsilon_i$, with ε_i i.i.d. $N(0, \sigma_\varepsilon^2)$. Let $R_i = y_{t_i} - y_{t_{i-1}}$.

(a) Suppose that time is equally spaced on $[0, 1]$, that is, $t_i = i/n$. Show that

$$\text{var}(R_i) = \frac{\sigma^2}{n} + 2\sigma_\varepsilon^2, \qquad \text{cov}(R_i, R_{i-j}) = \begin{cases} -\sigma_\varepsilon^2, & j = 1, \\ 0, & j \geq 2. \end{cases}$$

This is the covariance function of an MA(1) process, that is, we may write $R_i = U_i - \theta_n U_{i-1}$, where U_i is an i.i.d. mean-zero shock process and the parameters θ_n and σ_U^2 satisfy two restrictions: $\sigma_U^2 (1 + \theta_n) = (\sigma^2/n) + 2\sigma_\varepsilon^2$ and $\theta_n \sigma_U^2 = \sigma_\varepsilon^2$. Explicit solutions can be given for θ_n and σ_U^2 in terms of σ^2, σ_ε^2, and n, but note that

$$\theta_n = 1 - \frac{1}{\sqrt{n}} \left(\frac{\sigma^2}{2\sigma_\varepsilon^2} \right)^{1/2} + O\left(\frac{1}{n} \right).$$

This means that the process R_i is an MA(1) process and has a moderate deviation from the unit root process.

(b) Suppose that t_i are equally spaced on the interval $[0, \sqrt{n}]$, that is, $t_i = i/\sqrt{n}$. Derive the properties of R_i.

13 Forecasting

We consider the forecasting question, that is, how to forecast or predict future values of a time series based on currently available information. This is of considerable practical importance, and there exists a huge industry with many different approaches and methodologies. Given a specific model we can work out the optimal point and interval forecasts according to some criterion. There is also a lot of forecasting that eschews referring to specific models and rather points to certain principles (that may be established within certain restrictive models) that can be applied in general situations. It is important to evaluate the quality of a series of forecasts, which is called forecast evaluation. We first discuss this in a general setting without reference to a model.

13.1 Objective Measure of Forecast Performance

We suppose that the target is to forecast some future scalar outcomes $y_{T+1}, y_{T+2}, \ldots, y_{T+r}$ for some integer r given some sample information $\mathcal{F}_T = \{y_1, \ldots, y_T\}$. We first say what we mean by success and failure. We define a general loss function L that reflects the preferences of the user of the forecast over the errors that are made. Usually, we work with quadratic loss so that $L(x, y) = (x - y)^2$, where y is the variable to be forecast and x is the forecast, so that $x - y$ is the forecast error, but absolute loss is also common, that is, $L(x, y) = |x - y|$. Some authors have worried that both of these well-known loss functions are symmetric whereas policy makers may have an asymmetric valuation of the costs of positive and negative errors. The LINEX loss function $L(x, y) = \exp(a(x - y)) - a(x - y) + 1$ is a leading example of asymmetric loss function. Most loss functions have the property that $L(x, y) = L_0(x - y)$, where the function $L_0(t)$ increases as t increases.

We consider the quadratic loss function case, where $L(x, y) = (x - y)^2$. In the multivariate case one typically works with either the trace of $(x - y)(x - y)^\mathsf{T}$ or the determinant, but here we suppose reduction has occurred to a scalar loss function. We seek a forecast that minimizes the average or expected loss, which is the (conditional) mean squared forecast error, that is, we choose $h \in \mathcal{H} = \{h \colon h \text{ is a measurable function } \mathbb{R}^T \to \mathbb{R}\}$ to minimize

$$E\left[L\left(y_{T+j}, h(y_1, \ldots, y_T)\right)^2 \mid y_1, \ldots, y_T\right],$$

and let $\widehat{y}_{T+j|T} = h_0(y_1, \ldots, y_T)$ be the minimizing value. Here, the expectation is taken over the true conditional distribution of $y_{T+j} \mid y_1, \ldots, y_T$. In fact, the solution $\widehat{y}_{T+j|T} = h_{\mathrm{opt}}(y_1, \ldots, y_T)$ is the conditional expectation

$$\widehat{y}_{T+j|T} = E(y_{T+j} \mid y_1, \ldots, y_T).$$

In stationary environments we may also consider the hypothetical forecast $E(y_{T+j} \mid y_T, y_{T-1}, \ldots)$ that makes use of the infinite past of the data, although we expect in that case $E(y_{T+j} \mid y_T, y_{T-1}, \ldots)$ and $E(y_{T+j} \mid y_T, \ldots, y_1)$ to be close for large T. Finally, we may also calculate the unconditional mean squared forecast error,

$$E\big(E[L(y_{T+j}, h(y_1, \ldots, y_T))^2 \mid y_1, \ldots, y_T]\big) = E\big[L(y_{T+j}, h(y_1, \ldots, y_T))^2\big].$$

In fact, $E(y_{T+j} \mid y_1, \ldots, y_T)$ minimizes this criterion too.

In general, the expectation $E(y_{T+j} \mid y_1, \ldots, y_T)$ is a complicated nonlinear function of $y_1, \ldots, y_T$; we may instead restrict attention to linear or affine functions of the data, that is, we minimize the mean squared error over functions $h \in \mathcal{L}$, where $\mathcal{L} = \{h \colon h(y_1, \ldots, y_T) = b_0 + b_1 y_1 + \cdots + b_T y_T$ for some $b_j \in \mathbb{R}, j = 0, 1, \ldots, T\}$. The BLP usually exists and has a closed-form solution. For linear models, this seems like a good starting point. Note that for a stationary process,

$$\lim_{j \to \infty} E(y_{T+j} \mid y_T, y_{T-1}, \ldots) = E(y_t)$$

(where strictly speaking this convergence is in probability), so that long-term forecasts return to the unconditional mean.

We remark briefly on the Bayesian perspective. For a Bayesian, one must calculate the predictive density

$$f(y_{T+1} \mid y_{1:T}) = \int f(y_{T+1} \mid y_{1:T}, \theta) f(\theta \mid y_{1:T}) \, d\theta \tag{13.1}$$

from the posterior $f(\theta \mid y_{1:T})$, and perhaps report summary statistics from this distribution such as its mean or mode. This is a general framework that can be implemented for any non-Gaussian specification of $f(y_{T+1} \mid y_{1:T}, \theta)$ using the simulation methods described in Chapter 9. The main difference from the frequentist approach is that the density $f(y_{T+1} \mid y_{1:T})$ is derived from both the prior and the model.

We first give some of the main frequentist approaches to forecasting based on some model assumptions that allow one to determine the optimal forecasts.

13.2 Forecasting in ARMA Models

We first consider how to forecast when we maintain the linear ARMA process structure.

13.2.1 Forecasting in the AR(1) Case

Consider the scalar AR(1) process $y_t = \mu + \phi(y_{t-1} - \mu) + \varepsilon_t$, where ε_t is i.i.d. with mean zero and variance $\sigma^2 < \infty$. Provided $|\phi| < 1$, y_t is stationary and $E(y_t) = \mu$. We first assume that ϕ, μ are known. We have $y_{T+1} = \mu + \phi(y_T - \mu) + \varepsilon_{T+1}$. Therefore, we forecast y_{T+1} by

$$\widehat{y}_{T+1|T} = E(y_{T+1} \mid y_1, \ldots, y_T) = \mu + \phi(y_T - \mu).$$

The forecast error is defined as $e_{T+1|T} = y_{T+1} - \widehat{y}_{T+1|T}$, and in this case we have $e_{T+1|T} = \varepsilon_{T+1}$, which is a random variable that has mean zero (the forecast is unbiased) and variance σ^2 conditional on the data, that is,

$$v^2_{T+1|T} = \text{var}\left(e_{T+1|T} \mid y_1, \ldots, y_T\right) = \sigma^2.$$

Any other unbiased forecast of y_{T+1} using the sample information $\{y_1, \ldots, y_T\}$ will have larger variance. Notice that the analysis goes through more or less the same if y_t is a vector, that is, a VAR(1) process. The only difference is that $\widehat{y}_{T+1|T}$ is a vector and $\text{var}\left(e_{T+1|T} \mid y_1, \ldots, y_T\right) = \Omega_\varepsilon$ is a covariance matrix.

What about forecasting r periods ahead? We have $y_{T+r} = \mu + \phi(y_{T+r-1} - \mu) + \varepsilon_{T+r}$, and so we can write

$$\widehat{y}_{T+r|T} = \mu + \phi(\widehat{y}_{T+r-1|T} - \mu),$$

which gives a recursive formulation. We can likewise obtain $y_{T+r} = \mu + \phi^r(y_T - \mu) + \phi^{r-1}\varepsilon_{T+1} + \cdots + \varepsilon_{T+r}$, from which we see that

$$\widehat{y}_{T+r|T} = \mu + \phi^r(y_T - \mu). \tag{13.2}$$

The forecast error is

$$e_{T+r|T} = y_{T+r} - \widehat{y}_{T+r|T} = \phi^{r-1}\varepsilon_{T+1} + \cdots + \varepsilon_{T+r},$$

which has mean zero and variance $v^2_{T+r|T} = \sigma^2(1 + \phi^2 + \cdots + \phi^{2r-2})$; it is a moving average of order r (and so forecast errors are correlated across horizons). Note that if $|\phi| < 1$, we have $\widehat{y}_{T+r|T} = \phi^r y_T \to 0$ (the unconditional mean) as $r \to \infty$ and

$$v^2_{T+r|T} = \text{var}\left(e_{T+r|T} \mid y_1, \ldots, y_T\right) \longrightarrow \frac{\sigma^2}{1 - \phi^2},$$

which are the unconditional mean and variance of the stationary process y_t. On the other hand, if $\phi = 1$ and $\mu = 0$ then $\widehat{y}_{T+r|T} = y_T$ for all r and as $r \to \infty$, $\text{var}\left(e_{T+r|T} \mid y_1, \ldots, y_T\right) \longrightarrow \infty$. The same is true in the vector case.

In practice, we must use estimates of ϕ and μ, so we instead compute $\widehat{y}_{T+r|T} = \widehat{\mu} + \widehat{\phi}^r(y_T - \widehat{\mu})$, where $\widehat{\phi}, \widehat{\mu}$ are estimated from sample data. The forecast error is now

$$\widehat{e}_{T+r|T} = y_{T+r} - \widehat{y}_{T+r|T}(\phi, \mu) + \widehat{y}_{T+r|T}(\widehat{\phi}, \widehat{\mu}) - \widehat{y}_{T+r|T}(\phi, \mu)$$

$$= \phi^{r-1}\varepsilon_{T+1} + \cdots + \varepsilon_{T+r} + (\widehat{\phi}^r - \phi^r)(y_T - \mu) + (1 - \phi^r)(\widehat{\mu} - \mu) + \cdots$$

Provided $\widehat{\phi}, \widehat{\mu}$ are consistent estimators of ϕ, μ (the sample size is large), the second term disappears as the estimation sample size increases. That is, the estimation error is relatively small compared to the intrinsic forecast error. The forecast error variance becomes $\sigma^2(1 + \phi^2 + \cdots + \phi^{2r-2})$. No matter how much data we have, this part will not disappear.

We may provide a forecast interval around our point forecast under some conditions. Specifically, let

$$\widehat{\mathfrak{I}}_\alpha(r) = \widehat{y}_{T+r|T} \pm z_{\alpha/2} \times \widehat{v}_{T+r|T}, \quad \widehat{v}^2_{T+r|T} = \widehat{\sigma}^2\left(1 + \widehat{\phi}^2 + \cdots + \widehat{\phi}^{2r-2}\right), \tag{13.3}$$

where $\widehat{\sigma}^2$ and $\widehat{\phi}$ are estimates of σ^2 and ϕ constructed from the sample. This is to be interpreted like a confidence interval in the sense that approximately $1 - \alpha$ of the time the future realization y_{T+r} will lie inside this interval (provided T is large). This interval is symmetric around the point forecast because of the $\pm z_{\alpha/2}$ critical values. Notice that in large samples the interval becomes

$$\widehat{y}_{T+r|T} \pm z_{\alpha/2} \times \sqrt{\sigma^2(1 + \phi^2 + \cdots + \phi^{2r-2})}, \tag{13.4}$$

which does not shrink to zero. The forecast interval is asymptotically valid provided $\varepsilon_t \sim N(0, \sigma^2)$ in the sense that

$$\Pr\left(y_{T+r} \in \widehat{\mathfrak{I}}_{\alpha}(r)\right) \to 1 - \alpha. \tag{13.5}$$

We may further argue that, conditional on $y_1, \ldots, y_T$, the distribution of $y_{T+r|T}$ is approximately $N(y_{T+r|T}, v_{T+r|T}^2)$, which is the so-called **predictive distribution** and is estimated by $N(\widehat{y}_{T+r|T}, \widehat{v}_{T+r|T}^2)$. In the multivariate case we may construct the joint forecast region or marginalize to focus on specific components.

If the error distribution is not normal then this argument is not valid; at least, the confidence band is not valid in the sense of (13.5). Gaussianity is a strong assumption and we did not need it for any of the estimation and inference procedures we have discussed because the CLT guarantees approximate normality of estimators, but for the fixed step-ahead forecasting there is no CLT to fall back on and we have to hang our hat on this assumption; or do we? We could assume some other distribution like a chi-squared or a t-distribution and use that. In the next section we outline how to construct valid confidence intervals when the shocks are not Gaussian and are not parametrically specified based on the bootstrap principle.

13.2.1.1 Forecast Interval for a Nonnormal Distribution

Provided we maintain the assumption that the shocks are i.i.d., we may estimate the distribution or quantiles of the error distribution and use these in place of the quantiles of the normal distribution. The distribution estimator is consistent, and so with a large estimation sample size we might expect it to provide a good approximation. Define, for each t,

$$w_t = \phi^{r-1}\varepsilon_{t+1} + \cdots + \varepsilon_{t+r}, \qquad F_w(x) = \Pr(w_t \le x),$$

where $w_T = e_{T+r|T}$ is the random prediction error when the parameters are known and we suppress dependence on r. The stochastic process w_t is a moving-average process of order r and so stationary and weakly dependent for any finite r. We require the quantiles of its distribution. If we observed a sample of values $\{w_t\}$ we would just calculate the empirical distribution based on this data. We replace w_t by consistent estimates, specifically

$$\{\widehat{w}_t = y_{t+r} - \widehat{y}_{t+r|t}, \ t \in I_{T,r} = \{t : T_0 \le t \le T - r\}\}$$

for some $T_0 > 1$ or, equivalently, $\{\widehat{w}_t = \widehat{\phi}^{r-1}\widehat{\varepsilon}_{t+1} + \cdots + \widehat{\varepsilon}_{t+r}, \ t \in I_{T,r} = \{t : T_0 \le t \le T - r\}\}$ for some $T_0 > 1$. That is, we use the estimation sample to mimic the out-of-sample forecast errors. In the one-step-ahead case $\widehat{w}_t = \widehat{\varepsilon}_{t+1}$, which are just the in-sample residuals. We then estimate the distribution of the forecast errors by the empirical distribution of the available sample, that is,

$$\widehat{F}_{\widehat{w}}(x) = \frac{1}{T_{I_{T,r}}} \sum_{t \in I_{T,r}} 1\left(\widehat{w}_t \le x\right),$$

where $T_{I_{T,r}}$ is the number of observations in the available sample $I_{T,r}$ (of $\widehat{w}_t$). We then define the forecast interval,

$$\widehat{\mathfrak{I}}_\alpha(r) = [\widehat{y}_{T+r|T} + \widehat{q}_{\alpha/2}, \widehat{y}_{T+r|T} + \widehat{q}_{1-\alpha/2}], \tag{13.6}$$

where $\widehat{q}_\alpha = \widehat{F}_{\widehat{w}}^{-1}(\alpha)$ for any α. Notice that this interval is not necessarily symmetric around the point forecast because $\widehat{q}_{\alpha/2}$ is not necessarily equal to $-\widehat{q}_{1-\alpha/2}$. Provided $T \to \infty$, $\widehat{w}_t \to w_t$ with probability one and $\widehat{F}_{\widehat{w}}(x) \to F_w(x)$ with probability one uniformly over x, and the interval (13.6) will be asymptotically correct in the sense that $\Pr\left(y_{T+r} \in \widehat{\mathfrak{I}}_\alpha(r)\right) \to 1 - \alpha$. This method relies on the assumption that $w_t = \phi^{r-1}\varepsilon_{t+1} + \cdots + \varepsilon_{t+r}$ are stationary and mixing, and drawn from the same distribution as $w_{T+1}, \ldots, w_{T+r}$, but does not require normality or even i.i.d. shocks. The predictive distribution in this case is $\Pr(y_{T+r} \le y \mid y_T, \ldots, y_1) = F_w(y - \phi' y_T)$, which can be estimated by $\widehat{F}_{\widehat{w}}(y - \widehat{\phi}^r y_T)$.

A further issue is that we may care about the joint behavior of the forecasts $\widehat{y}_{T+r|T}$, $r = 1, \ldots, R$, say. The intervals we propose above are pointwise valid but they ignore the multiple testing issue. In that case we must estimate the joint distribution

$$F_w(x) = \Pr(w_t(1) \le x_1, \ldots, w_t(R) \le x_R), \quad w_t(r) = \phi^{r-1}\varepsilon_{T+1} + \cdots + \varepsilon_{T+r}.$$

This can be done using the multivariate empirical CDF.

13.2.2   Forecasting in the AR(∞) Model

We now suppose that the data are generated by a more general process with an AR(∞) representation,

$$y_t = \mu + \sum_{j=1}^{\infty} \gamma_j(y_{t-j} - \mu) + \varepsilon_t, \tag{13.7}$$

where γ_j are coefficients and ε_t are i.i.d. (or perhaps MDS). This is consistent with y_t being a stationary and invertible ARMA(p, q) process (including, for example, the MA(1) process). We would like to forecast y_{T+1} by its conditional expectation given the entire past,

$$E(y_{T+1} \mid y_T, y_{T-1}, \ldots) = \mu + \sum_{j=1}^{\infty} \gamma_j(y_{T+1-j} - \mu)$$

$$= \mu + \sum_{j=1}^{T} \gamma_j(y_{T+1-j} - \mu) + \sum_{j=T+1}^{\infty} \gamma_j(y_{T+1-j} - \mu).$$

In practice, we do not observe $y_0, y_{-1}, \ldots$, and we do not know the parameters μ, γ_j. We use only the first sum with estimated parameters

$$\widehat{y}_{T+1|T} = \widehat{\mu} + \sum_{j=1}^{T} \widehat{\gamma}_j(y_{T+1-j} - \widehat{\mu}) \tag{13.8}$$

to make the forecast. Of course, we need to have good estimates of $\widehat{\gamma}_j, j = 1, \ldots, T$, which generally require more structure such as provided by an ARMA(p, q) model in which the γ_j are functions of a small number of underlying parameters. We may have to further truncate, taking $k = k(T)$ lags, where $k(T) \to \infty$ and $k(T)/T \to 0$ as $T \to \infty$. For example, $k(T) = c \log(T)$ for some constant c can be sufficient for stationary and invertible ARMA processes, because they are geometrically mixing/ergodic.[1] For processes with slower decay, $k(T) = cT^\kappa$ for some $\kappa > 0$ may be appropriate. The above arguments apply equally to the multivariate case where $y_t, \varepsilon_t \in \mathbb{R}^n$ and the parameters are vectors or matrices. The forecast error is ε_{T+1} plus some other stuff that is to do with the estimation error and the truncation, both of which terms go to zero in probability under some conditions. We may apply normal forecast intervals or general nonnormal ones.

Higher-order forecasts can be made recursively. We have

$$E(y_{T+r} \mid y_T, \ldots) = \mu + \gamma_1 E(y_{T+r-1} - \mu \mid y_T, \ldots) + \cdots$$
$$+ \gamma_{r-1} E(y_{T+1} - \mu \mid y_T, \ldots) + \sum_{j=r}^{\infty} \gamma_j(y_{T+r-j} - \mu),$$

and so we can let, for $r = 1, 2, \ldots,$

$$\widehat{y}_{T+r|T} = \widehat{\gamma}_1 \widehat{y}_{T+r-1|T} + \cdots + \widehat{\gamma}_{r-1} \widehat{y}_{T+1|T} + \sum_{j=r}^{T} \widehat{\gamma}_j(y_{T+r-j} - \mu), \qquad (13.9)$$

with (13.8) as the starting value. The forecast interval can be constructed as for the AR(1) case.

Note that in some cases one may be willing to specify μ a priori. For example, central banks often have a mandate to achieve, say, a 2% inflation rate. In that case it is their common practice to assume that μ corresponds to this target rate rather than estimate it from the historical data, which contains all their past mistakes. This imposes that $\lim_r \to \infty \widehat{y}_{T+r|T} = \mu$ (in probability), and inside such forecasts the central banks happily achieve their target eventually. One may question whether this happy world is justified. Actually, it is not quite accurate, since even in that case the forecast uncertainty does not disappear; specifically, the long-horizon forecast is centered at μ but has variance equal to the unconditional variance of the process. On average, the central banks exactly meet their target in the long run with probability zero.

This methodology can be applied to GARCH models using the ARCH(∞) representation $y_t = \sigma_t \varepsilon_t$, where $\sigma_t^2 = \psi_0 + \sum_{j=1}^{\infty} \psi_j y_{t-j}^2$, that is, we let $\widehat{\sigma}_{T+1|T}^2 = \psi_0(\widehat{\theta}) + \sum_{j=1}^{T} \psi_j(\widehat{\theta}) y_{T+1-j}^2$.

13.2.3 Forecasting Transformations

We often take transformations of the data before applying a model, such as the logarithm. This can be justified in various ways. For example, if the original data are positive, such as a price series, then taking logarithms seems to make Gaussian-type models work better. In

---

[1] For the ARMA(p, q) model there are iterative algorithms that obviate the need to choose $k(T)$ and use all the data.

fact, this is pretty much the standard practice for price series. Taking logarithms can also attenuate any trend so that it does not overwhelm the other properties of the series. In that case, we naturally have a forecast for the transformed data, whereas we may ultimately be interested in forecasting the original data. For example, suppose that $y_t = \phi y_{t-1} + \varepsilon_t$, where $y_t = \tau(x_t)$, with x_t the raw series and τ a known monotonic transformation such as the logarithm or $\Phi^{-1}(F(\cdot))$ (see Section 10.4). We forecast y_{T+1} by $\widehat{y}_{T+1|T} = \widehat{\phi} y_T$, where $\widehat{\phi}$ is any consistent estimator of ϕ. We then may forecast x_{T+1} by $\widehat{x}_{T+1|T} = \tau^{-1}(\widehat{y}_{T+1|T})$. However, this is in general a biased forecast. Note that x_t is also a Markov process when ε_t are i.i.d., and indeed $x_{T+1} = \tau^{-1}(y_{T+1}) = \tau^{-1}(\phi y_T + \varepsilon_{T+1})$. We have

$$E\left(x_{T+1} \mid x_T\right) = E\left(\tau^{-1}(\phi \tau(x_T) + \varepsilon_{T+1}) \mid x_T\right) \neq \tau^{-1}(\phi \tau(x_T)).$$

Instead, we need to estimate the effect of the shock on the nonlinear transform. We let

$$\widehat{x}_{T+1|T} = \frac{1}{T} \sum_{s=1}^{T} \tau^{-1}(\widehat{\phi} \tau(x_T) + \widehat{\varepsilon}_s),$$

where $\widehat{\varepsilon}_s = y_s - \widehat{\phi} y_{s-1}$. For large samples, this provides a consistent and asymptotically unbiased forecast of x_{T+1}. For the logarithmic transform, this simplifies because $\tau^{-1} = \exp$ and $\exp(a + b) = \exp(a)\exp(b)$. If we ignore the estimation error we have

$$x_{T+1} - \widehat{x}_{T+1|T} = \tau^{-1}(\phi \tau(x_T) + \varepsilon_{T+1}) - \frac{1}{T} \sum_{s=1}^{T} \tau^{-1}(\phi \tau(x_T) + \varepsilon_s)$$

$$\simeq \tau^{-1}(\phi \tau(x_T) + \varepsilon_{T+1}) - E\left[\tau^{-1}(\phi \tau(x_T) + \varepsilon_{T+1}) \mid x_T\right].$$

Define $pe_{T+1} = \tau^{-1}(\phi \tau(x_T) + \varepsilon_{T+1}) - E\left[\tau^{-1}(\phi \tau(x_T) + \varepsilon_{T+1}) \mid x_T\right]$ and its distribution $F_{pe}(\cdot \mid x_T)$ conditional on x_T. The distribution F_{pe} can be estimated by

$$\widehat{F}_{pe}(t \mid x_T) = \frac{1}{T} \sum_{s=1}^{T} 1\left(\tau^{-1}(\widehat{\phi} \tau(x_T) + \widehat{\varepsilon}_s) - \frac{1}{T} \sum_{s=1}^{T} \tau^{-1}(\widehat{\phi} \tau(x_T) + \widehat{\varepsilon}_s) \leq t\right).$$

We then obtain the critical values $\widehat{q}_\alpha = \widehat{F}_{pe}^{-1}(\alpha \mid x_T)$ and the $1 - \alpha$ coverage prediction interval,

$$\widehat{\mathfrak{I}}_\alpha(1) = \left[\widehat{x}_{T+1|T} - \widehat{q}_{\alpha/2}, \widehat{x}_{T+1|T} + \widehat{q}_{1-\alpha/2}\right].$$

Again, this interval is not necessarily symmetric around the point forecast.

An alternative approach is to consider the symmetric forecast interval for y_{T+1} based on the normal critical values,

$$\left[\widehat{y}_{T+1|T} - z_{\alpha/2} \times \sqrt{\widehat{\sigma}^2(1 + \widehat{\phi}^2)}, \widehat{y}_{T+1|T} + z_{\alpha/2} \times \sqrt{\widehat{\sigma}^2(1 + \widehat{\phi}^2)}\right],$$

and then transform this interval to an asymmetric interval for x_{T+1},

$$\mathfrak{I}_\alpha(x_{T+1})$$

$$= \left[\tau^{-1}\left(\widehat{y}_{T+1|T} - z_{\alpha/2} \times \sqrt{\widehat{\sigma}^2(1 + \widehat{\phi}^2)}\right), \tau^{-1}\left(\widehat{y}_{T+1|T} + z_{\alpha/2} \times \sqrt{\widehat{\sigma}^2(1 + \widehat{\phi}^2)}\right)\right],$$

which retains its validity (under the assumption that ε_t is Gaussian) in the sense that $\Pr\left(x_{T+1} \in \mathfrak{I}_\alpha(x_{T+1})\right) \longrightarrow 1 - \alpha$ as $T \to \infty$. This is relying on the so-called equivariance of the monotonic quantile transformation.

13.3   Other Forecasting Methods and Contexts

We consider some other settings beyond the AR(∞) class of processes.

13.3.1   EWMA Forecasting

The exponential weighted moving average (EWMA) forecast method is due to Holt (1957) and Winters (1960). The idea is to use a recursive structure, which is very easy to update. It is quite widely used in many contexts and without reference to explicit models, which is why it is attractive for some.

Definition 13.1   For an observable series y_t and parameter α, for each $t \geq 1$ let

$$\widehat{y}_{t+1|t} = \alpha y_t + (1 - \alpha)\widehat{y}_{t|t-1} = \widehat{y}_{t|t-1} + \alpha(y_t - \widehat{y}_{t|t-1}), \qquad (13.10)$$

and let $\widehat{y}_{1|0} = y_0$ be some chosen initial value such as the sample average. Then $\widehat{y}_{t+1|t}$ is the EWMA forecast of y_{t+1} based on parameter α.

The parameter $\alpha \in [0, 1]$ determines the weight given to past observations. When $\alpha = 1, \widehat{y}_{T+1|T} = y_T$, while if $\alpha = 0, \widehat{y}_{T+1|T} = y_0$. In general, we have

$$\widehat{y}_{T+1|T} = \sum_{j=1}^{T-1} \alpha(1 - \alpha)^j y_{T-j} + (1 - \alpha)^T y_0.$$

Many applications of this method choose the value α from past experience or by trial and error so that it is not an estimated quantity. This is what makes the method simple and attractive to use. This approach is designed for data without a trend since the multiperiod forecast is $\widehat{y}_{T+k|T} = \widehat{y}_{T+1|T}$. There is a modification called double exponential smoothing designed for trend data and other modifications for seasonal data; see Hyndman and Athanasopoulos (2014) for an exposition of the full bag of tricks.

Note that the EWMA filter can be interpreted as a one-sided kernel smoother with an exponential kernel. Specifically, we have

$$\frac{1}{Th} K\left(\frac{j/T}{h}\right) = \frac{1}{Th} \exp\left(\frac{-j}{Th}\right).$$

Note that $(1 - a/n)^n \to \exp(-a)$ for any a as $n \to \infty$. Therefore, if we let $\alpha = 1/Th$, the two schemes give similar weights. Figure 13.1 shows the two weighting schemes.

The EWMA filter is at the heart of many "trading systems." For example, the **moving average convergence divergence** measure is defined as the difference of two moving averages of prices,

$$\text{MACD} = \text{EWMA}_{12}(P) - \text{EWMA}_{26}(P)$$

and the investor should compare this with the "signal," which is an EWMA of MACD, signal $= \text{EWMA}_9(\text{MACD})$. Figure 13.2 shows an example. These are referred to as 9-, 12-, and 26-day moving averages, but really they are EWMA forecasts with parameter $\alpha = 2/(n + 1)$, where n is the number of days, $n = 9, 12, 26$. That is, the "9-day moving

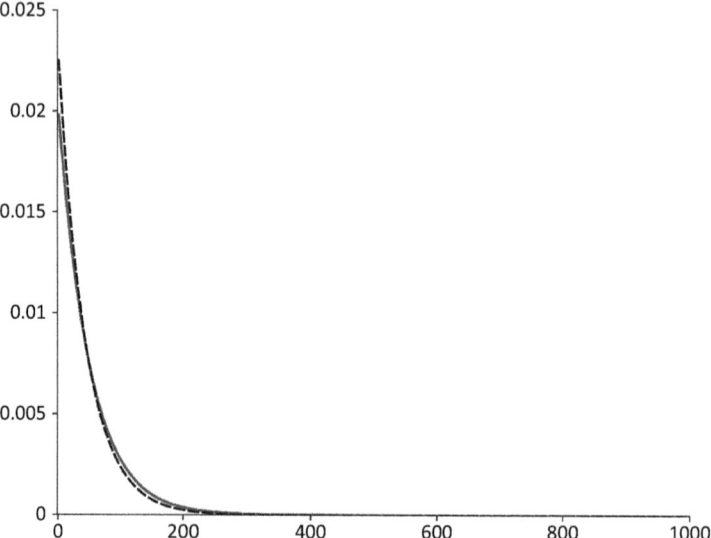

Figure 13.1 EWMA weights and exponential kernel.

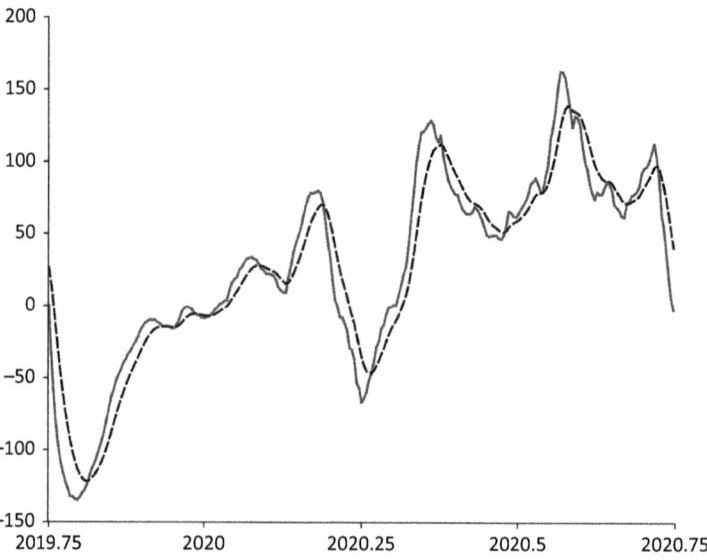

Figure 13.2 MACD (solid) and signal (dashed) for daily Amazon closing prices from 2020.

average" is actually an EWMA with parameter $\alpha = 0.2$. Perhaps the logic of this is that, as $n \to \infty$,

$$\left(1 - \frac{2}{n+1}\right)^{n+1} \to \exp(-2) \simeq 0.135,$$

a number that is mysterious and deep.

13.3.2 Regression Forecasting

Suppose that $y_t = Bx_t + u_t$, where $\{y_t, x_t, t = 1, \ldots, T\}$ are observed data with $y_t \in \mathbb{R}^n$, and $x_t \in \mathbb{R}^K$ are exogenous regressors, while u_t is an error term that satisfies $E(u_t \mid x_t) = 0$. For example, x_t could contain time trends and dummy variables, but it could also contain other stochastically generated variables. Suppose we want to forecast $y_{T+1}, \ldots, y_{T+R}$, and we observe additionally $x_{T+1}, \ldots, x_{T+R}$. We suppose first that u_t is a white noise process. In this case, the prediction is $\widehat{y}_{T+r|T} = \widehat{B}x_{T+r}$, where $\widehat{B}$ are the OLS estimators. The prediction error is

$$y_{T+r} - \widehat{y}_{T+r|T} = u_{T+r} - (\widehat{B} - B)x_{T+r}.$$

Under classical conditions one has the exact formula

$$V_r = E\big((y_{T+r} - \widehat{y}_{T+r|T})(y_{T+r} - \widehat{y}_{T+r|T})^\mathsf{T}\big) = \Sigma_u\big(1 + x_{T+r}^\mathsf{T}(X^\mathsf{T}X)^{-1}x_{T+r}\big),$$

where X is the $T \times K$ matrix of exogenous regressors. If the error term is normally distributed one can show that $\widehat{B}x_{T+r}$ is the BLP of y_{T+r} and is unbiased. If u_t is also normally distributed then $y_{T+r} - \widehat{y}_{T+r|T} \sim N(0, V_r)$ and one can obtain asymptotically valid prediction regions from consistent estimates of Σ_u. For large T the second term is of smaller order and can be dropped. This methodology can also be applied in the context where K is large, and even larger than the sample size T. In that case one first uses a selection method such as LASSO or SCAD to select the relevant covariates and then uses those with selected $\beta_{ij} \neq 0$.

If $x_{T+1}, \ldots, x_{T+R}$ are not observed at the time of forecasting, then one must predict them using some model. Let $\widehat{x}_{T+r|T}$ be such a prediction, and then let $\widehat{y}_{T+r|T} = \widehat{B}\widehat{x}_{T+r|T}$. An example might be if x_t contains lagged y_t (in which case one should think through the dynamic structure). An alternative approach is to run the so-called predictive regressions $y_{t+r} = B_r^\mathsf{T}x_t + u_{t;r}$, which deliver $\widehat{y}_{T+r|T} = \widehat{B}_r x_T$, where $\widehat{B}_r$ is the OLS estimator of B_r in this model. In this case, we may interpret B_r as the slope of the best linear predictor of y_{t+r} by x_t. Only in some special cases will it correspond to a proper regression. For example, if x_t satisfies a VAR process, $x_{t+1} = Ax_t + \varepsilon_{t+1}$, then

$$y_{t+r} = Bx_{t+r} + u_{t+r} = BA^r x_t + u^*_{t+r},$$
$$u^*_{t+r} = B\varepsilon_{t+r} + \cdots + BA^{r-1}\varepsilon_{t+1} + u_{t+r},$$

where $E(u^*_{t+r} \mid x_t) = 0$.

Figure 13.3 shows an application to UK COVID data with a global quadratic trend model ($x_t = 1, t, t^2$) for the log of cases, where the forecast is for cases and involves the back-transform procedure outlined in Section 13.2.3.

13.3.3 Nonparametric Case

In the case where $x_t = y_{t-1}$ we may forecast one step ahead by $\widehat{y}_{T+1|T} = \widehat{m}(y_T)$, with a forecast error that is

$$y_{T+1} - \widehat{y}_{T+1|T} = \varepsilon_{T+1} - (\widehat{m}(y_T) - m(y_T)).$$

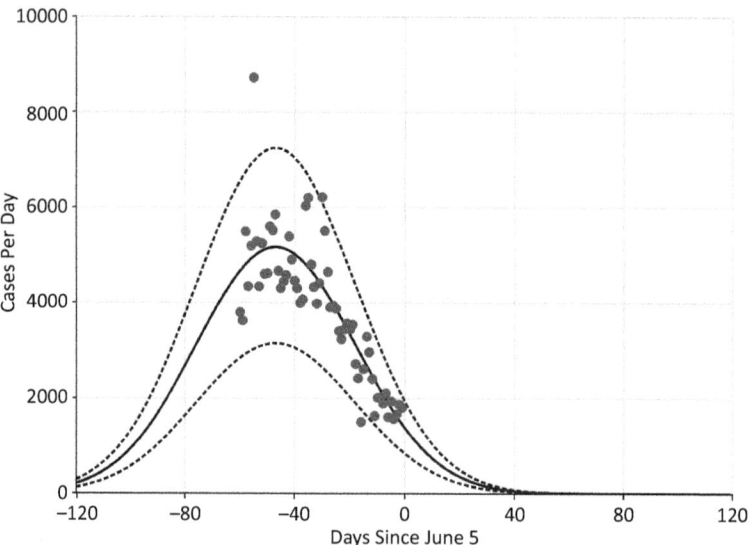

Figure 13.3 Forecast of COVID-19 new daily cases for UK made on June 5, 2020.

Here, we drop the explicit treatment of $\sigma(\cdot)$ and just assume that the distribution of $\varepsilon_{t+1} \mid y_t = x$ is denoted $F(\varepsilon \mid x)$.

The estimation error part is of small order in probability, as in the parametric case, and so to construct the forecast interval we just have to estimate the distribution $F(\varepsilon \mid x)$. In particular, a $1 - \alpha$ prediction interval is

$$\mathfrak{I}_\alpha(1) = \left[\widehat{Q}(\alpha/2 \mid y_T), \widehat{Q}(1 - \alpha/2 \mid y_T)\right],$$

$$\widehat{Q}(\alpha \mid x) = \widehat{F}^{-1}(\alpha \mid x), \qquad \widehat{F}(\varepsilon \mid x) = \frac{\sum_{t=1}^{T-1} K_h(x - y_t) 1(\widehat{\varepsilon}_{t+1} \le \varepsilon)}{\sum_{t=1}^{T-1} K_h(x - y_t)},$$

where $\widehat{\varepsilon}_{t+1} = y_{t+1} - \widehat{m}(y_t)$.

What about forecasting y_{T+2} given $\{y_1, \ldots, y_T\}$? There are two approaches. First, the iteration approach. Notice that

$$y_{T+2} = m(y_{T+1}) + \varepsilon_{T+2} = m(m(y_T) + \varepsilon_{T+1}) + \varepsilon_{T+2}.$$

First, forecast $\widehat{y}_{t+1|t} = \widehat{m}(y_t)$ for sample t. Then smooth y_{t+2} against $\widehat{y}_{t+1|t}$ (call this m_*) and forecast y_{T+2} by $\widehat{y}_{T+2|T} = \widehat{m}_*(\widehat{y}_{T+1|T})$. The second approach may loosely be called nonparametric predictive regression. Define the regression function $m_2(x) = E(y_{t+2} \mid y_t = x)$, and let $\widehat{y}_{T+2|T} = \widehat{m}_2(y_T)$. In this case we construct prediction intervals as in the one-step-ahead case. See Chen, Yang, and Hafner (2004) for a discussion of the relative merits of the two approaches.

We next consider explicitly the case where $x_t = t/T$, which has some special features. What is the forecast for $y_{T+1}, y_{T+2}, \ldots$ in this case? First, note that this regression has a compact support $[0, 1]$ and that estimation at the right boundary is needed for forecasting, so the local constant estimator should be adjusted with a boundary kernel although the local linear estimator is fine as is. In the case where the regression function is smooth (no structural breaks) we have $m((T + k)/T) = m(1) + (k/T)m'(1) + \cdots$, and so one can forecast future values using extrapolation basically: to first order the forecast is constant, to second order it is linear in the horizon, and so on. For the local linear method, we let $\widehat{y}_{T+k|T} = \widehat{m}(1) + (k/T)\widehat{m}'(1)$, where $\widehat{m}(1), \widehat{m}'(1)$ are the local linear intercept and slopes at the right boundary. This forecast is valid for any finite k, and even so for moderately large k such that $k < Th$, where h is the bandwidth. This method, however, does not apply for all horizons since there is no assumption of stationarity here and knowledge of $m(1)$ has nothing to say about $m(2)$, say.

13.4   Forecast Evaluation

Forecast evaluation is a very important activity. We would like to know how good a forecast is in some absolute sense and how it compares with other forecasts, especially if we are going to pay money for it. This is usually done by splitting the sample into an estimation sample and an evaluation sample.

Let the full sample be denoted $\{y_1, \ldots, y_n\}$ with $n = T+R$, let the estimation (**training**) sample be $\{y_1, \ldots, y_T\}$, and let the evaluation (**test**) sample be $\{y_{T+1}, \ldots, y_{T+R}\}$. We then calculate forecasts $\widehat{y}_{T+1|T}, \ldots, \widehat{y}_{T+R|T}$ for all the evaluation sample and compute some measure of performance based on the comparison with the outcomes $y_{T+1}, \ldots, y_{T+R}$. This is really a one-shot comparison. In some cases one cares about specific horizons and wishes to have several comparisons to evaluate. Suppose you are interested in the one-step-ahead forecast. In that case, one might compute $\widehat{y}_{T+1|T}, \widehat{y}_{T+2|T+1}, \ldots, \widehat{y}_{T+R|T+R-1}$, which allows for multiple comparisons. That is, one reestimates whatever model one is using with all of the available data $\{y_1, \ldots, y_{T+r}\}$ to forecast y_{T+r+1}. In this way one obtains R comparisons of the one-step-ahead forecast.

We may consider rolling or recursive "estimation" windows. That is, we may use data $\{y_{T+r-k}, \ldots, y_{T+r}\}$ to compute the forecast of y_{T+r+1} with k some integer such that $1 \leq k \leq T + r - 1$. The recursive window (or full-sample scheme) takes $k = T + r - 1$ and all the data is used. Alternatively, one may use, say, the most recent five years of data in a forecasting scheme, which we denote by $T + r - k : T + r$. This is called a rolling window scheme. It protects against parameter nonconstancy, as we have seen. Note that rolling windows overlap a lot, so that the evaluation errors $y_{T+r+1} - y_{T+r+1|T+r-k:T}$ will be highly correlated.

Define the performance measures

$$\text{MSPE} = \frac{1}{R} \sum_{r=1}^{R} (\widehat{y}_{T+r|T+r-1} - y_{T+r})^2, \quad \text{MAPE} = \frac{1}{R} \sum_{r=1}^{R} |\widehat{y}_{T+r|T+r-1} - y_{T+r}|,$$

which correspond to sample versions of $E(L(\widehat{y}_{T+1|T}, y_{T+1}))$, where $L(x, y) = (x - y)^2$ and $|x - y|$ respectively. In fact, it is common practice to also work with the RMSPE, the square root of MSPE. The interpretation of RMSPE is like a standard deviation. We can write $\widehat{y} - y = \widehat{y} - \overline{\widehat{y}} + \overline{\widehat{y}} - \overline{y} + \overline{y} - y$, dropping subscripts, and obtain the decomposition of the MSPE into

$$\text{MSPE} = \frac{1}{R} \sum_{r=1}^{R} \left(\widehat{y}_{T+r|T+r-1} - \overline{\widehat{y}}\right)^2 + \left(\overline{\widehat{y}} - \overline{y}\right)^2$$

$$+ \frac{1}{R} \sum_{r=1}^{R} (y_{T+r} - \overline{y})^2 - \frac{2}{R} \sum_{r=1}^{R} \left(\widehat{y}_{T+r|T+r-1} - \overline{\widehat{y}}\right)(y_{T+r} - \overline{y}).$$

The first term concerns the variability of the forecast itself around its average, the second captures any systematic bias within the forecast sample, and the third captures the variability of the forecasted outcome. The final term is the covariance of the forecast with the outcome. For a well-specified model we would expect $(\bar{\hat{y}} - \bar{y})^2$ to be small.

These measures depend on the scale of the data, which makes it hard to compare across series or across transformations of the same series. Some authors have advocated normalization by the target, that is, $\hat{y}_{T+r|T} - y_{T+r} \to (\hat{y}_{T+r|T} - y_{T+r})/y_{T+r}$, in which case the above measures are called percentage MSE and so on. This approach works well when y never gets close to zero, but otherwise it can perform poorly (Hyndman and Koehler, 2006). More acceptable is to work with performance measures that are normalized against some benchmark. For example, let $\hat{y}^*_{T+r|T}$ be a benchmark forecast such as the sample mean, then consider

$$\frac{\sum_{r=1}^{R} L(\hat{y}_{T+r|T}, y_{T+r})}{\sum_{r=1}^{R} L(\hat{y}^*_{T+r|T}, y_{T+r})}$$

for whichever loss function L. This is, by construction, between zero and infinity, with the smaller the value the better.

Campbell and Thompson (2008) proposed the out-of-sample R^2, which is defined in this case as

$$R^2_{\text{OOS}} = 1 - \frac{\sum_{r=1}^{R} (y_{T+r} - \hat{y}_{T+r|T})^2}{\sum_{r=1}^{R} (y_{T+r} - \bar{y})^2}, \tag{13.11}$$

where $\bar{y}$ is the sample mean of observations using the sample information. This is just a relocation of the general measure that is constrained to lie in $[0, 1]$, where the value 1 measures perfect performance. If we are considering one-step-ahead forecasts we may want to revise the estimation sample each time. That is, for forecasting $T + j$ we use the estimation sample $\{y_1, \ldots, y_{T+j-1}\}$ and compare with the mean $\bar{y}_{1:T+j-1}$ of the new estimation sample, that is,

$$R^2_{\text{OOS},j} = 1 - \frac{\sum_{j=1}^{R} (y_{T+j} - \hat{y}_{T+j|T+j-1})^2}{\sum_{j=1}^{R} (y_{T+j} - \bar{y}_{1:T+j-1})^2}.$$

The choice between these two methods depends on the purpose of the exercise.

It is not necessary to have a fully specified model to forecast. In fact, a model that fits the data well in sample may do poorly at forecasting **out of sample**. At the extreme case one may perfectly fit the sample data (the in-sample R^2 is one), but such approaches generally fail to forecast the future well. Unfortunately it is equally true that a procedure that forecasts well in one period is not guaranteed to forecast well in another period.

13.4.1   Record of Macroeconomic Forecasters

Macroeconomists regularly provide forecasts of output, inflation, unemployment, and interest rates. There is a long track record of some official forecasters like the Congressional Budget Office (CBO) and the Federal Reserve Board Federal Open Market Committee (FOMC) members; likewise private sector organizations like Blue Chip who aggregate private sector forecasts. The CBO reports the mean error and the RMSPE as

Table 13.1 Performance of difference central banks in forecasting inflation.

Horizon	Period	BoE	ECB	Riks	BoC	Norges	RBNZ
One year	2015–2019	0.64	0.67	0.38	0.41	1.02	0.65
	2020Q1–2021Q1	1.02	0.96	1.12	1.30	0.71	0.46
	2021Q1–2023Q2	4.60	4.99	5.01	3.07	3.63	4.22
One quarter	2015–2019	0.20	0.31	0.25	0.23	0.37	0.40
	2020Q1–2021Q1	0.38	0.46	0.81	0.42	0.71	0.56
	2021Q10-2023Q2	1.23	1.38	1.76	0.70	1.12	1.27

well as the "two-thirds spread" of forecast errors ($Q_{5/6} - Q_{1/6}$). The mean error is reported to capture systematic biases in their forecasts. A variety of structural and nonstructural time series methods are deployed to deliver forecasts (Diebold, 1998). There are many reasons why macroeconomic forecasts fail or appear to fail: turning points in the business cycle; changes in labor productivity trends; changes in crude oil prices; the persistent decline in interest rates; the decline in the labor share—that is, labor income as a share of GDP; and data revisions. Primiceri and Tambalotti (2020) drew attention to some specific issues in macroeconomic forecasting that arose out of the pandemic and the big changes in the economy that it delivered. Bernanke (2024) provided a detailed review of the forecasting methods of the Bank of England, focusing specifically on inflation (for which it has a target), unemployment, and GDP, and made some comparisons with other institutions. Table 13.1 is taken from his report and shows the RMSPEs of one-year-ahead and one-quarter-ahead inflation forecasts by different central banks since 2015 broken down into subperiods. According to this comparison the Bank of England did very well in terms of short-term forecasting until 2021, and somewhat less well in terms of annual horizon. All the institutions' forecasting methods suffered a substantial drop in performance in the most recent period. A 4.60 RMSPE performance compared with a target of 2% is clearly little more than guesswork. This also hides the fact that the forecasts were systematically lower than target rather than equally too high and too low.

The Bank of England is famous for its **fan charts**, which are essentially prediction intervals for different levels of α plotted together with different shading. These are constructed using the past history of forecast errors apparently with a split normal distribution, where the skewness parameter can be determined partially by human (i.e., the Monetary Policy Committee) input. The precise methodology is available in the R package `fanplot`.

Bernanke made a number of recommendations for forecast practice. For example, that longer-term inflation expectations should not be anchored to the central bank target rate. He is also not a fan of the fan chart, saying they have weak conceptual foundations.

13.4.2 Record of Financial Market Forecasters

Meese and Rogoff (1983) showed that it is very hard to beat the random walk model in forecasting monthly exchange rates by structural models or other time series models such as VAR using a number of predictors. Diebold and Nason (1990) showed the same results for weekly exchange rates and also compared with kernel smoothing autoregressions. Rossi (2013) reviewed the literature and concluded:

Overall, our analysis of the literature and the data suggests that the answer to the question: "Are exchange rates predictable?" is, "It depends" – on the choice of predictor, forecast horizon, sample period, model, and forecast evaluation method. Predictability is most apparent when one or more of the following hold: the predictors are Taylor rule or net foreign assets, the model is linear, and a small number of parameters are estimated. The toughest benchmark is the random walk without drift.

Similar results are available for stock returns – the historical mean model is hard to beat for stock returns. Patterns of autocorrelation seem to change over time. Pesaran and Timmermann (1995) considered monthly stock returns. There is a literature on long-horizon stock market predictability (Cochrane, 1999), but this evidence has been questioned by Goyal and Welch (2003). Every year analysts forecast the stock market level at the end of the following calendar year. For example (as of November 21, 2022) Barclays forecasted a 2023 year-end S&P500 of 3675, with the following comment:

We acknowledge some upside risks to our scenario analysis given post-peak inflation, strong consumer balance sheets and a resilient labor market. However, current multiples are baking in a sharp moderation in inflation and ultimately a soft landing, which we continue to believe is a low probability event.

The actual year-end value was 4770. Of course, others such as Deutsche Bank forecasted higher outcomes of 4500 (as of November 28, 2022). Overall there is a substantial dispersion in the forecasts issued by professional investors.

There is also extensive literature on forecasting listed companies' quarterly earnings announcements. Analysts constantly produce forecasts of company earnings and these are available on the I/B/E/S (Institutional Brokers' Estimate System) and Value Line websites, for example. They may use a variety of methods to do so and post forecasts for near-term and longer-term earnings, and common practice is to calculate the earnings surprise based on the consensus of the analysts' forecasts from the day before the announcement. Ball and Watts (1972) argued that earnings follow a random walk. Brown and Rozeff (1979) argued that analysts' forecasts outperformed "less naïve" time series models, especially at longer forecast horizons. Brown *et al.* (1987) argued that analysts' forecast superiority over time series models is due to a timing advantage and an information advantage. Nowadays many new sources of information are available, including some nonstandard ones like satellite pictures of parking lots. These new types of data require new tools for producing forecasts. Chen *et al.* (2022) applied machine learning to a large set of detailed financial information aimed at predicting the direction of future earnings changes. They obtained significant out-of-sample predictive power concerning the direction of earnings changes.

We close this discussion with a presentation of Amazon earnings per share estimates (from I/B/E/S) and the outturn during the pandemic of 2020 in Table 13.2. Clearly, analysts were consistently underestimating the earnings of Amazon during the first phase of the pandemic. In Figure 13.4 we fit a regression-based forecast to the earnings; this also fails to capture what is going on in 2020.

Table 13.2 Amazon quarterly earnings per share forecast and outturn.

Date	Actual	Estimate
Q1 2020	5.01	6.25
Q2 2020	10.30	1.46
Q3 2020	12.37	7.41
Q4 2020	14.09	7.23
Q1 2021	15.79	9.37

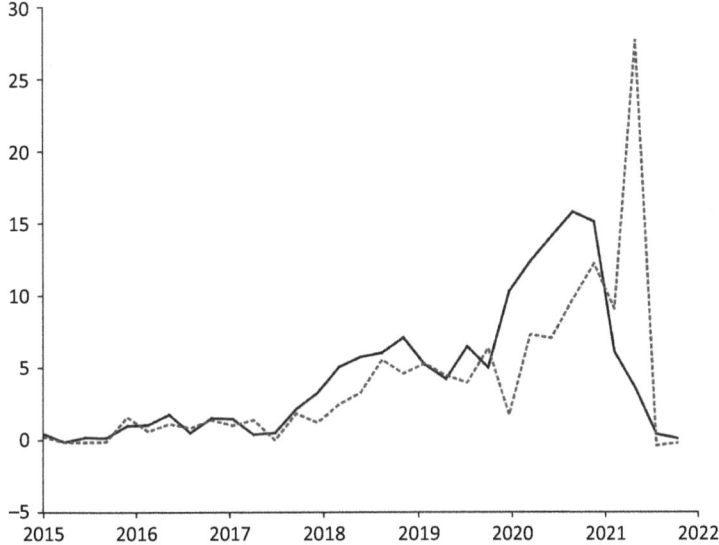

Figure 13.4 Quarterly Amazon earnings per share along with forecast based on quarterly dummies and quadratic trend. The solid line is the actual and the dashed line is the forecast.

13.4.3 Record of Weather Forecasters

The first ever daily weather forecast was published in *The Times* newspaper on August 1, 1861. Nowadays common practice involves large-scale models with hundreds of thousands of nonlinear partial differential equations solved by numerical methods based on real-time data recorded at many locations. There are several commonly used ways of evaluating the performance. The skill score,

$$\frac{\text{RMSPE}_{\text{norm}} - \text{RMSPE}}{\text{RMSPE}_{\text{norm}}},$$

where $\text{RMSPE}_{\text{norm}}$ is the root mean squared error based on a climate benchmark (such as the historical average temperature on that day, or yesterday's temperature). Trend correlation is measured by

$$\text{TC} = \text{corr}((\widehat{y}_s - \widehat{y}_{s-1}), (y_s - y_{s-1}))$$

for an outcome y with forecast $\widehat{y}$. The Brier score is widely used for probabilistic forecasts of precipitation, for example. The most common formulation of the Brier score is

$$\text{BS} = \frac{1}{N} \sum_{t=1}^{N} (p_t - o_t)^2 ,$$

where p_t was the probability that was forecast while o_t is the binary indicator of whether the forecast event occurred or not, and N is the number of forecasting instances. The Brier skill score (like an R^2) is defined as

$$\text{BSS} = 1 - \frac{\text{BS}}{\text{BS}_{\text{ref}}},$$

where BS_{ref} is the Brier score of reference or baseline predictions that the forecast seeks to improve on. Haiden *et al.* (2021) documented the improvements in European weather forecasting over time in terms of several metrics, including the Brier skill score.

13.4.4 Statistical Tests about Forecasts

These measures can compare the forecasting performance of different methods. An alternative way of comparing two forecasts is to carry out a statistical test of the null hypothesis that the two forecasts have equal predictive power against the alternative that one is superior.

Suppose that $\widehat{y}_{T+h|T}$ is a forecast of a variable y_{T+h}. We may be interested in whether this is an unbiased forecast. To test whether it is we may run the Mincer–Zarnowitz regression,

$$y_{T+h} = \alpha + \beta \widehat{y}_{T+h|T} + u_{T+h},$$

and test whether $\alpha = 0$ and $\beta = 1$. To do this effectively we need a large number of such forecasts, that is, for many T. We note that if this is carried out using all the in-sample observations one obtains $\alpha = 0$ and $\beta = 1$ with probability one. If $\widehat{y}_{T+h|T}$ is generated from some nonlinear method or we are using out-of-sample data then this is not necessarily true and the regression provides evidence about whether the forecast is unbiased or not.

Often, more than one forecast is available (for example, the Central Bank, the Treasury, the International Monetary Fund (IMF), and so on). Diebold and Mariano (1995) proposed a test of **equal predictive accuracy**. Let there be two forecasts of a series y_{T+j} with errors $\widehat{\varepsilon}_j$ and $\widehat{\varepsilon}_j^*$, $j = 1, \ldots, R$. We consider the null hypothesis that the two errors have the same mean. In practice, they may both be highly autocorrelated, which requires that one take account of this. Let

$$S = \frac{(1/\sqrt{R}) \sum_{j=1}^{R} d_j}{\sqrt{\widehat{\text{lrvar}}(d_j)}}, \tag{13.12}$$

where $d_j = \widehat{\varepsilon}_j - \widehat{\varepsilon}_j^*$ and $\widehat{\text{lrvar}}(d_j)$ is an estimate of the long-run variance $\text{lrvar}(d_j)$ of the series d_j. Provided the evaluation sample size R is large and provided the forecast errors are stationary or approximately so, S can be approximated by a standard normal random variable.

We have two forecasts, f_T and g_T, of an outcome at time $T + r$. We consider a loss function L_{T+r} such as the mean squared prediction error. We wish to test the hypothesis of equal predictive ability,

$$H_0: E\left[L_{T+r}(y_{T+r}, f_T) - L_{T+r}(y_{T+r}, g_T)\right] = 0,$$

which is the Diebold and Mariano framework.

Alternatively, given information $\mathcal{H}_t$, we may wish to test the hypothesis of equal conditional predictive ability,

$$H_0: E\left[L_{T+r}(y_{T+r}, f_T) - L_{T+r}(y_{T+r}, g_T) \mid \mathcal{H}_T\right] = 0,$$

with probability one.

We suppose that we carry out the forecasts over many, perhaps overlapping, periods.

13.5 Forecast Combination

Suppose you have multiple forecasts $f_{1,T+r}, \ldots, f_{K,T+r}$ of outcome y_{T+r} for $r = 1, \ldots, R$. We have discussed ways of comparing these forecasts according to some criterion function and testing whether they have equal predictive ability. This line of work leads towards a "best forecast." Instead, we consider here the concept of model averaging or forecast combination whereby one combines the forecasts of different models in some way; see Hansen (2007) for further discussion. For example, suppose that we consider all the univariate linear regression forecasts (short regressions) of the outcome y_{T+1},

$$\widehat{y}_{T+1|k} = x_{k,T+1} \frac{x_k^\mathsf{T} y}{x_k^\mathsf{T} x_k},$$

for $k = 1, \ldots, K$. Then let $\widehat{y}_{T+1|\text{MA}} = \sum_{k=1}^{K} w_k \widehat{y}_{T+1|k}$, where w_k are weights that satisfy $\sum_{k=1}^{K} w_k = 1$. By linear regression theory we can choose the weights so that $\widehat{y}_{T+1|\text{MA}} = \widehat{y}_{T+1|1,\ldots,K}$, but this involves inverting the $K \times K$ matrix $X^\mathsf{T} X$, so we might as well just fit the long regression. Instead, we might take $w_k = 1/K$ to avoid this matrix inversion. The real benefit of model averaging comes in nonlinear models, and this technology is widely used in combination with neural networks and other machine learning techniques. Chen *et al.* (2018) showed how to use model averaging to combine univariate kernel smoothing on different lags of different covariates to produce better predictions and to avoid the curse of dimensionality from high-dimensional nonparametric regression.

One common application is in weather forecasting where two models may be proposed for forecasting tomorrow's temperature: the long-term seasonal forecast, for example the average temperature based on the same day in the last T calendar years, or the short-term forecast from, say, an EWMA process fitted to historical data. We let

$$\widehat{y}_{T+1|T} = \lambda \widehat{y}_{T+1|T,\text{EWMA}} + (1 - \lambda)\widehat{y}_{T+1|T,\text{LR}}.$$

13.6 Application

We compare the random walk model versus the deterministic trend for the daily (logarithm of) S&P500 index. The random walk plus drift model is $y_t = \mu + y_{t-1} + \varepsilon_t$, where $y_t = \log(P_t)$ and ε_t is i.i.d. with mean zero and variance σ^2. This model is hard to beat. We estimate μ by $\widehat{\mu} = \sum_{t=2}^{T} \Delta y_t / T$ and σ^2 by $\widehat{\sigma}^2 = \sum_{t=2}^{T} (\Delta y_t - \widehat{\mu})^2 / T$. We forecast

Figure 13.5 Random walk forecast of log of stock prices.

future values by $\widehat{y}_{T+k|T} = y_T + k\widehat{\mu}$, which grows linearly with the horizon. The forecast error variance is $\sigma^2_{T+k|T} = k\sigma^2$ in the absence of parameter estimation, so we compute the prediction bands as $\widehat{y}_{T+k|T} \pm z_{\alpha/2}\sqrt{k}\widehat{\sigma}$. We take as our forecast evaluation period the days since the Trump inauguration of January 20, 2016, and we take as the estimation sample the period of equal length preceding that.[2] The forecast made on inauguration day was extrapolated from then to the end of his term, that is, we do not reestimate the model every day; this is shown in Figure 13.5. It seems that there was outperformance of the stock market during this period relative to what was predicted (despite the COVID-19 dip) but that this was within the range of uncertainty estimated from the data. The estimation period is relatively short here, or rather the prediction period is rather long. We did the same exercise using four presidential terms for estimation data and obtained similar results.

We next use a deterministic trend model. We modify the standard linear trend so that the trend must pass through the last observation, which makes the method more comparable with the random walk method. That is, we suppose that $y_T = \alpha + \beta T$, which leads to the regression of $y_t - y_T = \beta(t - T) + \varepsilon_t$. The forecast is

$$\widehat{y}_{T+k|T} = \widehat{\alpha} + \widehat{\beta}(T + k) = y_T + k\widehat{\beta},$$

which is shown in Figure 13.6. The error bands are based on the estimated standard deviation of the residuals from the estimation sample. The long-term forecast in this case happens to be quite similar to the random walk forecast. The main difference is in the error bands, which for the random walk model are much wider and growing (at a rate

---

[2] We could have taken the election day, the electoral college vote day, or a number of other starting points.

Figure 13.6 Trend forecast of log of S&P500.

of the square root of the horizon) with the horizon, whereas the error bands for the deterministic trend model are more optimistic. Consequently, the deterministic trend model suggests significant departures, whereas the random walk model does not support this. We also calculated the nonparametric bands that used directly the quantiles of the residual distribution, but in this case there was not much difference.

The MSPE of the deterministic trend model is 0.034 765 368 and of the random walk model 0.026 868 152, while the MAPE of the deterministic trend model is 0.175 010 50 compared with 0.154 092 44 for the random walk, so the random walk is marginally better than the trend model according to these criteria. The Diebold–Mariano test statistic (assuming i.i.d. errors) is 58.94, which is strongly against the null of equal predictive ability.

We now consider the implied forecast and error bands for the level of prices. We take

$$\widehat{P}_{T+k|T} = \exp(\widehat{y}_{T+k|T})\widehat{m}, \qquad \widehat{m} = \frac{1}{T}\sum_{t=1}^{T} \exp(\widehat{\varepsilon}_t)$$

as our point forecast, and the prediction bands are of the form

$$\left(\widehat{P}_{T+k|T} \exp(-z_{\alpha/2}c\widehat{\sigma}), \widehat{P}_{T+k|T} \exp(z_{\alpha/2}c\widehat{\sigma})\right),$$

where in the random walk case $c = \sqrt{k}$, while in the linear trend case $c = 1$. The forecasts and the forecast intervals are shown in Figures 13.7 and 13.8. In both cases the intervals are asymmetric because the exponential function transforms the symmetric interval for the log of prices in this way. It would be possible to construct a symmetric interval for prices, but then this would not respect the fact that prices are positive.

Figure 13.7 Random walk model forecast of stock price level.

Figure 13.8 Deterministic trend-based forecast of stock price level.

13.7   Summary

We considered the problem of forecasting future values of a time series based on a sample of data. We considered both model-based and model-free (or nonparametric) approaches. We considered different ways of evaluating forecasting performance and of comparing different forecast methods. The R language has several packages for forecasting, including `forecast`. Hyndman and Athanasopoulos (2014) is a practical introduction. The elephant in the room is Diebold (2017), which is a comprehensive treatment of all things forecasting.

13.8   Exercises

13.1 Suppose that $y_t = \phi y_{t-1} + \varepsilon_t$, where ε_t is i.i.d. with mean zero and variance $\sigma^2 < \infty$. Assume that ϕ is known and let $\widehat{y}_{T+h|T} = \phi^h y_T$. Consider $e_{T+h|T} = y_{T+h} - \widehat{y}_{T+h|T}$, $h = 1, \ldots, H$. For $k \neq h$, calculate $\text{cov}(e_{T+h|T}, e_{T+k|T})$.

13.2 Suppose that $y_t = \varepsilon_t - \theta \varepsilon_{t-1}$, where ε_t is i.i.d. with mean zero and variance $\sigma^2 < \infty$, and $\theta \in (-1, 1)$. Assume that θ is known. Define the optimal forecast of y_{T+h}, denoted $\widehat{y}_{T+h|T}$, based on data $\{y_1, \ldots, y_T\}$. Consider $e_{T+h|T} = y_{T+h} - \widehat{y}_{T+h|T}$, $h = 1, \ldots, H$. Calculate $\text{cov}(e_{T+h|T}, e_{T+k|T})$ for $k \neq h$.

13.3 Suppose that $y_t = \phi y_{t-1} + \varepsilon_t$, where ε_t is i.i.d. $N(0, \sigma^2)$. Derive the optimal forecast of the average future value $\bar{y}_{T|T+r} = (1/r) \sum_{j=1}^{r} y_{T+j}$. For example, we have daily data but we are interested in the average value of an outcome in the coming month that we expect to materialize.

13.4 Suppose that

$$y_t = \mu + y_{t-1} + u_t, \qquad u_t = \sigma_t \varepsilon_t$$

$$\sigma_t^2 = \omega + \beta \sigma_{t-1}^2 + \gamma u_{t-1}^2,$$

where ε_t is i.i.d. standard normal.
(a) How would you forecast y_{T+1} based on the sample $y_1, \ldots, y_T$?
(b) How would you forecast $x_{T+1} = \exp(y_{T+1})$ based on the sample $x_1, \ldots, x_T$?
(c) How would you construct a prediction interval for x_{T+1}?

13.5 Suppose that $y_t \in \mathbb{R}^n$ follows the VAR(2) process

$$y_t = \mu + A_1(y_{t-1} - \mu) + A_2(y_{t-2} - \mu) + \varepsilon_t,$$

where $\varepsilon_t \sim N(0, \Omega_\varepsilon)$. You have the sample $\{y_1, \ldots, y_T\}$, and the parameters μ, A_1, A_2, and Ω_ε are known. Explain how to forecast:
(a) $y_{1,T+r}$
(b) $y_{1,T+r} + \cdots + y_{n,T+r}$.
Provide forecast intervals for both cases.

13.6 Suppose that the monthly inflation rate $(\log(P_t) - \log(P_{t-1}))$ calculated from the dataset CPIAUCNS follows an AR(12) process. Estimate the model using data from 191901 to 201912. Forecast inflation for $202001, 202002, \ldots, 202012$. Now reestimate the model using data from 191901 to 202012 and forecast inflation for $202101, 202102, \ldots, 202112$. Now reestimate the model using data from 191901 to 202112 and forecast inflation for $202201, \ldots, 202212$. Now reestimate the model using data from 191901 to 202212 and forecast inflation for $202301, \ldots, 202312$. How did you do? Compute the RMSPE of your forecast.

13.7 Do the same exercise as in the previous question except you update the estimation sample monthly. That is, estimate the model using data from 191901 to 201912. Forecast inflation for 202001. Now reestimate the model using data from 191901 to 202001 and forecast inflation for 202002, and so on. How much does your performance improve? Do you want to be a central banker now?

13.8 Do the same exercise as in the previous question and for each forecast compute the 90% forecast interval (this is central bank standard) and count how many times the realization fell inside the projected forecast interval. Try two different intervals:
(a) assuming normal distribution
(b) assuming i.i.d. shocks and using the empirical distribution constructed from the sample.

13.9 Suppose that $y_t = \phi y_{t-1} + \varepsilon_t$, where ε_t is i.i.d. with mean zero and variance $\sigma^2 < \infty$. Assume that ϕ is known and let $\widehat{y}_{T+r|T+r-1} = \phi y_{T+r-1}$. Calculate the expected value of the components in the decomposition

$$\text{MSE} = \frac{1}{R} \sum_{r=1}^{R} \left(\widehat{y}_{T+r|T+r-1} - \overline{\overline{y}} \right)^2 + \left(\overline{\overline{y}} - \overline{y} \right)^2$$

$$+ \frac{1}{R} \sum_{r=1}^{R} (y_{T+r} - \overline{y})^2 - \frac{2}{R} \sum_{r=1}^{R} \left(\widehat{y}_{T+r|T+r-1} - \overline{\overline{y}} \right)(y_{T+r} - \overline{y}).$$

13.10 (Bayesian forecasting). Suppose that $y_t = \phi y_{t-1} + \varepsilon_t$, where ε_t is i.i.d. Gaussian with mean zero and variance 1. Suppose that the prior for ϕ is $U(-1, 1)$. Calculate the Bayesian predictive density (13.1) in the absence of any data. Now let $\{y_1, \ldots, y_T\}$ be the observed data. Calculate the Bayesian predictive density (13.1) based on the posterior density obtained from this data.

13.11 For the HAR model

$$y_t = \mu + \beta(y_{t-1} - \mu + \cdots + y_{t-10} - \mu) + \gamma(y_{t-11} - \mu + \cdots + y_{t-66} - \mu) + \varepsilon_t,$$

where $\varepsilon_t \sim N(0, \sigma^2)$, what is the optimal forecast $y_{T+r|T}$ and the forecast error $e_{T+r|T}$ for $r = 1, \ldots 66$ assuming knowledge of the parameters? Using $y_t = \log(\text{VIX}_t)$ from the dataset VIX, fit the model using the data up to 2023 and implement the forecast.

13.12 Suppose that $y_t = \phi_1 y_{t-1} + \phi_2 y_{t-2} + \phi_3 y_{t-3} + \varepsilon_t - \theta \varepsilon_{t-1}$ is a stationary and invertible ARMA(3,1) process with ε_t i.i.d. with mean zero and variance σ^2.
(a) Write an expression for $\widehat{y}_{T+1|T}$ that involves $E(\varepsilon_T \mid y_1, \ldots, y_T)$.
(b) Now write a recursive expression for $\widehat{y}_{T+r|T}$ that involves $\widehat{y}_{T+1|T}, \ldots, \widehat{y}_{T+r-1|T}$ only.
(c) How does one in principle obtain an expression for $E(\varepsilon_T \mid y_1, \ldots, y_T)$?
(d) Derive an expression for the prediction error variance for $\widehat{y}_{T+1|T}$.

13.13 Suppose that $y_t = \mu + u_t$, $u_t = \sigma_t \varepsilon_t$, $\sigma_t^2 = \omega + \beta \sigma_{t-1}^2 + \gamma u_{t-1}^2$. Show that, for $r = 1, 2 \ldots$, $\sigma_{T+r|T}^2 = \omega + (\beta + \gamma)\sigma_{T+r-1|T}^2$, where $\sigma_{T+r|T}^2 = E(\sigma_{T+r}^2 \mid y_T, \ldots, y_1, \ldots)$ and $\sigma_{T+1|T}^2 = \omega + \beta \sigma_T^2 + \gamma u_T^2$. Therefore, argue that $\sigma_{T+r|T}^2 = \delta_0 + \sum_{j=0}^{\infty} \varphi_j u_{T-j}^2$ and give the precise form of δ_0 and φ_j. Derive a forecast for future values of $(y_{T+r} - \mu)^2$ given $y_T, \ldots, y_1$.

13.14 Using the Covid19 dataset, extract the time series of cases and deaths from COVID-19 for France over the period 20200101–20201214. Use the EWMA forecasting model to forecast new deaths over the month of June given data from January to May, and evaluate the performance of this forecast. Try different parameter values and different estimation/evaluation samples.

APPENDIX A

Fourier Analysis

We first review a little of the background mathematics. For an integrable function $g \colon \mathbb{R} \to \mathbb{R}$, we may define its Fourier transform as

$$\widehat{g}(\lambda) = \mathcal{F}(g)(\lambda) = \int_{-\infty}^{\infty} g(t) \exp(-2\pi i \lambda t) \, dt, \tag{A.1}$$

where $\widehat{g}(\lambda) \colon \mathbb{R} \to \mathbb{R}$, and its inverse,

$$g(t) = \mathcal{F}^{-1}(\widehat{g})(t) = \int_{-\infty}^{\infty} \widehat{g}(\lambda) \exp(2\pi i \lambda t) \, d\lambda. \tag{A.2}$$

The Fourier transform possesses several useful properties. First, it is linear, that is, for real-valued α, β and functions g, h we have $\mathcal{F}(\alpha g + \beta h)(\lambda) = \alpha \mathcal{F}(g)(\lambda) + \beta \mathcal{F}(h)(\lambda)$. Second, the Fourier transform of a sinusoid with frequency λ_0 is the **Dirac delta** function δ at $\pm \lambda_0$, that is, for $g(k) = \exp(2\pi \lambda_0 k)$, $\mathcal{F}(g)(\lambda) = \delta(\lambda - \lambda_0)$. It follows that

$$\mathcal{F}(\cos(2\pi \lambda_0 \cdot))(\lambda) = \frac{1}{2} \left[\delta(\lambda - \lambda_0) + \delta(\lambda + \lambda_0) \right],$$

$$\mathcal{F}(\sin(2\pi \lambda_0 \cdot))(\lambda) = \frac{1}{2i} \left[\delta(\lambda - \lambda_0) - \delta(\lambda + \lambda_0) \right].$$

Third, a time shift induces a phase shift in the Fourier transform. For a function $g(\cdot)$,

$$\mathcal{F}(g(\cdot - k_0))(\lambda) = \mathcal{F}(g(\cdot)(\lambda) \exp(-2\pi i \lambda k_0).$$

Finally, the Fourier transform of the convolution is the product of the Fourier transforms, that is, $\mathcal{F}(g * f) = \mathcal{F}(g)\mathcal{F}(f)$, where $(g * f)(u) = \int g(t) f(u - t) \, dt$. These properties are shared with the characteristic function.

A.1 Complex Geometric Series

For any complex number z with $|z| < 1$,

$$\sum_{k=0}^{\infty} z^k = \frac{1}{1 - z}.$$

Therefore,

$$1 + \sum_{k=1}^{\infty} z^k + \sum_{k=1}^{\infty} \overline{z}^k = \frac{1}{1 - z} + \frac{1}{1 - \overline{z}} - 1 = \frac{1 - \overline{z} + 1 - z - (1 - z)(1 - \overline{z})}{(1 - z)(1 - \overline{z})}$$

$$= \frac{1 - z\overline{z}}{(1 - z)(1 - \overline{z})} = \frac{1 - |z|}{|1 - z|}.$$

If $z = \phi \exp(i\lambda)$, then $|z| = \phi^2$ and

$$|1 - z| = (1 - \phi \exp(i\lambda))(1 - \phi \exp(-i\lambda)) = 1 - 2\phi \cos(\lambda) + \phi^2. \tag{A.3}$$

APPENDIX B

Matrices and Multivariate Normal

For an $n \times m$ matrix A, we let $\text{vec}(A)$ denote the rowwise vectorization. For an $n \times n$ matrix A, we let $\text{vech}(A)$ denote the upper part of the matrix in a row vector. So, for

$$A = \begin{pmatrix} a_{11} & a_{12} \\ a_{21} & a_{22} \end{pmatrix},$$

$\text{vec}(A) = (a_{11}, a_{12}, a_{21}, a_{22})^{\mathsf{T}}$ and $\text{vech}(A) = (a_{11}, a_{12}, a_{22})^{\mathsf{T}}$. $\text{Tr}(A)$ is the trace (the sum of the diagonal elements) and $\det(A)$ is the determinant of a square matrix A. For two matrices A, B ($n \times m$ and $p \times q$), the Kronecker product $A \otimes B$ denotes the $np \times mq$ matrix with blocks $A_{ij}B$. A useful property is that $\text{vec}(ABC) = (C^{\mathsf{T}} \otimes A)\text{vec}(B)$. Magnus and Neudecker (1988) is the absolute gold standard for matrix calculations.

Definition B.1   We say that $X = (X_1, \ldots, X_k) \sim N(\mu, \Sigma)$ when

$$f_X(x \mid \mu, \Sigma) = \frac{1}{(2\pi)^{k/2} \det(\Sigma)} \exp\left(-\frac{1}{2}(x - \mu)^{\mathsf{T}} \Sigma^{-1}(x - \mu) \right),$$

where Σ is a $k \times k$ covariance matrix,

$$\Sigma = \begin{pmatrix} \sigma_{11} & \sigma_{12} & \cdots & \sigma_{1k} \\ & \ddots & & \vdots \\ & & & \sigma_{kk} \end{pmatrix},$$

and $\det(\Sigma)$ is the determinant of Σ. The characteristic function of X is

$$\varphi_X(t \mid \mu, \Sigma) = \exp\left(-t^{\mathsf{T}}\mu + \frac{1}{2}t^{\mathsf{T}}\Sigma t \right)$$

for any $t \in \mathbb{R}^k$.

Theorem B.1

(i) *If $X \sim N(\mu, \Sigma)$ then $X_1 \sim N(\mu_1, \sigma_{11})$, which is shown by integration of the joint density with respect to the other variables.*

(ii) *The conditional distributions of $X = (X_a^{\mathsf{T}}, X_b^{\mathsf{T}})^{\mathsf{T}}$ are Gaussian too,*

$$f_{X_a|X_b}(X_a) \sim N(\mu_{X_a|X_b}, \Sigma_{X_a|X_b}),$$

where the conditional mean vector and conditional covariance matrix are given by

$$\mu_{X_a|X_b} = E(X_a \mid X_b) = \mu_a + \Sigma_{ab}\Sigma_{bb}^{-1}(X_b - \mu_b),$$
$$\Sigma_{X_a|X_b} = \Sigma_{aa} - \Sigma_{ab}\Sigma_{bb}^{-1}\Sigma_{ba}.$$

In fact, in the bivariate case we may write

$$X_1 = \mu_1 + \frac{\sigma_{12}}{\sigma_{22}}(X_2 - \mu_2) + \varepsilon_1, \tag{B.1}$$

where ε_1 is independent of X_2 with mean zero and variance $\sigma_{11} - \sigma_{12}^2/\sigma_{22}$. Note that the conditional median is equal to the conditional mean.

(iii) *If and only if Σ is diagonal, then $X_1, \ldots, X_k$ are mutually independent. In this case, $\det(\Sigma) = \sigma_{11} \times \cdots \times \sigma_{kk}$ and*

$$-\frac{1}{2}(x - \mu)^\mathsf{T}\Sigma^{-1}(x - \mu) = -\frac{1}{2}\sum_{l=1}^{k}\frac{(x_l - \mu_l)^2}{\sigma_{ll}},$$

so that

$$f_X(x \mid \mu, \Sigma) = \frac{1}{\sigma_{11}^{1/2}\sqrt{2\pi}}\exp\left(-\frac{1}{2}\left(\frac{x_1 - \mu_1}{\sigma_{11}}\right)\right) \times \cdots$$
$$\times \frac{1}{\sigma_{kk}^{1/2}\sqrt{2\pi}}\exp\left(-\frac{1}{2}\left(\frac{x_k - \mu_k}{\sigma_{kk}}\right)\right).$$

Theorem B.2 *If $X \sim N(\mu, \Sigma)$ and $y \mid X \sim N(BX, \Omega)$ then*

$$\begin{pmatrix} X \\ y \end{pmatrix} \sim N\left(\begin{pmatrix} \mu \\ B\mu \end{pmatrix}, \begin{pmatrix} \Sigma & \Sigma B^\mathsf{T} \\ B\Sigma & B\Sigma B^\mathsf{T} + \Omega \end{pmatrix}\right).$$

Furthermore, $X \mid y \sim N(m, V)$ with

$$m = \mu + \Sigma B^\mathsf{T}\left(B\Sigma B^\mathsf{T} + \Omega\right)^{-1}(y - B\mu),$$
$$V = \Sigma - \Sigma B^\mathsf{T}\left(B\Sigma B^\mathsf{T} + \Omega\right)^{-1}B\Sigma.$$

Definition B.2 (Matrix normal distribution; Dawid, 1981) We say that $X \sim \mathbf{MN}(M, U, V)$ if and only if $\mathrm{vec}(X) \sim N(m, V \otimes U)$, where $m = \mathrm{vec}(M)$ and the density function of the matrix random variable X is

$$f(X \mid M, U, V) = \exp\left(-\frac{1}{2}\mathrm{tr}\left(V^{-1}(X - M)^\mathsf{T}U^{-1}(X - M)\right)\right).$$

Definition B.3 The Bartlett–Sherman–Morrison formula,

$$(A + UCV)^{-1} = A^{-1} - A^{-1}U\left(C^{-1} + VA^{-1}U\right)^{-1}VA^{-1},$$

is used in several proofs. Here, A, C, U, and V are conformable matrices, with A and C square and invertible.

Definition B.4 For a real symmetric $n \times n$ matrix A, we can write uniquely $A = Q\Lambda Q^\mathsf{T} = \sum_{i=1}^{n}\lambda_i q_i q_i^\mathsf{T}$, where λ_i are real numbers and $QQ^\mathsf{T} = Q^\mathsf{T}Q = I_n$. We can also write $A = PP^\mathsf{T}$, where P is lower triangular and P^T is upper triangular.

Definition B.5 (The Cholesky factor algorithm for a matrix A) Repeat the following steps until convergence:

for $i = 1, \ldots, n$,

$$P_{ii} = \sqrt{A_{ii} - \sum_{k<i} P_{ik}^2}$$

for $j = i+1, \ldots, n$,

$$P_{ji} = \frac{A_{ji} - \sum_{k<i} P_{jk} P_{ik}}{P_{ii}}.$$

APPENDIX C

Laws of Large Numbers and Central Limit Theorems

Theorem C.1 *Suppose that y_t is a stationary ergodic process with $E(|y_t|) < \infty$. Let $S_T = \sum_{t=1}^{T} y_t$. Then, as $T \to \infty$, $(1/T)S_T \xrightarrow{P} E(y_t)$, meaning that, for any $\epsilon > 0$,*

$$\lim_{T \to \infty} \Pr\left(\left|\frac{1}{T}S_T\right| > \epsilon\right) = 0.$$

Theorem C.2 (Marcinkiewicz–Zygmund law of large numbers for linear processes)
Suppose that $\{y_t\}$ is a linear process $y_t = \sum_{j=0}^{\infty} \psi_j \varepsilon_{t-j}$, where ε_t is i.i.d. with $E(\varepsilon_t) = 0$ and $E(|\varepsilon_t|) < \infty$, and $\sum_{j=0}^{\infty} |\psi_j| < \infty$. Then $(1/T)S_T \xrightarrow{P} 0$.

The identically distributed nature of the shocks can be weakened.

Theorem C.3 (Central limit theorem for linear processes; Phillips and Solo, 1992)
Suppose that $\{y_t\}$ is a linear process $y_t = \sum_{j=0}^{\infty} \psi_j \varepsilon_{t-j}$, where ε_t is i.i.d. with mean zero and variance σ^2, $\sum_{j=0}^{\infty} |\psi_j| < \infty$, and $\sum_{j=0}^{\infty} \psi_j \neq 0$. Let $S_T = \sum_{t=1}^{T} y_t$ and $\sigma_S^2 = \sigma^2 \left(\sum_{j=0}^{\infty} \psi_j\right)^2$. Then

$$\frac{1}{\sigma_S \sqrt{T}} S_T \implies N(0, 1).$$

We can equivalently (the supremum comes for free) say that

$$\lim_{T \to \infty} \sup_{x \in \mathbb{R}} \left|\Pr\left(\frac{1}{\sigma_S \sqrt{T}} S_T \leq x\right) - \Phi(x)\right| = 0,$$

where $\Phi(x)$ is the standard normal CDF.

Herrndorf (1984, Corollary 1) established the following result for a general sequence of random variables not necessarily stationary.

Theorem C.4 *Suppose that $\{y_t\}$ is an α-mixing sequence,*

$$\sum_{k=1}^{\infty} \alpha(k)^{\delta/(2+\delta)} < \infty.$$

Suppose that $E(y_t) = 0$ and $E(|y_t|^{2+\delta}) \leq C < \infty$ for some $\delta > 0$, $t = 1, 2, \ldots$, and suppose that, for some $\sigma^2 = \mathrm{lrvar}(y_t) > 0$, $(1/T)E(S_T^2) \to \sigma^2$. Then

$$\frac{1}{\sigma \sqrt{T}} S_T \implies N(0, 1).$$

This CLT is commonly used in econometrics. It embodies a trade-off between the moment conditions and the rate of decay of the mixing coefficients. If $\delta = \infty$, then we only need $\sum_{k=1}^{\infty} \alpha(k) < \infty$, which allows $\alpha(k) = (k \log k)^{-1}$ for example, a slow rate of decay. On the other hand, if δ is small, we require that $\alpha(k) \to 0$ fast as $k \to \infty$. For stationary processes that satisfy geometric mixing, that is, $\alpha(k) \leq C\rho^k$ for some $\rho \in (0, 1)$, then the moment condition can be weakened to $E(y_t^2 \log^+(|y_t|)) < \infty$, but no further (Doukhan, Massart, and Rio, 1994).[1] The Herrndorf result allows for nonstationarity of limited degree. For example, suppose that $y_t = \sigma(t/T)u_t$, where u_t is a zero-mean stationary and mixing process, while $\sigma \colon [0, 1] \to \mathbb{R}_+$ is a smooth function. Then, provided $\sum_{j=1}^{T} j|\gamma_u(j)|/T \to 0$, we have

$$\frac{1}{T} E(S_T^2) \to \int_0^1 \sigma^2(u)\, du \times \mathrm{lrvar}(u).$$

For regression, the following result is of use.

Theorem C.5 (Amemiya, 1985, Theorem 3.5.4) *Suppose that $y_t = \beta^\top x_t + u_t$, where u_t are i.i.d. with mean zero and finite variance, and indepdent of all x_t. Suppose further that, with probability one,*

$$\frac{\max_{1 \leq t \leq T} x_{kt}^2}{\sum_{t=1}^{T} x_{kt}^2} \longrightarrow 0$$

for $k = 1, \ldots, K$. Letting Δ be the $K \times K$ diagonal matrix with elements $\sum_{t=1}^{T} x_{kt}^2$, $k = 1, \ldots, K$, suppose that, with probability one, $\Delta^{-1/2} X^\top X \Delta^{-1/2} \to M$, where M is positive definite. Then $\Delta^{1/2}(\widehat{\beta} - \beta) \Longrightarrow N(0, \sigma^2 M^{-1})$.

In the univariate case, we have the result that

$$\sigma^{-1} \left(\sum_{t=1}^{T} x_t^2 \right)^{1/2} (\widehat{\beta} - \beta) \Longrightarrow N(0, 1).$$

This is true, for example, if x_t are polynomial trends. It is also true if x_t is stochastic, say $x_t = bt + z_t$, where z_t is standard Cauchy distributed.

Herrndorf (1984) gave an FCLT for the sum of α-mixing random variables. We give an updated version of this theorem due to Lin and Lu (1996). Define the partial sum process $W_T(u) = S_{\lfloor Tu \rfloor}/\mathrm{stdev}(S_T)$ and let $W(\cdot)$ be the standard Wiener motion. Define also the class of functions

$$G = \left\{ g \colon [0, \infty) \to [0, \infty),\ g \text{ is convex},\ g(0) = 0, \right.$$

$$\left. g(x)/x^2 \text{ is nondecreasing},\ \lim_{x \to \infty} \frac{g(x)}{x^2} = \infty \right\}.$$

Denote by g^{-1} the well-defined inverse of a function $g \in G$, and define the function $f_g \colon [0, \infty) \to [0, \infty)$ by $f_g(0) = 0$ and $f_g(x) = (g^{-1}(1/x))^2 x$ for $x > 0$. For example, $g(x) = x^2 \log(x) \in G$. If $g(x) = x^{2+\delta}$, then $f_g(1/x) = x^{\delta/(2+\delta)}$.

---

[1] There do exist CLTs for ρ-mixing sequences that require only second moments.

Theorem C.6   *Suppose that $\{y_t\}$ is an α-mixing sequence with $E(y_t) = 0$ and $E(y_t^2) < \infty$ for all $t = 1, 2, \ldots$, and suppose that, as $T \to \infty$, $(1/T)E(S_T^2) \to \sigma^2$ for some $\sigma > 0$. Suppose also that there exists a function $g \in G$ such that*

$$\sup_{t \geq 1} Eg(|y_t|) < \infty, \qquad \sum_{j=1}^{\infty} f_g(\alpha(j)) < \infty.$$

Then $W_n(\cdot) \Longrightarrow W(\cdot)$.

Hall and Heyde (1980) provided a comprehensive theory for martingale difference sequences, including laws of large numbers and central limit theorems.

Theorem C.7   *Let $\left\{S_{ni} = \sum_{j=1}^{i} X_{nj}, \mathcal{F}_{ni}, 1 \leq i \leq k_n\right\}$ be a zero-mean martingale for each $n \geq 1$. Then $\Pr\left(S_{nk_n} \leq x\right) \to E\left(\Phi(\eta^{-1}x)\right)$, where Φ is the standard normal CDF, provided the following three conditions are satisfied:*

(i) *For all $\varepsilon > 0$, as $n \to \infty$, $\sum_{i=1}^{k_n} E\left[X_{ni}^2 1\left(|X_{ni}| > \varepsilon\right)\right] \longrightarrow 0$.*
(ii) *As $n \to \infty$, $U_n^2 = \sum_{i=1}^{k_n} X_{ni}^2 \xrightarrow{P} \eta^2$, where the random variable $\eta^2 > 0$ with probability one.*
(iii) *The sigma fields $\mathcal{F}_{ni}$ are nested, namely, $\mathcal{F}_{ni} \subset \mathcal{F}_{ni+1}$ for all $i \leq k_n$.*

In the (very common) case that η^2 is constant, this is a standard CLT. But in some cases we should allow for normal mixtures in the limit.

Theorem C.8   *Suppose that y_t is a weakly stationary process with mean μ_y and auto-covariance function $\gamma_y(\cdot)$. Let $x_t = \sum_{k=-\infty}^{\infty} \psi_k y_{t-k}$, where $\sum_{k=-\infty}^{\infty} \psi_k^2 < \infty$. Then x_t is a weakly stationary process with mean $\mu_x = \mu \sum_{k=-\infty}^{\infty} \psi_k = \mu\psi(1)$ and autocovariance function*

$$\gamma_x(j) = \sum_{k=-\infty}^{\infty} R_k \gamma_y(j-k), \qquad R_k = \sum_{j=-\infty}^{\infty} \psi_j \psi_{j+k} = (\psi * \psi)(L).$$

If $y_t = \int \exp(it\lambda)\, dZ(\lambda)$, then

$$x_t = \sum_{k=-\infty}^{\infty} \psi_k \int \exp(i\lambda(t-k))\, dZ(\lambda)$$

$$= \int \exp(i\lambda t) \left(\sum_{k=-\infty}^{\infty} \psi_k \exp(-i\lambda k) \right) dZ(\lambda)$$

$$= \int \exp(i\lambda t) B(\lambda)\, dZ(\lambda) = \int \exp(i\lambda t)\, dZ_B(\lambda).$$

Theorem C.9   *If y_t is a stationary process with $T \times T$ covariance matrix Γ_T,*

$$\Gamma_T = \begin{pmatrix} \gamma(0) & \gamma(1) & \cdots & \gamma(T-1) \\ \gamma(1) & \gamma(0) & \ddots & \vdots \\ \vdots & \ddots & \ddots & \gamma(1) \\ \gamma(T-1) & & \gamma(1) & \gamma(0) \end{pmatrix},$$

then the vectors containing polynomial terms or trigonometric polynomials are approximate eigenvectors of Γ_T.

For example, $u = (1, \exp(i\lambda_1), \exp(i\lambda_2), \ldots, \exp(i\lambda_{T-1}))^\mathsf{T}$ satisfies $\Gamma_T u = cu + r$, where $c \in \mathbb{R}$ and r satisfies $i_T^\mathsf{T} r \to 0$ as $T \to \infty$.

APPENDIX D

Data and Data Sources

We supply the following datasets on the book website.[1]

Arbuthnot Yearly births in London, 1629–1710, by gender assigned at birth (male or female).

Arsenal20222023 Goals scored and conceded by Arsenal during the 2022/2023 Premier League season (38 matches). Shows Arsenal goals, opposition goals, home or away.

Cam30 Data from Cambridge weather station, 30-minute frequency, from 30/06/1995 15:00:00 to 07/03/2024 02:00:00. Shows temperature in centigrade ($\times 10$), humidity, dew point, pressure in millibars, wind speed in knots, wind direction (NE, NW, etc.), sun in hours, rain in millimeters, and maximum wind speed in knots.

CETD Central England temperatures, 165901–202003. Years by month with annual average.

cnyusd Daily Chinese yuan / US dollar exchange rate: date, opening price, closing price, intraday high price, intraday low price; other fields are void. Time period 20010625–20240308.

Covid19 Daily number of new cases and deaths from COVID-19 by country, 20200101–20201214.

CPIAUCNS Consumer price index for all urban consumers: All items in US city average, index 1982–1984 = 100, monthly, not seasonally adjusted. From 191901 to 202401.

Deadscots Total mortality in Scotland from 1974 to 2023 W5 by week (53 weeks potentially).

ffdaily Daily returns on the three Fama–French factors plus the one-month T-bill rate from 19260701 to 20240131. Downloaded from Ken French's website.

flash Transaction prices on the Emini S&P500 near futures contract on the day of the flash crash, 20100506.

FTSE Daily prices and trading volume on the S&P500 index. Shows date, opening price, closing price, intraday high price, intraday low price, adjusted price, and trading volume in GBP.

GME Gamestop. Shows date, opening price, closing price, intraday high price, intraday low price, adjusted price, and trading volume in USD from 2002 to 2021.

INDPRO US monthly industrial production index from 191901 to 202401 (seasonally adjusted). Shows date and index.

[1] www.cambridge.org/lintontimeseries

`INDPRON` US monthly industrial production ($2017 = 100$) from 191901 to 202401 (not seasonally adjusted). Shows date and index.

`marathon` Race times of male and female runners.

`OXMT` Monthly weather data from Oxford, UK, 1853–2024. Shows year, month, t_{max} (centigrade), t_{min}, af (frost days), rain in millimeters, sunshine in hours. Some missing data.

`PCE` Personal consumption expenditures, billions of dollars, monthly, seasonally adjusted annual rate. From 195901 to 202401.

`sp500` Daily prices and trading volume on the S&P500 index, which contains around 500 large stocks traded on the NYSE, NASDAQ, CBOE, and BZX exchanges. We show the daily closing price level (Monday through Friday), the date, the opening price, the intraday high price, the intraday low price, the adjusted price, and the trading volume in USD.

`sp500stocks` Daily dollar returns on 441 stocks of the S&P500 index between 2005 and 2015.

`Toronto` Monthly temperature from Toronto, Canada, 1840–2016.

`ukbirthday` Frequency of birthdays by day of year, average over the last 20 years.

`UNRATE` US monthly unemployment rate in percentage terms from 194801 to 202401 (seasonally adjusted). Shows date and rate. Downloaded from Federal Reserve Economic Data (FRED), Federal Reserve Bank of St. Louis.

`UNRATENSA` US monthly unemployment rate in percentage terms from 194801 to 202401 (not seasonally adjusted). Shows date and rate. Downloaded from FRED.

`usabirthday` Frequency of birthdays by day of year, average over the last 20 years.

`USGDPQSA` US gross domestic product, billions of dollars, quarterly, seasonally adjusted annualized rate, 1947Q1–2023Q4.

`VIX` Daily VIX rate from 19900102–20240307: date, opening price, closing price, intraday high price, intraday low price; other fields are void.

There are many entities that provide some data for free download.

- European Central Bank's Statistical Data Warehouse.
  http://sdw.ecb.europa.eu/
- St. Louis Federal Reserve Bank: Lots of freely downloadable macro and financial data.
  https://fred.stlouisfed.org/
- Federal Reserve Bank of New York. Regional economic data; markets operation data; national economic data. Note also electronic databases attached to published papers.
  www.newyorkfed.org/data-and-statistics
- US Treasury yield curves.
  www.treasury.gov/resource-center/data-chart-center/interest-rates/Pages/TextView .aspx?data=yield
- World Bank Open Data. Lots of data that can be browsed by country or indicator.
  http://data.worldbank.org/
- Bank of England statistical interactive database. Economic, financial, interest rate, and exchange rate data by country, financial instrument, business category, economic and industrial sector. Note also electronic databases attached to published papers.
  www.bankofengland.co.uk/boeapps/database/

- The IMF publishes a range of time series data on IMF lending, exchange rates, and other economic and financial indicators.
  www.imf.org/en/data
- Bloomberg and Datastream. Bloomberg provides current and historical financial quotes, business newswires, and descriptive information, research, and statistics on over 52 000 companies worldwide. You can only access the database from one of their terminals.
- WRDS (Wharton Research Data Services) provides the user with one location to access over 250 terabytes of data across multiple disciplines including accounting; banking; economics; finance; environmental, social, and governance; and statistics. WRDS provides access to S&P Capital IQ, CRSP, NYSE, Thomson Reuters, Bureau van Dijk, Global Insight, OptionMetrics, and other important business research databases. Using a standard query structure (for example company names, dates of interest, financial parameters) students can create customized reports. These reports can be stored, revisited and exported.
  https://wrds-www.wharton.upenn.edu/
- Fama–French data library. This site has a large amount of freely downloadable historical data compiled by Eugene Fama and Kenneth French. The data is updated regularly, and the Fama–French three-factor data is especially useful for analyzing fund and portfolio performance.
  http://mba.tuck.dartmouth.edu/pages/faculty/ken.french/data_library.html
- Robert Shiller data library. This site has Robert Shiller's PE10 data, used in the book *Irrational Exuberance*. The PE10 data is updated regularly.
  www.econ.yale.edu/shiller/data.htm
- William Schwert. Monthly stock returns from 1802–1925 and daily stock returns from 1885–1962.
  www.billschwert.com/gws_data.htm
- Yahoo Finance and Google Finance. Provide historical price information at daily frequency for thousands of assets, easy to download in CSV or Excel format, no login.
  https://uk.finance.yahoo.com/
  www.google.co.uk/finance?tab=ee
- Asset Macro. Historical macroeconomic data and market data (stocks indices, bonds, commodities, FX).
  www.assetmacro.com/market-data/
- OANDA. A great resource for historical FX rates that you can easily download.
  www.oanda.com/uk-en/trading/tools/
- Thinknum. US macro data at the zip-code level. Requires signup.
  www.thinknum.com/
- GitHub. This is an open-source community for programmers. You can find lots of useful software and tools there, and also public datasets. Need to create an account, but free.
  https://github.com/caesar0301/awesome-public-datasets#finance
  https://vincentarelbundock.github.io/Rdatasets/datasets.html
- LOBSTER. Trade and quote data from NASDAQ.
  lobsterdata.com

- Caltech Quantitative Finance Group. Gives some tips about data.
  http://quants.caltech.edu/research.html
- Quandl. Includes some free data but need to sign up.
  www.quandl.com/
- CME Group. High-frequency trade and quote data from their platforms (modest fees apply).
  www.cmegroup.com/market-data.html
- Things that R can do.
  https://cran.r-project.org/web/views/Finance.html
- Amit Goyal's website.
  https://sites.google.com/view/agoyal145
- Andrew Patton's website.
  http://public.econ.duke.edu/~ap172/
- Kevin Sheppard's website.
  www.kevinsheppard.com/

A Short Introduction to EViews

You can access most of the EViews functionality via menus. Just browse through the menus, and find the appropriate command. You will then be guided through several windows that prompt you for the information required to perform the command. The most important and difficult step (in any software) is to read in data. To do this you need to create a **workfile**. We show here how to do this for dated daily data. We assume here that you have downloaded a CSV file with seven columns with a header describing each (as one would have obtained from Yahoo finance).

1. Go to https://finance.yahoo.com.
2. In the "Quote Lookup" dialog box enter MSFT.
3. Click "Historical Data."
4. Change the time period to "Max," then enter "Done" and "Apply" in the right-hand box.
5. Click "Download data." You should now have an Excel file, MSFT.csv. It should have seven columns with a header describing each, and the first date being 03/01/1950 (January 3, 1950) or 20150103.
6. Open EViews 14 and create a new workfile: click File > New > Workfile.
7. Select the "Dated – regular frequency" option and further specify "Daily – 5 day week" frequency and the start and end dates using American dating convention (you may have downloaded in European dating convention).
8. The workfile is created with two preexisting variables, c and resid (coefficients and residuals). Every time you estimate something, the coefficients are stored in c and the residuals in resid.
9. Import the data (Select File > Import from File) and click the file on your drive; you should see a box with title "Text Read – Step 1 of 4." Click Finish (if you like, you may click Next and see the options available, which I don't think you need at this point). You should see a box with "Link imported series to external source." Click Yes, why not!
10. You now have a workfile (UNTITLED – you can save it later with a name) with eight named series: adj_close, c, close, high, low, open, resid, volume. Do a cross-check with your raw data file by clicking on the series names. Compare the number of observations, and check whether each series got the correct name. EViews should have transposed the dates into the right order. You should see a number of observations with NA (which means not available); these are mostly just holidays when the stock price was not returned. We have to eliminate these next.

11. From the workfile window, Proc > Copy Extract from Current Page (by value to new page or workfile). You then see a box called "Workfile copy by Value"; you enter the following into the open box headed "Sample – observations to copy":

$$\texttt{@all if close <> NA}$$

Then click Page Destination and New workfile. You now get to enter the name of the file you want to keep. Let's call it sp500daily. To be on the safe side use File > Save > sp500daily. The dates with missing observations have been eliminated.

12. You next want to create a new variable for return. Click the Genr button on the workfile window and then insert the defining equation of your new variable. For example,

$$\texttt{Ret=(adj\_close-adj\_close(-1))/adj\_close(-1)}$$

Note that when you write x(-1), EViews understands that you want x lagged one period. For logarithmic return, define

$$\texttt{r=log(close)-log(close(-1))}$$

13. Generating the day of the week dummy. Use the Genr command and enter D1=@weekday=1, which gives the Monday dummy; likewise for the other days of the week.

14. You can now get by with the menu-driven commands.

15. Exporting EViews graphs. EViews generates graphs, but they may not look the way you want them to. In order to use an EViews graph in another program you can save it as a Windows metafile (*.wmf). After generating the graph, click Object > View Options and then you may copy to clipboard or save to disk. If you choose save to disk you will be offered several formats.

Bibliography

Ai, C. and Chen, X. (2003). Efficient estimation of models with conditional moment restrictions containing unknown functions. *Econometrica*, 71(6), 1795–1843.

Aït-Sahalia, Y. (1996). Nonparametric pricing of interest rate derivative securities. *Econometrica*, 64(3), 527–560.

Aït-Sahalia, Y. and Jacod, J. (2014). *High-Frequency Financial Econometrics*. Princeton University Press.

Aït-Sahalia, Y., Mykland, P. A., and Zhang, L. (2011). Ultra high frequency volatility estimation with dependent microstructure noise. *Journal of Econometrics*, 160(1), 160–175.

Akaike, H. (1974). A new look at the statistical model identification. *IEEE Transactions on Automatic Control*, 19(6), 716–723.

Almon, S. (1965). The distributed lag between capital appropriations and expenditures. *Econometrica*, 33(1), 178–196.

Amemiya, T. (1985). *Advanced Econometrics*. Harvard University Press.

Andersen, T. G., Bollerslev, T., Diebold, F. X., and Labys, P. (2001). The distribution of realized exchange rate volatility. *Journal of the American Statistical Association*, 96(453), 42–55.

Andersen, T. G., Bollerslev, T., Diebold, F. X., and Labys, P. (2003). Modeling and forecasting realized volatility. *Econometrica*, 71(2), 579–626.

Andrews, D. W. K. (1984). Non-strong mixing autoregressive processes. *Journal of Applied Probability*, 21(4), 930–934.

Andrews, D. W. K. (1991a). Asymptotic normality of series estimators for nonparametric and semiparametric regression models. *Econometrica*, 59(2), 307–346.

Andrews, D. W. K. (1991b). Heteroskedasticity and autocorrelation consistent covariance matrix estimation. *Econometrica*, 59(3), 817–858.

Andrews, D. W. K. (1993). Tests for parameter instability and structural change with unknown change point. *Econometrica*, 61(4), 821–856.

Andrews, D. W. K. (1994). Empirical process method in econometrics. In R. F. Engle and D. L. McFadden (eds), *Handbook of Econometrics*, Vol. IV. North Holland, Amsterdam.

Andrews, D. W. K. and Ploberger, W. (1994). Optimal tests when a nuisance parameter is present only under the alternative. *Econometrica*, 62(6), 1383–1414.

Andrews, D. W. K. and Whang, Y.-J. (1990). Additive and interactive regression models: Circumvention of the curse of dimensionality. *Econometric Theory*, 6(4), 466–479.

Ansley, C. F., Kohn, R., and Wong, C. (1993). Nonparametric spline regression with prior information. *Biometrika*, 80(1), 75–88.

Baba, Y., Engle, R. F., Kraft, D. F., and Kroner, K. F. (1990). Multivariate simultaneous generalized ARCH. Mimeo, Department of Economics, University of California, San Diego.

Bai, J. (2003). Inferential theory for factor models of large dimensions. *Econometrica*, 71(1), 135–171. doi:10.1111/1468-0262.00392

Bai, J. and Ng, S. (2002). Determining the number of factors in approximate factor models. *Econometrica*, 70(1), 191–221.

Baillie, R. T., Bollerslev, T., and Mikkelsen, H. O. (1996). Fractionally integrated generalized autoregressive conditional heteroskedasticity. *Journal of Econometrics*, 74(1), 3–30.

Ball, R. and Watts, R. (1972). Some time series properties of accounting income. *Journal of Finance*, 27(3), 663–681.

Bampinas, G., Ladopoulos, K., and Panagiotidis, T. (2018). A note on the estimated GARCH coefficients from the S&P1500 universe. *Applied Economics*, 50(34–35), 3647–3653.

Bandi, F. M. and Phillips, P. C. B. (2003). Fully nonparametric estimation of scalar diffusion models. *Econometrica*, 71(1), 241–283.

Barndorff-Nielsen, O. E., Hansen, P. R., Lunde, A., and Shephard, N. (2008). Designing realized kernels to measure the ex-post variation of equity prices in the presence of noise. *Econometrica*, 76(6), 1481–1536. doi:10.3982/ECTA6495

Barndorff-Nielsen, O. and Shephard, N. (2002). Econometric analysis of realised volatility and its use in estimating stochastic volatility models. *Journal of the Royal Statistical Society, Series B*, 64(2), 253–280.

Barron, A. R. (1994). Approximation and estimation bounds for artificial neural networks. *Machine Learning*, 14, 115–133. doi:10.1007/BF00993164

Bartlett, M. S. (1948). Smoothing periodograms from time-series with continuous spectra. *Nature*, 161(4096), 686–687.

Bartlett, M. S. (1950). Periodogram analysis and continuous spectra. *Biometrika*, 37(1/2), 1–16.

Baumol, W. J. and Benhabib, J. (1989). Chaos: Significance, mechanism, and economic applications. *Journal of Economic Perspectives*, 3(1), 77–105.

Bauwens, L., Laurent, S., and Rombouts, J. V. (2006). Multivariate GARCH models: A survey. *Journal of Applied Econometrics*, 21(1), 79–109. doi:10.1002/jae.842

Baxter, M. and King, R. G. (1995). Measuring business cycles: Approximate band-pass filters for economic time series. NBER Working Paper 5022. National

Bureau of Economic Research, Cambridge, MA.

Bell, W. R. and Hillmer, S. C. (1984). Issues involved with the seasonal adjustment of economic time series. *Journal of Business & Economic Statistics*, 2(4), 291–320.

Belloni, A., Chernozhukov, V., and Hansen, C. (2014). Inference on treatment effects after selection amongst high-dimensional controls. *Review of Econonomic Studies*, 81(2), 608–650.

Bergstrom, A. R. (1984). Continuous time stochastic models and issues of aggregation over time. In Z. Griliches and M. D. Intriligator (eds), *Handbook of Econometrics*, Vol. II. North Holland, Amsterdam.

Bergstrom, A. R. and Nowman, B. (2007). *A Continuous Time Econometric Model of the United Kingdom with Stochastic Trends*. Cambridge University Press.

Bernanke, B. (2024). Forecasting for monetary policy making and communication at the Bank of England: A review. Available at www.bankofengland.co.uk/independent-evaluation-office/forecasting-for-monetary-policy-making-and-communication-at-the-bank-of-england-a-review.

Beveridge, W. H. (1921). Weather and harvest cycles. *Economics Journal*, 31(124), 429–452.

Biau, G. and Devroye, L. (2015). *Lectures on the Nearest Neighbor Method*. Springer, Berlin.

Bickel, P. J. and Bühlmann, P. (1997). Closure of linear processes. *Journal of Theoretical Probability*, 10, 445–479.

Bickel, P. J. and Freedman, D. A. (1981). Some asymptotic theory for the bootstrap. *Annals of Statistics*, 9(6), 1196–1217.

Bickel, P. J., Klaassen, C. A. J., Ritov, Y., and Wellner, J. A. (1993). *Efficient and Adaptive Estimation for Semiparametric Models*. Johns Hopkins University Press, Baltimore, MA.

Bickel, P. J., Ritov, Y., and Tsybakov, A. B. (2009). Simultaneous analysis of Lasso and Dantzig selector. *Annals of Statistics*, 37(4), 1705–1732. doi:10.1214/08-AOS620

Black, F. and Scholes, M. (1973). The pricing of options and corporate liabilities. *Journal of Political Economy*, 81(3), 637–654. doi:10.1086/260062.

Blanchard, O. J. and Quah, D. (1989). The dynamic effects of aggregate demand and supply disturbances. *The American Economic Review*, 79(4), 655–673.

Blanchard, O. J. and Watson, M. W. (1982). Bubbles, rational expectations and financial markets. In P. Wachtel (ed), *Crises in the Economic and Financial Structure*. Heath and Company, Lexington, MA.

Bollerslev, T. (1986). Generalized autoregressive conditional heteroskedasticity. *Journal of Econometrics*, 31(3), 307–327.

Bollerslev, T. (1990). Modelling the coherence in short-run nominal exchange rates: A multivariate generalized ARCH model. *Review of Economics and Statistics*, 72(3), 498–505.

Bollerslev, T., Engle, R. F., and Nelson, D. (1994). ARCH models. In D. F. McFadden and R. F. Engle (eds), *Handbook of Econometrics*, Vol. IV. North Holland, Amsterdam.

Bollerslev, T., Engle, R. F., and Wooldridge, J. M. (1988). A capital asset pricing model with time-varying covariances, *Journal of Political Economy*, 96(1), 116–131.

Bollerslev T. and Wooldridge, J. M. (1992). Quasi-maximum likelihood estimation and inference in dynamic models with time-varying covariances. *Econometric Reviews*, 11(2), 143–172.

Bosq, D. (1996). *Nonparametric Statistics for Stochastic Processes*. Springer, New York.

Box, G. E. P. and Cox, D. R. (1964). An analysis of transformations,. *Journal of the Royal Statistical Society, Series B*, 26(2), 211–252.

Box, G. and Jenkins, G. (1970). *Time Series Analysis: Forecasting and Control*. Holden-Day, San Francisco, CA.

Box, G. E. P. and Pierce, D. A. (1970). Distribution of residual autocorrelations in autoregressive integrated moving average time series models. *Journal of the American Statistical Association*, 65(332), 1509–1526.

Breidt, F. J., Crato, N., and de Lima, P. (1998). The detection and estimation of long memory in stochastic volatility models, *Journal of Econometrics*, 83(1–2), 325–348.

Brillinger, D. R. (1980). *Time Series, Data Analysis and Theory*. Holden-Day, Oakland, CA.

Brock, W. A. and Hommes, C. H. (1997). A rational route to randomness. *Econometrica*, 65(5), 1059–1095.

Brockwell, P. J. and Davis, R. A. (2006). *Time Series: Theory and Methods*, 2nd edition. Springer, Berlin.

Brooks, C., Burke, S. P., and Persand, G. (2001). Benchmarks and the accuracy of GARCH model estimation. *International Journal of Forecasting*, 17(1), 45–56.

Brown, L. D., Hagerman, R. L., Griffin, P. A., and Zmijewski, M. E. (1987). An evaluation of alternative proxies for the market's assessment of unexpected earnings. *Journal of Accounting and Economics*, 9(2), 159–193.

Brown, L. D. and Rozeff, M. S. (1979). Univariate time-series models of quarterly accounting earnings per share: A proposed model. *Journal of Accounting Research*, 17(1), 179–189.

Bühlmann, P. and van de Geer, S. (2011). *Statistics for High-Dimensional Data: Methods, Theory and Applications*. Springer, New York.

Cai, Z. (2002). Regression quantiles for time series. *Econometric Theory*, 18(1), 169–192.

Campbell, J. Y., Lo, A. W., and MacKinlay, A. C. (1997). *The Econometrics of Financial Markets*. Princeton University Press.

Campbell, J. Y. and Shiller, R. J. (1988). Stock prices, earnings and expected dividends. *Journal of Finance*, 43(3), 661–676.

Campbell, J. Y. and Thompson, S. B. (2008). Predicting excess stock returns out of sample: Can anything beat the historical average? *The Review of Financial Studies*, 21(4), 1509–1531.

Cantelli, F. P. (1933). Sulla determinazione empirica delle leggi di probabilitá. *Giornale dell'Istituto Italiano degli Attuari*, 4, 421–424.

Carrasco, M. and Chen, X. (2002). Mixing and moment properties of various GARCH and stochastic volatility models. *Econometric Theory*, 18(1), 17–39.

Cavaliere, G., Mikosch, T, Rahbek, A., and Vilandt, F. (2023). Asymptotics for the generalized autoregressive conditional duration model. Preprint, arXiv:2307.01779.

Chaudhuri, P. (1991). Nonparametric estimates of regression quantiles and their local Bahadur representation. *Annals of Statistics*, 19(2), 760–777.

Chen, J., Li, D., Linton, O., and Lu, Z. (2018). Semiparametric ultra-high dimensional model averaging of nonlinear dynamic time series. *Journal of the American Statistical Association*, 113(522), 919–932.

Chen, R., Yang, L., and Hafner, C. (2004). Nonparametric multistep-ahead prediction in time series analysis. *Journal of the Royal Statistical Society, Series B*, 66(3), 669–686. doi:10.1111/j.1467-9868 .2004.04664

Chen, S. X. (1999). Beta kernel estimators for density functions. *Computational Statistics and Data Analysis*, 31(2), 131–145.

Chen, X. (2007). Large sample sieve estimation of semi-nonparametric models. In J. J. Heckman and E. E. Leamer (eds), *Handbook of Econometrics*, Vol. IV B. North Holland, Amsterdam.

Chen, X., Cho, Y. H., Dou, Y., and Lev, B. (2022). Predicting future earnings changes using machine learning and detailed financial data. *Journal of Accounting Research*, 60(2), 467–515.

Chen, X. and Fan, Y. (2006). Estimation of copula-based semiparametric time series

models. *Journal of Econometrics*, 130(2), 307–335.

Chen, X. Hansen, L. P., and Scheinkman, J. (2009). Nonlinear principal components and long-run implications of multivariate diffusions. *Annals of Statistics*, 37(6B), 4279–4312. doi:10.1214/09-AOS706

Chen, X., Linton, O., and Robinson, P. M. (2000). The estimation of conditional densities. In M. L. Puri (ed), *Asymptotics in Statistics and Probability: Papers in Honor of George Gregory Roussas*. De Gruyter, Berlin. doi:10.1515/9783110942002-008

Chen, X. and Shen, X. (1998). Sieve extremum estimates for weakly dependent data. *Econometrica*, 66(2), 289–314.

Chicheportiche, R. and Bouchaud, J.-P. (2014). The fine-structure of volatility feedback I: Multi-scale self-reflexivity. *Physica A: Statistical Mechanics and its Applications*, 410, 174–195.

Chow, G. C. (1960). Tests of equality between sets of coefficients in two linear regressions. *Econometrica*, 28(3), 591–605.

Christiano, L. J. and Fitzgerald, T. J. (2003). The band pass filter. *International Economic Review*, 44(2), 435–465.

Chudik, A., Kapetanios, G., and Pesaran, M. H. (2018). A one covariate at a time, multiple testing approach to variable selection in high-dimensional linear regression models. *Econometrica*, 86(4), 1479–1512.

Cleveland, R. B., Cleveland, W. S., McRae, J. E., and Terpenning, I. J. (1990). STL: A seasonal-trend decomposition procedure based on LOESS. *Journal of Official Statistics*, 6(1), 3–33.

Cleveland, W. S. (1979). Robust locally weighted regression and smoothing scatterplots. *Journal of the American Statistical Association*, 74(368), 829–836.

Cochrane, J. H. (1999). New facts in finance. NBER Working Paper 7169. National Bureau of Economic Research, Cambridge, MA.

Cohen, A. (1966). All admissible linear estimates of the mean vector. *Annals of Mathematical Statistics*, 37(2), 458–463.

Conley, T. G., Hansen, L. P., Luttmer, E. G., and Scheinkman, J. A. (1997). Short-term interest rates as subordinated diffusions. *The Review of Financial Studies*, 10(3), 525–577.

Coppejans, M. (2004). On Kolmogorov's representation of functions of several variables by functions of one variable. *Journal of Econometrics*, 123(1), 1–31.

Corsi, F. A. (2009). A simple approximate long-memory model of realized volatility. *Journal of Financial Econometrics*, 7(2), 174–196.

Cox, D. R. (2006). Frequentist and Bayesian statistics: A critique (keynote address). In L. Lyons and M. K. Ünel (eds), *Statistical Problems in Particle Physics, Astrophysics and Cosmology*. World Scientific, Singapore.

Cox, J. C., Ingersoll, J. E., and Ross, S. A. (1985). A theory of the term structure of interest rates. *Econometrica*, 53(2), 385–407.

Cox, D. R. and Reid, N. (2004). A note on pseudolikelihood constructed from marginal densities. *Biometrika*, 91(3), 729–737.

Cox, D. R. and Snell, E. J. (1989), *Analysis of Binary Data*, 2nd edition. Chapman and Hall/CRC, London.

Craven, P. and Wahba, G. (1978). Smoothing noisy data with spline functions. *Numerische Mathematik*, 31, 377–403.

Dahlhaus, R. (1997). Fitting time series models to nonstationary processes. *Annals of Statistics*, 25(1), 1–37.

Dahlhaus, R. and Subba Rao, S. (2006). Statistical inference for time-varying ARCH processes. *Annals of Statistics*, 34(3), 1075–1114. doi:10.1214/009053606000000227

Davidson, J. (1994). *Stochastic Limit Theory*. Oxford University Press.

Davis, R. A. and Yau, C. Y. (2011). Comments on pairwise likelihood in the time series models. *Statistica Sinica*, 21(1), 255–277.

Dawid, A. P. (1981). Some matrix-variate distribution theory: Notational considerations and a Bayesian application. *Biometrika*, 68(1), 265–274. doi:10.2307/2335827

Dedecker, J. and Saulière, G. (2017). The Mann–Whitney U-statistic for α-dependent sequences. *Mathematical Methods of Statistics*, 26, 111–133. doi:10.3103/S1066530717020028

Delgado, M. A. and Hidalgo, J. (2000). Nonparametric inference on structural breaks. *Journal of Econometrics*, 96(1), 113–144.

Denton, F., Feaver, C., and Spencer, B. (2005). Time series analysis and stochastic forecasting: An econometric study of mortality and life expectancy. *Journal of Population Economics*, 18(2), 203–227.

Diebold, F. X. (1998). The past, present, and future of macroeconomic forecasting. *Journal of Economic Perspectives*, 12(2), 175–192.

Diebold, F. X. (2017). Forecasting in Economics, Business, Finance and Beyond. Available at www.sas.upenn.edu/~fdiebold/Teaching221/Forecasting.pdf

Diebold, F. X. and Mariano, R. S. (1995). Comparing predictive accuracy. *Journal of Business and Economic Statistics*, 13(3), 253–263.

Diebold, F. X. and Nason, J. A. (1990). Nonparametric exchange rate prediction? *Journal of International Economics*, 28(3–4), 315–332.

Diebold, F. X. and Yılmaz, K. (2014). On the network topology of variance decompositions: Measuring the connectedness of financial firms. *Journal of Econometrics*, 182(1), 119–134.

Dimson, E. (1979). Risk measurement when shares are subject to infrequent trading. *Journal of Financial Economics*, 7(2), 197–226.

Doan, T., Litterman, R. B., and Sims, C. A. (1984). Forecasting and conditional projection using realistic prior distributions. *Econometric Reviews*, 3(1), 1–100.

Dong, C., Gao, J., and Linton, O. (2023). High-dimensional semiparametric moment restriction models. *Journal of Econometrics*, 232(2), 320–345.

Doukhan, P. (1994). *Mixing: Properties and Examples*. Springer, Berlin.

Doukhan, P., Massart, P., and Rio, E. (1994). The functional central limit theorem for strongly mixing processes. *Annales de l'Institut Henri Poincaré: Probabilités et statistiques*, 30(1), 63–82.

Drost, F. C. and Nijman, T. (1993). Temporal aggregation of GARCH processes. *Econometrica*, 61(4), 909–927.

Durbin, J. (1953). A note on regression when there is extraneous information about one of the coefficients. *Journal of the American Statistical Association*, 48(264), 799–808.

Durbin, J. (1960). The fitting of time-series models. *Review of the International Statistical Institute*, 28(3), 233–244.

Durbin, J. (1973). *Distribution Theory for Tests Based on the Sample Distribution Function*. Society for Industrial and Applied Mathematics, Philadelphia, PA.

Dybvig, P. H. and Zhang, H. (2018). That is not my dog: Why doesn't the log dividend–price ratio seem to predict future log returns or log dividend growths? SFS Cavalcade Asia-Pacific 2017 Annual Meeting (Beijing), AFA 2019 Annual Meeting (Atlanta). doi:10.2139/ssrn.3123595

Efron, B. (1982). *The Jackknife, the Bootstrap, and Other Resampling Plans*. Society for Industrial and Applied Mathematics, Philadelphia, PA.

Efron, B. (1986). Why isn't everyone a Bayesian? *The American Statistician*, 40(1), 1–5.

Eicker, F. (1967). Limit theorems for regressions with unequal and dependent errors. In *Proceedings of the Fifth Berkeley Symposium on Mathematical Statistics and Probability*, Vol. I. University of California Press, Berkeley.

Elbadawi, I., Gallant, A. R., and Souza, G. (1983). An elasticity can be estimated consistently without a priori knowledge of functional form. *Econometrica*, 51(6), 1731–1751.

Embrechts, P., Klüppelberg, C., and Mikosch, T. (1997). *Modelling Extremal Events*. Springer, New York.

Engle, R. F. (1974). Band spectrum regression. *International Economic Review*, 15(1), 1–11. doi:10.2307/2526084

Engle, R. F. (1982). Autoregressive conditional heteroscedasticity with estimates of the variance of United Kingdom inflation. *Econometrica*, 50(4), 987–1007.

Engle, R. F. (1984). Wald, likelihood ratio, and Lagrange multiplier tests in econometrics. In Z. Griliches and M. D. Intriligator (eds), *Handbook of Econometrics*, Vol. II. North Holland, Amsterdam.

Engle, R. F. and Granger, C. W. J. (1987). Co-integration and error correction: Representation, estimation, and testing. *Econometrica*, 55(2), 251–276. doi:10.2307/1913236

Engle, R. F. and Russell, J. R. (1998). Autoregressive conditional duration: A new model for irregularly spaced transaction data. *Econometrica*, 66(5), 1127–1162. doi:10.2307/2999632

Engle, R. F. and Sheppard, K. (2001). Theoretical and empirical properties of dynamic conditional correlation multivariate GARCH. NBER Working Paper w8554. National Bureau of Economic Research, Cambridge, MA.

Eubank, R. L. (1988). *Smoothing Splines and Nonparametric Regression*. Marcel Dekker, New York.

Fama, E. (1970). Efficient capital markets: A review of theory and empirical work. *Journal of Finance*, 25(2), 383–417.

Fan, J. (1992). Design-adaptive nonparametric regression. *Journal of the American Statistical Association*, 82(420), 998–1004.

Fan, J. (1993). Local linear regression smoothers and their minimax efficiencies. *Annals of Statistics*, 21(1), 196–216.

Fan, J. and Chen, J. (1997). One-step local quasi-likelihood estimation. *Journal of the Royal Statistical Society, Series B*, 61(4), 927–943.

Fan, J. and Gijbels, I. (1996). *Local Polynomial Modelling and Its Applications*. Chapman and Hall, London.

Fan, J., Heckman, N. E., and Wand, M. P. (1995). Local polynomial kernel regression for generalized linear models and quasi-likelihood functions. *Journal of the American Statistical Association*, 90(429), 141–150. doi:10.2307/2291137

Fan, J. and Li, R. (2001). Variable selection via nonconcave penalized likelihood and its oracle properties. *Journal of the American Statistical Association*, 96(456), 1348–1360.

Fan, J. and Yao, Q. (1998). Efficient estimation of conditional variance functions in stochastic regression. *Biometrika*, 85(3), 645–660.

Faust, J. (1992). When are variance ratio tests for serial dependence optimal? *Econometrica*, 60(5), 1215–1226.

Feinstein, C. A. (2002). Seasonality of deaths in the U.S. by age and cause. *Demographic Research*, 6(17), 469–486.

Feller, W. (1965). *An Introduction to Probability Theory and its Applications*, Vol. II. Wiley, Chichester.

Findley, D. F., Monsell, B. C., Bell, W. R., Otto, M. C., and Chen, B.-C. (1998). New capabilities and methods of the X-12-ARIMA seasonal-adjustment program. *Journal of Business & Economic Statistics*, 16(2), 127–152.

Florens-Zmirou, D. (1993). On estimating the diffusion coefficient from discrete observations. *Journal of Applied Probability*, 30(4), 790–804.

Forni, M., Hallin, M., Lippi, M., and Reichlin, L. (2000). The generalized dynamic-factor model: Identification and estimation. *Review of Economics and Statistics*, 82(4), 540–554.

Foster, D. P. and Nelson, D. B. (1996). Continuous record asymptotics for rolling sample variance estimators. *Econometrica*, 64(1), 139–174.

Fuller, W. (1995). *Introduction to Statistical Time Series*. Wiley, Chichester.

Gabaix, X. (2008). Power laws. In S. N. Durlauf and L. E. Blume (eds), *New Palgrave Dictionary of Economics*, 2nd edition. Palgrave Macmillan, London.

Gabaix, X., Gopikrishnan, P., Plerou, V., and Stanley, H. E. (2006). Institutional investors and stock market volatility. *Quarterly Journal of Economics*. 121(2), 461–504.

Gabaix, X. and Ibragimov, R. (2011). Rank − 1/2: A simple way to improve the OLS estimation of tail exponents. *Journal of Business and Economic Statistics*, 29(1), 24–39.

Gallant, A. R. and Souza, G. (1991). On the asymptotic normality of Fourier flexible form estimates. *Journal of Econometrics*, 50(3), 329–353.

Gao, J. (2007). *Nonlinear Time Series: Semiparametric and Nonparametric Methods*. Chapman and Hall, London.

Gatev, E., Goetzmann, W. N., and Rouwenhorst, K. G. (2006). Pairs trading: Performance of a relative-value arbitrage rule. *The Review of Financial Studies*, 19(3), 797–827.

Giraitis, L., Li, Y., and Phillips, P. C. B. (2023). *Robust Inference on Correlation under General Heterogeneity*. Cowles Foundation Discussion Papers 2354. Cowles Foundation for Research in Economics, Yale University.

Giraitis, L. and Robinson, P. M. (2001). Whittle estimation of ARCH models. *Econometric Theory* 17(3), 608–631.

Glivenko, V. (1933). Sulla determinazione empirica delle leggi di probabilitá. *Giornale dell'Istituto Italiano degli Attuari*, 4, 92–99.

Glosten, L. R., Jagannathan, R., and Runkle, D. E. (1993). On the relation between expected value and the volatility of the nominal excess return on stocks. *Journal of Finance*, 48(5), 1779–1801.

Godambe, V. P. and Thompson, M. E. (1978). Some aspects of the theory of estimating equations. *Journal of Statistical Planning and Inference*, 2(1), 95–104.

Golub, G and van Loan, C. (1996). *Matrix Computations*, 3rd edition. Johns Hopkins University Press, London.

Goyal, A. and Welch, I. (2003). Predicting the equity premium with dividend ratios. *Management Science*, 49(5), 639–654.

Gozalo, P. and Linton, O. B. (2000). Local nonlinear least squares: Using parametric information in nonparametric regression. *Journal of Econometrics*, 99(1), 63–106.

Granger, C. W. J. (1969). Investigating causal relations by econometric models and cross-spectral methods. *Econometrica*, 37(3), 424–438. doi:10.2307/1912791

Granger, C. W. J. and Hughes, A. O. (1971). A new look at some old data: The Beveridge wheat price series. *Journal of the Royal Statistics Society, Series A*, 134, 413–428.

Granger, C. W. J. and Joyeux, R. (1980). An introduction to long memory time series models and fractional differencing. *Journal of Time Series Analysis*, 1(1), 15–29.

Granger, C. W. J. and Morris, M. J. (1976). Time series modelling and interpretation. *Journal of the Royal Statistical Society, Series A*, 139(2), 246–257.

Grenander, U. (1954). On the estimation of regression coefficients in the case of autocorrelated disturbances. *Annals of Mathematical Statistics*, 25(2), 252–272.

Grenander, U. and Rosenblatt, M. (1957). *Statistical Analysis of Stationary Time Series*. Wiley, New York.

Härdle, W. (1990). *Applied Nonparametric Regression*. Cambridge University Press.

Härdle, W., Horowitz, J., and Kreiss, J.-P. (2003). Bootstrap methods for time series. *International Statistical Review*, 71(2), 435–459.

Härdle, W., and Linton, O. (1994). Applied nonparametric methods. In R. F. Engle and D. L. McFadden (eds), *Handbook of Econometrics*, Vol. IV. North Holland, Amsterdam.

Härdle, W. and Marron, J. S. (1985). Optimal bandwidth selection in nonparametric regression function estimation. *Annals of Statistics*, 13(4), 1465–1481.

Haiden, T., Janousek, M., Vitart, F., Ben-Bouallegue, Z., Ferranti, L., and Prates, F. (2021). Evaluation of ECMWF forecasts, including the 2021 upgrade. ECMWF technical memorandum 884. European Centre for Medium-Range Weather Forecasts, Reading, UK.

Hall, P. (1992). *The Bootstrap and Edgeworth Expansion*. Springer, New York.

Hall, P. and Heyde, C. C. (1980). *Martingale Limit Theory and Its Applications*. Academic Press, New York.

Hall, P. and Yao, Q. (2003). Inference in ARCH and GARCH models with heavy-tailed errors. *Econometrica*, 71(1), 285–317.

Hall, R. E. (1978). Stochastic implications of the life cycle–permanent income hypothesis: Theory and evidence. *Journal of Political Economy*, 86(6), 971–987.

Hamilton, J. D. (1989). A new approach to the economic analysis of nonstationary time series and the business cycle. *Econometrica*, 57(2), 357–384.

Hamilton, J. D. (1994). *Time Series Analysis*. Princeton University Press.

Han, H., Linton, O., Oka, T., and Whang, Y.-J. (2016). The cross-quantilogram: Measuring quantile dependence and testing directional predictability between time series. *Journal of Econometrics*, 193(1), 251–270.

Hannan, E. J. (1970). *Multiple Time Series*. Wiley, Chichester.

Hannan, E. J. (1973). The asymptotic theory of linear time-series models. *Journal of Applied Probability*, 10(1), 130–145.

Hannan, E. J. and Quinn, B. G. (1979). The determination of the order of an autoregression. *Journal of the Royal Statistical Society, Series B*, 41(2), 190–195.

Hannan, E. J. and Rissanen, J. (1982). Recursive estimation of mixed autoregressive-moving average order. *Biometrika*, 69(1), 81–94.

Hansen, B. E. (1997). Approximate asymptotic p-values for structural-change tests. *Journal of Business & Economic Statistics*, 15(1), 60–67.

Hansen, B. E. (2007). Least squares model averaging. *Econometrica*, 75(4), 1175–1189.

Hansen, L. P. (1982). Large sample properties of generalized method of moments estimators. *Econometrica*, 50(4), 1029–1054.

Hansen, L. P. and Hodrick, R. J. (1980). Forward exchange rates as optimal predictors of future spot rates: An econometric analysis. *Journal of Political Economy*, 88(5), 829–853.

Hansen, L. P. and Singleton, K. J. (1982). Generalized instrumental variables estimation of nonlinear rational expectations models. *Econometrica*, 50(5), 1269–1286.

Hansen, P. R. and Lunde, A. (2005). A forecast comparison of volatility models: Does anything beat a GARCH(1,1)? *Journal of Applied Econometrics*, 20(7), 873–889. doi:10.1002/jae.800

Hansen, P. R. and Lunde, A. (2006). Realized variance and market microstructure noise. *Journal of Business and Economic Statistics*, 24(2), 127–161.

Harris, D., McCabe, B., and Leybourne, S. (2008). Testing for long memory. *Econometric Theory*, 24(1), 143–175.

Hart, J. D. (1991). Kernel regression estimation with time series errors. *Journal of the Royal Statistical Society, Series B*, 53(1), 173–187.

Hart, J. D. and Vieu, P. (1990). Data-driven bandwidth choice for density estimation based on dependent data. *Annals of Statistics*, 18(2), 873–890.

Harvey, A. C. (1989). *Forecasting, Structural Time Series Models and the Kalman Filter*. Cambridge University Press.

Hasbrouck, J. (2007). *Empirical Market Microstructure*. Oxford University Press.

Hastie, T., Montanari, A., Rosset, S., and Tibshirani, R. J. (2022). Surprises in high-dimensional "ridgeless" least squares interpolation. *Annals of Statistics*, 50(2), 949–986.

Hastie, T. J. and Tibshirani, R. (1990). *Generalized Additive Models*. Chapman and Hall, London.

Hastie, T., Tibshirani, R., and Friedman, J. (2009). *The Elements of Statistical Learning: Data Mining, Inference, and Prediction*. Springer, New York.

Hasza, D. P. (1980). A note on the maximum likelihood estimation for the first-order autoregressive processes. *Communications in Statistics: Theory and Methods*, 9(13), 1411–1415.

Hausman, J. A., Lo, A. W., and MacKinlay, A. C. (1992). An ordered probit analysis of transaction stock prices. *Journal of Financial Economics*, 31(3), 319–379.

He, C. and Teräsvirta, T. (1999). Fourth moment structure of the GARCH(p, q) process. *Econometric Theory*, 15(6), 824–846.

Herrndorf, N. (1984). A functional central limit theorem for weakly dependent sequences of random variables. *Annals of Probability*, 12(1), 141–153. doi:10.1214/aop/1176993379.

Heston, S. L. (1993). A closed-form solution for options with stochastic volatility with applications to bond and currency options. *Review of Financial Studies*, 6(2), 327–343.

Hidalgo, J. and Seo, M. H. (2013). Testing for structural stability in the whole sample. *Journal of Econometrics*, 175(2), 84–93.

Hill, B. M. (1975). A simple general approach to inference about the tail of a distribution. *Annals of Statistics*, 3(5), 1163–1174.

Hill, J. B. (2010). On tail index estimation for dependent, heterogeneous data. *Econometric Theory*, 26(5), 1398–1436.

Hillmer, S. C. and Tiao, G. C. (1982). An ARIMA-model-based approach to seasonal adjustment. *Journal of the American Statistical Association*, 77(377), 63–70.

Hodrick, R. (1992). Dividend yields and expected stock returns: Alternative procedures for inference and measurement. *Review of Financial Studies*, 5(3), 357–386.

Hodrick, R. and Prescott, E. C. (1997). Postwar U.S. business cycles: An empirical investigation. *Journal of Money,*

Credit, and Banking, 29(1), 1–16. doi:10.2307/2953682

Holt, C. C. (1957). Forecasting seasonals and trends by exponentially weighted moving averages. Office of Naval Research Memorandum 52. Reprinted in Holt, C. C. (2004). *International Journal of Forecasting*, 20(1), 5–10. doi:10.1016/j.ijforecast.2003.09.015

Hong, S., Linton, O., and Zhang, H. (2017). An investigation into multivariate variance ratio statistics and their application to stock market predictability. *Journal of Financial Econometrics*, 15(2), 173–222.

Hong, Y. (1996). Consistent testing for serial correlation of unknown form. *Econometrica*, 64(4), 837–864.

Howrey, E. P. (1968). A spectrum analysis of the long-swing hypothesis. *International Economic Review*, 9(2), 228–252.

Hyndman, R. J. and Athanasopoulos, G. (2014). *Forecasting Principle and Practice*. Otexts, Melbourne.

Hyndman, R. J. and Koehler, A. B. (2006). Another look at measures of forecast accuracy. *International Journal of Forecasting*, 22(4), 679–688.

Ibragimov, I. (2001). Estimation of analytic functions. *IMS Lecture Notes-Monograph Series*, 36, 359–383.

Ibragimov, I. A. and Hasminskii, R. Z. (1980). On nonparametric estimation of regression. *Soviet Mathematics Doklady*, 21, 810–814.

Imbens, G. W. and Lemieux, T. (2008). Regression discontinuity designs: A guide to practice. *Journal of Econometrics*, 142(2), 615–635.

Imbens, G. W. and Rubin, D. B. (2015). *Causal Inference for Statistics, Social, and Biomedical Sciences: An Introduction*. Cambridge University Press.

Jacod, J., Li, Y., Mykland, P. A., Podolskij, M., and Vetter, M. (2009). Microstructure noise in the continuous case: The pre-averaging approach. *Stochastic Processes and their Applications*, 119(7), 2249–2276.

Jacod, J. and Protter, P. (1998). Asymptotic error distributions for the Euler method for stochastic differential equations. *Annals of Probability*, 26(1), 267–307.

Jensen, S. T. and Rahbek, A. (2004). Asymptotic normality of the QMLE of ARCH in the nonstationary case. *Econometrica*, 72(2), 641–646.

Jiang, G. and Knight, J. (1997). A nonparametric approach to the estimation of diffusion processes with an application to a short-term interest rate model. *Econometric Theory*, 13(5), 615–645.

Joe, H. (1997). *Multivariate Models and Dependence Concepts*. Chapman and Hall, London.

Johansen, S. (1988). Statistical analysis of cointegration vectors. *Journal of Economic Dynamics and Control*, 12(2–3), 231–254.

Johansen, S. (1991). Estimation and hypothesis testing of cointegration vectors in Gaussian vector autoregressive models. *Econometrica*, 59(6), 1551–1580.

Johansen, S. (1995). *Likelihood-Based Inference in Cointegrated Vector Autoregressive Models*. Oxford University Press.

Jordà, Ò. (2005). Estimation and inference of impulse responses by local projections. *The American Economic Review*, 95(1), 161–182.

Kiefer, N. M., Vogelsang, T. J., and Bunzel, H. (2000). Simple robust testing of regression hypotheses. *Econometrica*, 68(3), 695–714.

Kilian, L. and Lütkepohl, H. (2017). *Structural Vector Autoregressive Analysis*. Cambridge University Press.

Kim, T. Y. and Cox, D. D. (1996). Bandwidth selection in kernel smoothing of time series. *Journal of Time Series Analysis*, 17(1), 49–63.

Koenker, R. (2005). *Quantile Regression*. Cambridge University Press.

Kolmogorov, A. N. (1957). On the representation of continuous functions of several variables by superposition of continuous functions of one variable and addition. *Doklady Akademii Nauk USSR*, 114(5), 953–956.

Koop, G. and Korobilis, D. (2010). Bayesian multivariate time series methods for empirical macroeconomics. *Foundations and Trends in Econometrics*, 3(4), 267–358. doi:10.1561/0800000013

Kreiss, J. P. and Franke, J. (1992). Bootstrapping stationary autoregressive moving average models. *Journal of Time Series Analysis*, 13(4), 297–317.

Kristensen, D. (2010). Pseudo-maximum likelihood estimation in two classes of semiparametric diffusion models. *Journal of Econometrics*, 156(2), 239–259.

Kristensen, D. and Linton, O. (2006). A closed-form estimator for the GARCH(1,1) model. *Econometric Theory*, 22(2), 323–327.

Kuznets, S. (1930). *Secular Movements in Production and Prices: Their Nature and their Bearing upon Cyclical Fluctuations*. Houghton Mifflin, Boston.

Kwiatkowski, D., Phillips, P. C. B., Schmidt, P., and Shin, Y. (1992). Testing the null of stationarity against the alternative of a unit root: How sure are we that economic time series have a unit root? *Journal of Econometrics*, 54(1–3), 159–178.

Lazarus, E., Lewis, D. J., and Stock, J. H. (2021). The size–power tradeoff in HAR inference. *Econometrica*, 89(5), 2497–2516.

Lee, S. W. and Hansen, B. E. (1994). Asymptotic theory for the GARCH(1,1) quasi-maximum likelihood estimator. *Econometric Theory*, 10(1), 29–52.

Leeb, H. and Pötscher, B. M. (2005). Model selection and inference: Facts and fiction. *Econometric Theory*, 21(1), 21–59.

Levy, H. (2006). *Stochastic Dominance: Investment Decision Making under Uncertainty*. Springer, New York.

Lewbel, A. (2007). A local generalized method of moments estimator. *Economics Letters*, 94(1), 124–128.

Li, S. and Linton, O. (2021). When will the Covid-19 pandemic peak? *Journal of Econometrics*, 220(1), 130–157.

Li, Y. (2024). Correcting the bias of the sample cross-covariance estimator. *Journal of Time Series Analysis*, 45(2), 214–247.

Li, Z. M. and Linton, O. (2022). A ReMeDI for microstructure noise. *Econometrica*, 90(1), 367–389.

Lin, Z. Y. and Lu, C. (1996). *Limit Theory for Mixing Dependent Random Variables*. Science Press, New York.

Linton, O., Maasoumi, E., and Whang, Y.-J. (2008). Consistent testing for stochastic dominance under general sampling schemes. *The Review of Economic Studies*, 75(1), 333–337.

Linton, O. and Mammen, E. (2005). Estimating semiparametric ARCH(∞) models by kernel smoothing. *Econometrica*, 73(3), 771–836.

Linton, O. B. and Nielsen, J. P. (1995). A kernel method of estimating structured nonparametric regression using marginal integration. *Biometrika*, 82(1), 93–100.

Linton, O. and Whang, Y.-J. (2007). The quantilogram: With an application to evaluating directional predictability. *Journal of Econometrics*, 141(1), 250–282.

Lipster, R. and Shiryaev, A. (2001). *Statistics of Random Processes*, Vol. I, *General Theory*. Springer, New York.

Litterman, R. B. (1986). Forecasting with Bayesian vector autoregressions: Five years of experience. *Journal of Business & Economic Statistics*, 4(1), 25–38.

Liu, L. Y., Patton, A. J., and Sheppard, K. (2015). Does anything beat 5-minute RV? A comparison of realized measures across multiple asset classes. *Journal of Econometrics*, 187(1), 293–311.

Lo, A. W. (1988). Maximum likelihood estimation of generalized Itô processes with discretely sampled data. *Econometric Theory*, 4(2), 231–247.

Lo, A. W. (1991). Long-term memory in stock market prices. *Econometrica*, 59(5), 1279–1313.

Lo, A. W. (2001). Risk management for hedge funds: Introduction and overview. doi:10.2139/ssrn.283308

Lo, A. W. and MacKinlay, A. C. (1988). Stock market prices do not follow random walks: Evidence from a simple specification test. *Review of Financial Studies*, 1(1), 41–66.

Lo, A. W. and MacKinlay, A. C. (1990). An econometric analysis of nonsynchronous trading. *Journal of Econometrics*, 45(1–2), 181–212.

Lobato, I. (2001). Testing that a dependent process is uncorrelated. *Journal of the American Statistical Association*, 96(455), 1066–1076.

Lumsdaine, R. L. (1996). Consistency and asymptotic normality of the quasi-maximum likelihood estimator in IGARCH(1,1) and covariance stationary GARCH(1,1) models. *Econometrica*, 64(3), 575–596. doi:10.2307/2171862

Mack, Y. P. (1981). Local properties of k-NN regression estimates. *SIAM Journal on Algebraic Discrete Methods*, 2(3), 311–323.

MacKinnon, J. G., Haug, A. A., and Michelis, L. (1999). Numerical distribution functions of likelihood ratio tests for cointegration. *Journal of Applied Econometrics*, 14(5), 563–577.

McQuarrie, A. D. and Tsai, C. L. (1998). *Regression and Time Series Model Selection*. World Scientific, Singapore.

Magnus, J. R. (1986). The exact moments of a ratio for quadratic forms in normal variables. *Annales d'Economie et de Statistique*, 4, 95–109.

Magnus, J. R. and Neudecker, H. (1988). *Matrix Differential Calculus with Applications in Statistics*. Wiley, Chichester.

Malinvaud, E. (1983). *Econometric Methodology at the Cowles Commission: Rise and Maturity*. https://cowles.yale.edu/sites/default/files/2022-12/50th-malinvaud.pdf

Mammen, E. (1992). *When Does Bootstrap Work? Asymptotic Results and Simulations*. Springer, Berlin.

Mammen, E. (1993). Bootstrap and wild bootstrap for high dimensional linear models. *Annals of Statistics*, 21(1), 255–285.

Mandelbrot, B. (1963). The variation of certain speculative prices. *Journal of Business*, 36, 394–411.

Masry, E. (1996a). Multivariate local polynomial regression for time series: Uniform strong consistency and rates. *Journal of Time Series Analysis*, 17(6), 571–599.

Masry, E. (1996b). Multivariate regression estimation local polynomial fitting for time series. *Stochastic Processes and their Applications*, 65(1), 81–101.

Masry, E. and Tjøstheim, D. (1995). Nonparametric estimation and identification of nonlinear ARCH time series: Strong convergence and asymptotic normality. *Econometric Theory*, 11(2), 258–289.

Meese, R. and Rogoff, K. (1983). Empirical exchange rate models of the seventies: Do they fit out of sample? *Journal of International Economics*, 14(1–2), 3–24.

Meijer, E. and Ypma, J. Y. (2008). A simple identification proof for a mixture of two univariate normal distributions. *Journal of Classification*, 25, 113–123. doi:10.1007/s00357-008-9008-6

Meitz, M. and Saikkonen, P. (2008). Stability of nonlinear AR–GARCH models. *Journal of Time Series Analysis*, 29(3), 453–475.

Mikosch, T. (1998). *Elementary Stochastic Calculus with Finance in View*. World Scientific, Singapore.

Mikosch, T. and Stărică, C. (2000). Limit theory for the sample autocorrelations and extremes of a GARCH(1,1) process. *Annals of Statistics*, 28(5), 1427–1451.

Müller, H.-G. (1992). Change-points in nonparametric regression analysis. *Annals of Statistics*, 20(2), 737–761.

Muth, J. F. (1960). Optimal properties of exponentially weighted forecasts. *Journal of the American Statistical Association*, 55(290), 299–306.

Mykland, P. A. and Zhang, L. (2006). ANOVA for diffusions and Itô processes. *Annals of Statistics*, 34(4), 1931–1963.

Nadaraya, E. A. (1964). On estimating regression. *Theory of Probability and its Applications*, 9(1), 141–142.

Nelson, C. R. and Plosser, C. R. (1982). Trends and random walks in macroeconomic time series: Some evidence and implications. *Journal of Monetary Economics*, 10(2), 139–162.

Nelson, D. B. (1990a). Stationarity and persistence in the GARCH(1,1) model. *Econometric Theory*, 6(3), 318–334.

Nelson, D. B. (1990b). ARCH models as diffusion approximations. *Journal of Econometrics*, 45(1–2), 7–38.

Nelson, D. B. (1991). Conditional heteroskedasticity in asset returns: A new approach. *Econometrica*, 59(2), 347–370.

Nelson D. B. and Cao, C. Q. (1992). Inequality constraints in the univariate GARCH model. *Journal of Business and Economic Statistics*, 10(2), 229–235.

Nerlove, M. (1964). Spectral analysis of seasonal adjustment procedures. *Econometrica*, 32(3), 241–286.

Newey, W. K. and Steigerwald, D. G. (1997). Asymptotic bias for quasi-maximum-likelihood estimators in conditional heteroskedasticity models. *Econometrica*, 65(3), 587–599. doi:10.2307/2171754

Newey, W. K and West, K. D. (1987). A simple, positive semi-definite, heteroskedasticity and autocorrelation consistent covariance matrix. *Econometrica*, 55(3), 703–708. doi:10.2307/1913610

Onatski, A. (2009). Testing hypotheses about the number of factors in large factor models. *Econometrica*, 77(5), 1447–1479.

Onatski, A. and Wang, C. (2018). Alternative asymptotics for cointegration tests in large VARs. *Econometrica*, 86(4), 1465–1478.

Pagan, A. R. (1984). Econometric issues in the analysis of regressions with generated regressors. *International Economic Review*, 25(1), 221–247.

Pagan, A. R. and Hong, Y. S. (1991). Nonparametric estimation and the risk premium. In W. Barnett, J. Powell, and G. E. Tauchen (eds), *Nonparametric and Semiparametric Methods in Econometrics and Statistics*. Cambridge University Press.

Pagan, A. R. and Schwert, G. W. (1990). Alternative models for conditional stock volatility. *Journal of Econometrics*, 45(1–2), 267–290.

Pakes, A. and Pollard, D. (1989). Simulation and the asymptotics of optimization estimators. *Econometrica*, 57(5), 1027–1057.

Parzen, E. (1957). On consistency of the spectrum of a stationary time series. *Annals of Mathematical Statistics*, 28(2), 329–334.

Patton, A. J. (2002). Applications of copula theory in financial econometrics. PhD dissertation, University of California, San Diego.

Patton, A. (2006). Modelling asymmetric exchange rate dependence. *International Economic Review*, 47(2), 527–556.

Patton, A. (2012). A review of copula models for economic time series. *Journal of Multivariate Analysis*, 110, 4–18.

Pearl, J. (2000). *Causality: Models, Reasoning, and Inference*. Cambridge University Press.

Peng, H., Wang, S., and Wang, X. (2008). Consistency and asymptotic distribution of the Theil–Sen estimator. *Journal of Statistical Planning and Inference*, 138(6), 1836–1850.

Peng, L. and Yao, Q. (2003). Least absolute deviations estimation for ARCH and GARCH models. *Biometrika*, 90(4), 967–975.

Perron, P. (1989). The great crash, the oil price shock, and the unit root hypothesis. *Econometrica*, 57(6), 1361–1401.

Pesaran, M. H. and Timmerman, A. (1995). Predictability of stock returns: Robustness and economic significance. *Journal of Finance*, 50(4), 1201–1228.

Pesaran, M. H. and Timmermann, A. (2007). Selection of estimation window in the presence of breaks. *Journal of Econometrics*, 137(1), 134–161.

Peters, O. (2019). The ergodicity problem in economics. *Nature Physics*, 15, 1216–1221. doi:10.1038/s41567-019-0732-0

Petruccelli, J. D. and Woolford, S. W. (1984). A threshold AR(1) model. *Journal of Applied Probability*, 21(2), 270–286.

Phillips, P. C. B. (1991a). Optimal inference in cointegrated systems. *Econometrica*, 59(2), 283–306.

Phillips, P. C. B. (1991b). To criticize the critics: An objective Bayesian analysis of stochastic trends. *Journal of Applied Econometrics*, 6(4), 333–364.

Phillips, P. C. B. and Jin, S. (2014). Testing the martingale hypothesis. *Journal of Business and Economic Statistics*, 32(4), 537–554.

Phillips, P. C. B. and Magdalinos, T. (2007). Limit theory for moderate deviations from a unit root. *Journal of Econometrics*, 136(1), 115–130.

Phillips, P. C. B. and Park, J. Y. (1999). Asymptotics for nonlinear transformations of integrated time series. *Econometric Theory*, 15(3), 269–298.

Phillips, P. C. B. and Perron, P. (1988). Testing for a unit root in time series regression. *Biometrika*, 75(2), 335–346.

Phillips, P. C. B., Shi, S., and Yu, J. (2015). Testing for multiple bubbles: Historical episodes of exuberance and collapse in the S&P 500. *International Economic Review*, 56(4), 1043–1078.

Phillips, P. C. B. and Solo, V. (1992). Asymptotics for linear processes. *Annals of Statistics*, 20(2), 971–1001.

Phillips, P. C. B. and Sun, Y. (2003). Regression with an evaporating logarithmic trend. *Econometric Theory*, 19(4), 692–701.

Phillips, P. C. B. and Yu, J. (2010). Dating the timeline of financial bubbles during the subprime crisis. *Quantitative Economics*, 2(3), 455–491.

Pollock, D. S. G. (2007). Wiener–Kolmogorov filtering, frequency-selective filtering, and polynomial regression. *Econometric Theory*, 23(1), 71–88.

Portnoy, S. (1984). Asymptotic behavior of M estimators of p regression parameters when p^2/n is large. I. Consistency. *Annals of Statistics*, 12(4), 1298–1309.

Portnoy, S. (1985). Asymptotic behavior of M estimators of p regression parameters when p^2/n is large. II. Normal approximation. *Annals of Statistics*, 13(4), 1403–1417.

Poterba, J. M. and Summers, L. H. (1988). Mean reversion in stock prices: Evidence and implications. *Journal of Financial Economics*, 22(1), 27–59.

Primiceri, G. and Tambalotti, A. (2020). Macroeconomic forecasting in the time of COVID-19. Northwestern University.

Protter, P. E. (2004). *Stochastic Integration and Differential Equations*, 2nd edition. Springer, New York.

Quandt, R. E. (1960). Tests of the hypothesis that a linear regression obeys two separate regimes. *Journal of the American Statistical Association*, 55(290), 324–30.

Resnick, S. and Stărică, C. (1998). Tail index estimation for dependent data. *Annals of Applied Probability*, 8(4), 1156–1183. doi:10.1214/aoap/1028903376

Robinson, P. M. (1983). Nonparametric estimators for time series. *Journal of Time Series Analysis*, 4(3), 185–207.

Robinson, P. M. (1988). The stochastic difference between econometric statistics. *Econometrica*, 56(3), 531–548.

Robinson, P. M. (1994). Semiparametric analysis of long-memory time series. *Annals of Statistics*, 22(1), 515–539. doi:10.1214/aos/1176325382

Rogers, L. C. G. (1997). Arbitrage with fractional Brownian motion. *Mathematical Finance*, 7(1), 95–105.

Roll, R. (1984). A simple implicit measure of the effective bid–ask spread in an efficient market. *Journal of Finance*, 39(4), 1127–1139.

Rosenblatt, M. (1956). Remarks on some nonparametric estimates of a density function. *Annals of Mathematical Statistics*, 27(3), 832–837.

Rossi, B. (2013). Exchange rate predictability. *Journal of Economic Literature*, 51(4), 1063–1119.

Rothenberg, T. J. (1973). *Efficient Estimation with A Priori Information*. Yale University Press, New Haven, CT.

Schwarz, G. E. (1978). Estimating the dimension of a model. *Annals of Statistics*, 6(2), 461–464.

Shephard, N. (ed). (2005). *Stochastic Volatility: Selected Readings*. Oxford University Press.

Shibata, R. (1981). An optimal selection of regression variables. *Biometrika*, 68(1), 45–54.

Shiller, R. (1973). A distributed lag estimator derived from smoothness priors. *Econometrica*, 41(4), 775–788.

Shorack, G. R. and Wellner, J. A. (1986). *Empirical Processes with Applications to Statistics*. Wiley, New York.

Silver, N. (2012). *The Signal and the Noise: Why So Many Predictions Fail – But Some Don't*. Penguin Press, London.

Silverman, B. W. (1984). Spline smoothing: The equivalent variable kernel method. *Annals of Statistics*, 12(3), 898–916.

Silverman, B. W. (1985). Some aspects of the spline smoothing approach to non-parametric regression curve fitting. *Journal of the Royal Statistical Society, Series B*, 47(1), 1–52.

Silverman, B. W. (1986). *Density Estimation for Statistics and Data Analysis*. Chapman and Hall, London.

Sims, C. A. (1972). Money, income, and causality. *The American Economic Review*, 62(4), 540–552.

Sims, C. A. (1974). Seasonality in regression. *Journal of the American Statistical Association*, 69(347), 618–626.

Sims, C. A. (1980). Macroeconomics and reality. *Econometrica*, 48(1), 1–48. doi:10.2307/1912017

Sims, C. A. (2015). *VAR System Properties from the Jordan Decomposition; Cointegration*. http://sims.princeton.edu/yftp/Times15/cointLect15.pdf

Sims, C. A. and Zha, T. (1999). Error bands for impulse responses. *Econometrica*, 67(5), 1113–1155. doi:10.1111/1468-0262.00071

Sklar, A. (1959). Fonctions de répartition à n dimensions et leurs marges. *Publications de l'Institut Statistique de l'Université de Paris*, 8, 229–231.

Slutzky, E. (1927). Slozhenie sluchainykh prichin, kak istochnik tsiklicheskikh protsessov. *Voprosy kon"yunktury*, 3, 34–64.

Slutzky, E. (1937). The summation of random causes as the source of cyclic processes. *Econometrica*, 5(2), 105–146.

Sornette, D. (2017). *Why Stock Markets Crash (Critical Events in Complex Financial Systems)*. Princeton University Press.

Stambaugh, R. F. (1999). Predictive regressions. *Journal of Financial Economics*, 54(3), 375–421.

Stock, J. (1994). Unit roots, structural breaks, and trends. In R.F. Engle and D.L McFadden (eds), *Handbook of Econometrics*, Vol. IV. North Holland, Amsterdam.

Stone, C. J. (1980). Optimal rates of convergence for nonparametric estimators. *Annals of Statistics*, 8(6), 1348–1360.

Stone, C. J. (1982). Optimal global rates of convergence for nonparametric regression. *Annals of Statistics*, 10(4), 1040–1053.

Stute, W. (1984). Asymptotic normality of nearest neighbor regression function estimates. *Annals of Statistics*, 12(3), 917–926.

Su, L. and Xiao, Z. (2008). Testing structural change in time-series nonparametric regression models. *Statistics and its Interface*, 1(2), 347–366.

Sutradhar, B. C. (1994). Moments of the sample autocovariances and autocorrelations for a general Gaussian process. *Sankhya B*, 56(2), 272–285.

Sutradhar, B. C. and Kumar, P. (2003). The inversion of correlation matrix for MA(1) process. *Applied Mathematics Letters*, 16(3), 317–321.

Taleb, N. N. (2010). *The Black Swan*, 2nd edition. Penguin, London.

Teräsvirta, T. (2018). Nonlinear models in macroeconometrics. *Oxford Research Encyclopedia of Economics and Finance*. doi:10.1093/acrefore/9780190625979.013.177

Theil, H. and Goldberger, A. S. (1961). On pure and mixed statistical estimation in economics. *International Economic Review*, 2(1), 65–78.

Tibshirani, R. (1984). Local likelihood estimation. PhD thesis, Stanford University.

Tibshirani, R. J. (1996). Regression shrinkage and selection via the lasso. *Journal of the Royal Statistical Society, Series B*, 58(1), 267–288.

Tong, H. (1990). *Non-Linear Time Series: A Dynamical System Approach*. Oxford University Press.

Tong, H. and Yao, Q. (1998). Cross-validatory bandwidth selection for regression estimation based on dependent data. *Journal of Statistical Planning and Inference*, 68(2), 387–415.

Van de Geer, S. A. (2008). High-dimensional generalized linear models and the lasso. *Annals of Statistics*, 36(2), 614–645. doi:10.1214/009053607000000929

Vogelsang, T. J. and Yang, J. (2016). Exactly/nearly unbiased estimation of autocovariances of a univariate time series with unknown mean. *Journal of Time Series Analysis*, 37(6), 723–740.

Wahba, G. (1990). *Spline Models for Observational Data*. Society for Industrial and Applied Mathematics, Philadelphia, PA.

Wang, Q. and Phillips, P. C. B. (2009a). Asymptotic theory for local time density estimation and nonparametric cointegrating regression. *Econometric Theory*, 25(3), 710–738.

Wang, Q. and Phillips, P. C. B. (2009b). Structural nonparametric cointegrating regression. *Econometrica*, 77(6), 1901–1948.

Watson, G. S. (1964). Smooth regression analysis. *Sankhya Series A*, 26(4), 359–372.

Watson, M. (1994). Vector autoregressions and cointegration. In R. F. Engle and D.L. McFadden (eds), *Handbook of Econometrics*, Vol. IV. North Holland, Amsterdam.

West, M. and Harrison, J. (1997). *Bayesian Forecasting and Dynamic Models*. Springer, New York.

Whang, Y.-J. and Kim, J. (2003). A multiple variance ratio test using subsampling. *Economics Letters*, 79(2), 225–230.

Whang, Y.-J. and Linton, O. (1999). The asymptotic distribution of nonparametric estimates of the Lyapunov exponent for stochastic time series. *Journal of Econometrics*, 91(1), 1–42.

White, H. (1980). A heteroskedasticity-consistent covariance matrix estimator and a direct test for heteroskedasticity. *Econometrica*, 48(4), 817–838.

White, H. (2000). A reality check for data snooping. *Econometrica*, 68(5), 1097–1126.

Whittaker, E. T. (1923). On a new method of graduation. *Proceedings of the Edinburgh Mathematical Society*, 41, 63–75.

Whittaker, E. T. and Robinson, G. (1967). *The Calculus of Observations: A Treatise on Numerical Mathematics*, 4th edition. Dover, New York.

Wiener, N. (1923). Differential-space. *Journal of Mathematics and Physics*, 2, 131–174. doi:10.1002/sapm192321131

Wiener, N. (1930). Generalized harmonic analysis. *Acta Mathematica*, 55, 117–258.

Winters, P. R. (1960). Forecasting sales by exponentially weighted moving averages. *Management Science*, 6(3), 324–342. doi:10.1287/mnsc.6.3.324

Wold, H. (1954). *A Study in the Analysis of Stationary Time Series*, 2nd edition. Almqvist and Wiksell, Uppsala.

Wu, W. B. and Pourahmadi, M. (2009). Banding sample autocovariance matrices of stationary processes. *Statistica Sinica*, 19(4), 1755–1768.

Yaglom, A. M. (1965). Stationary Gaussian processes satisfying the strong mixing condition and best predictable functionals. In J. Neyman and L. M. Le Cam (eds), *Bernoulli 1713 Bayes 1763 Laplace 1813*. Springer, Berlin. https://doi.org/10.1007/978-3-642-99884-3_14

Yakowitz, S. (1987). Nearest neighbour methods for time series analysis. *Journal of Time Series Analysis*, 8(2), 235–247. doi:10.1111/j.1467-9892.1987.tb00435.x

Zellner, A. (1962). An efficient method of estimating seemingly unrelated regression equations and tests for aggregation bias. *Journal of the American Statistical Association*, 57(298), 348–368.

Zellner, A. and Palm, F. (1974). Time series analysis and simultaneous equation econometric models. *Journal of Econometrics*, 2(1), 17–54.

Zhang, L. (2006). Efficient estimation of stochastic volatility using noisy observations: A multi-scale approach. *Bernoulli*, 12(6), 1019–1043.

Zhang, L., Mykland, P., and Aït-Sahalia, Y. (2005). A tale of two timescales: Determining integrated volatility with noisy high-frequency data. *Journal of the American Statistical Association*, 100(472), 1394–1411.

Zhou, B. (1996). High-frequency data and volatility in foreign-exchange rates. *Journal of Business and Economic Statistics*, 14(1), 45–52.

Index